Correspondence of James K. Polk

VOLUME VI, 1842–1843

JAMES K. POLK

From an 1846 painting by G. P. A. Healy
Copy in the Tennessee Historical Society Collections

Correspondence of
JAMES K. POLK

·····➤●◆●➤·····

Volume VI
1842-1843

WAYNE CUTLER
Editor

CARESE M. PARKER
Associate Editor

1983
Vanderbilt University Press
Nashville

Library of Congress Cataloging in Publication Data (Revised)
Polk, James Knox, Pres. U.S., 1795–1849.
  Correspondence of James K. Polk.
  Vol. 6 edited by W. Cutler.
  CONTENTS: v. 1. 1817–1832.—v. 2. 1833–1834.—v. 3. 1835–1836.—
v. 4. 1837–1838.—v. 5. 1839–1841.—v. 6. 1842–1843.
  1. Polk, James Knox, Pres. U.S., 1795–1849. 2. Tennessee—Politics and
government—To 1865—Sources. 3. United States—Politics and
government—1845–1849—Sources. 4. Presidents—United States—Correspondence.
5. Tennessee—Governors—Correspondence. I. Weaver, Herbert, ed. II. Cutler, Wayne,
1938–
  III. Title.
E417.A4 1969   973.6′1′0924   75–84005
ISBN 0–8265–1211–9

Sponsored by

Vanderbilt University

The National Historical Publications and
Records Commission

The Tennessee Historical Commission

The Polk Memorial Association

To

James F. Hopkins and Mary W. M. Hargreaves

PREFACE

Defeated in his 1841 bid for reelection to the Tennessee governorship, Polk retired to his home in Columbia to wait out his two-year sojourn in the political wilderness. He firmly turned aside suggestions that he stand for election to the United States Senate. By pairing his election with that of a prominent Whig, such as John Bell or Ephraim H. Foster, Democrats in the 1841–42 Tennessee legislature hoped to fill both vacant seats and thereby neutralize Whig charges of partisan obstructionism by the Tennessee Senate's "Immortal Thirteen" Democrats, who refused to meet in joint convention with the Whig-controlled lower chamber. Although Whig members of the legislature wanted to fill both U.S. Senate seats with members of their own party and although they could control by a narrow margin any joint convention of the two houses, they took full advantage of the election deadlock to divide the Democracy and ridicule its obstructionist and novel opposition to holding a joint convention. Of course, the Whigs avoided pairing Polk with one of their own leaders, for to do so would unite the Democrats and release them from their untenable position. Polk welcomed a compromise solution to this politically explosive issue; but the leader of Tennessee's Democracy neither desired nor needed to hold high elective office to secure his political future.

As principal executor of Andrew Jackson's political legacy to Tennessee, Young Hickory inherited the frustrating task of conserving the Old Democracy's future at both the state and national levels. If he would defeat the opposition at home, he must stress sectional and state issues at the expense of his mentor's long-standing coalition with the northern Democracy. On the other hand, if Polk focused attention on those questions that transcended sectional and state interests, he would render Tennessee Democrats vulnerable to Whig charges of being too radical, too impractical, and too insensitive in their anti-consolidationist approach to the general government. Many of Polk's advisers urged him to moderate his opposition to economic relief proposals such as those for a more protective tariff, a federal bankruptcy act, and a new national bank. It was ironic that the two major factions in the Tennessee Democracy, the Jackson loyalists and the John C. Calhoun nullifiers, both espoused Thomas Jefferson's radical political creed, but could not agree on the extent to which they might be bound by philosophical considerations.

Calhounites in Tennessee fought every effort to raise a protective tariff and on that issue could pass for Jeffersonian radicals without apology or exception. On the question of founding another national bank, they worried in private, but in public often chose to speak more quietly, if at all, against the measure. Calhounites preferred to talk about local and state issues in their contests for office. Polk had courted and won their support in his 1839 gubernatorial race. As governor he had named Calhounites to interim appointments in the United States Senate. He had brought them into the inner circle of political decision making in Tennessee. Those efforts at party unity notwithstanding, Polk would not support Calhoun for the 1844 presidential nomination. On the other hand, the Calhoun faction in Tennessee could unite with Polk on state issues, but would not back his coalition with Van Buren. It was one thing for Polk to sacrifice himself politically for the redemption of Van Buren's place in history; it was quite another to ask Calhoun's friends to do so. The harsh political reality was that Jackson would not assign his political movement to a former turncoat, and Tennesseans would not accept Jackson's choice for the assignment. Indeed, they had rejected the leader of the northern Democracy in four of the last five elections.

Almost evenly divided in its partisan preferences, the Tennessee electorate's voting habits encouraged office seekers of both parties to hold to the center of their party's ideological spectrum. Because election campaigns at the county and state levels were intensely partisan contests, their outcomes usually rested on arousing party spirit and getting party members to the polls, not on securing support from the small numbers of independent voters or on changing voters' party affiliations. The art of winning elections in Tennessee had become the artifice of avoiding divisive issues and at the same time exciting every member of the party to do his duty. In large measure the partisan mummery of the campaigns sought to innervate the faithful, not to convert the heathen. Stump speeches, torchlight parades, and newspaper propaganda changed the minds of but a few voters, for most party members knew their political arguments in great detail and often with as much sophistication as the candidates themselves. The decisive question in every poll was how many of each party would vote, and to that end party organizers staged mass rallies to reinforce the individual member's will to stand before the election judges and put his ticket in the box.

Voting in the early years of the young Republic was both a very personal and public act of familial pride. Sons generally voted for the party of their father and his father; and although party names might change from one generation to another, political perspectives passed intact from one generation to the next. Many younger voters traced their partisan inheritance back to their grandfathers and took great pride in affirming their family's political tradition. Political preferences, like those of religion, were more often than not questions of birth or marriage; backsliding generally proved more popular than converting to a new creed, particularly so if the lapse of faith could be redeemed in the next canvass by a happier choice of candidates.

Whigs in Tennessee could count themselves fortunate indeed that their party never nominated non-westerners for the presidency. The sectional distrust and conflict that regularly threatened to split the national Democratic coalition barely touched Polk's political adversaries, most of whom had left the Old Democracy in favor of the politics of moderation. By avoiding discussions of national issues Tennessee Whigs could concentrate on holding the middle ground in state elections and thereby could avert party schisms of the sort that had induced many Democrats to stay home on the past several election days. Martin Van Buren and James K. Polk were the two best friends against whom the Tennessee Whigs every campaigned.

Like so many young men of his day, Polk was born and bred to his partisan heritage. That he was dogmatic about his political convictions probably expressed something more of his temperament than his schooling. The content of his political creed closely followed that held by his grandfather, Ezekiel Polk, whose radical rejection of governmental control and religious conformity had led him to the Tennessee frontier. Like many radical partisans of the American Revolution, Ezekiel Polk never overcame his deep distrust of a strong general government; nor did his grandson, James K. Polk, who held to the same republican ideology with such tenacity that he devoted the whole of his adult life to the cause of diffusing political and economic power. Whether in office or not, Polk set aside the counsels of moderation, caution, and convenience, for Young Hickory was too self-disciplined, too self-righteous, and too self-willed to bend to the winds of political opportunism. He would defeat the Whigs on his own terms or not at all.

During his two years in the political wilderness Polk adopted a double-edged strategy for redeeming Tennessee and holding together the aging Jackson-Van Buren coalition. Political lieutenants throughout the state assumed that having come so close to reelection in 1841, Polk would run again for governor in the August 1843 election. His refusals to consider election to the U.S. Senate or solicit an appointment in John Tyler's

administration suggest that he wanted another chance at defeating the
Whigs of Tennessee. Of course, he could do no further combat in the
political arena until he had arranged his personal financial affairs, which
were greatly compromised by debts from his 1841 gubernatorial bid. To
that end he asked friends in Congress to secure loans and requested
agents in Tennessee to sell parts of his landholdings in the Western
District. In the summer of 1842 Polk traveled to Cincinnati, Washington
City, Philadelphia, and New York in search of cash loans as well as
currency of a more directly political nature. Financial pressures in the
money markets had not abated since the bank suspensions of late 1839;
Polk's loan applications met with failure in almost every quarter. He
likewise learned no more about Martin Van Buren's 1844 presidential
election plans than he had on the occasion of the ex-president's visit to
Columbia in early May. Polk had wanted assurances that if Van Buren
were nominated for president, he would insist that the convention settle
on a nominee for second place. In 1840 Van Buren had declined to name a
vice-presidential running mate; and the National Democratic Convention
had failed to make a selection for fear of dividing the party. As early as
1842 it was clear that Polk planned to run for governor in 1843 and for
vice-president in 1844; and no one had a more vital stake in Polk's success
than did Van Buren.

By the most deliberate of choices Polk continued to insist that Tennessee Democrats would conduct the 1843 campaign on national issues. He
did not wish to talk about James C. Jones' record as governor; nor did he
wish to promise economic recovery through governmental works projects. By focusing attention on federal questions Polk would identify himself and his state party with the Jackson-Van Buren coalition and its
return to power over the general government. The 1843 governor's race
would be run as a referendum on the 1844 presidential question. By
defeating the Tennessee Whigs, Polk would prove that Van Buren was
yet "available," that is, "electable," in a two-party, slave state. The example must be made, or Van Buren's standing must remain at the bottom
of the South's list of "available" candidates. In short, Van Buren's credi-
bility as a presidential candidate in 1844 rested largely on the question of
whether or not he could win in the South.

Polk's interest in running for second place on the party's 1844 ticket
involved political calculations of both state and national consequence. His
prospects for the vice-presidency could be used to maintain the loyalty of
the Tennessee Calhounites, whose votes in the 1843 state elections would
be needed and might be secured by holding out the possibility of an 1844
Calhoun-Polk ticket. Although party strategists understood that both
nominees could not come from slave states, the idea would appeal to
parochial prejudices, however improbable it might be. If Polk were to

carry Tennessee in 1843, he would render Van Buren's nomination all but certain and thereby demonstrate his own claims to a place on the ticket, not to mention future preferment. If Polk were to fail in his efforts to redeem Tennessee, he might yet through his vice-presidential bid so position himself as to become every faction's second choice for first place on the presidential ticket, should sectional divisions block the convention from making a choice. Above all other considerations, Polk needed to preserve the old Jackson-Van Buren coalition, for apart from it neither he nor any other leader of the party could hope to bridge the widening chasm of sectional jealousy and distrust. The one unavoidable risk assumed by Polk's strategy was that he and others loyal to Andy Jackson might lose control of the Tennessee Democracy should the Whigs win the state in the 1843 elections. He took that gamble; and had Van Buren's friends in the North financed Polk's third race for the governorship, they might have been more pleased with the results.

Although ostensibly at the close of his governorship Polk retired to private life and resumed the practice of law, he remained the working leader of the Tennessee Democracy. Of course, he would no longer give daily oversight to legislative and party affairs in Nashville, but he continued to offer a guiding hand in making major policy decisions. Unfortunately for his party the Whigs chose the legislative issues and labored successfully to force Democratic members into a corner on two important questions raised in the 1841–42 session. Playing on personal rivalries among the Democrats, the Whigs floated various unlikely compromise tickets for filling Tennessee's two vacant seats in the U.S. Senate. Frustrated by the threat to party unity, Democratic leaders in the upper house fell upon the unhappy expedient of arguing that the traditional mode of selecting senators in joint convention should be abandoned. Whig members answered the argument by turning the principle of majority rule against the Democrats, who could hardly deny the fact of Whig victories in the state elections of August 1841. With an equal measure of self-serving argumentation the thirteen Democratic members of the Tennessee Senate refused to investigate charges of fraud in the management of the Bank of Tennessee. Even worse, they declined to confirm the governor's appointments to the Bank's board of directors. The fraud charges had no basis in fact, but the rejection of Jones' appointments gave credence to more damning allegations of concealment and obstruction. Had not radical Democrats always opposed Whig programs for relief and improvements by raising the double phantom of minority rule through government corruption? The Whigs argued with great glee and some effect that the people need only turn the Democrats out of office to avert such spectral prophecies of republican doom.

Aware that obstructionist tactics might translate into Whig gains in

1843, Polk and his chief aides decided upon the strategy of securing conditional resignations from Democratic members of the legislature and challenging their Whig counterparts to do likewise. The resignation scheme would have required calling special legislative elections throughout the state to determine the electorate's specific wishes for ending the deadlock over choosing Tennessee's U.S. senators. Whig members countered the Democratic proposal with the argument that the previous year's elections had settled the question by giving their party a clear majority in the lower house and returning a Whig governor to office. The plebiscite plan went nowhere, and of necessity new stratagems surfaced when the legislature met in special session on October 3, 1842.

Tennessee's General Assembly gathered to consider legislation for the relief of debtors, to fill the state's two vacant seats in the U.S. Senate, and to draw new boundaries for legislative, senatorial, and congressional districts. Several experienced observers thought it unlikely that the legislature would agree on any measures, and predictions of an addled assembly came close to their mark. Majorities in both parties rejected banking and judicial schemes for easing credit and postponing foreclosures for nonpayment of debts. The "Immortal Thirteen" Democrats in the upper house refused to meet in convention with the Whig majority that controlled the lower house. Only on the redistricting questions could the arts of compromise be practiced with any concluding effects. The most efficient piece of management came in drawing off the congressional boundaries, and with a quick sleight of hand Andrew Johnson, chairman of the Senate congressional redistricting committee, gerrymandered three members of his own party out of their seats in Congress. By separating Abraham McClellan, Hopkins L. Turney, and Harvey M. Watterson from political alliances in neighboring counties, Johnson so arranged the new first and fifth districts as to facilitate congressional nominations for himself and his close friend, George W. Jones. Although Johnson and Jones both won their seats in Congress, the dislocation of incumbents occasioned severe intra-party fights in the new first, fourth, and fifth districts. The pattern for resolving those conflicts repeated itself in almost every instance: Van Burenites gave way to Calhounites for the sake of party unity and the hope of local and state victories.

As in previous state elections since 1835, Polk determined party strategy and directed party organizational efforts prior to the crucial canvass of 1843. Working in the Tennessee House through his brother, William H. Polk, and in the Senate through his closest confidant, Samuel H. Laughlin, the "retired" former governor arranged for the Democratic members of the special session of the legislature to hold a caucus and adopt a platform around which the party might unite. The resolves favored rigid economy in the general government and literal construction of the federal constitution; they denounced adoption of protective tariffs and internal improvements, creation of a national bank, distribution to the states of federal revenues from the sale of public lands, and provision for federal bankruptcy proceedings. Recounting the origins of the Whig party, these lengthy resolutions quoted a previous General Assembly's declarations alleging that in 1825 John Q. Adams and Henry Clay had made a corrupt bargain to steal the presidency; the platform then listed by name and current party affiliation those who had voted in 1827 to condemn Adams and Clay. The argument that many prominent Whigs initially had opposed the founders of their party was further supported by embarrassing quotations from letters written and published in 1827 by John Bell, then a strong supporter of Andrew Jackson. Taken together, the platform addressed national issues and called the party to unite against Henry Clay's election to the presidency. The caucus urged that Democrats hold their nominating convention six months earlier than usual and recommended that primary meetings be organized in each county to make plans for the 1843 elections. No mention was made of Polk's running for governor or for a place on the national ticket; however, the call for an early meeting in Baltimore passed for an informal endorsement of Van Buren, whose friends had taken that tack in several other states. Calhoun partisans discouraged the idea and held firm for a gathering of delegates in May of 1844.

Early in 1843 Polk launched new organizational efforts for promoting and financing party candidates in the forthcoming August elections. He used the Maury County Corresponding Committee as a model for building a more effective network of communications among party workers at the local and county levels. Within every civil district the county's corresponding committee would target and solicit prospective donors, identify by name and party preference each voter, and circulate campaign literature as might be generated locally or supplied by the Central Committee in Nashville. Polk urged the *Nashville Union* to publish a separate newspaper during the campaign, but projected costs proved prohibitive. Instead, the *Union* devoted its weekly edition to the state elections and offered it to subscribers at a special rate of $1 for those issues appearing between March 15 and election day. Having placed his party's election machinery in motion, Polk made his formal announcement for governor on February 10, 1843.

The 1843 gubernatorial campaign would take Polk and his opponent, James C. Jones, from the swamp lands of the Mississippi to the mountains of Carolina and Virginia. The candidates would debate in more than eighty counties during the four-month canvass, which opened on

March 24 in Springfield, a small village just north of Nashville. The schedule called for visits in the Western District before the onset of the summer heat and for appointments in the higher regions of East Tennessee during late June and July. Traveling by horseback in the morning hours, the candidates arrived at the speaking site by mid afternoon, debated for some five to six hours, dined with local politicians, attended to their correspondence, and retired late in the evening. The physical demands of riding and speaking, coupled with a chronic deficit of rest, rendered both men susceptible to recurring respiratory and intestinal complaints. Surviving the campaign with health intact represented something of a victory in its own right.

By the end of the first week of engagements either candidate could have made the other's speech, including anecdotes, hand gestures, and emphatic pauses. Smiling congenially through Jones' light-hearted discussion of serious issues, Polk tried relentlessly to expose the shallowness of Jones' facile explanations of complex questions. Only on rare occasions did Polk display his considerable talents for repartee and joke telling, skills that he had used so successfully against Newton B. Cannon in 1839. Whig newspaper editors proudly claimed that "Grinnin' Jimmy" Polk was but a poor match for "Slim Jimmy" Jones' power to entertain the large assemblies of fun-loving Tennesseans. Democratic polemicists generally decried Jones' showmanship and praised their candidate's definitive refutations of Whig doctrine and practice. As there were but few surprises in the daily rehearsal of this traveling debate, it must be assumed that the principals deliberately adopted and retained those roles that best served their election strategies. Polk probably played the straight man to his comic opponent because neither approach, nor any combination of the two, would have turned any large number of Tennesseans around in their opinions of Martin Van Buren. Perhaps Polk hoped to win an improbable victory; perhaps he did not. In any case, he changed neither the manner nor the substance of his oratory in his long journey to defeat.

Polk had made Henry Clay the straw man of his 1839 campaign for the governorship, and he did so again in 1843. At every opportunity, some ninety speeches in all, he pointed to Jones' open endorsement of Clay for the 1844 Whig presidential nomination and denounced the Sage of Ashland's projects for banking, taxing, and spending. A vote for Jones would be a vote for a national bank, a protective tariff, a larger federal debt, and a greater consolidation of power in the general government. Polk displayed the dreaded chains of tyranny at every stop and urged his hearers to free themselves from the lure of Whig promises to legislate the good life into existence. Unwilling to settle for a superficial statement on

Clay's measures, Polk detailed each piece of Whig legislation since 1841 and catalogued its most onerous provisions. Jones repelled Polk's arguments with barnyard humor and clever escapes to down-home issues. He hit hard at the obstructionist tactics of the "Immortal Thirteen," whose partisanship had prevented the election of U.S. senators, blocked examination of bank fraud charges, and denied appointment of new directors for the Bank of Tennessee. Jones demanded to know whom Polk would support for president in 1844; when Polk declined to make a public endorsement prior to the convention, Jones predicted that his opponent would be run for vice-president on a Van Buren ticket. Polk linked Jones to Clay, and Jones tied Polk to Van Buren. Thus the outcome of the race would rest largely on the size of the Democrat vote, for the Whigs were unified and the Democrats divided. Polk ran hard on his most vulnerable issue and lost.

Jones defeated Polk by a majority of 3,833 votes in an election that saw over 110,000 white adult males exercise their franchise. Although the Democrats held their ground in East Tennessee and registered small gains in the Western District, they failed to produce sufficiently large majorities in Middle Tennessee to carry the state at large. The General Assembly elections went against Polk's party as well, as the Whigs won control of both houses of the legislature. Only in the congressional results could Democrats take consolation, for in those races they won six of the eleven seats, a minimal gain considering that the Assembly would send two Whigs to the U.S. Senate. The Tennessee vote demonstrated rather convincingly that Van Buren could not carry the state in 1844 and that Tennessee Democrats must detach themselves from the Loco Foco influence if they would avoid future defeats.

Explanations and reactions to the Whig victory varied widely among Democratic leaders in Tennessee. On August 18 Polk wrote Van Buren that Tennessee Democrats had been "greatly embarrassed and weakened by local causes and questions of State policy." Polk labored with abandon to paint over all traces of the underlying causes of factional divisions in the Tennessee Democracy. Within weeks of the August election party newspapers in East Tennessee endorsed Lewis Cass of Michigan for president. Calhoun Democrats in Nashville organized a pro-Cass club that would appeal to younger voters impatient with the issues that had brought their party down. A. O. P. Nicholson, a Calhoun advocate of the Young Democracy, attempted to wrest control of the *Nashville Union* from the Van Buren wing of the party. Only by the strongest of exertions were Polk and his friends able to retain power over their most influential newspaper. The tide of disaffection crested in November at the state convention, which chose an anti-Van Buren slate of delegates to attend the presidential nominating convention. For most practical purposes the 1843 defeat had brought the Jackson party in Tennessee close to the edge of dissolution. All that remained of Jackson's influence rested with Polk's greatly embarrassed candidacy for the vice-presidential nomination. Incredulous that Tennessee Democrats might abandon the father of the Second Democracy, many Whig editors claimed that Polk had orchestrated the Cass movement in order to get Van Buren's attention and force his way onto the New Yorker's ticket. For his part, Van Buren wrote on December 27 that he viewed as "incomprehensible" Tennessee's rejection of its Jacksonian traditions, which had "within the last two or three years brought all the rest of the old Democratic States into their former, & true positions." Van Buren dryly concluded that "in good time" Polk must "seek out the cause and apply the remedy."

Polk's course of action in the fall of 1843 followed a narrowing channel of political choices that could not be widened or redirected. He turned his fullest attention to the task of making himself everyone's first choice for second place on the presidential ticket. Letters from the Hermitage and emissaries to party leaders in other states urged Polk's vice-presidential nomination. All factions of the party in Tennessee were asked to don this one remaining mask, behind which their divisions might be hidden. Several of Polk's closest advisors dared to hope that their efforts might place their friend in position to become everyone's second choice for first place on the national ticket. Inadvertently or otherwise, Polk's loss in Tennessee had enhanced Henry Clay's presidential prospects and diminished those of Martin Van Buren. In his defeat Polk had forced difficult questions of "availability," lost control of the Tennessee Democracy, and gained renown for his intrepid and uncompromising defense of political principles and alignments that would win but one more time the approval of the federal electorate.

This Volume

With this volume the reader will find one important addition to the series format. Fearful that diminished grant support might force suspension of the series, the editors have introduced a retrospective calendar of all Polk letters written from the earliest date, 1816, through the terminal year of the present installment, 1843. Entries for letters published or briefed in the series appear in *Italic* type and include only the documents' dates and addressees. Entries for unpublished letters appear in Roman type and include the documents' dates, addressees, classifications, repositories, and verbal précis. The use of brackets in the date column mark those elements supplied by the editors; the use of a question mark within a bracketed date indicates that some part or all of it is problematical. As in the assignment of captions to documents published or briefed, designations of addressees reflect the editors' styles of identification and not necessarily those of the signatories. Again, brackets signal an editorial hand in supplying information unstated in the documents. Letters, names, and subjects included in the calendar are indexed with the rubric *c* added to their page citations.

Continuing under the assumption that their primary responsibility is to assemble and make available the significant correspondence of James K. Polk, the editors have made no important changes in the editorial procedures adopted for the first five volumes. Selectivity has been necessary, but otherwise the editors have continued in their efforts to reproduce the correspondence in a form as faithful to the original text of each letter as possible; original spelling, punctuation, capitalization, and grammar have been preserved except where slight alterations have been required for the sake of clarity. Lowercase letters at the beginning of sentences have been converted to capitals. When it has been impossible at other places to determine whether the writer intended a capital or a lowercase letter, current style has been followed. Commas and semicolons have been inserted sparingly in sentences that lack clarity or are deficient in punctuation. Superfluous dashes have generally been deleted, and those that appear at the ends of sentences have been converted to appropriate punctuation marks. Words unintentionally repeated by the writers have been deleted. These minor changes have been made silently, without editorial indications of where they occur. Letters that were particularly difficult to decipher or those written by semiliterate persons have been given special attention, and that fact is indicated in the footnotes. Reliance on the ever-useful *sic* has been severely limited.

As all the letters printed are either to or from James K. Polk, his name will seldom be included in the headings that appear above the documents. Regardless of their position in the original manuscript, the salutation, provenance, and date will ordinarily appear on a single line just below the heading. Except in rare instances, complimentary closings have been omitted. An unnumbered note at the end of each letter or summary gives the document's classification, repository designation, place of address, authorial notations, endorsements, and notice of previous publication.

Numbered annotations follow the unnumbered note. Ordinarily a brief explanation or identification is given upon the first mention of a person or special subject. Later appearances of such persons or subjects are not usually accompanied by editorial comment. To identify everything is, of course, impossible; some items have been identified only tentatively. The editors thought that these tracings, however slight in some cases, might prove useful to the researcher. The names of some persons are marked "not identified further" either for want of sources of for lack of textual clarity as to which of two or more persons by the same name was intended. Unusual cases of the latter kind have been explained briefly. The index will be helpful in sorting references in which only a surname is given and in finding the location of the original explanation or identification.

The annotations often have been assembled from several sources. Frequently the sources are so obvious as to need no identification. These considerations, coupled with a desire to insure that the footnotes do not overwhelm the presentation of the textual material, have persuaded the editors to forego the citation of sources in footnotes.

Acknowledgments

In dedicating this sixth volume of the series to James F. Hopkins and Mary Wilma Hargreaves the editor respectfully celebrates the historical scholarship and professional dedication that his editorial mentors have brought to the first six volumes of *The Papers of Henry Clay*. Serving under their tutelege in the preparation of their fourth and fifth volumes provided invaluable opportunities for learning the purposes of their work as well as its erudition. That they gave more than they received in training their assistant attests to the depth of their concern for the future of our nation's program in historical editing, a commitment to which they have devoted a large part of their careers and of which this present Polk volume serves as letters testamentary.

It is again this editor's great pleasure to acknowledge the enormous contributions of those colleagues whose skills and labors have sustained the Polk Project through the last three years: Carese M. Parker, associate editor, has brought her critical insights and meticulous care to every page of this volume; research associates David W. Bowen, James P. Cooper, Jr., and Earl J. Smith have assisted, each for a year or more, in researching and annotating select portions of the correspondence; John H. Reinbold has worked parttime researching and bringing the note files up to date; and Leta R. Cutler, staff assistant, has seen the calendaring of documents through their several stages of composition and assembly.

Together we single out our collective thanks to the very able staffs of the Vanderbilt University Library, the Tennessee State Library and Archives, the National Archives and Records Service, and the Library of Congress. For their generous sponsorship of the Polk Project, special thanks go to members of the National Historical Publications and Records Commission and its staff, headed by Frank G. Burke; to members of the Tennessee Historical Commission and its staff, directed by Herbert L. Harper; and to members of the Polk Memorial Association and its Auxiliary. We also express our appreciation to the director of the Vanderbilt University Press, John W. Poindexter, and to members of his staff, Jane C. Tinsley and Gary G. Gore, for their continuing support of this series in matters of both production and distribution.

Perhaps our largest debt of gratitude belongs to the many friends of history who have urged public officials to sustain their commitment to the nation's cultural heritage. Countless expressions of public and private endorsement of the national and state programs in historical editing have encouraged the Polk editors to hold a steady course against the current drift of uncertain and inadequate funding for agency sponsors. To all who have spoken in behalf of the Polk Project, we extend these words of deep appreciation.

WAYNE CUTLER

Nashville, Tennessee
September 1982

CONTENTS

Contents

1843

Contents

SYMBOLS

Document Classification

AC	Autograph Circular
ACI	Autograph Circular Initialed
ACS	Autograph Circular Signed
AD	Autograph Document
ADI	Autograph Document Initialed
ADS	Autograph Document Signed
AE	Autograph Endorsement
AEI	Autograph Endorsement Initialed
AES	Autograph Endorsement Signed
AL	Autograph Letter
AL, draft	Autograph Letter, drafted by writer
AL, fragment	Autograph Letter, fragment
ALI	Autograph Letter Initialed
ALS	Autograph Letter Signed
ALS, copy	Autograph Letter Signed, copied by writer
ALS, draft	Autograph Letter Signed, drafted by writer
ALsS	Autograph Letters Signed
AN	Autograph Note
ANI	Autograph Note Initialed
ANS	Autograph Note Signed
C, copy	Circular, penned by person other than the writer; authorship attributed
CI	Circular Initialed
CS	Circular Signed
D, copy	Document, penned by person other than the writer, authorship attributed
DI	Document Initialed
DS	Document Signed

E	Endorsement, penned by person other than the recipient
EI	Endorsement Initialed
ES	Endorsement Signed
L, copy	Letter, penned by person other than the writer; authorship attributed
LI	Letter Initialed
LS	Letter Signed
N, copy	Note, penned by person other than the writer; authorship attributed
NI	Note Initialed
NS	Note Signed
PL	Published Letter; authorship attributed
Pvt Ms	Private Manuscript

Repository Designations

CSmH	Henry E. Huntington Library, San Marino
DLC–AJ	Library of Congress, Andrew Jackson Papers
DLC–AJD	Library of Congress, Andrew Jackson Donelson Papers
DLC–GW	Library of Congress, Gideon Welles Papers
DLC–HC	Library of Congress, Henry Clay Papers
DLC–JKP	Library of Congress, James K. Polk Papers
DLC–Johnson	Library of Congress, Andrew Johnson Papers
DLC–LW	Library of Congress, Levi Woodbury Papers
DLC–Misc. Coll.	Library of Congress, Miscellaneous Collections
DLC–MVB	Library of Congress, Martin Van Buren Papers
DNA–RG 15	National Archives, Records of the Veterans Administration
DNA–RG 28	National Archives, Records of the Post Office Department
DNA–RG 42	National Archives, Records of the Office of Public Buildings and Grounds
DNA–RG 45	National Archives, Naval Records Collection of the Office of Naval Records and Library
DNA–RG 46	National Archives, Records of the United States Senate
DNA–RG 49	National Archives, Records of the Bureau of Land Management
DNA–RG 56	National Archives, General Records of the Department of the Treasury

DNA–RG 59	National Archives, General Records of the Department of State
DNA–RG 60	National Archives, General Records of the Department of Justice
DNA–RG 75	National Archives, Records of the Bureau of Indian Affairs
DNA–RG 77	National Archives, Records of the Office of the Chief of Engineers
DNA–RG 92	National Archives, Records of the Office of the Quartermaster General
DNA–RG 94	National Archives, Records of the Adjutant General's Office, 1780–1917
DNA–RG 99	National Archives, Records of the Office of the Paymaster General
DNA–RG 107	National Archives, Records of the Office of the Secretary of War
DNA–RG 156	National Archives, Records of the Office of the Chief of Ordinance
DNA–RG 217	National Archives, Records of the United States General Accounting Office
Ia-HA	Iowa State Department of History and Archives, Des Moines
ICHi	Chicago Historical Society
KyLoF	Filson Club, Louisville
MHi	Massachusetts Historical Society, Boston
NcU	University of North Carolina, Chapel Hill
NHi	New-York Historical Society, New York
NjMoHP–LWS	Morristown National Historical Park, L. W. Smith Collection
NjP	Princeton University
NN–Kohns	New York Public Library, Kohns Collection
T–ARW	Tennessee State Library, A. R. Wynne Family Papers
T–GP	Tennessee State Library, Governor's Papers
T–JPH	Tennessee State Library, John P. Heiss Papers
T–JKP	Tennessee State Library, James K. Polk Papers
T–RG 5	Tennessee State Library, Internal Improvements Papers
T–RG 80	Tennessee State Library, Secretary of State's Papers
WHi	State Historical Society of Wisconsin, Madison

Published Sources
  ETHSP   *East Tennessee Historical Society's Publication*
  NCHR   *North Carolina Historical Review*
  THM   *Tennessee Historical Magazine*
  THQ   *Tennessee Historical Quarterly*

CHRONOLOGY

1795	November 2	Born in Mecklenburg County, North Carolina
1806	Fall	Moved to Maury County, Tennessee
1812	Fall	Underwent major surgery by Dr. Ephraim McDowell in Danville, Kentucky
1813	July	Began study under Robert Henderson at Zion Church Academy
1816	January	Entered University of North Carolina as a sophomore
1818	June	Graduated from University of North Carolina
	Fall	Began reading law in office of Felix Grundy
1819	September	Elected clerk of the senate of Tennessee General Assembly
1820	June	Admitted to the bar
1823	August	Elected to the lower house of Tennessee General Assembly
1824	January 1	Married to Sarah Childress of Murfreesboro
1825	August	Elected to United States House of Representatives
1827	August	Reelected to House of Representatives
	November 5	Death of his father, Samuel Polk
1829	August	Reelected to House of Representatives
1831	January 21	Death of his brother Franklin, aged 28
	April 12	Death of his brother Marshall, aged 26
	August	Reelected to House of Representatives
	September 28	Death of his brother John, aged 24
1833	August	Reelected to House of Representatives
	December	Became chairman, Ways and Means Committee
1834	June	Defeated by John Bell for Speaker of the House

1835	August	Reelected to House of Representatives
	December 7	Elected Speaker of the House over John Bell
1836	August 6	Death of his sister Naomi, wife of Adlai O. Harris
1837	August	Reelected to House of Representatives
	September 4	Reelected Speaker of the House
1839	August	Elected Governor of Tennessee over Newton Cannon
1841	August	Defeated in gubernatorial election by James C. Jones
1843	August	Defeated in gubernatorial election by James C. Jones
1844	May	Nominated for the presidency at Democratic National Convention
	November	Elected President of the United States over Henry Clay
1845	March 4	Inaugurated as President of the United States
1849	March 4	Yielded office to his successor, Zachary Taylor
	June 15	Died in Nashville

Correspondence of James K. Polk

VOLUME VI, 1842–1843

1842

FROM JOHN CATRON[1]

Dr Sir: Washington, Jny. 2d 1842

I have been here two weeks and learned very little else than you have heard through the newspapers, other than this, as I think, that say, Benton, Buchanan, Calhoun, and a few minor men, have taken ground against Mr. Foward's Treasury-Bank project, & pretty much against every part of it.[2] Why they did not let the Whigs lead off, they best know. The rank & file, I feel well assured thought differently to a great extent, and you are aware, that my opinion for five years has been, that amongst that rank & file were our safest thinkers, if they were allowed to think. My friend, I am no prophet. Still I'll hazzard the opinion, that if the Dem. party aid the Whigs in breaking down Mr Tyler, and drive to the old Whig set, the Tyler Whigs, we will again be beaten for the Presidency: and 2d, if our party, rejects all plans of a Bank, or Fiscal agent, and attempts to fight the Bank party with *nothing*, or with the *memory*, of that defunct shadow, the Sub-Treasury (a feeble thing, never felt by the People, known, nor cared for)[3] we shall again have a triumphant Bank party in power, and in four years we will have a U.S. Bank of the old stamp. The large majority of the American People look for somthing; and if the Democratick party could agree to a Fiscal Bank, pretty much as Mr Tyler, & the Secy. of T. recommend, striking off the Bill of exchange feature,[4] of course, and do Battle on it against a U.S. Bank, I feel very sure, we would be safe. The circulation of Treasury checks is not obnoxious to the Constitution, nor fraught with any danger of a serious character, as it seems to me and they would furnish a satisfactory circulation, of equal value everywhere, and one that would be felt, & recognized by the People as National, and one that a U.S. Bank would not be allowed to supplant. A *forestalling* substitute, is what we want, & I think must have, as a *repelling* force. To Tennessee friends I may talk plainly, without being suspected of Bank tendencies. The idea, of uniting purse & sword, is an absurd scare-crow. The *people* at large cannot keep the money—their agents must—and Human agents must be trusted: and where they are Subject to Congress, to the People, for Congress is the people, in this regard there can be as little danger of abuse, as there is in the Custom Houses, land offices &c. It is the best that can be done. The Whig party hold, that the money of the Nation cannot be entrusted to the hands of the Executive, or the agents of the Governmt, but should be kept by a private Corporation, distinct from the Executive, & Congress. In short, that the people dare not be trusted with their own money, nor its management in the Treasury. Such a distinct Treasury the Whigs offer. We offer *nothing* & with this nothing, set up to fight a system well understood & which will be taken, unless something else as a substitute is offered. That substitute must furnish a circulating Government *paper*; specie we have not, nor can we create it, nor draw it from the State Banks, nor could we circulate it over our wide-spread country if we had it. Paper we must have, & a paper backed with the credit of the U.S.; nor will less than fifteen millions answer. Less, would not be felt; & more would be useful, if the deposites of individuals, & the revenue should furnish a basis for the circulation.

I think the plan should be tested by a trial, and reformed, if it does not answer. Of one thing there can be no doubt, something should be done; nay, something *must be* done, or a U.S. Bank is the consequence.

The hard money plan is a Theory, & deemed a feeble, & exploded theory, by the People. It cannot longer be a principle of successful action by the Democratick party: Theory can never with numbers, be a principle of *continued* action. It is sapped by langour, & will fade into contempt, because it is an empty nothing in practice, and common-sense is asked to steadily to pursue a shadow, and *firmly* to maintain—*nothing*! This is indisputably, our present position; and the question for our friends to solve is, will they change their position? Mr. Tyler invites the trial, and submits himself to any change of the plan he proposes, that Congress may deem adviseable; & within limits that the democratick party would of course not transcend.[5] I am often asked, "What Sort of a party is this of yours, that rejects all plans of a fiscal agent, and offers none for itself?" A question so pertinent, & so withering, is unanswerable, unless we fall-back on the Sub-Treasury plan, and found ourselves on that infant scheme buried in its swaddling clothes, & if reproduced, would again die on our hands, & we again be laughed at, as idle dreamers: Can any thinking man doubt it?

Of one thing I have no doubt, the party that originates a Treasury

Bank (I will so call it, for such it must in a degree be) and founds itself on such a Bank, with a paper circulation of 15 millions, or more, will scatter to the winds the old U.S. Bank party, & will maintain itself with ease, and with credit before the People. A U.S. Bank they do not want (I mean the agricultural majority), but a substitute they will if possible have and ardently desire, not, at the hands of the Whigs, but furnished by their own natural friends, the democrats. And if these do not act, apathy, and eventual dispair, will overcome the sparse, & undisciplined majority; they will pursue the plough in peace, & let the Cities & Towns act, & Set up a U.S. Bank. Do you doubt it? A Treasury Bank may be an evil if you please. I dont think so, but it will resist a greater evil, and may be, the only means; it is, certainly an appropriate means, and one within our reach.

You know how I dislike extremes, how dangerous they are, we have learned, & the other side has learned, during the past summer. A moderate plan, & a *strong* plan, can be moulded out of Mr. Tyler's proposition. I pray you to think of it. But remember, our choice is, between *something*, & *nothing*.

Our Senators. On this subject, you know my opinion is, that the election in the ordinary form by convention should be gone into risking the consequences if no better could be done,[6] 2d, that a whig & democrat should be elected if possible & this is all that is possible, & 3d, that Tom Brown & Foster[7] be taken if this is the alternative, & I supposed such to be the fact when I left.

It would be very bad, for our friends to be thrown off, in the great contest in Augt 1843,[8] from the issues the calld. session of Congress furnished,[9] & to battle over the new issue of senators, or no senators from Tennessee. Who can support the new theory, that an election by joint ballot is unconstitutional? The assumption is nonsense, and the ground that Mr. Foster refused [to] answer questions, to 13 senators is one of no force;[10] certainly wholly unfit for a party to rest itself upon. I have not conversed with a single man of our friends who resided out of Tennessee, that did not feel sorely aggrieved, and alarmed at the position of our friends in the Senate. They all urge an election at any hazzard.

J. CATRON

ALS. DLC–JKP. Addressed to Columbia under the frank of Aaron V. Brown.

1. A strong political ally of Polk, Catron was appointed to the U.S. Supreme Court in the last days of the Jackson administration. A Tennessean, Catron helped the *Nashville Union* financially and served occasionally as an editorial writer.

2. Thomas Hart Benton, James Buchanan, John C. Calhoun, and Walter

Forward. Forward, a lawyer from Pennsylvania and former member of the U.S. House, 1822–25, headed the Treasury Department for almost two years, 1841–43; he frequently differed with President John Tyler in political and economic affairs. The administration's "Treasury-Bank" plan, submitted by Forward on December 21, 1841, called for the establishment of a Board of Exchequer at Washington City with agencies at important commercial centers as Congress might direct. Public creditors would hold the option of receiving payment in Treasury notes or in specie; note issues in excess of $15 million would be made only with specific legislative sanction; and notes would be convertible to specie only at their place of issue. The board and its agencies would receive private deposits of specie, issue certificates of deposit thereon, and sell domestic bills of deposit, redeemable at the place of issue. For additional details, see House Document No. 20, 27 Congress, 2 Session.

3. Proposed first by President Martin Van Buren in 1837, the Independent Treasury plan for excluding the banking industry from custody and management of U.S. Treasury funds became law on July 4, 1840. Whigs and Conservative Democrats combined in Congress to repeal the Independent Treasury by Act of August 13, 1841.

4. Section 11 of Forward's draft authorized the Board of Exchequer and its agencies to purchase and sell domestic bills of exchange; however, neither the Board nor the agencies could deal in discounts or accommodations.

5. Forward indicated in a cover letter transmitting his Exchequer proposal to Congress that the president would accept revision of the details, though not the general outline of the plan.

6. Tennessee's two seats in the U.S. Senate went unfilled for the period from February 7, 1842, until October 16, 1843. The "Immortal Thirteen" Democratic members of the Tennessee Senate held a majority in that branch of the 1841–42 General Assembly and refused to hold a joint election convention with the Whig-controlled House of Representatives. Knowing that on a joint vote two Whigs would be chosen, the "Immortal Thirteen" argued that the traditional joint-convention method of electing U.S. senators was unconstitutional and that a concurrent majority in both houses was required for election.

7. Thomas Brown and Ephraim H. Foster. Brown represented Roane County for two terms in the Tennessee House, 1817–19 and 1821–23; in 1839 he failed to win the Whig nomination in Tennessee's Fourth Congressional District. A Nashville lawyer and one of the founders of the Whig party in Tennessee, Foster served three terms in the Tennessee House, 1827–31 and 1835–37. Appointed to the U.S. Senate following the resignation of Felix Grundy in 1838, Foster won election to a full six-year term beginning March 4, 1839. Having pledged to resign should a Democratic majority be elected to the next legislature, he redeemed his promise in November of 1839.

8. Tennesseans would elect a new governor and a new legislature in August of 1843.

9. Controversial issues arising during the called session of the Twenty-seventh Congress, held in the summer of 1841, included the expense of the extra session itself, creation of a national bank, distribution of land-sale revenues,

preemption rights on public lands, and provision for bankruptcy proceedings in federal courts.

10. Democrats in the Tennessee Senate addressed a circular letter to the several U.S. senatorial candidates and requested their views on the principal issues raised at the special session of the Twenty-seventh Congress. The "Immortal Thirteen" specifically inquired if the candidate admitted the right of the legislature to instruct U.S. senators.

FROM HOPKINS L. TURNEY[1]

Washington City. January 2, 1842

Turney states that he has learned of a Whig scheme, devised in the spring of 1841, to prevent at that time the election of U.S. senators from Tennessee. Nicholson had informed Brown[2] late last spring that the Whigs would not attend a special session of the legislature, should one be called to provide senatorial representation in the called session of Congress. Turney adds that he is willing to yield his election to any other "Good & True democrat," but that "N. is not that man."

ALS. DLC–JKP. Addressed to Columbia.

1. A lawyer from Winchester, Turney served four terms in the Tennessee House, 1825–37; three in the U.S. House; 1837–43; and one in the U.S. Senate, 1845–51. He was Polk's political friend and spokesman in the Mountain District.

2. Aaron V. Brown and A. O. P. Nicholson. A resident of Pulaski, Brown was Polk's former law partner and longtime friend. He served in the Tennessee Senate and House, 1821–33, in the U.S. House, 1839–45, and in the governorship, 1845–47. From 1857 until his death in 1859, Brown was postmaster general in the administration of James Buchanan. A Democratic member of the Tennessee House from Maury County, 1833–37, and of the Tennessee Senate, 1843–45, Nicholson served an interim appointment in the U.S. Senate from December 1840 until February 1842. He moved to Nashville in 1844 and edited the *Nashville Union* before being named president of the Bank of Tennessee, 1846–47.

TO ANDREW JACKSON DONELSON[1]

My Dear Sir: Columbia Jany. 4 1842

I addressed a letter to Genl. Jackson on yesterday,[2] accompanied with the copy [of] one written by him to me in February 1838.[3] My letter to him will explain its own object; I think it probable that he may desire your assistance in preparing his answer. In that event I wish you to note the suggestions contained in my *private letter* to him,[4] which accompanied the one designed to call him out.[5] He will I have no doubt show them both to you.[6]

I see that his opinions continue to be quoted in favour of a *Bank of some kind,* and as I have said to him, I think it due to his own future fame, as well as to his principles, that he should while living put an end to all cavil or doubt in regard to them. It is the more especially necessary that he should do so now, because I see it insisted upon in some of the newspapers, that the Bank he suggested in some of his messages, was similar to Mr Tyler's Exchequer Bank.

I hope you will assist him in preparing his answer. It should be done with studied care.

JAMES K. POLK

ALS. DLC–AJD. Addressed to Nashville and marked *"Private."*
1. A nephew of Rachel Jackson, Donelson served as private secretary to Andrew Jackson while he was president, 1829–37. Donelson later guided negotiations for the annexation of Texas and was minister to Prussia.
2. Letter not found.
3. See Andrew Jackson to Polk, February 1, 1838.
4. Letter not found.
5. See Polk to Jackson, December 31, 1841.
6. On January 7, 1842, Jackson wrote that he had received Polk's three letters and would attend to them as soon as his own health would permit. ALS. DLC–JKP.

FROM WILLIAM H. POLK[1]

Dear Sir—   Nashville Tennessee Jan'y 6th 1842
The resolutions as introduced in the Senate by Mr. Laughlin electing Hopkins L Turney & Thomas Brown United States Senators,[2] come up for consideration in the House on yesterday. They were voted down. The resolutions were divided, and by that means we forced the Whigs to vote down the distinct proposition for *compromise.* On the Resolution nominating or electing Turney, the whole *Party* stood firm; but on the Resolution selecting Brown, three of the Democrats *bolted.* Rogers & Reece of Lincoln and Oglesby of Overton,[3] and I regret to say that Col. Dew[4] compromised the character of the democrats of Old Maury, by running out of the House and thereby *dodgeing* the question. He returned into the Hall as soon as the vote was anounced by the Speaker.[5] I moved that he have leave to record his vote. He declined, stating that his object in leaving the House was *to avoid voting.* There can be no difficulty in understanding the *influence* which opperated on him.

The Whigs to day when the Resolution was taken up, to go into the election of Comptroller and Treasurer, inserted an amendment, as was anticipated to elect United States Senators—which Resolution passed in its amended form. No difficulty is anticipated, with regard to the action on the part of the Senate. They will strike out the provision relating to U.S. Senators, and concur in the Resolution as originally introduced in the House. Our whole object is, to place them in the position of refusing to elect State officers, necessary and essential, to the proper administration of our State Government, because we prevent them from placing in the Senate men who stand *Mum*, virtually controverting and denying the right of the people to know the opinions and political *views* of their public servants. They will stand in the *indefensable* attitude, of having cloged the wheels, and prevented the necessary opperation of our State Government, because we would not passively surrender up the *rights* of the people, by *permitting* the election of Foster and Jarnigin.[6] If we can succeed in placing them in this light before the country our conquest will be easy. I will write you again in a fiew days.

WILLIAM H. POLK

ALS. DLC–JKP. Addressed to Columbia.

1. The only surviving brother of James K. Polk, William H. Polk practiced law in Columbia and served three terms in the Tennessee House, 1841–45 and 1857–59, and one term in the U.S. House, 1851–53. Young Polk went to Naples for two years as U.S. minister to that court, 1845–47; and he fought with the rank of major in the Mexican War.

2. Samuel H. Laughlin, a McMinnville lawyer and farmer, served three terms as a Democrat in the Tennessee Senate, 1839–45. On December 20, 1841, Laughlin introduced in the Tennessee Senate resolutions that the legislature should choose two U.S. senators and that those senators should be Hopkins L. Turney and Thomas Brown. The resolutions passed in the Senate on December 31, 1841, but failed in the House on January 5, 1842.

3. John C. Rogers, Joel L. Reece, and Hardin P. Oglesby. A Lincoln County lawyer and Democrat, Rogers served a single term in the Tennessee House, 1841–43. Reece, a Lincoln County farmer, served one term as a Democrat in the Tennessee House, 1841–43. Oglesby represented Overton County as a Democrat for a single term in the Tennessee House, 1841–43; he won election as sheriff of Overton County in 1844.

4. John H. Dew, a Wilson County lawyer, served as a Democrat in the Tennessee House, 1831–35; he moved to Columbia in 1836 and represented Maury County for one term in the House, 1841–43. Dew staunchly supported A. O. P. Nicholson's senatorial bid in the 1841–42 General Assembly.

5. Burchett Douglass represented Wilson County for four terms in the Tennessee House during the period from 1821 to 1833; after moving to Fayette County, he won two additional terms in the House, over which he presided when that body was controlled by Whigs, 1837–39 and 1841–43. Douglass also headed

the Somerville branch of the Bank of Tennessee and served as a Whig presidential elector in 1840.

6. Ephraim H. Foster and Spencer Jarnagin. Jarnagin studied law under Hugh L. White and practiced in Knoxville until 1837, when he removed to Athens, McMinn County, and became a leader of the Whig party. A Whig presidential elector in 1840, Jarnagin failed in his efforts to win a seat in the U.S. Senate in 1841. Two years later, however, the legislature elected him to that body; and he served from 1843 until 1847.

FROM JOHN H. DEW

Nashville, Tennessee. January 10, 1842

Dew reports that on January 8 the House voted 37 to 34 in favor of resolutions requiring the resumption of specie payments by the three stock banks and the Bank of Tennessee.[1] He predicts that these banks will resume without a court contest. Dew notes that on January 7 the House rejected the tippling bill because some of the repealers "would not agree to such an increase of tax . . . as would satisfy the party that were called modifiers. Consequently the modifiers united with the *anti* repealers." [2] Dew considers both House votes to be important victories. Also the House rejected a Senate resolution "choosing" Turney and Brown for the U.S. Senate.[3] Turney's defeat came on a strict party vote. Dew adds that he and several other Democrats opposed Brown because they had promised constituents not to vote for a Whig.

ALS. DLC–JKP. Addressed to Columbia and delivered by William H. Polk.

1. On December 28, 1841, Dew introduced a set of five resolutions aimed at forcing the resumption of specie payments by the state's three stock banks, the Union Bank, the Planters' Bank, and the Farmers and Merchants' Bank. The Internal Improvements Act of 1838 established the Bank of Tennessee and made it the government's agency for issuing some $4 million in internal improvements bonds; the first one-hundred thousand dollars in annual bank profits would go to the support of the state's common schools.

2. The 1842 House liquor bill, sponsored by Democrat Hugh L. W. Hill of Warren County, would have repealed an 1838 ban on retailing liquor by the drink and revived the acts of 1831 and 1835, which had provided for the taxing of liquor sales and licensing of saloons, commonly known as tippling houses. Radical "wets" amended Hill's proposal by removing all sales taxes on liquor produced in Tennessee; that provision led the "modifiers" to unite with anti-repealers who favored keeping the 1838 quart law, so called because it prohibited the retailing of liquor in quantities of less than a quart.

3. See John Catron to Polk, January 2, 1842, and William H. Polk to Polk, January 6, 1842.

FROM J. GEORGE HARRIS[1]

My Dear Sir,   Nashville [Jan.][2] 11. 1842

I have just opened and read yours of the 7th inst.[3]—and notwithstanding the weakness of my right arm occasioned by a lancet-letting of nearly a quart of blood within the last three hours, hasten to reply. You were right, of course in attributing the non-receipt of the Union[4] to the inadvertency of the clerk. He will forward back-numbers.

Yes; all our attempts to elect U. S. Senators have failed, and at present I see no light in prospect.[5] We ought to be represented, if possible—we ought at all hazards to elect men who will obey or resign. If I have religious devotion to any one principle of right, it is to that of the representative's unqualified accountability to his constituents.

A proposition has been secretly made by Bell's[6] friends, of which no doubt you are privately apprised. But it calls for too great a sacrifice of feeling. Perhaps you may not think so; at all events I give it you in confidence as it came to me—and respectfully ask your opinion at length.

Bell, through his friends (the delegations of Wilson and Rutherford) *intimates* that if the democrats will join them in electing him to the Senate, he will answer all the questions, and his friends will vote for any democrat in the State that the democrats may agree to run. This is the proposition as I understand it.

Now what are the considerations? We have a battle to fight next year for Governor. We can beat them—but be assured they are not intending to suffer it to go by default. The Senatorial Question is to be met on the stump. If we could now settle it by compromise, the question of itself falls, and the State is represented by one demo. & one whig, elected by the demo. party and a fraction only of the whigs. Thereby Foster is not only dead but forgotten. But this putting Bell in the foreground—*there's* the rub. Yet cannot we *match* him with an equal—and by elevating him *under the promise to obey*, shall we not increase our power to instruct him out? If *you* could only be his checkmate in the U. S. Senate, I should not fear him. I have received this through a private source and upon hearing it gave no opinion—for while I saw that many points could be made by us in acceding, still the price seems to be almost too high to pay. What do you think.

You will see that the Banks have been haltered up to law at last[7]—and I rejoice at it. No measure of our party in the legislature will prove more popular before the people.

The old hero[8] was here a day or two ago, and spent twenty-four hours in town. He was in high spirits. He gives a *Bear Dinner* to a few friends to-morrow, to which I have an invitation and shall attend. Gen Armstrong[9] & family go up.

Nothing doing in the House to-day. Dew is making a speech against note-shavers.

J. GEO. HARRIS

ALS. DLC–JKP. Addressed to Columbia and postmarked January 11.

1. A staunch New England Democrat, Harris had been associated with the New London *Political Observer* (Conn.), the *New Bedford Daily Gazette* (Mass.), the Boston *Bay State Democrat*, and the Boston *Morning Post* before assuming the editorship of the *Nashville Union* on February 1, 1839.

2. Erroneously dated "Dec. 11. 1842."

3. Letter not found.

4. Started in 1835 by Medicus A. Long, the *Nashville Union* was Tennessee's leading Democratic newspaper.

5. See John Catron to Polk, January 2, 1842, and William H. Polk to Polk, January 6, 1842.

6. John Bell of Tennessee.

7. See John H. Dew to Polk, January 10, 1842.

8. Andrew Jackson.

9. Robert Armstrong served as Nashville's postmaster from 1829 until 1845. An unsuccessful candidate for governor in 1837, he remained politically active and coordinated Polk's three gubernatorial campaigns. An officer in the War of 1812, Armstrong commanded a brigade of Tennessee militia in the Second Seminole War.

FROM JAMES WALKER[1]

Dear Sir,   Nashville Jany 13. 1842

I have seen Armstrong, Laughlin & Hardwicke[2] upon the matter we talked of. I find the Democrats will in no *way or shape* take up Bell[3]— they say it would be rewarding apostacy, and whitewashing the traitor who has caused all the trouble in Tennessee politics. In all this I heartily concur, and am satisfied that it is better to make no election than to take Bell under any circumstances. This is my feeling and judgement as to our political interests.

I find there is also a very great aversion to taking Foster under any circumstances, and it will be very difficult to induce the Democracy to agree to that compromise, even if he agrees to answer[4] & the election to be by concurrent vote. There is more difficulty on this subject than I apprehended. Laughlin talks about the impossibility of giving up

Turney—to this I replied hold on to Turney, if he is most satisfactory to our party.

I have not, nor will I use, or allow your name to be used, unless it can be done without in the least compromising you. The matter is very uncertain. Make no calculations on it. It is more than probable that no election will take place. I will however stay here several days, be governed by circumstances, and move as prudently as my judgement may dictate.

JAMES WALKER

ALS. DLC–JKP. Addressed to Columbia.
1. Walker, a prosperous Columbia businessman, was Polk's brother-in-law, the husband of Jane Maria Polk Walker.
2. Robert Armstrong, Samuel H. Laughlin, and Jonathan P. Hardwicke. A tavern keeper in Dickson County, Hardwicke served as a Democrat in the Tennessee Senate from 1837 until 1843.
3. See J. George Harris to Polk, January 11, 1842.
4. Reference is to Ephraim H. Foster's refusal to answer interrogatories submitted to the several candidates for election to the U.S. Senate by the Tennessee legislature. See J. George Harris to Polk, December 13, 1841.

TO SACKFIELD MACLIN[1]

My Dear Sir.   Columbia Jany. 17th 1842

I learned some days ago that overtures had been made by some of the friends of *Mr Bell*, to compromise the Senatorial question by electing him (Bell) and any Democrat who might be offered, and *in any mode* which might be preferred.[2] I am glad to learn that it met with no favour from our friends. It would not do to elect *Bell* by Democratic votes. It would not only be placing him in a position to do mischief but it would be rewarding his apostacy. This evening I learn that similar overtures have been made by some of Mr Foster's friends, and if this be so, it is a grave question what ought to be done. To no man in the State would it be more grating, than to myself, to be driven to the necessity of making a compromise by which he might obtain a seat in the Senate, and yet it is not impossible that our *safety as a party* in the State might require such a sacrafice. Having long since withdrawn any use of *my name & being wholly out of the question*, you will of course understand me as speaking solely in reference to our future ascendancy in the State, and without the slightest reference to myself personally. It would be a bitter pill to take *Mr F*. even upon a compromise, and yet if nothing else can be done I have been brought very seriously to doubt, whether we had not better take him with *some good & true Democrat* than to leave the State unrepresented in the Senate, & thus raise up a perplexing and troublesome issue *of Senators or no Senators* in the State, which may and probably will be the test question in our elections in 1843. Before you could compromise at all, either with him or any other *Whig*, they must yield to *your mode of election & agree to obey instructions*. If they will do this and agree to give us a Democratic Senator with him, my conviction is, that it is the course of safety to yield to it. I have no doubt if you adjourn without choosing, that a decided majority of our party will sustain you in the course you have taken: still *I know some* and fear there may be others who will not. It would be most unfortunate if by our divisions upon this local issue, when we are perfectly safe on the Federal issues of the Extra Session,[3] we should be overwhelmed in the State in 1843. *A small fragment* of our party, seceeding on this question & uniting with the Whigs would affect our overthrow. If a compromise is affected by which the *Whigs* choose their favourate candidate from the Middle Division of the State, then according to former usage, the Democratic candidate should come from *East Tennessee*. It would break down either party who would disturb this usage. If *both parties*, upon a compromise unite, for the time being in *breaking down the mountain* such would not be the effect. We have in East Tennessee among others *John Blair*, *Andrew Johnson* of your Senate, *Dr. Ramsey* & *Dr Lide* of Athens, either of whom would make respectable Senators.[4] If both Senators are taken from Middle Tennessee, then I think after what has occurred that the Democratic party are bound by every honorary tie to *Mr Turney*. It is *true* that he often said to me before he left & so has written since, that if the success or good of the party required it, he would cheerfully yield to any other *good & true Democrat*. He always made an exception of one man & has so written since. He does not regard Mr. N.[5] as being with us *in heart*, or further than it is his personal interest to be. He frankly declares that he would consider himself degraded and badly treated by his party, to be dropped for such a man as *N*. You know I agree with him in his opinion of *N*. and of his true position. Every day convinces me more and more, that he (N) is now travelling in the broad road, that *John Bell* travelled for several years before his apostacy, whilst he was making *loud professions* of his adhesion to our principles. We all know where *John Bell* now is. *And mark what I now say to you*, that five years, perhaps not one will pass, before he is found where *Bell* now is unless it shall be his personal interest shall make him *seem* to be otherwise. *I am not mistaken*. I speak from no personal or indignant feeling. I would prefer to day, an open opponent, to a hypocritical friend in disguise. Under no circumstances therefore would I compromise on *him*. I hope our friends may not be so far deceived as to think of such a thing for a moment.

I write you frankly and without reserve. My opinion is, that the course of safety is to choose Senators, provided you can do it, without a compromise of our principles or an abandonment, of the ground which the Democratic Senators have taken. God grant you a safe deliverance. When will your session close? Write to me.[6]

JAMES K. POLK

ALS. DLC–Johnson. Addressed to Nashville and marked *"Confidential."*
1. A Democrat, Maclin represented Fayette, Hardeman, and Shelby counties in the Tennessee Senate, 1841–43.
2. See J. George Harris to Polk, January 11, 1842.
3. See John Catron to Polk, January 2, 1842.
4. John Blair, Andrew Johnson, James G. M. Ramsey,and John W. Lide. A merchant, manufacturer, and lawyer in Washington County, Blair served as a Democrat in the U.S. House from 1823 until 1835; he lost his bid for reelection in 1834 to William B. Carter. Blair subsequently sat for one term in the Tennessee House, 1849–51. Johnson, seventeenth President of the United States, served one term in the Tennessee Senate, 1841–43. Knoxville physician, railroad promoter, and banker, Ramsey wrote one of the early landmarks in Tennessee historiography, *The Annals of Tennessee to the End of the Eighteenth Century.* Lide is not identified further.
5. A. O. P. Nicholson.
6. See Sackfield Maclin to Polk, January 26, 1842.

FROM WILLIAM H. POLK

Dear Brother,   Nashville Tennessee Jan'y 17th 1842
I this evening received your letters of the 15th[1] and was disappointed somewhat in the *verdict* as rendered in the case of Redding; though I doubted very much his *inocence.*[2] When you wrote me, you of course was not advised, of the proposition made by Mr. Foster, expressing an entire willingness to do "anything" or acceed to any terms the democrats, might choose to *precribe,* so as to enable him to obtain a seat in the U.S. Senate. Maj Hardwick wrote you, he informed me, fully on the subject last night.[3] I did not show your letter to any one but Mr Walker, and will consult him in the morning as to the propriety, under the new state of circumstances, of showing it to Johnson, Hardwick or Laghlin or McLin.[4] If any thing occurs to-morrow, I will write, and keep you fully advised of every movement.

Barkely Martin[5] returned from Columbia this evening; and informed me that there would be a meeting of a portion of the people of Maury County this day, in Columbia, to express their opinion, relative to the propriety of forcing a *resumption* of specie payments on the part of the several Banks in Tennessee. I did not give *him* to understand what would be my course, on the subject, in the event that the meeting should instruct the Maury delegation, and will not commit myself in any way, until I am clearly satisfied, as to the character of the meeting. But my impression is at this time, that some sinister design, on the part of certain individuals is at the bottom of the movement, and I will most certainly, unless *differently advised*, disregard the instructions eminating from a *Town meeting*, composed principally of the indebted portion of the community. I believe it to be my duty to force the Banks to act in good faith, so far as my individual exertions are concerned, and will so shape my course unless instructed to the contrairy by a majority of the people of Maury County. Mr Martin advocates the propriety of *requesting*, but not *forcing* the Banks to resume, by Sci. Fa.[6] against them, thereby occupying the position, in an *inexplicable betweenity*—and is in favour of extending the time for resumption until the first of January 1843. If I could discover any good or advantage that would arise from a postponement, until Jan'y I would willingly consent to the delay—but no advantage can be desired from delay, and much inconvenience and danger may be *incurred*, if the predictions of the opponents of Resumption are correct, that *hard times* and an increased oppression in the money matters of Tennessee, will necessarily follow such a movement on the part of the Banks. If the Banks resume in July, and this prediction is correct, the depression will have spent its force, and confidence will have been restored, before the August elections 1843. But if we delay the time of resumption until Jan'y we will have to fight the battle of 1843, in the midst of a panic.

Write to me by return mail, concerning the mee[ting][7] and advise me in full view of all the facts [what] course it would be best to persue. My own impression is, that the only course I can persue is to go *Jackson like* for what I believe to be for the best interest of the state, adhearing to principle, and not governed by any circumstances, which may exist at the time. I will oppose any alteration of the resolutions as they passed the House of Rep. unless you advise me to the *contrary*.

WILLIAM H. POLK

ALS. DLC–JKP. Addressed to Columbia. Polk's AE on the cover states that he answered this letter on January 19, 1842; Polk's reply has not been found.

1. Letters not found.

2. On September 17, 1841, the Maury County Grand Jury indicted Isaac Redding for the murder of Elizabeth Redding. On January 15, 1842, a Maury County Circuit Court jury acquitted him of the charge of murder in the first degree, but found him guilty of involuntary manslaughter. Redding secured a

retrial of his case at the May and September terms of the Circuit Court and won acquittal on the manslaughter charge.

3. On January 16, 1842, Jonathan P. Hardwicke wrote of "a great effort being made to carry out an unholy alliance between F[oster] & N[icholson]." ALS. DLC–JKP.

4. Andrew Johnson, Jonathan P. Hardwicke, Samuel H. Laughlin, and Sackfield Maclin.

5. A Columbia lawyer and politician, Barkly Martin served as a Democrat for three terms in the Tennessee House, 1839–41, 1847–49, and 1851–53, and sat for one term in the Senate, 1841–43. He subsequently won election to the U.S. House and served from 1845 until 1847.

6. Writ of scire facias.

7. A tear in the manuscript has obliterated portions of the sentence here and below.

TO JAMES WALKER

My Dear Sir.   Columbia Jany 17th 1842

On yesterday I wrote a full letter to William[1] & directed him to shew it to you. This evening I receivd yours of yesterday's date, and also one from my friend Hardwicke.[2] I have answered Hardwicke's.[3] He speaks of the possible necessity of my going to Nashville, to prevent my own immediate Representatives from compromising with Mr F's friends by taking him & N.[4] I have no doubt, that *Mr N.* is now in the broad road that *John Bell* travelled—for several years, before his apostasy became manifest; and in less than five years he will be where *Bell* now is, unless it is his personal interest to be otherwise. I would rather today see a Whig elected than him—for the reason that I have more respect for an open opponent, than a hypocritical friend in disguise. The course of M. & D.[5] is strange indeed, and I would think it not only proper but important, that you should before you leave Nashville have *a plain talk with them.* It can make matters no worse & would probably prevent them from doing mischief. If you know *Genl. Maclin,* it will be important you should talk freely to him as also to *Fentress,*[6] *Laughlin* & *Hardwicke.* If necessary stay a day longer to do this. The time has come when our friends should be undeceived as to *N.* You should see *Armstrong* & put him in motion. He can see *confidential friends* & do much. *Mr Rowles*[7] is my friend & unsterdands[8] him well. So does *Mr McGinnis* of Savannah.[9] *Hardwicke* thinks the party, may in the last resort be thrown back upon me. I have said nothing in my reply to him on that subject. That is a point on which I ought not to be consulted. *Turney* writes to me that he would cheerfully yield to any *good & true Democrat* but not to Mr N.[10] (because he has no confidence in him)—if the good of the party requires it. If a compromise is made & Mr F. is the *Whig candidate* from the west, then the *Democratic candidate* should come from E. Tennessee. If in the compromise *both parties*, should agree for the time-being to *break down the mountain* & take both Senators from the West, then the Democratic party, are bound in honour to adhere steadfastly to *Mr Turney*, & brother *William* can do this, with out any hazard to himself at home. I s[ay]¹¹ they are bound to adhere to *Turney*, unl[ess] some *as good and true a man*, as he who will be more available can be united upon. Mr N. is not that man, & I repeat that I would rather have an open opponent than him.

Show this to *William*. I enclose it to him lest you may have left & have said to him he could open & read it if he choses.

JAMES K. POLK

ALS. DLC–JKP. Addressed to Nashville and marked *"Confidential."*
1. Letter to William H. Polk not found.
2. On January 16, 1842, James Walker wrote from Nashville informing Polk of developments in the election of U.S. senators from Tennessee. ALS. DLC–JKP. Jonathan P. Hardwicke states in his letter of January 16, 1842, that Barkly Martin, a Nicholson supporter, is trying to block the election of Hopkins L. Turney to the Senate. ALS. DLC–JKP.
3. Polk's reply to Hardwicke of January 17, 1842, has not been found.
4. Reference is to Ephraim H. Foster and A. O. P. Nicholson.
5. Barkly Martin and John H. Dew, Maury County's representatives in the Tennessee Senate and House.
6. David Fentress, a lawyer in Bolivar, served one term in the Tennessee House as a Democrat, 1841–43.
7. A Bradley County lawyer and Democrat, George W. Rowles won election to two terms in the Tennessee House, 1841–43 and 1857–59.
8. Misspelling of "understands."
9. Christopher H. McGinnis, proprietor of Madisonville's first hotel, moved to Hardin County during the 1830's; he served as a Democrat in the Tennessee House from 1839 until 1847.
10. See Hopkins L. Turney to Polk, January 2, 1842.
11. Portions of two words have been obliterated by a tear in the manuscript here and below.

FROM JONATHAN P. HARDWICKE

Nashville, Tennessee. January 26, 1842

Hardwicke thinks that the Tennessee Whigs led by Foster have abandoned all expectation of electing a U.S. Senator during this session of the legislature. The Democrats must either "unite with the Bell party" ¹ or try to elect Adam R.

Alexander and Turney.[2] Alexander will cooperate with the Democrats, but Polk must "come to this place . . . with out delay," for several legislators are planning to go home soon.

ALS. DLC–JKP. Addressed to Columbia.
1. See J. George Harris to Polk, January 11, 1842.
2. Adam Rankin Alexander and Hopkins L. Turney. Alexander, a farmer, represented Maury County in the Tennessee Senate, 1815–19; served in the U.S. House as a Federalist from Madison County, 1823–27; and represented Shelby County as a Whig in the Tennessee House, 1841–45.

FROM SACKFIELD MACLIN

Senate Chamber
My dear Sir,   [Nashville] January 26th 1842
I had the pleasure of receiving yours of the 17th inst. in relation to the Senatorial election. It is true as you have heard (as I am informed) that some of Bell's friends made some overtures to the Democratic party.[1] It is equally true, (as I am informed) that Foster is willing to go to the Senate of the U S under any circumstances consistent with private honor. Consequently he would not object to an election by the seperate action of the two houses of the General Assembly.

Our friends are determined under no circumstances to vote for Bell, and it would be with much difficulty that they would vote for Foster.

Since the receipt of your letter I have talked with many of our friends upon the subject. I am well satisfied that the Democrats in the Senate would be willing to elect Foster and some *good and true republican,* provided he would answer those interogatories submitted to him at the beginning of the session, and pledge himself to be governed by instructions. But it seems that no one will move in this matter. I would do so if there were not so many older members, who must know better than myself the proper way to commence this matter.

I am pretty well satisfied that you are right when you say, that our safety may depend upon the election of Senators. However, my democratic friends in my District[2] will stand firm, notwithstanding a few of the *most consumate partisans* that ever breathed condemned my course in the Senate. Yet, if the Whigs should succeede in making the question Senator or no Senator, we might be defeated.

I conceive that it is a matter of very small moment either to myself or my country, whether I am defeated or not. But my great conscern is in relation to your success. It will not do for you to be defeated. I think it would be proper for you to visit the seat of government before we adjourn, and you can make these older members move upon the subject. If you think I am correct, I shall look for you in a few days. We will adjourn on the 7th Feburary.

SACKFIELD MACLIN

ALS. DLC–JKP. Addressed to Columbia.
1. See J. George Harris to Polk, January 11, 1842.
2. Maclin represented Fayette, Hardeman, and Shelby counties in the Tennessee Senate.

FROM THOMAS FLETCHER[1]

My Dear Sir,   Jackson Miss Jany 28th 1842
    Last evening,there was a political meeting at the capitol, and Martin Van Buren and R M Johnson[2] were nominated for President and Vice President. After the committee had reported, it was moved to strike out R M Johnson, and insert your name, which was after much confusion, and discussion, lost. I do not think that this meeting, expresses the true feeling of the people of the State, in regard to the Vice Presidency. Genl Foote[3] injured you by stating privately, that you had in your message condemned the course of Mississippi, in relation to the State bonds.[4]
    As I feel much solicitude in your political elevation, I will thank you to inform me, if in any message you have condemned the course of Miss. in regard to the State bonds. Such a report, industrously circulated among the anti Bankers, who constitute a large majority in this State, might affect your popularity, and I should be pleased to have it in my power, at a suitable time, to contradict it. I should be glad to hear from you, at Natchez.

THOMAS FLETCHER

ALS. DLC–JKP. Addressed to Columbia. Polk's AE on the cover states that he answered this letter on February 11, 1842; Polk's reply has not been found.
1. A Natchez lawyer and Democrat, Thomas Fletcher became commissioner of bankruptcy for Adams County, Mississippi, in 1842. He later served as marshal for the southern district of Mississippi.
2. Richard Mentor Johnson, a Kentucky lawyer and hero of the War of 1812, served in both houses of Congress before his election by the U.S. Senate in 1837 to the vice-presidency.
3. Henry S. Foote, a Mississippi lawyer and 1844 Democratic presidential elector, won election in 1847 to the U.S. Senate as a Unionist; he resigned from the Senate in 1852 to become governor of Mississippi.

4. In the election of 1841 Mississippi Democrats advocated solving the state's fiscal problems by repudiating $5 million worth of state bonds issued to the Mississippi Union Bank. Although Polk made no Mississippi references in his legislative message of October 7, 1841, he did argue that interest on Tennessee state bonds should be paid even if such payments required the levying of additional taxes.

FROM SAMUEL H. LAUGHLIN

My dear Sir,   Senate Chamber, Nashville, Jany. 29, 1842
By letters from H. L. Turney and Cave Johnson,[1] we learn that Mr. Johnson will arrive at home on this day. He wrote to Maj. Hardwicke from Louisville. I hope you will be here in a few days, and that you will write to Mr. Johnson to meet you here. For the cause, it is important. To me, personally, it is still more important. Mr. Johnson wrote me from Washington on 16th instant, that not having heard from me on the subject, and having also expected to hear some suggestions from you after your return from Mississippi, and which he had not received, that he had directed his friend T. H. Fletcher, that unless I gave security for the money advanced by him to Long, through me, to establish "Union," to sue me for the amount here on the spot.[2] Fletcher has called on me, and I promised him, which I must do, to acknowledge the service of a writ. The money was paid in the purpose of the original stock of the paper, the greater portion of which was burnt in Green's House.[3] That I was personally to be bound to pay it never entered my mind when I received it unless it was to apply it to purpose intended. Yourself, Grundy[4] and Donelson, to make more certain for my security, gave releases in 1837. The office, and its debts receivable passed out of my hands, and not a cent has been paid me of proceeds, by any subsequent holder of the books, leaving my loss over five times as much as Mr. Johnsons. Now, sir, he has elected to take his course, and to every other oppressive screw which has been put on me here during the session, as I wrote you, is now added the hostility of every bank striker on account of my course on resumption.[5] All these matters come well nigh driving me to madness. The political erenena[6] in which I receive nothing but hard blows, has become too hot for me. I must be off, and I most devoutly pray God to hasten the end of my service in this assembly, so that I may with honor, and justice to my constituents, retire to hard work, where I may ruminate at leisure upon my own past folly.
Gov. Jones[7] has nominated a list of Bank Directors[8] which meets no

approval, except of a few individuals, on either side. You will see the list. They will be rejected in the lump.

The latest scheme here in relation to senators, is a hope of electing Col. A. R. Alexander and H. L. Turney.[9] Dr. Hodsden has gone home.[10] Miller is about to go.[11] If we get clear of another, and East Tennessee dont ruin every thing, as she is likely to do,[12] and as she has done in regard to state debt and river bonds,[13] we may, possibly be able to elect this ticket in *our own way*, by concurrent seperate vote.

All these things premised, I do hope you will come to Nashville as early as possible, and that, if it meets your views, you will write to Mr. Johnson, or try to meet him here.

I see by the papers, that you are engaged in professional pursuits, I hope profitably, and that you find pleasure in it. Please make my respects to Madame Polk.[14]

S. H. LAUGHLIN

ALS. DLC–JKP. Addressed to Columbia and marked "Private."

1. One of Polk's closest friends and political allies, Cave Johnson practiced law in Clarksville and served in the U.S. House as a Democrat, 1829–37 and 1839–45. Polk appointed him postmaster general in 1845.

2. For more on Laughlin's financial problems at the *Nashville Union* and his debt to Cave Johnson, see Laughlin to Polk, January 11, 1839, and November 13, 1841; and Polk to Laughlin, December 29, 1841. Upon completion of his term as governor in October of 1841, Polk visited his cotton plantation near Coffeeville, Mississippi. Thomas H. Fletcher, a Nashville lawyer and unsuccessful merchant in his early years, represented Franklin County in the Tennessee House, 1825–27, and served as secretary of state from 1830 until 1832. Medicus A. Long published several newspapers in the 1830's, including the *Nashville Union* from 1835 until 1836.

3. Alexander Little Page Green, a Methodist minister, was instrumental in locating the Southern Methodist Publishing House in Nashville. Details about the fire, which destroyed the original press and paper stock purchased for the *Nashville Union*, have not been found.

4. Felix Grundy.

5. On January 8, 1842, the Tennessee House passed resolutions requiring that Tennessee banks resume specie payments on July 1, 1842; see John H. Dew to Polk, January 10, 1842. A few days later, however, the Tennessee Senate rejected those resolutions by a margin of one vote; the Senate favored a later resumption date.

6. Misspelling of "arena."

7. James Chamberlain Jones, a Wilson County farmer and one-term member of the Tennessee House, 1839–41, served as a Whig presidential elector in 1840. In 1841 and 1843 he defeated Polk in the Tennessee gubernatorial elections. In 1850 Jones moved to Shelby County and became president of the Memphis and

Charleston Railroad. He served as a Whig in the U.S. Senate, 1851–57, but supported Democrat James Buchanan for president in 1856.

8. Jones nominated Alexander Allison, Joseph W. Clay, William Williams, Andrew Ewing, Benjamin McCulloch, Mason Vannoy, M. M. Monahan, Peter Martin, William Maney, Thompson Anderson, Jonathan Currin, and Joseph W. Allen as directors of the Bank of Tennessee at Nashville.

9. See Jonathan P. Hardwicke to Polk, January 26, 1842.

10. Robert H. Hodsden, a Maryville physician, won election as a Whig to two terms in the Tennessee House and served from 1841 until 1845. In 1844 he moved to Sevier County and subsequently sat for one term as a Union Party member in the Tennessee House, 1861–63.

11. A lawyer from Sevierville, Isaac A. Miller won election as a Whig to the Tennessee House in 1839 and 1841.

12. Adam Rankin Alexander and Hopkins L. Turney were both from the western half of the state; Laughlin suggests that state sectional considerations might transcend partisan interests and thus defeat the compromise.

13. On January 25, 1842, five Democrats joined nine Whigs in giving Senate approval to legislation that cancelled some $300,000 in state bonds for river improvements authorized by the Internal Improvements Act of 1838. Under the new law, dated January 31, 1842, river projects in the Western District and in East Tennessee would receive a total appropriation of $200,000, funds for which would be advanced by the Bank of Tennessee pending receipt of a like amount from the general government under the Distribution Act of September 4, 1841. Senators from Middle Tennessee, sensitive to the termination of their section's share of the program, voted nine to four against the river bonds bill, senators from the Western District and East Tennessee voted ten to two in favor of it.

14. Sarah Childress Polk.

FROM JAMES M. HOWRY[1]

Oxford, Mississippi. February 15, 1842

Howry reports that a recent Democratic meeting at Jackson nominated Van Buren and Johnson. Its course of action "was all arranged and the Committee packed." A motion to substitute Polk's name for that of Johnson's failed, as did a proposition to postpone the nomination of vice-president. R. J. Walker[2] directed the meeting, the proceedings of which did not meet the approbation of "the rank & file." In northern Mississippi Calhoun's friends are mustering their forces. If Calhoun wins the nomination for president, the party will choose a northerner to balance the ticket.

ALS. DLC–JKP. Addressed to Columbia. Polk's AE on the cover states that he answered this letter on February 24, 1842; Polk's reply has not been found.

1. Formerly a resident of Hickman County, Tennessee, Howry moved in 1836

to Oxford, Mississippi, wher he continued to practice law. In 1840 he lost a special election for judge of the circuit court, but in 1841 won the regular election for that post.

2. Pennsylvania born, Robert J. Walker moved to Natchez, Mississippi, in 1826 and practiced law. He served in the U.S. Senate from 1835 until 1845, when he became secretary of the Treasury in Polk's cabinet. Subsequently, he served as governor of the Kansas Territory and as U.S. financial agent in Europe during the Civil War.

FROM JOSEPH W. HORTON[1]

Bank of Tennessee

Dear Sir   Nashville Feby 21. 1842

Yours of the 17 inst is recd with enclosures.[2] Agreeably to your request I have renewed your note and herein return you the old one.[3]

Jos. W. Horton

ALS. DLC–JKP. Addressed to Columbia. Polk's AE on the cover reads: "note $3000—at four months dated Feby. 21st 1842."

1. A Davidson County businessman and cashier of the Bank of Tennessee, Horton served several terms as sheriff of Davidson County.

2. Letter and enclosures not found.

3. Enclosure not found.

FROM ROBERT ARMSTRONG

Dear Govr,   Nashville Feby. 23d 42

Willo. Williams[1] will I think be Elected President of the Bank in the morning. Carroll[2] is *again* disapointed. You see from the Rejection of Barker that the Whigs of the Senate are united and will reject any Democrat offered.[3] Claiborne[4] will go by the board and they are determined to unite their party and fight.

Harris wants stiring up. With Van Pelt & Eastman[5] to back him we ought to be able to Keep the State in Ship Shape. No News. In haste.

R. Armstrong

[P.S.] Respects to Mrs. P. When will you be up?

ALS. DLC–JKP. Addressed to Columbia.

1. Directors of the Bank of Tennessee met in Nashville on February 24, 1842, and elected Willoughby Williams president in place of William Nichol, resigned. A

Nashville lawyer and former sheriff of Davidson County, Williams had served briefly as president of the Union Bank of Tennessee in 1837.

2. William Carroll, an elder statesman of the Tennessee Democracy, served as governor for six terms, 1821–27 and 1829–35.

3. On February 11, 1842, the U.S. Senate rejected the renomination of James N. Barker as first comptroller of the Treasury. An ardent Jacksonian, Barker served as mayor of Philadelphia, 1819; as collector of that city's port, 1829–38; and as first comptroller of the U.S. Treasury, 1838–41.

4. On January 18, 1842, Tyler nominated Thomas Claiborne to be U.S. marshal for the Middle District of Tennessee; the Senate rejected the nomination on March 9, 1842.

5. Henry Van Pelt and Elbridge G. Eastman. Van Pelt, who began his editing career with the Frankin *Recorder* in 1821, assumed direction of the Democratic *Memphis Weekly Appeal* on April 21, 1841; he remained with the *Appeal* for some ten years. Eastman established the Knoxville *Argus*, a Democratic newspaper, in 1839; he edited the *Nashville Union* from 1847 until 1849.

FROM HOPKINS L. TURNEY

Dear Sir   Washington Feb. the 24th 1842

This I believe is about the first time I have marked a letter to you private and my reason for doing so now is this. I am about speaking to you freely about certain of our prominent political friends. Before I do so, permit me to say I will send you as soon as it is printed the report & bill of the select committee on currency.[1] The Tyler men are willing so to amend the bill as to make it the Sub Treasury, with the deposite feature. This I think our friends ought to agree to, but I fear that Benton, Buckhannon,[2] and the other aspirants for the Presidency with a view to destroy Tyler, will then oppose the bill. After this bill shall have been thus amended would it not be better for us as a party to support it than to pursue a course of policy, that will leave things in the present deranged and disorganized condition. Upon this subject I would be glad to have your opinion. I believe our friends here from Tennessee all agree, but I will not seperate from my party unless there should be a division in our ranks. Then of course I cannot be with both divisions, which I fear will be the case on this important question. These leaders of ours, with a view to promote themselves, or which is the same thing, to prostrate Tyler to make way for themselves, will I fear do an essential injury to the country. It is certainly a verry small business, to make war on such a man. I would as soon make war on a woman in *labour*. If you were now here to lead off in this matter you could make yourself the prominant man of our party— Calhoun may lead off. I do not know what course he will take, but I think it likely Benton will carry the leaders in the Senate with him. Wright[3] with a view of promoting the views of little Van, Buck, and others are affraid, to set up for themselves in opposition to Benton and his forces. A majority of the democrats in the House if left to themselves would support the bill, but many of them have their favourites of the leaders whose prospects they desire to promote for the Presidency and will not therefore be likely to seperate from them unless they had some prominant man to lead off. This is one of the prominant questions that seperates the two parties and I shall regret verry much to see our party divided on it, which I fear will be the case. Let me hear from you on this subject.

H. L. TURNEY

ALS. DLC–JKP. Addressed to Columbia and marked "Private & confidential." Polk's AE on the cover states that he answered this letter on April 15, 1842; Polk's reply has not been found.

1. The U.S. House's Select Committee on Finance and the Currency, appointed on December 10, 1841, reported on February 17, 1842, a bill proposing a plan of finance similar to that recommended by Treasury Secretary Walter Forward. For details of the House bill, see House Report No. 244, 27 Congress, 2 Session. For the particulars of Forward's Exchequer Board, see John Catron to Polk, January 2, 1842.

2. James Buchanan.

3. Silas Wright, U.S. senator from New York from 1833 until 1844, backed Martin Van Buren for president in 1844, declined the second place on Polk's ticket, won election to the governorship of New York, and served from 1844 until 1846.

FROM CAVE JOHNSON

Dear Sir,   Washington Feby 27th 1842

Your two letters of the 7th & 9 inst.[1] I recd at Clarksville on the 16th just as I entered the Steamboat for my departure to this place. On my way I had no opportunity of writing. As to Laughlins debt to me[2] I had heard of the surrender of your & other claims & was applied to, to surrender mine thro Mr. G[3] which I declined doing & delayed pressing the claim upon Laughlin simply because I heard of his embarrassments & did not wish to press him. He now denies any *personal responsibility* & treats it as an advancement by me to the support of the paper. The original transaction was a mere loan to him of the money. Hearing of his embarrassment, I first wished security & you assured me it should be made safe by a lien on the establishment & you took from Laughlin a statement in writing that he would have the money secured by a lien on the establishment which was not done. I cannot afford to loose the money if it can be avoided & so soon as I found that Laughlin did not contemplate its payment I directed suit.

I do not consider it a hard case on Laughlin. He might & ought to have made money and his negligence ought to be visited on no one but himself. I regret his situation is such as to be harrassed by his opponents & to avoid any thing of the sort directed Mr. Fletcher to give indulgence upon the debt being secured. I have sacrificed much more than I ought to have done in these political contests and had I been as imprudent as Laughlin should have been as much embarrassed. I have today written him that I cannot surrender & shall collect it if I can. I regret to press him because I like him personally as well as his politics but I am too poor to make such a sacrifice & besides I have *Hickman & Dickson* to provide for as well as myself [and] wife.[4]

I do not think we have much to dread in the next election from the course of the "immortal thirteen." It seems to be approved rather than condemned in the section I was in. Fosters folly in refusing to answer[5] excuses it with all democrats & his *weakness* in answering after the adjournment only renders his position more ridiculous. An election of Senators[6] at the call session which is probable will make the whole pass into oblivion.

I approve your course in going to the Law tho you have some danger to apprehend from it. Your absence from the bar & devotion to other subjects will demand great exertion on your part to sustain your high reputation. You should have a partner to perform the drudgery & only appear in great cases. I have met none of the publications to which you allude except Fosters address.[7] Should not Turney[8] answer it?

I have yet met but few members & know but little of what has been going on in my absence. I think the Ten. democrats will vote for the fiscality if buying & selling Bills be stricken out.[9] I find that the inclination of their minds now. I have not had leisure as yet to examine the Report & Bills. All the Senators it is understood go against it, & it is now thought [it] will have but few supporters from either of the great parties.

It seems probable that Claiborne will be *rejected*—I suppose because Genl. Jackson recommended him.[10] If he does we shall again present Childress.[11] *Tyler* will do for us all he can I am sure. Yet he is so betwixt the parties that he is often troubled to know how to act. Houston of Alabama[12] says Tyler has played all his big cards without making a trick & now he wishes to comp.[13]

My health is better than it has been for years.

C JOHNSON

ALS. DLC–JKP. Addressed to Columbia and marked *"private."* Polk's AE on the cover states that he answered this letter on April 16, 1842; Polk's reply has not been found.

1. Letters not found.

2. See Samuel H. Laughlin to Polk, January 29, 1842.

3. Felix Grundy.

4. Johnson and his wife, Elizabeth Dortch Brunson Johnson, named two of their sons, James Hickman and Thomas Dickson, after counties in his congressional district.

5. See John Catron to Polk, January 2, 1842.

6. See Catron to Polk, January 2, 1842.

7. The Nashville *Republican Banner* of February 11, 1842, published Ephraim H. Foster's "Address to the People of Tennessee," which faults the thirteen Democrats in the Tennessee Senate for the Assembly's failure to fill the state's two vacant seats in the U.S. Senate.

8. Reference probably is to Samuel Turney, brother of Hopkins L. Turney. Formerly a member of the Tennessee House, 1829–35, Samuel Turney served six terms in the Tennessee Senate, 1839–47, 1855–57, and 1861–62. Democrats elected him Speaker of the Senate in 1841.

9. See Hopkins L. Turney to Polk, February 24, 1842.

10. See Robert Armstrong to Polk, February 23, 1842.

11. A resident of Williamson County and a cousin of Sarah Polk, William G. Childress had served one term as a Democratic member of the Tennessee House, 1835–37, and had run unsuccessfully for the U.S. House in 1839.

12. George Smith Houston, a lawyer, sat in the U.S. House as a Democrat, 1841–49 and 1851–61; represented Alabama in the U.S. Senate, 1874–78; and served as governor of his state from March of 1879 until his death nine months later.

13. Probably an abbreviation of the word *compound* or, possibly, *compromise*.

FROM ARCHIBALD YELL[1]

Sunday Evening

My Dear Govr.   Little Rock 6th March 42

I wrote you some few weekes since on the subject of the sale of your land in Arkansas.[2] The pressure is so deeply felt here by all Classes that no sales Can be made at any price and our only Currency is Arkansas rags, at ten for one.

But thank God at the next session of the Legislature we shall be able to put them into Liquidation. I have been heretofore in advance of public oppinion upon the subject of Banks & the Currency, but now I am over-taken & I fear shall be th[r]own in the back-ground. The people now see

& feel their Condition and they will act rather from feelings than Judgmt. My Doctrine has been from the start, "Pay up or Wind up." Nothing has been so fortunate to our party and so disastrous to the Feds as the blow up of the United Stats Bank. It has & will tend to establish the Bentonian Doctrine,[3] for I am very sure myself that, we must have either a *Sub-treasry* or some other Regulator to keep those rotten & Corrupt State Institutions from ruining the Country if it is not already done. I have no quarters to ask or give to the Banks either National or State; so its "War to the Knife." [4] The politics of Arkansas is Democracy on the increase. We shall have no difficulty in our State elections except we become *Weak* from our strength by too many anxious aspirnts for office.

She is as true to the needle in National Politics and she will support the Candidate of the Party be he whom he may; we will no doubt be as well Contented as any other State to take the Regular Nominee of a Convention. From Consideratns which I need not mention to you I think their first Choice would be R M Johnson. Next, *Yourself*, Benton, Buchannon & they will take VanBuren but not as a matter of Choice. Mr. Van Buren has the Confidence of our leading men here but they have no grate love for the man. They think him rather *Cold blooded*.

Should VanBuren be Selected by the Convention I am enclined to think they will also Nominate Johnson for Vice President so as to harmonize & to present the old and defeated ticket.

If it should be Mr Buchannon, then I think your Chance will be *first* for Vice President. Should however a man be Selected South of Masons & Dicksons line for Prest. then I presume we shall have to look to the Free States for a Vice President. Buchannon, Wright or Woodbury[5] would be very acceptable no doubt to our Party. What is Mr Calhoun about? Is he not in expectency, and will not he feel disappointed if not run? Is there any probibility or Contingency which would bring our party to Nominate Mr Tyler? He I believe will Join our Party before the end of this Session and a rumour is now rife here that he is about to reorganize his Cabanet & to bring in a godly portion of Democrats. Can that ultimately lead to his Nomination by our Party. It would seem from the devotion of Mr Clay's friends that they will make an effort to have him Nominated by the Whig Party but I still believe Genl Scott[6] will get the Nomination and that he has more strength than Mr. Clay. Upon all those Subjects I should like to have your oppinion as I have much confidence in your Judgment & Candour.

I became acquanted with Brother *Otey*[7] of your place who has been preaching to the Sinners of Little Rock. He is a Gentleman of fine Talents and has made a very favorable impreson here. He speaks so favorable of your Female Institute[8] that I have some Idea of placing my little daughters[9] at it. In that event *our* little Children Can become acquanted and I shall have the pleasure of visiting once more my old friends and acquantences in Tennessee, and perhaps I may stumble upon some old *Widdow* who would Come to Arkansas. Tell Madame Polk that If I visited Ten that I shall need and expect her influence in my efforts—so I desire her to look out. If I am to have any *say so* in the matter I desire them neither *too old* or *too young* not over 40 nor under *15*. As to size I am not particular—as to appearance I should not be overly nice, as I should have to make *profert of myself*!

I see you have had a deadly struggle in your Legislature and they have adjoirn & gone home to test the Correctness of their Cause before the People.[10] Since they defeated you, I have *disown* my State—& I now prefer to hail from *N. Carolina* a State that few will acknowledge to have given them birth.

Let me hear from you and be so good as to present my best & warmest Respects to Mrs. Polk and accept for yourself . . . .

A YELL

ALS. DLC–JKP. Addressed to Columbia. Polk's AE on the cover states that he answered this letter on April 18, 1842; Polk's reply has not been found.

1. A close personal and political friend of Polk, Yell practiced law in Fayetteville, Tennessee, until his appointment as judge of the Arkansas Territory in 1832. He won election to several terms in the U.S. House, 1836–39 and 1845–46, and served as governor of Arkansas from 1840 until 1844. Yell died in the Mexican War.

2. Yell had detailed his efforts to sell Polk's Arkansas lands in a letter dated January 22, 1842. ALS. DLC–JKP.

3. Thomas Hart Benton, who represented Missouri in the U.S. Senate for thirty years, strongly supported a hard money policy.

4. "War even to the knife!" was the reply of Palafox, governor of Saragossa, when summoned to surrender by French troops besieging that city in 1808.

5. James Buchanan, Silas Wright, and Levi Woodbury. Woodbury was secretary of the Treasury, 1834–41. Earlier he had served as governor of New Hampshire, Democratic senator from that state, and secretary of the navy. After heading the Treasury Department, Woodbury returned to the Senate and served there until appointed to the United States Supreme Court in 1846.

6. Winfield Scott, acclaimed for his completion of the Cherokee removal and the restoration of peace on the Canadian border in 1838, became ranking general of the U.S. Army in July 1841. Although regarded as a presidential prospect as early as 1839, Scott did not receive the Whig nomination until 1852.

7. Formerly rector of St. Paul's Episcopal Church in Franklin, James H. Otey was consecrated as the first Protestant Episcopal bishop in Tennessee in 1834.

8. Founded in 1835 by Leonidas Polk and James H. Otey and owned by the Protestant Episcopal Church of Tennessee, Columbia Female Institute sustained a large enrollment for almost a century.

9. Yell's daughters are not identified further.

10. Reference is to the General Assembly's failure to fill the state's two vacant seats in the U.S. Senate. See Sackfield Maclin to Polk, January 26, 1842.

TO SARAH C. POLK

My Dear Wife   Jackson March 11th 1842

I reached here on yesterday and will leave this evening. I find the waters so high as to prevent me from visiting some of the lands which I wished to see, until my return from the plantation.[1] I will examine our tract near *Denmark* on tomorrow, & go to *Dr Caldwell's* tomorrow night.[2] On the next day (Sunday) I will go to Bolivar, & from there to the plantation. I will be back here, at the meeting of the Supreme Court, on the 1st Monday in April, and in about ten days after that time I will probably be at home. I will write you again as soon as I get to the plantation. Let *Elias*[3] sow the oats & clover seed as soon as you return from Murfreesborough. It is time that they were in the ground.

JAMES K. POLK

P.S. I had no difficulty on account of high waters, in getting here, except a detention of five hours & ferrying 3½ miles at Tennessee River. J.K.P.

ALS. DLC–JKP. Addressed to Columbia.

1. Owner of considerable land in West Tennessee, Polk wished to inspect his properties there. Polk's plantation, however, was in Yalobusha County, Mississippi.

2. A Haywood County planter and physician, Silas M. Caldwell had married Lydia Eliza Polk Caldwell, Polk's sister, in 1817.

3. Elias was Polk's personal servant for many years.

FROM JOHN C. CALHOUN

My dear Sir   Washington 12th March 184[2]

I regret to inform you, that our most strenuous effort to save Mr. Claiborne failed. Party feelings triumphed over every other consideration. He was rejected by a strict party vote, every Whig present voting for the rejection, & every Republican against it. It will, however, be some consolation to him & his friends, that not the slightest effort was made to impeach his character.

You are right in supposing, that nothing that could be said would arrest the Whigs in their course. They seem bent on their own distruction and the country's too. Instead of holding back in consequence of the depressed state of the treasury, they appear more intent than ever on spending money. We already notified, that the five million of treasury notes[1] are exhausted, and an addition of several millions more are required; all this too when the paper of the government is under protest in N. York! To me it seems more like madness, than any thing I have ever witnessed in publick life.

In the mean time, the Republican party is quiet and composed, making no movement of its own, and supporting or opposing the measures proposed by their opponents, just as they accord with, or are in opposition to their principles & policy. During the long period I have been in publick life, I have never seen the party sounder in principles, or more harmonious in feelings. I hope it may continue.

I am glad to learn, that the indications are favourable with you. I do hope that you will be able to reverse the majority at the next trial of strength. There is much interest felt here to see Tennessee in her true position.

I send enclosed a copy of my speech on the veto.[2] It was well received by our friends and even a considerable portion of the Whigs. With kind remembrance to Mrs. Polk.

J. C. CALHOUN

ALS. DLC–JKP. Addressed to Columbia.

1. By Act of January 31, 1842, Congress authorized an issue of U.S. Treasury notes not to exceed $5,000,000; the note issue, which was patterned after that of 1837, would terminate at the end of one year.

2. On February 28, 1842, Calhoun made a Senate speech against Henry Clay's proposal to restrict the veto power of the president; enclosure not found.

FROM E. G. EASTMAN

Knoxville, Tennessee. March 18, 1842

Eastman recalls that when he was in Nashville the previous fall, Polk volunteered to visit East Tennessee. Eastman suggests holding a grand rally of the Democracy at Rogersville, which would be the best place because "friends in old Hawkins put more energy into a thing of this kind." Early August would be the best time, for that is "when the farmers have most leisure." General Fain[1] has consulted leading Democrats in Hawkins; all earnestly favor the idea. Sullivan, Washington, and Greene counties would each "turn out their thousand" to welcome Polk. Eastman confesses that he earlier feared the failure of the Senate to elect U.S. Senators "might produce a wavering among the weak." He is pleased to report that such is not the case. Eastman adds that he will be in Nashville for two weeks in May and hopes to see Polk at that time.

ALS. DLC–JKP. Addressed to Columbia. Polk's AE on the cover states that he answered this letter on April 15, 1842; Polk's reply has not been found.

1. A Rogersville merchant and postmaster, 1823–39, Nicholas Fain won election to the Tennessee House for two terms, 1839–43.

FROM AARON V. BROWN

Dear Sir   Washington March 22nd 1842

I have to enquire whether you have amongst your old congress papers, the claim of Maj Jno. & Capt Alexander Nelson for bounty land. Robt J Nelson has written me about it & I have searched the Pension office & the office of the clerk of the house for the papers in that case.[1] If you can find them please send them to me.

We have to day passed Resolutions of censure on the notorious abolitionist (Giddens) from Ohio. Where uppon he rose, passed through the Hall, shook hands with his friends & will be off in the morning.[2] I suppose his resignation will be handed in in the morning. The vote was a very strong one against him[3] several of our Southern Whigs thinking it was a fine opportunity to wipe off the stain of suspicion attached to them for former votes on the subject. Leave was unanimously given to him to speak in his defence, but being determined to be a martyr he remained obstinately silent. I suppose he will be a candidate for reelection & as his is a strong Whig district the only plan to beat him will be, for some acceptable Whig to become his opponent *not an* abolitionist & by the Democrats voting for him Giddens may be beat. Old Adams[4] and he shook hands—long & affectionately & it is said the former dropt a few tears at parting. Old Saltonstall[5] was quite moved on the occasion. I disliked the proceedings though I voted for them because we had let off old Adams—it seemed too much like worrying the Jackall when we should have hunted the Lion.

You no doubt notice the slow progress of business—without surprise after your Knowledge of such things. There is great disputing about who or which party shall be responsible for the acts of this administration. Tyler has no party beyond "The Guard" [6] & can it seems do nothing to augment the number. Mr Clay was to have made his great valedictory to day on his retrenchment resolutions, but it seems Allen during the morning hour, introduced certain resolutions or proceedings against him that so disconcerted him for the time, that he beg [a] day (tomorrow).[7] I cant say more because I have not yet seen Allens proceedings but they are said to be important. You will see them.[8]

Much of the delay & the difficulties here grow out of President making. Parties are evidently in motion, each endeavoring to do something for himself. Clay will be nominated very soon probably in N.C. in order to have the start of all others.[9] It is suspicioned here that he has bought off Scott[10] some how or other, but not *known* to be so. Calhoun & Buchannon are looking to it—Benton, if Van Buren dont & if "the old Hero" says it. It is thought Van Buren will. Now my earnest desire is that Genl Jackson will say nothing about it—nothing at all. I have contended valiantly for him twice & if it must be so would again, but he wants availability. It allways was and will be an uphill business to sustain him in Tennessee especially. My own opinion is that (Van Buren not offering) Silas Wright is the most available man in our ranks—less could be said against him by our enemies than against any body else. Calhoun would make the best *executive officer* perhaps of any of them, but I fear (much as I like him) would lack *availability*. But he has increased his popularity amazingly in the last few years & when the time comes for designating our Candidates, the question of availability may be greatly altered. Old Dick[11] can come it, no where, & if he could I could not exactly confide in him on several points.

As to the Vice Presidency not much is said except in connection with the nomination of Van Buren, Wright or Calhoun, in all of which events your name is freely used. The great mass of our friends still say it is too soon to move in the matter & I think Buchannons friends have ruined *him* by too early a presentation.

I have passed a very unhappy winter on account of the sickness of my family[12] & I think I shall return somewhat in advance of the close of the Session, which will scarcely take place sooner than the 1st or middle of July.

Your friends will be very happy to see you if you come to this City as you mentioned to be likely, & I think it would be very well to come on about all the month of May. Be pleased to present our best respects to Mrs Polk.

A V Brown

ALS. DLC–JKP. Addressed to Columbia. Polk's AE on the cover states that he answered this letter on April 20, 1842; Polk's reply has not been found.

1. On August 20, 1834, Robert J. Nelson had requested Polk's assistance in filing a claim in the name of his father, Alexander Nelson, who served as a captain of militia during the Revolution. Major John Nelson probably was Alexander Nelson's brother. A boyhood companion of Polk in Maury County, Robert J. Nelson moved to Mississippi, Arkansas, and then Memphis, Tennessee; he was a

surveyor, speculator, and farmer. On March 4, 1842, he again wrote to Polk on the subject of these claims. ALS. DLC–JKP.

2. A lawyer and abolitionist from Ohio, Joshua Reed Giddings served in the U.S. House from 1838 until 1859; during his lengthy congressional career he changed his party affiliation from that of Whig, to Free Soil, and finally to Republican. Giddings resigned on March 22, 1842, following the House's resolution of censure, but won reelection that same year and resumed his seat on December 5.

3. The censure motion passed by a majority of 125 to 69.

4. John Quincy Adams, the sixth president of the United States.

5. A lawyer from Massachusetts, Leverett Saltonstall served numerous terms in both houses of the state legislature before sitting as a Whig in the U.S. Congress from 1838 until 1843.

6. President Tyler's small group of followers in Congress earned the sobriquet, "Corporal's Guard" or "the Guard."

7. On March 22, 1842, Henry Clay announced that he felt too indisposed to address the Senate as scheduled, but hoped to present his views the next day on his retrenchment and reform resolutions. On March 23 Clay addressed the Senate for nearly three hours, arguing that his resolutions were not a violation of the Compromise Tariff of 1833, answering objections to an increase in tariff rates, and defending his proposed federal budget of $22,000,000. Of the eleven resolutions introduced by Clay on February 15, 1842, only three received Senate approval; they argued that the general government had a duty to provide adequate revenue for current expenses, that the government must abolish all useless offices and practice rigid economy, and that the executive departments should report on what retrenchments could be made.

Clay's famous valedictory address, unrelated to the retrenchment resolutions, came on March 31, 1842. On that occasion Clay formally announced his retirement from the U.S. Senate, apologized to any members whom he might have offended over the years, and wished the blessings of heaven upon all his colleagues.

8. Senator William Allen's actions, which reportedly disconcerted Clay on March 22, included presentation of the proceedings of a Democratic mass meeting in Muskingum County, Ohio; those resolutions condemned the measures of the recent extra session of Congress, attacked the general policy of the Whig party, and associated the abolitionists with the Whig members of the U.S. House. A lawyer, farmer, and stock raiser from Chillicothe, Ohio, Allen won election as a Democrat to one term in the U.S. House in 1833 and sat in the U.S. Senate from 1837 until 1849.

9. On April 4, 1842, North Carolina Whigs nominated Clay for president during their state convention at Raleigh.

10. Winfield Scott.

11. Richard M. Johnson.

12. On December 23, 1841, Brown noted in a letter to Polk that "Mrs. B. is in bad health." ALS. DLC–JKP. Brown's wife in 1842 was the former Sarah Burruss of Giles County.

FROM J. G. M. RAMSEY

My Dear Sir   [Mecklenburg, Tennessee. March 30, 1842][1]
I met several of our friends in town yesterday. The general topic now, is the succession.[2] Gentlemen that heretofore have maintained a perfect silence on that subject begin to speak out. The visit of several high ex-functionaries to the south & South West discloses its object to be *political*, & and has forced upon them the immediate consideration of the subject. Should Knoxville be a point in the route of Mr. V.B.[3] & those travelling with him we have determined that while he shall receive the attentions due to a great statesman & deserving citizen we will consider him as a *retired* politician—nothing more. I mingle necessarily freely & frequently with the Whigs & I hear their sentiments & I can assert positively that few very few of them will under any contingency support him. Many—most—of the Democrats believe him to be hopelessly prostrated. I will regret to see him again brought forward. It will throw us into a minority all over the country & especially in Tennessee. Our friends say so in Athens & Jonesboro, & I hear in Nashville too. Could my voice be heard by the Union Harris would say so aloud & at the present time. Such a declaration should be made by all our papers & meet Mr. V.B. on his Western tour. It might yet save us from incurable dissentions. His prospects at Charleston & in S.C. have been any thing but encouraging. The small fragment of the old Union party, still under the influence of Mr. Poinsett[4] is all that he can count on there. How it is in Ga. I do not hear. But if Al. & Tenn. will discountenance the effort just now he will at once foresee the certain issue of his effort to resuscitate his ruined fortunes. Some of our friends here still say the movement would be premature or before now Knox County would have spoken.
By a succession of failures of the Mail I am without a "Jeffersonian" for several weeks. I could judge from its editorials & selections how my letter was received.[5] I have but one No. since & it was favorable. More of this hereafter. I write this hasty note principally to acquaint you with the feelings of our friends hereabouts—& that is that we should avoid on the present visit of Mr. V.B. to Tennessee any step that would identify us with the attempt entertained elsewhere with too much favor, to bring him forward again.
I shall occasionally write you or Mr. Walker; but will not of course feel neglected or disappointed if you do not allways reply. Your other engagements & your *position* will prevent. Tell me tho, when I go wrong.

                                              J. G. M. RAMSEY

ALS. DLC–JKP. Addressed to Columbia. Polk's AE on the cover states that he answered this letter on April 16, 1842; Polk's reply has not been found.

1. Date and provenance of the letter is taken from Ramsey's postal cancellation written on the cover.

2. In letters to Polk of February 2 and 26, 1842, Ramsey discussed his efforts to promote a Calhoun-Polk ticket in 1844. ALsS. DLC–JKP.

3. Martin Van Buren, accompanied by James K. Paulding, made a tour of the South and Southwest during the spring of 1842. They arrived in Nashville from New Orleans by steamer on April 25th. Van Buren and Paulding first called upon Jackson at the Hermitage, visited Polk in Columbia for a couple of days beginning May 7, and returned to Nashville and the Hermitage for a week's stay. On May 16 Van Buren and his entourage left Nashville by stage for Lexington, Kentucky, where they were to be hosted by Henry Clay.

4. Joel R. Poinsett of South Carolina, the first U.S. minister to Mexico, 1825–29, served as secretary of war during Van Buren's administration.

5. In a letter to Polk dated February 26, 1842, Ramsey mentioned that he had written to J. W. Hampton, editor of the Charlotte *Mecklenburg Jeffersonian*, urging him to endorse a Calhoun-Polk ticket in the 1844 election. ALS. DLC–JKP.

FROM AARON V. BROWN

Dear Sir   Washington April 9th 1842

I enclose you for *confidential use* a pamplett[1] of which some 2 or 300 I expect have been sent out in different directions *as feelers*. It shews one fact that the friends of Mr Calhoun intend to present his pretensions to the public consideration.

Our friends in Tennessee have no objection to *such an experiment* on the public sentiment, especially if it is not contemplated to forestal the action of our party in its ultimate designation of the man of our choice. I send it to you as one of the occuring incidents of the day in reference to the succession but without desiring any publicity to the pamplet or wishing any use to be made of it which might seem inconsistent, with a friendly presentation of it to me by one of his friends.[2] It is too soon entirely too soon to bring up the Presidential question.

Wright is sometimes spoken of as suitable for the Vice Presidency on a Calhoun ticket. But I do not understand that *he* has ever favored any such idea.

Many here apprehend some demonstration of the Old General in favor of Van Buren, during or soon after the pending visit to the hermitage. Our friends here are getting much inclined to adopt the One term System

in practice & I have heard them run over arrangements like this—
Calhoun next 4 years, Wright Do.[3] Vice President. Wright next after &
you V.P. & the next turn they designate as *yours* for the Presidency. But
I think it pretty evident that if V.B. is run again that *your* relative
position would most probably bring you up on his ticket the next time. It
is said Ritchie[4] & others would try hard to put Stephenson[5] on the ticket
instead of yourself. But I tell you there is great aversion amongst our
friends *in Congress* to take up Van Buren again. They do not seem to
think favorably of his *availability*. From all the signs I fear very much
that we shall be much divided if not distracted in our next selection. I
dash these things down hastily for your own eye, under the belief that
you are entitled to know from me whatever is transpiring here on these
topics.

Our foreighn relations are involved in *serious* difficulties at the present moment & I learn from one in favorable position to Know[6] that there
is not much prospect of a satisfactory adjustment of the pending questions with G. Britain.[7]

A V Brown

ALS. DLC–JKP. Addressed to Columbia. Polk's AE on the cover states that
he answered this letter on April 20, 1842; Polk's reply has not been found.
  1. Francis W. Pickens, *A Brief View of the Present Position of the Republican Party* (1842).
  2. Not identified further.
  3. Abbreviation for "Ditto," meaning "next four years."
  4. Thomas Ritchie, editor of the *Richmond Enquirer* from 1804 until 1845,
unofficially directed affairs of the Democracy in Virginia.
  5. Andrew Stevenson, a lawyer, served several terms in the Virginia House
of Delegates before winning election to the U.S. House, where he served from
1821 until 1834. He presided as Speaker of that body during his last four terms of
service. Stevenson also served as minister to Great Britain from 1836 until 1841.
  6. Not identified further.
  7. Brown probably refers to the case of the *Creole* and the Northeastern
boundary dispute. In late 1841 slaves on the American brig *Creole* mutinied,
seized control of the ship, and sailed it to Nassau. British authorities resisted
Secretary of State Webster's demand for the return of the slaves and vessel; that
incident was not adjusted until 1855. Webster's Northeastern boundary negotiations culminated later in 1842 in the Webster-Ashburton Treaty, which fixed the
Maine-New Brunswick boundary along its present line.

FROM ROBERT ARMSTRONG

Nashville, Tennessee. April 13, 1842
Armstrong reports that General Jackson has received a letter from Martin

Van Buren at Columbia, S.C., estimating his arrival at the Hermitage sometime between the 20th and 25th of April. A committee will meet on the 14th to arrange a reception. Armstrong suggests that Polk might wish to escort Van Buren from Nashville to the Hermitage.

ALS. DLC–JKP. Addressed to Columbia and marked "*Private.*" Polk's AE on the cover states that he answered this letter on April 15, 1842; Polk's reply has not been found.

FROM ROBERT ARMSTRONG

Dear Sir,   Nashville 15 April 42

I have seen Doctr McNeill on the subject you wished me.[1] He says he has not the money on hand but that he has a right to expect it from several sources and that his friend Jimmy shall be accomodated, that he will not dispose of any money until you inform him further on the subject. In a few days he expects to be in funds. He spoke of leaving shortly for some place. He is in bad Health.

I think you had better write him a short note yourself. Say nothing of *Interest*, nothing of time. Only that you want it, so that your crop &c. will meet it & that you wish to pay some different a/cts, & preferd having your debts *Concentrated* &c &c. I told him you wanted some 3 or 4 thousand dollars. He will do any thing for you in *his* power.

R. ARMSTRONG

[P.S.] He says he may not be able to get in his money or collect any. If he does you will get the Refusal of it—*write him.*[2]

ALS. DLC–JKP. Addressed to Columbia.
1. Polk wished to borrow money, probably from William McNeill, a physician in Columbia for many years.
2. Armstrong's postscript written on the cover.

FROM J. G. M. RAMSEY

My Dear Sir   [Mecklenburg, Tennessee. April 18, 1842][1]

I wrote you some weeks since[2] informing you what I have written to Hampton the editor of the Mecklenburg Jeffesonian. I see from the last No. of that journal that he takes the same views I had expressed—so far at least as Mr. Calhoun is concerned (do you see his paper?) & I have just received a letter from him in which says "I entirely & cordially concur in your views & stand ready to advance them in every honorable way." He then goes on to express his regrets at the conflicting pretensions of several prominent men in our ranks—Col. Johnston[3] &c &c—& fixes down upon C. as the only one that can hope to succeed. He then comes to the V.P. & adds "The choice of a candidate for the V.P. (the history of whigery has proven) is of no little consequence. *Gov. Polk* would please me as well as any other man in the Union. I inclosed you[r] [l]etter[4] to Mr. Fisher of Salisbury.[5] He is cordially with your views. You need not be surprised if Mr. Calhoun is nominated at the Salisbury Convention the 20th May." [6] This letter is a long one & I have not time to copy the whole—but there is an omission in it to which I will call his attention. I will say by the next mail "that Tennessee will not respond to that nomination unless your name is presented at the same time—that with that arrangement C. may succeed—without it he cannot. The West has its claims & can not be expected to cooperate if they are disregarded & that the Sal. Con. may decide Mr. C's fate by coupling him with one not from the West." These views I will present to Fisher & others of the Con—& if Mr. C's friends will destroy him they shall do so with their eyes open. Hampton in his letter say nothing in favor of a Northern man for V.P. but mentions "I see an important article in the Albany Argus[7] which I think means more than meets the eye at a glance. It is a semi-biographical notice highly laudatory of Mr. Calhoun & at t[he] [s]ame[8] time coupling with it a very favourable notice of Senator Wright—thus placing them both prominently before the public eye." He does not mention him further as a candidate for anything but I will make an argument against him[9] by saying the South & West must go together or we must fall to pieces. I mention what I intend writing that if Graham or Walker[10] or any other has a single acquaintance in N.C. we should all write in the same strain—before the 20th May. My S.C. correspondents still insist that C. & P. be nominated in Tenn. this spring. We will find it impossible to send our daughter to Columbia—much as we had desired it.[11]

J. G. M. RAMSEY

ALS. DLC–JKP. Addressed to Columbia.

1. Date and provenance taken from Ramsey's postal cancellation on the cover.

2. See Ramsey to Polk, March 30, 1842, for notation of Ramsey to Polk, February 26, 1842.

3. Richard M. Johnson.

4. Manuscript torn.

5. Charles Fisher, a Democratic leader in western North Carolina, served several terms in the state legislature and two terms in the U.S. House, 1819–21 and 1839–41.

6. Reference to the meeting at Salisbury is not further identified; however, Democrats of Mecklenburg County did hold a convention in August of 1842 and on that occasion nominated John C. Calhoun for president.

7. The *Albany Argus*, edited by Edwin Croswell, was the leading newspaper of the northern Democracy.

8. Manuscript torn.

9. Here Ramsey interlined the abbreviation "W." for the name "Wright."

10. Daniel Graham and James Walker. Graham, formerly a resident of Murfreesboro, served as Tennessee's secretary of state, 1818–30, and state comptroller, 1836–43.

11. One of eleven children, Ramsey's daughter is not further identified. On February 2 and 26 Ramsey had discussed prospects for her attending the Columbia Female Institute. ALsS. DLC–JKP. See also, Ramsey to Polk, May 10, 1842.

FROM SAMUEL H. LAUGHLIN

My dear Sir,   McMinnville, April 19, 1842

In this quarter, democracy was never more completely in the ascendant than it is at the present moment. The course of the "13," [1] the course of the democracy in regard to bank Directors,[2] and in regard to the failure of the Representation Apportionment Bill,[3] meets the distinct approval of nearly the whole people of the Mountain District.[4] So far as the Senatorial Election question is concerned, we should have been cashiered to a man if we had suffered the election of Foster and Jarnagin, having the power to prevent it. On that subject the approbation of our constituents is not negative or tacit approval—it is affirmative, open approval by declarations promptly and everywhere uttered by our friends, and tacitly by hundreds of whigs who approve Tyler's course, and who are sorely disappointed in all the doings of the Called and present session of Congress. Jones nor no other Whig can run in this District in the next gubernatorial contest as well as Cannon[5] did in 1839. Jones has sunk out of all notice, and is only thought of or remembered because he is the *acting* executive. All men look to you in the next campaign, and all desire to have the privilege of voting directly for you for the office of Governor, though all would with equal zeal give you their votes as a candidate on the republican ticket for a higher office. Whatever you may be out for in 1844, or in 1843, the Mountain goes for *en masse*.

I am glad to see that Andrew Johnson has published his speech on the Senatorial election question.[6] It is in the Argus, and I think should be transferred to the Union.

Jacobs and his Railroad have gone to the Devil.[7] I have just seen young Brown the Clerk in the House,[8] and he informs me that the New President[9] and *present* board of Directors are about to press and sue the stockholders upon a call upon stock, and that there is a general repugnance to pay any more, believing what they have paid has been misspent, and that if the call is pressed by suits it will produce a general rebellion among the stockholders. The road was conceived in folly and has been brought forth in sin, and been conducted in fraud and inequity. The LaGrange road[10] is but little better.

When Mr. VanBuren comes to Nashville you will see him of course. Judge Ridley[11] and myself intend to pay our respects to him.

You will see that our old friend John Ford[12] here, keeps up a pretty good war. While we have a press, however retired I may live, I can have every thing straight as a shingle in this district.

Mr. Cave Johnson writes me that he has summoned you as a witness upon his claim against me, or will summon you when the cause is at issue in Davidson Circuit Court. He says he does not wish to distress me but that he must be paid. He admits that I have lost by the business, and that I have done some service, and that when our friends get into power, he will urge that something in the official line shall be done for me. All this is poor consolation to a man stuped to the eyes, aye, over head and ears in embarrassments—embarrassments incurred in a cause in which Mr. Johnson had so much more at stake than I had.[13]

Dr. Gwin[14] as well as Mr. Johnson have the same kind of demands, except that as to the Doctor, I am personally bound, and for the other I never was and at the time did not intend to be. I wish to be freed from both upon any terms of liquidation in my power, and will write to both on the subject in a few days proposing such compromise as I can make. I will also write to Mr. Turney. I will request them to place their claims in Turney's hands, or empower him to settle and compound the matter with me. I can procure lands, such as our Warren and Cannon County lands, and pay them at the lowest price—lands clear of all incumbrance and held under old perfect titles. I have friends who will furnish the lands, and allow me to work out the pay like a slave by what I can earn hereafter if I live—they running the risk of my dying. Mr. Turney is a perfect Judge of such property, its value and titles. I wish to deal fairly—do the very best I can—and finally. If you could drop a line to Dr. Gwin, Johnson and Turney or any of them, aiding me in my just purpose, you will greatly oblige me. I shall write to them when I return from Van Buren Court, about 27th or 28th inst.

S. H. LAUGHLIN

ALS. DLC–JKP. Addressed to Columbia, marked "Private," and postmarked "McMinnville Te. 2 May."

1. The "Immortal Thirteen."

2. On February 5, 1842, the Tennessee Senate considered Governor Jones' nominations for directors of the Bank of Tennessee, but the thirteen Democratic members of the Senate denied their confirmation. Again on February 7 the Democrats refused to agree to Jones' nominations.

3. On February 5, 1842, the "Immortal Thirteen" rejected a motion to appoint a conference committee for adjusting disagreements between House and Senate redistricting bills.

4. Tennessee's Fifth Congressional District included Franklin, Warren, White, and Overton counties.

5. Newton Cannon, a Williamson County planter and supporter of Henry Clay, lost races for the governorship in 1827 and 1839, but won bids for that office in 1835 and 1837.

6. Delivered in the Tennessee Senate on October 27 and 28, 1841, Johnson's speech appeared in the Knoxville *Argus* of April 13, 1842.

7. Solomon D. Jacobs, a Knoxville merchant and promoter of internal improvements in East Tennessee, became president of the Hiwassee Railroad Company in 1837. He served two years as mayor of Knoxville, 1834–35, and represented Knox County in the Tennessee House from 1839 until 1841. The Tennessee legislature incorporated the Hiwassee Railroad Company in 1836 for construction of a railroad from Knoxville through the Hiwassee District to the southern boundary of the state.

8. Thomas A. Brown won election as first assistant clerk of the House on October 5, 1841.

9. John McGaughey, former member of both the Tennessee House, 1827–33, and Senate, 1835–36, replaced Solomon D. Jacobs as head of the Hiwassee Railroad Company in 1842.

10. Chartered in 1835, the LaGrange and Memphis Railroad Company began construction in 1838. The railroad suspended construction in 1842.

11. Bromfield L. Ridley, a lawyer, represented Warren County for one term in the Tennessee House, 1835–37. He moved to Murfreesboro in 1840 and served as judge of the Chancery Court from 1840 until 1861.

12. John W. Ford, a Polk supporter, edited the McMinnville *Central Gazette* from 1835 until 1842; he served as postmaster at McMinnville during that same period of time.

13. Reference is to Laughlin's debt to Johnson for capital with which to establish the *Nashville Union*.

14. William M. Gwin, native Tennessean, physician, and staunch supporter of Andrew Jackson, served as U.S. marshal for Mississippi, 1833–41, and sat in the U.S. House for one term, 1841–43. In 1849 he moved from Mississippi to California and represented that state for portions of two terms in the U.S. Senate, 1850–55 and 1857–61.

FROM ROBERT ARMSTRONG

Dear Sir,   Nashville April 22d 42

I understand Haskill of Madison has resigned and I learn that McCallahan or McCorry either can most surely be Elected.[1] You Know more about this than I can tell you. One thing I Know that it is very Important that we should Elect a Democrat, and carry Madison. Would it not be well for you to write to those Gentlemen and other friends at Jackson before some of them engage in it and *spoil* it.

No further accounts of Mr Van Buren. Only that *all* New Orleans was engaged in giving him a warm Reception.

Our Committee started down this morning in the *Hermitage* with a party of Ladies and Gentlemen to meet him.[2]

Doctr. McNeill is waiting to receive money. If I see him to day I will Know his prospects &c &c. The Genl is well and expects you up when Mr Van Buren arrives. When you come bring all the force you can. I will write you by Monday nights mail if any News from him. Bring all our friends and let us Know when you will be up. I will give you the result of the New York City Elections on the back of this Letter if we receive it by the mail to night.[3]

I should have visited you for a day but I could not get off. Nothing would have been done toward Mr Van Burens reception. It looks well now and their is quite a good feeling even with the Whigs. Our respects to Mrs. Polk.

                                         R. ARMSTRONG

[P.S.] You have the correct view of Mr Van Burens visit and what ought to be the course of the Genl. and our friends. I have previously spoken to the Old Genl. and Donelson in the same way. Their is great scheaming going on and the sooner it is put down the better. The only fear of the Democratic party, is division and a split up about men. When I see you I have much to say to you.

Jones is just about closing a purchase of the Planters Bank for a Plantation in Miss and Negroes at 25 Thousand Dollars. This looks like *he* was off, preparing to "Slope."

ALS. DLC–JKP. Addressed to Columbia.

1. William T. Haskell, Samuel McClanahan, and Henry W. McCorry, Sr. Haskell, a leading Madison County Whig and son of Joshua Haskell, won election to the Tennessee House in 1841 and served as a presidential elector for Henry Clay in 1844. He later sat for one term in the U.S. House, 1847–49, and ran unsuccessfully for governor in 1859. McClanahan and McCorry were influential Madison County Democrats.

2. A committee of thirty-one citizens, including George W. Campbell, Andrew Jackson Donelson, J. George Harris, Felix Robertson, and Robert Weakley, was appointed on April 2, 1842, to plan a suitable reception for Van Buren in Nashville. A delegation from this committee sailed aboard the steamer *Hermitage* to meet the former president aboard the *Nashville* at Smithland, Kentucky.

3. Democrats elected Robert H. Morris mayor; the aldermanic races ended in one disputed contest and an even split between Democrats and Whigs for the remaining seats.

FROM ROBERT ARMSTRONG

Dear Govr.   [Nashville] 25 April [1842][1]

Mr Van Buren arrived to night 7 Oclk with a Large Escort and two steam Boats with Bands of music &c &c. We made truly a fine display. He goes up in the morning *early* to the Hermitage, an[d] will return here on Thursday next 28 to meet his friends. Show & Bring all the force; we will find room. I want to see you badly. You sent no letter by to nights mail for Horton.[2]

R. ARMSTRONG

ALS. DLC–JKP. Addressed to Columbia.

1. Year and provenance identified through content analysis.

2. Polk's note to the Bank of Tennessee for $331 fell due on April 25, 1842; probably Armstrong had endorsed the note and wished to remind Polk of its deadline. On April 25, 1842, Joseph W. Horton, cashier of the bank, acknowledged receipt of Polk's payment under cover of April 22; Polk's letter has not been found. ALS. DLC–JKP.

FROM HOPKINS L. TURNEY

Dear Sir   Washington April the [26]th 1842[1]

I this day received yours of the 16th of this month[2] and I am pleased to see that you agree with your friends here from Tennessee on the financial question,[3] though I cannot nor will not use your opinion in any way, as it is marked private and besides as there is likely to be a division in the democratic ranks on the question, it would not only be useless to identify you in the division but might at some future period prove prejudicial. For the presant I can see no necessity for your giveing any public opinion about it. I do not think Congress will adjourn before the 10th or 15th of July next. I would be pleased to see you here. I think A. O. P. N.[4] has put his foot in it. Can it be possible that He can longer deceive the democracy of Tennessee? His course as it seems to me is not only foolish but ridiculous, a mixed meeting to invite the Ex. President and do him honor, a man whom they had denounced as the most corrupt that lives, to honor him for what, true they do not say, but it cannot be for his faithful public services, nor for the measures of his administration—these the Whigs have condemned in the strongist termes.[5] Suppose he was to accept, what would be the character of the Tost, in what sentament of approbation of his public life could the Whigs agree? None.

It is roumerd here that Webster and Spencer[6] are to resign and that their places will be filled by the appointment of democrats. I have no faith in this roumer. Tyler would not appoint demo. even if the places were vacant, which I do not believe will happen.

The committee of the whole on the Union this day filled the blank in the appotionment bill with 50,079 which gives Tennessee 15 members and the house to consist of 288 members.[7] This I think is all wrong; the number ought to have been redused. I will write to my old friend Moore[8] again shortly, and I still hope he will come right. He certainly cannot be deceived by N. always.

There is now a strong talk here that Van and yourself will be our next candidates; the Idea is I think gaining strength. It is not exactly as it ought to be, but it may be the best we can under the existing circumstances do. You know my feelings and views, and here all agree you would be as strong if not stronger than Van. But if you or any other new man were taken up, there would not be a vacancy for the aspirants for the next eight years. Van can only serve foure. He therefore has the aid of many leading men, which I think gives him much strength in convention which he otherwise would not have.

I am pleased to see we are gaining in Tennessee. I have a corrispondance from one end of the state to the other, and they all give the same account from the differant sections that you give from Jackson. I have no doubt we now have a large majority in Tennessee if we could now have a recount.

Present my rispect to Mrs Polk, and accept for yourself my best wishes.

H. L. TURNEY

ALS. DLC–JKP.

1. Misdated "April the 25th"; date identified through content analysis.

2. Letter not found.

3. See Hopkins L. Turney to Polk, February 24, 1842, and Cave Johnson to Polk, February 27, 1842.

4. A. O. P. Nicholson.

5. The occasion of Nicholson's proposal to include Whigs on the arrangements committee for Van Buren's Nashville visit has not been identified; probably Nicholson suggested his idea to Polk, who in turn may have mentioned the matter to Turney in his letter of April 16, 1842.

6. Daniel Webster and John C. Spencer. Former legislator, congressman, and secretary of state of New York, Spencer served as U.S. secretary of war from October 12, 1841, until March 3, 1843, when he became secretary of the Treasury. He resigned from the latter post on May 2, 1844.

7. On April 26, 1842, the U.S. House amended the general apportionment bill by allowing one representative for each 50,179 people. The House sent the bill to the Senate on May 3, but the upper house changed the ratio to 70,680. On June 17, 1842, the House accepted the Senate version, which fixed the membership of the House at 233. Under the new formula Tennessee lost two of her thirteen seats.

8. Possibly Richard B. Moore, a resident of Maury County.

FROM CAVE JOHNSON

Dear Sir,   Washington 29th April 1842

I recd. today your letter[1] & was gratified to learn the prospects of the Democrats in the western district. If we cannot beat the whigs upon their measures we may give up. I consider that result as certain not only in Tennessee but throughout the Union. The Whigs here have recently made a singular movement & one which I think must seriously effet them if these designs should be carried out—an amendment to the apportionment Bill, to compel the states to adopt the district system,[2] with ulterior object it is believed, if they succeed in this, of districting the whole U.S. This movement was made by Hallstead & no doubt in consequence of the recent elections in Con., Rhod Island, New Jersey & Georgia—the only states which vote by Genl ticket.[3] Their recent elections indicate the success hereafter of the Democratic party in each & by districting *something may be saved* & besides the Districts could be laid off *here* by a reckless Whig majority & something saved in that way. I think it probable they cannot succeed in the first move & of course the latter falls. We voted first in Com. for 60.500, which was very unfavourable to the slave States—the fractions covering 8 members. Of course the southern members made a great struggle to get rid of it & succeeded in substititing 50.178 which is very favorable to us & increases the House to 306 members. A strong effort will be made in the House to get it to about 70.000.[4]

The Treasury has a new Tariff Bill to substitute in place of Saltonstalls which is said to be much better.[5] We expect it every day. The

Whigs by their retrenchment Committees[6] are making strong move-ments agt. Van Buren, by hunting up all the extravagance in Florida, in removing the Indians & in every other branch of the public service, & making their Reports silently & letting every thing pass without notice & the *Reports*, one sided, leaving [out] every thing that does not suit them, will come upon us as having had the sanction of Congress. A good thing occurred lately. Great efforts are making to impeach the integrity of Carey Harris[7] while acting as Commissioner of Indian Affairs, & the proof is a letter from Jeff. Porter,[8] proposing a partnership with him in purchasing Indian reservations & Harris to pay the money & decide the Cases & Jeff make the purchases.[9] Jeff is now here attempting to get the Committee to make a new Report so as to exculpate. This is the talk among the members. I have not examined the facts. Something of the sort caused the resignation of Harris. They believe that Van is to be our Candidate & these are the proofs of their former Charges agt him. There is no knowing what such men as Stanly[10] may do. We must counteract the movement in some way & how, it is difficult to say. The extravagance of the officers in Florida & in removing the Indians ought to cause their dismissal. I am now so far behind the oeconomical retrenchment men, tho I pursue my former course, I am hardly regarded as one of them. New Converts are always the most zealous as well as clamorous. What do you think of Briggs making retrenchment speeches! Everett talking of oecon-omy! & Slade denouncing the extravagance of the last adm![11] Their sollid effort is at Van Buren & some of our timid friends are afraid to meet their clamors but that we have a decided majority for him in Congress I have no doubt. I know but little of the movements of the friends of others. Now & then I hear a little by accident. An address has been for some weeks written intended to be sent every where privately by Pickens[12] to arouse his friends but rumor says, that they are afraid to make the movement lest the facts should be made public & bring down upon him, all the friends of others who have pretensions & thus break him down—& it is the prevailing opinion that all our aspirants will yeild to none but Van Buren. I may also add that I have met with no democrats except a few on the Ohio who does not wish that you should be on the ticket with Van & this will certainly be the case if he or Silas Wright is nominated unless it shall be again thought necessary to reconcile the Col[13] & keep him out of the way by placing him on the ticket. In my opinion there is no doubt of our success unless he should be taken up by the Whigs & Clay dropped. If Col will permit it, my opinion is that it will be done. Clay will be too flat in a year to make any thing of him. I see no reason why you should not call here going to or returning from N. York. Nothing more can be made of it than will be made of your trip to New York.

We had an angry discussion about Poindexters Report, which it is said will implicate Hoyt, Butler & Curtis and all others connected with the Custom House & Wise intimated to day that it would implicate in gross fraud many of the leading manufacturers of New England in a conspiracy with the collector to break up the trade in woolen goods.[14] The Pres was called on for the Report in Feby. Poindexter never made his Report until the 20th of April to the Treasury. Stanly called for it but could not get it, as it had not been examined at the Treasury or coppied to comply with the call. Stanly summoned Poindexter & got a coppy which he presented to the House for printing by order of his Committee. It will be soon published & it is supposed will have a tendency to injure Van Buren.

It is hardly probable that I can screw myself up to make a speech on the Tariff & Brown doubts whether he will. He & Habersham have proposed a counter report which he thinks will answer well for circulation better than a speech.[15]

I suppose Shepherd of Williamson recomended as a Tyler Whig will be appointed Marshall.[16] We recomended the renomination of Claiborne & if he did not do that, we then all united in recomending Wm G. Childress, Genl Clements or Matlock.[17] Genl J's[18] recomendation will carry Shepherd. The Genl ought not to interfere by recomending political opponents to the exclusion of his former & long tried friends. We should have had a democrat but for his recomendation. I think the Pres. is using every means to make capital by his patronage. It is believed, that as soon as Congress adjourns—the Clay whigs in office will be shoved overboard. They are now the most odious to the Pres. of all other cliques or parties. I do not see that he has or can make the slighest impression upon the Democratic. Benton & the Globe[19] are going to extremes agt. him and as I think acting unwisely. We ought certainly to support when we can & conciliate as much [as] possible. It was believed for some time here that Ewings Bank Bill *with the assent of the States*[20] would be taken up & passed instead of the Exchequer schemes proposed at the present session & make an issue with Clay upon that. The Madisonian[21] has recently denied any such project & so does his friends.

I know Jas M Howry well & occasionally correspond with him, send him documents &c. My impression is that no demonstration at this time in behalf of any of our candidates would operate favorably among our friends. They generally oppose the idea of any movement until next year & I am often censured for speaking freely upon the subject among our friends.

My impression is that I cannot remain longer than the close of the session. I have formed a partnership in the practice of the Law & my personal attention will be expected after this session.[22] I have written

Hardwicke to ascertain his views & wishes on the subject. I am very unwilling to do any thing that would seem unkind toward him or give any advantage to one friend over another. I must try & make some money for Hickman and Dickson[23] & besides we cannot with propriety have them here with us & we cannot leave them.

I should be glad if you & Nicholson could in some way become reconciled & move as harmoniously as here-to-fore. Tho I shall have but little to do with politics hereafter I shall feel as much anxiety as ever for the success of our cause & should deplore any misunderstanding which would tend to weaken us. We ought to bear & forbear much. Concession, harmony, everything for the cause. I have made similar suggestions to him. He speaks in kind terms of you—will support your re-election and is determined to adhere to our party.

The prevailing opinion here seems to be that our difficulties with England will be reconciled without difficulty. Lord Aberdeen you see renounces the right of search & rumor says Ld. Ashburton is ready to give an equivalent in Lands on the Coast for the mountain lands in dispute, which will be a good bargain for the state of Maine and as to the Creole I suppose there will be indemnity offered in the negotiation protracted or postponed.[24] Webster I suppose will settle as much as he can & leave the balance for future adjustment. We ought not settle one until the other is adjusted. Both questions, in the event of war, will unite the North & South. My respects to Madam.

C JOHNSON

[P.S.] My health is better than you ever knew it.

ALS. DLC–JKP. Addressed to Columbia and marked *"Private."* Polk's AE on the cover states that he answered this letter on May 10, 1842; Polk's reply has not been found.

1. Letter not found.

2. On April 27, 1842, William Halsted from New Jersey moved such an amendment in the U.S. House; that body concurred in the amendment on May 3. The final bill, which became law on June 25, 1842, omitted Halsted's wording, but incorporated the idea that members of Congress should be elected at the district level rather than state wide. A lawyer, Halsted served two terms in the House as a Whig, 1837–39 and 1841–43.

3. In recent elections Connecticut Democrats carried their gubernatorial and legislative tickets in every congressional district in the state. Early in 1842 Rhode Island's free suffrage advocates won a plebiscite on the adoption of their proposed constitution; under that authority they elected their leader, Thomas W. Dorr, governor of the new regime and gained majorities in both houses of their new legislature. Although the free suffrage issue cut across party lines, Dorr's "rebellion" received more support from Democrats than from Whigs. Democrats in New

Jersey scored significant gains in state elections held in October of 1841. In February of 1842 Georgia Democrats carried their ticket in a special election to fill three vacancies in that state's congressional delegation.

4. See Hopkins L. Turney to Polk, April 26, 1842.

5. On March 31, 1842, Leverett Saltonstall reported a tariff bill from the House Committee on Manufactures; that bill received little consideration. In response to a request from the House Committee on Ways and Means, Secretary of the Treasury Walter Forward transmitted a tariff proposal to the House on May 9. Forward's draft bill raised duties above the 20 per cent ceiling fixed by the Compromise Tariff Act of 1833, but did not mention distribution of the proceeds of public land sales. The general revenue bill, which was reported by the Committee on Ways and Means on June 10, 1842, proposed tariffs exceeding the 20 per cent level and provided for unconditional continuance of distribution; that bill passed the House on July 16 and the Senate on August 5. Tyler vetoed the legislation four days later and cited reasons similar to those he had given on June 29 for disapproving a temporary tariff bill, which would have extended the life of tariff and distribution laws due to terminate on June 30. Tyler argued that Congress should not violate the 1833 tariff compromise for purposes of distribution; nor should Congress borrow money for such purposes. Under great pressure to enact a general revenue act, Congress dropped its distribution clause, and Tyler accepted the revised bill on August 30, 1842. The Tariff Act of 1842 returned duties to their 1833 level, which had ranged from 23 to 35 per cent ad valorem.

6. Johnson's reference probably included the select Committee on Retrenchment, the standing Committee on Public Expenditures, and the six standing committees on expenditures in the five executive departments and on the public buildings. Johnson himself headed the Committee on Expenditures on Public Buildings and supported efforts to implement government economy.

7. Carey A. Harris, former resident of Williamson County, Tennessee, rose to the rank of chief clerk in the War Department; in 1836 Jackson chose him to head the Office of Indian Affairs, in which post he served until his resignation in late 1838.

8. Thomas Jefferson Porter of Columbia, Tennessee, succeeded his father, Joseph, as clerk of Maury County Court in the 1820's, served as an executor of Samuel Polk's estate, ran unsuccessfully for Congress in 1833, and acquired extensive land holdings in Tennessee's Western District.

9. On April 12, 1842, John T. Stuart, Whig member of the House Committee on Public Expenditures, reported committee findings that Harris had used his public office for private gain and that Van Buren had accepted Harris' resignation quietly rather than expose corruption in the administration. The committee report included evidence that Porter and Harris had collaborated to secure certain Indian lands in Mississippi for personal benefit. The contents of Porter's 1838 letter to Harris, upon which the accusation was founded, was known to the committee only through the testimony of government clerks claiming to have read the document. In a letter dated May 16, 1842, and addressed to the chairman of the committee, Porter used evidence from the General Land Office to support his argument that his land claim had required Treasury Department action and

had involved no connection with Harris' Office of Indian Affairs. Porter further explained that because of illness he had been unable to travel to Washington City to press his claim in person. See House Report No. 640, 27 Congress, 2 Session.

10. A lawyer from North Carolina, Edward Stanly served several terms as a Whig member of the U.S. House, 1837–43 and 1849–53. In 1857 he ran unsuccessfully as a Republican for the governorship of California; during the Civil War he held the post of military governor of eastern North Carolina.

11. George Nixon Briggs, Horace Everett, and William Slade. Briggs, a lawyer, served as a Whig congressman from Massachusetts, 1831–43; as governor, 1844–51; and as judge of the state's Court of Common Pleas, 1853–58. Everett, a lawyer and prominent Vermont Whig, won election to seven terms in the U.S. House, 1829–43. Slade, a lawyer and editor, served as Vermont's secretary of state, 1815–22; sat as a Whig in Congress, 1831–43; and won election as governor, 1844–46.

12. Francis W. Pickens, a South Carolina lawyer and planter, first won election to Congress as a nullifier and sat from 1834 until 1843. A member of the Nashville Convention of 1850, he served as governor of South Carolina from 1860 until 1863. On Pickens' pamphlet urging Calhoun's nomination, see Aaron V. Brown to Polk, April 9, 1842.

13. Richard M. Johnson.

14. On April 28, 1842, Edward Stanly from the House Committee on Public Expenditures submitted to the House George Poindexter's report to Secretary of the Treasury Walter Forward. In 1841 Tyler had appointed Poindexter, a former congressman, senator, and governor of Mississippi, 1819–21, as one of three commissioners to investigate the U.S. customhouse in New York City. Poindexter's minority report concurred with the majority report of Commissioners William M. Steuart and Alfred Kelley in revealing pervasive corruption in the customhouse under Collector Jesse Hoyt, 1838–41. Poindexter's report went further, however, by adding a severe condemnation of the Whig, Edward Curtis, who had succeeded Hoyt. Poindexter also implicated Benjamin Franklin Butler, a former law partner of Van Buren and U.S. attorney general, 1833–38, for his actions as U.S. attorney for Southern New York, 1838–41; Butler served in the latter position again, under Polk, 1845–48. See House Report No. 669, 27 Congress, 2 Session.

15. On May 5, 1842, Richard Wylly Habersham submitted to the House a minority report from the Committee on Manufactures protesting against the high protective duties urged by the committee's majority; Aaron V. Brown and Patrick Calhoun Caldwell of South Carolina joined Habersham in signing the minority report. A lawyer from Savannah, Georgia, Habersham served in the U.S. House as a State Rights Democrat from March 4, 1839, until his death on December 2, 1842.

16. Before serving as U.S. marshal in Middle Tennessee, Benjamin H. Sheppard had co-edited the Jackson *District Telegraph and State Sentinel*, 1837–38.

17. Thomas Claiborne, William G. Childress, Jesse B. Clements, and, possibly, Gideon C. Matlock. Clements, a planter in Lincoln County, had ad-

vanced to the rank of brigadier general in the Tennessee militia in 1836. Matlock took an active part in Democratic party affairs in Wilson and Smith counties.

18. Reference is to Andrew Jackson.

19. The Washington *Globe*, founded in 1830 and edited by Francis P. Blair, had become the leading national newspaper of Jacksonian Democrats.

20. Thomas Ewing, an Ohio lawyer, sat as a Whig in the U.S. Senate, 1831–37 and 1850–51. He served as secretary of the Treasury under Harrison and Tyler, March 5 to September 13, 1841, but resigned in protest against Tyler's opposition to a national bank. On June 3, 1841, Ewing had sent to the U.S. House a report recommending repeal of the Independent Treasury Act and creation of a fiscal agent of the United States. As reported to the Senate on June 12, Ewing's "Fiscal Bank" scheme provided for a central bank in the District of Columbia with branches, or offices of discount and deposit, located in the several states whose legislatures did not object. Ewing's plan received the endorsement of Tyler, who had objected to the creation of a national bank on constitutional grounds; Ewing's plan removed these objections. Tyler urged, but failed to receive, Henry Clay's support.

21. Established in 1837 with Thomas Allen as editor and publisher, the Washington *Madisonian* initially backed conservative Democrats. In the spring of 1841 the newspaper suspended publication, but in September of that year Tyler revived it. Allen retained his post as editor.

22. Johnson's partner is not identified.

23. Reference is to Johnson's sons, James Hickman and Thomas Dickson.

24. Reference is to the Northeastern Boundary Dispute, which was settled by the Webster-Ashburton Treaty in 1842. George Hamilton Gordon, fourth Earl of Aberdeen, was secretary of state for foreign affairs in the British cabinet. Alexander Baring, first Baron Ashburton, served as commissioner procurator and plenipotentiary to the United States; his instructions from Lord Aberdeen gave him authority to settle all outstanding disputes with the United States. See Aaron V. Brown to Polk, April 9, 1842.

FROM LEVIN H. COE[1]

Dear Sir   Somerville Apl. 30th 1842

Your favor of the 19th Apl.[2] was to hand by last Sundays mail. An unusual press of such buisiness as could not be postponed has delayed my reply until to day.

I have mailed a letter written at some lenth to Judge Howry at Oxford—Throwing upon him the onus of a proper move in that state & suggesting that it be made promptly & giving the reasons for it. He will also write to Mr Claibourne.[3]

I have also written to my old Friend James E. Saunders at Courtland[4] urging him to make a move and telling him that his own Statesman K.[5]

stands no chance [and that] to hold back for him will defeat him & you both and saddle us with old *Dick*.[6] I will hear from him in a few days and write you the result. The first move made elsewhere I think should be promptly followed by the hoisting Van[7] & P.—*unconditionally*. In this way alone can we hope not to be juggled off. I have written to Judge Howry & Saunders both that *to that* we intend to come, for that we cannot & will not carry Dick. I have suggested to Judge H. the partiality for Calhoun with some of our Democrats at H Springs[8] so that he might sound there before he leaps.

L. H. Coe

ALS. DLC–JKP. Addressed to Columbia.

1. Coe, a popular lawyer and Democrat from Somerville, served in the Tennessee Senate, 1837–41, and held the office of Senate Speaker during the latter part of his second term.

2. Letter not found.

3. John F. H. Claiborne, a Mississippi Democrat and newspaperman, served one full term in the U.S. House, 1835–37, and part of a second; he lost his seat in 1838 to Sergeant S. Prentiss in a special election required by the House. Claiborne moved from Madison County to Natchez and edited his hometown newspaper, the *Mississippi Free Trader*.

4. James E. Saunders, a member of the 1840 Alabama legislature, moved from Courtland to Mobile in 1842 and engaged in the mercantile business. In 1845, Polk appointed him collector of the port of Mobile, a position he held until 1849.

5. Reference is to William Rufus King, whose public career included service as U.S. Senator from Alabama, 1819–44 and 1848–53; as minister to France, 1844–46; and very briefly as vice-president of the general government in 1853.

6. Richard M. Johnson.

7. Martin Van Buren.

8. Holly Springs, Mississippi.

FROM ARCHIBALD YELL

My Dear Sir   Little Rock 30th Apl. 1842

Your verry acceptable letter of the 19th Inst.[1] was recieved last evening, for which you will please accept my thanks.

The political information Contained in your letter is no doubt a verry Correct history of the movements of the seviral aspirents to the *Presidency*. It is the first reliable information which I have recieved this winter or spring, but is pritty much in accordince with the impresion made upon my mind, through the mediam of the News Paper and my

Knowledge of most of the leaders of the seviral aspirents. Things so far are unsittled, and it is extreamly doubtful who may be the Nominees of the Party. Each of the aspirents will Continu to feel and make interest for themselves until the meeting of the Convention, who will I hope make the most available selection and one that will again ensure our success. But I am one of those who have but little Confidence in the *patriotism* of the grater body of the members of Conventions and they are not always a fare exponant of popular oppinion.

Those Conventions are too often Composed of political aspirents whos patriotism never extends beyond a good fat office eithr for thirselvs or frinds. Hince the peopls favirte may be bortered away. A Combination of Interests may be formed to place the weakest & most objectionable Candidate before the Nation. To make Clearer my views I refer you to the Whigs Harrisburgh Convention wheir Tip & Tyler riceved the nomination. Our Party are not always exempt from like errors. I their fore Consider the *Prise* as now in markiet. He that bids higheist will Win; or rather he that Can be able to Combine the strongest Ticket for Presidet & Vice Presidet will receive the Nomnation.

Buchannon[2] I have no doubt has risked his Nominatin upon his & *Kings* strength and King will stand no Chance with any other aspirnt. If Calhoun should receive the Nominatin I should think Wright or Woodbury would be united with him from the Free States, and they would form a strong Tickett. Uncle *"Dick"* [3] will take any man that will give him strength & he will strive to Coalace with Porter, Wilkins or Dallis of Pensyla[4]; that will tend to weaken both *He & Buchannon*. Should Mr. Van Bern[5] or Wright get the Nominatin, then I Consider the Contest betwn *you* & *Stevenson* of Virginia for the Vice Presidency. Your Claims being about equal, it may depend in some degree upon the prospect of your respective states. Tennessee being the most doubtful will not lessen your Chance, but It will be important to have in the Convention some of your ablest & best Diplomatists. I am not sure If I shall not attend myself. I am however so much of a Novice in such matters I may decline the Honor. I have a fare prospect in Arkansas to Conquer the Soless Corporations here. The next Legislature will settle this matter with the banks.[6] I shall be then Content. I have but one other object to accomplish and I shall retire sattisfied. It is to give the [Ind]ians[7] a good drubing which we will do [soon]er or later. Have you seen my "Canterous" [cor]respondence with *"Earl Spencer."* [8] What a scamp he is!

Now for the *Widdow*.[9] I think I recollict her. She was (if I mistake not) with her Farthr in Nashville during the Session of the Legislatu of 1827. I was also a member. She was large good looking but rather sallow

Conplected; she is of good age, First rate Family & pritty enough for *me*. I have 4 childen in Arkansas & one in Tennessee, *5*. How many has *she*? We may be overstocked, but I should not be the first to object. With such *advantages* would she have me & come to Arkanis? If she would I would then say she is also a *sensable woman*. Say to Mrs Polk if she expects me to go for you for *Presidet* or Vice P., she must shew her frindship.

You say Mrs P. is in "good earnest, no Joke," Nor am I a joking. I Can not come this year to Tennessee. I have this 500,000 acrs of Land to Locate. This must not be neglected. Then our Legislature convens in Nov., but I Can keep up a correspondence with you & learn sompthig of my prispects. What is the *widdars* name? Where does she live?

If D Webster was out of the Cabint I should say we stood agood Chance for a War with England & Mexico, but that fellow will Cheat us out of it. I hope the *Texians* & *Mexicans* will keep it up until our *Indians* takes sides & then we will thrash them. Nothing short of a war Can get us out of Debt.

Present me kindly to Mrs Polk and bilieve me as evr . . . .

A. YELL

ALS. DLC–JKP. Addressed to Columbia.

1. Letter not found.
2. James Buchanan.
3. Richard M. Johnson.
4. David R. Porter, William Wilkins, and George M. Dallas. Porter, an iron manufacturer, served as governor of Pennsylvania from 1839 until 1845. Wilkins, first president of the Bank of Pittsburgh, served in the U.S. Senate, 1831–34; went to Russia as Jackson's minister plenipotentiary, 1834–35; sat in the U.S. House, 1843–44; and headed the War Department under Tyler, 1844–45. Dallas, a Philadelphia lawyer, served as mayor of Philadelphia, 1829; U.S. Senator, 1831–33; minister to Russia, 1837–39; vice-president under Polk, 1845–49; and minister to Great Britain, 1856–61.
5. Martin Van Buren.
6. Reference is to Arkansas' two state banking systems, both of which were closed by 1844.
7. Manuscript mutilated here and in two lines following.
8. In early 1842 Yell exchanged with Secretary of War John C. Spencer a series of letters in which the Arkansas governor argued the pressing danger of Indian raids and protested the secretary's refusal to reinforce regular army troops on the frontier. The use of the title "Earl" probably alludes to the name similarity between the American secretary of war and his contemporary, John Charles Spencer, 3rd Earl Spencer and leader of the Whig Party in England.
9. Not identified further. See Yell to Polk, March 6, 1842.

FROM HARVEY M. WATTERSON[1]

Dear Sir.   Washington City. 2d May 1842

I was gratified to learn on yesterday from our friend A V Brown, that you would probably visit this City some time during this or the next month. I hope you will not abandon that intention. Your friends here would like very much to see you.

You remarked to me in your last letter that you would like for me to inform you from time to time of such *matters of general interest* as do not make their appearance in the Newspapers. I presume you wish to know what the leaders of the Democratic and Whig parties are saying and doing in regard to the next Presidential election. Thus supposing, I will briefly give you what I have seen and heard, and my own impressions founded upon the same.

It is perhaps needless for me to say that it is now the settled purpose of the Whig party to make Mr Clay their candidate at all hazards, and a Bank or no Bank is to be the main issue. It is the hobby on which he calculates success. President Tyler has "headed" himself by retaining Webster in his Cabinet and his "fishy" course generally[2] and is not seriously thought of for the succession or re-election, or whatever you may call it, by any respectable number of either party. He will "evaporate" at the end of this term a striking monument of the folly of attempting to establish a third or "Patriot Party" as his friends style themselves in this country.

Now for the Democrats. Buchannon is so anxious for the nomination that he has *almost* turned *cross-eyed!*[3] But it wont do. He can not even unite the entire Democratic Delegation in the House of Representatives from Pennsylvania. I regard his prospects as peculiarly gloomy, but not more so than those of his friend Col King of Alabama who would like the best of all things in the world to be run upon *his* ticket for Vice President.

Benton you know has declared for Mr Van Buren, and is considered out of the scrape. This *seems* to be very disinterested patriotism indeed, and it *may* be.

Mr Calhoun's friends are pressing his claims warmly. I have seen a small pamphlet said to be and no doubt written by Pickens urging many reasons why he should be taken up as by the Democratic party.[4] This pamphlet has not yet met the "public eye" and perhaps will not, as the move is deemed impolitic by Dixon H. Lewis,[5] and other friends of Mr Calhoun. They think it would be calculated to array against him at too early a period the particular friends of the other aspirants. Personally Mr

Calhoun is very popular with a large majority of the Democratic members of Congress, but many doubts are entertained on the subject of his *availability* by a number of those who would zealously support him, *if* he were the nominee of the party. That he will get the nomination—the chances are now against him.

Silas Wright, in my humble opinion, could be nominated by the Democratic members of the present Congress. But his partiality for Mr Van Buren is such, that he is supposed to be out of the question.

The conclusion which I draw from all the signs of the times at present is, that Van, that "used up man" is to be our party candidate. If so no man, I think, has a fairer prospect for the Vice Presidency than yourself.

I would be glad to hear from you.

H M WATTERSON

ALS. DLC–JKP. Addressed to Columbia and marked "Private."

1. Watterson, a lawyer and founding editor of the Shelbyville *Western Freeman*, served one term in the Tennessee House, 1835–37, and two terms in the U.S. House, 1839–43. Elected to one term in the Tennessee Senate, 1845–47, he presided over that body as its Speaker. From 1847 until 1851 he edited the *Nashville Union*; in 1851 he became editor of the *Washington Union*.

2. Possibly an allusion to administration support of New England fishing interest against British encroachments.

3. James Buchanan suffered muscular disability in one eye.

4. See Aaron V. Brown to Polk, April 9, 1842.

5. A Montgomery lawyer and member of the Alabama House, 1825–27, Dixon H. Lewis sat in the U.S. House from 1829 until 1844, when he resigned to fill the U.S. Senate seat vacated by William R. King.

FROM ROBERT ARMSTRONG

Dear Sir,   Nashville 4 May 42

I am at a loss to know what to say to you. I can learn nothing or understand Donelson; he will go out with Mr Van Buren and continue on to his Mississippi place.

Mr. Van Buren seems disposed to say nothing on the subject we spoke of when I last saw you.[1] I made an effort through Donelson again this evening, but it is all *Mum* with kind feelings, &c &c. It may be that he will say to you what he will not say to any other person. The old Genl. will *Tell him before leaving the Hermitage*, to have a conversation with you.

Their is now a Committee here from Huntsville who insist on his going there from Columbia. If he does, our friends in Giles, Lincoln, Bedford &c

&c. ought to know it.[2] The greater the show *now* he is here, the better for our cause. The old Chief is very Ill, somewhat Improving, but feeble and very weak.

R ARMSTRONG

[P.S.] Doct. McNeill has Just *returned.*

ALS. DLC–JKP. Addressed to Columbia.

1. Reference probably is to the 1844 Democratic vice-presidential nomination.

2. Armstrong informed Polk on May 7 that Van Buren had left that morning for Columbia and would return to Nashville on May 9. ALS. DLC–JKP. Van Buren did not include a visit to northern Alabama on his 1842 tour.

FROM HARRY[1]

Dear Master State of Miss. Carroll County May 10th 1842

As a sevent I want to subcrib my friendship to you & famley as I am still in Carrollton yet & doing Good Labor for my imployer, but tho I am feling[2] in some degree, my Eye site is falling of me, I am well Trated by my imployer. He feeds well & dont worke me Tow Hard. I would wish to be Remembrd to all of my people, Old Mistrs[3] aspshenly.[4] Tell the old Lady Harry is hir Sevent untill dath & would be Glad to see Hir one mor. I Expect to come out a christmust to see you.

The Hardness of Times & casness[5] of mony is Her & will Reduce wages. Deer Master I looked for you of Febuary but you never come up to Carrollton. Deer Master I have Eleven children. I have ben faithful over the anvill Block Evr cen 1811 & is still old Harry. My childrens names [are] 1 Daniel 2 Morcel 3 Ben 4 Elis 5 Carrell 6 Charles 7 Eleeshee 8 David 9 Morning 10 Carline 11 Opheelia. Som Resquest from you please to Send me a Lettr How all of the people ar doing in your country.

HARRY

[P.S.] Direct your Lettr to—Mr Edward P. Davison[6] Carrollton Miss.

L, written and signed in unknown hand. DLC–JKP. Addressed to Columbia.

1. One of Polk's duties as executor of Samuel W. Polk's estate was the oversight of the slave, Harry, who was hired out as a blacksmith in Carrollton, Mississippi.

2. Probably a misspelling of "failing."

3. Jane Knox Polk, Polk's mother, resided in Columbia.

4. Probably a misspelling of "especially."

5. Probably a misspelling of "scarceness."

6. Not identified further.

FROM J. G. M. RAMSEY

My Dear Sir   Mecklenburg May 10. 1842

I wrote you recently giving you the substance of an answer I had recd. from the Editor of the Meck-Jeff.[1] & remarked at the time that I would soon reply, &c. This I have since done after the following manner. "I am glad to hear you say that as to the V.P., Gov. Polk would please you as well as any other man in the Union, but you then ask the question "might not a ticket of both Southern men lose us the victory?" This is a most significant & important question, but without entering at length into its investigation I would barely remark that there is little force in the objection that neither of the two candidates is from the North. Considered *sectionally* our party is in an admitted minority in both branches of the Legislature & it is therefore not unfair that we should have the Executive—but theory aside you will recollect that in 1828 the West & South gave the P. & V.P.[2] & they were sustained not only with unanimity but with enthusiasm. New England now except Mass. & Vt. would do so again, & the question at issue being radical & essential with the Demo. party sectional influences would yield or be inoperative. N.Y., Pa. & the Middle States would unite upon our candidates & blessed with such an administration as has not been since that of Washington the whole country would once more harmonise perfectly. I beg leave to add that my acquaintance with the feelings & preferences of the people of N.C. & especially of Tenn. & her co-terminous Western States, enables me to say *who ought to be nominated at Salisbury for V.P.* All admit that it will be a close race in N.C. & T. under the most favorable circumstances. We have a majority *if* the materials can be brought *to combine.* Gov. Polk is a native of your State & the name is closely identified with the lofty spirit of independence that characterised the Whigs of 1775. He is moreover an adopted son of Tennessee & has added lustre to the State & she is justly proud of his purity—his virtue—his abilities & his services. She appreciates as she ought the manly & self-sacraficing devotion he has manifested for our principles & his disinterested & laborious defence & advocacy of them. These claims of his to the consideration & confidence of his countrymen should not be—must not be over-looked on the 20th May. That day cannot be consecrated to a more hallowed purpose than his nomination to the second station in the Gt.[3] To do otherwise would have a very bad effect elsewhere & especially in Tennessee—upon the prospects of whomsoever is the Pres. nominee of the Bal. Con.[4] That nominee could not but derive a vast acquisition of strength by having Gov. P. associated with him as V.P. I hazard little in saying that thus associated he would certainly carry N.C., Tenn., Al., & Miss. Without this association the result in all these States I consider doubtful—very. You requested me to write fully & freely. I have done so. I cannot be mistaken. You ought at once to nominate Polk. He will help you even in your approaching state elections—more than you have conception of. Especially will you need him as an auxilliary to carry Mr. C.[5] in N.C. & Tenn. These remarks are my own. Take them only for what they are worth. They are neither suggested or authorised by another. They are my honest convictions & I thought some member of the Convention should know them." Thus for my answer. It will be showed to Fisher, & to others in higher stations. It shows earnestness, but not more temper I think than the occasion required.

Yours of Apl. 16. is recd.[6] The extract you sent me from a Washington Cor.[7] coincides with my accounts from other places & persons. Whether V.B.[8] or C. runs—or if both do you ought to be the V.P. in either case. Ill keep up the fire in the South.

We are much gratified at the arrangements permitted by the Rector & suggested by the kindness of Mrs. P. & yourself in relation to our daughter.[9] At this time we find it impossible for her to attend—desirable as it otherwise would be. She is called unexpectedly to Ky. on an *affair of honor* with a female friend & she must forego for the present the advantages of the Institute & the civilities of your family. Present our thanks & best regards to Mrs. Polk—& my own to your excellent mother.

I was at Rogersville, Greeneville &c a week ago. Our friends are in fine spirits up there. I expected to have a county meeting to invite you among others in Aug. I will expect the Vol. you mention by Major Graham or Humphreys.[10]

A strong Whig told Bass (J.M.)[11] & myself the other day in town that you were the only one that could beat Clay for the Presidency.

J. G. M. RAMSEY

P.S. I intimated to Bass that the Bank of Tennessee had not been sufficiently cautious in some of its late *decisions* & doings & that it might thus injure you & your friends.[12]

ALS. DLC–JKP. Addressed to Columbia.

1. For Ramsey's brief of the answer he received from J. W. Hampton, editor of the Charlotte *Mecklenburg Jeffersonian* (North Carolina), see Ramsey to Polk, April 18, 1842.
2. Andrew Jackson and John C. Calhoun.
3. Abbreviation for "government."
4. Reference is to the 1844 Baltimore Convention.
5. John C. Calhoun.
6. Letter not found.

7. Polk's Washington correspondent may have been Aaron V. Brown or Cave Johnson. See Brown to Polk, March 22, 1842. In a lengthy letter of March 20, 1842, Johnson recounts political speculation on the 1844 Democratic ticket quite similar to that reported by Brown. ALS. DLC–JKP.

8. Martin Van Buren.

9. See Ramsey to Polk, April 18, 1842. Franklin G. Smith headed the Columbia Female Institute from 1836 until 1852.

10. Daniel Graham and West H. Humphreys. A lawyer from Somerville, Humphreys won election to a single term in the Tennessee House, 1835–37; served as state attorney general and reporter, 1839–51; and presided over the U.S. District Court for West Tennessee from 1853 until 1861, in which latter year he accepted the position of C.S.A. judge for Tennessee. The volume expected by Ramsey is not identified further.

11. John M. Bass, a son-in-law of Felix Grundy, served as president of the Union Bank of Tennessee in the late 1830's and early 1840's; he won election as mayor of Nashville in 1833.

12. Banking transactions not identified further.

FROM FRANKLIN H. ELMORE[1]

My Dear Sir   Charleston May 12, 1842

The recent decisive triumphs of our party & principles over the Whigs is a subject of such gratulation to every patriot that I cannot forbear to seek you out in your retirement to express to you the profound satisfaction which we all feel in this quarter on the happy prospect that seems again opening upon our country. The rebukes they are daily meeting at the hands of an abused & repentant people are the most signal ever witnessed in our history. To good old Virginia, the glorious mother of so many states & of that still more glorious creed of principles for which we contend, how much of gratitude do we owe for her last & most triumphant vindication of her principles & the constitution![2] If North Carolina does but assume a position at our side, never will the whole south have presented so firm & united a front. But be that as it will, Whig folly & wickedness have numbered its own days & nothing can prevent the reestablishment of the Government on true republican principles unless there be a falling out by the way in our own Democratic ranks. So far, harmonious concert has given unity to us & an irrisistible career, but it has also conquered so many into our ranks, that we are in danger of falling to pieces by our own weight. I do not mean in immediate, but prospective danger of it. The Whigs are so sensible of their desperate condition that they already are counting on this hope for Mr. Clays success—so writes Preston to his friends here.[3] As a good cause, holy principles & the irrisistible vigor of truth & our friends have won the battle, so it becomes their prudence & patriotism, with forecast & decision, to take timely steps to secure for ourselves & posterity its legitimate results. The battle has been won on *Principles* not on men & we cannot be too careful not to let its trophies be snatched away in the very moment of victory, by allowing the influence of the latter to modify the support of the former, so as to impair the union & power of our party. It does seem to me that there never opened a fairer prospect for settling, for a long succession of years, the character of our administrations & giving permanent ascendency to the Democratic construction of the constitution, and of consolidating the prosperity of the whole country. Having secured the almost certain assurance of a victory in the last struggle which ejects the Whigs & restores the Democrats to power, our only danger is in our dissensions in selecting the leader who is to be the exponent of our principles. If we unite on one judiciously selected & fairly chosen, there can be no doubt of a glorious triumph & a long ascendency—while on the other hand it is impossible to foretell all the calamities that may fall on us as a party or a people, by a mistake in this particular.

In the future movements of our party, much will depend on you & your immediate friends. Your long services & prominent position at Washington & at home, have given you friends & influence that may be exercised for great good. Many of us who have known you, have not forgone the hope of seeing you again performing your part for the public welfare, & giving your services to the country. And if our party is reinstated in power, let who may be chief, I trust your voice will [be] heard in its administration and such I may safely say is the public feeling here.

In the selection of a candidate for the Presidency, you know what would be the voice of So Carolina. The long services & brilliant talants of Mr. Calhoun has for a long time made him her favorite. And his glorious services since Whig ascendency, have made him even dearer to their affections. The choice of a candidate may be said to rest between him & Mr. Van Buren. On the spot where his talents & service are most seen & felt, there is no doubt Mr. Calhoun is greatly preferred—I mean at Washington, amongst the Representatives who have been fighting by his side, and amongst whom he has been a leader. With the people he has gained immensely & is daily adding to his popularity. He has been in the thickest of the fight & on every occasion has exhibited in the service of the country the most distinguished abilities.

Mr. Van Buren has great claims on our confidence & gratitude. He undoubtedly fell a martyr to our principles & if it were a mere question of reward, he is intitled to all the support we have warmly given him & even more. But to me, it seems, the question is rather, is it wise & expedient to risk a great cause again on him who has lost the battle before? Do we see such prospects of success in his leading, as to induce us to risk *all* again upon his banner? It cannot be unknown that in all the south he has had great difficulty in procuring a warm support, while he has met with a more unrelenting opposition than any public man of the times. Very many persons of intelligence who agree with us in principles, have never been able to give him confidence or support. The Whigs in the late election gained thousands who felt so while they were Democrats at heart & we had thousands who then voted with us, but who would now resist his being our candidate all of whom could be got for Mr Calhoun. They say that he has had a fair trial & it was clear that he is not one to get up a warm feeling for—that he has too much weight to carry. In short that in the popular feeling there are prejudices too powerful to be overcome & that if he be run, we may look for certain defeat.

It is understood here that Mr. Stevenson of Virginia is to be insisted on as his vice. The Richmond Enquirer it is said stipulates for it as the sine quo non—how truly I cannot say. He then is put in the line of succession, & after him of course a northern man as it would now seem to be necessary to alternate, between the slave & non slave holding sections. The overwhelming rout of the Whigs in that state may precipitate this arrangement & if it is to be counteracted it does seem to me that no time should be lost. If acquiesed in, we cannot know it too soon.

Amongst other matters connected with this subject, is the question of how many terms a man should serve. The Whigs go for one term—Mr. V.B. has had one term. I am not a one term man, but if the Party adopt it, I shall acquiese. I understand that there is a strong disposition that way at Washington, and that Mr. Calhoun is not disposed to be out for more than one, not, at his time of life, having more time to allot to the public service.

In regard to Mr. Van Buren, you know what has been my course. I entered Congress with every prejudice against him, and when I eventually gave him my support, it was you know with every possible reservation. Slowly but surely my convictions were attained on which I gave him my confidence, & I do not know any public man of the day, except Mr. Calhoun, to whom I feel we owe more. I should feel perfectly safe in his hands—and if he is elected President, unless he turn upon his own principles I shall be prepared to do as I have done before, give him both confidence & support. But while I feel thus towards him, I also feel that we owe as much to say the least to Mr. Calhoun, & that we cannot postpone the acknowledgement. I believe too that he will unite far more of the elements of power & success in the coming struggle & that our party will act more wisely to risk the great cause to which we are devoted, on his leading rather than anothers.

I will my Dear Sir be pleased to hear from you, if you have leisure & to interchange views upon these & such other public topics as may be agreeable to you.

I pray you present my most respectful regards to Mrs. Polk . . . .

F. H. ELMORE

ALS. DLC–JKP. Addressed to Columbia. Polk's AE on the cover states that he answered this letter on June 13, 1842.

1. Franklin Harper Elmore, South Carolina lawyer and supporter of John C. Calhoun, sat in the U.S. House, 1836–39; presided over the bank of the State of South Carolina, 1839–50; and served briefly in the U.S. Senate in 1850.

2. In the Virginia legislative elections of April, 1842, Democrats carried both houses by sizable majorities.

3. William C. Preston, a strong advocate of states' rights, won election to the U.S. Senate in 1833 as a Calhoun nullifier and gained reelection in 1837. Becoming an anti-Jackson Whig, he resigned his seat in 1842 rather than follow the instructions of the South Carolina legislature.

FROM CAVE JOHNSON

Dear Sir,   Washington May 20th 1842

Yours of the 10th[1] was received this morning. I was somewhat uneasy lest Van Burens appearance might not operate favorably for him in Ten. Our people have so often looked on the old Genl. whose personal appearance was so much better that I thought it probable his trip[2] would be of no advantage. I had supposed Van Buren would have mentioned the subject of the next elections and I think he should have done so and that you & he should have conferred freely. All the injury will arise from such charges without any benefit derived from it, tho it is probable any understanding between you & him would have but little influence on the future movements of our party, without you both had taken a more active Stand for each other than would have been prudent. I think a serious & powerful effort will be made by some Southern Democrats to thrust him aside upon the pretence, that having been beaten, he is not safe for another race—that old charges will be revived—the trouble of explanation &c & he thrust aside there will be room for another. Hence the secret pamphlet was written which I have never seen and which it is said has not been circulated for fear of exposure & the consequences which might result.[3] The Index is supposed to be in that interest, but no developments have been made in that quarter as far as I can see. The prospectus of a New Paper The Spectator has been recently issued, edited by Doct. Martin (the author of the index who was removed from the Chief Clerkship of the State Department).[4] This it is said will be a Buckhanon paper. These things indicate pretty strongly a setled determination in high quarters to thrust him aside.[5] I should think Gov W—ry[6] of N.H. could not be induced to lend himself in any way to any such project. The friends of Van say openly here, if he is not run that Silas W.[7] is the man. These things will annoy us exceedingly and particularly if another Congress comes here without our candidates being setled on & I think it would be good policy in us to have that matter setled next year.

I shall not be surprised if the condition of Rhode Island[8] should have much influence on the future action of our party. Senator Allen made a bitter speech the other day, denouncing the conduct of the Pres. in strong terms & among other things insisting upon the principle that a majority of the people of any State has the right to alter, to amend &c & to my surprise some of the States right men give into this view.[9] It is said Allen is acting upon consultation with Benton & if the debate goes on in the Senate & the views of Allen are sustained by some of our leaders, it may make a serious division in our rank. I learn that Calhoun will to day or tomorrow make some conciliatory movement & so pass by the difficulty, such as the Senators interposing, urging the adjoining States to do so & thus settle the difficulty or thus delay the action of parties in that State for a while, hoping that reason may regain the ascendency & that some project may be devised which will be agreeable to both parties. We are expecting every arrival of the mail to bring us intelligence of a battle or row of some sort. The Charter men are urged *to a perseverance* by the course of the Pres. who most unwisely as I think told them what kind of a case he would act on & how he would act. They are thus induced to persevere under the expectation of drawing their opponents to such a state as will induce the Pres. to act. In my opinion if he had simply said, no case is made out for the interposition of the Executive as Van did to the Buck-shot-war heroes,[10] the difficulty would now have been over. This movement excited the Democracy of New York, who generally act on impulse & without much reflection. They have promised assistance to the other side, who are as much encouraged if not more so by it than the other side by the letters of the Executive. So the matter now stands. The Senate went into Executive session at an unusually early hour as some suppose on the Rhode Island difficulties. I have not seen the official Comments & cannot of course give any opinion. I understand the difficulty to arise in this way. The Original Charter was a corporation of land holders, giving the land holders the right of voting &c and which was fair & equal & gave general satisfaction & on account of this no constitution was formed at the termination of the Revolution. Recently the manufacturing interest has acquired the ascendency in point of numbers & the struggle now is which party shall rule? The latest intelligence says the reform Gov. has possession of the State House & two canons and an attack was hourly expected to be made on the Arsenal in the possession of the old Gov. There is no knowing what influence or to what lenth, this difficulty may produce. A blow struck may give rise to a civil war. It is a great misfortune to the country that Van is not now the Pres. His coolness, discrimination & good sense would have passed such an event without difficulty.

The Clay men of the West have become thorough reformers, [and] leave me in the shade altogether. I am in hopes we shall now be able to do some good & make some useful reforms. The Navy Bill will be cut down some two or three millions.[11] I rather think we could now repeal the Home Squadron which only lost 8 votes at the Extra Session.[12]

You will regret to learn that Gov Thomas & lady have seperated probably forever[13]—some foolish jealous fit of his, for which there was not the slightest cause—even worse than Houstons.[14] I think he is a ruined man in every point of view. I have not seen him. They tell here some strange anecdotes of his conduct. His wife is in Va. I hope you will visit the city. It will be of service rather than injury to you. We shall not probably get away before the middle of Augt. or September. The Whigs never expect to get back & must make the most of their time.

C JOHNSON

[P.S.] No duel yet between Wise & Stanly.[15] One is expected notwithstanding Wise is bound to keep the peace in the District. Stanly has been out of the City for a week & rumor says in practising with Reverdy Johnson one [of] his balls rebounded & struck Johnson about the eye & there is some danger of his loosing it.[16] The papers next morning said he had fallen from his horse. Brown talks of leaving here next week for Ten. with his family.

ALS. DLC–JKP. Addressed to Columbia and marked *"private."*

1. Letter not found.

2. Reference is to Martin Van Buren's visit to Nashville and the Hermitage in late April of 1842.

3. See Aaron V. Brown to Polk, April 9, 1842.

4. The Alexandria *Index* (D.C.) began publication in April of 1841 and issued its last number in August of 1842. Chief clerk of the State Department in 1840 and 1841, Jacob L. Martin had declined an offer in 1838 to edit the *Nashville Union*. In March of 1843 Calhoun interests acquired the financially troubled *Spectator* and ran it as Calhoun's national newspaper until its demise in late 1844.

5. Reference is to Van Buren.

6. Levi Woodbury.

7. Silas Wright.

8. Popular dissatisfaction with suffrage restrictions led to Rhode Island's "Dorr Rebellion" of 1841–42. In late 1841 a popular, but extralegal convention framed and ratified a "People's Constitution," which provided for white manhood suffrage and called for new state elections. The legislature declared the new constitution illegal and sponsored a regularly scheduled spring election under authority of the colonial charter of 1663. Thomas W. Dorr won the new constitution's gubernatorial election; and the incumbent governor, Samuel W. King, gained reelection under the old charter. Both Dorr and King applied to Tyler for military aid. In a letter dated April 11, 1842, Tyler assured King that if an actual insurrection were raised against the charter government, the general government would furnish that protection guaranteed to each state under Article 4, Section 4 of the U.S. Constitution. In a private letter of May 9, 1842, Tyler urged King to exercise conciliation and restraint, including a general amnesty and a new constitutional convention. On May 18 the Dorrites attempted and failed to seize the state's militia arsenal; the "rebellion" rapidly lost support thereafter. Dorr received a sentence of life imprisonment, but won release in 1845.

9. On May 17, 1842, William Allen made extended remarks introducing two resolutions affirming the right of Rhode Island citizens to establish a constitutional republican form of government and enjoining the general government from blocking the people's efforts to establish such a government in Rhode Island. On the following day the Senate tabled Allen's resolutions.

10. In 1838 both Democrats and Whigs claimed control of the Pennsylvania House of Representatives in a dispute over the election of House Speaker. A threatening mob forced several legislators to flee. Failing to receive assistance from the general government, Joseph Ritner, the governor, called out the state militia and equipped the troops with buckshot cartridges. The conflict ended when Democratic members, aided by three Whigs, organized the House.

11. Congress reduced the 1842 estimates for naval expenses by approximately two million dollars.

12. On July 21, 1841, the U.S. House authorized creation of a Home Squadron by a vote of 184 to 8. Tyler approved appropriations for eight additional naval vessels and contingent expenses on August 1, 1841.

13. Francis Thomas, a leading lawyer from western Maryland, won five terms as a Democrat in the U.S. House, 1831–41; he served as governor from 1841 until 1844. In 1841 he had married Sally Campbell McDowell, twenty-year-old daughter of James McDowell of Virginia and favorite niece of Thomas H. Benton.

14. Married on January 22, 1829, Sam Houston left his wife, Eliza Allen, in April of that same year.

15. On May 7, 1842, Edward Stanly and Henry A. Wise had an altercation in which Wise struck Stanly with a cane; two days later Stanly challenged Wise to a duel. Word of the impending duel led to the arrest of Wise, who was released on bond to keep the peace and remain in the District; Stanly had already left Washington for Baltimore. Seconds for the two men settled the matter peacefully. Wise, a lawyer from Virginia, sat in the U.S. House from 1833 until 1844. Originally a Democrat, he broke with Jackson over the U.S. Bank issue; in 1841

he became leader of the Tyler Whigs in the House. Wise subsequently served as governor of Virginia from 1856 until 1860.

16. Reverdy Johnson's injury resulted in a loss of sight in his left eye. Johnson sat in both the Maryland Senate, 1821–29 and 1860–61, and in the U.S. Senate, 1845–49 and 1863–68. He also served as U.S. attorney general, 1849–50, and as U.S. minister to Great Britain, 1868–69. A noted constitutional lawyer, Johnson argued the Dred Scott case in 1856 for the defense.

TO SAMUEL H. LAUGHLIN

My Dear Sir: Murfreesboro' June 1st 1842

I see in the Nashville Banner[1] of Monday last, a communication over the names of four of the Whig Senators, addressed to *"The Thirteen,"* but more especially to yourself *Hardwicke, Johnson* and *Powell* proposing that the Senators shall resign and submit the matters in dispute to their respective constituents.[2] They take especial care not to include in their proposition the House of Representatives in which the *Whig party* hold an accidental majority. They modestly propose that the Democrats shall surrender their power in the Senate, whilst the Whigs shall retain theirs in the House. In this way they doubtless calculate that they have every thing to gain and nothing to loose. Suppose the Democratic Senators accede to their proposition, and the elections, to supply the vacant places shall result as they did in August last, with perhaps an addition of one or two Democratic Senators, still the Whig party by retaining their power in the House would be in no worse condition than they now are. Now my first impression is, that the proposition of the four Whigs should be promptly and boldly met by one on our part, that all the members of both Houses, shall resign, and all go again before the people. If they agree to this, I shall rejoice in it, & shall have no fears of the result. If they decline it, it will prove, what I believe to be true—that they do not really mean or desire to submit their cause to such a test. I think they should be told distinctly that the Democratic Senators will cheerfully accept their proposition and resign provided the members of the House will do so also.

By a reply of this character, you will prevent them from making a false impression on the public mind, such as their address unopposed is calculated to make. By that address they manifest a seeming desire, to submit existing differences to the people. Their insincerity will be exposed by their refusal to include the House also. I verily believe if the House resigns that we should gain in another election not less than a dozen members, whilst the peculiar arrangement of Senatorial Districts might make the result more doubtful in that Branch.

It will not do, to suffer the address of the four Whigs to go unanswered. My judgment is that the answer should be forthcoming without delay, and as you are so much dispersed, that it will be impossible for you to be together. I suggest for your consideration that you should prepare and publish over your individual signature a proper reply, such as you are so well able to prepare, & send copies of the paper containing it, to each of the Democratic Senators accompanied by a short note to each requesting him, through the newspaper nearest him, to signify his assent to it, which I have no doubt all would do. If you approve the views herein suggested, the newspapers, should without delay present them to the people. I am so well satisfied of their correctness, that I have written to the *Argus*, the *Union* & the *Appeal*³ suggesting them. If our friend *Ford* concurs he can print them through his paper.⁴ If in addition to what I have here suggested, half a dozen Democratic members of the House could be got together, & make an address to the four Whig Senators, proposing that all the members of the House as well as the Senate shall resign it would be an admirable movement.

I am here with my wife on a visit to her relations and to attend the marriage of Dr. Rucker's Eldest daughter⁵ this evening. I will leave for Columbia in the morning.

JAMES K. POLK

ALS. DLC–JKP. Addressed to McMinnville. Laughlin's AE on the cover states that he answered this letter on June 18, 1842, and enclosed a reply to the Whig senators; Laughlin's letter to Polk has not been found. Published in Joseph H. Parks, ed., "Letters from James K. Polk to Samuel H. Laughlin, 1835–1844," *ETHSP*, XVIII, 159–60.

1. Felix K. Zollicoffer edited the Nashville *Republican Banner*, a major Whig organ in Tennessee, from January 1842, to August 1843.

2. Four Whig senators, Henry Frey, Joseph H. Peyton, Robert C. Foster, and Thomas R. Jennings, attacked the "Immortal Thirteen" in a letter published in the Nashville *Republican Banner* of May 30, 1842. An open letter addressed to the "Citizens of Tennessee" from four Democratic senators, Samuel H. Laughlin, Jonathan P. Hardwicke, Andrew Johnson, and Robert W. Powell, had occasioned the Whig attack.

3. Reference is to three Democratic newspapers, the Knoxville *Argus*, the *Nashville Union*, and the *Memphis Appeal*. Henry Van Pelt edited the *Memphis Appeal* from 1841 to 1851.

4. Reference is to John W. Ford's McMinnville *Central Gazette*.

5. Elizabeth Childress Rucker, daughter of William R. and Susan Childress Rucker, married Lunsford P. Black of Rutherford County. William R. Rucker was a Murfreesboro physician; his wife, Susan, was the sister of Sarah Childress Polk.

FROM GEORGE R. POWEL[1]

Rogersville, Tennessee. June 2, 1842

Powel writes that he has received Polk's letter[2] and that the local "committee of correspondence" has selected August 11 as the most suitable day to have Polk speak in Rogersville.

ALS. DLC–JKP. Addressed to Columbia.

1. Powel represented Hawkins and Sullivan counties in the Tennessee House, 1835–37, and served as circuit court clerk for Hawkins County, 1835–37, as well as clerk and master of the chancery court, 1855–59.

2. Letter not identified further.

TO FRANKLIN H. ELMORE

My Dear Sir: Columbia Tennessee June 13th 1842

My absence from home has prevented an earlier acknowledgement of the receipt of your esteemed letter of the ultimo.[1] I need scarcly assure you, that it gave me sincere pleasure to receive it. I remember with deep gratitude that disinterested act of personal friendship—voluntarily performed on your part—near the close of my service as Speaker of the House of Representatives, when I was violently assailed by a political faction, who could have had no higher aim than to affect me injuriously before the public, and especially in the then approaching political canvass in my own state, in which it was known I was to have a prominent part.[2] I gladly avail myself of this first appropriate occasion which has offered to thank you for the part which you acted on that occasion. I rejoice with you at the increased and increasing strength of the Democratic party, and at the certain prospect that our principles are to be re-established in the Government, at the close of the present Presidential term. How could it have been otherwise. Our opponents succeeded to the possession of the Government by means most extraordinary, and without any common or avowed political principles, upon which they were united. Now that their obnoxious and ruinous policy has been developed, it does not surprise me to witness the overwhelming revolution in the public sentiment which is every where manifest. That the days of their power are numbered if we act with common prudence I think certain, absolutely certain. I concur with you in opinion that the greatest danger which we have to apprehend is, that we may become weak from our great strength, and the divisions which may unfortunately grow up in reference to the succession.[3] We are united upon the great & leading *doctrines* which divide the country, whilst men are but the instruments through whom our views of the public policy are to be carried out. I should feel that our principles were perfectly safe under the lead of either of the two distinguished gentlemen whom you name, and of whom you are of opinion will probably be selected as our candidate. For Mr. Calhoun I entertain the highest personal and political regards. I have been at all times on personal good terms with him, and though for a season, as you know, we did not act together politically, yet the subjects upon [which] we differed either involved no essential principle, or have passed off, and are not now before the country. That he possesses talents and extensive acquirements that fit him for any station is admitted by all, and it gives me pleasure to accord to him prominent public services in the recent and pending struggles of principles, with the common adversary. To Mr Van Buren too I accord talents of the first order, and have unabated con[fi]dence in his political firmness and integrity. As you say truly, he "undoubtedly fell a martyr to our principles" in the last contest, and this will naturally attract to him the sympathies of many political and personal friends. Between men of the same principles, either of whom are suited to the station, the question of availability will certainly become material in any selection which may be made. For myself living in retirement, as I have been for near a year past, I have not been consulted by any of the aspirants or their friends, and can only form opinions from what I see passing before the public, and the occasional speculations of correspondents. Mr Van Buren as you know has recently paid a visit to the Hermitage and spent some time in the state. You have doubtless observed the idle speculations of the Whig press in this quarter, in regard to what they chose to consider the object of his visit, and especially as connected with my name; and yet I solemnly assure you, that not a word either verbaly or in writing, has ever up to this hour, passed between us on the subject.[4] If he conversed with any other person, in the state, upon the subject I have no knowledge of it, and do not believe that he did. What the Whig press, therefore attributes to him, was undoubtedly no part of the object of his visit to this state. This I deemed it proper to mention, not that it was perhaps of the slightest importance to do so. My great desire is, that in the selection of the candidate who is to be the exponent of our principles there shall be union, harmony and concord. Whoever may be thus freely selected in a general convention in which the body of the people shall be truly represented, I will cheerfully support. The insight and influence which you ascribe to myself and my friends is probably greatly overrated, but whatever it may be, it will I trust be exerted in a manner to promote the success of our common principles. I thank you for the desire which you kindly express,[5] to see me again performing a part in public life. How that may be, is in the future. I have all my life relied for the little political preferment which I have obtained, upon the people and the people alone, unless my station as Speaker of the House may be regarded an an exception. I have never desired or sought place or station from any other power that had it to bestow, and I am very sure I never shall. Should I ever come into public life again, it is most probable that I shall look for my advancement to the same source I have heretofore done.

You give me the first information I had (except from rumour) that Mr S. of Va.,[6] was to be insisted on in certain quarters, as the candidate for V.P. if Mr V. Buren was nominated for the first office. This may be so, and it looks probable; still, a few leading politicians cannot & should not control the real choice of the people, should that choice be manifested in their primary assemblies, through their delegates in convention or otherwise. The same remark may be made in regard to the selection of the candidate for the first office also. I have never, Mr Dear Sir, during my whole public life, and much as I have mingled with public men, had any thing to do with political combinations or arrangements, such as are often said to take place among political leaders, by which they seek to produce the desired results, and know nothing of the means in which such things are accomplished. I have no doubt however that a few leading men, do often give direction to the course of their party & perhaps secure their own elevation making that seem to be public opinion, which is really not so.[7] This is all wrong and whenever it is attempted, the people should take the matter into their own hands.

I will add a word only in regard to this state, and her probable future course. Parties have been for some years very equally balanced. I have fought two hard battles, gained one and lost the other, by about equal majorities. I have no doubt however but that the Democracy are now in a handsome majority. The same causes, which have added to our strength elsewhere, have operated here. The Whigs will contest every inch of ground in our next contest; still I am confident we will carry the state, unless indeed we should by possibility be so unfortunate as to be weakened by an unacceptable or unpopular ticket. Our divisions are so equal that a small floating body of voters, such as are to be found in all the states, may control the result.

I shall be pleased, my Dear Sir, to hear from you again and as often as your leisure may permit, and shall take great pleasure in adding you to the number of my valued correspondents.

James K. Polk

ALS, draft. DLC–JKP. Addressed to Charleston and marked *"Copy"* and *"Private."*

1. Reference is to Franklin H. Elmore to Polk, May 12, 1842.

2. Immediately prior to the Tennessee gubernatorial canvass of 1839, Elmore introduced a resolution in the U.S. House asking that the thanks of the house be extended to the outgoing Speaker, James K. Polk, "for the able, impartial, and dignified manner" in which he had presided. A few Whigs, led by Sergeant S. Prentiss of Mississippi, tried unsuccessfully to amend the resolution by striking the word "impartial."

3. Here Polk cancelled the following words: "This I think we cannot too soon guard against."

4. Both the *Nashville Whig* and the Nashville *Republican Banner* speculated that during his visit to Tennessee Van Buren discussed the vice-presidential question with Polk.

5. Here Polk cancelled the following words: "that I may be in the next administration—whatever may be its shape. I have to say what my intimate friends have long known, that at no period would I have consented to fill a cabinet or other subordinate executive station. I shall certainly never seek such a station and should the tender of it now be made which is not probable, I do not think it likely that my firm opinion and views will undergo any change."

6. Andrew Stevenson.

7. Here Polk cancelled the following words: "My desire in reference to the Vice Presidency as well as the Presidency is that there should be union, harmony, and concert in its selection, and that the people and not a few politicians should make the selection." Polk then interlined above the cancellation the paragraph's last sentence.

FROM SARAH C. POLK

Dear Husband   Columbia June the 24th 1842

I received your letter to day from Louisville[1] and was pleased to hear from you. Leaving home in rather feeble health, I feel much solicitude to hear from you often.[2] We have no news here. Your visit to the East begins to excite some interest. The *Observer* [3] is out with some of its low wit, and the question is often asked where you are and for what? The Banner has not missed you yet, but is much troubled about your going to East Tennessee to eat a dinner.[4] William[5] has gone to Nashville. I will ask him to write you on his return. I have received a letter for you from Irwin[6] at Savannah containing $50 in Alabama money the balance he says on your note. I suppose half is Knox's[7] though I have not said any thing to him on the subject. If I must give him his portion you must so write me.

You did not write me, or tell me, how often for me to write would be agreeable to you. I am affraid of being troublesome in my communications as I have written twice this week.[8] I hope to hear from you soon.

SARAH POLK

ALS. DLC–JKP. Addressed to Washington City. Published by Sarah Agnes Wallace, ed., "Letters of Mrs. James K. Polk to Her Husband," *THQ*, XI (September, 1952), pp. 282–83.

1. Letter not found. Polk wrote to Sarah from Cincinnati on June 22, 1842, advising her of his progress on his journey. ALS. DLC–JKP.

2. Reference is to Polk's departure, not that of his wife. In June and July of 1842 Polk traveled to Washington City, Philadelphia, and New York for purposes both political and financial.

3. Established in 1834, the *Columbia Observer* soon became a Whig newspaper. A. M. and J. B. Rosborough assumed the editorship in the spring of 1841.

4. See George R. Powel to Polk, June 2, 1842.

5. William H. Polk.

6. A Democrat from Hardin County, James Irwin acted as Polk's agent for land transactions in that area. Irwin's letter has not been found, but Polk did receive his letters of February 21 and March 18, 1842. ALsS. DLC–JKP.

7. Joseph Knox Walker, third son of James and Jane Maria Polk Walker, served as private secretary to Polk during his presidency. Walker later practiced law in Memphis and represented Shelby and Fayette counties as a Democrat in the Tennessee Senate from 1857 until 1859.

8. On June 19 Sarah wrote to Polk at Washington City. Sarah's "second" letter was written Tuesday evening, June 21, as a continuation of the letter of June 19. ALS. DLC–JKP.

FROM ARCHIBALD YELL

Dear Govr.   Little Rock 25th June '42

I wrote you a long letter some weeks since[1] and have recieved no answer. As I have a little leisure from the drudgery of the office I have concluded to give you a short history of the doings on this side of the great Watters.

We have Unfortunatly four Democratic Candidates for Congress, which I fear is to give us some trouble. However the moment the Whigs bring out a Candidate we will unite upon Judge Cross who is our most prominent Candidate,[2] and they will unquestionably do so. In our strength we have become weak—too many great men for the few places.

The only question in relation to state policy is the Winding up of our Banks. I have been Waring upon them ever since I have been in office; they are difficult to manage as all moneyed Corporations are but if I am not verry much mistaken we shall be able to put them into Liquidation, beyond the posibility of a doubt. It will be to me a Victory & a blessing to the Country. Your old friends Col Jo W McKain [and] Genl. A. Whinny will both be in the next Legislature[3] and [are] strong Anti Bank & Yell men—"Distructers as we are called." E H Fletcher[4] is in Ark and one of my Locating Agents to select the 500,000 acres of land. So is Jo McKain another. So you see I am pretty clanish, & so they charge me. Your old friend McKisick[5] is in Washington Co & a doing well. Just as Clever as ever. Old Billy Gilchrist[6] is here driving a way at the Law & a little farm. I accationaly appoint him a special Judge to help him a long. He is a thorough Democrat & warmly your friend. Indeed all your old Tennessee acquantences are as boistrous for you now as they were ten years ago. You are as well known in Ark as Genl Jackson. The Democrats are for you & the Whigs *hate* you!

We shall reelect Col Sevier[7] to the Senate without trouble. What I shall or Can do two years hence is wholy Uncertain. I am not now in-clinced to run for reelection, tho that must depend upon Circumstances.

If I should be pleased with (Mrs. Polk's) *Widdow*[8] & she with *me*, she may talk me back to old Tennessee! Would not that present a strange history in my life and who knows but it may hapen. I am now quite in Love with the Widdow & if I am not mistaken in her appearence for I knew her in 1827, she is large & fine looking & she must be amiable. Her Father was one of the best men that ever lived. Tell Mrs Polk she has set me half crazy, & now I can not abandon the *Claim* until the matter is farther investigated. But my Dear Sir I am now up to *near* 40 & she can not be more than 33 or 35 at fartherst. She will be detered too, from this Land of *Bowie knives*, I fear, and aga[in][9] how presumptuous in me to make a tour to Tennessee to see a Lady without some hope or expecta-tions of success?

Say to Mrs P.—or you must give me a minute detail of her appear-ence, Inteligence, age & *No. of Children* & such other perticulars as may interest me, &C. Old Widdows[10] are the greatest fools on earth; I shall therefore close this subject. Let me hear from you & how things progress in Tennessee. Present me to Mrs. Polk . . . .

A. YELL

ALS. DLC–JKP. Addressed to Columbia.

1. Possibly Yell to Polk, April 30, 1842.

2. A native Tennessean, Edward Cross moved to Arkansas in 1826. Having served as U.S. judge for the Arkansas Territory, 1830–36, and as U.S. surveyor general for Arkansas, 1836–38, he won election as a Democrat to the U.S. House and served from 1839 until 1845. The other three candidates are not identified.

3. Abraham Whinnery and probably Joseph W. McKean. A resident in Polk's congressional district and a colonel of the Tennessee militia during the late 1820's, Whinnery moved to Arkansas and served several years in the territorial legislature. Formerly of Columbia, Tennessee, McKean moved to Sevier County, Arkansas, where he was a merchant and postmaster; he also served in the Arkansas territorial legislature.

4. Formerly a merchant and resident of Fayetteville, Tennessee, Elliot H. Fletcher experienced bankruptcy in the mid 1830's; he has not been identified further.

5. A good friend both to Yell and Polk, James McKisick served as court clerk of Bedford County, Tennessee, before moving to Arkansas about 1836.

6. Previously a resident of Shelbyville, Tennessee, and Yell's former law partner, William Gilchrist moved to Arkansas about 1837.

7. Ambrose H. Sevier, a native Tennessean, served as delegate from the Arkansas Territory from 1828 until 1836; he won election as a Democrat to the U.S. Senate in 1836 and served until 1848.

8. See Yell to Polk, March 6 and April 30, 1842.

9. Part of one word obliterated by sealing wax stain.

10. Probably misspelling of "widowers."

TO ANDREW JACKSON

My Dear Sir: Washington City July 1st 1842

I have seen Mr Kendall[1] and delivered to him, the package of papers with which you entrusted me, relating to the declaration of martial law &c. at New Orleans. He will without delay, make out an abstract of them for public use. Having ascertained that Mr Ingersoll of Phila.[2] had recently made a Report, and that a Bill is now pending in the House of Representatives in reference to the fine,[3] I thought it proper to advise him, as also *Dr. Gwynn*[4] and a few others of your friends of the existence of these papers, as furnishing important information, when the discussion comes up in the House. *Mr Kendall's* abstract will be furnished to them, to be used in debate. *Dr. Gwynn* is exceedingly indignant, as indeed are all your friends, at the outrageous statements of the Senator from Louisiana,[5] and will avail themselves of the first possible opportunity to expose them to the public. They think they will be able to get up Mr Ingersoll's Bill in the House, and if they can reach it, they have but little doubt but that they will pass it through that body.

The President's Veto of the *Little Tariff Bill* [6] as it is called here, settles this question: that the *Distribution* shall cease, whenever the duties exceed 20 percent, being the maximum duty of the compromise act.[7] It has produced great confusion and excitement among the Whigs, and an animated debate upon the subject is now going on in the House. The Democracy will generally sustain the veto.

I will leave here in two or three days for New York, & think after spending a short time there I will return home.

JAMES K. POLK

ALS. DLC–AJ. Addressed to the Hermitage.

1. Amos Kendall, a newspaperman and member of Andrew Jackson's "Kitchen Cabinet," served as postmaster general from 1835 until 1840. In 1842 he edited a Washington biweekly, *Kendall's Expositor*.

2. Charles J. Ingersoll, a Pennsylvania Democrat, served five terms in the U.S. House, 1813–15 and 1841–49.

3. In 1815 Dominick Hall, U.S. district judge for Louisiana, fined Andrew Jackson one thousand dollars for contempt of court, the citation for which had been issued after Jackson arrested Hall for defiance of orders issued under authority of martial law. In 1842 Jackson's friends in the U.S. House backed Ingersoll's bill to refund the fine; Whig opposition blocked that measure and subsequent refund proposals until February of 1844.

4. William M. Gwin.

5. Charles Magill Conrad, a former Jacksonian Democrat who became a Whig over the national bank issue and served in the U.S. Senate for Louisiana from April 14, 1842, to March 3, 1843, delivered a speech on May 18, 1842, opposing the Senate's version of the Jackson relief proposal and defending Hall's contempt citation. A subsequent Whig amendment to the bill stipulated that congressional remission of the fine would be made without reference to the equity or legality of its imposition. Opposed to any measure that did not exonerate Jackson, Democrats defeated the amended legislation.

6. Reference is to the Temporary Tariff Bill of 1842.

7. Reference is to the Tariff Act of 1833.

FROM SARAH C. POLK

My dear Husband   Columbia July 1st 1842

Your letter from Cincinatti I received a few days ago.[1] But you do not write me how you are? If you have company, what kind of company &c. All that you say to me [is that] I am here or at such a place. I flatter myself to get a longer history of yourself soon. William[2] promised me to write you all concerning the public affairs, and I suppose that he has done it. I would judge from the tone of the *Whig papers* that there will not be a general resignation of the Legislature.[3] They intend to get out of it in some way. I have heard very little individual conversation since you left. Weddings, examinations &c. seem to occupy the whole attention of every one here at present. No politics, no pary feeling but every thing quiet as far as I know. *Jane* is married—large wedding.[4] John Williams gave a large party, Mrs. Dr. Polk a small one and I gave them a dinner on yesterday.[5] Had Mrs. Claiborne & Mrs. McNeal here.[6] And your name sake Mr. Helms little son died yesterday suddenly.[7] This is all the news we have or all that I know. Do write me often. I feel more anxious than usual to hear from you. I will be thankful even for one line from you.

SARAH POLK

ALS. DLC–JKP. Addressed to Washington City.

1. Polk to Sarah C. Polk, June 22, 1842. ALS. DLC–JKP.

2. William H. Polk.

3. See Polk to Samuel H. Laughlin, June 1, 1842.

4. Jane Clarissa Walker, fourth child of James and Jane Maria Polk Walker, married Isaac Newton Barnet of Rutherford County on June 22, 1842.

5. References are to John Williams, a Columbia merchant, and to Mary Rebecca Long, wife of William Julius Polk. A son of William Polk of North Carolina, William Julius Polk practiced medicine in Maury County and served as president of the Columbia branch of the Bank of Tennessee from 1838 until 1840.

6. Probably Sarah Martin Lewis King Claiborne and Clarissa Polk McNeal. Sarah Martin Lewis, daughter of Joel Lewis of Davidson County, was the widow of James King of Sullivan County and later the wife of Thomas Claiborne, member of the U.S. House for one term, 1817–19, and leading Nashville attorney. Clarissa Polk, wife of Thomas McNeal of Hardeman County, was Polk's aunt and Jane Clarissa Walker Barnet's great-aunt.

7. Meredith Helm's four-year-old son, James K. Polk Helm, died on June 30, 1842. An early Maury County settler, Meredith Helm established a tannery in Columbia in the early 1820's. He served nine terms as mayor of Columbia between 1829 and 1852.

FROM HENRY HORN[1]

My Dear Sir   Philadelphia July 6th 1842

In accordance with your request made to me on the evening of the 4th I made inquiry among many of my friends in relation to the subject matter of our conversation and regret to find that my anticipations have been realised.[2]

As I remarked to you at that time many of our capitalists have been much crippled in their finances and others who may not eventually lose much have their funds at present compleatly locked up in dead investments from which they cannot withdraw them without sacrafises of a most ruinous character which they are unwilling to make.

Besides there is a strong indisposition on the part of those who may still have any surplus funds remaining on hand, against making investments in real estate out of our immediate vicinity, while they have so many and such frequent opportunities of making profitable investments here.

With much regret that I cannot be serviceable to you in the present emergency, and a fervent hope that you may be successful in N York.

HENRY HORN

ALS. DLC–JKP. Addressed to Astor House, New York.
1. A Philadelphia hardware merchant and friend of Polk, Horn served as a Democrat in the U.S. House for one term, 1831–33.
2. See Sarah C. Polk to Polk, June 24, 1842.

FROM HOPKINS L. TURNEY

My dear Sir,   Washington July 17th 1842
    I have been quite engaged since my return from New York, in feeling certain men and endevouring to assertain all I possibly could of their feelings and views in relation to our next candidates for the P. & V.P. of the united states, and among others I had a long talk with Allen of Ohio, and after persueing the course with him you suggested, and finding it had the effect you supposed but to a much greater degree than was expected, I introdused the subject of the V.P. with a remark, that a false step in this matter would have a Tendancy to throw him back. He declard to me that he had not nor would not in any way interfear in the selection of the candidate, that he would support the nominee be him whom he may, & that he hoped a good and judicious selection would be made. He was then sincear but I know not how long he may remain in this opinion. Madill and Wellar are the mear index of Allens wishes.[1] It is currently roumerd here and generally believed that Calhoon & Woodbury have formed a union, and Bentons friends are exerting themselves to procure his nomination. I have not heard who they want with him but am inclined to think it would be Wright. But this will be no go. He has plased himself behind Van Burin.

    I have frequently been enquired off by Bentons friends to know what was the state of feeling between you and B. and have unaformly answerd that the best of feelings existed at least on your part, and when pressed for the reason for such an enquery, I was informed, that there was a democratick paper in Mosouri urgeing your claimes that was constantly denounceing Benton.[2] I have replied that I did not suppose that you even knew of it, much less to encourage it.

I have writen to So. C. fully on this subject. Parmentur assures me that himself and Hallet will have all things arranged right in the Bay state.[3] You will go into convention with moore states and by far a larger electorial vote than any other one man and if the people should be fairly represented as the others drop off you would be taken up as the second choice. But as this thing will be greatly under the controle of politicans, and will therefore be subject to the intreagues of designing men I cannot now conjecture the probable result. Judgeing however from presant appearances your chance is decidely the best. Calhoon is here and he entertains I think kind and friendly feelings for you and when he is out of the way I think if nothing happens to mar his feelings he will be for you, as in that event the candidate for the V.P. must come from the South.[4]

I will Start your Books in the course of the ensueing week.[5] Congress will not adjourn before the 15th of august if then.

H. L. TURNEY

ALS. DLC–JKP. Addressed to Columbia.

1. William Medill, John B. Weller, and William Allen. An Ohio lawyer, Medill served as a member and Speaker of the Ohio House, 1835–38, before winning election in 1839 as a Democrat to the first of two terms in the U.S. House. He subsequently held a position in the Post Office Department, 1845, and served as commissioner of Indian affairs, 1845–50, before winning election to one term as governor of Ohio in 1853. Also an Ohio lawyer, Weller served three terms in the U.S. House, 1839–45, and represented California in the U.S. Senate from 1852 until 1857. He fought with the rank of colonel in the Mexican War, won election to one term as governor of California, 1858–60, and went as U.S. minister to Mexico in 1860.

2. Missouri newspaper not identified further.

3. William Parmenter and Benjamin Franklin Hallett. A pioneer in the glass industry and president of the Middlesex Bank, Parmenter served as a member of the Massachusetts House in 1829 and the Massachusetts Senate in 1836; as a Democratic congressman, 1837–45; and as naval officer at the port of Boston, 1845–49. A lawyer, editor, and Democratic party manager, Hallett merged his *Boston Daily Advocate* with the *Boston Post* in 1838; during the Pierce administration, he served as district attorney of Boston.

4. Turney assumes that Martin Van Buren will receive the Democratic presidential nomination in 1844.

5. Polk probably had asked Turney to send him some government documents.

FROM CAVE JOHNSON

Dear Sir,   Washington 20th July 1842

I enclose you another letter which I recd this evening just as I enclose it & of course without reading it.[1] Turney & myself this evening walked in the public grounds & met D. H. Lewis, Gwin & Caldwell[2] and had a good deal of conversation with them. The sum and substance was this. The north had a candidate for the last 8 years. We first elected Van. He could not sustain himself notwithstanding all our efforts. It is now due to the South that we should have a candidate who of course should be C. & Wright.[3] Then (after one term) Wright to come up & Gov. P.[4] from the South, & after that term then Gov. P. would be of the right age &c & besides all the usual arguments agt. Van were repeated. We spoke in the highest terms of Calhoun but I thought it due to frankness to say, that, notwithstanding my great respect for C. & the cheerfulness with which I would support him if selected by our party, that I thought the true policy of the South, whilst the abolition question & tariff were unsettled, that we should strengthen ourselves in that quarter which I thought could be more certainly affected by running Van &c & arguments of similar character.

Your position is a delicate one. I look upon Buch & King[5] as unfriendly to your prospects. I suspect Benton & Allen also. Of course Calhoun & friends must go to the north.[6] I hear some talk recently, that Bentons friends are making movements for him, notwithstanding his letter,[7] acting upon the idea, no doubt, that if Van is to be shoved aside he ought to stand next. Turney & myself are compelled to be cautious for whatever we say is attributed to you. Gwin said this evening that Van could get Miss. if you was on his ticket & not without. I do not know whether he talks so to others. I do not like such movements as I hear going on & think but little will be gained by the movers. My dislike is so great that I avoid rather than seek to know any thing about them.

I think I shall leave here as soon as the Tariff, Army & Navy Bills are disposed of [8]—pair off with some whig. I suppose we shall have a Bill soon to pay ourselves until the *15th of September*. We are very well.

                                                                        C JOHNSON

ALS. DLC–JKP. Addressed to Columbia. Polk's AE on the cover states that he answered this letter on July 29, 1842; Polk's reply has not been found.

1. Earlier on July 20 Johnson had written Polk a similar letter with enclosure. ALS. DLC–JKP. One of the enclosures, Lawson Gifford to Polk, July 7, 1842,

requested Polk's assistance in securing government contracts to supply federal forces in Florida. ALS. DLC–JKP. The other letter forwarded to Polk has not been found.

2. Dixon H. Lewis, William M. Gwin, and Patrick Calhoun Caldwell. A lawyer, Caldwell served in the South Carolina House, 1836–38; in the U.S. House as a state rights Democrat, 1841–43; and in the state Senate, 1848.

3. John C. Calhoun for president and Silas Wright for vice-president.

4. Polk as Wright's vice-president.

5. James Buchanan and William R. King.

6. Sectional politics would force Calhoun to select a vice-presidential candidate from a northern state.

7. In a letter to Moses Dawson, dated December 6, 1840, Benton had endorsed Van Buren for president in 1844.

8. For passage of the 1842 tariff, see Cave Johnson to Polk, April 29, 1842. Army appropriations for 1842 received final congressional approval on August 6; naval appropriations on July 30.

FROM ROBERT ARMSTRONG

Dear Govr,   Nashville 22d July 42

I differ with you as to the Whigs Resigning.[1] Bell and the Banner are for it. Foster and the Whig against it. *See the Whig of 21s.*[2] All shall be done that can be done. I have not seen Harris since William Polk left here. I have received the Resignations of B. Martin of Maury & Gardner of Weakly and Buchannon of Giles since your Brother left.[3] Please say so to him.

Report says if a Resignation that Bell will be a candidate in this County. If so, we will make a case of him.

R ARMSTRONG

ALS. DLC–JKP. Addressed to Columbia.

1. See Polk to Samuel H. Laughlin, June 1, 1842.

2. Nashville *Republican Banner* and *Nashville Whig*. The *Whig* of July 21 carried an article suggesting that Whigs might agree to a special election of the whole legislature if Democrats would pledge to allow the election of U.S. senators from Tennessee by joint ballot of both houses of the new legislature.

3. Barkly Martin, John A. Gardner, John Buchanan, and William H. Polk. A Weakley County lawyer, Gardner served three terms as a Democrat in the Tennessee Senate, 1841–47, and a single term in the House, 1879–81. A farmer, Buchanan represented Giles County as a Democrat in the Tennessee House, 1835–37, 1839–43, and 1845–47.

TO SAMUEL H. LAUGHLIN

My Dear Sir: Columbia July 22nd 1842

I wrote you a very hasty line on yesterday.[1] I am satisfied that the Whigs yet hope that some *one or more* of the Democratic members will fail to have their *actual resignations* at Nashville on the 1st of August, and in that event, I strongly suspect that they will avail themselves of that flimsy pretext to decline the proposition for a general resignation.[2] They must if possible have no such apology left to them. I have written many letters since my return home on monday with a view if possible to have all the resignations in, at the time.[3] I have more fears that *Grisham* of Fentress, *Col. Wan* of Meigs, *Hembree* of Roane, *Walker* of McMinn & *Lane* of Claiborne[4] may not be heard from in time than any others. I have written to East Tennessee to have *Lane* certainly seen.[5] And now my Dear Sir, let me urge upon yourself, *Hill* & *Hopkins*,[6] to send special messengers if necessary, to see *Grisham* & *Wan* & if possible *Walker* of McMinn. The latter you know is a slow man in his movements & though he has announced his willingness to resign he has not I understand, sent in his *actual resignation*. If you have any possible opportunity to have him seen or written to in time, do so. If you write to some friend at Kingston, on the main stage line, he could send a messenger to see both *Wan* & *Walker*, neither of whom lives more than forty miles from that point. See *Hopkins* & *Hill* if convenient, show them this letter, & be certain at all events that *Grisham* & *Wan* at least are seen. I have written to *Col. Hembree*.[7] I suggest that you do so also. I will be at Nashville on the 1st of August & hope to meet you there on that day. Let me hear from you by return mail.

JAMES K. POLK

P.S. Fearing that possibly you may not be at home, I address this jointly to yourself and *Mr Ford*, who resides [in][8] town, will get the letter on its [arriv]al, & who is requested to see H[ill and] Hopkins, if you are absent. J.K.P.

ALS. NN–Kohns Collection. Addressed to McMinnville and marked *"Private."* Laughlin's AE on the cover states that this letter was answered on July 29; the reply was dated July 28, 1842.

1. Letter not found.
2. See Polk to Laughlin, June 1, 1842.
3. Letters not found. See Alexander O. Anderson to Polk, July 24, 1842, and E. G. Eastman to Polk, July 25, 1842.
4. Thomas Grisham, William Wann, Joel Hembree, James Walker, and Isaac

C. Lane were Democratic members of the Tennessee House. Grisham of Fentress County served one term, 1841–43; Wann, a former sheriff of Meigs County, served three terms, 1839–45; Hembree, a farmer from Roane County, served four terms, 1839–43, 1845–47, and 1849–51; Walker, a farmer from McMinn County, served three terms, 1837–43, and sat one term in the Tennessee Senate, 1849–51; and Lane, a farmer and sheriff from Claiborne County, served two terms, 1841–43 and 1853–55.

5. Letter not found. See E. G. Eastman to Polk, July 25, 1842.

6. Hugh L. W. Hill and Thomas H. Hopkins. Hill, a farmer, school teacher, and distiller from Warren County, served three terms in the Tennessee House as a Democrat, 1837–43, and won election to one term in Congress, 1847–49. Hopkins, originally from Mississippi, practiced law in McMinnville and served one term in the Tennessee House, 1841–43.

7. Letter not found.

8. Manuscript mutilated here and on line below.

FROM ALEXANDER O. ANDERSON[1]

At Home Near Knoxville

My Dear Sir   July 24th 1842

Mr Eastman & myself have mounted a Messenger upon one of my horses, & started him for the residence of Wan. I have written to Wan & if he has not already resigned,[2] he will I have no doubt forthwith. If the Messenger returns with the news that Wan hesitates, I will go to his house immediately myself, & Lane will be attended to by Mr Reynolds.[3]

I believe my last letter[4] you never answered, but as I have never had any ceremony with my old friends, at a crisis such as this, I wou'd not forego the opportunity of assuring you that we are fully alive to all that ought to be done. I shou'd have been glad to have heard from you upon the present occasion, and expect the pleasure of joining you at Rogersville.[5]

I wou'd be glad to hear from you at what day you expect to leave Nashville, and at what day you will probably reach this foot of the mountain, & by what route.

I have been struggling this spring, or rather winter, spring & summer, to repair my shattered finances, which have suffered during the last ten years of political Struggles, but my eye has not been wholly withdrawn from the scenes around me, and I have looked with anxiety to the struggle you wou'd repeat as I believed, triumphantly, in Tennessee, in the next year, as an event in itself important, and as tending to higher results.

Be pleased to present me most respectfully to Mrs Polk.

A ANDERSON

P.S. I was in Athens a few days since & my Brother Pierce[6] vowed he wou'd have a Polk meeting there while you were in East Tennessee, and I think it will be done.

ALS. DLC–JKP. Addressed to Columbia and marked *"Private."* Polk's AE on the cover states that he answered this letter on July 29, 1842; Polk's reply has not been found.

1. A Knoxville lawyer, Anderson headed the U.S. land office in Alabama in 1836 and served in 1838 as a federal agent for removing the Indians from Alabama and Florida. He won election as a Democrat to the U.S. Senate in place of Hugh L. White, who resigned in 1840. In 1849 Anderson moved to California, where he served in that state's Senate, 1850–51, and on its Supreme Court, 1851–53.

2. See Polk to Samuel H. Laughlin, July 22, 1842.

3. Robert B. Reynolds, a Knoxville lawyer and Democratic party worker, was attorney general for Tennessee's Second Judicial District from 1839 until 1845.

4. Probably a reference to Anderson's letter of October 6, 1841.

5. Polk planned to attend a Democratic meeting at Rogersville in Sullivan County on August 11, 1842.

6. An Athens lawyer, Pierce B. Anderson represented McMinn County as a Democrat in the Tennessee House from 1843 to 1847.

FROM E. G. EASTMAN

Knoxville, Tennessee. July 25, 1842

Eastman acknowledges receipt of Polk's letter[1] and reports efforts to secure resignations from Wann of Meigs County and Lane of Claiborne.[2] Reynolds has seen Hembree on this same subject. The barbecue at Rogersville will attract a large crowd, including many former Whigs. Eastman urges Polk to bring Governor Carroll and to remind William H. Polk that Pate[3] expects him to call when he comes to Knox County. Pate plans to attend the barbecue and, if encouraged, might switch party affiliations. Local Whigs are speculating about the Democratic presidential and vice-presidential nominations and are wondering about the meaning of the Rogersville barbecue in that regard.

ALS. DLC–JKP. Addressed to Columbia. Polk's AE on the cover states that he answered this letter on July 29, 1842; Polk's reply has not been found.

1. Letter not identified further.

2. See Polk to Samuel H. Laughlin, July 22, 1842.

3. John F. Pate, a Knox County Whig, won election to a single term in the Tennessee House in 1841.

FROM J. G. M. RAMSEY

My Dear Sir   Mecklenburg July 25, 1842

I do not know where this may reach you, but as I have kept you advised heretofore of the state of public opinion in the Carolinas in reference to the succession I extract from a letter recd. yesterday from a leading gentleman in S.C.[1] a portion of his letter bearing on that subject.

"Van B.[2] is out of the question. If he runs the Democratic party is broken up—himself is broken down—& Clay elected President. Calhoun, Buchanan, Wright—any leading democrat in preference to him. Calhoun is strong & daily growing stronger notwithstanding the apathy of his friends & the absence of any thing like management in any quarter. I believe the people will elect him by a spontaneous unpremeditated effort of their own. Polk I think is determined to run for V.P. with some body—Calhoun in preference I think—but V.B. from circumstances probably is most likely. Vans vice however must & will come from Virginia & it will be so decided at the Convention. Polk may be held up till then but not longer. Who Calhoun friends will put up for Vice I do not know. N.Y. & Pa. seem to be considered the States to furnish him. The feeling of all is strongly with Polk & if he could be elected with Calhoun I think he would be prefered. If Calhoun is elected I am confident any place in the cabinet Polk might desire would be cheerfully accorded to him & at the expiration of 4 years which would be as long as Mr. C. would serve he might enter for the stakes if he chose & I am sure no man would be more acceptable to the whole party than himself. A short time however will make all the developments in prospect for the next 3 or 4 years. The politicians appear all afraid to make a move at present."

Thus for my correspondents letter. Make what you can from it. He is a shrewd observer, a true friend of yours, a deliberate calculator & is *truly* advised from all parts of the country.

If you visit Rogersville *from the West* we will of course see you at Knoxville on your way. If *from the East*, on your return home. I must *see* you, but I fear that I can scarcely get to the barbacue tho I will if I can. Knox will be well represented there. If a resignation takes place we will revolutionise E.T.[3] Even Knox will make something by the Bankrupt law[4] & other Whig measures.

I have had but 20 minutes to copy from my letter & the mail can be detained no longer.

J. G. M. Ramsey

ALS. DLC–JKP. Addressed to Columbia.
1. Not identified further.
2. Martin Van Buren.
3. See Polk to Samuel H. Laughlin, June 1, 1842.
4. Passed in August of 1841, the second federal bankruptcy law permitted voluntary bankruptcy, but allowed creditors to proceed against traders; Democrats repealed this law in 1843. An earlier bankruptcy law, passed by Congress in 1800, had been repealed in 1803.

FROM SAMUEL H. LAUGHLIN

My dear Sir,   McMinnville, Tenn. July 28, 1842

Your letters from Columbia, of the 21st and 22nd instant, the first postmarked Spring Hill,[1] have been before me for some days. I returned home from Winchester on Monday last, to the Chancery Court here, and met our friend Col. Waterhouse,[2] who is now here, and learn that Mr. Wann had written and deposited his resignation[3] in the post office in time for it to be now in Nashville. Of any action on the part of Mr. Walker, of McMinn, he has no knowledge, though he thinks it probable his resignation has been forwarded.

It has been impossible for me to go to Fentress. Mr. Hopkins could not go, but he wrote on monday last, a pressing letter to Grisham, and inclosed him the form of a letter of resignation. I had previously written him in June, pressing him to send it to Genl. Armstrong. I think he will send it.

I have written to Mr. Hembree. Lane I have scarcely any acquaintance with, but I hope the steps taken will insure his concurrence with his breathern.

It is most manifest from the tone of the last Nos. of the Banner and Whig[4] of this week, that the Whigs will not stand up to the rack. They have now agreed, after the Banner had publicly declared itself in favor of resignation, to unite in defeating the measure upon every futile and ridiculous pretext they can devise. There will be no resignations, but the necessity of a *unanimous* tender of them on our part is not lessened. I therefore earnestly hope, that our friends will *all* send them in.

I have no time to write in detail. I would be most glad to see you, but my engagements at Court for two or three weeks to come, will prevent me from meeting you at Nashville on 1st. prox. I will write to you there, as I wish you to see a gentleman there for me on a matter you will know to be important.[5]

S. H. Laughlin

ALS. DLC–JKP. Addressed to Columbia and marked "Private."

1. Polk's letter of July 21, 1842, has not been found.

2. A large landholder and former justice of the peace in Rhea County, Richard G. Waterhouse won election in 1841 as a Democrat to one term in the Tennessee Senate.

3. See Polk to Laughlin, July 22, 1842.

4. The Nashville *Republican Banner* and the *Nashville Whig*.

5. No Laughlin to Polk letter addressed to Nashville in August of 1842 has been found.

FROM LEVIN H. COE

Somerville, Tennessee. July 30, 1842

Coe reports that he has written to James E. Saunders of Courtland, Alabama, urging open support for a Van Buren-Polk presidential ticket. Van Buren and Calhoun may now be considered the only candidates for the first office, and Calhoun will have to give way. The selection for the second office narrows down to Polk and Johnson. Polk's friends, however, will have to break their silence soon, or Johnson will be saddled upon the party. Coe will write a similar letter to Judge Howry of Oxford, Mississippi, and may risk such a letter to Claiborne of the Natchez *Mississippi Free Trader*. Also, Coe fears that the continued pretensions of Benton, who wants Wright for his "second in command," may blow up the party. If there is a general resignation of the Tennessee legislature,[1] Democrats in the Western District will be prepared; Polk may depend upon a considerable gain in the District.

ALS. DLC–JKP. Addressed to Columbia. Polk's AE on the cover states that he answered this letter on September 1, 1842; Polk's reply has not been found.

1. See Polk to Samuel H. Laughlin, June 1, 1842.

TO WILLIAM McNEILL

Dear Sir: Nashville Augt. 2d 1842

I called at your house to see you, on the matter of business[1] about which we conversed a few weeks ago, but did not find you at home. I have requested my friend *Genl. Armstrong* to see you on the subject, and shall be greatly obliged if you can make the arrangement desired, and which Gen. A. will explain to you.

JAMES K. POLK

ALS. DLC–JKP. Addressed locally.

1. See Robert Armstrong to Polk, April 15 and 22, 1842.

FROM DANIEL GRAHAM

Dear Sir   Nashville, Tenn. 11 Augt 1842

This is the immortal 'leventh[1] here, and the day opened finely. The promise was, that you would have a fair field at Rogersville, but at 20 to three Oclock a heavy cloud came from the South and has been deluging us for an hour now at 4. It has probably been a showering day to some distance and we feel that the good democrats of East Tennesse have had a damper.

No positive developments of Whig news since you left, but the inferences are strong that the leaders here are uncertain as to the final *action* of the members, and the papers are holding themselves open to proclaim loudly for either event as it may turn up.[2] A solemn conclave was held yesterday at Ephs.[3] Bell was there. Bob[4] was also in from Franklin, and the Demos have guessed that they are concocting two proclamations to be used as occasion might require. A confident opinion also prevails that Bell is likely to succeed in impressing upon Foster[5] that he is the only man who can save the party for Governor and that he must be ready to start against you in time to open the campaign with the candidates for special election, if there should be a resignation. I cannot trace this opinion to any official source, and it may be that it has originated merely in the reasonableness of the conjecture. It would be feasible enough that Bell should operate on Foster through Clay & others of the Bell Whigs, and that Clay might promise Foster, that if he would let Bell go to Senate and save, or not save, the State by running for Gov. that Clay would give him a mission, or any thing else that might suit when Clay got to be President. It is more and more manifest that they are keeping Jones for a "hand plant," to be used or not as they may desire. If they can make any more eligible arrangement, they are maintaining him in so weak a manner now, that they can at any time shake him off without the loss of a dozen adherents; but if they can do no better, they are so training him, that they may present him fairly for the party strength, at any time.

The Banks sustain themselves so well and there is so little call for specie that Caleb[6] & the ultra Clay bank men are very uneasy. Caleb spends all his ingenuity in making daily & imaginary changes in the rates of all the paper of the Banks & their branches. He was evidently elated with the hope that he could produce such confusion in the rates of the State Circulation that he would disgust the public & turn their expectations to Clay & his remedy, but in that he has been a good deal defeated. The paper calling the Clay meeting for Saturday next[7] has been pressed with the zeal of desperation on the old legion, and in most cases they have succeeded, but some stood out. All who put their names down, are considered as in *"for during the war."* Some will doubtless be secured in that way who might otherwise have dropt out. Coleman,[8] the Butcher banker, refused to sign, and is out for Mayor against Stout[9] the incumbent, who is the Whig proper and will probably on that account be called to the chair at the Whig meeting of Saturday. Coleman has more personal strength than Clay or Stout, and will most probably be supported by the entire democratic strength.

Claiborne is looking for his dismissal by every mail. Caruthers[10] has written that Shepherd has been nominated to the Senate & will be confirmed.[11]

Carroll has received an invitation to the Athens dinner[12] and thinks he will go. Armstrong finally declined going to Rogersville. It was best not to leave here, and I so thought but gave no solemn adjudication that way.

Ben Motley[13] has resigned Senator from Wilson. Jones' brother-in-law Munford will probably be elected in his place.[14]

The great Nashville Camp meeting[15] has been on hand all last week. Bell attended closely, staid there one night with Harry Hill[16] and was in the altar looking devoutly. Some one said he made fifty votes.

Daniel Donelson will be elected easily in place of Barry.[17] Some fellow named Daughtry[18] is running against him. The County trustee of Rutherford[19] was here today & says that the democrats will carry that County if the Whigs resign. You passed through there however & know what is calculated on. Humphreys has drawn a Bill agt. the Hiwassee Road. Atty Allen has sued Caleb & the other Brokers.[20]

GRAHAM

ALS. DLC–JKP. Addressed to Knoxville and forwarded to Athens under cover of Robert B. Reynolds to Polk, August 16, 1842. ALS. DLC–JKP. Graham noted at head of his first page, "not much in it, and need not be read until not much engaged with Company."

1. Graham probably refers to the date of Polk's speaking engagement at Rogersville.

2. See Polk to Samuel H. Laughlin, July 22, 1842, about the proposed resignation of members of the Tennessee legislature.

3. Reference is to a Whig meeting held at the home of Ephraim H. Foster.

4. Robert C. Foster, Jr., son of Robert C. Foster, Sr., and brother of Ephraim H. Foster, represented Williamson County in the Tennessee House for three terms between 1829 and 1841 and in the Senate for one term, 1841–43, during which service he presided as Speaker; he practiced law in Franklin and in Nashville.

5. Ephraim H. Foster.

6. Caleb C. Norvell edited the *Nashville Whig*, which supported Henry Clay and advocated formation of a third Bank of the United States.

7. In the *Nashville Whig* of July 30, 1842, Norvell called for a meeting of local Whigs on Saturday, August 13, to promote the election of Henry Clay to the presidency. "The call has already been numerously signed, and every hour swells the list with the names of those who are determined to nail their colors to the mast."

8. Thomas B. Coleman, a merchant, served as mayor of Nashville, 1842–43; he was the son of Joseph Coleman, the first mayor of Nashville.

9. Samuel Van Dyke Stout, a merchant, served as mayor of Nashville, 1841–42.

10. Robert L. Caruthers, a Whig lawyer in Lebanon, represented Wilson County for one term in the Tennessee House, 1835–37, and sat in the U.S. House for a single term, 1841–43.

11. On August 6, 1842, the U.S. Senate confirmed the appointment of Benjamin H. Sheppard to be U.S. marshal for the Middle District of Tennessee.

12. En route home from Rogersville, Polk spoke at a political dinner in Athens on August 18, 1842.

13. Benjamin T. Motley, who raised blooded horses in Wilson County, resigned from the Tennessee Senate in 1842 after serving as a Whig for two and a half terms, 1833–37 and 1841–42.

14. Thomas J. Munford, a farmer, won Motley's seat and served as a Whig for the remaining year of the term. Munford's sister, Sarah Watson Munford, married James C. Jones in 1829.

15. Reference is to a revival meeting held at Nashville's Methodist Episcopal Church.

16. Harry R. W. Hill, a wealthy Nashville commission merchant, was a prominent Methodist layman.

17. Daniel Smith Donelson and Thomas R. Barry. A West Point graduate and farmer in Sumner County, Donelson served two and a half terms as a Democrat in the Tennessee House, 1842–43 and 1855–59; he ran unsuccessfully for Congress in 1843 and served as a C.S.A. general during the Civil War. Also a Democrat and lawyer from Sumner County, Barry served two and a half terms in the Tennessee House, 1839–42 and 1851–53; he resigned in 1842 and ran unsuccessfully for Congress in 1849 and 1853.

18. Not identified further.

19. Not identified further.

20. George W. Allen of Sumner County served as attorney general of Tennessee's Sixth Judicial District from 1841 until 1849; his prosecution against Caleb C. Norvell et al. has not been identified further.

FROM SAMUEL H. LAUGHLIN

My dear Sir   McMinnville, August 11, 1842

Mr. Hopkins left Smithville for Fentress the same evening our messenger found him (Friday) and after obtaining Mr. Grishams resignation in proper form, brought it to Sparta and enclosed it to Gen. Armstrong in time for it to have reached Nashville on yesterday (Wednesday) at "High Meridian." Grisham said he had sent his resignation by mail the day before Mr. H. found him—or, at least, had put it in the hands of a friend to carry to Jamestown to be mail'd. It is now no matter whether this is true or not. Mr. Walker's resignation has also gone to Nashville in duplicate, and is undoubtedly there.[1] So you see, as far as these cases are concerned, we are safe. I have seen your letter to Ford,[2] and am aware that Mr. Hembree's resignation is also in the proper place.

You will see that the last Banner is silent, editorially, on the subject of resignations, but gives place to Burchett Douglass' long and angry reply to Turney's alternative proposition.[3] Douglass pretends not to know any thing about what Marable will do. This is *prima facie*, a lie. D's reply was either written in Nashville or by directions from Nashville by McMahon at Memphis.[4] The whigs are bent, or I mistake the sign, on trying to escape the general proposition by making a false issue with Sam Turney on his very unwise proposal to Douglass and Marable. I have written to him, since I saw the Banner, to remain silent, or reply to Douglass in a short pointed card, holding him and his party to a final decision on the general proposition, which is a state question between the two great parties, and to deny his right to accept or reject the individual proposition made to himself and Marable until the whigs as a party have finally acted on the proposal for a general resignation. This is the previous question to be settled according to Turney's letter. I hope Turney will do what is proper. The whigs would gladly get him into a newspaper war, in order that they may traduce and destroy him, and wound the democratic party through him.

The Chancery Court at Winchester interferes with my intended trip to Nashville. I have however sent a power of attorney, or the same thing in effect, to Gen. Armstrong, Mr. Kezer[5] or W. H. Polk, to put my name to a note notifying Jennings[6] &c. that the resignations are in hand. I did this, fearing Hardwick might not be present, or any other democratic Senator.

You will see that Ford takes the true and only proper and safe ground as I conceive in relation to the Turney and Douglass question. We are glad to see that you will pass through Hiwassee and Ocoe before you return home. The foolish whigs here believe that we sent old Argo[7] over the mountain to make the appointment for you, and say it has been very quickly arranged.

Please present me respectfully to Gen. Anderson and Mr. Eastman.

S. H. LAUGHLIN

ALS. DLC–JKP. Addressed to Knoxville and marked "Private."

1. See Polk to Laughlin, July 22, 1842.

2. In a letter of August 11, 1842, John W. Ford acknowledges receipt of a letter from Polk dated August 7, 1842; Polk's letter has not been found. ALS. DLC–JKP.

3. In a public letter to John W. Ford of July 5, 1842, Samuel Turney, Democratic Speaker of the Senate, proposed his own resignation and that of House Speaker Burchett Douglass and one other Whig representative, Henry H. Marable of Humphreys County. By that stratagem "the fate of the State" could be decided "by single combat." See the *Nashville Union*, July 15, 1842. Douglass answered with a public letter to the *Memphis Enquirer*, subsequently printed in the Nashville *Republican Banner* of August 8, 1842. Marable, a physician and farmer, won election to a single term in the Tennessee House in 1841 and returned to that body for one session in 1865.

4. Jesse H. McMahon, a prominent Whig and former editor of newspapers in Franklin, Jackson, and Nashville, joined the *Memphis Enquirer* in 1838 and remained as editor of that newspaper throughout the 1840's.

5. Timothy Kezer, a Nashville merchant and hatmaker, was Laughlin's son-in-law.

6. Thomas Reid Jennings, a Nashville physician and member of the medical department of the University of Nashville, served as a Whig member of the Tennessee Senate from 1839 until 1845.

7. W. H. Argo, a minor Democratic political operative in McMinnville, was related to Laughlin through the marriage of Thomas P. Argo to Mary Laughlin Argo, both of McMinnville. The kinship tie between W. H. Argo and Thomas P. Argo has not been identified.

FROM CAVE JOHNSON

Friday morning

My dear Sir   Washington Augt. 19 [1842][1]

We shall leave here tomorrow or next day & I write you a line to give you a brief sketch of the state of things here. And brief it must be as we are packing up preparatory to our movement. The Whigs are divided without the possibility of reunion—the tariff men proper, wishing tariff without distribution about 75 or 80; the distribution men the balance of the Whigs. The Democrats cannot go with the high tariff men & they will accept nothing that we can offer. Nor can they go with the distributionists, nor they with us, so that nothing can be done—a triangular warfare & not a great difference in the numbers of either. The votes you will see in the morning papers & can easily trace those who go for Clay—the White Charlies[2] & those who go for a tariff. The vote of yesterday[3] is a death blow to Clay & demonstrates that nothing can or will be done this session & we shall adjourn as soon as the Senate will allow us. They now have up the British treaty.[4] Rumor says Benton, Buckhanon[5] & Calhoun take ground agt it. Yet it is believed it will be ratified. The final vote will probably take tomorrow. We shall leave the Captain[6] with 20 pCent Tariff & distribution & 30,000,000 in debt. We have passed nothing of consequence but private claims, some (Deane[7] heirs) outstanding for 60 years—others grossly fraudulent which have been over & over rejected. They must have something to brag of, & pass every thing. Bell's course as Sec. in paying Ross, Clinch & others will disgrace him forever unless he is grossly misrepresented.[8] Both are now before Committees and reports expected.[9]

Among our friends the difficulties are equally as great if not worse. Calhoun & friends are pressing on with great zeal & in my opinion will never yield to any Convention or any thing else. I think the split inevitable. It is known that Wright cannot be seduced. Woodbury seems standing still watching the signs. The better *opinion* is that he will not yield. *Clifford*[10] is to be made their speaker and Maine secured. Yet he is *still* watching the signs.[11] I think their prospects will all fail. Yet they seem bright here and great confidence is felt.[12] Mr Buckhanon will yield to the embrace, hoping no doubt [for] the succession, unless better prospects are hereafter holden out for the present term. Benton is of course firm for Van & I fear for Col RMJ,[13] tho I can learn nothing distinct, except an occasional expression slipping out in my presence, that he will be satisfied with the Vice presidency. You will understand that I have studiously avoided seeking or receiving communications in relation to these matters further than to let my position be distinctly known & which forbids the approval of those who are maneuvering in such matters & of course the little I learn is mere accidental.

You will see Benton & Calhoun have a issue in the Tariff—Calhoun for a *horizontal tariff*, Benton for discrimination (I have not read his speech)[14] & Calhouns friends of course say for Tariff. Their feelings toward each other are as bitter as those of Clay & Webster. B. talks openly. C. never mentions the former. All N.C. is for C—except Genl McK[15]—all Al. & Mississippi & a great part of V.[16] New H & Maine are neutral & go for the nominee. We need make no calculation of Penn. if the Tariff is kept open which Clay and his friends determine shall be the case and in that event N.Y. shivers in the wind. Ohio is safe for us and I think Indiana & Illinois. I yet am of opinion that RMJ will not yield & that he will be taken up by the whigs. His friends in Ky studiously avoid saying he is agt a U.S. Bank. All the Dem. North will be for a Ten. Vice[17] unless policy induces them to avoid competition by selecting another & I have no doubt that effort will be made. Bell is not regarded by the friends of Clay here as a reliable man.

But I must go to the labors of the day—& try & be ready for my departure tomorrow.

C JOHNSON

ALS. DLC–JKP. Addressed to Columbia and marked "private."

1. Year identified through content analysis.

2. "Charley" is a slang expression meaning "watchman." The "White Charlies" reference is to Speaker John White's followers. White, a lawyer, served in the Kentucky House in 1832 and as a Whig in the U.S. House from 1835 until 1845, during which period he was elected Speaker of the House for the Twenty-seventh Congress.

3. On August 18 the House rejected a Ways and Means Committee resolution proposing that the vetoed tariff bill be modified in such manner as to obviate Tyler's opposition to its 27th section, which provided for the repeal of restrictions on the distribution of land revenues.

4. The Webster-Ashburton Treaty.

5. James Buchanan.

6. John Tyler.

7. In pursuance of his duties as an agent for the United State in France from 1776 to 1778, Silas Deane performed services and incurred expenses for which he failed to obtain satisfactory compensation prior to his death in 1789. By Act of August 11, 1842, Congress allowed payment of Deane's claims.

8. John Bell, John Ross, and Duncan Lamont Clinch. Shortly before his resignation from the Cabinet on September 11, 1841, Secretary of War Bell authorized payment of over $500,000 in claims pressed by Chief Ross in behalf of fellow Cherokee tribesmen. In April of 1841 Bell settled the claim of Duncan Lamont Clinch for corn and sugar cane destroyed on his Florida plantation in 1836 by U.S. troops; Bell allowed nearly $26,000. Clinch, who attained the rank of brigadier general in 1829, fought against the Seminoles in 1835; he won election to Congress as a Georgia Whig in 1844.

9. On August 27, 1842, the Committee on Indian Affairs submitted to the U.S. House Report No. 1098, which related to claims arising from the removal program. The War Department reported the Clinch settlement on July 26, 1842. House Document No. 276, 27 Congress, 2 Session.

10. A lawyer and two-term member of the Maine House, 1830–34, Nathan Clifford won election as a Democrat to the U.S. House in 1839 and 1841; served as U.S. attorney general under Polk, 1846–48; and sat as an associate justice on the bench of the U.S. Supreme Court from 1858 until 1881.

11. Reference probably is to Levi Woodbury.

12. Reference is to the Calhoun faction of the Democratic Party.

13. Martin Van Buren and Richard M. Johnson.

14. Benton addressed the Senate on the tariff question on July 5, 1842.

15. James I. McKay, a lawyer and Democrat from North Carolina, served in

the U.S. House from 1831 until 1849; earlier he had won election to several terms in the state senate and had served as U.S. attorney for the district of North Carolina.

16. Virginia.

17. Reference is to Tennessee's candidate for vice-president, James K. Polk.

FROM J. GEORGE HARRIS

My Dear Sir,   Nashville Aug 24, 1842

I am at a little loss how to temper my course on the subject of the Presidency and Vice Presidency. You know Clay is *urged openly* by his leading friends; and Dick Johnson's friends are *indecently* pressing *his* claims. Meantime we are doing nothing. The conflicting aspirations at Washington I need not speak of. The *ultimate* action of our party in favor of N.Y. and Tenn. I cannot doubt. *But when is it time for us to act in our Tennessee papers, and how far ought we to go in the onset are considerations which should not be disposed of with too much haste. A little modesty* on our part at this time I have thought was *becoming* at least; and accordingly I have adopted your advice in my editorial conduct, "holding the ship close to the wind" of democratic principles, filling her sails with the breezes of the democratic triumphs, and said little or nothing with reference to her officers for the next voyage. This was Van Buren's advice in his letter to Missouri,[1] quoted and approved by us, and advised as a worthy saying by you in our conversations.

I have a letter from Greene, "the democracy of New England" as he has been called,[2] and though he speaks less definitively touching the future than he might have done, still he says "V.B. & P are our choice and we shall press their claims with all prudence." But *the best* intelligence that I have from the northward, is a letter from Mr. Croswell of the Albany Argus.[3] After two or three pages on private and personal affairs he says: "Politically the aspects are favorable. All the indications throughout the Union point to the democratic ascendency, and as we think to certain restoration. While the Republicans of this State and of this section of the Union prefer (as I cannot doubt) to recal Mr. Van Buren and to do justice to an administration and to public views which have proved to be founded on wisdom and patriotism; and which the people are daily giving signal manifestations of their approval of, they are prepared to support with the utmost cordiality any democrat who shall be the choice of the National Convention."

So much for Mr. Croswell's sentiments on the subject of the Presidency. But, he continues:

"So also (says he) respecting the Vice Presidency. The preferences of this State *and of this region* are with *great unanimity* for Gov. Polk. *No man stands higher* or *stronger in the confidence of the Democracy and no one would call out their suffrages in his support with greater alacrity than he. But these are matters* (he adds) *which we, as well as our friends in Tennessee desire to treat with all delicacy*; and to leave to the unbiassed decision of a National Convention, the assembled delegates of the whole party."

There *is* delicacy at this embryo stage of the matter, so far as Croswell and myself on the one hand and yourself and Van Buren on the other are concerned. While the Argus is regarded abroad as enjoying the full and entire confidence of Mr. Van Buren, the Union is looked upon as being the guardian of your particular interests, the repository of your confidence. And while both of us may by private conference effect much and all that is necessary in moving the democratic press, our editorials though decided should in my judgment be carefully tempered and not importunate. Croswell further says—all in connexion:

"Combinations, and possibly intrigues may be started to prevent what now seems to be *the natural*, if not *the inevitable* tendency of things; but if those should be I have little belief or fear that they will seriously obstruct the course of the popular feeling."

I give Croswell's letter the weight that would be due to one from Van Buren's own hand. Under all the circumstances it is *oracular*. Van Buren has few confidants, but he has prudent and effective ones from whom he reserves nothing. There is more in his late still-hunts throughout the Union than any of us have dreamed of. He has been badly and unfairly beaten and his own personal pride, to say nothing of his devotion to his principles, is actively at work. *I am more than ever convinced that he will be the nominee of the Convention*; and in my reply (privately) to Croswell I have endeavored to convince his understanding that we are willing to sink or swim with him, *looking* of course to, or rather hinting at, the *guid pro quo*. I have referred him to that long letter which I wrote him on the subject of the Vice Presidency two-and-a-half years ago (in your office) and sent him a copy of the old Voice of the Southwest[4]; have informed him that you jeoparded and as I believe lost your reelection as Governor because you made such bold and vigorous efforts in Van Buren's election by barbecue speeches &c.; have told him that our party in this State comprise that portion of the Tennesseans who *do not change from slight and trivial causes*—thro' that ordeal we have passed unscathed. I think I know your sentiments well enough to protect your interest in that quarter as you would have me—though I must at our next interview confer with you more freely upon some points of the future. With reference to the N.Y. State election[5] Croswell says: "Our contest in this State will be sharp and active—more so, perhaps, than some of our friends now imagine—but I cannot doubt that the democratic party will fully sustain itself. We shall be able to judge more fully at the extra session next month." [6]

But to return to you: a week or two ago I received a long letter from Mr. Coe, of Fayette. It was in reply to one I had previously written him in reply to a previous one. In short: some five months ago & after a conversation with you I took the ground very modestly and by way of approving the remarks of other papers, that the true policy of the democratic party was to adhere to advocate and defend their cherished principles, and not volunteer their various preferences for the succession so long before-hand; advising patience until the National Convention. A week or two afterwards I received a letter from Mr. Coe, in terms somewhat unexpected, complaining of my course in that behoof. I replied very kindly that I had acted in accordance with my own best judgment, gave my reasons, and stated that I had not acted contrary to the counsel of those who he himself is in favor as well as myself of elevating to the two highest offices in the government. After three months he wrote me in reply, which I found in the post-office on my return from E. Tenn, reiterating that I had "done *us* much damage" by the article before adverted to, advising me to "dry your blankets" [7] and stating that *a vigorous* move was forthwith contemplated upon the chess-board. I paid no attention to the *chafing* parts of his letter but replied kindly, although I confess that I felt deeply injured at being accused of a lack of *zeal in your behalf*, and especially by *him* whom I have not only uniformly defended in my paper but personally quarrelled with deadly weapons upon the square in defence of his reputation.[8] It is pretty tough—but Mr. Coe is the best architect of his own future, I suppose.

In the next Union I shall publish the article that appears in the Alabama papers; with such remarks as prudence may dictate.[9] I would like to see you very much or to hear from you at length.

I have written this letter at night while awaiting at the bed-side of my sick sister-in-law;[10] and owing to the quiet of the hour I have made it more prolix than I intended.

J. Geo. Harris

[P.S.] If you think it advisable to send this letter to Dr. Ramsey you are at liberty to do so. I may perhaps throw a little north-eastern light in his mind.[11]

ALS. DLC–JKP. Addressed to Columbia and marked "*Private*." Polk's AE on the cover states that he answered this letter in August, 1842; Polk's reply has not been found.

1. On March 6, 1841, Martin Van Buren wrote a public letter thanking the Missouri legislature for resolutions praising his administration and nominating him for the presidency in 1844. The ex-president urged that the presidential question be left to the future and that principles ever be given priority over personal considerations.

2. Charles G. Greene, influential leader in the New England Democracy, founded the *Boston Morning Post* in 1831 and remained its editor for forty-eight years.

3. Edwin Croswell edited the *Albany Argus* from 1823 to 1854.

4. Not identified further.

5. Reference is to New York's legislative and gubernatorial elections, which were scheduled for November 8, 1842.

6. On August 16, 1842, the New York legislature met in special session to apportion congressional districts under the Census of 1840.

7. Coe's complaint was that Harris had put a wet blanket on local efforts to promote Polk's vice-presidential candidacy.

8. References by J. George Harris in the *Nashville Union* of July 13, 1840, and by Levin H. Coe in the same of August 3, 1840, indicate that Harris and Edwin H. Ewing, a prominent Whig, engaged in a fistfight during the second week of July. In a public speech on June 20, 1840, Ewing had rebuked Coe and Harris for publishing partisan attacks on William Henry Harrison in the *Union*.

9. On August 26, 1842, the *Nashville Union* carried an article from the *Huntsville Democrat* supporting Van Buren as the Democratic nominee and reprinting a Van Buren-Polk endorsement appearing in the Tuscumbia *Franklin Democrat*.

10. Mary Kent McGavock, daughter of James McGavock, was the youngest sister of Harris' wife, Lucinda McGavock Harris. The Harrises were married on May 5, 1842.

11. Harris wrote his postscript in the left margin of the last page.

FROM WILLIAM M. GWIN

My dear Sir   Washington City Augt. 27th 42

We have had an Extraordinary scene enacted here today in the passage of the Tariff bill through the Senate. The vote was 24 to 23, Messrs Wright, Buchanan, Sturgeon & Williams of Maine voting for it.[1] It must be fatal to Wright & Buchanan's future position in the Democratic party, nine tenths of whom are anti protective as to a tariff. This is the most odious protective tariff ever passed. This move on the political chess board must Seriously affect Mr. Van Buren. All of his confidential friends in Congress have gone for this tariff—the Representative from his district, McLellan, his relative Van Buren & his chief counsellor Wright.[2] The inevitable result must be in my opinion to make Mr. Calhoun the Democratic candidate for the Presidency. I acknowledge that I am anxious for it as matters now stand & most anxious for you to take the same position. It must put you next to him in the South & in his place when he leaves the political stage. If you do not move now & take this position others must. The force of events will so order it. With the South united upon you as the leader next to Mr. Calhoun, nothing can prevent your elevation to the highest station known in our country. Do write me to Vicksburg fully & openly on this subject.

W. M. GWIN

ALS. DLC–JKP. Addressed to Columbia and marked "Private." Polk's AE on the cover states that he answered this letter on October 14, 1842; Polk's reply has not been found.

1. Silas Wright, James Buchanan, Daniel Sturgeon, and Reuel Williams. Sturgeon, a physician, won election to several terms in the Pennsylvania House and Senate, 1818–30; served as state auditor general, 1830–36, and as state treasurer, 1838–39; and sat two terms in the U.S. Senate, 1839–51. Williams, a lawyer, won election to several terms in the Maine House and Senate between 1822 and 1832; he served in the U.S. Senate as a Democrat from 1837 to 1843.

2. Robert McClellan, John Van Buren, and Silas Wright. A New York lawyer, McClellan served two terms as a Democrat in the U.S. House, 1837–39 and 1841–43. Also a lawyer, Van Buren won election to the New York Assembly in 1831 and served as a Democrat in the U.S. House for one term, 1841–43.

FROM CAVE JOHNSON

Dear Sir,   Washington Augt 28th 1842

I wrote you a line last night & under the excitement of the moment produced by the vote on the Tariff in the Senate, in which I said some things of our friends rather harsher perhaps than is prudent and therefore re-write this morning tho in but little better mood than last night.[1] But before I enter in that, I must explain some papers which accompanies this letter in another envelope.[2] Sec. B. allowed Jno. Ross 587,000 on a claim disallowed by Crawford, Poinsett & Van Buren—revised & reversed their decision contrary to all usage & law.[3] Many harsh things are said here, as to the *Sec's* integrity. The papers on a call made by me were referred to the Com. of Ind Aff & Harris reported in part on yesterday[4] & the papers were ordered to be printed. I mention this to direct your attention to it when published. Another, Genl. Clinch's account has been disallowed for 25,000. The decision was reversed & the money paid & I enclose you the opinion of Bell & Poinsett. I enclose you this because the damages alledged & paid for were produced by the Conduct of the Ten. Volunteers. If all the allegations were true the decision of B. is an outrage upon common sense & honesty too. But as they are wholy untrue as you will see from Poinsetts opinion & as will be proved, as W.B.C.[5] tells me, by every volunteer, he may & ought to be made to feel their indignation. I had first thought of sending them to Genl. Armstrong but thought it more prudent to submit them to your examination & let you give directions if they ought to be used & how. In the case of Ross, Mathew St Clair Clarke[6] was Ross' lawyer (in whose house the Sec. lived). He brought it up & argued it & Bell gave the very learned opinion which I enclose. Ross & Clarke squabbled about the fee as rumor says, & the Sec. wrote Ross he ought to pay the lawyer (some say) 20 or 30,000 & others 50,000, as he had saved such a sum. This is rumor. I suppose the printed papers will make some startling disclosures, as even the Whig Cooper of Penn.[7] is shocked at the startling facts disclosed. The examination will be resumed next winter. The Report *is a part*.

We have had a sort of shufling in politics which has made a very deep impression on my mind & I must add a very unfavorable one as to many of our leaders. I informed you of the *irreconcilable* squabble between the Tariff Whigs & the distribution Whigs. It was kept up every night in caucus until all parties were satisfied that no reconciliation would ever take place & we voted for adjournment on the 22nd (the Democrats & distribution Whigs) & sent it to the Senate. This evidenced discord irreconcilable among them. The distribution Whigs of the Senate were for uniting with the Democrats & adjourning—and we should have adjourned on that day without a Tariff without any Whig reconciliation & the Whig ranks forever broke up but alas for poor human nature. The Whig squabble created hopes among *our leaders* of using the Tariff Whigs in the presidential election for their *own benefit* & at the expense of other democrats. The Tariff Whigs were in *truth in market*, put up to the *highest bidder*. Ingersol's *amendment*, drawn up by Buckhanon, who is thought by many to represent J.C.C.[8] proposed to take the Tariff of 1 Jany 1840 (6/10), Cash duties & home valuation—a pretty fair bid equal at least to the Tariff of 1832. It seemed for a while that it would take but when it came to be voted on, it was too low for Tariff men & too high for Anti tariff but many of our Van B friends would not be outbid and was disposed to give no advantages to the other branch of democrats. It was even hinted that J.C.C. would vote for it as a temporary measure. It was soon given out that Wright would go for it too and such things were said too of Benton. A project was then started in the same quarter to begin at the Tariff of 1840 & let it gradually come off by tenths until 1845 thus to shove it out of the presidential election. This proposition was so little favored as never to have been presented to the House. This state of things seemed likely to secure the Tariff Whigs to others. Then the great champion Clay & his friends set to work & bid up at last the big Tariff without distribution upon condition that a separate distribution Bill should be sent to the Capt[9] for another veto. This was of course accepted, having that confidence in each other which exists among pickpockets, when their union is necessary for their own preservation or being identical in principle, having no other than to secure money on one side & political promotion on the other. But all could not be lost in that way. Van's friends would not be outbid so the N.Y. Dems. in the House (many of them) & Wright in the Senate gave way & agreed to the same bid, whilst Buckhanon & Sturgeon & R[e]uel Williams united. I have no doubt the Whigs were detailed in both Houses, so as just to make enough to pass the Bill in both Houses, getting as many of Van's friends with them as possible—and we were then beaten 2 votes in the House and one in the Senate. The Bill was engrossed in the Senate yesterday by 24 to 23. Buckhanon, Sturgeon, Wright & Williams among the yeas—and Archer, Berrien, Clayton, Graham, Henderson, Mangum, Merrick, Preston, Rives among the nays.[10] It will come to us tomorrow & of course be a law. They could have had us easily 8 or 10 majority in either House if desirable. We have sent the Senate the Bill for repealing the proviso to the distribution Bill of the call session,[11] which will probably pass tomorrow & we shall adjourn on Wednesday, leaving the Capt. to pocket the distribution if he chooses. What effect this state of things may hereafter have is still very uncertain. Van's friends are much hurt & many will probably desert to Calhoun. Clays friends in the north are not less hurt & many may go to Van. I fear it will result in the formation of a Northern & Southern party. Bucks[12] position seems not clearly understood. Some consider him as acting for Van, others for J.C.C. and I suspect [he] is in truth playing a double game, ready to go with that side which will help him most. Many of Van's friends suspect Woodbury of being willing to be the Vice for J.C.C. tho I do not. Some suppose that Buck will finally yield to that with the reversionary prospects. If Clay is ruled off which I think by no means improbable or strange as you may think it I shall not be surprised to find this zealous friend rallying in support of Van. J.C.C. acquires favor with the politicians & may be the formidable opponent of Van. One thing you may consider certain—the hostility between their friends is irreconcilable & the friends of J.C.C. will not yield to a convention. Our friends are much chagrined. I fear A.V.B.[13] is gone from Van. Turney is dissatisfied with every body & I am not much better tho I am not disposed to think that Van gives countenance to such movements & to hold him responsible for them. I cannot think he will yield to the protective policy. But little has been said of late as to the Vice Presidency further than is connected with the elevation of J.C.C. Van's friends are for abiding by the convention & having one fairly selected. When we were informed in the House of Wrights speech,[14] I never witnessed so many doleful countenances, among the friends of J.C.C., who could not conceal their delight at the supposed advantage which it gave him over Van. One says well what shall we do, C.? Another says, this is horrible! Another, we are betrayed! Another, I suspected as much from his vote in 1828![15] I could see that many thought I *would of course give up Van* & were anxious to know. I only replied to them, that I believed I should join the Whigs. They paid higher than any body else. I may say *to you* that I have been deeply mortified and am now, particularly at the course of Wright— which will be an additional reason for having nothing further to do with politics. You need expect nothing except upon the ground of securing the vote of Ten. Every thing of the sort is a mere calculation of interest. I shall leave here tuesday or wednesday. My health is very good.

C JOHNSON

ALS. DLC–JKP. Addressed to Columbia and marked *"private."*
1. Johnson's initial draft of this letter has not been found.
2. Not found.
3. John Bell, John Ross, Thomas Hartley Crawford, Joel R. Poinsett, and Martin Van Buren. Crawford, a lawyer from Chambersburg, Pennsylvania, sat in the U.S. House from 1829 until 1833; he served as special Indian commissioner in the 1836 fraud investigation and subsequently as commissioner of Indian affairs from 1839 until 1845. See Cave Johnson to Polk, August 19, 1842.
4. William A. Harris from the Committee on Indian Affairs reported to the House on August 27 about the removal of the Cherokees under Chief John Ross; see Johnson to Polk, August 19, 1842. Harris, a lawyer and editor, served in the Virginia House, 1830–31; sat one term in the U.S. House, 1841–43; went as chargé d'affaires to the Argentine Republic, 1846–51; and edited the *Washington Union*, 1857–59.
5. Probably William Bowen Campbell, Johnson's Whig colleague from Carthage. Campbell, a lawyer, served in the Tennessee House, 1835–36, and in the U.S. House, 1837–43; he had fought as a captain in the Seminole War during which Clinch's Florida plantation allegedly suffered nearly $26,000 in damages by U.S. forces.
6. A Pennsylvanian, Matthew St. Clair Clarke served as clerk of the U.S. House from 1822 until 1833 and won election again in 1841.
7. A lawyer, James Cooper served two terms in the U.S. House, 1839–43; several terms in the Pennsylvania House; and then a single term in the U.S. Senate, 1849–55.

8. Charles J. Ingersoll, James Buchanan, and John C. Calhoun. Ingersoll's amendment is not identified further.

9. President Tyler.

10. Reference is to William S. Archer (Va.), John M. Berrien (Ga.), Thomas Clayton (Del.), William A. Graham (N.C.), John Henderson (Miss.), Willie P. Mangum (N.C.), William D. Merrick (Md.), William C. Preston (S.C.), and William C. Rives (Va.); all were Whig members of the U.S. Senate.

11. On August 26, 1842, the House voted to repeal the 1841 proviso that distribution should cease when import duties exceeded twenty per cent of value.

12. Reference is to James Buchanan.

13. Aaron V. Brown.

14. On August 27, 1842, Silas Wright announced to the U.S. Senate his reluctant support for the tariff bill on grounds that a defective bill was better than no revenue bill at all.

15. On April 22, 1828, Silas Wright, then a member of the U.S. House, voted for the "tariff of abominations."

FROM J. GEORGE HARRIS

My Dear Sir: Nashville, Aug 30, 1842

Yours, in confidence, of the 26th is at hand.[1] I have been necessarily absent so much of late and my attention at my post is so much needed at this time that it is next to impossible for me to visit you this week as invited through your letter. I have the heartfelt gratification of saying that I have received a good letter from our mutual friend in the West. Dist., and good relations are fully restored.[2]

You will have seen how I have treated the subject matter under consideration. It is well at this juncture to conciliate So: Caro: if possible, by some private demonstration from your hand to a friend at Washington. Can you say, so that it may reach the *metaphysician's*[3] ear that "Tennessee and So: Caro: have run together *one* successful race, and may run another," [4] or something like it. Members of Congress are *too* busy. I could not refrain from rapping their knuckles with the club of the Detroit Democrat.[5] How do you like our present position?

No further demonstrations of the intentions of the Whigs on the subject of resignation are apparent.[6] I shall watch the movements day after tomorrow, and if they do not come up to the mark shall file a *closer* upon them.

Why is it that Sherrell resigned?[7] Was it not produced by the Fosterians? Did they not persuade him or provoke him to it? It is at least presumable for he bolted on some of their test-questions at the last session. Gov. Jones has appointed the 22d Sept as the day on which his vacancy is to be filled.[8] You know Jones had only about 310 maj. in Bledsoe, and cannot some governing influence be exerted there by our friends? I have tried to persuade Col Foot[9] to go there on "a trip to the mountain" springs but I fear I shall not succeed. He says if he could go he would not go in vain. It is *very* important. Any effort that is made should be made quickly and without much noise.

J Geo Harris

ALS. DLC–JKP. Addressed to Columbia.

1. Letter not found.

2. Reference is to Levin H. Coe, who resided in Tennessee's Western District; see J. George Harris to Polk, August 24, 1842.

3. Reference is to John C. Calhoun.

4. Jackson and Calhoun headed the Democratic ticket in 1828.

5. In the *Nashville Union* of August 30, 1842, Harris printed an excerpt from a Detroit *Constitutional Democrat* article arguing that the preferences of congressmen for the Democratic presidential candidates mattered very little; Congress should pass wise laws and leave the election of the president to the people. The *Constitutional Democrat* was the semiweekly edition of the Detroit *Daily Constitutional* from May through September, 1842, and the weekly edition from October of 1842 through about July of 1844.

6. See Polk to Samuel H. Laughlin, June 1 and July 22, 1842.

7. A Bledsoe County farmer, Cravens Sherrell served three terms as a Whig in the Tennessee House, 1841–45 and 1851–53.

8. Harris' reference to Jones' calling a special election has not been identified. Sherrell attended a special session of the legislature that met on October 4, 1842.

9. Not identified further.

FROM HOPKINS L. TURNEY

Dear Sir   Louisville Ky. Sept. 4th 1842

I arrived here last evening on my way home in company with Mr. Watirson,[1] and we are detained for want of a stage, none leaving on Sundays. Bad luck this for home sick Devils.

You have doubtless been advised of the unfortunate division of our friends in congress on the passage of the last Tariff bill.[2] It was unfortunate truly, but I hope and believe it will finally result in no mischivious consequences to our party, or to the country. Calhoon and his friends are makeing it the occasion of denounceing Van Burin and his friends as high tariff men, in order to thurst *him* Calhoon at the head of the party. The truth of this matter is that while the Clay wing of the whig party were opposing the tariff without distribution and thereby produceing a division between the distribution and tariff men which threatened to prove fatal to the whig party, Calhoon and his friends with a view no doubt of secureing the support of the Northeran Federalist were makeing propositions of compromise of a tariff embraceing all the objectionable principles in the bill which are to [be] found in the bill that finally passed. *Wright* discoverd this movement of Calhoon and resolved not to be out bid. So he went to work, in the same way and committed himself and his friends in the house for the bill. The Clay men however seeing what would inevitably be the result of their course that it would effectually distroy Clay, finally gave their support to the measure. As soon as this was done and the whig party thereby reunited, Calhoon returnes to his free trade doctring and raises the hugh and cry against Van, Wright &c. and are now labouring to rise upon their downfal, when in fact *he* is guilty of the same offence, except he displaid moore judgement in his retreat from a measure which he would doubtless have supported but for the reunion of the whigs. Wrights public reasons for supporting the bill are that it is intended as a temporary measure, that it defeats distribution, and that something was indespencierble for the government, and that this was the only thing he could get. These are pausible though not substancial reasons. Now the next congress will meet before a nomination will be made, and the Van Burin men with a view to reinstate him and themselves in the south and thereby to secure his nomination & election will go far to modify the tariff and make it accepterble to us. Benton has great feelings on this subject, and I think he is now looking to you as the most available man to counteract the effects of the manuvers of C.s friends in the south. They are resorting to all sorts of means to accomplish their object. While Gwinn is writeing to you that you are to be run for the Presidency,[3] Lewis and the other Calhoon trainors are writeing letters to every other section that Calhoon is the only man of our party that can be elected as these other men are now prostrated by their course, and that this has done moore for Calhoon than his friends could have done in years. Now sir I do not think that Gwinn is incincear to you, but I do think he is deceived by these men, for I do know they are looking alone to C's interest. Vans friends every where will now take a stronger stand for you than they otherwise would have done. I think our friends from Tennessee acted with great prudence and discression on critical occasion so as to preserve the friendship and good feelings of both Calhoons and Van's friends.

H. L. TURNEY

ALS. DLC–JKP. Addressed to Columbia.
1. Harvey M. Watterson.
2. See Cave Johnson to Polk, August 28, 1842.
3. See William M. Gwin to Polk, August 27, 1842.

FROM JAMES M. HOWRY

Oxford, Mississippi. September 9, 1842

Howry reports on Democratic presidential politics in Mississippi. Since last May he has favored pressing Polk's vice-presidential claims publicly, but cannot move the party, as Calhoun's presidential candidacy necessitates a "Northern man" to fill out the ticket. At present Calhoun controls the most active portion of the state's Democrats and also the newspapers in Northern Mississippi. Howry is anxious to take action in Polk's behalf before the state's congressional delegation returns home because "they *can & will throw cold water*" on any movement that would hurt Calhoun's prospects. Thompson[1] has distributed Calhoun letters and speeches throughout the state. Gwin is friendly, but may oppose Polk's nomination if Calhoun should choose either Wright or Woodbury to form a ticket.

ALS. DLC–JKP. Addressed to Columbia. Polk's AE on the cover indicates that he answered this letter on September 23, 1842; Polk's reply has not been found.

1. A lawyer from Oxford, Mississippi, Jacob Thompson sat in the U.S. House as a Democrat from 1839 until 1851; he served in Buchanan's cabinet as secretary of the interior from 1857 until 1861.

FROM SAMUEL H. LAUGHLIN

My dear Sir, Nashville, Sept. 9, 1842

You will have seen by the course of the whigs for a month past, as indicated by their papers and conduct, and finally, by the Governor's proclamation,[1] that there is to be no resignations. After Douglass replied to Turney, I feared they intended to make some movement in regard to Turney's challenge to Douglass and Marable, and instantly, while you were in East Tennessee, sent to Turney and dictated the substance of a short answer to Douglass,[2] which he adopted except in the addition of some foolish words about *sacrifices* &c. His answer held and still holds Douglass and Marable in the wrong.

Our course will, I think, now be plain, not to give an inch of our former ground in regard to Senators and districts. Turney, however, and another Senator[3] who, perhaps, ought to remain nameless, will require vigilant watching. The whigs evidently hope for *something*, and there are but two quarters from which they can possibly obtain help. If they expect it from Turney it will be because he has been very badly used in his connexion with the bank at Sparta,[4] and it must spring from revenge. Some men would sacrifice their party for the sake of individual revenge; and there are others who would do it to promote their personal political purposes—such as having a way opened to a seat in Congress. I hope we have none such in the ranks of the "immortal 13." In this my wishes are so strong that I am willing to hope against hope. Let the strongest appliances by instruction and admonition, from the proper quarters, be applied to any case nearest your home, and I will see that Hop[5] and every other force shall be applied in my country to our Speaker.[6]

You will have seen some small speculations, by way of preliminaries and feelers in Ford's paper[7] on the Presidency and Vice Presidency in prospect. I have deemed it best to *speak out*, but in terms of conciliation and submission to a Convention. Something of the same kind shall be kept up both before and after the meeting of the legislature—unless it shall prove to be improper or premature.

I came here on last Thursday night and go home tomorrow. I have seen no person out of Mr. Kezer's family and house. I have not gone to town although I have some pressing private business. I have been in the midst of deep sorrow and affliction. On Sunday last, I burried my infant daughter,[8] aged three years, who departed this life the night before. My head is sick and my whole heart faint within me. Every day some fond tie is being broken which bound me to life and its objects. It is true I have six surviving children,[9] but this last stroke, depriving me of the last pledge of wedded affection, has affected me deeply—so deeply, that I fear I shall never know comfort or happiness more. Were it not for my helpless orphan boys, I should wholly withdraw to solitude, and renounce every worldly pursuit.

Let me hear from you at your leisure . . . .

S. H. LAUGHLIN

ALS. DLC–JKP. Addressed to Columbia, marked "Private," and postmarked "September 8, 1842."

1. On September 1, 1842, Governor James C. Jones issued a proclamation convening an extra session of the legislature to meet on October 3, 1842.

2. Samuel Turney's reply to Burchett Douglass appeared in the *Nashville Union*, August 26, 1842. See Laughlin to Polk, August 11, 1842.

3. Andrew Johnson.

4. Samuel Turney's connection with the Sparta branch of the Bank of Tennessee has not been identified further. The Bank of Tennessee opened its branch office in Sparta in 1840 with John Jett as its first president.

5. Hopkins L. Turney.

6. Samuel Turney.

7. John W. Ford's speculations in his McMinnville *Central Gazette* have not been identified further.

8. Cora Kezer Laughlin, Laughlin's youngest child, died on September 3, 1842. Her sister, Isabella Laughlin, age seventeen, had died three months earlier.

9. Samuel Houston, John James, Andrew Jackson, Ellen (Mrs. Timothy Kezer), Sarah Louise (Mrs. Thomas Calhoun Smartt), and Mary (Mrs. T. P. Argo).

FROM JONATHAN P. HARDWICKE

D Sir,   Charlotte Sept 11th 1842

It is now known that the Legislature will soon be in session again.[1] We may suppose we will be called to elect Senators and lay off the State into Congressional, Senatorial and Representative Districts. How far we may succeed none can now tell. For myself [I] think it very doubtful whether we can do either, and I would respectfully ask you in the event of a failure what will be the effect. By what Law or clause in the Constitution can members be elected to the Legislature here after, or the members to the Congress of the U. States. I would also be pleased to know your opinion on the late law of Congress requiring the States to vote here after by Districts alone.[2] I have very much questioned the act upon Constitutional grounds. If I was fully sattisfied upon that point, I could now marke out my course at the call session; as the only remedy in the Congressional question I would be in favour of the General Ticket sistem, for the next election of members in our state. I hope you will give me your views on these as well as all other subjects likly to be before us at that time.

Purmit me here to remark that I very much fear we are getting behind again upon the Presidential election. The Whigs of Tenn. and of several other states are out in bold relief for Clay, and tauntling asking the Democrats to pick their man. For my self I fear most of all other evils some internal dissentions, for it is obvious that several of our distinguished men are becoming restless for preferment.

I have no doubt from what I have herd from Washington & else where, that the Democrats were prepared months ago for the nomination of Van Buren and your self. Without the least intention to flatter you, I will here remark that from the most reliable surces of all my information you were the favourite of the party at Washington, two months ago. Now Sir if the delay on our part[3] is likly to produce your nomination for the first office, I cheerfully forego all my fears, and assure you I would have much stronger hopes of success, than I have ever had for Van Buren. Of these things you must be abler to judge than I am having so lately been at the City. Write me as early as you can. I did receive your letter written just after your return[4] but it was one month & a day on the road.

J. P. HARDWICKE

ALS. DLC–JKP. Addressed to Columbia and marked "*Private.*" Polk's AE on the cover states that he answered this letter on September 22, 1842; Polk's reply has not been found.

1. On September 1, 1842, Jones issued a gubernatorial proclamation convening the Tennessee legislature in special session on October 3, 1842.

2. See Cave Johnson to Polk, April 29, 1842, for information about Halsted's amendment to the apportionment bill; the law received approval on June 25, 1842.

3. Polk probably had suggested that in the forthcoming special session of the legislature Democrats should avoid making any nominations for the 1844 presidential contest.

4. Letter not found. Having visited Washington City, Philadelphia, and New York, Polk returned to Tennessee in the middle of July.

FROM ALEXANDER O. ANDERSON

My Dear Sir   At Home[1] Sepr 14th 1842

The whigs will not resign, nor can they be goaded to it by any movement in the H.R. to that end.[2] Nevertheless, I think it highly adviseable that you shou'd see that a prudent & well-timed movement of that character shou'd be made.

Since the gov's proclamation,[3] I am satisfied another attempt will be made to elect Senators. As matters stand, & with the vantage ground we occupy, in every respect, as to issues & the conduct of our Party in the recent matter of resignation, I think it will be a suicidal policy to submit to any compromise whatever, and, therefore, our Senators shou'd be exhorted to stand firm.

After our state affairs it is highly important that your attention shou'd be directed to national politics, for at this movement,[4] the movements commenced sometime since, are being continued with renewed effort. Whatever others may feel, I have no sympathy in common with those who are ready & willing to sacrafice Tennessee to any quarter of the Union. I am not. And such are my feelings and determination, equally, upon the ground that it is due from me to you, & from Tennessee to you. In the north they do not know how to appreciate such efforts as you have made, or the idea that you have thrown yourself into the breach, and

gathered together the shattered fragments of the Republican Party.
They entertain the opinion there that our revolution here was under very
different auspices, because they have no just conception of *the power and
effect of a true Republican* intercourse with the people, & the public
discussions from day to day before their assembled masses; but to come
more directly to the point, the true question which presents itself, when
stripped of the drapery of humbuggery, is whether we shall, in a mad and
unwise devotion to any man, in the ensuing Presidential contest, bind
ourselves hand & foot, without regard to what Tennessee has a right to
expect, & justly to claim. The moment Tennessee does that she will be as
powerless in all movements of whatever character, whether in convention or elsewhere, as a ten year-old Child, and treated with about the
same ceremony—made to wait, and get nothing, except some fragment
which may be left! Let us look how much reason there is in the proposition that Tennessee shou'd make herself a slave to the will of any Clique.
Who was it that restored Tennessee? Who fought the great Battle? Who
roused up her dispirited Democracy? Who, in one word, has created the
Party here? You—& you alone Singly moved upon that mass, & gave it
form, & heat, & life & motion! & who broke it down by a series of
blunders, that very Clique & that very Head of the Clique,[5] who I know
had prepared to sacrafice you—& will do it again, & again, if Tennessee
can be so reckless as to be committed without regard to you! The reason
for all this is obvious, and is *absolutely irremoveable*! It is that your
position for the future is an object of irreconcileable envy, & inexpressi-
ble apprehension. In this I am right—I know that I am not mistaken—but
if Tennessee will be true to herself, she can dictate who may be the next
President, & who shall be his successor. But if she acts with pusillanimity
her actors, & especially her great Leader, will be treated as mere instruments, while the three or four ini[ti]ated smile in their Sleeves, at her
pretensions. Let Tennessee be true to herself, & the Union will be true to
her, and at a moment when we have a just right to struggle for Suprema-
cy, it astonishes me that any leading Press in the State shou'd *by every
possible indirection*, endeavor to commit her, or *indicate* her in the Presidential Contest.[6] Perhaps, I ought to make some allowances. They do
not feel as I do. I have staked my political fortunes with you. Your
friendly hand has been with me—and I am willing to stake all for the sake
of your success, in connexion with the great principles for which we
contend, for I verily believe the time is coming when fewer, & yet fewer
of our public men can be trusted to stand, in all times of imminent trial,
by the great principle of our Constitution. And I verily believe if Tennessee will be true to herself that the day will come when your position, &
your rigid principles will be looked to for the highest office, as essential to

promote our great National Interests. This will be, as certain as I write, as far as human foresight can go, the result, if Tennessee does not now act a suicidal part, and sacrafice you to the north—not to the Party—for there is much danger that the Party will be sacraficed too!

This is in substance what I said to you when we were last together. And as to our public men, that they will not stand the test thro' the trying years that are coming, look at the recent desertion of their Party principles by Mr. Buchanan & Mr. Wright, in the passage of the last Tariff Bill. A Bill viler & more abominable than any thing which has ever been placed upon the national Statute Book.[7] Their Apology was any thing but satisfactory.[8] Both those Gentlemen look forward to the Presidency. The first will agree to a contingent remainder, if he can do no better. The last looks complacently upon a vested Right if the power of his great prototypes shall be in the ascendant! Will such men do thro the times that are coming? No! They have not the nerve, and they are behind the age. They lack forecast. The Time is coming when monopolies will go down in the North, the Middle, the West & the South. Their desertion was at a moment when we had the Whigs upon the hip—the hip—and the law of the Compromise Still in force. And they started back at the sight of Whig protests against the payment of duties—& had Mr. Benton, tho voting for his Party, apologizing for their course![9] The Sagacious man who Sees all this shou'd remember that the action of Tennessee, of this day, is to have a decided effect upon the state of things to be produced for the future, by just such movements. And if she is true to herself, the Union will be true to her—& not otherwise!

In my opinion, therefore, unless Tennessee designs to abandon you, which she will not do, *if allowed* to speak & to act, her voice must be wholly uncommitted upon the subject of the Presidency. She must be free to Choose & to Act—and this not seemingly but in reality—& her leading Presses here must indulge themselves in no unworthy indirection. In regard to this I think you ought to give a very decisive tone to things at Nashville, & if you feel any delicacy in a direct expression of your views to Eastman, when you mention the subject refer him to me. As matters at present stand our public Press, at Nashville,[10] especially, is in a fair way to have us committed to Mr. Van Buren, without once looking to the true position of Tennessee or to the Vice Presidency, or great future results.

For myself, as to the Presidency, I am for the man who may be finally nominated, by whatever mode our Party may agree to—altho I believe, if Mr. Van Buren shou'd be the man, the struggle will be doubtful in Tennessee—and can only be successful by the aid of your name—because first, the prejudices are greater against him, than any enthusiasm that exists for him—or ever can! He is not a man to excite enthusiasm. The range of his affections is limited to the circle of three or four.[11] And Secondly, the iron—the very iron has entered the heart of the people against the principle of the second term Service, and there is no instance of a man having been run three times for the Presidency—successfully. I learn by my correspondents that it was much talked of, at an early part of this Session, to nominate by the Democratic members of Congress—and as our conventions are constituted—much the fairest mode! The opinion was well founded, as I am informed that if that shou'd be the method that you wou'd certainly be preferred—but the idea was made war upon by New York! She wou'd have no room to play—& drew off from the advocacy of it some of the friends of Col. Johnson. That plan of action ought to be revived, at least conversationally, next Session, and advocated by the Tennessee Delegates. It is the only mode in which the west can be fairly heard—for the Federal states of Vermont & Massachusetts are equally heard in Convention, as heretofore constituted. But if the Democratic members are allowed to vote individually, you will go ahead of any Candidate two to one.

Let me hear from you. I have much more to write, but I find I have already lengthened this beyond my expectation when I sat down.

The Treaty which has been made[12] I feel satisfied is honorable to our Country, or such men as Calhoun, King, & Sevier, & the great majority of Republican Senators wou'd not have supported it. I see Mr. Buchanan's favorite Press in Pa is coming out against it in advance, for the purpose of holding him up.[13] [. . .][14] also does Webb with his Courier take ground against it.[15] It is desirable that the Tennessee Press shall not blunder upon this subject.

As to the new Tariff our Tenn. papers shou'd open their batteries upon it fiercely & unsparingly. Have the example set at Columbia & Nash[ville].[16] It is important in more ways than one to Tennessee.

A ANDERSON

ALS. DLC–JKP. Addressed to Columbia and marked "*Private & Confidential*." Polk's AE on the cover states that he answered this letter on October 15, 1842; Polk's reply has not been found.

1. Anderson resided near Knoxville, Tennessee.

2. See Polk to Samuel H. Laughlin, June 1 and July 22, 1842.

3. See Laughlin to Polk, September 9, 1842, and Jonathan P. Hardwicke to Polk, September 11, 1842.

4. Anderson wrote "movement," but probably meant "moment."

5. Reference is to Martin Van Buren and his close advisers.

6. Reference is to the *Nashville Union*, which had encouraged the idea of a Van Buren-Polk ticket without actually making a formal endorsement.

7. See Cave Johnson to Polk, August 28, 1842, and Hopkins L. Turney to Polk, September 4, 1842.

8. On August 27, 1842, James Buchanan and Silas Wright each explained to the U.S. Senate that his vote for the tariff bill was given reluctantly; each argued the necessity of passing some sort of revenue bill.

9. On August 26, 1842, Thomas Hart Benton stated in the U.S. Senate that he had voted against several Democratic tariff bills because the Whig majority ought to have the general conduct of measures for which they were responsible, including those means by which the government would be kept alive.

10. *Nashville Union*.

11. Van Buren's inner circle included such New York party stalwarts as Silas Wright, John A. Dix, Azariah Flagg, William L. Marcy, Edwin Croswell, Churchill C. Cambreleng, and Benjamin F. Butler.

12. Webster-Ashburton Treaty.

13. Reference probably is to the *Lancaster Intelligencer*, edited by John Forney.

14. A tear in the manuscript renders one word illegible.

15. James Watson Webb, publisher of the *Morning Courier and New York Enquirer*, supported Andrew Jackson and the Democratic Party until 1831; the newspaper changed its political views following Webb's receipt of a $50,000 loan from the Second Bank of the United States. Webb's editorial stance on the Webster-Ashburton Treaty is not identified further.

16. A tear in the manuscript renders a portion of this word illegible.

FROM HOPKINS L. TURNEY

Winchester, Tennessee. September 20, 1842

Turney writes that he has received Polk's letter of September 10,[1] but explains that family obligations prevent his being able to attend the Pulaski dinner or meet with Polk at this time.[2] Recalling that at their last meeting he had expressed his determination not to stand for reelection to Congress, Turney asks Polk to keep that decision private, as circumstances might require a change of mind.

ALS. DLC–JKP. Addressed to Columbia.

1. Letter not found.

2. Pulaski Democrats had invited Polk and other party leaders to attend a barbecue on September 27, 1842.

FROM ABBOTT LAWRENCE[1]

My Dear Sir: Boston Sept 21st 1842

I have your favor of the 9th[2] this morning, and in reply beg to state, that such as the condition of the public mind in regard to securities at a distance, that I do not believe it possible at this time to obtain the loan you desire. We have the Loan of the U States at 20 years bearing an interest of 6 per cent,[3] which has absorbed considerable surplus money, that together with the impetus given to business from the passage of the Tariff bill[4] has taken up most of the *floating* capital in this City. If I had the money on hand I would lend it myself, but the condition of things has been such for the last year or two that I have had but little surplus income. Another year I hope and trust will bring to us a more prosperous state of affairs. I pray you to make my kind regards with those of Mrs Lawrence[5] to Mrs Polk . . . .

ABBOTT LAWRENCE

ALS. DLC–JKP. Addressed to Columbia.

1. Abbott Lawrence, a Boston importer and merchant, served two terms as a Whig in the U.S. House, 1835–37 and 1839–40. He declined a cabinet position in the Taylor administration, but accepted appointment later in 1849 as minister to Great Britain, where he served for three years.

2. Letter not found.

3. By Act of July 21, 1841, Congress authorized the Treasury to issue up to $12 million in government stock. In a supplemental Act of April 15, 1842, Congress increased the authorization by $5 million. By Act of August 31, 1842, Congress allowed the Treasury to issue up to $6 million in Treasury notes for purchase of previously issued stock, the market value of which had fallen below par.

4. Tariff of 1842.

5. Abbott Lawrence married Katherine Bigelow, daughter of Timothy Bigelow, on June 28, 1819.

TO SAMUEL H. LAUGHLIN

My Dear Sir: Columbia Sept 23rd 1842

Having engaged to attend a Public Dinner at Pulaski on the 29th and another at Lynnville on the 30th Instant, I cannot be at Nashville before the first day of your Extra Session.[1] On some accounts I regret this. My brother[2] will be there on wednesday next, and I think it important, that Hardwicke, yourself and one or two others should meet him there two or three days before the meeting of the Assembly. He is fully in possession of my views, upon several matters of importance which will come before you. We must have the proper understanding among friends at the outset & act in concert.

JAMES K. POLK

P.S. I will be at Nashville if possible on the Sunday evening before your meeting. J.K.P.

ALS. DLC–JKP. Addressed to McMinnville and marked *"Private."* Published in *ETHSP*, XVIII, pp. 160–61.
1. The extra session of the Tennessee General Assembly convened on Monday, October 3, 1842.
2. William H. Polk.

FROM ROBERT ARMSTRONG

Dear Sir,   Nashville 27th Septr. 42
Find enclosed your note to William Nichol[1] and Cash balance proceeds of your Bill. "Statement Below."

Nett Proceeds of Bill[2]   960.00
Note to Nichol $800
Int. on debts & Exchange on *Branch* Notes   35.40
Cash herewith enclosed   124.60 $960.00

The Bill was discounted and paid in the Notes of the Athens Branch Bank.

I wish you may have but little more of this kind [of] business. It is all wrong, and I hope you will soon be in a Situation to take nothing from Banks &c.

Come in as Soon as you can. I know it will be Important for you to be here at the *Coming in* of our friends.

The Election of Coleman Mayor has given the leading Whigs *Trouble.* Can't account for it. We can.

R Armstrong

ALS. DLC–JKP. Addressed to Columbia.
1. Note not found. William Nichol, son of Josiah Nichol, operated a steamboat line and commission business in Nashville, served as mayor of the city for two years, 1835–36, and became president of the Bank of Tennessee in 1838. On July 31, 1842, Nichol had written Polk requesting payment of the note and explaining his need to apply those funds to the purchase of a new residence. ALS. DLC–JKP.
2. Polk's discounted note to the Athens branch of the Bank of Tennessee has not been found.

FROM WILLIAM WALLACE[1]

Maryville, Tennessee. September 27, 1842

Wallace writes at the request of Knoxville Democrats to solicit Polk's aid in securing the removal of Knoxville's postmaster[2] and his replacement by William Lyon, Jr., son of an old friend.[3] Such an appointment would help sow division among area Whigs; young Lyon is popular and well connected.[4]

ALS. DLC–JKP. Addressed to Nashville. Polk's AE on the cover states that he answered this letter in October 1842; Polk's reply has not been found.

1. William Wallace, a native of Sevier County and an active railroad promoter, served many years as sheriff of Blount County, 1820–42, and sat one term in the Tennessee House, 1853–55.

2. James W. Campbell was postmaster of Knoxville from March 1841 until January 1845.

3. William Lyon, Jr., was the son of William Lyon, a leading Knoxville Democrat.

4. Susan P. Washington Ramsey, daughter of James Trimble of Nashville and wife of W. B. A. Ramsey, was a cousin to William Lyon, Jr. Young Lyon's sister, Susan, married Campbell Wallace, brother of William Wallace.

FROM WILLIAM H. POLK

Dear Sir   Nashville Sept. 30th 1842

The members still come in, slowly. In addition to those mentioned in my letter of last evening,[1] are Sevier & Foster & Maclin of the Senate, Pate, Scruggs, Standerfer, Green of the House.[2] All of the E. Tennessee delegation of our party, will be here before *Monday* Standerfer informed me—passed them, he in the Stage, they on horseback. I cannot as yet see any urgent necessity for your being here before Tuesday. The members seen to regard the subject of *relief*, with more interest than any other. But little talk and apparently less interest manifested concerning the election of Senators. From the information received here, it is very probable that Douglass will be unable to reach Nashville during the Session, and very certain that he cannot preside as Speaker. Eph. Foster is behaving himself with remarkable modesty, but seldom in Town, and then seems to avoid being about the Taverns. Anderson Hilliard[3] is here from Columbia, and will return on Sunday. I will write you again by him.

WILLIAM H. POLK

ALS. DLC–JKP. Addressed to Columbia.

1. In his letter of September 29 William H. Polk named the few members of the Tennessee Assembly already in Nashville and reported several indications of Whig interest in a compromise on the election of U.S. senators. ALS. DLC–JKP.

2. Valentine Sevier, Robert C. Foster, Jr., Sackfield Maclin, John F. Pate, James Scruggs, William Standifer, and James L. Green. All except Maclin and Green were Whigs.

3. Anderson W. Hilliard was a merchant in Columbia.

FROM LEVIN H. COE

Somerville, Tennessee. October 1, 1842

Coe explains that he was unable to attend the Pulaski dinner[1] for reasons of court business and personal illness. Local Democrats learned yesterday of Douglass' resignation[2] and decided to run William Ruffin,[3] who is popular with the Whigs. Coe agrees with Ruffin that the Democrats should conduct a quiet race. Polk's appearance might cause Ruffin to lose Whig votes.

ALS. DLC–JKP. Addressed to Nashville.

1. See Hopkins L. Turney to Polk, September 20, 1842.

2. James C. Jones announced Douglass' resignation to the Tennessee House on October 4, 1842. Apparently Douglass resigned because of poor health.

3. In 1838 William Ruffin founded the West Tennessee Silk Company, which endeavored to cultivate silk in Fayette County; Ruffin, a cousin of Thomas Ruffin of North Carolina, resided in Memphis in the 1850's.

FROM SAMUEL H. LAUGHLIN

My dear Sir, Nashville, Tuesday Ev. 9 oclock, Oct. 11, 1842

We have just concluded our meeting. We had our papers all in order, and the scraps[1] were destroyed from which the last sheets were prepared, and at precisely 7 o clock to-night the Court room being the place, we had a very full meeting, and according to the organization of the meeting and preliminaries which I had also drawn up and *unanimously* adopted our Preamble and resolutions which are now in the hands of Col. Harris for next Union.[2] Every thing was harmonious. Mr. Martin I think was off making a temperance speech. Mr. John[3] I believe was absent. S.M.[4] was not present I believe. But the vote was unanimous, but it was casually said by myself and others for the lobby, that such of our friends as were absent, know the contents of our reports, and that we were in perfect harmony. The vote of adoption is entered *unanimous* and the proceedings are signed by the Chairman and three Secretaries.[5] The account of meeting names all the Committeemen, motions &c. and by whom made. Dew moved the adoption &c. All I have time to say is, that I go to bed better satisfied and in better spirits than I have been in for the last week.

Great difficulties however are likely to arise in the Congressional district committee.[6] Copeland[7] and Maclin wish to begin in the East, and proceed west, making all the districts as near the ratio as may be, so as to leave the fractional district in the west, to secure the benefit of it to the west alone. Copeland seems to be deranged upon it. He proposes a district including Warren, which is to include Hamilton and Marion, leave out Coffee, and run across the state from Georgia to Kentucky and include Jackson on the Kentucky line. Its population is over the Congressional ratio, and to include Jackson and White makes it Whig by seven or 8 hundred. He presses this district. He and Dew on the Committee, effect to take the lead, and both, so far, act like fools.

Remember me respectfully to Mrs. Polk . . . .

S. H. Laughlin

ALS. DLC–JKP. Addressed to Columbia and marked "Private."

1. Reference is to the working drafts of the resolutions.

2. The *Nashville Union* of October 13, 1842, carried an account of the Democratic legislative caucus held in Nashville on October 11, 1842. The meeting recommended that Democrats hold their national convention in Baltimore on the fourth Monday of November, 1843.

3. Probably a reference to Andrew Johnson.

4. Sackfield Maclin.

5. Richard Warner was named chairman, and Sam Milligan, Christopher H. McGinnis, and John A. Gardner were elected secretaries. Warner, a farmer from Bedford County, won election to two terms in the Tennessee House, 1833–35 and 1837–39, and served three terms in the Tennessee Senate, 1839–43 and 1845–47. Milligan, a lawyer from Greene County and close associate of Andrew Johnson, sat three terms in the Tennessee House, 1841–47.

6. On October 11, 1842, the General Assembly set up a joint select committee, equally divided between the parties, to lay off the state into congressional districts. On October 20, the committee reported that it was unable to reach agreement and submitted two separate bills, one from each party. Not until the last day of the called session, November 16, 1842, did the two houses of the legislature agree to the final bill for redistricting the state.

7. Solomon Copeland, a Democrat from Henry County, won election to one term in the Tennessee House, 1841–43.

FROM WILLIAM H. POLK

Dear Sir,   Nashville Oct. 12th 1842

The meeting of the democratic members of the Legislature, was held according to previous arrangement, last evening in the Court Room.[1] Nearly all the members were present, and the meeting went off as was desired by all, without a single disenting *voice*. Andrew Johnson was not present, but the circumstance seemed to be noticed by none—both his colleagues[2] were in attendance. I have not heard a single member mention the circumstance of his absence, none seeming to regard it as a matter of the least *consequence*.

I have had occassion to be with him frequently in the last day or two, he being Chairman of the Committee to prepare a Bill laying off the state into Congressional districts; his manner and feeling as far as I can judge, [have] *been* unusially *frindly*. The Committee will not be able to agree, and will in a few days ask leave to be discharged. The main difficulty presenting itself is in the Eastern division of the State. The result may be, that the democratic party will frame and present a fair bill, doing justice to both parties as far as practicable, and adhere to it throughout, unless the action of the House where it is under consideration can make such amendments, as to concilliate the support of a sufficient number of Whigs to ensure its passage. There has been no developments touching the Senatorial election, since you left; I will keep you advised from time to time of the progress of things here.

The *Post note* plan for *relief* appears to be gaining strength among the members.[3] I am inclined to take strong ground against it. I would like to have your views of the question, at length, if it is convienent.

                                                        WILLIAM H. POLK

ALS. DLC–JKP. Addressed to Columbia. Polk's AE on the cover states that he answered this letter on October 14, 1842; Polk's reply has not been found.

1. See Samuel H. Laughlin to Polk, October 11, 1842.

2. Reference is to Sam Milligan and John Jones. Jones, a close associate of Andrew Johnson from Greene County, served one term in the Tennessee House, 1841–43.

3. Reference is to a Senate bill requiring the Bank of Tennessee to issue $2 million in post notes payable in twelve months. Introduced on October 8, 1842, the measure met strong opposition from banking interests and failed to receive majority support from either party.

FROM J. G. M. RAMSEY

Mecklenburg, Tennessee. October 12, 1842

Ramsey renews an earlier recommendation of William Lyon, Jr., for postmaster at Knoxville,[1] suggests the intercession of Cave Johnson and Robert Armstrong with a postmaster general,[2] and reports the receipt of a letter from a Calhoun supporter recently returned from a northern tour.[3] Ramsey's correspondent depreciates Van Buren's election chances while giving "very flattering representations" of Calhoun's prospects; in New York, Pennsylvania, and New Jersey "the young Democracy & all the mercantile interests not connected with & dependent upon the manufacturing interests" are for Calhoun.

ALS. DLC–JKP. Addressed to Columbia.

1. Ramsey and William Lyon, Sr., wrote on September 24, 1842, and recommended William Lyon, Jr., to be postmaster at Knoxville. ALS. DLC–JKP. See William Wallace to Polk, September 27, 1842.

2. Charles A. Wickliffe, a former congressman and governor of Kentucky, served as postmaster general from 1841 to 1845.

3. Not identified further.

FROM WILLIAM C. TATE[1]

Dear Sir   Morganton No Ca. Octr 13th 1842

I received your letter some time since[2] and would have answered you sooner, but I concluded not to write until Mrs. Tate would decide whether or not she would be willing for Marshal and Eunice to go to Tennessee. I urged upon her the propriety of leting them both go, as soon as I received your letter, and I think by next spring she would have consented for you to have them and superintend their education, but for the sad event I will now communicate to you. The congestive fever appeard in my family the latter part of last month in a most agravated and dangerous form. Marshal and Eunice were attacked about the same time. Marshal is now out of danger entirely, but poor little Eunice fell a victim to it. She died on the 8th Inst. 12 o'clock at night. Several of my negroes have been low with the same fever but are now convalesent. Eunice was a lovely interesting child and expressed a great wish to see her friends in Tennessee since we recvd your last letter. Mrs. Tate will not consent for Marshal to leave her soon. I think myself he is most too small and young. He is quite delicate and his habits and health have to be watched very particularly. I think in a few years she will give her consent. I will keep him at school as much as I think he is able to bear without injuring him by confinement. Mrs. Tate wishes to be kindly remembered by you.

Wm. C. Tate

ALS. DLC–JKP. Addressed to Columbia.

1. William C. Tate, a physician in North Carolina, married Laura Wilson Polk, the widow of Polk's brother and the mother of Roxana Eunice Ophelia Polk and Marshall T. Polk, Jr.

2. Letter not found.

FROM HARVEY M. WATTERSON

Dear Sir   Beech Grove Coffee Co. Oct 16. 1842

I send you one of the handbills announcing the Barbacue at Davis' Mills on Friday next.[1] I shall be greatly disappointed if there is not an immense number of persons present on the occasion. I was at the Mills at Meeting today and I found the ditches already dug to barbacue their meats in. Dr. Norton[2] says several Whigs in his neighborhood have subscribed a shoat or two each. The Democrats have gone into the matter in the right spirit—all are anxious for it. I want you to make them just such a speech as you made at Pulaski and Lynnville.[3] I wrote a pressing letter to Turney to come, and I have some hope that he will do so, as he may be on his way to Nashville about that time. If you come by Nashville you could come to Father's[4] in the stage the evening before the Barbacue. I will meet you on next Thursday night if I can hear where you will be. I would like very much for you to reach Father's. In haste.

H M Watterson

P.S. I have just received your letter of the 14th.[5] I will meet you at Shelbyville on next Thursday and will expect you to go with me to Fathers that night. HMW

ALS. DLC–JKP. Addressed to Columbia.

1. Enclosure not found. Watterson also wrote Polk on October 6 and 11 about the barbecue at Davis' Mills, which was a post village in the eastern part of Bedford County next to the Coffee County line.

2. Probably William B. Norton, an active Democrat in that eastern part of Bedford County which in 1836 was detached to form Coffee County.

3. Polk had spoken at public dinners in Pulaski on September 29 and in Lynnville on September 30.

4. A planter, railroad promoter, and large landholder in western Coffee County, William S. Watterson of Beech Grove served one term in the Tennessee House, 1823–25.

5. Letter not found.

FROM WILLIAM H. POLK

Dear Sir   Nashville Oct 18th 1842

The news from Ohio this evening is most *glorious*.[1] Shannons majority cannot be less than 10,000. This blow was not expected by the Whigs, and they *die* very hard. They begin to express some doubts as to the *availibility* of Mr. Clay, and are beginning to canvass the propriety of starting Genl. Scott, who I fear will be more formidable, as they will spring the *drum and fife* on us.

The meeting here on Saturday week,[2] it is thought will be very large. I saw Harris & Genl. Armstrong, and *hand-bills* will be struck and circulated in the morning—and preperations made for a grand affair. Nothing new. The releif Committee reported a bill this morning reorganizing the whole Judiciary system, restricting the courts to two terms anually,[3] which with other provisions is equal to the suspension of all debts, judgements, and executions for 18 months or 2 years, which I think will pass without much opposition.

WILLIAM H. POLK

ALS. DLC–JKP. Addressed to Columbia.

1. On October 11, 1842, Ohio Democrats elected Wilson Shannon to a second term as governor and increased their majorities in both houses of the legislature. An Ohio lawyer, Shannon enjoyed a varied political career, which included service as Ohio's attorney general, 1835; governor, 1838–40 and 1842–44; U.S. minister to Mexico, 1844–45; Democratic congressman from Ohio, 1853–55; and governor of the Kansas Territory, 1855–56.

2. James K. Polk spoke at a Democratic meeting in Nashville on October 29, 1842.

3. After reversing itself several times, the Tennessee House on October 26, 1842, passed a relief bill that reduced the frequency of circuit court meetings in each county from three to two. William H. Polk opposed the relief measure and raised constitutional objections to it in a speech before the Tennessee House on October 21. On November 9 the Tennessee Senate rejected a much amended version of the House bill.

TO SAMUEL H. LAUGHLIN

My Dear Sir: Columbia Oct. 19th 1842

I see that the Nashville Whig papers, have at length broke ground upon the Democratic Preamble and Resolutions.[1] It is manifest from the tone of their articles that they are at fault in knowing how to meet them. The *Banner* I see promises to make startling developements, and to demolish you hereafter. I hope you will give attention to what they may say, and as *Harris* must be very busy, in attending to other duties, that you will assist him in refuting or answering what may appear. Do not suffer them to depart from the issues, which your Resolutions present. They will probably attempt to get up an angry discussion, with you, upon some immaterial collateral matter. This should not be allowed. Hold them on, to the old records,[2] which you have brought forward; and compel them to justify and defend the Bankrupt law, and other odious measures of the party in power.

There was a *Clay* meeting here on monday concerning which I wrote to brother *William* on yesterday.[3] It was thinly attended and went off heavily. It produced not the slightest effect, except to rouse up the Democracy. A number of our Whig's will not vote for *Mr Clay*. We have called an *anti-Clay* meeting for the 31st, at which there will probably be a very large crowd. I leave this evening to attend the Barbecue at *Davis's Mills* in Bedford on the 21st & will be at home again on sunday evening. This is great labour, but some one must do it & I submit to it cheerfully. Now is the time to prostrate *Clay* in the State. It may be more difficult next spring.

I have received a letter from *Col Yoakum*,[4] expressing deep solicitude that Rutherford may not be sacraficed in the arrangement of Congressional & Senatorial Districts. I know the difficulties attending the subject, but still hope, that she may be saved, in one if not both. The Central position of that County makes it more important that we should preserve our strength there, than in any other County in the State. Do what you can, consistently with your duty to others, for our Rutherford friends. We have heard nothing here from the Fayette election.[5] The election news from abroad is indeed most cheering.[6]

JAMES K POLK

ALS. DLC–JKP. Addressed to Nashville and marked "*Private.*" Published in *ETHSP*, XVIII, p. 161.

1. See Samuel H. Laughlin to Polk, October 11, 1842.

2. The Democratic legislators' "Preamble and Resolutions" of October 11, 1842, contained a list of those members of the 1827 General Assembly who had voted for a resolution condemning Henry Clay's "corrupt bargain" with John Q. Adams. Many of those voting for the 1827 resolution supported Clay in 1842.

3. Letter not found.

4. Henderson K. Yoakum wrote Polk on October 8, 1842, urging that Rutherford County not be assigned to a predominantly Whig congressional or legislative district. ALS. DLC–JKP. Yoakum, a graduate of the U.S. Military Academy,

served as mayor of Murfreesboro, 1837–43; won election to one term in the Tennessee Senate, 1839–40; moved to Texas in 1845; and authored a two-volume *History of Texas*, which was published in 1855.

5. Reference is to a special election to fill Burchett Douglass' seat in the Tennessee House. Erastus T. Collins, a Whig, defeated William Ruffin, a Democrat, on October 13, 1842.

6. Reference is to recent elections in Maryland, Ohio, Delaware, and Georgia.

FROM ADAM HUNTSMAN[1]

Jackson, Tennessee. October 20, 1842

Huntsman reports that Polk will receive an invitation to speak at a public dinner in Memphis.[2] Huntsman already has indicated that Polk will accept an appointment fitted to his fall trip to or from his Mississippi plantation.

ALS. DLC–JKP. Addressed to Columbia. Published by Emma Inman Williams, ed., "Letters of Adam Huntsman to James K. Polk," *THQ*, VI (December, 1947), p. 355. Polk's AE on the cover states that he answered this letter on October 24, 1842; Polk's reply has not been found.

1. Born in Virginia, Adam Huntsman had moved by 1809 to Overton County, where he practiced law and engaged in extensive land speculations until 1821. He sat three terms for Overton County in the Tennessee Senate, 1815–21, and later represented Madison County in the Senate for two terms, 1827–31. A loyal Jacksonian Democrat, he defeated David Crockett for a seat in Congress and served one term in the U.S. House, 1835–37.

2. Letter not found. See Sackfield Maclin to Polk, December 23, 1842.

FROM CAVE JOHNSON

Dear Sir,   Clarksville October 21st 1842

I recd your letter[1] enclosing one of Doct. Ramsey.[2] If I am not mistaken the Doct. & Eastman sent on strong recomendations to us for the appointment of one of the Crosiers (A. J. Crosier[3] I think) & my recollection is that most of us upon their recommendation united in recomending Crozier, if Mr Lewis[4] was not appointed. I have however written Mr. W.[5] a private letter making the suggestions. It is however a great mistake in supposing that I have "his ear." So far from it I have been treated worse since he has been in than I was before tho I do not suppose he knew it. At Dover a most violent, *Clay, Bank, Bell man* was appointed over my recomendation of a most gentlmanly whig & I suspect upon the secret recomendation of Bell, as the new P.M.[6] was formerly one of the clerks at the rolling mill.[7] I have however written, strongly urging the removal of Campbell and have also written Doct. Ramsey as you request. I enclose you the Doct. letter. The tour of his southern friend[8] to the north only repeals the impression that some southern politicians wish to make. It is probable the idea of placing Wright or Buckhanan as vice on the ticket was given up long before their votes on the Tariff & for a better reason. Theres not a doubt in my mind that Van[9] will recive the nomination without difficulty and from the recent proceedings in Charleston[10] & the course of the N Y Post,[11] I suppose his (Calhouns) friends will yeild & support the nominee. The only question which we have to guard agt. is, will it be deemed necessary to buy off R.M.J.?[12] The recent elections will demonstrate that Clay can do nothing. The Whigs proper have no confidence in Scotts sense or pliability. I cannot but think they will be driven to look to some pliant democrat. If we have any difficulty it will arise from southern obstinancy.

The Resolutions at Nashville[13] will do much good, if they are properly circulated. It should be done in pamphlet form with your speech at Pulaski. It is important I think that our convention should decide upon our candidates before the meeting of the next Congress to avoid all intrigue &c among the members. I should have preferred, if it could have been done, that the nomination had been made before the election. Tho we might have lost in the elections something, yet we should have had a more firm & better setled majority & would have suppressed any political movements among the Democrats. We are in great danger from too large a majority.

It is hardly probable I suppose that Congressional districts will be laid off but if it is I suppose my district will be cut to pieces for fear that I might wish to run again. In the Legislative districts, Montgomery & Robertson should be separated, and *the family connexion*[14] will be brok up, & we shall certainly have a Senator or two more. It will be difficult to beat them united. You ought if possible to suppress any debate among the Democrats upon the proposition to disregard the slave population in laying off districts.

If I go to Nashville it will be on the 29th. My time will be fully occupied with my little matters at home & have no time to attend the Courts. I have just removed to my new building a mile from town.

C JOHNSON

[P.S.] I think we will make Genl McKay speaker in the next Congress.

ALS. DLC–JKP. Addressed to Columbia and marked "private."
1. Polk's letter is not identified further.
2. See J. G. M. Ramsey to Polk, October 12, 1842.

3. Reference to "A. J. Crosier" is probably Arthur R. Crozier, son of John Crozier, Knoxville's postmaster from 1804 to 1838.

4. Isaac Lewis, a Knoxville Democrat, wrote Polk on May 4, 1842, requesting help in securing the Knoxville postmastership. ALS. DLC–JKP.

5. Charles A. Wickliffe.

6. Anthony Rogers was appointed postmaster at Dover on July 6, 1842.

7. Reference is to the Cumberland Iron Works in which John Bell acquired an interest through his marriage to Jane Erwin Yeatman. The Works expanded its operations in the 1840's and in 1852 held assets in excess of $500,000.

8. Ramsey's "southern friend" is not identified further.

9. Martin Van Buren.

10. On September 22, 1842, a meeting of Charleston Democrats nominated John C. Calhoun for president, but indicated a willingness to support Martin Van Buren "should he be designated by a National Convention."

11. Reference is to Parke Godwin's New York *Morning Post*; Godwin was the son-in-law of William Cullen Bryant, editor of the New York *Evening Post*. In the fall of 1842 the *Morning Post* endorsed John C. Calhoun for the presidency; it also indicated a willingness to support the nominee of a national Democratic convention.

12. Richard M. Johnson.

13. See Samuel H. Laughlin to Polk, October 11, 1842.

14. Reference is to the relationship between Richard Cheatham, one of Robertson County's most prominent Whigs, and his Whig brothers-in-law, William K. Turner and Mortimer A. Martin of Montgomery County.

FROM ALEXANDER O. ANDERSON

Near Knoxville, Tennessee. October 27, 1842

Replying to a letter from Polk of October 15, 1842,[1] Anderson recalls that very early in their acquaintance he thought that Polk's position was "such that it wou'd be just as easy to advance, in the end, to the highest honors of the Country, as to effect a landing upon the second *platform*." In order to enhance the future of both Polk and the Tennessee Democracy, Anderson recommends that the state party express no preference among current presidential aspirants. If Tennessee enters the convention with Polk's "name *alone* inscribed upon her banner," his nomination as vice-presidential candidate is certain no matter who wins first place on the ticket. Anderson also warns against factional fights within the party over the treaty vote in the Senate.[2]

ALS. DLC–JKP. Addressed to Columbia and marked "*Confidential*." Polk's AE on the cover states that he answered this letter on December 16, 1842; Polk's reply has not been found.

1. Letter not found.

2. Reference is to the Webster-Ashburton Treaty, ratified by the Senate on August 20, 1842.

FROM WILLIAM M. GWIN

My dear Sir   Vicksburg November 5 [18]42

I have recd and read with great pleasure your letter of the 14th Ult.[1] My letter to which it was an answer[2] was written in undue excitement which probably caused me to lay more stress upon the Democratic Votes in Congress for the Tariff bill than in a calmer moment I other wise should. I acknowledge that I had no patience with some of our friends who voted for the bill because their votes were necessary as they declared to pass it when the fact is the Whigs could & would have passed it without a Democratic vote in either House as they afterwards boasted they could.

On the subject of the Presidency I am altogether in favor of a National Convention. It is the only legitimate mode by which we can concentrate strength for the coming contest. My support of Mr. Calhoun is attended with no feeling against Mr. Van Buren. On the contrary I shall if he is the nominee of the Convention give him as ardent a support as I did in 1832, 1836 & 1840. I have thought & still think that Calhoun & some acceptable Northern Democrat would be stronger than Van Buren & Johnson. With your name on the ticket with Mr. V. Buren we would be equally as strong in the South as if Mr. Calhoun were the nominee especially in this state, No. Carolina, Georgia & Tennessee. These states are all doubtful if V. Buren & Johnson are our candidates. They are certain for us if you are associated with V. Buren or if Calhoun is the candidate for the Presidency. This is the debateable ground in the South. I am firmly convinced that a plan is forming to force Johnson on us again if Van Buren is nominated. His recent Tariff Speech in Pensylvania was intended to catch N. York & Pensylvania.[3] Extras of the Kentucky Gazette[4] have been circulated all over the Union nominating him for the Presidency. This state has been flooded with them. This is intended to put him in so prominent a position that the Convention will be forced to nominate him for the Vice Presidency if V. Buren is nominated to keep him from running as an independent candidate for the Presidency and he will run for the Presidency if not nominated for the Vice Presidency and the principal reason that will be urged in favor of such a step will be that he has been badly treated by being abandoned by the Democratic party and a Stigma attempted to be cast upon him by nominating his associate in 1836 & 1840 & dropping him. Altogether he is the weakest man for the Vice Presidency that was ever thought of by the Democratic party. He is a tariff man, Bank man & in favor of internal Improvements by the General Government.

The time selected by the Legislature of Tennessee for the convention to meet is a very good one the very best that could be selected.[5] I would prefer its assembling at Cincinnatti so that the South & West could have a fair chance to send their delegates. Your personal friends should be cautious not to induce the belief by their acts that you are opposed to Calhouns nomination. *Now* his friends are yours. They are most enthusiastic in his support and look upon you as the next leader in the South. If he can get the votes of the Southern states his nomination is certain for Pensylvania is certain to vote for him in convention in preference to V. Buren between whom & Buchanan the master spirit of that state there is no good feeling. Calhoun' friends intend to press his claims for a nomination before the Convention with unabating zeal; nor do they intend to flinch from its decision. If he can only maintain his present ground he must get the nomination for he has every advantage as his friends can urge him with an earnestness that could not becomingly be exerted in favor of an ExPresident. Yet it will & must be done with good feeling on both sides.

I shall be most happy to hear from you at Washington. I will with pleasure give you all the news from that place this winter if you desire it.

WM. M. GWIN

ALS. DLC–JKP. Addressed to Coffeeville, Mississippi. Polk's AE on the cover states that he answered this letter on December 15, 1842; Polk's reply has not been found.

1. Polk's letter has not been found.
2. See Gwin to Polk, August 27, 1842.
3. Richard M. Johnson, an advocate of protection, spoke in Harrisburg, Danville, and Southwark during his October travels in Pennsylvania and New York, which also included visits to Pottsville, Reading, Philadelphia, Allentown, Wilkesbarre, Williamsport, Troy, East Smithfield, Towanda, Montrose, Oswego, and Elmira.
4. The *Kentucky Gazette* "Extra" is not further identified. A Democratic newspaper, the *Kentucky Gazette* was published in Lexington from 1787 until 1848.
5. See Samuel H. Laughlin to Polk, October 11, 1842.

FROM SARAH C. POLK

My dear Husband   Columbia Nov. 7th 1842

Your *order* to write you on the sunday following your leaveing, I did not comply with for the reason I had nothing to communicate. This being the day of the Whig meeting here I awaited for the occasion to be over. E. J. Sheilds[1] did not make his appearance. *Cahal* answered your speech of last monday, & Greenfield, Nicholson [made a] few remarks.[2] They were the only speakers. There was a good many people in town it being court. But the court house was never filled while the speaking was going on, and I am told there was not fifty persons there who were attending when Cahal finished. S. P. Walker[3] says the object of Cahal seemed to do away the effect of your speech on the Whigs. Notice was given that E. J. Sheilds would be here and address the people on next Saturday if it did *not rain.*[4] The Democrats has called or will call a meeting for the first monday in December, when the members of the Legislature will be at home. Sam Walker thinks Nicholson is anxious to make a talk himself, gives evidence of a strong desire to take a active part and get in favour with your friends. N. came over a few days ago to borrow some of your Journals. He had Milton Browns answer to your Tarriff votes in his hand.[5] I infered he intended to answer Brown. I suppose of course you saw his answer[6] as it came out just after you left. You would see it in the District on your way.[7]

The Nashville papers take but little notice of the meeting here last monday. And the speeches of to day made no impression here. I believe this is all the political news I have. Elias brought the sheep home, went to Oliphants,[8] who says he will start in a week or two, and will let me know precisely what day. I will have to defer my visit to Murfreesboro' until the Sheep & Hogs are started on their journey, and I fear that I will be kept waiting all the month, by the Sheep, Hogs, Mitchel & the Corn.[9] I have given you all the domestic matters and I do not know that I have any thing else to say at present.

SARAH POLK

ALS. DLC–JKP. Addressed to Coffeeville, Mississippi.

1. A lawyer from Pulaski, Ebenezer J. Shields represented Giles County for one term in the Tennessee House, 1833–35, and served two terms as a Whig in the U.S. House, 1835–39; late in 1842 he moved to Mississippi and thereafter to Memphis.

2. Terry H. Cahal, Gerrard T. Greenfield, and A. O. P. Nicholson. Cahal, a prominent Columbia Whig and lawyer, served twice in the Tennessee Senate, 1835–36 and 1837–39; he became mayor of Columbia in 1840. Greenfield, a Democrat and gentleman farmer, earned the reputation of being one of the state's most skilled physicians.

3. Samuel P. Walker, the eldest son of James and Jane Maria Polk Walker, was Polk's nephew. Young Walker subsequently moved to Memphis where he became a successful lawyer.

4. On November 17, 1842, Sarah wrote to Polk that "*Sheilds* spoke here last Saturday to a few persons." ALS. DLC–JKP.

5. On November 2, 1842, the Nashville *Republican Banner* published a letter written to the Jackson *West Tennessee Whig* by Milton Brown, a Whig congressman from Jackson. Brown accused Polk and Cave Johnson of voting both ways on the tariff question. Brown originally had adopted that line of attack in a speech in the U.S. House on July 7, 1842. On that occasion he had charged that Polk, who professed to be anti-tariff, had voted for a duty on tea and coffee in the tariff debates of 1832–33. Polk answered Brown's speech in remarks made in Giles County on September 29 and 30, 1842. Polk explained that his vote was part of an anti-tariff strategy. Brown's published letter attempted to answer Polk's defense. Born in Ohio, Brown moved to Tennessee and lived in Nashville and Paris before settling permanently in Jackson. A member of the Madison County bar, he served as chancellor of West Tennessee, 1837–39, and sat in the U.S. House for three terms, 1841–47.

6. Reference is to Brown's letter to the Jackson *West Tennessee Whig*.

7. Polk was traveling to his plantation in Mississippi.

8. Not identified further.

9. Reference is probably to James Mitchell, who rented Polk lands in Maury County; Mitchell had sent corn to Polk as a rent payment in November of 1839.

FROM MARTIN VAN BUREN

My dear Sir   Lindenwald Nov 11th 1842

Our returns are not all in but sufficient is known to make our complete success certain.[1] A majority of more than 15000 for Gov,[2] 7/8ths of the senate elected this year. Much more than two thirds of each branch of the legislature with about 3/4ths of the members of Congress may be safely set down as the fruits of our great victory.

Remember me very kindly to Mrs. Polk & to my good friend Mrs. Lucius Polk[3]. . . .

M VAN BUREN

ALS. DLC–JKP. Addressed to Columbia. Polk's AE on the cover states that he answered this letter on December 8, 1842.

1. Reference is to the New York state elections of November 8, 1842.

2. New York Democrats elected William C. Bouck of Schoharie County.

3. Mary Eastin Polk, niece of Rachel Jackson, married Polk's cousin, Lucius J. Polk.

FROM JONATHAN P. HARDWICKE

Sunday A M

My Dear Sir,   Nashville Nov 13th 1842

We have agreed to adjourn to morrow the bill to lay off the state into

Congressional Districts.[1] The compromise bill, reported by Ewing of Davidson and Campbell of Washington,[2] was rejected in Senate yester-[day] on its first reading by the twelve Whig senators & Ross[3] from Lincoln, the 12 other D's voting for it. It proposed six W Dts & five D. Dts. A motion to reconsider is now pending. Our policy is to reconsider & pass the bill with out amendments, send it back, & let the Whigs reject it in the House. No Senators yet nor is there any strong probability that we will elect any. The relief measures are all laid upon the shelf, having been rejected by about an equal number of each party. An attempt will be made in both Ho's to recind the adjourning resolution to morrow; the result is doubtfull. Times and things seem to be going on pretty well so far as I can judge, *Except* as to Mr *Van Buren.* I assure you Sir, there is a plain disinclination on the part of our friends to take up Van Buren again. I have taken some pains to arrive at this conclusion. At our little caucus's and incidental meetings, the matter has been discussed incidentally. At all times none is on principal opposed to him but all express fears, some that the old prejudices may & will be brought up & others that with him you will fall &c. &c. &c. A few evenings since some 12 Senators were at my room. An election was had between Van Buren, Calhoun, Cass,[4] Dick Johnson, and Buchannon,[5] S Wright, &c. Cass was evidently the favourite. Johnson of Green & some others for Calhoun, against all others, &c. &c.

Our friends in many sections were divided upon the subject of relief. It is posible, if not probable, that some colision may arise amongst our friends upon that subject at home, and in no event can we be bettered by it. It was no party question here nor can it be so construed. My own opinion is that every step should be taken to prevent any dispute espicially in our ranks. I would only remarke that a word from you might do good to William H. Polk. Martin was a great relief man tho he voted against the Court bill.[6] He prayed all mighty God it might pass. Dick Warner was a relief man, William H. anti relief, &c. &c. Look to it and do say what you think best.

J. P. HARDWICKE

ALS. DLC–JKP. Addressed to Coffeeville, Mississippi. Polk's AE on the cover states that he answered this letter on December 15, 1842; Polk's reply has not been found.

1. Hardwicke's syntax is garbled; he means that Senate consideration of the compromise redistricting bill has been postponed until the next day.

2. Edwin H. Ewing and Brookins Campbell. Ewing, a lawyer from Nashville, served as a Whig in the Tennessee House, 1841–43, and in the U.S. House, 1845–47. Campbell, a lawyer from Washington County, served as a Democrat in the Tennessee House, 1835–39, 1841–43, 1845–47, and 1851–53; he won election to the U.S. House in 1853 and served until his death in December of that year.

3. William T. Ross, a Fayetteville criminal lawyer, served as a Democrat in the Tennessee Senate, 1841–45.

4. Lewis Cass, lawyer and Democrat, served as governor of the Michigan Territory, 1813–31; U.S. secretary of war, 1831–36; U.S. minister to France, 1836–42; U.S. Senator from Michigan, 1845–48 and 1851–57; and U.S. secretary of state, 1857–60. In 1848 Cass ran unsuccessfully as the Democratic candidate for president.

5. James Buchanan.

6. See William H. Polk to Polk, October 10, 1842.

FROM W. L. D. EWING[1]

My Dr Sir.   Hillsborough Ills. Novr 14th 1842

Politicians of the same school, use little ceremony in corresponding, or conversing with each other. You will perhaps, on a moments reflection, recollect me. I formed an acquaintance with you at Washington in the ever memorable years of 1836 & '37, and have appreciated that acquaintance and my knowledge of your public career, so highly, that, in common with all my friends in this Country, I feel solicitous that your name, should be before the American people for the office of vice president. I take the liberty to address you this note on that subject. In a few days our Legislature, which is largely democratic, will be in session, and I intend to make an effort to secure your nomination for the vice presidency by resolution of that body. I believe it can be done. Your extraordinary efforts to effect the redemption of Tennessee have been witnessed with profound admiration. This, together with your congressional career, has made you eminantly popular in this section of the Union. Besides, your locality in references to Mr Van Buren is precisely as it should be. For the next contest, no person is thought of here for the presidency, but the above named gentleman. Your Tennessee and other western friends are very numerous in the 'prairie' state, and are as enthusiastic as the most ardent and devoted of your own state. *We* are strong enough at any time, and with any name to carry the democratic ticket for those high offices, but I am very free to say that yours would add essential weight to it in connection with that of Mr Van Buren's, who is not as strong in Illinois as some other prominent democrats. I flatter myself, that I shall receive an answer in due course of mail; which answer shall be for the inspection of the public or not, just as your notions of propriety may direct you to enjoin upon me.

                                        W. L. D. Ewing

N.B. If you think worth while to answer me address me at Springfield, Illinois, where I shall be during the session.

ALS. DLC–JKP. Addressed to Columbia. Polk's AE on the cover states that he answered this letter on December 7, 1842; Polk's reply has not been found.

1. William Lee Davidson Ewing, a native of Kentucky and a prominent Illinois Democrat, won election to several terms in the Illinois legislature and served as Speaker of the House for sessions held in 1830, 1838, and 1840; in 1832 the Illinois Senate elected him president pro tempore for one term. In 1833 he became lieutenant governor, served briefly as governor in 1834, and the next year went to the U.S. Senate to complete two years of an unexpired term.

FROM JONATHAN P. HARDWICKE

My Dear Sir   Nashville Nov 20th 1842

By this you will see I am yet in the City of Rocks. I have been the last few days attending to private business. If there were some few more States to be herd from I dont know when I should get a way, especially if they came in like New York, Misshigan & Deleware too.[1] As old Gollahorn[2] said, its parfactly amasin. You will have seen from the papers before you see this, the glorous results. I hope this will reconcile our friends to Mr Van Buren, & produce fresh courage in all our ranks. Our friends here and else where are truly sanguyne in the hope, of carrying eight of the eleven Congressinal districts next summer. H. L. Turney says the Nox District[3] is ours beyond all doubt, if we run a candidate. Macklin thinks the same for his.[4] If the Whigs run a man from Davidson, & the Democrats one from Smith, I think our chance is good, but to reverse it, we cant come it.[5] If this reaches you as is intended try by all means to set Coe & Maclin right before you leave them if posible. It does seem that we are doomed to destruction, by the very silly if not downright foolishness of our own friends. Andy Johnson & Brookins Campbell, Coe & Macklin & how many more feuds I cant tell have sprung up this fall. If they can be controled, and every man does his duty, our friends in New York, and else where, win next summer, drink of the fountain that now gladden the harts of all good and true Democrats in Tennessee. Yes sir if our folks will do their duty Whigery, in the language of Daniel the great,[6] will be Obseleete. The Whigs here say they will haul down the Clay flag, but they dont say whos they will run up. Our true friends cant conqir doubt, nor hesitate to take up Van Burin if he should be the nominee of the Convention. No sir, they wont nor ought they to think of another after this good news. We come in one of making Senators but as usual failed. We went it strong for relief, repealed the Ca. sa.[7] law and gave eight months stay on the Judgments of Justices of the Peace &c &c.[8]

                                      J. P. HARDWICKE

P.S. There is an under currant working here to get the Seat of Government. If our friends in old Reatherford[9] will take fresh Courage and manage to advantage we will have a decided majority in the next Legislature. It is said the Whigs wont run but one Candidate in this County and he is Ephraim.[10] A majority is all important to us and equally so to the Whigs as the Districts will certainly [be] laid off anew at the next session. Wilson, and Wiliamson[11] may be bidders at the great sale; if so, they may fall in to the compromise also.

ALS. DLC–JKP. Addressed to Somerville. Polk's AE on the cover states that he answered this letter on December 15, 1842; Polk's reply has not been found.

1. Reference is to recent Democratic election victories.
2. Not identified further.
3. The Third Congressional District of Tennessee, as established by the General Assembly in November, 1842, consisted of Knox, Roane, McMinn, Rhea, Bledsoe, Meigs, Polk, Bradley, Hamilton, and Marion counties.
4. The Tenth Congressional District of Tennessee, as established by the General Assembly in November, 1842, consisted of McNairy, Hardeman, Fayette, Shelby, Tipton, Haywood, Lauderdale, and Dyer counties.
5. The Eighth Congressional District of Tennessee, as established by the General Assembly in November, 1842, consisted of Smith, Sumner, and Davidson counties.
6. Probably Daniel Webster.
7. Abbreviation for *capias ad satisfaciendum*. On November 5, 1842, the Tennessee General Assembly repealed all laws authorizing the issuance of a writ of *capias ad satisfaciendum*, which allowed imprisonment for debt.
8. On November 14, 1842, the Tennessee General Assembly passed a relief act that allowed an eight-month stay of execution on all judgements issued by justices of the peace.
9. Rutherford County.
10. Ephraim H. Foster of Davidson County.
11. Wilson and Williamson counties.

FROM J. G. M. RAMSEY

My Dear Sir   Mecklenburg Nov. 29. 1842

Another letter from a South Carolina correspondent[1] says "The election in New York & Massachusetts[2] confirms all we have heretofore heard about the spread of the principles of Mr. Calhoun & of Free trade. It is all the achievement of the young democracy whose polar star is J.C.C. The nominations are about to commence now either directly or indirectly in the Legislatures or conventions of the party in Ga., N.C., Al., Mi. &c &c."

"I had the article you alluded to put in the Mercury relating to Polk.[3] We are all sensible of Polks merits but it does not become us to go vice-president making. We should be content with the compliment paid us by the nomination of C. for President. As regards myself if J.C. were not a candidate for the Py.[4] I would be glad to see Polk nominated by the State for the V.P. & for one would be willing to move in it but not now, circumstanced as we are. If the Conventions do it there will be no sacrifice of feeling in supporting him in S.C."

Thus far my correspondent. Set it down for what it is worth.

The members of the Leg. have returned home—Some of them ashamed of what they have done & already making exculpatory statements about their conduct. The Con. districts do not give satisfaction. Arnolds friends are blustering that he has been legislated out of Congress & the dissatisfaction extends to a part of this his old district—& it is the more general as Williams friends make the same complaint about himself—he has been legislated out for the purpose of making a District to suit T. J. Campbell, a modern Clay man.[5] Some of my neighbours who were aspiring to Williams seat are joining in the same cry as their chance is now hopeless. I hear that Campbell will be a candidate—& I expect that Blackwell[6] will be so certainly. He will get a good many Whig votes if W. does not run as it is probable he will not. We fan the flame & will make the most of it.

The Whig papers here[7] made a furious onset on you about a speech (reported in the Whig & Banner[8] & distorted still more by letter writers from Nashville & published at Knoxville) of your Brother on the River Bill.[9] I have no doubt his remarks were perverted but I think his vote for the bill has counteracted all your opponents were making of his remarks. Reneau & Senter will lock horns in the 2nd. Dist. & Wheeler or Frazier or Wallace have some chance.[10] Above we will have a difficulty with Johnson & Campbell,[11] but I hope it may be healed. Here we are sanguine of carrying our member.[12] Campbell[13] as he passed through was clear for the Tariff & I doubt not will make it his hobby.

J. G. M. RAMSEY

[P.S.] Richie did not (of course) write me but an Editorial about the last of Sep leads me to think he approves of my suggestions.[14]

ALS. DLC–JKP. Addressed to Columbia. Polk's AE on the cover states that he answered this letter on December 14, 1842; Polk's reply has not been found.

1. Not identified further; this correspondent, however, may be the same person to whom Ramsey referred in his letters to Polk of July 25 and October 12, 1842.

2. In an extremely close election, held originally on November 14, 1842, but not decided until January of 1843, Democrats won a majority of the seats in the

Massachusetts Senate, lost in the House, but elected Marcus Morton governor on a joint ballot of the two houses; the Whigs won seven of ten congressional seats.

3. The article on Polk is not identified further. The *Charleston Mercury*, 1822–68, was edited at this time by John A. Stuart, who supported John C. Calhoun for the presidency.

4. Abbreviation for "Presidency."

5. Thomas D. Arnold, Joseph L. Williams, and Thomas J. Campbell. A Whig, lawyer, and bitter opponent of Jackson and Polk, Arnold represented the Knoxville district for one term in the U.S. House, 1831–33; he moved to Greenville and represented Tennessee's First Congressional District for one term, 1841–43. Williams, a Knoxville lawyer and the son of former Senator John Williams, represented Tennessee's Third District as a Whig in the U.S. House for three terms, 1837–43. Campbell, a Whig and member of the Athens bar, represented the Fourth District in Congress for one term, 1841–43.

6. Julius W. Blackwell, a Democrat from Athens, won election to the U.S. House from the Fourth District in 1839 and from the Third District in 1843.

7. The Knoxville *Post* and the *Knoxville Register*. The *Post*, a Whig newspaper first issued in April 1841 by James Williams, was published in Knoxville until 1848, when Samuel P. Ivins relocated and published it as the *Athens Post*. The *Register*, an influential newspaper established in 1816 by Frederick S. Heiskell, became the leading newspaper for the Hugh Lawson White faction of the Whig Party.

8. The *Nashville Whig* and the Nashville *Republican Banner*.

9. On November 5, 1842, the Tennessee House began consideration of a bill to pay $200,000 to East Tennessee and the Western District in discharge of their claim for river bonds under an act of 1838. On November 5 William H. Polk argued in the House that payment of that obligation should be suspended temporarily in order to grant financial relief to the people and to the Bank of Tennessee. On November 12 he attempted to answer criticism of his earlier remarks and announced he would vote for the river bill. See Samuel H. Laughlin to Polk, January 29, 1842.

10. Lewis Reneau, William T. Senter, John R. Wheeler, Julian Frazier, and William Wallace. A Whig and a lawyer from Sevier County, Reneau served three terms in the Tennessee House, 1823–27 and 1835–37, and two terms in the Tennessee Senate, 1839–43. Senter, a Methodist minister and farmer in Grainger County, won election as a Whig presidential elector in 1840 and represented Tennessee's Second Congressional District in the U.S. House for one term, 1843–45. Wheeler, a Democrat and a lawyer from Campbell County, served one term in the Tennessee Senate, 1839–41. Frazier, a Democrat from Grainger County, served as quartermaster general of the Tennessee militia during Polk's governorship.

11. Andrew Johnson and Brookins Campbell were Democratic rivals in the First Congressional District.

12. Julius W. Blackwell.

13. Thomas J. Campbell ran unsuccessfully against Blackwell.

14. The editorial in Thomas Ritchie's *Richmond Enquirer* is not identified

further. In a letter to Polk of September 22, 1842, Ramsey advised that he had urged Ritchie's support of Polk for the vice-presidency. ALS. DLC–JKP.

FROM WILLIAMSON SMITH[1]

Dear Sir.   Madison Cty. Miss. 8th Decemr. 1842

Agreeable to promise, I write you on my return home. 2 or 3 days after my return I ralied my friends, and made a desent upon our friend Handy of the Independant,[2] and he forthwith agreed to place your name at his Masthead for Vice P. It to is due to him to say it was not hard to do, when properly laid before him. We have called a County meeting on the 2nd day of Jany and made out our Committees &c. They will be instruted to urge your Claims as strong as it can be done. I have had certain Men put on who will do their duty. Our Court was still in session on my return, and I made it my business to talk with very many of the leading Democrats, and I did not meet with a dissenting voice to your Claims. Every Man save one will advocate your claims, and that man only on the ground that your location and Mr. Calhouns does not suit.

I saw Mr Totten[3] at Oxford. He told me he would go home & set the Ball in Motion. I did not get to see Judge Howry, as there was company at his House which prevented my seeing him, but Totten promised me he would see him and attend to matters.

I incline to think Calhoun will be the nominee of the state convention here; that is the delegates to the Genl. Convention will be instructed [to] support his claims. I did not oppose it strensously as I thought it most prudent not to do so. As all seem so cheerfully to give in to Idea of your claims, I have written to Sterling Lester[4] and requested him to show my letter to Kincannon,[5] and suggested to him the importance of calling a Meeting.

I regret very much it will not be in my power to be at either of our meetings. Since I saw you, I have determined to start to Washington City in a few days, on the business of my claim.[6] Gov Morehead[7] of Kentucky wrote me he had examined my claim and he had no doubt but if I would go to Washington, this winter, that his influence with the Whigs & mine with the Democrats we would [be] able to get it passed. He had examined the claim and the only difficulty would [be] in reaching it, which he thought could be done if it was started in time.

If there are any of your particular friends that you think you could render me any service by giving me a letter to them at Washington it would be acknowledged as another favour added to the very many already confered. I should start in 2 or 3 days. My Brother Gabriel[8] has just returned from Kentucky. He says it is very clearly understood there that Mr. Clay will not be run for President and that the Democrats of Kentucky are for Dick Johnson for President. That will do very well. It will perhaps put [him] out of the way. I should be pleased to hear from you at Washington. Any thing I can do for your success while there, it is unnecessary to say shall be done. I will perhaps be able to get the hang of things to some extent.

Please present my respects to Mrs. Polk, and say to her I shall notice who I take in the stage with me this trip.[9]

WILLIAMSON SMITH

ALS. DLC–JKP. Addressed to Columbia. Polk's AE on the cover states that he answered this letter on December 15, 1842; Polk's reply has not been found.

1. A lawyer and former resident of Columbia, Smith completed the unfinished term of Terry H. Cahal in the Tennessee Senate, 1836–37, and won election to one term in the Tennessee House, 1839–41. In the early 1840's, he moved to Mississippi and eventually settled in Canton.

2. Reference is to the Canton *Independent Democrat*, probably edited by Alexander H. Handy. A native of Maryland, Handy subsequently practiced law in Canton and served on the Mississippi Supreme Court.

3. James L. Totten, a lawyer and native of Tennessee, served one term in the Tennessee Senate, 1835–37, representing Dyer, Carroll, and Gibson counties; he subsequently moved to Marshall County, Mississippi, where he won election to one term in the Mississippi House, 1844–46.

4. Sterling H. Lester, a former resident of Giles County, Tennessee, moved to Mississippi in the middle 1830's.

5. Andrew A. Kincannon was a former resident of Lincoln County, Tennessee, where he served as sheriff and delegate to the Tennessee Constitutional Convention of 1834. In the late 1830's he moved to Columbus, Mississippi, and in 1844 won election to the Mississippi House.

6. On October 24, 1837, Smith contracted with the U.S. government to transport six-thousand Cherokees west of the Mississippi by steamboat. Not permitted to complete the contract because of a change in governmental planning, Smith claimed that he sustained considerable monetary loss. In the course of his first attempt to win legislative relief, the Committee on the Judiciary of the U.S. House referred his case to Secretary of War Joel R. Poinsett. On June 17, 1840, Poinsett wrote a letter acknowledging the justice of the claim to the Committee on Ways and Means of the House. On the strength of that recommendation, the Bank of the United States advanced Smith the full amount of his claim, $35,327; and, in early 1843, officers of the bank petitioned Congress for payment. On February 14, 1843, a majority report of the House Committee on the Judiciary recommended that the bank's request be refused.

7. James T. Morehead, a Whig lawyer and legislator, won the lieutenant governorship of Kentucky in 1832; he became governor on the death of John Breathitt in 1834. After presiding over Kentucky's Board of Internal Improve-

ments from 1838 until 1841, Morehead won election to the U.S. Senate, where he served one term.

8. Gabriel Smith, brother and business partner of Williamson Smith, moved to Mississippi from Maury County, Tennessee, in the late 1830's or early 1840's.

9. Smith had traveled to Washington City in March of 1840 to press his claim before the House Committee on the Judiciary; his traveling companion on that earlier occasion is not identified.

FROM HOPKINS L. TURNEY

My Dear Sir   Washington City Dec. the 8th 1842

On my arrival at Nashville when on my way to this city I learned for the first time the congressional districts as laid off by the legislature. The one in which I live includes Waterson, and George W. Jones.[1] The former you know is not acceptable to me as my representative nor never was and much less so now, for the very good and sufficient reasons which I under existing circumstances ought not to mention. He however is in the district and you know he is willing to sacrefice any and every thing to sustain himself; Jones is a good democrat a worthey and tallented gentleman and I would be perfectly willing for him to represent the district. Waterson has promised me to abide by the decision of a convention, relying no doubt upon cearrying Bedford and Marshal, two of his old counties, and there by to secure for himself the nomination. Jones could cearry Lincoln. I could get Lincoln and Franklin against W. if Jones was out of the way, or if I was out of the way Jones could get Franklin. Now Sir I wish to accomplish two things. 1st. there must be but one democratick candidate, and secondly, he must not be, H.M.W. if it can be avoided. For myself I am willing to run, or not, as circumstances may require. Maney of my friends think I will still be thought of for the senate,[2] in which event it would be better for me and for the district, that I should not run for the House. In no event however will I be the meanes of produceing discensions or divisions in our ranks either for the H. or S. By a union with Jones I could give him the nomination. But sir I am out of business, have not a case on the docket, a large family and really need some ready money. This I could make by remaining here annother congress, enough to support my family until I could get into a practice. Yet this shall not enduce me to Stand in the way of any party arrangement or from sacrefic-cing my views and wishes on the alter of the public good. I am therefore willing that Jones shall run, rather than produce any diffaculty, and to take my Chance before the legislature, and if I should shear the same fate there, I will modistly retire to my private life still adheaering to and on all proper occasions Sustaining democratick principles and men.

I would be much pleased to have your opinion freely exspressed on this Subject. It cannot, or if it could it should not effect you in any way whatever, for no human being shall ever know it except ourselves. I do therefore rispectfully soliset your opinion and advice in relation to this to me important matter.

You and Van[3] are identified. Your fates will inevitably be the same. I have not had a full talk with Benton but He has requested me to call on him for the express purpose, which I will do in a day or two the result of which I will advise you. All seem to agree, that the contest will be between Van & you, against Calhoon & Woodbury, in which contest you will have, Benton & Allen, and also, a large majority of our friends in the presant Congress.

H. L. Turney

ALS. DLC–JKP. Addressed to Columbia. Polk's AE on the cover states that he answered this letter on December 17, 1842; Polk's reply has not been found.

1. Turney, Harvey M. Watterson and George W. Jones lived in the Fifth Congressional District, which included Franklin, Lincoln, Bedford, and Marshall counties. A native of Virginia, Jones became a saddler in Fayetteville. He served two terms in the Tennessee House, 1835–39, and sat one term in the Senate, 1839–41. A candidate for presidential elector on the Van Buren ticket in 1840, Jones first won election to the U.S. House in 1843 and served until 1859.

2. U.S. Senate.

3. Martin Van Buren.

TO MARTIN VAN BUREN

My Dear Sir: Columbia Tenn. Decr. 8th 1842

On my return home from a visit to my plantation in Mississippi, a few days ago, I received your letter of the 11th ultimo, announcing our great victory in New York. I had been prepared to anticipate success in that State, but not by so overwhelming a majority as the result proves. The triumph of our principles in New York, Ohio and other states during the present year,[1] has given the Democracy of this State fresh courage for the contest which is before us. Ours as you are aware may be fairly regarded as debateable ground. We will have a bitter and a hard struggle during the next summer, but confidently hope to be able to number Tennessee among the Democratic States. Our habit is, to meet and address the people in public assemblies. I have done so, in several of the Counties recently, and am satisfied that we have increased and are increasing our strength. I have not yet been announced as the Democratic

Candidate for Governor, though all my friends insist that I shall be in the spring. The labour of canvassing a State like this, of more than six hundred miles in extent, and reaching from the mountains of Virginia & Carolina to the Swamps of the Mississippi, and of visiting and addressing the people in more than eighty Counties, is greater than can be estimated by any one who has not performed it. It requires four months of unceasing riding and speaking. I have twice performed it, and standing in the relation which I do to the Democracy of the State, I must undertake it again. We will do our duty, and I think will give a good account of ourselves in August next, as well as in the great contest of 1844. I shall be pleased to hear from you, as your leizure may permit, and to receive any suggestions—which you may deem it important to make.

JAMES K. POLK

ALS. DLC–MVB. Addressed to Kinderhook, New York.

1. See William H. Polk to Polk, October 18, 1842; Polk to Samuel H. Laughlin, October 19, 1842; and J. G. M. Ramsey to Polk, November 29, 1842.

FROM ROBERT ARMSTRONG

Dear Sir.   Nashville 12th Decembr. 42

If you can spare time I think a few days here would be well and profitable spent. Every thing looks well from every quarter. Doctr. Young[1] says *Jones* will be the Whig Candidate.[2] If he is not they will have *none*. I think Guild[3] will agree to run in this district[4] for Congress. If he does we will "get our freedom."

There is several matters to arrange that the sooner done the better, and when you come you must stay a few days.

Verry close in Massachusetts.[5] Our friends think Morton safe.[6] Laughlin is here—no News.

R ARMSTRONG

ALS. DLC–JKP. Addressed to Columbia. Polk's AE on the cover states that he answered this letter on December 14, 1842; Polk's reply has not been found.

1. John S. Young, a native Virginian, settled in Warren County, Tennessee, about 1830; he practiced medicine prior to moving to the Cherokee agency at Calhoun in 1836. The General Assembly elected him secretary of state in 1839, and he held that position until 1847.

2. Reference is to the Tennessee gubernatorial election of 1843.

3. Josephus C. Guild, a Gallatin lawyer, served three terms in the Tennessee House, 1833–36, 1845–47, and 1851–53, and sat for one term in the Senate,

1837–39. He was a presidential elector in 1844 on the ticket of Polk and George M. Dallas.

4. Tennessee's Eighth Congressional District.

5. Reference is to the Massachusetts elections of 1842. See J. G. M. Ramsey to Polk, November 29, 1842.

6. Marcus Morton, a lawyer, represented his Massachusetts district in Congress for two terms, 1817–21, and sat on the state Supreme Court from 1825 until 1840. Elected governor as a Democrat in 1840, he narrowly won reelection in 1842. In 1845 Polk appointed Morton collector of customs in Boston, where he served until 1849.

FROM LEVIN H. COE

Dear Sir   Somerville Decr. 14. 1842

Your favor is to hand by yesterdays mail.[1] I owe you an apology for not having written before this. I reached home from Winstons[2] with high inflamation of the breast. I have had an attack of it every time I have been subjected to the least exposure since. I start N. Orleans in the morning & hope the trip may be of advantage to me.

I was at Jackson last week and even the leading Whigs there admit we are gaining.

I have written to Judge Dunlap[3] by to days mail asking him to say to his confidential friends that he is a candidate for Congress. I have the Demos. of this County & the adjoining ones expecting & anxious to hear it.

I have also suggested an 8 Jany meeting in Hardeman. It will be court week and the meeting would be large. The Whigs hold a meeting in Memphis in a few days.[4] One will probably follow here—then we will follow that. I hope we will get suitable candidates out in due time for all the offices & have no fear of the result. Party machinery cannot reanimate & bring up the rank & file of the Whig party & the effect of the new Tariff upon the price of Cotton about Apl & May next in further reduction of price will have much effect in this part of the State. Maclin is about to settle in Somerville to practice law. He is here now.

L. H. Coe

Van of the . . .[5] is acting a little strangely at times of late. Write nothing confidential to him.[6]

ALS. DLC–JKP. Addressed to Columbia.

1. Polk's letter not found.

2. Probably Thomas J. Winston, a Democrat residing in La Grange, Tennessee.

3. A lawyer from Bolivar, William C. Dunlap served two terms as a Democratic congressman, 1833–37. He held a circuit judgeship in Tennessee from 1840 until 1849; in the 1850's he won seats in both the Tennessee House and Senate.

4. Not identified further.

5. Probably Henry Van Pelt, editor of the *Memphis Appeal*.

6. Coe wrote this admonishment of caution on a separate sheet.

FROM JONATHAN P. HARDWICKE

My Dear Sir   Charlotte Dec 18, 1842

Your favour of the 15 Inst. was recvd by due course of mails yesterday.[1] I had previously recvd flattering accounts of your labours in the District. Maclin says you made havock amongst the Mechanicks in his neighbourhood and that things are working well. He tels me he is of[f] the track entirely, and that Judge Dunlap, & Dr. Searcy[2] will probably be the Candidates in that district, for Congress. You will see from the Union,[3] that we are ever mindfull of our duty. We had a Democratick meeting here yesterday, preparitory to a Convention to be held at Dover, in Feby, to nominate Candidates for Congress & the Senate. Who they will be I cant tell, but hope the nominations will be made with out regard to men, and for the good of the cause and our party. I have every reason to beleive our friends generally expect and desire my nomination for Congress.

I must say to you what I have not said to any other save S. Maclin, that I dont expect to be a candidate again for any office. In a word if my present plans go into effect, I shall leave the State by or before the first of April next. Of that I shall determine in a short time. If I should leave as I now expect to do, *Cave Johnson* will be nominated again and *Maj. Gray*[4] for the Senate &c.

I was at the Circuit Court in Humphreys. From all I could learn there, Wily[5] will be the Democratic Candidate for that district. If so, he will be elected, and is good and true. Eubank[6] wont run again, but Dickson[7] will send some one that will give a good account. We doubtless are better organized and things are working more smoothly than in most other Co.s or Dsts. of the State.

What ever I do, or where ere I go, I will cast in my mite, by both handing and holding to further the cause we have been battling for. There are three reasons for the course, I have marked out for my future actions. First, increase of years, bodily afflictions, and a desire to give my attention to my domestick affairs, which, [I] have greatly neglected for the last six years. I am not imbarassed, nor do I intend to be, but I have not made what I should under other circumstances.

I shall be pleased to here from you at all times and much more so to know that you are successfull in your labours.

J. P. HARDWICKE

ALS. DLC–JKP. Addressed to Columbia.
1. Polk's letter not found.
2. "Dr. Searcy" is not identified further; reference probably is to Granville D. Searcy. On December 9, 1842, John H. Bills wrote to Polk that Granville Searcy was a possible Whig candidate in the Tenth Congressional District. ALS. DLC–JKP. Granville D. Searcy represented Tipton County in the Tennessee House for one term, 1835–37, and Shelby County for one term, 1849–51.
3. *Nashville Union.*
4. A farmer, hatter, Free Will Baptist minister, and Democrat from Stewart County, James Gray served in both the Tennessee House, 1827–33, and Senate, 1835–37; a veteran of the War of 1812, Gray later held the rank of major in the Tennessee militia.
5. A farmer from Benton (previously Humphreys) County, James Wyly served three terms as a Democrat in the Tennessee House, 1837–39, 1843–45, and 1847–49.
6. A tailor and farmer from Dickson County, John Eubank served six terms as a Democrat in the Tennessee House, 1839–49 and 1861–63.
7. Dickson County.

FROM CAVE JOHNSON

Dear Sir   Washington Dec 18th 1842
I recd your two letters of the 8th & 9th[1] on yesterday. I had never before met Milton Browns letter.[2] It is a foolish contemptible thing no doubt designed to make an other issue. If a suitable opportunity presents I will not fail to expose it. He will have enough to do to manage his other votes at the call session[3] & if Gardner runs he will be fully occupied without troubling you. I have changed my opinion of him very much since he has been here. I will send you the Documents[4] you desire in a few days.

I have recd letters from Fitzgerald & Jas T Dunlap[5] wishing to know whether I would be a candidate &c written before my card appeared in the Union[6]—also from Majr H.[7] The two latter wishes to be candidates & Fitzgerald intimates that several others in Henry desire it, tho not himself. I have urged all of them to have a convention and thus avoid running more than one. If that can be effected, I think we will be certainly safe. Judge Martin[8] will probably be the whig candidate. If in your way you had better press the matter. Any division may be disastrous.

I shall not be surprised if we have new parties & new issues before the Presidential election. Recent publications in The Mercury[9] induce the belief that Calhoun is a candidate any how. They talk here of submitting to a convention *if fair*— that the members should be *elected* by *districts* &c.[10] If the convention decides agt. him, they will complain *of its unfairness* and intend to run him any how. This is in my opinion their setled determination, & I fear Woodbury is in it, & they will try & get Maine by intimating that Clifford is to be Speaker. The new issue I think will be the British Treaty.[11] Benton's speech you will see.[12] The greatest effort of his life & I shall not be surprised if it prevents any appropriation to carry it into effect. Woodbury & Calhoun voted for it denouncing the treaty but public faith requires its execution. The defence of this measure will secure them the aid of the Pres. & his friends. Van Buren will go into the Convention with more than two to one, if there be any thing like a fair representation. It seems impossible to ascertain their views as to the Vice Presidency. They are however evidently greatly dissatisfied with efforts Old Dick[13] is making to get uppermost & we can hear it occasionally said that Polk or King is the man. McKay is very desirous of your nomination—I think the only Van B. man in the delegation of his State. The Calhoun men are acting very badly. You remember the election of Speaker,[14] how it was managed, the same game is going on in the Legislature of N.C. Some 10 or 12 his friends refused to vote for Bedford Brown because *his first* choice is Van, & vote for Saunders. The whigs are by degrees coming to Saunders & will probably elect him.[15] The same game is expected in Alabama, & finally to be played out over the whole union in the presidential election. Cass has come out in substance declining to run for the Presidency unless nominated by a democratic National Convention.[16] As he hails from Ohio, I shall not be surprised if an effort should be made to put him on as Van's Vice President for fear the whigs might present him a nomination. Genl Anderson is here full of *secrets of state* of immense importance—will rather do harm than good. He has but little prudence & not much judgement. King refuses to go for Van if old Dick is on the ticket. Buckhanon[17] has given up hopes I think & stands with Benton agt. the Treaty. The Guard has still hopes that the Democrats will take up Tyler. I have not yet visited him. He was unwell when I got here & I have for several days been very unwell—a slight return of my old complaint—swelled face & shoulders so much affected that I could not put on or off my coat. Williams[18] of Maryland died on his way. Habersham is probably dead.[19] Judge Young[20] of Illinois had an appoplectic fit a few days ago. He will probably recover. Brown, Turney, & myself are together on Missouri Avenue.[21] Caruthers, Gentry, W B Campbell, & C H Williams[22] decline. Jeff Campbell and Arnold will be probably choked off.[23] I shall not be surprised if there should not be returned (20 men) twenty men of the present Congress. I have been able to go about but very little. We shall not fail to note every thing interesting to you & give you an account of it. My respects to Madam.[24]

C JOHNSON

ALS. DLC–JKP. Addressed to Nashville.

1. Letters not found.

2. See Sarah C. Polk to Polk, November 7, 1842.

3. Reference is to the special session of the Twenty-seventh Congress, which met in the summer of 1841.

4. Not identified further.

5. William Fitzgerald and James T. Dunlap. Fitzgerald served as circuit court clerk in Stewart County, 1822–25, sat one term in the Tennessee House, 1825–27, and held the position of attorney general of the Sixteenth Judicial Circuit, before winning election in 1831 to a single term in the U.S. House. He moved to Henry County in the late 1830's and in 1841 became judge of the Ninth Judicial Circuit. Dunlap, a member of the bar in Paris, Tennessee, won election to one term in the Tennessee House, 1847–49, and sat two terms in the Tennessee Senate, 1851–55; he served as Democratic presidential elector in 1852 and comptroller of Tennessee, 1857–62.

6. Cave Johnson's card, which was addressed to the citizens of the Ninth Congressional District, announced that he would not run again for Congress; he published his declination in the *Nashville Union* on December 6, 1842. Johnson subsequently changed his mind and won reelection to the Twenty-eighth Congress.

7. Jonathan P. Hardwicke.

8. Mortimer A. Martin, a Whig lawyer in Clarksville, served as judge of the Seventh Circuit from 1836 to 1850.

9. *Charleston Mercury*.

10. Reference is to U.S. congressional districts.

11. Webster-Ashburton Treaty.

12. On August 18, 1842, the U.S. Senate met in executive session to debate the Webster-Ashburton Treaty; Thomas Hart Benton made a speech opposing ratification. On August 30, 1842, the Senate adopted a resolution removing its injunction of secrecy subsequent to the exchange of ratifications; those deliberations, including speeches, began appearing in the public press in early December of 1842.

13. Richard M. Johnson.

14. Reference is to the election of Robert M. T. Hunter as Speaker of the U.S. House of Representatives in 1839.

15. Reference is to the election of a U.S. Senator for North Carolina to replace the incumbent Whig, William A. Graham, upon the expiration of his term, March 3, 1843. The Democratic majority in the legislature divided between Bedford Brown and Romulus M. Saunders. Both candidates finally withdrew and

allowed the election of William H. Haywood, a Democrat and former Speaker of the North Carolina legislature's lower house. Brown, a planter in the vicinity of Greensboro, served in both houses of the North Carolina legislature before representing his state in the U.S. Senate, 1829–40. He had resigned in 1840 rather than follow the instructions of a Whig dominated legislature; he won election to the state senate in 1842. Saunders, a lawyer active in North Carolina politics since 1815, lost his bid for the governorship in 1840; having previously served three terms in the U.S. House, 1821–27, he returned to that body and served two more terms, 1841–45.

16. The Washington *Globe* of December 17, 1842, printed a letter that Lewis Cass had written in Paris, August 19, 1842, answering questions about his presidential aspirations. Cass had claimed that he did not wish or expect to be president, but should the majority of the Democratic party feel his nomination "necessary" and should he receive the endorsement of a national convention, he would "yield with reluctance."

17. James Buchanan.

18. James W. Williams, former Speaker of the Maryland House of Delegates, won election to the Twenty-seventh Congress as a Democrat, but died on December 2, 1842.

19. Richard Wylly Habersham died December 2, 1842.

20. Richard M. Young served in the Illinois House, 1820–22; sat as judge of the Fifth Judicial Circuit, 1825–37; won election as a Democrat to the U.S. Senate in 1836; and went to the bench of the Illinois Supreme Court in 1843. Polk appointed him commissioner of the General Land Office in 1847.

21. Johnson and his two Democratic colleagues from Tennessee apparently resided at Mrs. Thompson's boarding house in Washington.

22. Robert L. Caruthers, Meredith P. Gentry, William B. Campbell, and Christopher H. Williams were Whig members of the Tennessee congressional delegation. Gentry, a member of the Williamson County bar, served as a Whig in the Tennessee House, 1835–39, and won election to several terms in the U.S. House, 1839–43 and 1845–53; he ran unsuccessfully for governor in 1853 on the American party ticket. Williams, a lawyer from Lexington, Tennessee, represented his district for five terms in the U.S. House, 1837–43 and 1849–53.

23. Reference is to the recent congressional redistricting in Tennessee, which placed the seats of Thomas J. Campbell and Thomas D. Arnold in jeopardy.

24. Sarah C. Polk.

FROM E. G. EASTMAN

Dear Sir—   Knoxville, Dec. 19, 1842

I recd. your favor of the 14th[1] on Saturday, and hasten to answer. I have not, since its reception, had an opportunity of conversing with any of our friends—Mr. Reynolds and Gen. Anderson being absent from town; and having been too unwell for a week past to be at my office, I have not seen either of our other active friends.[2] The subject on which you write is one, however, on which we have frequently conversed, and on which we are cordially agreed. I have written to several of our leading friends in other counties on the same subject, and have urged upon them the vital necessity of speedy and efficient organization. I have also written an article for my next paper, borrowing nearly all its suggestions and a large part of its language from your letter, in which I urge the immediate call of county meetings. You will see the article in the next Argus,[3] and I trust will approve it. I shall use my most strenuous exertions, by articles in the Argus, by conversation with our friends as opportunity offers, & by letters to see that an anti-Clay and anti-any-other Whig Meeting is held in every county in East Tennessee within the ensuing three months at the latest, and I have sanguine hopes that when you visit us in the spring, as I suppose you intend doing, you will find, what you have never yet found, our party here efficiently and thoroughly organized.

Our party here are in the finest spirits, and our opponents utterly disheartened. Great as may have been the changes in the Western District, I do not believe them equal to those in our section of the State. I have lived here near four years, and my business, even if I had not the inclination, has forced me to calculate, until I believe I can do it with tolerable accuracy, the ebbs and floods of the political tide. I never was a sanguine calculator, as on at least two occasions, you have seen. Yet I do most sincerely believe that if the election for Governor were to come up today you would receive a decided majority in this section of the State, and we are daily and hourly gaining strength. This the Whigs themselves freely admit.

Johnson will probably be our candidate for Congress in the 1st district.[4] His foolish and uncalled for quarrel with Campbell may injure him some.[5] Still he will be easily elected. I have no doubt that the Whigs will run two candidates in the 2d district.[6] Reneau has already announced [. . .][7] candidate, and will not back out for any body. The leaders are dissatisfied at this; and are urging Gen. Brazelton[8] to run. If he should decline, of which I do not think there is any prospect, then Wm. Williams or Parson Lewis[9] will be the second man. I repeat that there is no doubt in my mind that two Whigs will run, and, if so, Gen. Frazier can be easily elected. In this district[10] Blackwell will run, and will be elected. His opponent is not yet determined on. Hints are thrown out that it will be Luke Lea,[11] but I do not believe it. He is their strongest man, but Blackwell can beat him. Neither Williams nor Campbell will be willing to back out, and the Democrats, perfectly united among themselves, are anticipating great sport from the contest.[12] Campbell, as he passed through here on his way to Washington, said to our friend Dr. Ramsey, "The Whigs will have to run me in preference to Williams," for said he, "although I voted for the bankrupt law, I also voted to repeal it, while Williams voted for it and against its repeal." They dread the bankrupt law, and well they may! We intend to contest every inch of ground in E.T. both for Congress and the Legislature. Even where success is hopeless, the beneficial effect of such a contest on the vote for Governor will more than repay the exertion.

You may have seen my notice of the Clay meeting in this place.[13] Strange as the account may have seemed, it was no exaggeration. They had runners out for six weeks in this and the adjoining counties—notices were published in their papers weeks in advance—and hundreds of printed handbills were circulated and posted up at all the cross roads and at all the public places in this and the adjoining counties. Yet, although it was court day, and a very fine day, at the most leisure season of the year, there were not two hundred persons—men, hogs, and Democrats—present! Less than the number of votes given against you in this town alone at the last election. Is not this *a sign*? I believe, you know *Ham Scott.*[14] Ham was one of "the runners" sent out to bring the people in to the meeting. He rode two weeks, Sundays not excepted. I saw him on the morning of the meeting, and asked him if they expected a large crowd. "Why, said he, there's no use in telling a lie about it, for you'll soon see. There'll be but dam'd few here—not *twenty* who don't come on other business. Two years ago, you could ride through the county and just shake a coonskin and draw the farmers from their corn fields; but now, they would not walk ten steps to see Jesus Christ himself if they thought he was a Whig." If you know Scott, you can imagine the energy with which he would make such a speech.

I hope to hear from you as often pending and during the canvass as you can find it convenient. Your hints and suggestions would be valuable to me under any circumstances, but are doubly so situated as I am, with scarcely one safe prudent counsellor to consult with. Editors usually complain of being troubled with *too much* advice. This is not, and never has been, my case. In reply to inquiries as to the best course to pursue in important matters, I have so long been accustomed to the reply, "O. I don't know—use your own Judgment," that I have long since ceased to ask advice here. I have long thought that the Democracy of the different sections of the State did not act with sufficient concert. Would not the appointment of corresponding committees at Knoxville, Nashville, and Jackson do much to remedy the evil?

I shall be at Nashville about the 10th of Feb. If I have time I intend to visit your town if it were only to see your brother,[15] to whom I beg you give my kindest regards.

E. G. EASTMAN

ALS. DLC–JKP. Addressed to Columbia. Polk's AE on the cover states that he answered this letter on December 24, 1842; Polk's reply has not been found.

1. Letter not found.

2. Probably J. G. M. Ramsey and Arthur R. Crozier.

3. Reference is to an article addressed to the "Democrats of East Tennessee" and published in the Knoxville *Argus* on December 21, 1842.

4. The First Congressional District of Tennessee, as established by the General Assembly in 1842, consisted of Johnson, Sullivan, Carter, Washington, Hawkins, Greene, and Cocke counties.

5. The immediate quarrel between Andrew Johnson and Brookins Campbell involved Johnson's charge that Campbell, as a member of the joint select committee on legislative redistricting of the Twenty-fourth General Assembly, failed to protect the interests of upper East Tennessee. Johnson, however, held a grudge of long standing against his fellow Democrat, who had defeated Johnson in a heated campaign for the legislature in 1837. See Jonathan P. Hardwicke to Polk, November 20, 1842, for further comment on party quarrels.

6. The Second Congressional District of Tennessee, as established by the General Assembly in 1842, consisted of Hancock, Grainger, Jefferson, Sevier, Blount, Monroe, Claiborne, Campbell, Anderson, and Morgan counties.

7. Faded manuscript renders at least two words illegible.

8. William Brazelton, a farmer and merchant from Jefferson County, served as major-general of the East Tennessee militia from 1839 until 1847.

9. William Williams, a Whig from Grainger County, served one term in the Tennessee House, 1839–41, and one term in the Tennessee Senate, 1841–43. Parson Lewis is not identified further.

10. The Third Congressional District of Tennessee.

11. Luke Lea, from Campbell's Station, Knox County, won election as a Democrat to two terms in the U.S. House, 1833–37, and served a partial term as Tennessee's secretary of state, 1837–39. An early advocate of Hugh Lawson White's presidential candidacy in 1836, Lea became a leading supporter of the Whig party.

12. Two incumbent Whig congressmen, Joseph L. Williams and Thomas J. Campbell, were placed in the Third District by the congressional reapportionment of 1842.

13. The Knoxville *Argus* of December 7, 1842, contains an account of a Whig meeting held in Knoxville on December 5, 1842.

14. Reference probably is to Hampton S. Scott, a Knox County resident listed in the 1840 census.

15. William H. Polk.

FROM ROBERT ARMSTRONG

Dear Sir. Nashville Decr. 20th 42

I send you the enclosed that you may see what we will have to contend with in Sumner.[1] Guild is yet here. I have said nothing to him of Barrys course or Trousdales expectations.[2] If we wish it, Guild will be our Candidate. He is the man and the only man that Campbell fears. Barry wishes Donelson to run for the Senate (that he may be beat). He (Barry) will run for the lower House with out opposition. This will Elect Doctr. *Peyton* to the Senate and all of which Bailey has arranged before leaving for New Orleans.[3]

I am not sure of the propriety of a compromise now. Some of our friends are for it, but they are those who want to get in to place without fighting and do as *they please when in*. We will succeed in this County and District if we can hold together and not have a brake up. Things are in a very delicate condition all over the State & it is only so since the rise of the Legislature. Their is great dissatisfaction and Distrust of some of our leading men. If we get these Knotty points settled all will go well and we shall have an easy time. Your majority will be 12 to 20 thousand.

Suffer me to say to you to avoid as far as possible in mixing up in local matters. I hope you will come in soon and remain long enough to put things all right.

Our old friend The Doctr[4] has not done as I expected in the money affair. I will see him and loock round and write you in two or three days. Perhaps I may hear of it in some other quarter. He has it and must loan it.

R. ARMSTRONG

[P.S.] I have much to say to you on many subjects. The manner of conducting the Union[5] &c &c.

ALS. DLC–JKP. Addressed to Columbia and marked "*Private*." Polk's AE on the cover states that he answered this letter on December 21, 1842; Polk's reply has not been found.

1. On December 15, 1842, Thomas R. Barry wrote Armstrong that "there is a move making to bring out Col Guild for Congress vs Campbell." Barry states that some three hundred Democrats will not vote for Guild because he had supported creation of the Bank of Tennessee. Guild's nomination would be a great injustice to Trousdale, "who has nearly broke himself in the Democratic cause." ALS. DLC–JKP. Barry's reference is to the 1843 election in Tennessee's Eighth Congressional District.

2. Thomas R. Barry and William Trousdale. Barry had recently resigned

from the Tennessee House; Daniel S. Donelson succeeded him as Sumner County's representative for the second session of the Twenty-fourth General Assembly. Trousdale, a Gallatin lawyer, won election to the Tennessee Senate, 1835–36, but resigned to serve in the Seminole War. After losing races for Congress in 1837, 1839, and 1845, he won the governorship of Tennessee and served from 1849 until 1851.

3. Joseph H. Peyton and Balie Peyton. Joseph H. Peyton, a Sumner County physician and Whig, served one term in the Tennessee Senate, 1841–43, before winning election to a single term in the U.S. House in 1843. Balie Peyton, a lawyer from Gallatin and the brother of Joseph H., sat as a Whig in the U.S. House for two terms, 1833–37; declined appointment as secretary of war under Tyler; became U.S. district attorney for eastern Louisiana in 1841; remained at New Orleans until the outbreak of the Mexican War; served as aide-de-camp for General W. J. Worth during the Mexican War; went to Chile as U.S. minister, 1849–53; and sat one term in the Tennessee Senate, 1869–70.

4. Reference is to William McNeill. See Armstrong to Polk, April 15, 1842, and Polk to McNeill, August 2, 1842.

5. *Nashville Union.*

FROM WILLIAM C. DUNLAP

Dear Sir   Bolivar Decr 20th 1842

Yours of the 15th Inst was received by the last mail.[1] I regret that both my health & pecuniary circumstances will prevent me from being a candidate for Congress in this District.[2] I am wholly unable to ride about and make speeches. I could travel to the Courthouses in the District but I do not believe that I could make speeches. The injury I received was much greater than any of my friends believed it was. I do candidly believe that we can elect a Democrat from the District if we will all act in concert; I will have this attended to on the Circuit in January next.

You are very much mistaken in Coe's aiding any of our candidates by being one himself; there is a deep rooted hatred by all the Whigs to Coe and he is so bitter in his speeches that if he was a candidate he would draw the party lines so strong that no Democratic candidate could get any Whig votes; we want a man to go and attack their measures with reason & to pursuade the people that they have been imposed on by the Whigs. Stanton of Memphis[3] is the man to run and he can unite Shelby County on the National Armory & Naval Depot being located at Memphis.[4]

I want J. J. Potts to run for the Senate; Geo. W Smith as the floating Member from this, Fayette, & Shelby; Edwin Hickman for Rep. of Shelby; Wm A Jones for Fayette; and Austin Miller or Edwin Polk for Rep of Hardeman.[5] With such a ticket we can increase the Democratic vote five hundred in this Congressional District. I believe they all can be got to run. I would willingly give up my office if I could serve the Democratic cause better than any other Gentleman in the District; But my honest opinion is that Stanton can serve the party as well if not better than myself; he speaks well, is personally popular and mixes finely with the people.

I find in my intercourse with the people in this Circuit that there are many Whigs who will not act any longer with their party and all they want is a Democratic candidate, against whom they have no prejudice, to vote the ticket; I have not the least doubt that at this time there is a democratic majority in this Congressional District. I know of one District in this County where they vote 85 votes and only 7 Democratic that I confidently believe a large Majority would now vote with us; the only men of influence in the District—to wit the McKinnie's,[6] five in number, told me last week when I was at thier house (where I stayed two day *hunting*) that they would not vote for Clay or any person who advocated his principles; these are some of the strongest US Bank men in the District that have changed against it and although they do not say they have abandoned the Whigs, they must vote for us. There are fewer changes in Fayette than either of the other counties.

I regret very much that I was from home when you were here that I could have had a full & free conversation with you; My Mother[7] was in Miss. and detained me attending to her. I will write you from Raleigh in February next by which time I can know the views of all our friends.

W C DUNLAP

ALS. DLC–JKP. Addressed to Columbia.

1. Polk's letter not found.

2. Tennessee's Tenth Congressional District.

3. Frederick P. Stanton, a Memphis lawyer, served as a Democrat in Congress, 1845–55, and as governor of the Kansas Territory, 1858–61.

4. In March of 1843 Congress passed an act authorizing the secretary of the navy to examine and survey the harbor at Memphis for the purpose of establishing a naval depot there. Senator Alexander Barrow of Louisiana and Representative John C. Clark of New York, both Whigs, had sponsored the legislation.

5. John J. Potts, George W. Smith, Edwin Hickman, William A. Jones, Austin Miller, and Edwin F. Polk were all Democrats; only Miller won election to the Tennessee General Assembly in 1843.

6. The 1840 census listed five Hardeman County residents with variant spellings of the surname, "McKinney." Three heads of households, Michael, Richard and William P. "McKinne," resided in the same district.

7. Susannah Harding Gilliam Dunlap.

FROM J. GEORGE HARRIS

My Dear Governor: Nashville Dec. 20. 1842

Your several letters of late date[1] are received; and I have given them all consideration. The proceedings of the Anti-Clay meeting at Columbia were deferred from day to day, but you will see that I have published them at last and shall forward 100 copies to the committee as directed.[2]

With reference to the National Convention, there seems to be a difference of opinion so wide as to make it quite improbable, in my judgment, whether it would be possible to bring about a union in favor of the day designated by the democratic members of our Legislature.[3] I wrote my friend Greene on the subject a month ago, but I see by a late paper (Post)[4] that he takes ground in favor of having the time and place fixed by a Congressional Caucus. You know we are not in favor of this, but if it cannot be remedied, it must be regarded as *the best we can do*. Why Blair came out openly in opposition to the resolution of our democratic members,[5] when no *other* move had yet been made upon the subject, I cannot divine. Owing to his *position* a great many papers have adopted his notions, and it would seem useless in my opinion, therefore, to *persist*. Still if your judgment is otherwise, inform me so by return mail, and I will most cheerfully prepare as forcible an article as I can in favor of our first proposition.[6]

I thank you for calling my attention to the article in the Lynchburg Virginian on the subject of the Tariff.[7] The manifest object of the leading Whig papers which publish articles of that character is to divide and conquer. They magnify the slightest apparent differences in sentiment into impassable gulfs, and by the policy of hair splitting endeavor to show that differences exist where in reality the text itself shows that there is no difference. I thank you for giving a sketch of the ground you occupy, and am happy to find that it strictly accords with my own views of the subject. In no respect, not upon a single point laid down, do we differ.

If I understand the Jefferson, Jackson, Van Buren and Polk doctrine it is this:

1st That we should have a Tariff of duties on imports just sufficient for defraying the annual expenses of the General Government, and no more.

2d That this Tariff should be laid by Congress with the most careful discrimination *incidentally* or *accidentally* releaving such necessaries as salt, tea, sugar, &c from taxation, and protecting, as a matter of course and as far as may be, such American interests as Congress may decide to need it most.

3d That the principle of protection is recognised so far only as it is accidental in levying duties to raise the *necessary revenue.*

Am I right? These are the *cardinal* points, and if I have not a correct view of the subject, I ask you in all candor and fact and true friendship to show me wherein I have misunderstood the doctrines of *our old school.*

This is a question which I have rarely ventured to touch *in the detail.* For I know that while there is a wide difference between our general doctrines [on] the subject and Clay's American System, the field is broad enough to fight against Clay's High Tariff without becoming entangled. But among our own prominent friends you know there are so many different shades of opinion when we approach *discrimination* that it were impossible to do justice to all and injustice to none *in the detail,* and yet have harmonious union. My object is, has been, and will continue to be, to unite with you and your friends, upon the subject; and I do most [. . .][8] regret that I was not more thoughtful than [. . .] any remarks upon the article that I copied approvingly from the Albany Argus subject to such an inference as is drawn by the Lynchburg Virginian.

It is the object of such papers to drive us either upon Scylla or Charybdis. They do not intend we shall ever have the benefit of the word *judicious.* They would wreck us upon doubtful doctrine of *Direct Taxation,* upon the rather unpopular (but too just) provisions of a *horizontal Tariff,* or swamp us in the dangerous sea of a *Protective Tariff.* It is their mode of electioneering, at this moment, and such articles as that which the Virginian copied from the Mercury[9] is calculated to do us no good at this jucture.

I have written hastily, and have been somewhat more explanatory than usual—but I am writing *a confidential letter to you.* Be kind enough at some moment of leisure to state wherein (if at all) I have erred in the text, as touching our position on the Tariff.

J. GEO. HARRIS

[P.S.] The Dicks[on][10] resolutions will appear in the next Union.[11]

ALS. DLC–JKP. Addressed to Columbia. Polk's AE on the cover states that he answered this letter on December 22, 1842; Polk's reply has not been found.

1. Polk's letters not found.

2. The proceedings of an anti-Clay meeting, held at Columbia on October 31, 1842, appeared in the *Nashville Union* on December 20, 1842. The committee to which Harris sent copies was probably the Democratic corresponding committee of Maury County.

3. See Samuel H. Laughlin to Polk, October 11, 1842.

4. References are to Charles G. Greene and the *Boston Morning Post.*

5. A journalist and member of Jackson's "Kitchen Cabinet," Francis P. Blair

established the Washington *Globe* and served as its chief editor from 1830 until 1845. The *Globe* of October 28, 1842, carried an editorial objecting to the November 1843 date selected by the Tennesseans for the National Democratic Convention. The editorial suggested that a date closer to the election would be better and that the traditional May date would be most suitable.

6. No article in defense of the November date has been found in the late December or January issues of the *Union*.

7. Richard H. Toler, a prominent Virginia Whig, edited for many years the *Lynchburg Virginian*, 1822–1893. The article on the tariff has not been identified.

8. One or more words, or parts of words, in three consecutive lines of the manuscript have been obliterated by a tear in the document or by the sealing wax.

9. The *Charleston Mercury*.

10. The same obliteration, as noted above, has rendered part of this word illegible. The *Nashville Union* of December 23, 1842, carried an article on a meeting of Dickson County Democrats at Charlotte on December 17. The Dickson County resolutions called for early organization of Democrats in the Ninth Congressional District, selection of legislative candidates for the state legislature and nomination of a single candidate for Congress.

11. Harris wrote his postscript in the left margin of the final page.

FROM HENDERSON K. YOAKUM

My Dear Sir,   Murfreesboro' Decr 22, 1842

You are fully advised of matters in these parts. And of the almost hopeless position into which we are thrown by false friends & far sighted federalism. Yet we are too proud to complain, and I hope, too patriotic to surrender. I have watched with some attention the course of some of our friends in the Legislature on the question of districts—and have come to the conclusion that they were more particular to secure & guard their own particular interests than to provide for the general welfare. They have acted the part of Webster in the Ashburton treaty—in securing their own sections, they have left to the enemy other sections that justice, services rendered, and sound policy required should be protected.

But we love our country better than our own local advantages. We fight for the good doctrines still—they are our doctrines, we cherish them, and hope to live to see their triumph in every part of our country. We place you high in the list of our good friends, & will not forget the good you have tried to do us.

The seat of Government will be a serious question with us. Yet we will not be foolish about it—we will go for the location at some central point,[1] first, to have it out of the commercial influence; secondly, to place it where, in the language of Mr Madison, it can look with the most "equal eye" over the whole country.[2]

Capt. James S. Smith and David M. Currin Esq. will be our candidates for the lower house.[3] Further we say nothing, and know nothing, and, I fear, can do nothing.

We are looking for you here, to take Christmas with us. We have much to say to you, and to hear from you. You will not disappoint us, but will accompany Mrs Polk to see her friends.

H. YOAKUM

ALS. DLC–JKP. Addressed to Columbia and marked *"Private."* Polk's AE on the cover states that he answered this letter on December 24, 1842; Polk's reply has not been found.

1. Tennessee's Constitution of 1834 required that the General Assembly designate and fix the state's seat of government in 1843. Nashville and Murfreesboro were prime contenders for the permanent seat of government.

2. The quotation is from James Madison's speech to the Constitutional Convention on August 11, 1787. Notes on the speech have been published in Robert A. Rutland et al., eds., *The Papers of James Madison* (12 vols.—; Charlottesville: University Press of Virginia, 1962—), X, 145–46.

3. Smith, a Rutherford County Democrat, served one term in the Tennessee House, 1839–41. Currin, a Murfreesboro lawyer and Democrat, moved to Memphis and served one term in the Tennessee House, 1851–53.

FROM SAMUEL H. LAUGHLIN

My dear Sir,   McMinnville, December 23, 1842

On my return home from Woodbury, on yesterday, where I had been since Monday last, I received your letter of the 15th inst.[1] and hasten to reply to it by to-day's mail. I am greatly pleased to hear of the favorable appearance of matters in the Western District. I had previously been informed by your brother[2] in Nashville, during the first week of the Supreme Court, that you had returned from the South to Columbia, and that there was a good prospect of some favorable arrangements as to candidates in the West, especially in the Hardeman Congressional district.[3] On the whole, I think our political affairs in Tennessee wear a good aspect. In the Congressional districts we have been wronged. I voted against the whole arrangement. Even in this district Turney contrived to do us great injustice.[4] He united with the Whigs in putting Cannon to the Rutherford district,[5] making its population 72,000 and leaving this district but 61,000. Whereas, if Cannon had been left where she desired to be placed, one district would have had 65,000 and the other 68,000. He did this to give the preponderance in the number of votes in this district to the Country east and north of the Caney fork, intending to be a candidate in time to come. Hop[6] did not get to Nashville in time, or this would have been prevented. Sam now intends to run for the Senate, and is the only democrat in his district who can be elected. He is pledged to Hop and myself to run for the Senate—and will help me for Congress with all his might against anybody, but especially Cullom[7] whom he hates, if Cullom should become a candidate which I hope he will not. He has strong *inclinations* however, although he confidentially informed me long before any bill passed,[8] that he had not the slightest wish to offer in any possible event. I had consulted him as a friend, and informed him in confidence, that I expected to be a candidate, and desired to be in the next Congress, but believed that I should not desire a re-election. He is a selfish man, and the Whigs of Jackson and White are pressing him hard. He says the democrats in his quarter are dissatisfied at my becoming a candidate to soon. The time I left to Hill, Locke, Gen. Smartt, Ford and other friends in Coffee &c.[9] They announced me before I came home from Nashville at the close of the session; and deemed it absolutely necessary to do so to prevent Mr. Hopkins and possibly others from popping out before me—things which would have produced perfect distraction in the district. Hopkins of course will not interfere with me. I am not sure that Cullom will stand back. He has literally done nothing since 1835. The Whigs of course hate him less than they do me. Judge Caruthers[10] and his strikers, who wish to remove him as a candidate for Judge next fall are pressing him—and with the Whigs, and a wing of the democracy in Overton, Jackson and Fentress, he may beat me. The leading democrats of White are for me to a man—on this side of the Caney fork he cannot get 50 democratic votes. The democratic majority in the district is about 1100—and the majority of the entire vote of the district above the Caney fork is about 1000. So stand matters. Some of our friends have, I believe, written to Cullom to try to keep him back and prevent a split. Others will do so; I hope how many. He still says he dont wish to offer, but I dont believe it. If he does, the Whigs can elect a man by a plurality. I have no wish or desire to serve in but one Congress. I shall want something else afterwards or nothing.

Ford's paper alludes to a young man named Minnis, living at Sparta, formerly of Jackson.[11] He is nobody—but he is in correspondence with Cullom. I have my spies on all of them—as far as is proper for my own safety and government. I wish you could see Cullom. You have promoted him—and a word from you, predicated on his declarations to everybody that he does not wish to run *now*, would settle him—a word deprecating the evils of a split. I am in great trouble about the business.

In this county we have no candidates. In Cannon, H. Trott[12] will be elected without opposition. Northcutt[13] is removing from the state. In DeKalb, two Whigs are out.[14] The County is nearly balanced between the parties. In due time our folks will start a man—I think Col. Tubbs[15] living in the Smith portion of the County. It is possible Hopkins will offer for the Senate here, but Lowry or Gen. Patton will most likely be the Senator.[16] In White, England and Gen. J. B. Rodgers, Whigs, are said to be candidates for floater from White, Fentress & Van Buren.[17]

I have visited DeKalb to advise our friends. I shall go to Van Buren next week. I have written to Batey and Gresham in Fentress,[18] advising them to harmonize with the democracy of the district, and act in concert as we have much at stake. If Fentress or Van Buren, on agreement, shall run a democrat, in harmony, he will be elected. Blackwell is out in 3rd district.

If I was clear of Cullom, I could with the aid of Sam Turney, carry everything in the district except the two representatives from White and Jackson. I wish I was clear of him. Can you devise no plan. He has lately, as he came to Nashville, visited Gen. Jackson. He pretends to reverance him greatly. I wish to[19] old Chief had admonished him of the evil of splits, and of the[20] greater evil of being taken up by the Whigs. If he had done so, it would have been of powerful influence. A word from him would settle it now.

S. H. LAUGHLIN

N.B. Write as often as convenience may permit.[21]

ALS. DLC–JKP. Addressed to Columbia and marked "Private."

1. Letter not found.
2. William H. Polk.
3. Tennessee's Tenth Congressional District.
4. References are to Samuel Turney and Tennessee's Fourth Congressional District, which included Warren, Coffee, Van Buren, White, DeKalb, Jackson, Overton, and Fentress counties.
5. The Seventh Congressional District, which included Rutherford, Cannon, Wilson, and Williamson counties.
6. Hopkins L. Turney, the brother of Samuel Turney.
7. Alvin Cullom, a lawyer and a Democrat, represented Overton County for one term in the Tennessee House, 1835–37, and served two terms in the U.S. House, 1843–47. He was judge of the Fourth Judicial Circuit of Tennessee from 1850 until 1852.
8. Reference is to congressional redistricting legislation.

9. Hugh L. W. Hill, William C. Smartt, and John W. Ford; Locke is not identified further. A farmer in Warren County since 1806, Smartt attained the rank of brigadier general in the militia following the War of 1812; he served one term in the Tennessee House, 1817–19, and two terms in the Senate, 1821–23 and 1825–27.

10. Abram Caruthers, a brother of Robert L. Caruthers, was judge of Tennessee's Fourth Judicial Circuit from 1836 until 1847.

11. John A. Minnis, a Democrat and lawyer at Sparta, formerly from Gainesboro in Jackson County, represented White and other counties for one term in the Tennessee Senate, 1847–49; later he moved to Chattanooga and won election to the Senate for a second term, 1859–61. The appropriate issues of the McMinnville *Central Gazette* have not been found.

12. A farmer and merchant in Woodbury, Henry Trott served as the first clerk and master of the Chancery Court in Cannon County, 1836–42, and represented that county as a Democrat for two terms in the Tennessee House, 1843–47.

13. Woodson Northcutt, a farmer, represented Warren County in the Tennessee House as a Democrat from 1833 until 1841; he moved to Alabama and served in that state's legislature from 1845 until 1849.

14. Not identified further. Daniel Coggin, a Whig and lawyer from Smithville, won the DeKalb County race for the Tennessee House in 1843.

15. Possibly James Tubbs, who resided in Smith County prior to the creation of DeKalb County in 1838; Tubbs was a native of South Carolina.

16. Thomas H. Hopkins, William A. Lowery, and Alexander E. Patton. Lowery, a farmer and saddler in Warren County, served one term as a Democrat in the Tennessee Senate, 1837–39. Patton, a resident of Pelham in Franklin County, is not identified further. Laughlin dropped his congressional bid and won reelection to the Tennessee Senate in 1843.

17. John England and John B. Rogers. England, a White County farmer and horse-breeder, served a single term as a Whig in the Tennessee House, 1841–43. Rogers, a lawyer at Sparta, represented White, Fentress, and Van Buren counties for one term as a Whig in the Tennessee House, 1843–45; later residing in McMinnville, he won election to one term in the Tennessee Senate, 1867–69.

18. Batey and Thomas Grisham. Batey, a Democrat, resided in the Obey and Wolf rivers area of Fentress County; for an earlier reference to him, see Laughlin to Polk, June 21, 1840.

19. Laughlin wrote "to" for the word "the."

20. The remainder of this paragraph, the closing, and the signature are written in the right margin of the document's final page.

21. Laughlin's postscript is written in the left margin of the first page.

FROM SACKFIELD MACLIN

La Grange, Tennessee. December 23, 1842

Maclin states that the gentlemen of Memphis who invited Polk to speak in that place feel neglected and would appreciate an answer to their letter, which Maclin says he handed to Polk.[1] Polk's recent speech at La Grange converted some of the Whigs.[2] In Maclin's opinion Polk can beat Jones by five thousand votes; however, Dunlap's efforts to have Fentress or Miller[3] run for Congress will endanger the election of Democratic legislators in the area. Maclin has written Dunlap encouraging him to run, for he can defeat J. B. Ashe, the probable Whig candidate.[4] The recent dissatisfaction by "merchants, Shavers, and money dealers" over Maclin's vote for the court bill[5] has subsided, and the local Democrats will come out for the bill since four-fifths of the people in the area favor the measure.

ALS. DLC–JKP. Addressed to Columbia and marked *"Private."*

1. Letter not found. Polk probably declined the invitation through Adam Huntsman. See Huntsman to Polk, October 20, 1842.

2. Polk took advantage of a trip to his plantation in Mississippi to make several political speeches, at least two of which were in late November at La Grange and Jackson.

3. David Fentress and Austin Miller. Miller practiced law in Bolivar; served as Eleventh Circuit Court judge, 1836–38; and won election as a Democrat to three terms in the Tennessee House, 1843–47 and 1861–63.

4. John B. Ashe, member of a prominent North Carolina family, practiced law in Brownsville and served as a Whig in the Tennessee Senate for two terms, 1839–43.

5. See William H. Polk to Polk, October 18, 1842.

FROM JOHN CATRON

My dear Sir.   Washington Decr 25th, 1842

Our frd. A. V. Brown informs me you wish a negotiation for 4000 d. at N. York, to right up your affairs, & put you in comfort. I know no one in N. York save a few lawyers, who will be here in a few days, when I will give any aid in my way. Now my frd. the little sums you got fr. me you need not provide for, as I am free from debt, well sheltered, & well salaried. In the next place, If you want a sponsor, I will be one, & A. V. Brown says he'l be another, which is all needed for 4000 d.

Nothing is yet settled here—Congress sober, & at work—scared by the charge of idleness during the last session. The Whigs are depressed at all points I have seen, & are disponding of Mr. Clay's prospects; still they cannot induce his numerous & rich friends to agree but that he is the stronger "Richmond."[1] The mass think Scott is, & Buchanan says in the end he thinks that Clay & Scott will give way & that Judge McLean[2] will be run. Now I don't think Clay will ever assent; he would prefer Scott. Judging from what I have heard from the Ky people and from the same authority, I think Mr Clay will not withdraw, let what will come. Certain it is his especial Ky frds must change their minds, that agst. a very fixd. purpose to the Contrary.

I think the indications here too strong to admit of doubt that Mr. Van Buren will be run. It seems now to lie between him & Mr. Calhoun.

Old Te-cumseh[3] says he'l go in for the race—wears a red Jacket, & looks the warrior. But he is for the old place of Vice. How he stands I have not yet learned sufficiently to give a fair guess. Buchanan also said to me he thought the indications were *now* for Van B. & yourself. This is a ground, if as well defined as Mr. B. thinks, of course, will be pressd. V.B. is weak before the people; but as a man of established doctrines strong. More of this anon.

Should be happy to hear from you, & the news at home.

No Whig West of the mountain[4] will again run for Congress, says A. V. Brown, except Milton B.[5] All in health & well housed at Brown's.[6]

My sincere regards to Mrs P. For yourself accept my best wishes.

J CATRON

ALS. DLC–JKP. Addressed to Columbia. Polk's AE on the cover states that he answered this letter on January 3, 1843; Polk's reply has not been found.

1. Allusion is to a line from William Shakespeare's *King Richard III*, act 5, scene 4 and refers to Henry, Earl of Richmond, afterwards Henry VII. "I think there be six Richmonds in the field: Five I have slain today instead of him."

2. John McLean of Ohio served four years in the U.S. House, 1812–16, and five years on the Ohio Supreme Court, 1816–21; he was appointed postmaster general by Monroe in 1823 and was reappointed by President John Q. Adams. Declining a place in Jackson's cabinet, McLean became an associate justice of the U.S. Supreme Court in 1829 and served until his death in 1861. During his years on the federal bench he was often mentioned as a possible presidential candidate.

3. Richard M. Johnson.

4. Reference is to the Cumberland Plateau of Tennessee.

5. Milton Brown.

6. Reference probably is to Brown's Hotel in Washington.

FROM JOHN W. CHILDRESS[1]

Murfreesboro, Tennessee. December 26, 1842

Childress recalls Polk's earlier offer to purchase a saddle horse needed for the 1843 campaign; now in need of extra money Childress agrees to sell. Henderson's reinstatement as postmaster[2] has not excited the Whigs; all of the Democrats are pleased, except Keeble,[3] who denounces his party and may join his wife's Whig kin.[4] Childress accepts the loss, which some Democrats would encourage. Rutherford County Whigs will field a strong ticket for the state legislature; Democrats will run candidates for the lower house, but none for the state senate or congressional seats. Some observers think that a bi-partisan effort to make

Murfreesboro the state capital might produce a compromise ticket, but Childress thinks that "party feelings will in all probability overcome their sense of interest." Nicholson likely will stand for the legislature from Maury County. Reportedly Watterson's friends in Bedford County are displeased with Polk, for they suspect that he favors Long over Watterson in that congressional district.[5]

ALS. DLC–JKP. Addressed to Columbia. Polk's AE on the cover states that he answered this letter on January 2, 1843; Polk's reply has not been found.
1. A younger brother of Sarah Polk, Childress lived in Murfreesboro where he practiced law.
2. Greenville T. Henderson served as postmaster of Murfreesboro from December 2, 1840, until June 4, 1841; he won reinstatement on December 13, 1842.
3. Edwin A. Keeble, editor of the Murfreesboro *Monitor*, served as mayor of Murfreesboro in 1838 and again in 1855; he won his race for presidential elector on the Buchanan ticket in 1856. Keeble's wife, Sally, was John Bell's daughter.
4. On December 29, 1842, Childress again advised Polk of Keeble's hostility and his plans to work against the Democratic party. ALS. DLC–JKP.
5. Under the terms of the 1842 redistricting legislation Tennessee's Fifth Congressional District included Bedford, Lincoln, Marshall, and Franklin counties.

FROM AARON V. BROWN

Dear Sir   Washington Decr. 27th 1842
    Your late letters[1] have come safely to hand & I now proceed to answer them. On the arrival of Judge Catron a consultation was held as to the best mode of ascertaining whether a loan could be negotiated for you or not.[2] Catron will see Butler of N.Y. so soon as he reaches here. Johnson will try through Vanderpoal, whilst I will try to do something through Faris of N.Y. & Ingersall (C. J.) of Philadelphia.[3] I do not think we constitute a good board of commissioners, but we will not fail to do our best. I have had an interview with some of the money dealers of this City, who express the opinion that such an arrangement could be hardly made in this City.
    In relation to the other matter, I have to say that though at a distance, you have formed a very just opinion of the present position of parties & your relation to them on reference to the Vice Presidency. If Van Buren gets the nomination—your position, will place you on the same ticket—with Johnson[4] your only competition. The fact of his having *campaigned* for the first office—against Van Buren, Buchanon, Calhoun & all others will probably cancel his claims on the score of restoration & make no one interest anxious to take him up. At least such is the present

appearance of things. Van Buren I think will be the nomenee, & if your present friendly relations with Mr. Calhoun & his friends can be preserved, I think there is no doubt in the case. This will be very difficult to be done. His friends are zealous & when we answer that we are for the nominee, then they want to know how Tennessee will vote in the convention. Evasion of that question leads to suspicion that Tennessee is for Van B. & that the fact is suppressd. from *policy.* Did you ever correspond with Ellmore?[5] Pickens told me today that he had seen it & that it was perfectly non committal. He did not speak of it complainingly in other respects but still I wanted to know how *he* became acquainted with the fact, if it were so.

Mr C's friends want the convention postponed untill spring 12 months—to give time they say for a full expression of the party wishes in the case. We still insist on the time fixed by our friends in the Legislature.[6] They[7] insist not only on the furthest time, but wish it to be one of the principles of action in the convention that each Congressional district shall have a vote & that it shall be given directly as the vote of that district & *not* by the delegates getting together & balloting amongst themselves & which ever shall get the majority carry the vote of that state. They plead intensely for this & as the news papers will presently be full of it, I submit it early for your consideration. I do not see at present how such a rule would hurt *you* & if it did not I should not care to dissent from Mr. C's friends in establishing it. I do not think any rule or mode of voting would Save him—but I want him to have as little cause of complaint as possible. I do not think any thing is to be apprehended from Stephenson or King.[8]

In relation to myself & whether I shall be again a candidate, I am in much perplexity. If possible I should like very much to be in the 28 Congress, in reference to the subject about which I am now writing—but the number of my children—the feeble health of my wife[9] & the almost total neglect of my private affairs for several years past—admonish me of the difficulties in the way of my offering. But I will take my position in a few weeks one way or the other & I desire you to say to your Brother[10] that such will be the case & that I hope the delay will not incommode him in his views.

I have a strong inclination to settle at Columbia for the Education of my children—renting first & buying after my means would enable me to do so with convenience. It is a position more elegible than Giles for purposes of education or of politics—for you must remember *the state must have governors after your time & all* my colleagues here insist that I shall *keep in position,* whether I offer for Congress or not. Moving objects are however the only ones that catch the public eye & it is therefore probable that if I retire for two years however essential to my private affairs—the democracy of the State would learn to do without me & leave me to that obscurity, to which my necessities might have driven me. On the whole I must beg of my friends to give me a little more time to make a decision of so important a matter as this is growing up to be in my future destiny.

My best regards to Mrs. Polk with the assurances that I should be very happy to continue in Congress, untill I saw her safely installed for 4 years in the house right opposite the Presidents lately occupied by Lrd. Ashburton. The very one in which "the mistress Vice President" should reside.

A V BROWN

ALS. DLC–JKP. Addressed to Columbia. Polk's AE on the cover states that he answered this letter on January 13, 1843; Polk's reply has not been found.

1. Letters not found.
2. See John Catron to Polk, December 25, 1842.
3. Cave Johnson, Aaron Vanderpoel, Charles G. Ferris, and Charles J. Ingersoll. Vanderpoel, a lawyer, served in the New York Assembly, 1826–30; in the U.S. House, 1833–37 and 1839–41; and on the Superior Court in New York City, 1842–50. Ferris, a native of the Bronx, practiced law in New York City and won election twice to the U.S. House, 1834–35 and 1841–43.
4. Richard Mentor Johnson.
5. See Franklin H. Elmore to Polk, June 13, 1842.
6. See Samuel H. Laughlin to Polk, October 11, 1842.
7. Reference is to Calhoun's friends; see Cave Johnson to Polk, December 18, 1842.
8. Andrew Stevenson and William R. King.
9. Sarah Burruss Brown, the mother of Brown's five children by his first marriage.
10. William H. Polk.

FROM J. G. M. RAMSEY

Mecklenburg, Tennessee. December 28, 1842

Ramsey recalls what he has written to Col. McMullen at Richmond,[1] presenting Tennessee's views in regard to the next National Democratic Convention and campaign: the Tennessee Democracy's position should be made known at the Virginia Democratic convention in March and in the Virginia legislature during the winter of 1842–43; the National Democratic Convention should be held in November of 1843 rather than May of 1844[2]; Johnson's name on the Democratic ticket would threaten the success of that ticket all over the union and especially in

Tennessee; the Democratic party in the union owed much to Polk; the party in Tennessee owed him everything; and Polk would bring stronger support to the ticket in 1844 than would any other man in the union. Ramsey concludes his letter to Polk by reporting the names and prospects of several East Tennessee candidates in the 1843 elections.

ALS. DLC–JKP. Addressed to Columbia.
1. Fayette McMullen, a teamster, farmer, and banker, served as a Democrat in the Virginia Senate, 1839–49, and sat in the U.S. Congress, 1849–57. He was governor of the Washington Territory from 1857 until 1861.
2. See Samuel H. Laughlin to Polk, October 11, 1842.

FROM WILLIAM FITZGERALD

Dr. Sir   Paris Decr 29, 1842
Since writing to you a few days since[1] I have rec'd a letter from our friend C. Johnson & regret to say that he most positively declines a reelection. So we must do the best we can. There is to be a convention for the purpose of nominating a candidate for Congress at Dover on the 18th Feb. next. I reckon Mr. Hardwick[2] will be the nominee. There is already a candidate out here, Mr. James T Dunlap. I have not learned whether he will be willing to rest his pretentions with the convention. I will try to get him to do so.

I think we have a fair prospect for collision in our ranks for the presidency. I apprehend a breaking up of our party so soon as a nomination is made. I fear Calhoun's friends will not yield to a nomination. If so the south will separate from us. I am decidedly for Calhoun but will leave him if he is not the choice of a fairly gotten-up convention of Democrats. I am for the principles of our party whether to be administered by a Northern or a Southern man—yet I prefer the Southern be run.

                                                          WM FITZGERALD
NB. I think the Whigs here are about bringing out Judge Martin of Clarksville for Congress. W.F.

ALS. DLC–JKP. Addressed to Columbia.
1. On December 25, 1842, Fitzgerald wrote Polk that Cave Johnson would probably decline to run for reelection to Congress. Fitzgerald recommended Judge William R. Harris as Johnson's successor and urged Polk to write Harris and recruit him for the Democratic ticket. ALS. DLC–JKP.
2. Jonathan P. Hardwicke.

1843

FROM TIMOTHY KEZER

Dear Sir   Nashville Jan. 1—[1843][1]

I Rcd. last night a list of the Several County Committees, together with a communication from the Maury Committee, and your letter advising us that the document intended for general circulation was also forwarded.[2] The latter however did not come, and the object of this letter is to notify you of that fact. We would have supplied the deficiency, by writing one ourselves, but deemed it advisable to wait for your plan, knowing that it would be better addapted to the end in view. We hope therefore to receive it by tuesdays mail, that we may be enabled to send them to all parts of the state by saturday night.[3] The Committee[4] met, last night, and matured some plans for a more vigorous action in future. We made out a list of all the persons in our County, to whom we are to apply for money, to set our War in motion.

I have had a talk with Col. Guild, and assured him that the whole democracy of Davidson would support him to a man, with enthusiasm. He says he could beat any Davidson County Whig. Tomorrow we intend to call on him—all of us together—and endeavour to obtain his consent to run. Not letting it be known that we have anything to do with it, he making the announcement at Gallatin. We will then write letters to the Sumner and Smith Committees expressive of approval, and entire willingness to unite on him. Our County Candidate will be attended to this week if possible.

The Whigs are already before hand of us in this county. They are—as we have learnt since you left us—perfectly organized. Every civil district has four men, whose duty it is to register and report an exact state of the two parties—names and politicks.

Rest assured however that we will give them the best fight, they ever encountered in this County.

I have Rcd. a letter from Col. Laughlin informing me that he had sent two of his warm and influential friends—one from Coffee the other from Warren—to Mr Cullum,[5] offering to submit his claims to a District Convention, pledging himself and friends to support Mr Cullum, or any third person selected, provided Mr Cullum will promise the same on his part.

T. Kezer

ALS. DLC–JKP. Addressed to Columbia. Polk's AE on the cover states that he answered this letter on January 2, 1843; Polk's reply has not been found.

1. Kezer wrote "1842"; year identified through content analysis.
2. Polk's letter is not identified further; the document "intended for general circulation" has not been found.
3. A general circular, attributed to the Maury County Democratic corresponding committee, was sent to county corresponding committees throughout the state, suggesting organizational plans for the state elections in August. See Polk to Samuel H. Laughlin, January 6, 1843, and Thomas Hogan to Polk, January 17, 1843.
4. The Davidson County Democratic corresponding committee.
5. Alvin Cullom.

FROM CAVE JOHNSON

Dear Sir,   Washington 4 Jany 1843

I recd. yours of the 27th[1] today from Nashville. I recd. a letter from J. T. Dunlap shortly after my arrival & also one from Fitz[2] to both of which I answered urging them to have a Convention & but one Candidate run. In all my correspondence I have urged the same thing & I hope they will settle it amicably. I do not see how I am to run under any circumstances—a wife & two & prospects for a third[3]—poor & sickly & getting old. I cant upon my pay support them here if I could get them along safely & to leave them, I had as well be divorced. After being here 20 mo. out of 24 how can I spend all my time traversing hills & dales only again to be absent nearly all the time & make nothing. I am convinced our friends will have patriotism enough to run but one & I can do them perhaps more good as a private gentleman than a Candidate.

Foster has been to Springfield—and shortly after petitions were in circulation begging the Genl.[4] to run for the lower House—so as to secure Henry[5] in the Senate from Robertson & Montgomery. If that should be the movement I have urged J. W. Judkins (Cross plains) to run for Robertson—Dr P F Norfleet for the Senate (of Port Royal)) and Joseph

Sturdevant (Clarksville 7 miles below) to run for Montgomery.[6] That ticket will secure us Robertson & Montgomery in the Senate & the House in Montgomery. Sturdevant is a Virginia lawyer, democrat & Methodist, of good sense & unexceptionable character. Norfleet is a man of fine sense, speaks well and a Baptist. J. W. Judkins is a merchant active, keen & shrewd & personally beloved by every one except the Cheatham gang. I mention these things to you that you may not press W. B. J. or Jas Dortch, neither of whom tho personally popular would do as well as the others.[7] They have been too much identified in all my races. I have written them to use all proper means to get the others out. With that ticket we can not be beaten for the Senate or in Montgomery. In all the other Counties we are safe. Cherry[8] should be made to run in Stewart. I fear some difficulty, tho no danger in Dickson. Majr. Young (Yellow Creek) is violently opposed to Hardwicke & Eubanks & wishes to run himself.[9] I fear his personal popularity is not sufficient. Robert McNeily[10] is our best man in that County tho not so popular as Eubanks. He discusses the questions well. If Hardwicke runs for Congress I presume Gray will run for the Senate. The people of Humphreys & Benton will never be fooled again. Wiley[11] will do very well.

So much for home affairs. Here we hear nothing of political movements except from the friends of Calhoun. They are unwilling to [agree to] a convention before the next Congress for obvious reasons. Calhoun's treaty speech[12] looks a little squally. He contrasts with evident pleasure, the course of Webster & himself with the conduct of the preceding Administrations greatly to the disadvantage of the latter upon the slavery questions arising from the Capture of some of our ships. Would you be surprised to see him & Webster fighting side by side in the next presidential Campaign? Suppose they make a treaty with Mexico & Texas & acquire Texas for us. How will that work? especially if they can show as is hinted, that Van B.[13] & his Cabinet opposed any treaty or purchase. Whatever can be done by the Executive to operate in the next elections will be done & when they Cease to hope for themselves will be thrown on that side. I have been greatly disgusted with the course of his friends in defeating Bedford Brown[14]—just as they did in defeating J W Jones[15]— and just as they will do if they can in the presidential race. The Mercury[16] justifies the Course of his friends in defeating Brown. In the same way Rhett was defeated by Pickens friends voting for Huger, an old Federalist & latitudinarian, more recently however a Union Man.[17]

Cass is here. I think there is more danger of his being taken up for Vice than old Dick notwithstanding the Missouri nomination.[18] We are exceedingly cautious here, lest the friends of Calhoun hold the balance on that question in the Convention after his claims are rejected.

I am prepared the first chance to say a word about Milton Browns letter.[19] We expect a Coffee Bill brought in. From your speech you had forgotten some important facts. Jackson reco. reduction in Coffee & Teas Dec 8' 1829.[20] McDuffie reported a Bill & passed it[21]—all voting for it in the spring of 1830. In the Bill of 1832, which you advocated it was made free.[22] We voted for it. Verplanks Bill is now copying for you & be soon ready for you—in which a duty of a Cent was laid—& we voted agt. the motion to strike out.[23] Brown has made a most infamous perversion of our Course which I will endeavor to expose. He made a speech agt. repealing the Bankrupt Law & perverted Bentons speech and Walls report as much as he has our Course.[24] He is a vain, silly, weak no account sort of man. I have pressed AVB[25] very much to offer & I think he will tho still hesitating.

I am to be mesmerized by Theo. Fisk[26] in a few days. I wish to see if it will have any effect on my nervous system. Fisk says it will cure me. Tho I keep about the pain in my shoulder & left arm is very bad. I am very much troubled to get my coat off or on and shall not be surprised if I loose its use altogether. Owing to this I seldom leave my room except going to the Capitol.

I doubt whether we could all agree on a circular.[27] We will however try. We talk of a caucus to recomend *the time* & place for a convention & *the manner*. The G[l]obe is much urged to still insist on the Spring of 1844 but he[28] declines & expressed himself satisfied with the Ten. recomendations[29] yet will not come out. He fears the South is the next election for printer.

We ought to make McKay speaker next time. J. W. J.[30] has been silent—could not be kicked into our defence.

C. JOHNSON

ALS. DLC–JKP. Addressed to Columbia and marked *"Private."* Polk's AE on the cover states that he answered this letter on January 14, 1843; Polk's reply has not been found.

1. Letter not found.

2. William Fitzgerald. See Cave Johnson to Polk, December 18, 1842, and Fitzgerald to Polk, December 29, 1842.

3. Cave and Elizabeth Dortch Brunson Johnson had three children who survived. James Hickman and Thomas Dickson Johnson were born in 1840 and 1842, respectively. Polk Grundy Johnson was not born until November 2, 1844.

4. Reference is to Richard Cheatham, a Springfield merchant and farmer. He represented Robertson County in the Tennessee House for five terms, 1825–33 and 1843–45, and won election as a Whig to one term in the U.S. House, 1837–39.

5. A Kentucky lawyer and businessman, Gustavus A. Henry served one term

in the Kentucky legislature, 1831–33, before moving to Clarksville, Tennessee. An active Whig, Henry won election to the electoral college in 1840, 1844, and 1852, but lost bids for a seat in Congress in 1841 and for the governorship in 1853.

6. John W. Judkins, P. F. Norfleet, and Joseph Sturdevant. Judkins was a justice of the peace in Robertson County from 1840 until 1848. Norfleet and Sturdevant appear in the 1840 census in Montgomery County, but are not identified further.

7. Willie B. Johnson and James N. Dortch. Johnson, Cave's younger brother and a Clarksville lawyer, sat in the Tennessee Senate for one term, 1835–37, and served twelve years as attorney general for the Seventh Judicial District, 1839–51. Dortch, brother-in-law of Cave Johnson, ran unsuccessfully for a seat in the Tennessee House in 1841.

8. William B. Cherry, a farmer, represented Stewart County in the Tennessee House as a Democrat for three terms, 1839–45, and served as sheriff of that county from 1837 until 1840.

9. Jonathan P. Hardwicke, John Eubank, and probably William B. Young. Young, a Dickson County Democrat, is not identified further.

10. Robert McNeilly, a lawyer, farmer, and mill operator, represented Dickson County as a Democrat in the Tennessee House for one term, 1837–39, and served as circuit court clerk for twenty years, 1842–62.

11. James Wyly.

12. In August of 1842 Calhoun analyzed the proposed Webster-Ashburton Treaty, which was before the Senate in executive session; he pronounced it, on balance, favorable to the United States. Calhoun focused criticism on the treaty's failure to protect American slave property from search and seizure by the British navy. Calhoun did give Secretary of State Webster credit for having reviewed U.S. claims in certain slave cases and claimed some credit himself for having championed that interest during the previous decade.

13. Martin Van Buren.

14. See Johnson to Polk, December 18, 1842.

15. John W. Jones, a lawyer from Virginia, won election in 1835 to the U.S. House, where he served five consecutive terms; he was Speaker during his last term. In 1839 House Democrats had nominated Jones to succeed Polk as Speaker of the House; several Nullifiers refused to support the caucus nominee and thus defeated Jones' bid.

16. *Charleston Mercury.*

17. Robert Barnwell Rhett, Francis W. Pickens, and Daniel E. Huger. An extreme advocate of states' rights and a South Carolinian loyal to John C. Calhoun, Rhett served in the U.S. House from 1837 until 1849. He succeeded Calhoun in the U.S. Senate in 1850, but resigned his seat two years later. Through his newspaper, the *Charleston Mercury*, Rhett espoused the right of secession and inveighed against the South's reliance upon the Democratic party. He was at the head of those who led South Carolina out of the Union in late 1860. Huger, a Charleston lawyer, sat in the South Carolina House, 1804–19 and 1830,

and served as circuit court judge, 1819–30; on December 15, 1842, the South Carolina legislature chose Huger over both Rhett and Pickens to complete Calhoun's term in the U.S. Senate. Calhoun had announced in November his resignation from the Senate, effective at the end of the session.

18. The anti-Whig members of the Missouri legislature recently had nominated Martin Van Buren for president and Richard M. Johnson for vice-president; they also recommended the third Monday in November of 1843 as the date for the National Democratic Convention.

19. See Sarah C. Polk to Polk, November 7, 1842.

20. Reference is to President Jackson's First Annual Message.

21. George McDuffie, a lawyer, sat in the South Carolina House, 1818–1820; won election to seven terms in the U.S. House, 1821–34; served as governor of South Carolina, 1834–36; and won election twice to the U.S. Senate, 1842–46. On February 5, 1830, McDuffie, the chairman of the House Ways and Means Committee, reported a bill "to reduce the duties on tea and coffee"; the act was approved on May 20, 1830.

22. The tariff act of July 14, 1832, imposed no duty on coffee; some teas were free, others not. 4 U.S. Stat., 589, 590.

23. Gulian C. Verplanck, a New York lawyer, sat in the U.S. House as a Democrat, 1825–33, and in the New York Senate, 1838–41. Serving as chairman of the House Ways and Means Committee, he introduced the compromise tariff legislation of 1832–33. On February 21, 1833, in accordance with Democratic strategy, Polk and Johnson voted against an amendment to strike out the duty of one cent on coffee.

24. In his U.S. House speech of January 3, 1843, Milton Brown defended the Whigs' Bankruptcy law of 1841 against Democratic repeal efforts. Brown argued that portions of the law now under Democratic attack had been supported by the Democrats in 1840. He cited Benton's Senate speech of May 27, 1840, and the Democratic minority bill reported to the Senate by Garret D. Wall on May 12, 1840, as evidence of the Democrats' stance in 1840. Wall, a lawyer, sat in the New Jersey General Assembly in 1827, served as U.S. district attorney for that state in 1829, won election as governor but declined to serve in 1829, sat in the U.S. Senate as a Democrat, 1835–41, and served as judge of the Court of Errors and Appeals of New Jersey from 1848 until his death in 1850.

25. Aaron V. Brown.

26. Possible reference to Theophilus Fisk, who with A. F. Cunningham published the Portsmouth and Norfolk *Chronicle and Old Dominion* from 1839 until 1845. Fisk's "medical practice," if any, has not been identified.

27. Polk wanted the Democratic members of the Tennessee delegation to circulate a letter of rebuttal to Milton Brown's charge that in 1833 the Democrats had favored an import duty on coffee.

28. The Washington *Globe*'s editor, Francis P. Blair.

29. See Samuel H. Laughlin to Polk, October 11, 1842.

30. John W. Jones.

FROM HOPKINS L. TURNEY

Dear Sir   Washington Jan. the 4th 1843

Since I wrote,[1] I have visited Mr Benton several times in order to assertain, if I could, his feelings in relation to the Vice Presidency, but have never yet had a free conversation with him on the subject, for the reason that there was always some pearson there to prevent it. But from his B's general conversations I still think he is for you or at least that he is not for Johnson, the proceedings of the democratick members of the legislature of Mosouri to the contrary not with standing.[2] I have conversed freely with a large majority of the democrats of N.Y. including Mr Wright, and if there is truth in men, N. York will not only suport you in convention, but will exercise her influence beyond the limits of that state. They all give me every assurance that you are exclusively looked to by the friends of Mr. V. Burin[3] in New York and they further add that Van is decidedly for you. Then in convention you will certainly get New York, Maine, New Hampshire, Massachusits, Merriland, Virginia, North Carolina, Georgia, South Carolina, Alabama, Tennessee, Mississippa, Louisianna. Johnson cannot count sertin on moore than Kentucky, Illanois, Indianna & Mosouri, even if Benton and Buckannan[4] both do their best for him. Then you would stand the best chance for Connettacut, New Jersey, Rhode Island, Vermont, & Delaware, and an eaquil chance for Arkansas. Thus you will see that from my estimates you are almost certain to receive the nomination, and in fact, all here agree that if Van should be successful, that you as a matter of course will be the man. Now Sir I have given you a full and canded statement thus far, but Calhoon[5] is the competetor of Van for the nomination and if he should be successful it is your defeat. C. and his friends are making tremendus exertions but I think he is sinking rapidly. But there is a third party being made—it is the Tyler party. This party is composed of the *office seekers*, and a class of politicians who have no fixed political principles, but are for a *Sound Currency*. The most dangerous men of all others, they call themselves the moderate men of all parties—and besides it is roumerd here that Tyler will make a Treaty for the annexation of Texas to the United States. This is likely true, and if he does it will give him some strenth in the South. If he has any sense he will do it as he has all to gain and nothing to loose. However, whatever strenth he may buy up with his patronage, or acquire in any other way, will I think innure to the benefit of Calhoon.

Would it not be well if such a Treaty should be made to address a letter to Van and if you please to Calhoon also, calling for their opinions on the subject.

Waterson[6] now says he will not be a candidate for Congress. Jones I understand is verry anxous to run; in fact he writes so himself, and I know not what to do. I dislike to be in his way.

H. L. TURNEY

ALS. DLC–JKP. Addressed to Columbia. Polk's AE on the cover states that he answered this letter on January 14, 1843; Polk's reply has not been found.
1. See Hopkins L. Turney to Polk, December 8, 1842.
2. See Cave Johnson to Polk, January 4, 1842.
3. Martin Van Buren.
4. James Buchanan.
5. John C. Calhoun.
6. Harvey M. Watterson.

FROM GEORGE W. ROWLES

Most Esteemed Governor,   Cleveland, Tenn: January 5th 1843

On my return from the Circuit Court for McMinn County, I found your very acceptable communication of the 8th ult.[1]

Your views in relation to the objections that may be urged against the bounds of the second Congressional District, are undoubtedly correct. That physic is already operating—by August its results will be both felt and seen in a political point of view. The Bill was the base thing of our opponents; they passed it through the Senate and House by nearly a party vote. The journals demonstrate their responsibility.

I have seen from the public press that you are still making bold and fearless attacks on the strong holds of our opponents; I doubt not but the result will manifest itself in an increase of democratic strength.

You have before this seen my formal announcement "that private business" would prevent my being a Candidate for Congress or either branch of the Legislature.[2] It is unnecessary to assure you that this step was taken under circumstances which *no personal or political* friend could censure me for conforming to. Believing, that I shall have the pleasure of seeing you in the Spring, I shall say no more on the subject until then. Mr. Blackwell has *announced himself*.[3] He, or any other democrat, sound in principle and firm in his course, as I know him to be, shall receive my *warm* and *zealous* support. Mr. Torbitt I hope will have the field alone for Senator.[4] But in relation to senator there is different opinions, but these *will be* all reconciled. Torbitt must be the man. James Lauderdale[5] will run for county member for this county; Col. McMillin,[6] wishes to run. A convention perhaps will be called, if necessary, to settle the matter between them. Mr. Stevens, or Vaughn[7] will run I think it likely for Monroe County; it is uncertain who will run in McMinn.

The spirit of democracy here is looking *onward*. In August her old legion throughout all East-Tennessee, will again plant their banner on its former proud eminence. Under the lead of a tried Captain, who before has led them to victory, they will again enter the field of battle, to make another glorious struggle for their ancient faith.

Please have the goodness to present my kindest remembrance to your brother Maj. Polk,[8] and retain for yourself considerations of my highest regards and esteem.

GEO. W. ROWLES

P.S. I was married on the 2 inst. Mrs. Rowles[9] was a whig; she declares now though, she is "neither Loco nor whig, but for Maj. Rowles in all cases." G. W. ROWLES

ALS. DLC–JKP. Addressed to Columbia.

1. Letter not found.

2. Rowles' "formal announcement" has not been found.

3. Julius W. Blackwell announced as the Democratic candidate for Congress in Tennessee's Third Congressional District.

4. Granville C. Torbett, a Monroe County lawyer, served one term in the Tennessee House, 1841–43, and sat two terms in the Senate, 1843–47. In 1852 he moved to Nashville where he practiced law and in association with E. G. Eastman published the *Nashville American*.

5. James Lauderdale, a farmer and railroad promoter in Cleveland, served as sheriff of Bradley County from 1838 until 1842 and won election to two terms in the Tennessee House, 1843–47.

6. Joseph W. McMillin represented Bradley County in the Tennessee House for one term, 1839–41.

7. Henry H. Stephens and James Vaughn. Stephens, a member of the bar in Madisonville, won election to two terms in the Tennessee House, 1845–47 and 1851–53, and ran as presidential elector on the Democratic ticket in 1848. Vaughn, a resident of Madisonville, served as sheriff of Monroe County from 1834 until 1838.

8. William H. Polk.

9. Rowles married Mary Adelia Stout, daughter of Dr. Benjamin C. Stout.

FROM JULIUS W. BLACKWELL

Athens, Tennessee. January 6, 1843

Blackwell writes that he has announced for Congress and will probably face

Luke Lea. Blackwell believes that he can defeat "old Uncle Luke," and reports that Whig ranks have thinned since Polk spoke near Athens last August.[1] Democrats should run candidates for every office, even in strong Whig counties, in order to maximize the Democratic vote. If that course had been followed before, Knox County "would not have been so *Blue* in 1840 & 41."

ALS. DLC–JKP. Addressed to Columbia. Polk's AE on the cover states that he answered this letter on January 17, 1843; Polk's reply has not been found.
1. See Alexander O. Anderson to Polk, July 24, 1842, and Daniel Graham to Polk, August 11, 1842.

FROM AARON V. BROWN

Dear Sir   Washington January 6th 1843

On my return from Missii. I staid but a few days at Pulaski & these were devoted almost entirely to business. I then had but little idea of being a candidate. But sence my arrival here, the applications have been such as to induce me to write my Brother & Thos. Martin[1] on the subject of the effect of such a step on my private affairs, which they know as much about as I do and which are somewhat involved as you may well immagine. If they write favorably I expect to offer; otherwise, if they do not. In the mean time if it be injurious to our party interest to let the matter lay over so long, rather than do that injury I would rather you would set me aside at once & take measures to start some body else. If however such delay will do no special harm I will "try to come it" on reaching replies from my friends which I suppose will not be very long, if those replies will allow of it. I dislike this hesitation & delay as much as any body can do, but I cannot prevent it, but by stepping aside & opening the way to somebody else, which I am perfectly willing to do.

You see the Missouri nominations.[2] Sevier[3] I understand says that *Johnson* will not accept a nomination for *Vice*. This however I can hardly credit.

The under currents begin to run pretty rapidly & the parties shew a good deal of anxiety about the nomination, & many doubt (of our friends) whether a convention *can* be *so* held so as to give satisfaction.

I think Tyler's notion now is not to build up a special or third party, but so to manage as to come in *as one of the Democracy* for a nomination by the Convention. Try for that & if he cant succeed for himself, he & most of his friends go for Mr. Calhoun—vain hope! Write to me about the *time* & manner of voting in the convention as mentioned in my last letter.[4]

Who lives in the house *north* of Judge Macks[5] & *South* of where Mrs. Rivers or Mrs. Booker lives?[6] I think someone said it had been purchased by the Bank.[7] Could it be rented? If not what other comfortable establishment convenient to the Academy[8] could be rented, and where on your street between the square & the academy. Whether I offer or not, I have pretty well concluded to come to Columbia in order to educate my children.

A. V. BROWN

ALS. DLC–JKP. Addressed to Columbia. Polk's AE on the cover states that he answered this letter on January 17, 1843; Polk's reply has not been found.

1. William R. Brown and Thomas Martin. Brown, a well-to-do farmer in Giles County and older brother of Aaron V. Brown, served one term in the Tennessee House, 1837–39. Martin, a Giles County businessman who later became president of the Louisville and Nashville Railroad, staunchly supported both Jackson and Polk; he declined appointment as secretary of the Treasury in the Polk administration.

2. See Cave Johnson to Polk, January 4, 1843.

3. Ambrose H. Sevier, U.S. senator from Arkansas married the niece of Richard M. Johnson, Juliette Johnson Sevier, in 1827.

4. See Brown to Polk, December 27, 1842.

5. Robert Mack, lawyer, poet, and member of one of Maury County's pioneer families, served on the Circuit Court bench from 1822 until 1828; he was related by marriage to Aaron V. Brown.

6. Myra Rhodes Rivers and Cynthia Holland Rhodes Booker. Myra, widow of John H. Rivers and later wife of Joseph H. Trotter, was the daughter of Tyree and Cynthia Holland Rhodes. Cynthia Rhodes subsequently married Peter R. Booker of Columbia.

7. Reference is to the Columbia branch of the Bank of Tennessee.

8. Reference is to the Columbia Female Institute, founded in 1835 and located west of Polk's residence on West Market Street, now denominated, "West Seventh Street."

TO SAMUEL H. LAUGHLIN

My Dear Sir,   Columbia Jany 6th 1843

Our committee here, have addressed a letter of which the enclosed[1] is a copy to every County in the State, except some four or five, where they could not learn the names of suitable persons to whom to address. They request me to forward the enclosed one for Van Buren[2] to you with a request, that you will address & forward it to the proper persons. They request also that you will furnish me with the names of the persons to whom you may address it. They have sent none to the new County of *Putnam*. If you think they should do so, send me the names and it will be attended to.

I regret exceedingly that any collision among friends has arisen in the mountain District,[3] and hope as you have been announced that it may be amicably arranged & that you may run without opposition. Mr. Kezer writes to me that a proposition had been made by your friends to leave the matter to a District Convention.[4] This is right, and was the only prudent course left, after it became certain that there would otherwise be a conflict among political friends. The proposition is such an one as cannot be declined. I would do anything in my power to reconcile these differences, but really I do not know what it is in my power to do more than has been done. There is danger that any attempted interference on my part might be construed into *Dictation* and still widen the breach. The letter of our committee here, which has been sent, will I hope have a happy influence.

I send you below, the names of the persons in the several Counties in your District[5] to whom it has been sent.

JAMES K. POLK

P.S. The following are the names & Counties referred above, viz:[6]

ALS. DLC–JKP. Addressed to McMinnville and marked *"Private."* Laughlin's AE on the cover states that the enclosure was sent to "Worthington and others." See notes 1 and 6 below. Published in *ETHSP*, XVIII, pp. 161–62.

1. Enclosure not found. See Timothy Kezer to Polk, January 1, 1843, and Thomas Hogan to Polk, January 17, 1843.

2. Reference is to Van Buren County.

3. See Laughlin to Polk, December 23, 1842.

4. See Timothy Kezer to Polk, January 1, 1843.

5. The Fourth Congressional District of Tennessee.

6. Polk's postscript includes the following list: Liberty, DeKalb County, Thomas W. Duncan, Thomas Whaley, Thomas Durham, and William H. Judkins; Hillsboro, Coffee County, Archibald Price, Alexander E. Patton, Isaac H. Roberts, Reuben Price, Lecil Bobo, and William S. Watterson; Sparta, White County, Isaac Taylor, Samuel Turney, Robert L. Mitchell, Henry Lyda, and J. C. Davis; Livingston, Overton County, Alvin Cullom, Hardin P. Oglesby, Creed Taylor Huddleston, Landon Armstrong, and Hiter; Jamestown, Fentress County, David Beaty and Thomas Grisham; and Gainesboro, Jackson County, Alexander Montgomery, Amos Kirkpatrick, Absolom Johnson, James Smith, and Matthew Cowen. Van Buren and Putnam counties are left blank; Laughlin's AE on the cover indicates that William Worthington was the Van Buren County recipient.

FROM WILLIAMSON SMITH

My Dear Sir,   Washington City 10th Jany 1843

Yours of the 15th Ult.[1] was received on my arrival here, on the 31st and in obedience to your request I sit down to give you a sketch of matters and things here. I am not likely to succeed in any portion of my business here. My claim is before the Judiciary Committee and the party lines are strictly & tightly drawn upon me. I had reason to believe Gov. Morehead from Kentucky could & would render me important service in the matter[2] but the lines are so tight drawn they cannot be broke. Judge Milton Brown from Ten. being one of the principal actors in the play, perhaps the time may come when he will be out of my way. I shall in a day or two leave for Miss. as nothing can be done here, in my business.

I will now give you what information I have gathered on the Presidential Election and in doing this I wish it to be strictly confidential, as I shall name certain men & their course which might throw me in Collision with at home.

The Calhoun Party here are moving heaven and earth to fetch about his nomination. There is a portion [of] the Ala. delegation with D. H. Lewis at their head, the Miss. delegation (a letter which I have seen from one of them to the Contrary Notwithstanding), and perhaps some others from the south, which I do not know as my means of information are very limited having but few acquaintants here. They are using every means in their power to Stave off the National convention, insisting on me when I go home at all events to have it put off until may or June 1844. Our friend Genl A. Anderson is here. He boards with Mr. Calhoun and is very much wrought up to the belief that your future prospects are Identified with Mr. Calhoun, that you have no chance to be Vice President on the Van Buren Ticket, that Johnson will be the nominee. Your Ten. friends here think differently. Mr. Calhouns friends here say that you cannot be the Vice President under Calhoun owing to locality, but the[y] seem to feel no hesitation in saying, to your friends if he can be the President, you can have any thing at home or abroad under him. That is not my feelings in this matter. This inducement will be held out to you by the Calhoun party. Doct Gwin, Thompson, & Genl. Anderson have all taken particular pains to tell me these things since I came here. They are all boarding with Calhoun. And have no doubt but he has given such intimations. I think the Democrats of Ten would think you rather a Qere[3] fellow, to see you on the Stump now supporting Mr. Calhoun, when they reflected what you said about 5 or 6 years ago. I wonder some of your friends here dont see and know that wont do.

Mr. Van Burens friends I think are laying Quiet rather than other wise. Your friends here particularly the Ten delegation appear sanguine that your name will be placed on the Ticket with V.B. I must confess I have some doubts. The Missouri Nominations[4] dont look exactly right; perhaps they may get better. It is understood here it was a very close contest whether Van Buren or Johnson should be nominated in the Missouri Convention, for the Presidency. Waterson[5] told me that Sevier (senator) told him that Johnson would not permit his name to be run for the Vice Presidency. Whether he has any authority for that I dont know.

The friends of Mr. Calhoun and those who profess to be your friends, that are Calhoun Men, say that you are two young, [that] your friends should not urge your claims, or rather that you should not permit them to do it, that it will be plenty time [for] you when Mr. Calhoun shall retire &c. I am at a loss what opinion to form in relation to the course that will be pursued by Mr. V. Buren & his friends between Johnson & yourself. You no doubt are better informed on that than I am. Should Johnson Decline, there would then be no doubt.

I believe all has been said that occurs to me now. I shall be at the Convention in Miss.[6] From what I could learn before I left home Calhoun will be nominated and you will be nominated for the Vice Presidency. If nothing better can be done, that we must submit to. Would that be best or make no nomination at all in Miss?

I fear I shall tax your time & patience in reading this letter, as I have no doubt you are receiving letters every day from other friends much better informed than I am, and can give you much more information than I can, but none who feels a deeper interest in the matter than I do.

I wrote you Mr. Handy, the Editor of the Independent democrat had promised me he would place your name at the head of his Column for the Vice Presidency.[7] I have received one of his papers, and I see he has not done it. I cannot tell the reasons.

Jany 13th. Since writing the above I have visited Mr. Benton in company with Lynn Boyd,[8] Cave Johnson, Genl Houston of Ala. Your name was not mentioned. Benton spoke slightly of R. M. John,[9] said he had better take a Mission off some where with a good salary &c &c. Boyd thinks you will be certain to be the nominee if John is not; thinks that doubtful. It will be hard to leave him off, if V. Buren is taken up. My own opinion now is that Calhoun will have no chance for the Nominations, as he will only be able to carry some 4 or 5 of the southern states. From the tone of his friends here he intends to run any how, and split off a portion of the Democratic party. That is Bentons opinion.

I shall leave the day after tomorrow for Miss. and would like to hear from you before our state convention. Be assured however of one thing. Nothing shall be left undone by me to promote your nomination. I see that North Miss. is moving and will come thru strong, for Van Buren and yourself, so says Genl Gwin & Thompson both, and both of them will be willing to give you up for Calhoun, I think. My room is out.

WILLIAMSON SMITH

ALS. DLC–JKP. Addressed to Columbia. Polk's AE on the cover states that he answered this letter on January 26, 1843; Polk's reply has not been found.

1. Letter not found.
2. See Smith to Polk, December 8, 1842.
3. Probably a misspelling of "queer."
4. See Cave Johnson to Polk, December 4, 1842.
5. Harvey M. Watterson.
6. Reference is to the State Democratic Convention, which met at Jackson on February 22, 1843, and nominated a slate of candidates for state office; the meeting made no recommendation on the Democratic presidential or vice-presidential ticket for 1844.
7. See Smith to Polk, December 8, 1842.
8. Linn Boyd, a Democrat from Kentucky, served several terms in the U.S. House, 1835–37 and 1839–55.
9. Richard M. Johnson.

FROM J. GEORGE HARRIS

My Dear Sir,   Nashville Jan. 16. 1843

I leave for the north to-night, and shall probably be absent five or six weeks. I shall attend with all due faithfulness to the subject matter of our late conversation, and write to you from Washington. I have, according to your suggestion, conversed with Messrs. Hogan & Heiss.[1] To publish a magazine like that of the Avd. Guard,[2] would be attended with an amt of expenditure which they think they would be unable to raise. This is no doubt the fact. They are desirous of getting subs. to the Union say for 15th March to 15th Aug at $1 only, and I think that our party cannot do themselves more substantial service than to take the matter in hand throughout the State. You shall here from me at Washington certain.

J. GEO. HARRIS

ALS. DLC–JKP. Addressed to Columbia.
1. Thomas Hogan and John P. Heiss became publishers of the *Nashville Union* in late April, 1842. J. George Harris continued as editor until March 31,

1843, when Hogan and Heiss assumed total control. Hogan, a native of Pennsylvania and former editor of the Murfreesboro *Weekly Times*, remained connected with the *Union* until his death on May 11, 1844. Heiss, also a native of Pennsylvania, had been employed as financial officer of the *Union* in 1840; he managed the newspaper's business affairs until May of 1845, when he became business manager of the *Washington Union*.

2. Reference is to the *Advanced Guard of Democracy*, a Democratic campaign paper published weekly in Nashville by J. George Harris from April 23, 1840, through the following October.

FROM HENRY SIMPSON[1]

Dear Sir.   Philada. 16th Janry 1843

I have to acknowledge the receipt of your favor of the 4th Inst.[2] and take pleasure in communicating with you at this important period of our election affairs. We had a glorious meeting of the friends of Mr. Van Buren on the 7th Inst. and our celebration of the 8th Janry. 1815 passed off with a public sentiment in his favor for the next presidential term.[3] It appears to be the general wish here, that you should be the candidate for the vice Presidency on the ticket with Mr. Van Buren, and if your state, as I have no doubt it will, should show a Democratic triumph at the ensuing elections, we can elect our candidates in 1844 & carry twenty out of the six and twenty states. Your being elected Govr. of your state, may not interfere with this arrangement, & from letters received from our friends lately at Washington City, it appears almost certain that you will be settled upon as the candidate for V.P. Col. Benton, Messrs. Allen, Tappan and Wright of the Senate,[4] all go in warmly for Mr. Van Buren, as the candidate for the Presidency in 1844. Besides which, the preference given to him by our friend the Hero of New Orleans will make and now does make, a rally in his favor somewhat like the Jackson fever of 1824, 1828 & 1832. The Tyler men here are few and far between; but, I suppose that in your state they are more numerous, and that many stray sheep will return to the fold. Our friends Geo. M. Dallas, Henry D. Gilpin, Dr. Petrikin[5] & others all favor the re-nomination of Mr. Van Buren, and although Mr. Buchanan has many friends in Penna. our state will ultimately go for Mr. Van Buren's being the nominee of a Democratic national Convention, to be held in this city & in *Independence Hall*, next 4th July, or some time next fall,[6] and it is proposed, should the health of ex-President Jackson permit (and he be *a delegate*, that he [be] made President of said Convention). You will see from our proceedings at our late celebration, that you have been noticed for the vice Presidency and I can assure you, that you have very many friends in our city, county and state. Poor degraded Penna, lost as she is in the state of her finances,[7] can never again be cheated out of her genuine vote for President and vice President, as in 1840.[8] All parties here, strange as it may appear, seem to be anxiously waiting for the period to arrive, when they shall be under the rule of a democratic administration of the general government, being satisfied that the Federal whig party does not know how to administer it, so as to produce general prosperity and happiness. I shall always be pleased to hear from you . . . .

HENRY SIMPSON

ALS. DLC–JKP. Addressed to Columbia.

1. Henry Simpson, brother of a noted Philadelphia editor and author, Stephen Simpson, served as alderman of Philadelphia, member of the Pennsylvania legislature, and appraiser of the port of Philadelphia. A nominal Democrat, Simpson enjoyed a long and often controversial career in Philadelphia politics.

2. Letter not found.

3. The friends of Martin Van Buren met at the Masonic Hall in Philadelphia on January 7, 1843. Andrew Jackson sent a message commending Van Buren for his faithful service; and Henry Horn, the presiding officer, toasted Polk as the next Democratic vice-presidential candidate. The celebration on January 8 commemorated Jackson's victory at the Battle of New Orleans.

4. Thomas Hart Benton, William Allen, Benjamin Tappan, and Silas Wright. A lawyer in Steubenville, Ohio, Tappan served as judge of the Fifth Ohio Circuit Court of Common Pleas in 1816 and as U.S. district judge of Ohio in 1833; he won election as a Democrat to one term in the U.S. Senate, 1839–45. He opposed slavery, but unlike his brothers, Arthur and Lewis, he rejected the abolition movement.

5. George M. Dallas, Henry D. Gilpin, and David Petrikin. A Philadelphia lawyer and Democrat, Gilpin was U.S. attorney for eastern Pennsylvania, 1831–36; solicitor of the U.S. Treasury, 1836–40; and U.S. attorney general, 1840–41. A physician in Danville, Pennsylvania, Petrikin served as a Democrat in the U.S. House for two terms, 1837–41.

6. Although at this time Polk, Simpson, and other Van Buren supporters favored holding the National Democratic Convention in the fall of 1843, party leaders acceded to Calhounite demands for a later date. Convention delegates assembled in Baltimore on May 27, 1844.

7. Having borrowed large sums for the construction of its canal system, Pennsylvania struggled to service its $40 million debt, the annual interest on which amounted to $2 million. Additonal loans with which to pay interest and to make further improvements on the canals increased the state's debts and brought its treasury to the edge of bankruptcy. In 1842 and 1843 Pennsylvania defaulted on its debt payments, but in 1844 the state paid its arrears as well as its current obligations.

8. Martin Van Buren lost Pennsylvania in 1840 by less than four hundred votes; Van Buren's Pennsylvania friends blamed the defeat on the apathy of those Democrats favoring additional bank loans for new public works programs.

FROM THOMAS HOGAN

Dear Sir.   Nashville, Jan. 17. 1843

I received your friendly letter last evening[1] and take pleasure in answering your inquiries. The letter of our committee[2] has been sent already to nearly sixty counties, including the extremes of the State. Why you have not received a copy at Columbia I cannot divine. I wrote a short reply to the Maury letter[3] about ten days ago, and handed it to Mr. Kezer to obtain the names of the committee. It should have reached you some days ago, unless he has mislaid it. The annunciation of candidates is not so easy a matter as we supposed. Maj. Claiborne will run for the senate, but prefers being called out by the *County* Committee,[4] feeling some delicacy I suppose in accepting what might be regarded a nomination from one of his own choosing. We also addressed a letter to Col. Guild urging him to come out, but he has thus far declined answering. From his hesitating I should infer his willingness to run. If Peyton is to be the Whig candidate, I doubt not he[5] will enter the lists. We are in a strait to procure candidates for the lower House. Connor on whom the duty devolves has not yet obtained Coleman's consent,[6] though we hear from various sources that his democracy is of the right order. Nor have we been eager to bring our whole ticket in this county for another reason. It is rumored that Trimble, Foster 3d and another weak one will be the Whig ticket.[7] These can be beaten, but if the Whigs had an idea of our being able to obtain strong men, they would make a better ticket. This is the reasoning of the older heads on our committee. Ewing, Rains, and Hollingsworth positively decline.[8]

Respecting the Extra paper, I have to say that your suggestions are *good* and *true*. I know that a separate paper would commend a larger subscription list than the Union, but there are some insuperable objections in the way. The expense to us would be greater on account of making it up and getting material. Besides—we would necessarily be obliged to purchase more type, as we have not enough to keep the matter for an extra standing. Not only the expense but the length of time in procuring it would be in the way. We propose however to issue a prospectus for the Union, offering the Weekly paper at $1 from the 15th of March till the election, and we doubt not will get a large circulation by enlisting in our behalf the Cor.[9] & County Committees. As soon as all our letters to the various counties have had time to reach their destination, we will start out our prospectus.

Capt. Jas. S. Smith will be out in Rutherford in a week or so. I saw him the other day. He feels sanguine.

They are rousing the "generals" in Cave Johnson's district. Gen. Cheatham runs in Robertson and Gen. Henry in Montgomery.

THOMAS HOGAN

ALS. DLC–JKP. Addressed to Columbia. Polk's AE on the cover states that he answered this letter on January 26, 1843; Polk's reply has not been found.

1. Letter not found.

2. Probably the Democratic corresponding committee of Davidson County. Letter not found.

3. See Timothy Kezer to Polk, January 1, 1843. The letter was from the Maury County Democratic Corresponding Committee.

4. On March 11, 1843, delegates from the civil districts of Davidson County met in convention at Nashville, nominated candidates for the state legislature, and appointed a county committee to oversee the forthcoming campaign.

5. Josephus C. Guild.

6. Thomas B. Coleman and probably Cornelius Connor, a Nashville businessman and Democrat.

7. John Trimble and Robert C. Foster, III. A wealthy Nashville lawyer, Trimble served as a Whig in the Tennessee House, 1843–45, and in the Tennessee Senate, 1845–47 and 1859–61. Foster, son of Ephraim H. Foster and nephew of Robert C. Foster, Jr., was also an attorney. Davidson County's Whig slate, announced in March of 1843, included Thomas R. Jennings for the Senate and Trimble and Charles W. Moorman for the House. All three won seats in the legislature.

8. Andrew Ewing, Felix R. Rains, and Henry Hollingsworth. Ewing, a Nashville Democrat, shared a legal practice with his Whig brother, Edwin; Andrew won election to one term in the U.S. House, 1849–51. Rains, a Nashville businessman, served as sheriff of Davidson County, 1838–43, and as a director of the Bank of Tennessee. Hollingsworth, a lawyer, served as mayor of Nashville from 1837 until 1839.

9. Corresponding.

FROM JOHN A. THOMAS[1]

My Dear Sir,   West Point, N. Y. Jan. 20. 1843

I had the pleasure to receive your letter of the 25th of Dec.[2] several days ago, and desired to reply immediately, but in order that I might communicate the standing of Cadets Armstrong and Couts,[3] I have delayed my answer until the close of the January examination. Your letter was received before they were examined, and I took occasion to make known to each, your renewed solicitude for his success, and hoped this would stimulate them to acquit themselves well, but I regret to add, such was not the effect. Mr. Armstrong is near the foot of nineteen of his class who are deficient in mathematics; he is also found deficient in English Grammar, and is very low in French and drawing. He is a young man of good moral character, and since I have been in command of the cadets, I have employed him in my office to write for me, and excused him from a part of his military duty. I shall continue to encourage him, but I ought to tell you candidly that unless he evinces more talent than he has heretofore, he cannot go through the Institution. This is offered as *my* opinion, judging from what I know of him.

Mr. Couts was also found *deficient*, but only in one branch, Engineering, the most important, however, pursued by the class of which he is a member. He is *very low* in *all* his studies and I am persuaded that this is chiefly owing to idleness; he might stand higher. His conduct, I regret to say has not been good, and in order that you may know how reprehensible it has been I beg leave to give you an account of his course in reference to a cadet who was detected in the act of *stealing* a *Turkey*. A cadet who had been but a few months in the Academy, was seen by one of the Professors to knock over a turkey and put it into a bag. This cadet was seized by the professor & though he denied that there was a turkey in his bag, his assertion was shown to be false by its being emptied out of the bag. Cadet Couts who was near, and apparently in company with this young man, was called on to give his name, which he refused to do, and plead for him and requested the professor not to report him, although he had seen the whole transaction. The next day, I was directed by the Superintendent[4] to order him to tell the name of the cadet, but he replied at once, that he had consulted with his friends in the Corps and had determined not to do it. I admonished him, & asked him if he was aware what he was doing. He not only disregarded my admonition, but proceeded to maintain that it was not dishonourable to "forage a turkey or pig, or indeed any poultry," and that it was not so considered by the cadets, nor by the students of any college in the country. I will not now detail all the aspersions he cast upon his comrades to shield himself, but would add that he took this course with deliberation, for, ten days after the interview I had with him, he forwarded to the Chief Engineer[5] a defence of his conduct, in which he avowed the most offensive principles. It is perhaps not unreasonable that we should sometimes find in the Academy cadets who would be fitter inmates for a house of correction, for, they come from all classes of society, and must necessarily bring with them the view of that society of which they have been members; but I confess I was amazed that Cadet Couts, who has been here nearly five years, and who is within six months of being graduated, should not only refuse to tell me the name of a cadet guilty of a disgraceful act but avow a code of morals fitted only for those who intend to lead lives of infamy. He has consulted his uncle Cave Johnston,[6] and has f[orwarded to][7] the Secretary of War[8] a letter acknowledging his error, and I suppose he will be merely reprimanded. This the Chief Engineer has already done in the most severe manner. I suppose Mr. Couts will be graduated but you must see that he has done himself an irreperable injury. The cadet who committed the act was found out & immediately dismissed.

I am charged with the most responsible duty, the *discipline* of the Academy, and it behoves me to use my best exertions to maintain it in a manner creditable to the country, and this I am determined to do. It is perhaps not too much to say *to you*, that a great deal is expected of me, for I am enjoying the command & emolument of a Major, tho I am still a Lieut., and I was selected for the station, and without any application of mine. And if I had no higher motive, I ought not disappoint the expectations of my friends. *By the time you will be President I hope to qualify myself* for promotion. The army regrets most sincerely that it ever, even in feeling, favored Whigery, and if it can only be forgiven this time, such a thing will surely never happen again. I met many of your friends when I was stationed at Troy, and they all seemed anxious that you should be the candidate for Vice President, Henry Vail[9] in particular. You could surely get the vote of N.Y. If I can serve you *in any* way I hope you will command me, and if Genl. Armstrong or any of your friends wish any thing done in my power it will give me great pleasure to comply with their wishes.

J. ADDISON THOMAS

ALS. DLC–JKP. Addressed to Nashville.

1. John A. Thomas, a son of Isaac J. Thomas of Columbia, was graduated from the U.S. Military Academy in 1833, was appointed to the Academy as a professor of ethics, geography, and history from 1834 until 1841, and was assigned commandant of cadets from 1842–45. Thomas practiced law in New York City until 1855, when he became undersecretary of state in the administration of Franklin Pierce.

2. Letter not found.

3. James Trooper Armstrong and Cave J. Couts. Armstrong, son of William Armstrong and nephew of Robert Armstrong, entered West Point in 1841. Although he did not graduate, he did serve in the Confederate army. A nephew of Cave Johnson, Couts was appointed to the military academy in 1838 and was

graduated in 1843. He remained in the army until 1851, when he resigned and moved to San Diego, California.

4. An 1814 graduate of West Point, Richard Delafield served as superintendent of the Military Academy from 1838 until 1845.

5. Joseph G. Totten served as chief of engineers from 1838 until his death in 1864.

6. Cave Johnson.

7. Deterioration of the manuscript in the crease of the fold has obliterated part of one word and probably all of a second one.

8. John C. Spencer.

9. A businessman from New York, Henry Vail served in the U.S. House of Representatives as a Democrat from 1837 until 1839.

FROM JOSEPH R. A. TOMKINS[1]

Dear Sir   Post office at Nashville Jany 20th 1843

Being here partly on business of a political nature—& being informed by Gen. Armstrong that you would like to hear how all things were going on in Sumner I cherfully comply with his suggestion & commence with the business that brought me here.

Doct Peyton as you no doubt have seen came out for Congress one week Since[2]—at which we were all well pleased being as we supposed the most vulnerable & easiest to beat of any in his ranks. But to our great surprise & mortification on Wednesday morning last Thos. Barry also came out. This movement on his part was discountenanced by *all* the true friends of Democracy in Sumner & we immediately determined on holding a convention & ruling him out. Our reason for this was first his known opposition to Benton who he openly cursed in the streets & yourself & also Harris which made us question his Sincerity as a Democrat & besides, he is an advocate of the bankrupt law. But fortunately for him & us he saw at once the current was so strong against him he withdrew the next day after I left. It hapened that there was some five or six in this place from Sumner & we have determined to go on with the convention & nominate candidates for all the offices. Mr Barry as I understand from Majr Burford[3] is willing to submit his claims *which are but small.*

After consulting our friends here & viewing the whole ground we have come to the conclusion that Guild is the man for Congress—although he would be making a great Sacrifice. But he has said to me that he perhaps might run if he had a fair field (this was said after Barry announced himself). Whilst on the subject of Guild, the Genl. was kind enough to let me see your letter to him written yesterday.[4] I am pleased at your writing him (Guild). It will have weight.

For the senate I think Burford is the only man that can beat Collum[5] if we can prevail on him to run. He is now here & does not positively refuse—write him if you think with us & urge him to come out. Campbell would not take an active part against him. Neither would Goodall.[6]

As for the lower house we have two candidates[7] which *perhaps* will do. They are right, but can't Speak. I think that Barrys move will do good for we will not go on to organise & you may rely old Sumner will do things worthy of herself. I am pleased to find the people of Davidson so united in favour of Guild. I do not doubt but he can beat Peyton if we can get him out. Guild or myself will write you more particularly after monday next the day on which we have a meeting at Gallatin preparatory to a convention.[8]

I am requested so say to you by Genl. Armstrong that the people of Davidson are in motion & the best will be done. Excuse the intrusion on you of this letter.

J. R. A. TOMKINS

ALS. DLC–JKP. Addressed to Columbia. Polk's AE on the cover states that he answered this letter on January 21, 1843; Polk's reply has not been found.

1. Tomkins, a prosperous merchant and Polk supporter, served as postmaster at Gallatin from 1837 until 1841.

2. See Robert Armstrong to Polk, December 20, 1842.

3. A tanner and merchant in Carthage, David Burford served as sheriff of Smith County, 1827–29; moving to Dixon Springs, also in Smith County, he engaged in agriculture and raised blooded stock. He won three terms in the Tennessee Senate, 1829–35, and presided over that body from 1833 to 1835.

4. Letter not found.

5. A lawyer at Carthage and Alvin Cullom's brother, William Cullom served two terms as a Whig in the Tennessee Senate, 1843–47, and two terms in the U.S. House, 1851–55; he won election to one term as clerk of the U.S. House in 1856.

6. Isaac Goodall, a farmer, represented Smith County as a Whig in the Tennessee House, 1837–39 and 1841–44.

7. Elijah Boddie and Stephen H. Turner won nomination as the Democratic candidates for the Tennessee House from Sumner County at a convention held in Gallatin on February 20, 1843. A lawyer in Gallatin, Boddie served four terms in the Tennessee House, 1827–29, 1831–33, 1835–37, and 1843–45. A justice of the peace in Sumner County and owner of considerable property, Turner sat for one term in the Tennessee House, 1843–45.

8. Meeting at Gallatin on Monday, January 23, 1843, party leaders called for a convention to be held at Gallatin on the third Monday of February to nominate Democratic candidates for the U.S. Congress, the Tennessee Senate, and the Tennessee House. No follow-up letter from Tomkins or Guild to Polk has been found.

FROM CAVE JOHNSON

Dear Sir,   Washington 22nd Jany 1843

I sent to your address the other day, the Journal of the Call Session & Verplanks original Bill reported in Dec. 1832.[1] The Journals of the last session are not yet all bound & of course there is as yet some difficulty in getting a coppy. I will send you the first I can get. I begin to fear if I make a speech on Browns letter,[2] I shall have to draw it in by the rush sheets[3] as every body else does. I have been expecting a Bill as recomended by the Sec of Tre.[4] leaving Tea & Coffee[5] but none as yet has been reported & I begin to doubt whether the Whigs intend to make any further provision for the Capt.[6] The high Tariff, Cash duties[7] &c has reduced importations to about one half what they were in the corresponding quarter of the last year, & of course we must have new duties or a new Treasury note Bill[8] or leave the Capt. to starve. An opinion now prevails that the Whigs intend to leave him with what he has got & can get from the Loan, which cannot be made available,[9] so as to force him to have a call session next summer—hoping no doubt that we will butt out our brains as they did.[10] If it should so turn out I think we might make it greatly to our advantage. If we could reduce the duties to a revenue standard, trade would revive and hard times pass away, without a Bank, and under the operations of the Subtreasury.[11]

The pamphlet I sent you, of Rhett, will show you the feelings of our Southern brethern.[12] The truth no doubt is they want the longest time for management here & the shortest time left us for making an exposure, if they leave us. As matters now stand, they know they would have no chance here or in a convention and therefore they loose nothing by delay.

If they desert us, & I think they will, they will go off *upon some great principle* & make a *terrible noise* & we shall have but little time for a proper exposure. The Mercury is now writing that Van is not to be trusted on the Negro question or Tariff.[13] You will begin to think that Drumgoole, Thomas, Turney & myself were right in not submitting in the Speakers election.[14]

It is a prevailing opinion I find that the influence of the friends of Calhoun, Buchhanan, Johnson & Cass, Woodbury, Wall, Gov. Porter will all be used in opposition to Van's nomination. Whatever they do is done in the dark & cannot seriously affect Van. He is much stronger now than at the last session. I was glad to see the nomination for Vice P. at Philadelphia by Henry Horn.[15] It is strong evidence of the democratic feeling there agt. the course of R.M.J.[16] The nomination in Missouri does not meet the approbation of the delegation here & I have the strongest reasons to believe will be opposed by T.H.B.[17] I have called twice to see him so as to draw him out but company always prevented. We are talking of a caucus to recomend a time for the Convention which will probably take place before we adjourn & I think there is no doubt that we shall select the 4 Mon in Nov. Rhetts pamphlet produces a good deal of talk & increases the desire for having it over. *Every step they* take increases the suspicion that we are to be deserted, if they have enough for the balance of power. I trust these suspicions may not be verified. It is proper however that you should know & think of them.

Brown[18] mentioned to me that you said we must raise money for you before we left. I wrote a line to Vanderpool to know how matters were now in N. York & also spoke to Rosevelt.[19] From what they say, there will be no chance of getting money in N.Y. for a Western man—U.S. stock 6 p cent is under par and any quantity to be obtained thru the loan *at par.* All say there is plenty of money but no confidence in any body. It was suggested to me that Reeves (Blair's partner) was the best chance.[20] I had a conversation with him. He talked doubtfully about it—no chance now but possibly there might be some before the adjournment. If there be any, it will be attended to.

I regret to learn that Hardwicke has sold out and is about to leave the State. I fear it will increase the chances of my nomination at Dover, against which I have earnestly protested. I do not see how I can take another canvass or how I can return here. I have been from home about 20 out of 24 mos. I could not ride over the hills & hollows as I use to do.

Jeff. Campbell[21] wishes to run. Jo. L. Wms.[22] declines & Luke Lea is said to be on the field. You ought to prevent if possible Andrew Johnson from running at McClelan.[23] Arnold declines. (Only watching for live democrats.)

Willie L. Norfleet will give Genl C. a race in Robertson.[24] My declining will give us strength in Montgomery. Some Whigs hope to get along better as there is more room in the democratic ranks than the other. It is said Kimble (author of J.O.)[25] to join us & run for the Senate. It is thought also that N. H. Allen[26] Will do so likewise & on no better grounds.

My health is somewhat better. We had 7 or 8000 people assembled today to hear Miller preach at the patent office—it turned out a hoax[27]— only one fight. We hear to night, that a British Steamer fired a shot into the Falmoth (Capt McIntosh) in the Gulph. The Falmoth gave her a *Broadside* with her Paixian guns & very seriously injured her if not destroyed her.[28]

C. Johnson

ALS. DLC–JKP. Addressed to Columbia and marked *"private."*

1. The Twenty-seventh Congress met in special session from May 31 to September 13, 1841. For background on the bill introduced in 1832 by Gulian Verplanck, see Cave Johnson to Polk, January 4, 1843.

2. See Sarah C. Polk to Polk, November 7, 1842.

3. "Rush sheets" were advanced or pre-publication copies of speeches scheduled for inclusion in the appendix to the *Congressional Globe*. Johnson planned to base his rebuttal on the written version of a speech that Milton Brown had delivered in the House on July 7, 1842.

4. Walter Forward of Pennsylvania served as secretary of the Treasury from September 13, 1841 to March 3, 1843.

5. Johnson's reference is to anticipated proposals retaining a tariff on tea and coffee.

6. Reference is to the president, John Tyler.

7. The compromise tariff of 1833 specified that after June 30, 1842, import duties would be collected in "ready money," and that all credit on duties would be abolished. In 1842 Congress allowed importers the right to warehouse their goods for sixty days, at the end of which grace period the duties would be paid in cash or the goods confiscated for sale at public auction.

8. See John C. Calhoun to Polk, March 12, 1842.

9. See Abbott Lawrence to Polk, September 21, 1842.

10. Whig splits during the 1841 special session of Congress denied Henry Clay the necessary votes to override Tyler's national bank vetoes.

11. Although repealed by the Whigs in 1841, the Independent Treasury system operated informally for want of a national bank through which to conduct the general government's fiscal affairs.

12. Published anonymously as a pamphlet in Washington City and reprinted in the *Charleston Mercury* of January 25, 1843, Robert B. Rhett's treatise, "An Appeal to the Democratic Party," promoted the presidential aspirations of John C. Calhoun and opposed the nomination of Martin Van Buren. Rhett argued that convention delegates should be elected by congressional districts and that the convention should meet in 1844 rather than in 1843. Rhett also urged discontinuance of the convention practice of voting by states under the unit rule.

13. Possibly Johnson refers to an editorial in the *Charleston Mercury* of January 19, 1843.

14. George C. Dromgoole, Francis Thomas, and Hopkins L. Turney joined Johnson and seven other Democrats in electing Robert M. T. Hunter, a Whig, to the House Speakership in 1839. South Carolina Democrats had refused to support the candidate of the House Democratic caucus, John W. Jones; and Johnson accordingly rejected South Carolina's first choice, Dixon H. Lewis. See Cave Johnson to Polk, December 18, 1842. Philip F. Thomas, a first-term Democrat, also voted for Hunter, but Johnson's reference probably is to Francis Thomas, who had served with Polk in the House since 1831. Dromgoole, a lawyer from Virginia, served five terms in the U.S. House, 1835–41 and 1843–47.

15. See Henry Simpson to Polk, January 16, 1843.

16. Richard Mentor Johnson.

17. Thomas Hart Benton. See Cave Johnson to Polk, January 4, 1843.

18. Aaron V. Brown.

19. Aaron Vanderpoel and James I. Roosevelt. Roosevelt, a Democrat and lawyer from New York City, won election to the state assembly in 1835 and 1840 and to the U.S. House in 1841, sat on the state's supreme court, 1851–59 and on the court of appeals, 1859, and served as U.S. district attorney for Southern New York, 1860–61.

20. A shrewd businessman, John Cook Rives shared the ownership of the Washington *Globe* with Francis P. Blair from 1833 until 1845. Rives reported congressional debates in the *Congressional Globe* for the period 1833 to 1864.

21. Thomas Jefferson Campbell.

22. Joseph L. Williams.

23. Abraham McClellan, a Sullivan County farmer, served numerous terms in the Tennessee House and Senate before going to the U.S. House for three terms, 1837–43.

24. Willie L. Norfleet and Richard Cheatham. Norfleet, a Democrat and resident of Robertson County, was a son of James Norfleet, a former member of the Tennessee legislature.

25. Herbert S. Kimble, a lawyer in Clarksville, sat one term in the Tennessee House as a Whig, 1849–51, and served ten years as Montgomery County judge, 1852–62; Kimble had published a pamphlet attacking Cave Johnson under the pseudonym, "J.O."

26. Nathaniel H. Allen, a Clarksville lawyer and a Whig, ran unsuccessfully for the U.S. House in 1841, but won election in 1843 to the Tennessee Senate and served one term.

27. Reference probably is to William Miller's prophecy that the Second Coming would occur in 1843.

28. Reports of a naval engagement between a British steamer and the American steamer *Falmouth*, captained by James M. McIntosh, have not been identified further. In the 1830's Henri Joseph Paixhans, a French inventor, developed a naval cannon shell designed to penetrate its target before exploding.

FROM GRANVILLE C. TORBETT

Madisonville, Tennessee. January 26, 1843

In reply to Polk's letter of the 16th instant,[1] Torbett reports that Monroe County is trying to organize for the legislative elections. A district convention has been recommended, and numerous "leading Democrats" have asked Torbett whether or not he would accept a Senate nomination.[2] Though he expects to seek reelection to the House, he would accept a Senate nomination if tendered. Torbett knows little of election prospects in surrounding counties, but writes that Polk should get a majority in Hamilton County. He hears little from Waterhouse's district, but expects him to run for reelection.[3]

ALS. DLC–JKP. Addressed to Columbia.
1. Letter not found.
2. McMinn, Bradley, Monroe, and Polk counties composed Torbett's senatorial district.
3. Richard G. Waterhouse represented Rhea, Bledsoe, Hamilton, Marion, and Meigs counties for one term in the Tennessee Senate, 1841–43.

TO SAMUEL H. LAUGHLIN

My Dear Sir: Columbia Jany 27th 1843
    I am anxious to hear how the difficulties which have unexpectedly sprung up in the Mountain District are about being adjusted. Does *Mr Cullom* desire to run for Congress, or will he insist upon it? Will it be necessary to call a District Convention? If so have any steps been taken to fix upon a time and place?[1] The matter will be much more easily settled now, than it will be after the canvass opens—and the public becomes excited. I should think there would be no difficulty now, but if it is postponed for two months there may be. I have only time to call your attention to the matter, and to ask for information. Who will be the Democratic candidates for Representative in the Legislature from *De-Kalb*, and from *Fentress, White* and *Van Buren*? Both these are debateable Districts and with proper candidates we can carry them. Who are likely to be the candidates for the Legislature in each of the other counties of your Congressional District?[2] It is very important in my judgment that all our candidates should be announced at the earliest practicable period. Give me all the information you have upon this, and other matters, connected with the approaching contest. In haste . . . .
                                      JAMES K. POLK

ALS. DLC–JKP. Addressed to McMinnville and marked "*Private.*" Published in *ETHSP*, XVIII, p. 162. Laughlin's AE on the cover states that he answered this letter on February 1, 1843.
1. See Laughlin to Polk, December 23, 1842; Timothy Kezer to Polk, January 1, 1843; and Polk to Laughlin, January 6, 1843.
2. In addition to the four counties named by Polk, Tennessee's Fourth Congressional District included the counties of Coffee, Jackson, Overton, and Warren.

FROM CAVE JOHNSON

Dear Sir,   Washington Jany 29th 1843

I recd. yours several days ago[1] but having just written you[2] I delayed hoping to get something that would interest you. You are mistaken in supposing the nomination in Missouri a pre-concerted movement, evidencing the course we are hereafter to pursue. Gov. M. informs me, that Mr. C—n. & Col RMJ[3] both had a few friends in the Legislature for Pres & they insisted that if a *restoration* was to take place, it should be complete & to gratify them & to secure the desired unamimnity, he was nominated as Vice. The Ca—n men here take the same ground as well as the Buck—n[4] men to *us Tennesseans* hoping that our friendship for you, under such circumstances would throw us against Van.[5] I had a long conversation with Col B.[6] on the subject. He will not commit himself for *any one* now but denounces Col RMJ as the damndest political wh—e in the Country—and stands committed agt. him—& said without hesitation, the position he now assumed made it the duty of the party to drop him. He informed me that the Miss. M.C.[7] had written home to make no nomination for Vice but that their letters had not reached there before the resolutions were adopted.[8] I think Gov. W—ry[9] is now rectus in curia.[10] The M.C. from N.H.[11] talk strongly of the impropriety of his course—not so much because he said or done any thing as because he believed & gave countenance by his silence to the idea, that he might be Vice for C—n Southern men certainly believed so. It is probable the Gov. who you know is cool, cautious & selfish had no favorable opinion of the availability of C—n but in the conflict between him & Van, the mantle of old Jackson might fall on other shoulders, perhaps his own—perhaps some others—and probably thought it best to stand still and let things take their own course and then do what suited him best. Buck. I think is leveling off a little, first for the want of C—[n]s availability—and secondly on account of the treaty.[12] He you know reported the resolution adopted by the Senate unanimously, in relation to slaves driven into the island by stress of weather, mutiny &c.[13] *The treaty approved* by C—n now leaves him in a delicate position in the *free states*. He will be kept up & get probably the nomination of Penn. as a compliment, afterwards all will go right. Mr. C—d of Maine[14] for similar reasons is probably right now. I may be wrong in my conjecture about Genl. C.[15] He now occupies the neutral territory—ready to serve one or the other—& will be the most dangerous man, if he turns his back on us. He will reside in Cincinatti. RMJ was taken up before from fear [of] his military popularity.

There is more & better reason to fear the other. Same reasons may have a similar influence *on our Convention*. This is what we have to guard against. I think the influence of the Admn. & *the Sec of State*[16] will be united with C—n agt. us & we have some reason to fear that Gov. Porter will lend himself to that concern. All united however cannot in my opinion affect Van. R.B.R.[17] entreats a postponement of the Convention to May 1844—gives the strongest assurances that they will not separate—that public opinion will settle the matter before that time & we will all move on harmoniously as he says. I think his pamphlet[18] *ensures* us *the Convention in Nov.* The prevailing opinion is that they will go off & if so, the *sooner* the *better* for *us*. If we delay until '44 and they have *enough* to hold *the balance*, we will be again treated as we were about the Speaker & as Bedford Brown was in N.C.[19]

I think you will need no defence after M. Browns late letter. Of all the nonsensical attacks I have ever witnessed—this exceeds all. I am however ready & shall avail myself of the first opportunity to say a word or two to him. He has treated Benton & Wall about Bankruptcy as bad as he has us by garbling & misrepresenting their speeches.[20] If I have leisure I will look into that also. I have been so little able to read or write from continued pain that I have not yet done any thing, & I must write a circular you know.[21] We expect some movement on Monday on the Tariff & I expect a chance within the next 10 days. I fear you will suffer in your next election from so many Whig M.C. omitting to run. Whoever runs in their places will repudiate all the proceedings of the Extra Session & we shall have the more difficulty in making the Whig Measures tell on them.

It is understood, that immediately on the adjournment of Congress, the Clay office-holders will be washed up & I suspect the Democrats also who refuse adhesion. He[22] dislikes one as bad as the other. But two Democrats voted for his exchequer—Caldwell (Conner's successor) & Bowne of N.Y.[23] Cushings Bill approaches so nearly the sub-treasury, that if taken up, it will receive a good many democratic votes.[24]

My health has improved slightly. Dixon Lewis is said to be very sick. We hope not dangerously so. Ben Howard succeeds Peters as Reporter[25] & he tells some pretty tales of the improper expenditure of the Contingent fund of the court. I have it in writing & may use it. My respects to Madam.

C. JOHNSON

ALS. DLC–JKP. Addressed to Columbia and marked *"private."*
1. Letter not found.
2. See Cave Johnson to Polk, January 22, 1843.
3. John Miller, John C. Calhoun, and Richard M. Johnson. Miller served as

governor of Missouri from 1825 until 1832 before winning election as a Van Buren Democrat to the U.S. House, where he served from 1837 until 1843.

4. James Buchanan.

5. Martin Van Buren.

6. Thomas H. Benton.

7. John C. Edwards and John Miller were Missouri's members in the U.S. House. Edwards won election as a Democrat to the U.S. House, where he served from 1841 until 1843. The following year he became governor of Missouri and served in that post until 1848.

8. See Cave Johnson to Polk, January 4 and 22, 1843.

9. Levi Woodbury.

10. "Rectus in curia," a Latin phrase, translates "legally right."

11. Charles G. Atherton, Edmund Burke, Ira A. Eastman, John R. Reding, and Tristram Shaw represented New Hampshire in the U.S. House in the Twenty-seventh Congress, 1841–43.

12. Buchanan opposed the Webster-Ashburton Treaty in part on grounds that the Treaty did not prevent seizure and manumission of slaves aboard distressed American vessels landing in British colonial ports. Although Calhoun also had defended such protection under the law of nations, he supported the Webster-Ashburton Treaty and left Buchanan to explain why northern Democrats should uphold slave interests abandoned by southern members of the party.

13. As chairman of the Senate Foreign Relations Committee Buchanan had reported favorably Calhoun's resolutions of March 4, 1840, which claimed protection of the law of nations for slaves aboard American vessels landing under stress in British colonial ports.

14. Nathan Clifford of Maine.

15. Lewis Cass.

16. Daniel Webster.

17. Robert Barnwell Rhett.

18. See Cave Johnson to Polk, January 22, 1843.

19. See Cave Johnson to Polk, December 18, 1842.

20. See Sarah C. Polk to Polk, November 7, 1842, and Cave Johnson to Polk, January 4 and 22, 1843.

21. See Cave Johnson to Polk, January 4, 1843.

22. John Tyler.

23. Greene W. Caldwell, Henry W. Connor, and Samuel S. Bowne. On January 27, 1843, Caldwell and Bowne voted against a resolution from the House Committee on Ways and Means opposing the creation of an exchequer bank, the plan for which had been proposed by Treasury Secretary Walter Forward at the previous session of Congress. For more on Forward's plan, see Hopkins L. Turney to Polk, February 24, 1842. Caldwell, a North Carolina physician, won election as a Democrat to the Twenty-seventh Congress and served from 1841 until 1843. Connor, a North Carolina planter, served ten terms as a Democrat in the U.S. House, 1821–41. Bowne, a New York lawyer, won election in 1841 as a Van Buren Democrat to a single term in the U.S. House.

24. Caleb Cushing, a Massachusetts lawyer and Whig, won election to four terms in the U.S. House, where he served from 1835 until 1843. Subsequently, he was appointed minister to China by Tyler and served from May 1843 until his resignation in March 1845. Cushing's bill is not identified further.

25. Benjamin C. Howard and Richard Peters. Having won four terms as a Maryland Democrat to the U.S. House, 1829–33 and 1835–39, Howard served as reporter for the U.S. Supreme Court from 1843 until 1862. Howard succeeded Richard Peters, who had compiled the reports from 1828 to 1842.

FROM THOMAS R. BARRY

Dear Sir,   Gallatin Jan 30th 1843

When I saw you last in Nashville you requested me whenever I had anything of importance to write you. There is much excitement in this county[1] relative to an appraisement Law. Five sixths of the voters in this county are in favour of it. Misouri Ohio and other democratic States have passed such Laws. The Globe is strongly in favour of the policy. See the Globe of Jan 19th.[2] Such laws are better calculated to defeat the Whig Candidate for the Presidency in 1844 than other policy—because when he proposes his great measure of Relief, a U.S. Bank, the people will say the Democrats have already given us a much safer and a more direct plan of Relief by enabling us to pay our debts with our property at fair evaluation. I believe if the Democrats were to come out boldly in favour of this policy it would give them possession of the State government for 20 years—besides as the Globe says it is perfectly right upon *Republican and moral principles*. It will not do for the Democracy to separate itself from the weak or poorer side; if it does it is certain *to be defeated*. It is wrong for a man to entertain unfounded suspicions against those with whom he is politically associated. I have for the last 2 years believed that Guild (the Col) by false misrepresentations induced you to believe that I would not have voted for you for U.S. Senator in 1841. I wish to know of you if this is so. I have no confidence earthly in him. And think the *wire-workers* of Davidson and Sumner[3] will some day regret having used their influence to promote his claims over those of Trousdale and my own.[4] I know with the genuine democracy of Sumner I can beat him 2 votes to one for any thing. But as it is likely that the nominee no matter who will be beat and as I was commited to Trousdale, who I found had not abandoned the idea of runing entirely I positively refused to let my name be used in competition with Trousdale's or to be canvassed before the delegates of the Convention. At the same time I am perfectly conscious that I am 300 votes stronger than any Democrat in the district oweing to the decided stand I took for the Relief Laws. Let me hear from you.

THOMAS BARRY

ALS. DLC–JKP. Addressed to Columbia.

1. Sumner County.

2. Editorials in the Washington *Globe*, January 16–19, 1843, denounced excessive note issues by state banks and supported Democratic proposals for a return to the Independent Treasury system. On January 17 the *Globe* argued in favor of the evaluation principle, which required that creditors accept arbitration of property appraisements rendered in foreclosure actions. In Massachusetts the evaluation law provided that the creditor, debtor, and county sheriff would each appoint one arbitrator and that the creditor would accept the mortgaged lands, as appraised, without benefit of a forced sale and in lieu of a cash settlement for that portion of the debt covered by the appraisement.

3. Reference probably is to members of the Democratic Corresponding Committees of Davidson and Sumner counties.

4. On January 20, 1843, Robert Armstrong wrote Polk that Barry had announced "three days ago" that he would run for Congress, but "today he is *off*." ALS. DLC–JKP. See also Joseph R. A. Tomkins to Polk, January 20, 1843.

FROM HOPKINS L. TURNEY

Dear Sir   Washington Jan. the 31st 1843

I on yesterday had a conversation with Mr. Benton, which confirmed in the opinion I had expressed to you, to wit, that He is decidly opposed to Col. R. Johnson. In this I am not mistaken. The conversation was rather casual. He commenced it, by enquireing about Tennessee. I told him our fate depended on the candidate for the Vice Presidency; that if Johnson was run we would be beaten beyond a doubt, and that it was cruel to Sacrifice us a third time[1] for a man who could not bring a single electorial vote to the concern. He agreed with me and said further, that Old Dick had loaned himself to Tyler & Calhoon to defeat our party, and that he would stand no possible chance for the nomination, and further that he was not to be relied on as a man or as a polition, and cursed him for a political hore. B. entertains bitter feeling for him—Johnson. I cannot be mistaken in this. In the conversation your name was not mentioned for the reason, that Here there is no other pearson Spoken of but you and Johnson, and I thought it best to put Johnson out of the way if possible without exsposeing any personal, or local, preferance. Benton says that Johnsons prospects will rapidly decline, and that he will finally Sink in the estimation of our friends, and likely Join the enemy.

Van is gaining ground, Calhoon looseing.[2] In a word I have Strong faith that we will be triumphant in the convention.

H. L. TURNEY

ALS. DLC–JKP. Addressed to Columbia.

1. Tennessee Democrats failed to carry their state in 1836 and 1840 elections.

Hugh L. White captured 57.9 percent of Tennessee's vote in 1836; William H. Harrison received 55.7 percent four years later.

2. Martin Van Buren and John C. Calhoun.

FROM SAMUEL H. LAUGHLIN

My dear Sir,   McMinnville, Feb. 1, 1843

I received yours of the 27th ult.[1] last night and hasten to reply to it. Mr. Cullom does desire to run for Congress—is urged to do so by the Whigs universally in White, Overton and Jackson—and by his democratic kin and friends in Overton who are willing to coalesce with the Whigs to insure his success. Three fourths of the democracy of the district[2] are for me. We have a thousand majority in the district. More than two thirds of the whole democracy are on this side of the Caney fork.[3] If he takes off a thousand above, and all the Whigs he will beat me with 5000 democratic votes for me. If a Convention takes place, his friends will insist that the vote must be by counties—giving the 4 or 500 democratic votes in Jackson, the same influence as 1400 in Warren or 1200 in Coffee. They will insist on this or Convention without regard to party.[4] In fact the first proposition is the same thing. If the first method is adopted, White County will hold the balance of power, and may decide against me, though the best men there, Isaac Taylor[5] &c. are for me. If we have a Convention, My friends will insist that the vote in Convention shall be according to the wishes of the majority of democratic voters in the district as represented, and this will decide it for me. If Putnam claims and has a County representation—then there are 5 counties above the river and four below.[6] But that county by law votes with the counties she is taken from. With her, counted as a seperate county, there are *nine* counties in this district— without her eight. Voting by Counties, it will therefore require 5 to be a majority of either 8 or 9. White must therefore decide it—as I expect majorities of the delegations of Jackson, Overton and Fentress will be fixed by himself and the Whigs to vote for him.

If Gen. Armstrong, Jos. W. Horton, who is the uncle or cousin of A. L. Davis of Sparta,[7] and other friends at Nashville would write to Isaac Taylor, Davis, &c. urging them, if they think it right, to secure the nomination for me, it would have great influence.

Cullom, on enquiries made by me, and informing that I wished to run in accordance with the wishes of many friends, if I could do so without interfering with his wishes, wrote to me in answer, about three weeks before my name was announced, that he had no wish to run—that under no circumstances would he run at the next election—and thanking me for my frank Communication of my wishes and views. What am I to think of him now?

If he runs—and the Sparta Whig paper[8] is out for him on that ground—he will take open ground against the course of the democracy, in the Assembly at the last and previous session, for not electing Senators to Congress as the Whigs desired—for not letting the election take place.[9] I am sure he will do this, and I care more for the evil effect it may have on your election, and the state election, than I do for myself. He will be quoted as democratic authority against us all over the state. When you made him special Judge (and I advised you to do it) and made him a Colonel,[10] a cold blooded viper was hatched, who cares for nothing and for nobody but himself.

In this county[11] we have Armstrong & French, candidates for House, and Locke coming out.[12] There is no candidate for Senate. In VanBuren & Fentress, the floating Rogers Whig—and Worthington of VanB. democrat are candidates.[13] In DeKalb two Whigs[14] are out, but no democrat as yet. One will run—and I think be elected. In Coffee Wm H. Coulson (Dem.) is out, but W. S. Waterson[15] or somebody else will be most likely to be selected. In the upper counties no candidates are out. Sam Turney says a Democrat named Green[16] will run in White.

If Dr. Robertson, Horton, Armstrong and our friends at Nashville were to send letters to their friends in White and Jackson, it would help me.[17] I wrote Cullom a friendly letter last week, when I published my proposal for a convention,[18] and quoted the words of his letter, which I received at Nashville in November. I did this, because his complaint is that I came out to soon—and he and his strikers say, to forestall him. I am to see him at Sparta next Monday & will write you from that place. If he has a spark of honor, he will be off without a convention—but I fear he has not. Our friends here are angry, but I cause him to be treated in papers and by myself with great respect. In haste . . . .

S. H. Laughlin

ALS. DLC–JKP. Addressed to Columbia and marked "Private."

1. See Polk to Samuel H. Laughlin, January 27, 1843.

2. Tennessee's Fourth Congressional District.

3. A branch of the Cumberland River, the Caney Fork rose in Warren, White, and Jackson counties, flowed northwest into Smith County and fell into the Cumberland at Carthage.

4. On February 5, 1843, John W. Ford wrote Polk that Laughlin favored an allocation of votes in the district convention based on "the Democracy of Numbers" rather than on an equal vote for each county. Alvin Cullom countered with

the suggestion that the convention votes be allotted on the basis of each county's total voting population, including Whigs as well as Democrats. Ford notes that Laughlin never thought of factoring the Whig voting strength into the allocation of convention votes. ALS. DLC–JKP.

5. An early White County settler, Taylor served as sheriff from 1812 until 1814 before winning four terms in the Tennessee House, where he served from 1817 until 1823.

6. Fentress, Jackson, Overton, Putnam, and White counties were north of the Caney Fork River; Coffee, DeKalb, Van Buren, and Warren counties were below.

7. Robert Armstrong, Joseph W. Horton, and A. L. Davis. Horton was married to Sophia Western Davis, daughter of John Davis of Davidson County. The exact degree of kinship between Horton and A. L. Davis, cashier of the Sparta branch of the Bank of Tennessee in 1840, is not identified further.

8. Reference is to the Sparta *Jeffersonian Whig*.

9. See John Catron to Polk, January 2, 1842.

10. Appointments not identified further.

11. Warren County.

12. Probably Hugh Armstrong, William M. French, and Jessee Locke, none of whom is identified further.

13. John B. Rogers and William Worthington. A native of Tennessee and a Van Buren County Democrat, Worthington lost his legislative race to Rogers. The 1842 redistricting plan for the Tennessee House placed the more populous part of White County in a single district and "floated" the remaining portion with Van Buren and Fentress counties.

14. Daniel Coggin and Pleasant A. Thomason. Thomason, a North Carolina native, was one of the early sheriffs of DeKalb County, which was formed in 1838.

15. William H. Coulson and William S. Watterson. Coulson is not identified further.

16. Not identified further.

17. Felix Robertson, Joseph W. Horton, and Robert Armstrong. A son of James Robertson and a popular physician, Felix Robertson served as mayor of Nashville in 1818, 1827, and 1828.

18. On January 27, 1843, Laughlin published a letter in the McMinnville *Central Gazette* calling for a convention, "based upon the true principle that the Democracy of numbers shall govern." John W. Ford to Polk, February 5, 1843. ALS. DLC–JKP.

FROM AARON V. BROWN

Dear Sir   Washington Feby. 4th 1843

As you might well suppose from my former letters I find myself extremely reluctant to offer for Congress.[1] I will not say any thing now about the "whys & the wherefores." I send you my letter of declination.[2]

Consult with your Brother[3] & who ever else you please & if you shall believe that my *not* running will do any material harm to our party burn the letter I send you & request the news papers to announce me forthwith. If on the contrary, we can run somebody else without danger or detrement, publish my letter & let them take the field.

You see that there is but one condition on which I am willing to run & that is that it is material to the success of our cause. If it is not I sincerely desire to be off. Your Brother having views it would be politic in evry respect, not to let it be known that I had thrown the whole subject so exclusively under *your* control. I am forced however to do this by the supposed necessity that exist for me to decide one way or other before I return. If the presumption now existing is strong enough that I will be a candidate, what harm would it do to let every thing stand so, untill I do come which will be by the 12 or 15 March? But I dont ask this if you think it would do harm. Do as you think best, without any delicacy in the case—with the certain assurance that that decision of the matter 'which lets me off from the service & leaves me to have some chance to enjoy the society of my family & to attend to my farm below will be most agreeable to me.

A V Brown

[P.S.] Feby 8th. I have retained this letter now 3 or 4 days expecting the letter from my Brother & Mr Martin[4] stating the result of their consultations, but it has not arrived & I am very uneasy at the consequent delay in the annunciation of my final decision.

What is the difficulty in the way of your Brother? As to the Grand Jury nomination of Maury that is nothing[5]—even if he had responded to it favorably & publickly. The only thing I can think of is the rivalship of B. Gordon.[6] *That* however stands on as good a foot as it would have done if I had declared off last fall. But I cant Jud[g]e at this distance, of all these matters & so conclude again—to let *him* run—to let Gordon run or any other approved man whose success is certain & let me off. As to the role of *Giles*[7] for the *Assembly* I will be responsible for that though I be off of the field.

But if none of these things will do—withhold my letter & have me announced as a candidate. A.V.B.

ALS. DLC–JKP. Addressed to Columbia and marked *"Confidential."*

1. See Brown to Polk, December 27, 1842, and January 6, 1843.
2. Enclosure not found.
3. William H. Polk.
4. William R. Brown and Thomas Martin.
5. In a letter published in the Columbia *Tennessee Democrat* on January 26, 1843, the Democratic members of the Maury County grand jury publicly recom-

mended William H. Polk and Powhatan Gordon for election to the Tennessee House of Representatives and Richard A. L. Wilkes for election to the Senate to represent Maury and Giles counties. Letters of acceptance from each appeared in the *Democrat* on February 16, 1843.

6. Boling Gordon, a Hickman County planter, served three terms in the Tennessee House, 1829–35, and two terms in the Senate, 1835–37 and 1843–45.

7. Giles County.

FROM CAVE JOHNSON

Dear Sir, Washington Feb 5th 1843

I recd. yours last evening.[1] I have taken proper means to have our candidates brought forward early but fear we shall have some difficulty. In Dickson, W. B. Young *is a candidate* & would be beaten by a Whig if he is run. He will not decline or submit to a convention. The Democrats will therefore if they succeed have him & a Whig to beat. This probably will be done but there is some danger. Vhories wishes to run for the Senate & so does Gray[2] & Stewart will not again yield to Dickson[3] I fear. I have written to such men as I thought could settle it. I have also written to Benton & Robertson.[4] I fear Doct. Norfleet cannot be prevailed on to run. Nor have I heard whether Sturdevant can. Willie Norfleet will run in Robertson, particularly if I should be nominated at Dover, which I fear will be the case. He wishes help in Robertson in making speeches.

I sent you some ten days ago the Journals of the Call Session & Verplanks Bill,[5] & started last night the Journals of the House. I could not get a copy of the Journals earlier. G. & S. is not so prompt in public printing as the Globe was formerly.[6] I shall not be surprised if the half the printing ordered at this session is done after we leave.

I know of nothing new to inform. I am so much confined on account of my health that I see nobody except in the House. The opinion is gaining ground & I think certain that if we hold a Convention in the faul that the friends of C.[7] will not go into [it]. This is fairly inferable from Rhetts pamphlett & strongly intimated in the Mercury.[8] I do not think Van's friends will postpone longer than the 8th of Jany.

A circular letter[9] signed by us all would no doubt be most advantageous but then we could not probably agree. When I finish mine I will submit it & see who will.

We are in the appropriation Bills & I suppose most of our time will [be] occupied with them—no modification of the Tariff, no Treasury notes, spoken [of]—& it seems now generally believed that the Whigs wish to make Tyler have a call session. He will not if it can be avoided *as he now says.* The making of the loan & the Tariff[10] will not keep him half thru the year & if he keeps up until the regular session he must do so or trip.

I think my rheumatism is better tho I have nearly lost the use of my left arm. I have however but little pain. I shall with great reluctance enter upon another canvass even if nominated. I dont see how I am to ride over the hills & hollows as will be expected. Nor do I see how I am to get my family here & keep even if I should get them here. I still hope however that Hardwicke will re-consider & accept the nomination. There is a general feeling, I think without foundation, in Robertson & Montgomery, that he could not be elected. That together with the desire of my aid in Robertson & Montgomery, has made them talk more of me & press me more than elsewhere and I fear that, he has been hurt by the imprudence of some of my over-zealous friends.

Your election will suffer from so many whigs declining because those who run will repudiate the acts of the call session & still be whigs.

I suppose AVB[11] will run tho he has not yet said so. J. G. Harris is here but I learnt nothing from him.

C. JOHNSON

ALS. DLC–JKP. Addressed to Columbia and marked *"private."*
1. Letter not found.
2. Jacob Voorhies and James Gray. A Dickson County merchant and farmer. Voorhies represented Dickson, Benton, Humphreys, and Stewart counties as a Democrat in the Tennessee Senate from 1843 until 1847.
3. Reference is to Stewart and Dickson counties.
4. Reference is to Benton and Robertson counties.
5. Gulian C. Verplanck. See Cave Johnson to Polk, January 4, 1843.
6. Joseph Gales and William Seaton, editors of the Washington *National Intelligencer*, succeeded Francis P. Blair and John C. Rives, editors of the Washington *Globe*, as printers to the U.S. House on June 11, 1841.
7. John C. Calhoun.
8. Robert B. Rhett and the *Charleston Mercury*. See Cave Johnson to Polk, January 22, 1843.
9. See Cave Johnson to Polk, January 4, 1843.
10. See Abbott Lawrence to Polk, September 21, 1842, and Cave Johnson to Polk, January 22, 1843.
11. Aaron V. Brown.

FROM JOHN A. GARDNER

Dresden, Tennessee. February 8, 1843
In response to Polk's letter of the "28th of last month,"[1] Gardner informs Polk

that conflicting claims to office among Democrats in his county[2] have become "irreconcilable." Unless a single candidate can be chosen, Etheridge,[3] the Whig candidate will win. Gardner has consented reluctantly to seek reelection to the Senate, probably without opposition. He does not know the extent of division in the Whig ranks, but declares that the Whigs are "more skillful in healing divisions" than are the Democrats. Having discussed the prospects of the several candidates in his own district,[4] as well as those surrounding him, Gardner writes that Polk's chances were "Never more cheering in this quarter."

ALS. DLC–JKP. Addressed to Columbia.
1. Letter not found.
2. Weakley County.
3. A Weakley County lawyer, Henry E. Etheridge won election to a single term in the Tennessee House in 1845. Subsequently, he served three terms as a Whig and American Party candidate in the U.S. House, 1853–57 and 1859–61; he became clerk of that body in 1861. In 1869 Etheridge won election to a single term in the Tennessee Senate.
4. Tennessee's Eleventh Congressional District.

TO E. G. EASTMAN

My Dear Sir: Columbia Feby. 13th 1843
In the Nashville Union of friday last,[1] it was announced upon my authority, that I would be a candidate for Governor and that I would open the canvass at Jackson on the first Monday in April. It is my purpose first to visit the Counties West of the Tennessee River. This I can do by the 1st or 10th of May, and can then go to any other part of the State, where my presence may be most needed. After my notices for the Western District shall be published,[2] you will know my whereabouts from day to day. If my friends in East Tennessee shall advise me that they think it important that I should come to that Division of the State, before I canvass Middle Tennessee, I will do so; and I can I think reach E. Tennessee by the 15th of May. If on the other hand my friends in E. Tennessee think I had better be there late in the canvass, I will in that event canvass Middle Tennessee, before I cross the Mountain.[3] When I go to E. Tennessee had I better cross the mountain at *Morgan* State, or at *Marion* & go up South of the River?[4] After you have consulted our friends at Knoxville, write me on these points.

I hope our party will be thoroughly organized & have candidates in the field, in every District & County in the State, and that they will be out by the 1st monday in April at furthest. Let the whole party present an unbroken front & move boldly on that day.

JAMES K. POLK

P.S. I wish you to procure and forward to me the *Knoxville Post*, containing the answer of its Editor to *Mr A. R. Crozier's* of 8th February 1842,[5] in relation to the Declarations made by *Gov. Jones* on the subject of the Senatorial election, whilst at Knoxville, immediately after the last election. I do not know that it will be necessary to use it, but if the subject should be discussed by him in the canvass, I wish to be prepared. I wish to have it in the *Post*, because that is *Whig authority*, which cannot be denied. If you have not preserved a copy of the *Post* containing it, it is probable Mr. Crozier has. J.K.P.

ALS. NHi. Addressed to Knoxville and marked *"Private."*
1. The February 10, 1843, issue of the *Nashville Union* has not been found. On February 24, 1843, the *Union* stated that Polk would attend the appointments of Governor Jones, commencing in Springfield on March 24, as "published in the *Banner* of Friday last." However, Polk's campaign would begin at Jackson on the first Monday in April, where nothing would give Polk "more sincere pleasure than to have his competitor with him."
2. The *Nashville Union* of March 7, 1843, carried a list of Polk's appointments for the campaign.
3. Reference is to the Cumberland Mountain.
4. Reference is to the Tennessee River.
5. The issue of the Knoxville *Post* in which its editor, James Williams, responded to Arthur R. Crozier's certificate has not been found. Crozier's certificate, addressed to E. G. Eastman and dated January 24, 1842, appeared in the Knoxville *Argus* of Januray 26, 1842. Crozier certified that soon after the governor's election of August 1841, James C. Jones had remarked to him that "the Senate would be justified in refusing to go into convention with the House for the purpose of electing U.S. Senators if he was elected Governor, as he considered that election a test between the two parties and would look upon his success as evidence that the people of Tennessee desired Whig Senators." In his reply, reprinted, in part, in the *Nashville Union* of March 31, 1843, Williams noted that Jones' statements were public and "his opinions were founded upon the express supposition that the Whig party had a majority in the State." See Robert Armstrong to Polk, March 31, 1843.

FROM WILLIAM H. POLK

Dear Brother   Nashville Feb 14th 1843
    I received your letter this evening[1] and would leave in the Stage for home in the morning, but that Rufus Polk is not so well as he was a day or two ago[2]—and I would dislike very much to leave him at this time, when the turn his disease may take is very doubtful. He has not had one of his suffocating spells since last night at 11 O'Clock, but is much weakened

from the last attack. It would I think be wrong for me to leave him, although I cannot be of any use or advantage to him, until his case results either in death or recovery, or until his Brothers shall arrive.[3]

As to the political movements in Maury, I have had my fears, that Mr. N. in his sly, sneaking way would create some confusion for the present[4]—not that I beleive he can in the least distroy the harmony of the party in the end. He may give trouble, but can inflict no injury. Tell my Wife[5] to send me the letter, she mentioned in her letter, from Mississippi concerning my Tanner claims.[6]

Make what use you please of the communication enclosed.[7]

WILLIAM H. POLK

[P.S.] You may make what alterations you please in my letter. You will discover I made some. If wrong correct them. The time is so short, I have no time to consider or reflect.

ALS. DLC–JKP. Addressed to Columbia.

1. Letter not found.

2. Rufus King Polk, third son of William and Sarah Hawkins Polk of Raleigh, North Carolina, died in Nashville of a "violent affection of the lungs" on February 25, 1843. Owner of a large plantation located in Maury County on the Mount Pleasant turnpike, Rufus King Polk was buried nearby in St. John's churchyard on February 27, 1843. He was a third cousin to William H. and James K. Polk.

3. Reference probably is to Rufus King Polk's brothers from Maury County, Lucius J., George W., and Andrew J. Polk; his fourth brother, Leonidas Polk, resided in New Orleans and served as bishop of the Episcopal diocese of Louisiana.

4. See Aaron V. Brown to Polk, February 4, 1843, and Sarah C. Polk to Polk, March 29, 1843. For William H. Polk's further analysis of A. O. P. Nicholson's part in county politics, see William H. Polk to Polk, April 10, 1843.

5. Belinda G. Dickinson was the daughter of William G. Dickinson, a prominent surgeon in Franklin, Tennessee.

6. Not identified further.

7. Enclosure not found.

FROM AARON V. BROWN

Dear Sir   Washington Feby 15th 1843

From mere *habit* I write you another of my *daily bulletins*. Johnson is to have an interview tomorrow with one of the Banks here to see what can be done in your case. No name will be disclosed unless the arrangement can be made. The renewals required say every 120 or 160 days could be made through the agency of *Rives* of the Globe[1] & may need a power of atto from you—of all which I will advise you in my next.

I got a letter today from Leatherman,[2] stating amongst other things—that Shields was gone to Memphis in search of a new home. Now what I fear is that the publication of *either of my letters of declination*[3] might enduce him to change his purposes. If you were to enquire & [a]scertain whether he was going & if going whether shortly it might be politic to delay a little "untill he had too far consummated the act to give it up." [4] It is desirable that he should go as it would help us some in Giles & Wayne & perhaps elsewhere. You must not except to the responsibility I have thrown upon you in my two last letters[5]—for you may be assured that I will not complain of the exercise of your judgment in the matter— whatever it may be.

A. V. BROWN

ALS. DLC–JKP. Addressed to Columbia.
1. Washington *Globe*.
2. Daniel Leatherman, a resident of Giles County, is not identified further.
3. Reference to one letter of declination, but not to two, has been found. See Brown to Polk, February 4, 1843.
4. Quotation not identified.
5. See Brown's letter of February 4, 1843, and the note dated February 8 and enclosed with same. On February 10 Brown wrote to Polk, but did not mention the political decision entrusted to Polk on February 4 or 8. ALS. DLC–JKP.

FROM ROBERT ARMSTRONG

Govr.   Nashville 16 Feby [1843][1]

Guild you will see from the cover page is off.[2] Trousdale is the man if he will accept. Donelson would do far better. All this is mixed up with a little low Intrigue but no matter. It will tend to Keep Peyton on the Tract and we can surely beat him.

Eastman is here and gives a good account of your prospects in East Tennessee. You will beat Jones 10 or 20 Thousand in the race. You will give Aid and Support to every Democratic Candidate in the field and none will increase Your Vote. I Sicken when I think of their treatment two years ago. We Must Succeed in the Members for the Legislature (I mean a Majority). It is so Important in Carrying Out other views and Matters before the Presidential Convention. In haste.

R. ARMSTRONG

ALS. DLC–JKP. Addressed to Columbia.
1. Year identified through content analysis.
2. Armstrong covered his letter to Polk with a second sheet on the reverse

side of which was written the text of a letter received from Josephus C. Guild; Armstrong wrote the text of his letter to Polk on the reverse side of Guild's cover sheet. Writing on February 13, 1843, Guild advises Armstrong that personal and financial considerations prevent his running for a seat in Congress and that his friends must be reconciled to his decision. ALS. DLC–JKP.

FROM JONATHAN P. HARDWICKE

My Dear Sir,   Charlotte Febry 16 1843
     Your favour of the 11th Inst[1] came to hand yesterday. I presume from the tennor of it, you were not in receipt of my last note, to you,[2] in which I made Known to you my intentions to retire from Publick life and the probability of my leaving the State in a few weeks &&. L. B. Chase[3] a Delegate to the Convention from this Co left to day for Dover. Before he started he called upon me to Know if I would under any circumstances accept a nomination, by that boddy. I told him I would upon two conditions: first, that he should in my name sincearly declare to the convention that I did earnestly desire they would agree upon some other good and true man and excuse me for the future; then if they should think that our cause and party would be endangered, with out my feeble efforts, and give me the nomination I would accept and forego all the evils that might attend me. I have recd. the warmest solicitations from every Co. in the District,[4] & none more warm than from Henry. I saw the Shff.[5] & some three other men from Henry some ten or 12 days ago and they assured me none but my self were spoken of. Since that I saw a friend of ours from Nashvl. who travelled through Henry & Benton, and said the same. That is the tone in which I have been addressed from each Co. and section of our District, Montgomery not excepted. Genl W.B.J.[6] might have gotten his information from E. H. Foster for whose sayings, opinions and person he has a higher regard than any man now living. Nothing but a sence of duty and my attachment to our cause and party could have induced me to change my determinations formed upon mature reflection. I still hope the Convention will settle upon another; if so it will I hope be C. Johnson. A few days will however, disclose the whole matter.

                                              J. P. Hardwicke

ALS. DLC–JKP. Addressed to Columbia. Polk's AE on the cover states that he answered this letter on February 20, 1843; Polk's reply has not been found.
     1. Letter not found.
     2. See Jonathan P. Hardwicke to Polk, December 18, 1842.
     3. Lucien B. Chase was a Charlotte lawyer. Later in 1843 he removed to

Clarksville, where he practiced law with Willie B. Johnson. Chase won election as a Democrat to two terms in the U.S. House, 1845–49. He removed to New York City at the end of his second term.

4. Reference is to the Ninth Congressional District of Tennessee.

5. John H. Warren served as sheriff of Henry County from 1840 until 1844.

6. Willie B. Johnson.

FROM CAVE JOHNSON

Dear Sir,   Washington 17th Feby. 1843

I recd. yours from Nashville on yesterday.[1] The House Journal will reach you before this.[2] I begin to fear that no legitimate excuse for replying to M.B.[3] will be presented. No Bill connected with the Tariff will come up. A Bill authorizing a re-issue of Treasury notes is the only measure in contemplation. So that if I do answer I shall have to get at it upon some amendment or pull it in neck & heels without regard to order or propriety. I shall try & do so. I have a half written circular[4] but doubt whether I shall finish it. I am on Somers Com.[5] & up to our eyes every day investigating the petty Larcenies about the House & shall not be surprised if it results in a dismission of Clark[6] & during the sitting of the House we have to watch very close to expose wholesale plunderings. They have actually a *project* on hand urging it as *a party measure* to buy the book of debates Gales & Seaton—*$150,000 to sustain that press.*[7] Some Whigs *back from it* & have disclosed *to me* as one of the watch dogs. If the effort is made we shall have some rare sport. I keep myself busy day & night but will try & finish my circular. Finding that we were not likely to make any arrangement with Reeves,[8] I called this morning to see Smith[9] Cashr. of Metropolis Bank[10] & had a good deal of conversation with him. He submitted my suggestions to the Board & writes me that nothing can be done. They are discounting freely but only on short paper & are afraid to put their funds beyond their reach for any time—so he writes me. I should have got Catron to go up. I have voted so much agt. their Bank Bills that they feel no inclination to do any thing that would oblige me. I suspect Reeves is shaving deeply. We will keep a look out & see what can be done.

We have heard but very little of late until yesterday as to elections. A pamphlet appeared in answer to Rhett[11] & was secretly handed about—denouncing Calhoun strongly. His friends attribute it to Benton—without any reasonable grounds. It is thought to be a forced immitation of his style & probably had its origin with the Whigs. This has produced a good deal of talk. I have not seen it nor could I get a coppy. If I get a coppy I will send it to you. Calhoun's friends say, that Benton has said, he would not support Mr. C. if nominated. Like Achilles[12] he would retire &c. This produces much talk. I am inclined to think these things are talked of & greatly exagerated preparatory to their leaving us if necessary. There is no doubt that Col B. talks strongly, if not very imprudently agt. both C. & RMJ.[13] Graham[14] of N.C. had a long & very friendly talk about you today—calls you Cousins &c & believes that you will certainly & ought to be nominated with Van.[15]

I hear but little further as to the Convention. The N. Yorkers approve our time[16] but are afraid to move—waiting for Va. If we fix on Nov. C–s friends will decline going into the Convention I think. Rhett is now at home canvassing I suppose. He & Trotti[17] are put in the same district— Rhett living in the negro region & Trotti among the whites & rumor says Rhett is likely to be beaten which I shall regret. Holmes is likely to be defeated by Rhetts brother.[18]

It will be very unfortunate if I am again nominated. I do not see how I can again run. I doubt whether I shall be able to go over the district. I think I shall loose the use of my left arm. We have cut down all salaries by a vote of the H.[19] without much rhyme or reason. It will do much good & a good deal of harm—but upon the whole we thought it advisable to vote it.

Rumor says that Webster will go out & become the agent of the holders of the State Bonds & head the assumption party. It will be made a great question in the next elections—that or the issuance of stock based on the public Lands—about the same thing.[20] Our friends are generally very well.

C JOHNSON

ALS. DLC–JKP. Addressed to Columbia. Polk's AE on the cover states that he answered this letter on March 10, 1843; Polk's reply has not been found.

1. Letter not found.
2. See Cave Johnson to Polk, January 22, 1843.
3. Milton Brown. See Sarah C. Polk to Polk, November 7, 1842.
4. See Cave Johnson to Polk, January 4, 1843, and February 5, 1843.
5. The House passed a motion by Johnson on February 3, 1843, to appoint a select committee to investigate the degree of compliance with retrenchment resolutions adopted at the previous session. George William Summers, a Whig from western Virginia, chaired the Select Committee on the Retrenchment of Expenditures of the House.
6. Matthew St. Clair Clarke. In its report dated February 23, 1843, the Summers Committee indicated that all House officers had complied with the retrenchment resolutions except Clarke, who had not reduced his staff as instructed. Clarke continued to serve in his post, but lost his bid for reelection on December 6, 1843, to Caleb J. McNulty of Ohio.

7. On February 16, 1843, William Woodbridge, a Michigan Whig on the Library Committee, introduced a bill in the Senate to publish "the debates and proceedings of Congress." The measure provided for a congressional subscription of 1,000 copies at a price of $5.00 each, of all volumes in a projected three-part series. Part one would cover the period March 1789 through May 1824. Part two would consist of the volumes in Gales and Seaton's *Register of Debates in Congress* from December 1824 through October 1837. The final segment would include the *Congressional Globe* and *Appendix* from December 1837 through March 1843. Gales and Seaton were named publishers of the first two segments and Blair and Rives, of the final one. After heated debate the measure died in the Senate.

8. John C. Rives.

9. A native of Maryland and a major in the militia, Richard Smith served as cashier of the Washington branch of the Second Bank of the United States prior to assuming the cashier's post in the Bank of the Metropolis.

10. The Bank of the Metropolis, established during the War of 1812, became a federal depository in 1833 after deposits were withdrawn from the Second Bank of the United States.

11. See Cave Johnson to Polk, January 22, 1843. On February 17, 1843, the editors of the Washington *Globe* noted a recently issued pamphlet entitled, "A Warning to the Democracy." According to their report, the pamphlet speculated that John C. Calhoun would lead his supporters into the Whig ranks if he did not receive the Democratic presidential nomination in 1844.

12. The hero of Homer's *Iliad*, Achilles, was the handsomest and bravest of the Greeks who fought in the Trojan War. An intense quarrel with Agamemnon caused him to retire to his tent, and the tide of battle turned decisively against the Greeks until Achilles returned to slay Hector, the Trojan leader.

13. Richard M. Johnson.

14. Reference probably is to James Graham, a lawyer and Whig congressman from North Carolina, 1833–43, or to his brother, William Alexander Graham, who served as a Whig in the U.S. Senate, 1840–43, and as governor of North Carolina, 1845–49. One of Polk's great aunts, Susan Polk, married Benjamin Alexander of North Carolina, whose son, William, may have been related by marriage to James and William Alexander Graham.

15. Martin Van Buren.

16. See Samuel H. Laughlin to Polk, October 11, 1842.

17. A lawyer from Barnwell and former member of the South Carolina House, Samuel Wilds Trotti served one session in the U.S. House from December 1842 to March 1843.

18. Isaac E. Holmes and James S. Rhett. A Charleston lawyer, Holmes served in the South Carolina House, 1826–33, before winning election as a Democrat to the U.S. House, where he served from 1839 until 1851. Rhett, a planter and lawyer, represented Christ Church Parish in the South Carolina Senate, 1837–48. He was a brother to Robert Barnwell Rhett.

19. On February 15, 1843, the House approved a bill, introduced by Thomas D. Arnold, that would have reduced compensation and allowances of members of Congress, civil servants, and military personnel. The measure failed to win Senate approval.

20. Federal financial relief to the states, as in previous sessions, sparked lively debate in Congress and the press. The Senate debated assumption of state debts and finally postponed further consideration until the next session. In the House a measure promoted by William Cost Johnson, a Maryland Whig, drew the greatest attention. He advocated the distribution of $200 million in four-percent government stock to the states based upon their proportionate representation in Congress. The public lands were to be pledged as security until the stocks were redeemed by the government.

FROM ROBERT M. BURTON[1]

Dear Sir   Lebanon 18th February 1843

I received your letter of the 30th of January[2] and should have replied before this but I have [been] prevented by my engagements at the Courts up to the present day. Previous to the reception of your letter I had attended a court at Decalb and made the proper enquiry as to the candidate who should be selected to run upon the Democratic ticket: Colo. Floyd of Alexandria[3] is the best choice and it is admitted by some sagacious Whigs that he can be elected. I am well acquainted with him. He promised me he would come out at the proper time and I think he will be elected. There are two Whigs out[4] both of whom are determined to run. Let this be as it may Floyd can be elected.

The dificulty between Laughlin & Cullum for a seat for Congress in the mountain District I fear cannot be adjusted.[5] Cullum is unwilling to submit the matter to a Convention unless the Whigs in the district are permitted to vote in the Convention which proposition is ridiculous and unheard of before. Judge Ridley staid with me last night on his way from one of his courts and I requested him to write to Laughlin and advise him to decline which he promised me he would do. I fear if this is not done it will damage our party materially and in the end drive Cullum over to the Whigs. Sam Turney I think from the last interview I had with him is opposed to Laughlins declineing but it is doubtless upon the ground that in future it would leave the way open for him. Cullum certainly will beat Laughlin with the aid of the Whig vote which he will get and you must see at once the propriety of Laughlins declineing. Guild I think will be the nominee for Congress in the Sumner District[6] and if he will consent to run he can be elected and he is the only man of our party that can, as I think. He is much opposed to becomeing a Candidate and I fear if nominated he will not run. The next best chance is Genl. Donelson. If Guild is nominated you must urge strongly upon him to run and it is possible he may be induced to do so.

Your friends every where within my range are certain of your success and I can confidently assure you that your vote in this and the adjacent counties will far exceed your vote in the contest with Govr. Cannon. I have heard none express a believe that Jones can be reelected. So to the charge and the victory is ours.

ROBERT M. BURTON

ALS. DLC–JKP. Addressed to Columbia.

1. A Lebanon lawyer, Burton represented Wilson County in the Tennessee House, 1827–29, and in the Constitutional Convention of 1834. He ran unsuccessfully for Congress in 1839.

2. Letter not found.

3. William Floyd, a native of Tennessee, ran one of the earliest mercantile establishments in Alexandria and attained the rank of colonel in the DeKalb County militia.

4. Daniel Coggin and Pleasant A. Thomason. See Samuel H. Laughlin to Polk, February 1, 1843.

5. Samuel H. Laughlin and Alvin Cullom. See Laughlin to Polk, February 1, 1843.

6. Reference is to the Eighth Congressional District of Tennessee.

FROM ISAAC TAYLOR

Sparta, Tennessee. February 18, 1843

Taylor informs Polk that both Laughlin and Cullom probably will run in the Fourth Congressional District. Neither man will withdraw in favor of the other, nor can they agree upon the composition of a district convention that might resolve the issue. Cullom wants the Democratic delegates apportioned according to each county's total voting population, and Laughlin prefers an apportionment solely by Democratic voting strength in each. Taylor favors Laughlin's approach because it follows traditional practices. He thinks both men will continue as candidates regardless of the decision of the convention, which is to be held in March. The Whigs probably will bring out a candidate later. Taylor believes Whig strength in the district is declining.

ALS. DLC–JKP. Addressed to Columbia.

FROM ANDREW JOHNSON

Dear Sir   Greeneville February 20 1843

I received your letter some few days since,[1] and in reply have to say, that all is right in Greene & Hawkins. We now have these two Counties

Completely organized, and ready for the Contest. The only difficulty we have to contend with is that Bagh[2] wants to run in Hawkins, and the democrats in the main are determined not to go for him. How the matter will be finally arranged I cannot tell. I am well assured of one thing, that it will not affect you in the slightest degree. As to the senate, it is now thought that Col Critze[3] will be the strongest man we Can run, for floater over Greene Hawkins & Washington. Dr. Kinney[4] will be the man, for Greene. Milligan is now a Candidate. For Congress Col McLelland[5] wants to run. I am a Candidate subject to a decission of the democratic party through a Convention. The truth is that our democratic friends want him to yeald the field without a Convention, and thereby save his feelings. It is thought here by some of our friends, that a letter from you would have more influence with him than any thing that Could be done. We have been trying to get Col Robertson[6] to run in Cock & Sevier. I fear we can not succeed. I saw him yesterday & talked with him on the subject. As to your election, from all the information I can obtained [it] is beyond doubt. The whigs here look upon your election them selves as being sure.

In Cock your vote can be increased 200 votes, in Greene 300 votes, in Hawkins 250 votes, in Sullivan 100 votes, in Washington 150 votes, in Johnson & Carter 200 votes, in all making 1,200 votes. If this congressional district[7] is canvassed as it should be, I am certain that your vote can be increased 1,000 votes. Your election I put down as an absolute Certainty, and Just in this connection you must permit [me] to remind you of what I told you in your own House fall befor last, that your true position was to remain befor the people, that you could Carry the state at a propper time, to Give you prominence befor the whol nation, & that in case Mr Vanburen was nominated for president you would be put upon the ticket for the vice presidency. Your position gives you another advantage also. I have all ways felt a deeper interest in your political advancement than perhaps you ever supposed I did; during the last canvass I made more speechs for the purpose of advancing your election than I did for my own, and would have prefered defeat my self, if it would have saved your election. I was induced to think last fall, that perhaps you had been some what soured at me. In this I am in hopes I was mistaken. I did not know but what some of Nicholson enemies had made a false impression upon your mind. I knew that there was a coldness between you and Nicholson, and was resolved on being the last man to widen the breach. I was a friend to both of you, and wanted to soothe insted of exciting and widening the misunderstanding. I thought and believed we were not in a condition to loose prominent men. You have allways been my first Choice for any thing, and I am especially frank in saying that Nicholson has been my second, and I am in hopes by this time that you and him are on good terms.

A. JOHNSON

P.S. Let me hear from [you] on the receipt of this. Please give my best respects to Mrs Polk &c. A. JOHNSON.

ALS. DLC–JKP. Addressed to Columbia and marked "Private."
1. Letter not found.
2. Michael Baugh, a Rogersville silversmith, served a single term as a Democrat in the Tennessee House, 1839–41. He was a Hawkins County justice of the peace from 1839 until 1848.
3. Philip Critz, a Hawkins County farmer, miller, and tanner, served in the Tennessee House, 1841–43 and 1859–61, and in the Senate, 1843–47.
4. Daniel Kenney, a Jonesboro physician and merchant, represented Greene, Hawkins, and Washington counties for one term in the Tennessee House, 1843–45.
5. Abraham McClellan. See McClellan to Polk, February 20, 1843, and Sam Milligan to Polk, February 20, 1843.
6. Not identified further.
7. Tennessee's First Congressional District.

FROM ABRAHAM McCLELLAN

My Dear Sir   Washington City Febry. 20th 1843
     Yours of the 8th Instant[1] has been recd. I feel grateful for your condolince in my late affliction.[2] It was so sudden and unexpected that it well near prostrated me at the time. I have a vary bad cold—or I would have wrote you Sooner.
     You wish to know the State of things in our Congressional Districte[3]—of which I Know but litle. The nuse of the Districts being laid of[4] only reached Blountville the day I left for this place—and since I have not heard much except of late. There is several asperents in our party—and I fear things are working badly from what I hear. Theire is to be divitions in our ranks. *Johnson* and our friends in Hawkins County, have been making arrangements for him to be the candidate for *Congress*,[5] so that Hawkins Co. can get the Senate, in his place. This they have don without consulting our friends in the other *Counties*. I understand *Johnson* has ere this or will in the next *Sintnal*[6] anounce him Self as a candidate subjecte to the desition of a convention. I think that Steps wrong for I am informed that our friends think that him and some of the Polititians of Hawkins have been manageing the mater so as

to have a pacte convention to nomanate him. My opinion is if they attempt to have a convention and have Strife in that convention between different men which is to receive the nomanation that it will do more harm then good for our people do not understand much about conventions and are not vary partial to them. So I fear that theire is to bee som disagreeable feelings and vary likely two or more Demacratic candidates and in that event you know a *Whig* would be elected. True as you say I did express a disare not to run at the last election owing to my health and my wife not wishing me to be so much from home. I did then wish our friends in Hawkins Co. to run a man and let me of—but they would not. Indead every time I have run it was because no other Demacrat would. But this winter owing in part to the Sudin change in my Situation at home and understanding that theire was so many asspirents in our ranks that would not give way to each other and that all would yeld to me perhaps—I wrote to som of my friends that if this could be brought about I would like to be in *Congress* once more. I am told that *Col A. Johnson* said if I wished to run that he would not but he after that knowing I had consented still was going on making arangements to have a pact convention. If him and our desining friends from *Hawkins Co.* would have consented for me to run I would have had no opposition. But I am not going to let my name be brought before a conventi[on][7] where theire is to be strife and unc[ertain]ty—no, but if Johnson and his [friends] will [not consen]t for me to be nomanated, up [on the] whole I can but think they treate[d me] badly. They it seems took som pains to tell the people of Hawkins that I would not run—and there by got them to be for his nomanation. I suppos they think now that they can do without me. They will se. I can retire to privet life concious that my motives have been for the good of my country not *Selfish*.

I hope you will be out soon. The sooner the better. I hope as you say that you think we will cary the State. I Should [say] so that you may cary it. I have said too much upon this subject but it is to you as a friend. Excuse my hast. I have not time to look over this. Remember me kindly to your Lady and be assure of my sincere wishes for your well fare and the cause in which you are labouring.

                                                      A. McClellan

ALS. DLC–JKP. Addressed to Columbia.

1. Letter not found.

2. McClellan's "late affliction" probably refers to a death in his immediate family, most probably that of his wife, Nancy Ann Moss.

3. Reference is to the First Congressional District of Tennessee.

4. See Samuel H. Laughlin to Polk, October 11, 1842.

5. See Andrew Johnson to Polk, February 20, 1843, and Sam Milligan to Polk, February 20, 1843.

6. The Jonesboro *Tennessee Sentinel*, established by Lawson Gifford in 1835, served the Democracy of Washington, Sullivan, Greene, and Hawkins counties. No 1843 issues of the *Sentinel* have been found.

7. Manuscript mutilated here and below as indicated by brackets; wording supplied by the editor from context.

FROM SAM MILLIGAN

Dear Friend,   Greeneville February 20. 1843

I would have replied to yours of the 27th ult[1] at an earlier day, had I not supposed I would be able to give you more information, touching the several matters of inquiry made in your letter, after the term of our circuit Court[2] which was held in this place last week. During which time I had an opportunity of confering with many of our political friends from the adjoining counties, as well as those from every part of Greene, for there were an unusual number of persons attracted to this term of the court in consequence of some very exciting criminal cases that were pending; and I am happy to say, that I found much more solicitude among our political friends for the success of our cause at the approaching election, than I believed myself at all authorized to expect from the low ebb at which politics seem to stand. I also found our opponents more sadly disappointed and more deeply mortified at the course pursued by their leaders since they came into power, than I really had immagioned. They feel they had been duped—decieved—and missled by those upon whom they looked as their friends; and, therefore, they are under no obligations to support them. But whether they will turn round and support those whom they have been taught to regard as enemies is still a debatable question. I am, however, judging from circumstances, forced to the conclusion that "there are hundreds of the more moderate Whigs in E. Ten. who will not hesitate a moment to change their politics—acknowledge their error—and come up to the poles" and do their duty by voting for democratic men & measures.

Before this reaches you, I presume, you will have seen in the Ten. Sentinel of the 18th inst. the announcement of Col. A Johnson as a candidate for congress, *subject to the decision of a convention.*[3] This announcement was not made, as I understand it, with the view to supersede the necessaty of calling a convention, if the people desire it, or to forstall the claims of other aspirants, but merely to set himself properly before the people of the district[4] and to satisfy the urgint solicitations of his friends.

Col. A. McClelan[5] also desires to become a candidate. He has many warm and zealous friends who are unwilling that he should yield to Johnson or any other man in the district. On the other hand Johnsons friends are unwilling that he should yield to McClelan or any other man. In order therefore to settle this vexed s[t]ate of things, Johnson has in his announcement expressed his willingness to submit his pretentions to a convention. And it is understood that McClelan will do likewise. I think from these circumstances we will be compelled to have a district convention, and by it, I entertain no dout, but we can amicably adjust the whole matter and avoid a collision among our selves from this quarter.

I can not certainly inform you who will be the candidate for the senate in this district, but it is generally understood that Col. Critz of Hawkins will be run, and if so I think he will be quite acceptable to the party.

Neither can I certainly inform you who will be run for floater. But Dr. D Kinny[6] of Jonesboro is spoken of, and I now think it most likely he will be the candidate, as there are no other aspirant for that office that I now am aware of. He will be an efficient and acceptable man.

For county representative, there are some three or four aspirants, but they all have mutually agreed to submit their claims to a county convention—which will meet on the 6th of march next. You will perceive we are making every effort to avoid a collision between friends. And I think we have things in such a train as will enable us to succeed in this most desirable thing without giving serious offence to any.

We have taken measures in "old Greene" for a thorough, and I hope, an efficient organization. And we are now standing *"erectis auribus"*[7] waiting to catch the sound of the word *Charge* from our *file leader*[8] in M. Ten. and we will be down upon the whiggers with a vengeance. I speak without flattery, but the general feeling in E Ten is, *that you must not be beaten this race.* The people are ready to do battle for you with more energy and zeal than they ever have done before.

S. MILLIGAN

[P.S.] I would be happy to hear from you at all times.

ALS. DLC–JKP. Addressed to Columbia.
1. Letter not found.
2. Greene County was in Tennessee's First Judicial Circuit.
3. See Abraham McClellan to Polk, February 20, 1843, and Andrew Johnson to Polk, February 20, 1843.
4. Tennessee's First Congressional District.
5. Abraham McClellan.
6. Daniel Kenney.
7. Latin phrase meaning "with attentive ears."
8. Reference is to Polk.

FROM ROBERT B. REYNOLDS

My dear Sir   Knoxville February 20th 1843

Before and since the receipt of your favor of the 19th ult.[1] I had & have busied myself in organising our forces, (by bringing out candidates & reconciling feuds), for the coming election. That too much apathy pervades our ranks, I am too well convinced—but a more general indifference exists among our opponents. Our friends will be animated sufficiently ere the day of the trial. Already do I see evidence of zeal in our ranks.

I concur with you that we ought to run candidates in every county and district where parties are nearly ballanced. In Roane Co. Col. Hembree will without doubt be reelected as the friends of Major Sevier[2] have declared for him & places his election beyond a doubt. In that senatorial district,[3] I do not believe that a suitable person can be found to take the field on our side. Col. Wheeler has joined the Methodist Church & refuses to run. Major Jarnagin is very easy on the subject & does not seem willing to make one effort to aid us—Major Burrus does not feel willing to enter the field.[4] These are our only materials in that district & all of them refuse to make the necessary effort to secure the district. However by running Major Sevier we secure Hembree's election & get at least a Tom Brown Whig[5] in the Senate—so that arrangement is the best we can make. Major Brown goes into it with a great good will.[6] In Blount, we are looking every day for the announcement of Jas Gillespie Esq[7] (the father of Findly)[8] to run for the House on the dem. Ticket. It is the opinion of Gen. Wallace that he can be elected. In Monroe our friends will run Torbitt or H. H. Stephens.[9] Torbitt's friends are endeavoring to obtain for him the nomination for the senate. If that fails, he will run for the County. In Hamilton Col. Shepherd[10] is out & will stand a good chance of success. I do not know who will run for Ham. & Marion, but some one must be brought out. Our friends are all satisfied that Anderson can be elected in McMinn. That we count as a gain. In Campbell & Anderson, R. D. Wheeler[11] is out. Peterson, Tyler Whig & Sharp dem. also in the field.[12] Old Col Tunnel[13] will be out and I fear be elected. If Sharp would withdraw there would be a good chance to elect Oliver or Col. Petree.[14] In Claiborne I hear that our friends are up and a doing & will increase their majority next summer. In Grainger either Col. McGinnis or Col Jas W Lafferty[15] will run for the House. In Cocke, Doct. Ramsey is trying to get Squire Wilson to run.[16] John Baker is a candidate in Jefferson.[17] He will run as the independent Whig & if elected go for us. These three last named counties I do not calculate on carrying, but we stand some chance in Grainger & will certainly have a candidate there.

Col. Johnson will shortly be announced as a candidate for congress, subject, however, to the decision of a convention. He is the man who should go to Congress in the first district.

I have the pleasure to say that we are rapidly gaining, even in old Knox, altho. we cannot hope to over come the majority against us. Yet, we will greatly reduce it; and as to East Tennessee, if the election was to take place to morrow, I do not believe the Whigs would beat us one vote, in her borders. I feel sanguine that we shall be able to make large gains in every county where the proper efforts are made. We intend to have candidates in *Knox*—though She be the Vanguard of whiggery.

You have no doubt Seen by the Argus the proceedings of our meeting here.[18] They take well amongst the people & will open the eyes of many hitherto led by the nose, as it were, to support the Whig party. I have no fears but that we shall gain several members in E.T. & overcome the Whig majority of 1841. I see by the Union that you commence the campaign at Jackson &c.[19] This is as it should be, as I believe it will be best to wind up the race in this division of the State. It will be early enough to reach here by the first of June & I think you ought to commence at Montgomery & go up the northern side of the State—touching at Campbells Station & then to Clinton & as you return visit Knoxville.

R. B. REYNOLDS

ALS. DLC–JKP. Addressed to Columbia.

1. Letter not found.

2. Probably Elbridge Gerry Sevier, a Roane County Whig who had been defeated for a seat in the Tennessee House by Joel Hembree in 1841. Sevier was married to Mary Caroline Brown, daughter of Thomas Brown.

3. The senatorial district was composed of Anderson, Campbell, Morgan, and Roane counties.

4. Probably John Jarnagin and Lewis Burris. Jarnagin, a merchant and hotel keeper in Clinton, served as clerk of the Anderson County Court, 1834–36, and as a clerk of the circuit court for Tennessee's Second Judicial District, 1836–44. Burris held the sheriff's post in Roane County from 1838 until 1844.

5. Thomas Brown, father-in-law of Elbridge Sevier, was a pioneer settler of Roane County. Brown served two terms in the Tennessee House, 1817–19 and 1821–23, and was clerk and master of Roane County Chancery Court, 1834–48.

6. Brown's agency in the attempt to place Hembree in the Tennessee House and Sevier in the Tennessee Senate is not further identified.

7. Virginia born, James Gillespy migrated early to Blount County, Tennessee, where he built a mill on Pistol Creek in 1803 and engaged in farming. He served two terms in the Tennessee Senate, 1821–25. Gillespy was the father of four sons, one of whom was John Finley Gillespy.

8. A Madisonville lawyer, John Finley Gillespy served three terms in the Tennessee Senate, 1829–33 and 1839–41.

9. Granville C. Torbett and Henry H. Stephens. A Madisonville lawyer, Stephens represented Monroe County for two terms in the Tennessee House, 1845–47 and 1851–53.

10. Lewis Shepherd, a Hamilton County Democrat, wrote Polk on March 5, 1843, that he was "again" a candidate to represent his county. ALS. DLC–JKP.

11. A merchant and farmer, Richard D. Wheeler represented Campbell County in the Tennessee House from 1837 until 1845 and from 1853 until 1855.

12. Reference possibly is to Joseph Peterson and William D. Sharp. Peterson served as sheriff of Campbell County, 1825–26, and later as one of the circuit court clerks for Tennessee's Second Judicial District, 1826–40. Sharp was register of Campbell County, 1841–42. Peterson and Sharp had both run for a seat in the Tennessee House in 1841.

13. William Tunnell, an Anderson County farmer, won five terms in the Tennessee House, 1819–23, 1825–27, 1835–37, 1839–41, and a single term in the Tennessee Senate, 1849–51.

14. Richard Oliver and Petree. Oliver, sheriff of Anderson County from 1834 until 1835, ran unsuccessfully for the Tennessee House in 1841. Petree, also an unsuccessful candidate for the Tennessee House in 1841, is not identified further.

15. McGinnis and Lafferty are not identified further.

16. Not identified further.

17. On February 6, 1843, J.G.M. Ramsey described Baker to Polk as "a kind of a Democrat." ALS. DLC–JKP. Baker is not identified further.

18. On February 15, 1843, the Knoxville *Argus* printed the proceedings of the Democratic meeting held in Knoxville two days earlier. The meeting appointed delegates to attend a national convention, established support for the platform of the Democratic Party, and endorsed Polk's bid for the governorship.

19. See Polk to E. G. Eastman, February 13, 1843.

TO JOHN C. SPENCER

Columbia, Tennessee. February 23, 1843

Polk introduces J. G. M. Ramsey and recommends him as being "well qualified to discharge the duties of a visitor to West Point." [1]

ALS. DNA–RG 94, Records of the Adjutant General's Office, 1780's–1917. Addressed to Washington City. AE on the cover states that Spencer answered this letter on March 13, 1843; Spencer's reply has not been found.

1. On February 17, 1843, Ramsey wrote Polk that as he needed to visit Raleigh and "some Eastern City" before publishing his *Annals of Tennessee*, he would be pleased to combine his private business with "some public duty." ALS. DLC–JKP.

FROM ROBERT ARMSTRONG

Govnr.   [Nashville] 24th Feby [18]43

At Dover Cave Johnston was nominated and a Letter read from him saying that he would serve &c.[1] Copeland is now here. Says that Johnston nomination puts all to rest and makes every thing great in that district. Gardner will run for the Senate again. I see Andrew Johnston[2] *is Out* for Congress. I Knew he would be from what Eastman said a few days ago. He is devoted to Johnston. McClennon[3] ought to press him off. Their is danger in him.

All I can say to you in relation to your appointments from Jackson[4] is that *you make them*, let them be *yours*. Keep Jones following. He will soon see *Sights* and Fly home for advise. The Whig leaders are making a Stir. I see a Fluttering and I think Peyton will be rushed off and Campbell put On *as* Johnston[5] is Out, what I told you when here.

Write me often. I will try and make Burton pay us now.

R. ARMSTRONG

ALS. DLC–JKP. Addressed to Columbia.

1. On February 18, 1843, county delegates to a Democratic district convention unanimously chose Cave Johnson to run for reelection in Tennessee's Ninth Congressional District.
2. Andrew Johnson.
3. Abraham McClellan.
4. See Polk to E. G. Eastman, February 13, 1843.
5. Cave Johnson.

FROM W. L. D. EWING

Hon & Dr Sir   [Springfield, Ill. Feb. 24, 1843][1]

I was very much flattered at the receipt of your kind favour of some weeks since.[2] I declined writing, in answer, immediately, in order, that I might sound the feelings of the Democratic portion of our Legislature and other democratic gentlemen in attendance at the Seat of Government.[3]

I take great pleasure in announcing the not unpleasant inteligence (I hope) to you, that you are the universal democratic favorite for the vice presidency of the Nation. I went to work, immediately, on my arrival here in December to ascertain the truth on this subject—and to my very agreeable (I can't say surprise) I found every body with whom I conversed (and I conversed with all the democrats in & out of the Legislature at the Seat of Government) for you. There were some for Col. Johnson but these were pleased that he had put his name forth for the Presidency, relieving them thereby from any obligation to vote for him for the Viceship. He has not many friends here. Indeed no one can make a show of strength against. Carolinian, Tennessean, Kentuckian & Yankee, are all for you. If I live I shall be in the convention, whenever it may be held,[4] if I live. I send you a half sheet of Illinois State Register containing a brief account of a very large & influential meeting of the democrats then at the Seat of Government,[5] at which, I had the honor to preside. You will see the mode proposed for raising our delegation in the National Democratic Convention.[6] This was done in order to propitiate what here was understood to be *extreme* Southern predeliction. But they will all be *on our side*. For Van Buren & James K. Polk, at the convention and at the polls. The Senator recently elected (Judge Breese) and his Colleague (McRoberts) are for you & V.[7] Both of whom will be in the convention.

So, my Dr Sir, in your reflections about your prospects (and no man can be without those reflections) put down the Prairie State[8] unanimously for Van Buren & Polk. Calhoun has many friends, but let him bide his time.

W. D. L. Ewing

ALS. DLC–JKP. Addressed to Columbia.

1. Letter dated by the author below his signature.

2. Letter not found. Reference probably is to Polk's letter of December 7, 1842; see W. L. D. Ewing to Polk, November 14, 1842.

3. Reference is to Springfield, Illinois.

4. The National Democratic Convention assembled in Baltimore on May 27, 1844, and concluded its deliberations five days later.

5. Enclosure not found. The *Illinois State Register*, a Democratic newspaper published in Springfield, was edited by William Walters and George R. Weber.

6. Each judicial district in Illinois would select one delegate to the national convention.

7. Sidney Breese, Samuel McRoberts, and Martin Van Buren. An Illinois lawyer who sat on the state supreme court in 1841 and 1842, Breese won election as a Democrat to the U.S. Senate in 1843 and served until 1849. A Danville, Illinois lawyer, McRoberts held several local, state, and federal positions before winning a single term in the U.S. Senate, where he served from 1841 until his death in 1843.

8. Reference is to Illinois.

FROM JONATHAN P. HARDWICKE

My Dear Sir   Charlotte Febry 25th 1843

You will have seen ere this reaches you the result of the Dover Convention which I have no doubt is sattisfactory to you at least so far as Cave is concerned.[1] Our man Voorhies is doubtless the ablest Polition amongst us, and will I hope be acceptable to our friends in the District. Eubank will run on our side in Dickson, for the Lower Branch. Our Circuit Court is just over. It is believed by Caves nearest friends that he will not accept the nomination. In that event, I have very reluctantly agreed if the Convention men will upon his declining it, call me out in a proper manner [I will] take the field.

I do and will continue to hope he will accept and run till the contrary is made to appear. Nothing in my opinion but his bad health will cause him to decline it, and to the latest dates from him his health was improving. Judge Martin will be the Whig Candidate if one they have, and will run upon the Bank and Tariff alone. He expects to make a great change in Our district, on account of the great Iron Interest, here. The Judge cant come it, nor can any other Whig in our district if we do as we should & I hope we will.

Nothing but our cause could induce me again to enter the field. The Convention I learn were unanimously in favour of me next to Cave, or in the event he could not run. I do not want to run at all but if our folks do as they say they will, as before remarked I shall forego all the consequences, and meet you perhaps in Robertson at the Gov's first appointment.[2]

J. P. HARDWICKE

ALS. DLC–JKP. Addressed to Columbia.

1. Reference is to Cave Johnson. See Robert Armstrong to Polk, February 24, 1843.

2. James C. Jones and Polk opened the gubernatorial campaign in Springfield on March 24, 1843.

FROM SACKFIELD MACLIN

My dear Sir,   Memphis Tennessee February 27th 1843

We are much pressed in this district for candidates—no one to run for Congress, for the Senate, or for the house of representatives.[1] However, David Fentress of Hardeman wishes (as I believe) to run for Congress, and some of our friends think he would run well. But I have no such idea.

The truth is, I apprehend he will injure our success. This belief is founded upon the fact that we were both electioning before the last election; and the result was, that he did not get the party strength in Hardeman, as you and myself both beat him; and he was running against an unpretending stranger, tho a man of good sense.[2] Fentress does not make a good speech before the people—his address is uncouth and rough, and in my opinion would not suit a large portion of this district. But the probability are in favour of his being our candidate, and if so, we will do our best to elect him. He is a true Democrat and party man. I have done all in my power to get those to become candidates who would assist you in your election, but I have thus far failed. But be assured, that we will run those for the Legislature who will succeed. At the last election you beat Jones in Hardeman 229 votes. You will at the next election beat him not less than 300 votes. In this county Jones beat you about 96 votes, and at the next election I had rather have your chance than his for the majority. I am firmly of the opinion, from all the information I can get from all parts of this division of the state, that Jones can not beat you as far as did Gov Cannon.[3] I have heard from some of our leading friends in E Tennessee and they assure me that you have gained ground there.

I will have the pleasure of seeing you at Jackson the first of April,[4] and may possibly want a few letters of introduction from you, as I am going west and south this spring.

Henry Clay is in this town, and the Whigs are doing their utmost for him. They appointed 25 to visit him at New Orleans and invite him to call at this place on his return home, and only one out of the 25 went down, and he reached here last Saturday. He was recd at the river[5] with more or less pomp & circumstance. From thence he we[nt][6] to the Exchange Hotel; and Leroy P[ope][7] flattered him; and he replied in a speech of one hour long, declaring himself for his old "American System." I was not present, but the Democrats say, it was a perfect failure. He is still in town going from house to house, but he makes no changes, and a splendid defeat awaits him in 1844. I have spoken free of Mr Fentress, but not with malice, for we are friendly, and if by accident he was to hear the contents of this letter, it would offend him. Therefore it with you.[8]

Sackfield Maclin

ALS. DLC–JKP. Addressed to Columbia.

1. Shelby County was part of Tennessee's Tenth Congressional District.

2. Contemporary election returns identified Fentress' Whig opponent only by his surname, "Jones"; he is not identified further.

3. Newton B. Cannon received approximately 1,900 more West Tennessee votes than did Polk in the gubernatorial election of 1839.

4. See Polk to E. G. Eastman, February 13, 1843.

5. Reference is to the Mississippi River.

6. Part of this word and that of one below were obliterated by the seal of the letter.

7. A native of Georgia, Leroy Pope, Jr., resided in Madison County, Alabama, before settling in Memphis, where he later served as superintendent of the city schools, 1857–61. The Nashville *Republican Banner* of March 8, 1843, carried a lengthy account of Clay's visit and Pope's welcoming address.

8. The syntax of Maclin's final sentence is garbled.

FROM CAVE JOHNSON

My dear Sir,   Washington Feby 28th 1843

I know you will be vexed when you find that we have not made a speech for circulation or written a circular.[1] I delayed making a speech upon M.B.[2] hoping for a chance upon a tariff Bill but none has been introduced & since the intention not to report such a Bill was made known, there has been no opportunity without thrusting it upon the House out of order and at the hazard of being coughed down. Brown[3] has had a tariff speech ready for a month but I think has given up all hopes. As to the circular I had one half done but found that it would occupy so much space as to be unmanageable & gave it up & prepared myself for a speech on the expenditures but have not delivered it & probably will not. Times are not as formerly, when the Com. of the Whole afforded an opportunity of general discussion, particularly on the civil & diplomatic Bill.[4] We took it up, had a slight discussion on Hasler[5] for an hour or two on two days; then came the resolution to take it out of Com.; an half an hour after voting on Amendments without debate—& it was done; the previous question instantly called & voted thro. in half the time it would take a modest man to read it. I dont think five hours were spent on the whole Bill. So it is with every Bill. The freedom of debate is litterally crushed beneath the previous question and the res. to take Bills out of Com. We lacked but a few votes to day of taking an appropriation Bill[6] out of Com. without its having been ever taken up in Com. The remedy we must adopt is this—when I get home whether a Candidate or not I will make my speech on M.B. in *self defence* & have it published. I will send it to you before publication. I must also make a speech on the Expenditures & publish it. B.[7] must make & publish his speech on the Tariff—& so we must go thro all the questions, Tariff, distribution, assumption, Banks & Bankruptcy. I will do my part whether upon the field or not. I trust sincerely our friends may be able to unite on Majr. H.[8] or some other available Democrat but chances are judging from my last letters that I shall be nominated.[9] If I have to continue in politics, which I did not intend when I left home I shall avail myself on the solicitations of many friends recently & become also a candidate for the Senate unless some better & older soldier than myself should be selected by our friends. Whilst I am perhaps more indifferent to such honors than almost any other, yet if I have to bear the burthen I see no reason why I should not share the honors.

I see no prospect of a convention in the faul. Our N.Y. friends all wish it but are afraid to move lest C.[10] & his friends should be driven off & they hope, that with a little delay his weakness will be so manifest, that they will yield & fall in. In this they are mistaken. They will hold the balance in Va. N.C. Geo. Alabama & Miss. & as sure as we are living, if it is postponed until May 1844, they will *leave us & ruin us*. It will be then too late to meet & overcome such opposition. I tell them so—but still they are not inclined to move—are *afraid* of a Congressional Caucus. My only hope rests upon the Va. State Convention in March.[11] If that body selects our time, N.Y. & N. England follows & the Convention will be holden & C. & his *friends go off*. But then we shall have time to beat them. Hopkins[12] takes the same ground & is active & doing all that he can. Jones[13] is *positively still* & no body knows how he is. All I believe of the other Va Democrats are inclined in favor C. & yet Hopkins tells me that there is now two to one in Va Legislature for Van.[14] In N.C. none stands firm but Genl McK.[15] who is too timid to say any thing. It is a general opinion here, if Van gets the nomination that you will be placed on the ticket. Abijah Mann[16] was here the other day. He is decidedly for it.

I have Judge C's promise to see Van Ness[17] on your monied business.[18] That is now the only hope. Van Ness would do nothing to oblige any of us, because we vote agt. his Bank, unless he thought we could be bought up by it.

We passed a Bill to day which keeps old Amos out of Jail[19] but few of the Whigs knew it & they did not wish to interpose. Only 40 voted agt. the appropriations for the Ashburton treaty.[20] Peel's speech[21] created a good deal of sensation here & should have delayed any appropriation until it was understood. If the weather is tolerable I shall leave thursday or friday morning.

C. JOHNSON

[P.S.] I hope you will find it convenient to meet his excellency[22] at Springfield, Clarksville &c. If you cannot you must let me know & I will be with him. I hear favorable news from Robertson. Our friends think they can beat the Genl[23] but in this they are mistaken. If he does not run, we shall be apt to get that Co. & the Senator. We shall secure Montgomery any how.

ALS. DLC–JKP. Addressed to Columbia. Polk's AE on the cover states that he answered this letter on March 10, 1843; Polk's reply has not been found.

1. See Sarah C. Polk to Polk, November 7, 1842.

2. Milton Brown.

3. Aaron V. Brown.

4. On February 24, 1843, the U.S. House took up the bill making appropriations for the civil and diplomatic service of the U.S. for the next fiscal year. Discussion continued on February 25 and 27, 1843. Francis Mallory of Virginia offered an amendment providing an appropriation of $100,000 for continuing the survey of the U.S. coast. Charles Brown of Pennsylvania opposed that and suggested a $60,000 reduction. Brown further urged that the House dispose of Ferdinand R. Hassler's office as head of the survey and assign the survey to other officials in the general government. On February 27, Brown's amendment was defeated, and an appropriation of $100,000 was passed.

5. Ferdinand R. Hassler was professor of mathematics at West Point, 1807–09; first superintendent of the U.S. Coast Survey, 1816–18 and 1832–43; and superintendent of weights and measures, 1830–32.

6. Reference probably is to a resolution proposed by the Committee on the Library and presented by Joseph L. Tillinghast. That resolution would have authorized the purchase of so many volumes of the U.S. laws as might be necessary to complete the sets then in the Library. Cave Johnson tried to refer the matter to the Committee of the Whole, but his motion was ruled out of order. Johnson then moved to table the proposal and the House concurred.

7. Aaron V. Brown.

8. See Jonathan P. Hardwicke to Polk, February 25, 1843.

9. See Robert Armstrong to Polk, February 24, 1843. In a letter of February 4, 1843, Willie B. Johnson expressed his fears to Polk that Democrats would split into factions at the Dover Convention. ALS. DLC–JKP.

10. John C. Calhoun.

11. The Virginia State Democratic Convention, held at Richmond on March 2–4, 1843, recommended that the National Democratic Convention be held at Baltimore on the fourth Monday in November, 1843.

12. A lawyer and Democrat, George W. Hopkins of Virginia won election to seven terms in the U.S. House, 1835–47 and 1857–59.

13. John W. Jones.

14. Martin Van Buren.

15. James I. McKay.

16. A New York merchant, Abijah Mann, Jr., served two terms in the U.S. House as a Jackson Democrat, 1833–37.

17. John Catron and John P. VanNess. A New York lawyer, VanNess won election as a Democrat to one term in the U.S. House, 1801–03. He remained in Washington to accept an appointment as major in the District of Columbia militia. VanNess served as mayor of Washington, 1830–34, and as president of the National Metropolitan Bank in Washington, 1814–46.

18. See John Catron to Polk, December 25, 1842.

19. On February 28, 1843, the U.S. House passed a Senate bill amending the laws regulating imprisonment for debt in the District of Columbia. That legislation provided that a debtor could not be placed in confinement pending an appeal or for one year after a final judgment by the U.S. Supreme Court. Amos Kendall, U.S. Postmaster General from 1835 until 1840, was placed under the imprisonment for debt law for a judgment given against him in the case of *Kendall* v. *Stokes*.

20. On February 28, 1843, the U.S. House passed an appropriation bill to implement the Webster-Ashburton Treaty, which required $217,728 to carry out the sixth article of the treaty and an additional $300,000 to "pay and satisfy the States of Maine and Massachusetts for the expenses incurred by them in protecting and surveying the disputed territory."

21. Prime Minister Robert Peel's speech of February 2, 1843, concerned the reciprocal right of maritime search. Sir Robert claimed for Britain a right to visit, as distinct from the right to search, vessels suspected of being engaged in the slave trade.

22. James C. Jones.

23. Richard Cheatham.

FROM GEORGE W. SMITH[1]

My Dear Sir,   Memphis March 2nd 1843

Your esteemed favor of the 26th Jany.[2] came duely to hand. I have delayed my answer untill I might be able to give you the desired information. I agree with you, that much depends in the approaching Canvass, upon the organization & concert of the Democrats. Up to the present time, there has been but little doing on either side in the way of organization. Though our friends are now begining to bestir themselves & I think in a few weeks, will have our ticket complete. There is no doubt but our end of the State will be as you say the "battle ground" & therefore the more necessity for harmonious & energetic action. I have no doubt the Democrats will vote stronger at the next August election in the District[3] than they have ever done before. And this opinion is based upon my personal knowledge of *many Whigs who will not sustain Mr Clay*, and when the questions are argued with which he is identified, they will not support the men who support him. We have had much difficulty in selecting our candidate for Congress. We would have selected by a convention, but thought it useless to go th[r]ough a public nomination, unless the nominee, would accept. Judge Dunlap was our choice, & would undoubtedly make the best run, & could unquestionably be elected but he declines the canvass, alledging many reasons which it would seen ought to excuse him. We then selected judge Wm T. Brown,[4] but I do not think it likely he will be a candidate. Fentress will be the next choice (& with many the first choice) & I am informed he will be announced in the next paper. He is a good selection, & I think will beat Mr Ashe with great ease, if he & his friends use the proper exertion. Mr Stanton will probably run for the Senate, as Judge Brown, with whom he is associated in the practice of Law, declines becoming a candidate for Congress. Or Stanton will be a candidate for Floater, in case, Mr Monroe Williamson[5] of Fayette is a candidate for the Senate, which I think most likely will be the case. These are among our most talented men & very able debaters, will do the cause justice I think, and we have no doubt of their election. As to our Representative from Shelby—we have some difficulty. We have some looking (in this way). Charles J. Nelson[6] a plain farmer, a good Democrat, is anxious to run, & the great majority of our party oppose it, not believing, he can be successful. He has some strength in his neighborhood, & the matter is to ease him off, without offending him, & his friends & then we will start an available candidate. I am not disposed to engage in politics, and can not consent to become a candidate unless it is to save the county—though I think we will give a good account of Shelby. And Nelson out of the way, we will start Maj Edwin Hickman[7] or some other Democrat who can be elected. I think the Democrats are greatly indebted to you. They feel it sensibly and you may have no fears, as to their giving you their aid. Since I received your letter, I have seen Gov Jones *"flourish"* and your response—am glad you have opened the canvass there early.[8] I will be at Jackson, by which time we will have our candidates all in the field & I will be able to give you more definite information. Many of the most intelligent Whigs have acknowledged to me that you would beat Jones—of which fact I do not permit myself to doubt.

I see that their only hope is to make capital, out of the course [of] the "immortal thirteen Democrat Senators." Say they will call you or Gov Jones out upon that *subject.* They attribute the fail[ure][9] to elect Senators to the Democrats, and will try t[o make] capital in that way. I believe they would be perfectly willing to say nothing about Federal politics. They dread to meet us upon these questions. You have no doubt seen an acct of Mr Clays grand entry, sojourn, & departure from our City.[10] He disappointed his friends very much. Gave us a *political speech,* of an hours length, which you see reported in the *Enquirer* & Appeal.[11] He made no political capital by his visit—made a very weak speech, and as to his oratory, which we all were expecting to hear, we heard nothing of it. I will probably write you again in a few days, if anything transpires worthy of notice. I will give you all the aid in my power, and wish you great success in the approaching canvass, having no doubt but that you will succeed in your present undertaking, and wish, that your life & health, may continue, to enable you to reap the great reward which the people have in store for you.

GEO W. SMITH

ALS. DLC–JKP. Addressed to Columbia.

1. A young Shelby County lawyer, Smith lost a bid for a seat in the Tennessee House to Adam R. Alexander in 1841.

2. Letter not found.

3. Reference is to the Western District.

4. William T. Brown, formerly a law partner of James P. Grundy in Nashville, served as judge of Tennessee's Sixth Circuit Court, 1836–38, before establishing a legal practice in Memphis.

5. James M. Williamson, formerly a resident of North Carolina and a member of that state's House of Commons, 1834–36, moved in 1838 to Somerville in Tennessee's Fayette County and took up the practice of law. He served in the Tennessee Senate from 1845 until 1847.

6. Not identified further.

7. Edwin Hickman, a Memphis merchant, served six terms as mayor of that city.

8. See Polk to E. G. Eastman, February 13, 1843.

9. A tear in the manuscript has obliterated parts of words here and below.

10. See Sackfield Maclin to Polk, February 27, 1843.

11. Reference is to the Memphis *Enquirer* and the *Memphis Appeal*, copies of which for March 1843 have not been found.

FROM JAMES M. HOWRY

My Dear Sir,   Oxford [Mississippi] 3 March 1843

Since I saw you I have had a severe attack of piles which have rendered me unfit for business, or even writing to my friends. I have post poned from week to week writing to you & as I commence my circuit next monday I must drop you a line giving you the state of affairs here *in short*.

There is likely to spring up a family quarrel among our party here, owing to several reasons.

Our Southern friends have *trifled* with the North in forcing upon them a day for the State Convention which did not meet our approbation, and the Convention has been holden & 37 Counties represented—21 not represented.[1] The Convention gave our present Gov Tucker the go bye and nominated Gen Brown,[2] who was in Congress 2 years ago. If the 21

Counties had been there, Tucker would have been renominated. But—1st Brown is a staunch *Van Buren man* (so is Gov Tucker) & made a speech a few weeks ago at a Dem meeting in his favor. 2nd He is a Dick Johnson man & last winter made a speech in his favor for V.P. 3. In his (Br's) section of the State recently R J Walker[3] was nominated for V.P. on V. Burens ticket & I think in Browns county.[4] The Convention refused to nominate candidates for Pres & V. Pres by 49 to 9, and for the present the rupture which we anticipated between V.B.[5] & Calhouns friends has passed by. But at some of the county meetings there was exhibited a good deal of acrimony between the friends of these Gentlemen—a very imprudent & thoughtless step of our friends. Some even went so far as to allow Mr V.B. & others recriminated upon his Southern competitor.

The nominations to Congress, Dr Hamet & Col Stone & the present incumbents,[6] will be well recd., but I think Stone & Hamet are V.B. but not certain. The others are Calhoun as you know. The conclusions of my mind are that Mr V. Buren is the choice of a majority of the Democracy of Mississippi and nearly all admit, that if he is chosen that you are their choice for the 2nd Office. But in the South, our leading men are against you in general. One very favorable sign is that in several of the counties you were nominated on both tickets—V.B. & Calhoun. Will not this have a salutary influence in your favor in a Natl. Convention? I See Col Johnson[7] has been invited to Natchez & says he will accept this Spring. The counties most friendly to you refused to go into Convention & thus many did not speak at all. From all I can learn Mr V. Buren will be the candidate as he should be before *all others*, and from Washington I learn our friends look for a difficulty growing out of the rival claims of yourself & Col Johnson. Our county held a meeting. I was from home. Calhoun was nominated by a close vote, & you were unanimously nominated for V.P. Our strength was not present. It is close here however between V.B. & Calhoun if all were to vote.

I hear nothing about a day for the Natl. Convention. The Hon Milton Brown I See, is anxious to change the venue. I have no doubt the Nashville Junta would like to change the venue & they could combine a tremendous force against you through the press & send Jones around to keep you engaged before the people. How many would you have to fight in this way? Hard to tell. If the Banks had money to spare & the paper money gentry had the funds to write & print & spend in electioneering they would give you trouble. I think as far as their means will go they will do so any how. Get strong men out for *all* offices is the plan as you well know. *Let old Cave*[8] be renominated. I am sorry to press a *fair nag* "but once more to the breach, dear friends, once more" [9] & this controversy is setled for years. Cave is too much interested in the result to refuse unless his equal could be found & that you know [cannot][10] be done. I think Harry Brown will best Milton.[11] [As for] the Legislature in that District the best men [will be] run. We will hold on for you, & every hope is [extend]ed for your triumphant success.

Clay has been among us. He cant keep from entering into politics, altho Democrats join in doing him honor. I've no news here of a local character. Some portion of our party are trying to stir up the question of repudiating the Planters Bank Bonds[12] but it will not take. But there is danger in the question.

I know you are & will be busy, but if any thing occurs worth writing drop me a line.

I fear the seat of Govt question will do harm some where, but I dont know where it will fall, in your state.

J. M. Howry

ALS. DLC–JKP. Addressed to Columbia.

1. See Williamson Smith to Polk, January 10, 1843.

2. Tilghman M. Tucker and Albert Gallatin Brown. A planter and lawyer, Tucker served as a member of the Mississippi House, 1831–35 and Senate, 1838–41; as governor, 1841–43; and as a Democratic congressman, 1843–45. Brown, a lawyer, served as a member of the Mississippi House, 1835–39; as a Democratic congressman from Mississippi, 1839–41 and 1847–53; as a circuit court judge, 1842–43; as governor, 1844–48; as U.S. Senator, 1854–61; and as CSA Senator, 1861.

3. Robert J. Walker.

4. Copiah County.

5. Martin Van Buren.

6. William H. Hammett, William A. Stone, William M. Gwin, and Jacob Thompson. A Methodist minister, Hammett served one term as a Democratic congressman, 1843–45. Stone, a lawyer in Lawrence County, sat in the Mississippi Senate, 1848–49, 1852, and 1856–58.

7. Richard M. Johnson.

8. Cave Johnson.

9. Quotation from William Shakespeare, *Henry V.*, act 3, scene 1.

10. Manuscript mutilated here and below. Wording in brackets supplied by the editor.

11. Henry Hill Brown and Milton Brown. A resident of Henderson County and a veteran of the War of 1812, Henry Hill Brown served four terms in the Tennessee Senate, 1823–25 and 1835–41.

12. Established at Natchez in 1830 by act of the Mississippi legislature, the Planters' Bank of the State of Mississippi reserved two-thirds of its capitalization to the state, which subsequently issued bonds to pay for its stock subscription.

FROM SARAH C. POLK

My dear Husband   Columbia March 3rd 1843

Agreeable to your order (or request) I write you to day. I have heard but little since you left on the subject of Politicks or candidates. The Observer[1] of yesterday, did not have one paragraph in it to your notice. The Democrat[2] contained McCay Cambell's letter announcing himself a candidate for the Senate, subject to a convention. His letter *I do* not like, and I have not seen any one to talk with since the paper came out. Dickerson is also out in the same paper, with a piece of writing, *to the people* of Maury, saying he had numerous personal solicitations to become a candidate, and takes that mode of thanking his friends, and that he had been fighting as a private and for *two long years* had been a daily labourer in the cause, says he is parentless & pennyless &c. All such stuff concludes, that if he is the choice of the convention he will serve. In the same paper, Dew, declines the solicitations of Many voters, and thinks his law office demands more of his attention. There has come no letter from Brown since you left. But one from Andy Johnson, Millegan,[3] and some others all giving a good account of things. Johnson writes in good feeling, but like a *skulk*. The Nashville papers are attacking you, about your denunciations of the Bankrupts, in your speeches a[t] different places.[4] From the tenor of these articles they hope to prejudice all the Democrats who have taken benefit of the Bankrupt law. They appeal to them, will you vote for a man who has no feeling or sympathy for the oppressed—who [would] call you dishonest for taken benefit of law that will relieve your distresses and all such stuff and I fear they may effect something with some persons. This is about all the Nashville papers have said of you since you left. Zollicoffer is yet sick and I reckon Jones writes himself. Democrat yesterday has an aritcle headed, Gov. Polk & the Vice Presidency, noticing, an article from the *Lebanon Spy, Ohio,*[5] suggesting your name for the V.P. This is all that I know of Politics at present.

Rufus Polk died last saturday and was intered at the Polk chapel on Monday.[6] Old Mrs. Lewis[7] died Tuesday. And this is all that has transpired since you left. The last three days has been intensely cold here, and I have thought much of you haveing to travel such weather. We are all getting on as ususal.

SARAH POLK

[P.S.] M. D. Cooper & Co. acknowledges the rect. of 90 Bales of cotton.[8] Horton renewed your note & returned the old one.[9]

ALS. DLC–JKP. Addressed to Bolivar and returned to Columbia.

1. Reference is to the *Columbia Observer.*

2. The Columbia *Tennessee Democrat* of March 2, 1843, contained the letters of McKay W. Campbell, C. J. Dickerson, and John H. Dew. Campbell was a Columbia lawyer. Dickerson was editor and publisher of the *Democrat.*

3. See Andrew Johnson to Polk, February 20, 1843, and Sam Milligan to Polk, February 20, 1843.

4. The Nashville *Republican Banner* of February 27, 1843, and the *Nashville Whig* of March 2, 1843, each carried an article or editorial denouncing Polk's position on the bankrupt law.

5. The *Spy* was a Democratic newspaper published in Lebanon, Ohio, from September 1842 through 1843.

6. See William H. Polk to Polk, February 14, 1843.

7. Mary B. Lewis, wife of James M. Lewis and mother of Micajah G. Lewis, died on February 27, 1843.

8. Matthew D. Cooper and Madison Caruthers were cotton factors active in the New Orleans export trade. The receipt from Cooper & Co. has not been found.

9. On March 1, 1843, Joesph W. Horton, Cashier of the Nashville Branch, Bank of Tennessee, renewed Polk's note, for an unknown amount, and returned his old note to him. ALS. DLC–JKP.

TO SARAH C. POLK

My Dear Wife: Somerville March 3d 1843

I have had exceedingly cold weather since I left Jackson. *Dr. Caldwell* whose house I left on yesterday, has agreed to go to the plantation and attend to my business for me as soon as the weather moderates. He can do all my business there as well [as] I can, if I were there. I will start home this evening, but will be delayed a day or two on the way. I will probably be at home on Wednesday next.

JAMES K. POLK.

ALS. ICHi. Probably addressed to Columbia.

FROM THOMAS MARTIN

Dear Sir   Pulaski March 7th 1843

Your several communications from Columbia came duly to hand. I regret to find Brown so fickle but it is in perfect keeping with his manner of think[ing]¹ and acting on most subjects.² I hope that when he reaches home that he will consent to remain a candidate; if so we shall have but little difficulty in this district. Brown is fearful of opposition, does not like to go thro the fatiegues of a warmly contested campaign, but indeed opposition is the life of the man if he could only believe it. I have written to him at Louisville and will also take care to have a letter for him at Nashville in due time. Yesterday we had a fine meeting³ and things passed off well. Rowles made a warm an animated speach and we have managed to get him off of the course without wounding his feelings materially.⁴ I am sorry for Rowles; he is anxious for distincting and his pecuniary matters will not permit him to remain quite,⁵ thin[kin]g that he could bring himself favourably before the public by political discussion which I belive he could do. He possesses much information on many subjects and could he only condesc[end] himself his information could be made valuable to himself and others. On some suitable occassion I think it would be well to write him giving him such assurances of friendship and consideration as you may think politic and reasonable. I should be glad to see him promoted and kept in a pretty good humor. This is rather a digression. We adopted at the meeting yesterday some pretty spirited resolutions, some complamentary notices of some of our prominent men yourself amongst the number. We have placed Calhoun & Van Buren on equal footing. Buford and Buchanon⁶ we recommend for Representatives and we confirmed the nomination of Colo Wilkes.⁷ The anunciation of Brown for Congress and the prompt and fearless presentation of candidates for the Legislature will do us good and we hope to keep the ball rolling—rolling—untill a hapy consummation.

THOMAS MARTIN

ALS. DLC–JKP. Addressed to Bolivar and returned to Columbia.

1. Brackets here and below enclose parts of words for which Martin failed to render complete spellings.

2. Reference is to Aaron V. Brown's candidacy for reelection to the U.S. House from Tennessee's Sixth Congressional District. Having been asked by Brown for an opinion on the subject, Thomas Martin wrote Polk on January 17, 1843, of his plans to write Brown and "give him the necessary impulse" to communicate at once with Polk on the subject. ALS. DLC–JKP. See Aaron V. Brown to Polk, February 4, 1843.

3. On March 6, 1843, Giles County Democrats met at Pulaski. They resolved to support Polk for the governorship, A. V. Brown for reelection to the U.S. House, Richard Wilkes for the State Senate, James Buford for the Tennessee House, and John Buchanan for floating candidate for the House. Further, they resolved to support Calhoun or Van Buren for the presidency, should either be nominated by the National Democratic Convention.

4. William P. Rowles, an educator, clergyman, and newspaperman, edited the Gallatin *Union* from 1839 until 1841. By 1843 he had removed to Pulaski, Giles County, where he was an instructor at Pulaski Female Academy. On February 20, 1843, Rowles wrote Polk that he had announced his candidacy for the Tennessee Senate for Maury and Giles counties, but was willing to "fight as a private soldier," if the Democrats had a "better & abler man" to "assume the batton." ALS. DLC–JKP.

5. Martin probably meant "quiet."

6. James Buford and John Buchanan. A prominent farmer, Buford represented Giles County in the Tennessee House, 1839–43.

7. Richard A. L. Wilkes, a Democrat, served in the Tennessee House, 1845–49, and sat in the Senate, 1849–51.

FROM JOHN BLAIR

Dr Sir: Jonesborough March 11 [1843][1]

I recived your communication of the 23d Decr. last[2] & expected to have had a favourable opening to reply with some degree of satisfaction to myself & interest to you, but such has been our unfortunate condition here oweing to the *number* of our *great men*, that every thing was deemed in danger of being lost again. We had a meeting of a number of the most leading & influential men of our County[3] on Saterday last & happily we removed the collissions between the aspirants to the House & for Floater & so settled the strife as to loose nothing from any one seeking to be a candidate nor their friends. We yet have another & still greater matter to settle & one which I fear will baffle our skill to manage it—I mean the selection of a Congress Candidate, or in other words to keep down the running of two or more democrats, for that appointment. A. Johnston[4] has declared himself some time since subject to the action of a convention *fairly* got up & properly conducted. J. A. Aiken[5] has declared himself under the like restrictions. Johnstons friends in Green & Hawkins have moved with hot haste & selected their delegates to meet at Jonesborough with the other County Delegates 1st May or thereabouts, but instructed to vote for Johnston. McClelland has not returned but writes to his friends that he wishes to be considered a candidate when he shall have returned.[6] Brookins Campbell is exceedingly sore toward Johnston & will not vote for him under any circumstances.[7] He does not wish to run save against Johnston, & only against him, to repel Johnstons attacks upon his public conduct as well as personal integrity. He is willing to be dropped in the District[8] provided Johnston is subjected to the same ordeal & thereby give to the District a candidate who is exempt from all collissions with other aspirants. Brookins Campbell is certainly the most popular man liveing in this County & whilst our primary meeting did not think proper to nominate him, until McLelland[9] had returned home & the whole ground explored. Still we as a salve to his feelings under Johnstons protest & charges, in the Legislature, unaminously recommended him to the consideration of the Voters of the District should he permit his name to be used. In any event this must work well for if Campbell should be nominated hereafter it will sustain him, if on the contrary he should not run, he has the gratification to know from his immediate County men that they do not endorse Mr. Js. charges of bargain sale corruption &c. We adjourned to meet again on the 1st Saterday in April next, that period being anterior to the time at which Greene & Hawkins propose to hold a convention in Jonesborough, to nominate a candidate for Congress. We in this quarter have nothing to *fear, save* from our *friends*. Docr. Kenney is the nominee for the floating member, & William Crouch for Representative.[10] Docr. Martin & Kenney had become irritated each at the other & it was somewhat difficult to extinguish the spark. Our general prospects here are indeed very flattering. I must think a great increase will be shewn at the next ballot box, provided well enough be let alone, & we sustain no loss by the conduct of our own prominent men. *Clay cannot go it* in this County even to the *Whig* [. . .][11] & that [. . .] has been considerably circumscribed since you & Jones had your contest. I am gratified to see Cave Johnston again nominated by his freinds; he is best calculated to keep up the party in that District[12] & is trust worthy in his stand in Congress. I write you this hasty scrawl at present that you may not imagine I have given up correspondence, & promise when future developements shall enable me, to write more at large. The people here on both sides are entirely free from excitement & it would be an extraordinary occasion on which they could be induced to turn out. The Democrats are more stedfast than ever, & the Whigs *cry from fear*, & seem unwilling to get into discussion on the dividing topics. In our divided condition it has been thought most adviseable to avert a line being drawn through o[u]r Democratic ranks before calling upon the people to express disapprobation to Clay & Co. If it should turn out that we can silence oposition in the congressional convass we will then be ripe for attack at any quarter. With either Johnston Campbell or McLelland *alone* the people would be satisfied & go into battle but with two or more, & a whig opposeing them would be a failure of energy & forebodeing of defeat. Our Ticket now is such as will be popular so far as adopted. Polk governor, Powel Senate,[13] Kenney floater & Crouch repr. With either of the persons before named for Congress, we need not fear a rapid increase. When the issue of our adjourned meeting shall be known, I will write you again, & I hope will then be enabled to give you a tighter picture upon which to look. I know not how our West Tennessee friends feel in reference to Clays being the preferred Whig candidate, but I know here the wish is that he should run, as we can stick to his skirts the authorship of most of the wild & reckless schemes of Whig policy. I cannot be mistaken when I say that Clay would combine less Whig strength in this part of Tennessee than most others. John McLean would be the man most to be dreaded on account of his being the idol of the Methodist. I see that your appointments have been published, for the most of your time which will intervene between this & the Election. I would have preferred your being East of the Mountain before the last of June but if your presence elsewhere is more requisite, we can forego the pleasure of seeing you until that period. When did you see the old cheif & how is he? I would be pleased to see him before he is called home & give him a parting shake of the hand at least. I recieved from C Johnston a prospectus of Kendle for publishing his life[14] which I think will be patronized. Remember me to Mrs Polk. & accept for yourself my assurances of friendly regard.

JOHN BLAIR

ALS. DLC–JKP. Addressed to Columbia.

1. Year written above the dateline, probably in Blair's hand.

2. Letter not found.

3. Washington County.

4. Andrew Johnson.

5. A Jonesborough lawyer, John A. Aiken served two terms in the Tennessee House, 1827–29 and 1839–41.

6. Abraham McClellan, an incumbent congressman, had not returned from Washington City.

7. See E. G. Eastman to Polk, December 19, 1842.

8. Tennessee's First Congressional District.

9. Abraham McClellan.

10. Daniel Kenney and William H. Crouch. Crouch, a native of Tennessee's Washington County, served one term in the Tennessee House, 1843–45.

11. This word and one on the line following are illegible.

12. Cave Johnson represented Tennessee's Ninth Congressional District.

13. A native of Maryland, Robert W. Powell practiced law in Elizabethton and represented the counties of Carter, Johnson, Sullivan, and Washington in the Tennessee Senate for two terms, 1841–45.

14. Reference is to a prospectus by Amos Kendall for a biography of Andrew Jackson; for details see the *Nashville Union*, March 24, 1843.

FROM WILLIAM G. CHILDRESS

At Home

Dear Sir.   [Franklin, Tennessee] March 13th 1843

I avail myself of the present occasion to give you the outline or a rough skeleton of a speech delivered in Franklin today by your competitor Gov. Jones. It may be of some little interest to you & if it should not I hope it will not prove injurious. He addressed the citizens (a good crowd) more than two hours upon the various subjects or topicks of the day. He said he had seen a notice in the newspaper (Review[1] I suppose) that the county candidates would address the citizens of this county on to day it being the first day of the circuit court & on Saturday but he resolved to avail himself of the opportunity of meeting and addressing the citizens of Williamson county fearing he would not have an opportunity of doing so before the first thursday in August next as Govr Polk his competeteor had made a long list of appointments covering the State except this & Maury County.[2]

1st. He attempted to render as he said an act of his stewardship. He refered to his promise in the last canvass that if elected he would exert his feeble abilities to have the laws faithfully executed & to sustain in the best possible manner the Bank of the State althoug he had no confidence in the ability or practicability of such an institution to afford the great benefit not only deserved but expected by the people. Nothing short of a National Bank could suffice and that it was in redemption of those pledges that he had made a nomination of the two boards of Directors both of which was rejected by the democratic Senate.[3] He also refered to his Message at the extra Session[4] recommending the appointment of three men to examine the Bank which was also rejected by the same body because they prefered darkness to light, & said not so with the Bank of the U.S. or as termed by the democrats the Marble place. When called upon by congress through their committee for examination they made a surrender of their books. They made an expose as honest men should do.

2. He next refered to the election of Senators to Congress & his recommendation &c & charge the defeat to the democrats.[5] Spoke of the long usage & custom of the country &c. and that a portion of those same democrats but two years before had gone into convention with him for the election of Senators & at a time when there was a less majority for them than he had in 1841. Charged the democrats of 1839 & 40 of having instructed the Venerable White & the *Galant* Foster out.[6] Then entered national politicks. Advocated a Bank of the U.S. Said Washington Madison Monroe & Grundy admitted the constitutionality of it & charged

the democrats of having seduced Tyler or the people would have had what the whigs promised in 1840. That Tyler admitted at the Harrisburg convention he had undergone a change in relation to a Bank. He next named the distribution act. He was for it and contended it furnished the only means of paying off our State Bonds save that of direct taxation. That the lands belonged to the States &c.

He was opposed to the Bankrupt law. That he advised his representative in congress[7] to vote against it and charged that the law would have been repealed before it went into operation but for the democrats in the Legislature refusing & preventing the election of two Senators in the Congress of the U.S. That Foster was against it which fact was known by a portion of the democratic members. He charged that the democrats were at heart & in feeling opposed to the repeal because they desired to make political capital out of it. He knew it had relieved many poor honest industrious labourers honourable worthy men with an enuendo as to the charge of all being dishonest (I fear they are making something out of this falsehood). Went on with the usual slang that Vanburen was for a Bankrupt law &c & of T. Bentons dodging on the final vote after his great parade & that he was the greatest humbugger of the day.

Next the Tarriff, alleging that the democrats charge the whigs as the tariff party and that since the formation of our Government it has been the sole mode of raising revenue and that if the democrats are opposed to this they must be for direct taxation or as they term it free trade. Some he said had thrown off the mask & come out boldly for it to wit, McDuffee a great leader, Rhett & a small democratic journal printed at Jackson.[8] Then went on in rather a low manner depicting the odious system & the great & Horrid manner of executing it. Described the tax gather[er] & assessor passing through the country seeking whome they may devour. Gave an instance that occured in the regn of Alfred (I presume before his began) when a Black Smith was called upon to tax his property when the assessor was about to levy a tax upon the Black Smith's daughter, when her father alleged she was not old enough, then the tax gatherer or assessor was about exposeing of her by making an examination to asertain her age when the father slew him with his hammer, scattering his brains over the floor. He made this a most glorious act &c. He was in favour of a tariff only for revenue purposes & so far as that operated as an incidental protection it was right, and charged the protective tariff upon the democrats—that it commenced with them in 1816—J. C. Calhoun then the leader (and yet in another part of his speech he said this New-fangled democratic party had not existed more than five or six years— they had a short pedigree). He charged that Jackson Vanburen & Benton & he could name others but would not as they were not present, we had voted for a protective tariff. Yes he could mention other items besides tea & coffee[9]—that the protective tariff consisted in the levying of the duty on the minimum principle of an article costing less than thirty cents supposed to cost thirty. Named the tariff of 1824 & 28 & 32. All those acts had recd the support of many leading democrats. He would refrain from giving the names of some as they were not present. He scorned to assail an enemy behind his back.

He charged that the act of 1832 levied a higher & heavier duty on all the articles of necessity than the act of 1842. He had compared them together item by item & he pledged himself to prove it if denied & made many insinuations as to the act of 1832.

He said the whigs had been charged & he really believed many democrats honestly believed the charge that the whigs were Federalist. Yes it had been said they were sailing under piratical colours all of which was untrue but more correctly applied to themselves & thus to the proof. What is a Federalist? It is the building up a strong federal Government, the power of the Government centering in one man. In a word it is taking from the many & giving to the few & then cited to the veto power in the president that the democrats were in favour of it. He said Alexander Hamilton was an avowed federalist & that he was for the veto power. Therefore the democrats were federalist. Again he said the democrats were for placing both purse & sword in the hands of the President by virtue of the Independent Treasury & finally stooped to the Hoe case[10] & Vanburens giving a preference to free Negros over white men, the old slang over again. Such is a rough sketch of the Governor's speech. I look upon it considering every thing as being one of the lowest & smallest things of the kind I ever heard from any man of the least pretentions to fill his station with that dignity that properly belongs to it.

Next followed Mr Sneed[11] from Rutherford who is a candidate to represent the two counties in the Senatorial branch of our legislature. There seemed to be great commotion among the whigs before he was done, saying give me a Williamson democrat before him. One came to me that I had considered more bitter towards me than any other & said I know you are astonished when I call upon you to come out, but now says he, if you will run you may vote for who ever you please but do not discuss national politicks in this county. Yet the leaders are active trying to get the rank & file satisfied. A few weeks will show their success & the prospect on our part. Call if you can when on your way to Robertson.

W. G. CHILDRESS

[P.S.] All in great hast as you may discover.

ALS. DLC–JKP. Addressed to Columbia.
1. The Franklin *Western Weekly Review.*

2. See Polk to E. G. Eastman, February 13, 1843.

3. See Samuel H. Laughlin to Polk, April 19, 1842.

4. In his legislative message of October 4, 1842, James C. Jones suggested amending the charter of the Bank of Tennessee and recommended the appointment of three commissioners as a board to investigate the affairs of the Bank and its branches. On October 31, the Senate Bank Committee, chaired by Samuel H. Laughlin, refused to support the governor's recommendations. On November 9, 1842, Franklin M. Buchanan offered an amendment in the House providing for the election by joint ballot of the legislature of three commissioners to investigate the Bank. Two days later, the bill passed the House but was indefinitely postponed by the "Immortal Thirteen" in the Senate on the following day.

5. See John Catron to Polk, January 2, 1842.

6. Hugh L. White and Ephraim H. Foster. See J. G. M. Ramsey to Polk, August 20, 1839, and John Catron to Polk, November 19, 1839.

7. Meredith P. Gentry.

8. George McDuffie, Robert B. Rhett, and the Jackson *District Telegraph and State Sentinel*. See Cave Johnson to Polk, January 4, 1843.

9. See Sarah C. Polk to Polk, November 7, 1842.

10. Naval Lieutenant George M. Hooe, court-martialed on charges of insubordination, disobedience of orders, and flogging of two men, was reprimanded in general orders by Secretary of the Navy James K. Paulding and dismissed from the West India squadron in June 1839. Hooe objected at his trial to the admission of testimony of two colored men in proving the charges of flogging against him. When submitted to the U.S. district attorney for an opinion, Hooe's objection was overruled; the testimony of free Negroes was admissible under U.S. law and could be changed only by Congress. Hooe submitted a memorial for review of his case to President Van Buren in December 1839. Upon review, Van Buren found nothing in the proceedings of the trial which required his interference. On June 14, 1840, John M. Botts, Whig congressman from Virginia, called for a House investigation of the Hooe case on grounds that colored persons were not competent witnesses in court. However, attempts in June and July 1840 to legislate on that subject proved unsuccessful. See House Document No. 244, 26 Congress, 1 Session.

11. A Murfreesboro lawyer, William H. Sneed won election to a single term in the Tennessee Senate, 1843–45. Before his senatorial term expired he moved to Greene County, 1844, and then to Knoxville the following year. Subsequently, he won election as a Know-Nothing candidate to the U.S. House, 1855–57.

FROM CAVE JOHNSON

Dear Sir,   Clarksville 16th March 1843

I recd yours[1] upon my return & will meet you at Springfield the evening of the 23rd (the day before you speak & will return to Clarksville with you & possibly go to Henry). I find a good deal of confusion in this district[2] but hope to be able very soon to settle every thing. But I fear it cannot be done without my becoming a candidate. I see your notices[3] & would not perform what you have undertaken, to be the King of the Jews. I should never be able to do it and I doubt your ability. As far as I can learn every thing looks well for the success of our cause.

I write merely to say, if you can, you had best come to Springfield the evening before. You will have a hard ride to Clarksville the day after.

The more I have thought of the suggestions in my last,[4] the more I approve of them. Let us write out our speeches on different points & at different times & have them printed in detached parcels, so that all may read. If we can confine them to the new issues in their conduct we have them. AVB[5] approves & will do a full share.

C. JOHNSON

ALS. DLC–JKP. Addressed to Columbia.
1. Polk's letter of March 10, 1843, has not been found.
2. Tennessee's Ninth Congressional District.
3. See Polk to E. G. Eastman, February 13, 1843.
4. See Johnson to Polk, February 28, 1843.
5. Aaron V. Brown.

FROM GEORGE C. CONRAD[1]

Dr Sir   Springfield March the 19th 1843

The Whigs had a meeting here on the 1st Monday in this month, and nominated Genl Cheatham for the Legislature, Mr. Henry for Congress, & Hockett Allen Esq. of Montgomery for the Senate. It is thought Allen will run & *perhaps* Henry will. Cheatham accepted the nomination and made a Speech, commencing and almost ending with the U.S. Bank question. He how[ev]er abused the Democratic Senators in the Legislature for not electing Whig Senators,[2] and for not confirming Gov. Jones' batch of Bank directors[3]— charging that they refused to confirm, in order to prevent detection of Corruption in the banks &c. His main argument was that we could not get along with out a bank. That in consequence of the *traitor* Tyler they could not get one immediately. That the Senate (U.S.) being democratic if the democrats had the majority in our State Senate, they could not get a bank, but if the Whigs had a majority in the next legislature, they would elect 2 *Whig* Senators & they could get a Bank &c. He said nothing about the Bankrupt law or Mr Clay. Felix Parker Jr. Esq. of Common School fund Memory,[4] followed Genl Cheatham & Hurrad. for Mr Clay against the field &c. I did not expect to say so much when I commenced writing my object being merely to inquire of you in behalf of your friends here at what time you would arrive, at this place, in attending to your appointment on the 24th Inst.? What rout will you come? Or will you come in company with Gov Jones? I presume the Bank will be the main hobby with the Whigs & I think the currency question will be the most important one to discuss here. It will be well to show that the Bankrupt law was purely a Whig measure & how many democrats & how many Whigs voted for it & that it would not have went into operation, but for Mr Clay. Also to Show the Constitutionality legality & consistency of the 13 Demo. Senators refusing to Elect U.S. Senators on the Whigs own terms &c. Has not the Whig Senate in Maryland refused to go into the election on the same terms?[5] If you can lay your hands on the journals of the legislature wherein Adams & Clay were Charged & Convicted of corruption intrigue &c bring it with you.[6] Please inform me at what time and by what rout you will arrive here. We would like to have your company to spend the evening with us. Can you reach here on thursday evening? If so stop at our house and remain while you stay here if you think it will not interfere with your arrangements &c. I would *like to have company*. If the weather is good perhaps I may go to Clarksville with you.

G. C. CONRAD

ALS. DLC–JKP. Addressed to Columbia.

1. A Springfield merchant and Democrat, Conrad had written Polk on February 21, 1843, concerning political movements of his own party; he "earnestly and most respectfully" urged Polk to debate James C. Jones at Springfield in March and invited Polk to stay at his home on that occasion. ALS. DLC–JKP.

2. See John Catron to Polk, January 2, 1842.

3. See Samuel H. Laughlin to Polk, April 19, 1842.

4. A Gibson County lawyer, Felix Parker, Jr., served four terms as a Whig in the Tennessee House, 1835–41 and 1847–49. Parker served on the Joint Committee on Education and the Common Schools and supported in 1838 the enactment of a system of common schools in Tennessee.

5. The Maryland legislature adjourned on March 10, 1843, without filling the Senate seat of John L. Kerr, a Whig whose term had ended on March 3. On a joint ballot by the two houses Democrats would have outnumbered Whigs by a vote of 55 to 48; the Whig-controlled Senate declined to meet with the House of Delegates and thus left the choice to the next legislature.

6. Reference not identified further.

FROM JOHN A. THOMAS

My Dear Sir,   West Point, N.Y. March 19th 43

In my last letter to you,[1] I was obliged to give such an unfavorable account of cadets Couts, & Armstrong, that I embrace the first opportunity, afforded by them, to make known to you, that their prospects are much fairer than at the date of my letter. Mr. Couts was released from arrest, with a reprimand from the Sec. of war,[2] and some punishment by the Superintendent,[3] & since has behaved very well. He will be graduated, I have no doubt.

Mr. Armstrong has improved in his studies, decidedly, and it is the opinion of his instructor in Mathematics,[4] that he has the ability to get through, if [he] will apply himself. This I am pleased to hear, for I was under a different impression. I would suggest that his Father[5] urge him to exert himself. I loose no occasion to impress upon him the advantages he is enjoying, and that he ought not to let them pass unimproved, but I fear he does not heed my admonitions.

I have learned from the papers that you are a Candidate for Govenor. I wish you success, altho, I know you have no need of my wishes. Your opponent I suppose is a whig.

Our Secretary of War, you will have learned has left us, and I must add that I am sorry we have made such a poor exchange. Mr Spencer is a man of great ability and indefatigable in exertion, and commanded the respect of the Army, at least; but Mr Porter![6] Alas. I am informed *by good authority* that while an officer in the militia during the last war, he was tried for cowardice and *cashiered*. What a grand fight we would make with such a leader!

We are so much out of the way of politics here, that I am at a loss to know who to select for my candidate for President. If I were near you, I suppose I could settle the question. Nullification excepted, & I would be a Calhoun man; but the convention is to dispose of all doubts. For my own part, I would rather fight a real battle, than to undertake the political one in which you are about to engage. The bitterness with which the press attacks public men is past endurance. This letter is longer than it should be.

JNO. ADDISON THOMAS

ALS. DLC–JKP. Addressed to Columbia.
1. See Thomas to Polk, January 20, 1843.
2. John C. Spencer.
3. Richard Delafield.
4. Not identified further.
5. James Trooper Armstrong was the son of William Armstrong, who served as Indian agent for the southern agency of the Western Territory, 1836–39, and subsequently, as agent for the Choctaws west of the Mississippi River.
6. James M. Porter, a Pennsylvania lawyer, jurist, and brother of David R. Porter, served as ad interim Secretary of War from March 8, 1843, until January 30, 1844. Porter's militia command is not further identified.

FROM TIMOTHY KEZER

Dear Sir   Nashville March 20, 1843

I am now fully convinced that Col. A. Cullom, intends to be a candidate whether he is the choice of the convention[1] or not. This I believe is settled beyond all contingency. Col. Laughlins friends are pressing his claims, with much zeal, and feel sanguine of being able to elect him, over all the combinations at work to defeat him. Under this state of affairs, there will [be] many things conspire to injure the party, and doubtless make a serious change against you. Though I would be proud to have Col. Laughlin elected to Congress, or to have a fair fight for a seat there, in opposition to any acknowledged Whig, I am yet unwilling that any local district election, should be the means of endangering our common cause, or opperating to injure your election, on which the Unity of the party in this state now hangs.

I am sure of one thing, that Col. Laughlin would make any reasonable—if not unreasonable—sacrifice to secure your election. I have therefore concluded, without consulation or advice from any one, to visit McMinville and if possible to get him to withdraw from the canvass. This I think can be done upon high and honorable grounds, for the convention will surely nominate him. We can then base his withdrawal upon the ground to avoid dividing the party—for Cullom will still be in the field. And further, he can with great truth, plead the embarrasd state of his private affairs and that they require his personal and undivided attention.

I am not sure that his declining, would be agreeable to you—but I believe it would prove a real benefit to you in the end. Still it would be quite humiliating to withdraw and leave one, who has acted so treacherous a course as Cullum, to a clear field. I am also aware that he would subject himself to great injustice and misrepresentation, as to the cause of his withdrawing. But in view of all these, I think the result will fully justify such a procedure.

I do not believe it will be difficult to get him to take down his name as a candidate. I feel confident it is not his own wish, nor never has been to be a candidate. He has consented to it from the solicitation of others. And believing as I do, that it is of but small importance, who represents that district,[2] compared with who shall be our next Governor, I am therefore willing to yield my personal and still warmer feelings in the first case, even to have a chance of securing, or benefiting the latter.

In all this I am as sincere, as I have been frank in suggesting to you the motives which influence me, in the course I intend to persue.

You have of course, seen both tickets of our county candidates.[3] I think we have nothing to fear on the score of personal, qualifications, or mental acquirements. We intend that they shall have no advantage of us, in point of marshalling forces, or of chargeing in a close fight.

T. KEZER

ALS. DLC–JKP. Addressed to Columbia.
1. For the Democratic convention held at Smithville on March 20, 1843, see Samuel H. Laughlin to Polk, March 27, 1843.
2. Tennessee's Fourth Congressional District.
3. Davidson County.

TO SAMUEL H. LAUGHLIN

My Dear Sir: Columbia March 20th 1843

I will set out on tomorrow for Springfield in Robertson County, where the canvass will open on friday next. You will see from the list of appointments as published in the newspapers, that I will not be in your part of the State until July. I start under the most favourable prospects. That we have greatly increased our strength in the State since the last election I have not a doubt; nor can I doubt our complete success, if we use the proper energy, and can preserve harmony in our ranks. Nothing but a want of harmony and unfortunate collisions between friends can possibly endanger our success. I have silently looked on, upon the State of things in your part of the State, in the anxious hope that Col. C.[1] and yourself, might be enabled to arrange the matter amicably and satisfactorily to both, and so as to avoid that division among our political friends, which I fear must follow if you are both candidates for Congress. You will I know my Dear Sir fully appreciate the reasons for my solicitude that perfect harmony and concert may be preserved in the action of our party in every part of the State. When I have expressed this solicitude I have done all I can do, and still hope that the threatened competition between friends may be avoided. I will only add that I have to day written a precise copy of this letter to Col. C.[2] intending in no possible manner to interfere in the matter, further than to express my deep anxiety on the subject, and to tender to both of you my friendly advice. I shall inquire for letters at all the places where I have appointments, and will be happy to hear from you at Jackson, or at such other point, as you may think a letter will reach me. Give me your opinion of our prospects as far as you may have information.

JAMES K. POLK

ALS. DLC–JKP. Addressed to McMinnville and marked *"Confidential."* Laughlin's AE on the cover states that he answered this letter on March 27, 1843. Published in *ETHSP*, XVIII, pp. 162–63.

1. Alvin Cullom.

2. Polk's AE on the cover of his letter to Alvin Cullom reads as follows: "Precise copy of this letter—written to Col. S. H. Laughlin & both mailed at Columbia Tenn March 20th 1843." ALS. DLC–JKP.

FROM ADAM HUNTSMAN

Jackson, Tennessee. March 25, 1843

Huntsman informs Polk that Milton Brown will meet Polk at Trenton "to discuss the sugar and Coffee vote." [1] Huntsman recommends that Polk be prepared with printed copies of his speeches and votes on the tariff issue.

ALS. DLC–JKP. Addressed to Paris. Published in *THQ*, VI, p. 356.

1. See Sarah C. Polk to Polk, November 7, 1842.

FROM WILLIAM WALLACE

Maryville, Tennessee. March 25, 1843

Wallace again urges Polk to switch his speaking engagement in Blount County from Louisville to Maryville, pleading that without that change Polk's supporters "will neither go to hear you nor vote for you." [1] Wallace notes that Hodsden, Hamil, and Gillespy are all candidates; he has "no fears of Gillespies success." [2] Wallace predicts that the Whigs in his district[3] will nominate Senter for Congress.

ALS. DLC–JKP. Addressed to Columbia.

1. Wallace had appealed to Polk earlier, on March 19, 1843, to move his speaking engagement to Maryville. The Louisville appointment was, Wallace claimed, "injudicious as it will prevent hundreds from attending that would do so if the speaking be at Maryville." ALS. DLC–JKP.

2. Robert H. Hodsden, Hamil, and James Gillespy. Hamil is not identified further. On March 15, 1843, Wallace wrote Polk, in some detail, concerning county elections. ALS. DLC–JKP.

3. Tennessee's Second Congressional District.

FROM SAMUEL H. LAUGHLIN

My dear Sir,   McMinnville, Tenn. March 27, 1843

I have received your letter of the 20th instant, dated Columbia, and one from our friend Kezer of the 23rd written after his interview with you in Nashville.[1] It needed no assurance from him or you either to convince me of the real state of your solicitude in regard to our troubles in this district,[2] or of your friendly feelings and wishes, present and prospective towards me personally. I had finally determined on my course of action here before I received either of your letters—and Waterson, Patton, Mercer and other Delegates who called on me on their return from the Smithville Convention, which met on Monday the 20th, concur with me in believing the course I had determined to take, in the event of my nomination.[3] Before stating what I am about to do, let me premise, that the Convention met. About 3400 of the democrary were represented—being Warren, Coffee, Dekalb and Van Buren. About 23 to 24 hundred were not represented. Those represented are unanimous—those not represented are divided. A majority of the real democracy of White and Fentress are for me—and a minority of those of Overton and Jackson for Cullom. In the whole district, I would get perhaps 4 or 5 hundred Whig votes only—but so many of the democrats in Overton and Jackson, are daily becoming disgusted at the signs of a Whig alliance that I would get a majority of them even in Cullom's strongest counties, and I have no doubt I could and would beat him, but in the end, the cards are so stacked that our party would suffer a great falling off in the Governors and County elections, especially endangering the election of the floating members from Fentress, White and Van Buren. Already Cullom and his Whig friends, and personal friends and Kindred in Overton, have got out Micajah Armstrong a rank whig, and younger brother of Landon Armstrong[4]—to all of whom Cullom is nearly related by intermarriages—who is running for the House upon the amalgamation and no-party hook—to put down party strife as is said—and who promises to vote the will of a majority of Overton for U.S. Senator. McCormack is running for the Senate on the same hook—put up by Ned Cullom, a rank Whig, for Alvans benefit,[5] because he is a pliant tool, and because he is supposed to be strong in Jackson where he once got a strong vote against Isacks[6] for Congress. He now lives, a poor creature at his coal mines on Obed's river in Fentress, but in that County, where I have lately been he has no strength. John B. Rodgers[7] is running for floater and now lives at Bon Air in White. He, Ned Cullom, Judge Caruthers (who wants Cullom out of the way of a renewal of his Judgeship), Dibrell, Quarles of Jackson, Brooks and others have put all these plans in motion.[8] A. Cullom tries to appear passive in the eyes of the democracy. The Whigs have two purposes in view. To run a candidate for Congress of their own, if they can see a hope of success; and if they cannot, then to injure us as much as [possible] in the manner above stated—and in which it will be impossible, if a split and conflict takes place to prevent the barter and changing of hundreds and hundreds of votes in the Governors and County elections. In a close contest between you and Jones, and between Rodgers and Worthington (a first rate friend of ours in Van Buren) irreparable injury, ruin and loss to our party may ensue. No sacrifice on my part shall be wanting to prevent it. No exertion I can make by myself or friends shall be pretermitted. I will look for justice and justification to our party hereafter. If I mistake the best course, it shall not be an interested and selfish mistake. I have not hesitated to sacrifice all I had to put on the altar heretofore, and I will do it again.

My plan. I am about to enclose the proceedings of the Smithville Convention, nominating me unanimously, in complimintary terms, with the correspondence which you will see accompanying it, to Col. Cullom. I will also enclose him a copy of the letter he wrote me, in answer to one from me, before my name was announced as a candidate last fall, in which he assures me, in terms of compliment and flattery that he would not, and did not desire to become a candidate. I will release him from every obligation implied by that letter. I will ask him to decide absolutely whether he is determined to run—and that if he will, seeing the state of the feelings of a majority of the party, that then, to avoid the evils which he must know will result from the split, that I will not—that for the sake of union—the sake of harmony—I will, at whatever sacrifice of my own personal wishes and the earnest wishes of my friends, decline the nomination and not run, and leave my justification to the judgment of my friends and the democratic party. This will submit the whole matter to his own discretion (honor he has none) and will enable me to stand *rectus in curia*, in all time to come. He will determine that he will run—for he has no sense of delicacy or honorable policy. I have no doubt of his having always concealed the fact from Landon Armstrong and others, that he assured me, when applied to as a friend, that he would not run. My course is, I hope right. I would not run the risk of loosing the Governors election, and majorities in the Gen. Assembly for a seat in either House of Congress or any other office. If he elects to run, as he will, I cannot and will not have the slightest agency in starting any other candidate. Mr Turney or any body else. You will see the result in the papers. May heaven prosper you in your labors. Although a private combatant, I can become neither a silent nor idle member of the democratic family while I have a pen or tongue. Respects to Fentress, Coe, Maclin, Gardner, Copeland &c.

S. H. LAUGHLIN

ALS. DLC–JKP. Addressed to Savannah and marked "Private."

1. See Timothy Kezer to Polk, March 20, 1843.
2. Tennessee's Fourth Congressional District.
3. William S. Watterson, Alexander E. Patton, and L. D. Mercer. A native of Kentucky, Mercer was a Democrat and a successful McMinnville merchant.
4. Micajah Armstrong and Landon Armstrong are not identified further.
5. McCormack, Edward N. Cullom, and Alvin Cullom. Edward N. Cullom was clerk and master of Overton County Chancery Court, 1834–47. McCormack is not identified further.
6. Jacob C. Isacks, for Winchester, won election to five terms in the U.S. House and served from 1823 until 1833. He died in 1835.
7. John B. Rogers.
8. Edward N. Cullom, Abram Caruthers, Anthony Dibrell, James T. Quarles, and Richard P. Brooks. A White County farmer and county court clerk, 1814–35, Dibrell served as a Whig in the Tennessee House, 1845–47, and as state treasurer, 1847–55. A Gainesville lawyer and Whig, Quarles represented Jackson County in the Tennessee House, 1845–47. A Jackson County farmer and Whig, Brooks served two terms in the Tennessee House, 1841–45.

FROM J. G. M. RAMSEY

My Dear Sir   Mecklenburg March 27. 1843

I had written to Nashville about the same time & on the same subject I wrote to you last.[1] It had given some of us here very serious trouble. But E.[2] has at length returned. I went to see him immediately & told him that he had returned just in time to give a new impulse to the cause—that we needed it—& that we depended upon him & would not allow ourselves to question the same active agency he had heretofore given us. He needed some such encouragement & evidence of full confidence on our part—& it has had a very happy effect. You see his last paper proves it. It is the best one for months back. I believe he will continue *himself*. No efforts of mine shall be wanting. He has had an offer to sell out half his interest in the paper—he to be sole Editor. I believe a partner who has business habits & one that could manage the fiscal department of the establishment would be of essential advantage to him. Our friends rather advise the sale. E. is a New Englander but no Yankee & needs some one to look at the profits & disbursements of the Press. His health is better & he is now every way better than we could have expected.

I have a letter from Col. Blair—written just after their county Convention.[3] He says it has had the happiest effects on their Assembly aspirants. Harmony is restored & conflicting pretensions reconciled. Col. Crouch is nominated for the county. Doctor Kenney for Floater. Powell

Senator. An[d] a preference was manifested for Campbell for Congress should he be proposed by the Convention shortly to meet in the 1st Congressional District. B. thinks that matter not yet satisfactorily arranged & the Argus of last week makes an appeal to them that I think must have some influence.[4] Here at home we hope similar dissentions among the Whigs may enable us to reap a countervailing advantage. They have five candidates for the House in Knox & 2 Senators. If they all run we can return two Democrats. But they have taken the alarm. An election of delegates to a County Convention was held or appointed to be held in each civil Dist. last Saturday—for the purpose of concentrating on one candidate for each station. It is too soon to tell to day what has been done or how it will work, but I believe we will be able to make something out of it, & also out of their Con. Con. shortly to meet at Athens.[5] Till then we are upon our oars & will watch the course of things & act accordingly. Our friends report favorably from all the surrounding country. In Sullivan we are perfectly without discipline. Some six of our people running on the same side. A letter from a friend at Nashville says your competitor[6] is in poor spirits, his friends not zealous.

I had written this far when I received your other letter[7] requesting the Post containing the Posts admissions about Jones declarations two years ago at the Mansion House.[8] Reynolds was here when it arrived & he has gone to town to procure it so as to send it by this days Mail to Jackson. He assured me it should be sent if a copy was in the county.

As to the change from Dandridge to New-market I know you would do more good at the latter place. From L.[9] to N.M. is about 20 miles across Pigeon & French Broad Rivers & a bad road. From N.M. to New Port 28 miles & you would have to go through Dandridge at last & might disaffect a few friends there. The distance & character of the roads will make it fatiguing on you & I have therefore not made the change. You have time enough to write me again if you still think it best to change the appointment.

Can you have us informed how unlucky Friday went off?[10] Edwin Polk[11] of Bolivar has sent me a request for a Vol. on the Mecklenburg Inde.[12] I can hear of no one but my own. Tell him if an opportunity offers I will send it, but he must consider it as a jewel & return it.

J. G. M. RAMSEY

ALS. DLC–JKP. Addressed to Jackson.

1. On February 6 and 17, 1843, Ramsey wrote Polk concerning elections in East Tennessee and a visitor's appointment at the United States Military Academy. ALsS. DLC–JKP. No other letters in late February or early March 1843 have been found.

2. Reference is to E. G. Eastman, editor of the Knoxville *Argus*.

3. For details of the Democratic convention in Washington County, see John Blair to Polk, March 11, 1843.

4. Reference not identified further.

5. On March 30, 1843, a Whig convention held at Athens unanimously nominated Thomas J. Campbell as the Whig candidate for Congress from Tennessee's Third Congressional District.

6. James C. Jones.

7. Letter not found.

8. See Polk to E. G. Eastman, February 13, 1843. On March 27, 1843, Eastman wrote Polk that the "Whigs always looked upon that admission of the editor as a gross *faux pax*, and it was utterly impossible to find a copy, except in my file." Eastman sent the Knoxville *Post* article to Robert Armstrong for Polk's use. ALS. DLC–JKP.

9. Louisville, Tennessee.

10. Polk opened his gubernatorial campaign in Springfield on Friday, March 24, 1843.

11. A Hardeman County lawyer and farmer, Edwin F. Polk was the youngest child of Ezekiel Polk and was twenty-two years younger than his nephew, James K. Polk.

12. On May 1, 1775, Thomas Polk, commanding officer of the Mecklenburg County regiment of North Carolina militia, called for the election of two representatives from each of the county's nine militia districts to assemble and consider the troubled state of the country. Delegates convened at Charlotte on May 19 and on the following day declared their constituents' independence. Ramsey's "volume" on the Mecklenburg Declaration of Independence is not identified further.

FROM SARAH C. POLK

Dear Husband   Columbia March 29, 1843

According to your instructions I write you to Jackson. Though I have nothing that is worth communicating. Matters stand here pretty much as you left them. The anticipated meeting or convention of the people here on Saturday last nominated William & Gordon,[1] but did not settle the matter between Campbell & Wilkes.[2] Campbell's friends wished no action on the matter promising that he, Campbell, would volentarily be out of the way in a few days. *Bob Campbell*[3] has not acted up to what you or his friends had a right to expect from him. As well as I can learn he caused much of the difficulty. But I suppose that William will write you, all, on the subject,[4] for you know that my opportunities for information of the kind is limited in your absence. The Observer of course poured out a new vial of wrath against you, after you left.[5] But I think that it will be like Jones *fidlers*, tire and break down before August. Too much of a flourish to hold out. The Nashville Whig, not the Banner[6] came out with the notice of the meeting at Springfield,[7] a long sketch of Jones speech and a short one of yours, rather fairer than expected from such a quarter. Though you must have seen it before this. There has not come to you many letters since you left. I sent some to Nashville, which I suppose you received. One from the secretary of War,[8] stating that the visiting board at West Point was done away, Which I enclosed to Dr. Ramsey. I send two to Jackson which I deem necessary for you to see. You gave me no directions where to send any letter to you after you leave Jackson. If you did I have forgotten. They may come something of importance that I ought to send to you and I am at a loss to know how or where to send them.

I must confess that I feel sad & melancholy at the prospect before me, or I should say before you. The fatigue exposure and absence for four months can not present to me a bright prospect. I have not the assurance that the body and constitution can keep up under such labours as you have to go through, and it is only the *hope* that you can live through it that gives me a prospect of enjoyment. Let me beg and pray that you will take care of yourself, and do not become to much excited. Don't think that I am down in the *celler*, for as soon as I am done writing I am going to dress and go out visiting as this is the first good day we have had since you left. I received your letter from Clarksville.[9] Do write me as often as you can find time to do so.

SARAH POLK

ALS. DLC–JKP. Addressed to Jackson.

1. William H. Polk and Powhatan Gordon. Brother of Boling Gordon, Powhatan Gordon won election to two terms in the Tennessee House, 1843–47.

2. The Maury County Democratic meeting on March 25, 1843, nominated candidates to represent the county in the "lower branch of the next Tennessee Legislature," but did not nominate candidates for the Senate. For the competition between McKay Campbell and Richard Wilkes, see Aaron V. Brown to Polk, February 4, 1843; Sarah C. Polk to Polk, March 3, 1843; and William H. Polk to Polk, April 10, 1843.

3. A cousin of Polk's, Robert Campbell, Jr., was a son of John and Matilda Golden Campbell. His mother was the eldest daughter of Ezekiel Polk.

4. See William H. Polk to Polk, April 10, 1843. See also Sarah C. Polk to Polk, April 17, 1843.

5. No March 1843 issues of the *Columbia Observer* have been found.

6. Nashville *Republican Banner*.

7. The *Nashville Whig* of March 28, 1843, carried a lengthy article entitled, "Opening of the Campaign—First Engagement."

8. Letter not found. Reference probably is to John C. Spencer, who was succeeded as secretary of war by James M. Porter on March 8, 1843. See Polk to John C. Spencer, February 23, 1843.

9. Letter not found.

FROM ROBERT ARMSTRONG

D Sir.   Nashville 31 March 43

I send you herewith a sheet of the Post sent to me from Knoxville by Eastman.[1] If this matter is properly handled, it will tell in East Tenss. See the Union[2] of to day which I send you with an extract from this sheet and Editorial remarks, &c.

Harris has secured his appointment,[3] is pleasd and flat[tered]. It is as well so. He has lost his usefulness to our party; the Whigs have taken great pains to effect his standing and injure his influence &c.&c.

Hogan is a very true man with more care about him—and will be advised. We will get a long verry well, perhaps better than before.

Take a little time and write to Hogan. *Address* the *firm.*[4] Urge them to keep us disconnected from Mr. Tyler, to endorse nothing or in any [way] to commit the *party* by what the[y] say in their paper &c.&c.&c.

All is going on well here. Donelson has been up in Smith and is highly pleasd with his prospects. So is Burford. The accounts from all Quarters is cheering. In Wilson, Jones[5] is becoming very unpopular and I heard last night from a friend that his vote will fall off 500 to 700.

Laughlin is still trying to ease off Culloum.[6] If he cannot he will with draw to save a division of our friends. Laughlin will then come to the *Senate* from his old district.[7] Turney has declined and Long it is said will be sustained by Franklin, Bedford & Marshal. I want Jones[8] to be rebuked. He is a good fellow but wants to go his own way. Turney *may* come to the Legislature.

At no time have I seen things look better and unless we injure ourselves we have nothing to fear. Keep the Prest. & his Cabinet and the *last* Congress *Whig,* Elected by the Whigs &c.&c.

Urge Our Candidates in the different Counties to press Home Fosters Refusal to answer Questions &c. No Whig will attempt to sustain him in their speeches, but will join in condemning him and *slide* off to some one else, for Senator. The object of Fosters friends will be as usual to get them committed to *him* on the stump &c.&c.

Waterson will succeed Hall.[9] This appointment & Harris's is realy more than poore frail Whiggery Can beare. I am fierfull that they will *hang* Tyler again for it.

R. ARMSTRONG

ALS. DLC–JKP. Addressed to Jackson.
1. See J. G. M. Ramsey to Polk, March 27, 1843.
2. The *Nashville Union.*
3. J. George Harris received a commission from Secretary of State Daniel Webster to be a commercial agent of the United States, with special reference to the sale of American tobacco in Europe.
4. See J. George Harris to Polk, January 16, 1843.
5. James C. Jones.
6. Samuel H. Laughlin and Alvin Cullom. See Laughlin to Polk, March 27, 1843.
7. Warren and Franklin counties.
8. George W. Jones.
9. Allen A. Hall was appointed chargé d'affaires to the Republic of Venezuela on March 15, 1841. Harvey M. Watterson was sent on a diplomatic mission to the Republic of Buenos Aires by John Tyler in March 1843. On February 16, 1844, Tyler appointed him chargé to the Republic of Buenos Aires; that appointment was rejected by the U.S. Senate on June 5, 1844.

FROM HOPKINS L. TURNEY

My Dear Sir.   Winchester April 1st 1843
In this District,[1] M. A. Long is the only candidate for Congress. On my return home Jones and Long were both in the field. I instantly declined and set about Settling the matter between them. Jones refused to submit to a convention, which [refusal] dambed[2] him and he has withdrawn from the contest leaveing no person but Long in the field. I could have gotten the nomination against either but not against both. I was the Strongest man single handed, but double and I was perhaps the weakest. Laughlin will decline and thus we will have no diffaculty or division in the mountain division. Jones and Cullom have both acted badly. I leave in the morning for Shelbyville court. If anything occurs I will write you again.

H. L. TURNEY

[P.S.] We have a considerable gain in this region.

ALS. DLC–JKP. Addressed to Savannah.
1. Tennessee's Fifth Congressional District.
2. Misspelling of "damned."

FROM HENDERSON K. YOAKUM

Dear Sir   Murfreesboro Tenn April 3 1843

You are now about to hold forth among the good people of Jackson. Success to you & the good old cause! I am so anxious to hear from you that I am prompted to write. You have laid off such a wide row to be weeded out between this and August that I expect not to see you except on the wing. I will give you the news. We have waited here with sanguine hopes that Williamson would put forth a candidate for senate. She has failed to do that, & the Whigs here having put forth Mr Sneed (who has little or no personal popularity), we have given a loose rein to Crockett,[1] who is a good hand for electioneering, and who, at the same time that he will be beaten, will greatly diminish the Whig majority in this district.[2] This is my honest opinion. Our great object is to give all hands a *majority in this county*. And will not that be doing something! We consider that the democratic is far superior to the Whig metal in this county and district. The announcement of Sneed as a candidate produced a better feeling towards Crockett among our friends. I had a conversation the other day with a gentleman who knows, and he informed me that Webster was losing cash with Tyler—Bob Tyler[3] said he was a traitor, & was trying to get himself up as a candidate on the assumption question. "Is the president aware of it?" said the gentleman to Bob. "He is," said he, "& Webster goes out of the cabinet in one month." You may rely upon this as authentic. Another thing you may rely on; by the month of June the missions at Sardinia, Portugal, Russia, & Venezuela will be recalled.

I enclosed a copy of the proceedings of our meeting here to Mr Van Buren, and took occasion to say, that we had expressed no preference for the men we wished to fill the two high offices, because we had a partiality for one of our own citizens, &c. He replied to my letter, & amont other things said, "The eyes of the democracy of the Union are upon the Tennessee election to a greater extent than usual. The condition of your representation in the senate, the feelings of the old chief, and a very proper desire to see Gov. Polk's praiseworthy exertions crowned with success are among the prominent causes of this general anxiety. I sincerely wish you success and have but little doubt of your obtaining it." [4] In my humble opinion more depends upon our success in this state in August next, than upon any election for the last ten years. Will you not feel this in every speech. It seems to me there is little doubt; yet I feel that we should be safe. I think that Hogan will fight well. Since 1839 Harris' influence has been paralized. Drive Jones off of that distribution question. To obtain the little that was distributed before the repeal took effect, the govt had to borrow the money. This view strikes everyone.

You will excuse the haste & plainness of this letter. There is a contest in Turney's Congressional Dist.[5] I fear that it will do us harm in Lincoln. Be careful how you write to Jones[6] or his friends on the subject. If you have time, I would like to have your honest opinion of the prospect. Any thing I can do for you name it. I am told that Laughlin will decline his nomination & run for Senate.

H. YOAKUM

[P.S.] Crosthwaite[7] is appointed Clerk & master here.

ALS. DLC–JKP. Addressed to Perryville.

1. Granville S. Crockett, a Murfreesboro farmer, served as sheriff of Rutherford County, 1834–36. A Democrat, he won election to the Tennessee House, served from 1835 until 1837, and subsequently became clerk of that body for one term in 1839.

2. Rutherford and Williamson counties.

3. Robert Tyler, eldest son of John Tyler, served in the Land Office at Washington during his father's term as president. Later he practiced law in Philadelphia, served as register of the Confederate Treasury, and was editor of the Montgomery (Alabama) *Mail and Advertiser*.

4. Neither the Democratic meeting in Murfreesboro nor this exchange of correspondence has been further identified.

5. Tennessee's Fifth Congressional District. See Hopkins L. Turney to Polk, April 1, 1843.

6. George W. Jones.

7. A physician, George D. Crosthwait served as clerk and master of Chancery Court at Murfreesboro, 1844–49; won election to one term in the Tennessee House, 1849–51; and sat in the Iowa Senate, 1852.

TO SARAH C. POLK

My Dear Wife   Jackson April 4th 1843

I reached here on sunday evening, having had no opportunity to write to you after leaving Clarksville. Yesterday and to day have been very important days in the canvass. The meeting at *Phillippi*[1] is over, and has resulted as all concede most gloriously. Yesterday was Jones's day to speak first. He declined it & I addressed a very large crowd including in the number the leading men of both parties from every part of this division of the State.[2] I spoke 3 1/2 hours. In my speech I went fully into the *Milton Brown* matter.[3] When I was done *Jones* took the stand and replied in which he took up the cudgels for *Brown* & boasted lustily that he was *my man*, but before he was done announced that *Brown* would also address the people on the next day (to day) at 11 O'Clock. 11 O'Clock came and he did not make his appearance. At 1 O'Clock the bell rang, and the crowd repaired to the Court House, & I with them. *Brown* made his appearance in a few minuts loaded with documents & Seated himself on the stand with old *Pleasant Miller* & Old *George W. Gibbs*[4] by his side. He made a speech of two hours—at which his friends stamped and applauded as much as they could. I followed, and I suppose it will not be immodest for me to say to *my wife*, that my speech was perhaps the happiest effort of my life. I drove him to the wall upon the facts and the argumnt, and as in his speech he had made a great effort to turn the occasion into a frolic, I concluded to close my speech by fighting the *old boy* with fire, and accordingly I turned the laugh upon him—& almost laughed him out of the Court-House. Without going into further details the result is, that my victory is the most trimphant I have ever achievd. The democrats to night are all rejoicing whilst the leading Whigs are sullen & melancholy. My friends say that I have made a great & decided gain among the masses & I have every reason to believe it. I will remain here three days more & then proceed on the canvass, in the highest spirits. I am satisfied that there are very decided gains in every County through which I have passed, less perhaps in *Gibson* than any other.

I receivd your letter to day. I will be at Savannah on the 14th at which point I shall expect to receive another letter from you. After that the points which are on the main-stage route & where letters will reach without delay are *Somerville, Memphis,* & *Camden,* and I shall hope to hear from you at each of these places. If any letters come which you think important enclose them to me. I was never in better health & stand the canvass exceedingly well. I have not time to write to brother *William,*[5] but you can shew him this letter. I will write you again before I leave here.[6]

JAMES K. POLK

ALS. DLC–JKP. Addressed to Columbia.

1. When James C. Jones refused to let Milton Brown debate with Polk at Trenton on April 1, Polk declared that "the Spectre should meet Brutus (alias Brown) at the appointed time at Philippi, nothwithstanding the generous interference of Gov. Jones." *Nashville Union.* April 7, 1843. Polk's classical reference was to a spectre's appearance to Brutus at Abydos, 42 B.C., an omen that Caesar's murder was not pleasing to the gods. Brutus answered boldly, "I shall see thee there"; and when the spectre reappeared at Philippi, Brutus, having

been defeated, "put his naked sword to his breast and so died." Plutarch. *Lives*: *Caesar*. chapter 69, section 7.

2. Western District of Tennessee.

3. See Sarah C. Polk to Polk, November 7, 1842.

4. Pleasant M. Miller and George W. Gibbs. Miller served as chancellor of West Tennessee from 1836 until 1837. A lawyer, Gibbs served single terms in the Tennessee Senate, 1813–15, and in the House, 1825–27, before removing to Obion County in 1829. He served briefly as chancellor of West Tennessee in 1839.

5. William H. Polk.

6. See Polk to Sarah C. Polk, April 7, 1843.

FROM SARAH C. POLK

My dear Husband   [Columbia] Friday April 7th 1843

As Mr. Walker leaves in the morning for Jackson, and expects to be at Perryville on sunday night, where I thought it likely he would meet you, I concluded to write you, though I am not able to give you much information about any thing. Mr. Walker has promised me if he does not meet you to leave a letter for you giving all political news from this county.[1] There seems to be fresh troubles concerning the Senatorial matter. I send you the Democrat[2] and refer you to Mr. W. as all my knowledge on such matters is from that source. *William* is at Pulaski[3] and no one has come from there since monday so we have as far as I can learn, no light on the subject. Our *kin*[4] thinks Houston Thomas[5] will not do and I know no other one's opinions but theirs. I was disappointed to day that I did not hear from you at Jackson. I am affraid that I shall have cause to complain of you if your letters are so few and far between. I think you told me to write you to Savannah which will do if I have any worth writing about. I send you a Letter & the Democrat.[6] Do take care of yourself.

SARAH POLK

ALS. DLC–JKP. Addressed to Perryville.

1. Maury County.

2. Columbia *Tennessee Democrat*. Enclosure not found.

3. See William H. Polk to Polk, April 10, 1843.

4. James Walker and Robert Campbell, Jr.

5. James Houston Thomas, Columbia lawyer and district attorney, 1836–42, prosecuted the state's indictment of William H. Polk in 1839 for the murder of Robert H. Hayes. Later a law partner of James K. Polk, Thomas won election as a Democrat to three terms in Congress, 1847–51 and 1859–61.

6. Enclosures not found.

TO SARAH C. POLK

My Dear Wife: Jackson April 7th 1843

I will leave this morning for Pleasant Exchange. Since I wrote you[1] I have been exceedingly busy in preparing my speech for the press, and finished it late last night.[2] Since the speaking on monday & tuesday, the Democracy have kept up a constant rejoicing; *Mr McClannahan*, who is the strongest man of the Democratic party in this County,[3] has been so much encouraged, by the events of the week, that on yesterday he announced himself a candidate for the Senate in this District. *Mr Ewell* (Democrat) who is also a talented, energetic & a fine debater announced himself as a candidate for the House.[4] *Coe* and all our leading friends from the District[5] are here, & I have never witnessed such zeal in the cause in any part of the State before. If the matter has not been settled between Campbell & Wilkes,[6] I hope for the sake of the cause that it will be without delay. If you see Robert Campbell urge him to attend to it, & impress upon him the vast importance of having perfect harmony in the County of my residence.[7] I will write you again at *Savanah*. In great haste.

JAMES K. POLK

ALS. DLC–JKP. Addressed to Columbia.

1. See Polk to Sarah C. Polk, April 4, 1843.

2. Polk reported his speech of April 4 at Jackson in the *Nashville Union* of April 11, 1843. Published as a letter dated April 4 and attributed to "A Spectator," Polk's report was captioned "The Canvass for Governor."

3. Samuel McClanahan, a Madison County lawyer, is not identified further.

4. Thomas Ewell, a Jackson lawyer, wrote Polk on April 13, 1843, that McClanahan had withdrawn from the Senate race; however, "for myself though the motive that induced me to offer (McClannahan's running) no longer operates, yet that the Whigs may not have further cause for boasting, I am determined to run." ALS. DLC–AJD.

5. Reference is to the Western District.

6. McKay W. Campbell and Richard A. L. Wilkes. See William H. Polk to Polk, April 10, 1843, and Sarah C. Polk to Polk, April 17, 1843.

7. Maury County.

FROM JOHN J. GOODMAN[1]

Worthy Friend   Huntsville Texas April 10th 1843

I seat myself to write you a line which I flatter myself you will not take a miss. I further flatter myself that you will respect this communication, and give me inteligence of all the viewes, both personal & political, that is convenient for you to do and who is, or will be the candidates for the next Chief Magistrate of the United States. This I wish to know because we feel mutch Interested In the Prosperity of your national affairs. We take mutch Interest in your willfare, as well as our own for the feelings and kindred bind us together all most as one people &c.

I will now say something of our dificulties with Mexico. We have had some fears of mutch hard fighting but we now believe all the threats of that black Hartet Despot Santaana[2] is a Hoax; he has long since bin satisfied that Anglo saxons were thorns in Texas and it was Truly re-marked by that despot in '36 that Texas was to Mexico as a fractured limb to the human boddy, that it was only calculated to destroy the hole body, and that Texas was only a bead of Thorns. Well a bed of Thorns it is to him and I am of opinion if he ever tryes the Experiment again of recon-quering Texas again he will be taught to believe that Texan valor is a perfect Toronado, for if it were not for our Cautious and Patriotic President[3] we would of had before this time a considerable force on the west of the Rio del nort.[4] We fear not Mexicans which has bin farly prooveen, by the fact of the small band of Texans only 280 in number attacting Near where they knew there was a Mexican force of near 3000 but what was the result—11 Texans killed 18 wounded, that of the enemy 602 killed and 251 wounded, but alass at the eve of conkering the hole Mexican force at that place their amunition failed and they were bound to surrender but Coln Fisher[5] their Comander did not consent to surrender until certain conditions were entered into by the Mexican commanders. After enter into the proposed agreement our brave Commander held his Sword over his head and broke it in Thre peices and throwed it on the ground. His men all did likewise with there rifles by beting them on the corners of the Houses and throwing them on the ground &c. It is rumored that those prisoners rebeled against their guard at Saltillo and made their escape and are on their way back.[6] I also have Just received inteligence that there is a Mexican in Washing[7] baring dispatches to this Goverment, from the Goverment of Mexico[8] thought to be of a caracter that we possess all the privaleges we have as a republic, but to consent to remain as a state of Mexico. This cannot winn for Two reasons. First this Goverment has declared herself Free and Independant of Mexico and never will submit to hover under that tryanical flag. In the 2d Place she has bin Acknowledge a free and independant nation by the most Powerful nations of the earth by which she has contracted national debts, and cannot and will not forfit an honest Contract.

I must conclude by a remark or Two in regard to the advantages of this Delightful Country. It presents at this time the most beautiful seanery to the eye that was ever beheld. In her wide spread praries and all over her Timbered lands all presents that beautiful Green as if it all ware an oats field in Tennessee in the month of May. Our Cattle our hogs and all are fat on what nature has done for this Country and every thing we plant in the soil flourishes and grows Luxurieusly even more so than in any Country I ever have seen. I am mutch pleased with my moove &c.

JOHN J. GOODMAN

[P.S.] Since closing this I have received oficially that our prisoners taken at Mier is free from Mexican Cruelty and has had an unparaled battle in which the enemy lost in Killed 700 [and] our loss 25 Killed. In the battle were 2000 Mexicans and 150 Texans. Mr. Walker[9] will tell you the particulars. J.J.G.

Permit me to introduce you to My Friend Mr. Walker who will hand you this in person. JOHN J. GOODMAN

ALS. DLC–JKP. Addressed to Columbia.

1. A Mount Pleasant hotel keeper, Goodman removed to Texas in the early 1840's.

2. Antonio López de Santa Anna, Mexican revolutionary soldier and military leader, headed the central government on four occasions: 1833–36, 1841–44, 1847, and 1853–55.

3. Sam Houston, a former Tennessean, served two three-year terms as president of the Republic of Texas, 1836–38 and 1841–44. After Texas' annexation to the United States, Houston served as U.S. Senator from Texas, 1846–59, and as governor, 1859–61.

4. Reference is to the Rio Grande River.

5. The Texan forces on the Mier Expedition, December 25 and 26, 1842, were commanded by Colonel William S. Fisher. Fisher was forced to surrender on the second day of the battle to the Mexican commander, General Pedro de Ampudia. Thomas J. Green in *Journal of the Texan Expedition Against Mier* states that 261 Texans engaged in the battle of Mier; 10 were killed and 23 badly wounded. Mexican casualties were thought to exceed 700.

6. General Ampudia was ordered to send the Texan prisoners to Mexico City. On the way they made a break for liberty at Salado on February 11, 1843, killed some of their guards, and escaped; the Texans were later recaptured in the mountains and a tenth of them shot. The survivors were eventually imprisoned in Castle Perote.

7. Washington-on-the-Brazos, capital of Texas.

8. On January 9, 1843, James W. Robinson, a Texan prisoner at the Castle of Perote, proposed to Santa Anna the basis for an agreement to reunite Mexico and Texas. On February 18, 1843, Santa Anna conferred with Robinson and arranged nine articles of agreement to be dispatched to Texas for its pacification and reincorporation in the Mexican Republic.

9. Walker is not identified further.

TO SARAH C. POLK

My Dear Wife: Perryville April 10th 1843

I received your letter by Mr. Walker last night.[1] The meeting at Pleasant [. . .][2] former years been almost unamiously Whig, but now such have been our gains that there are great divisions, & my vote will be greatly better than it has ever been. In this county[3] we will speak to day. My friends give me very favourable accounts. The contest is becoming warm. I find it to be necessary to expose *Jones's* gross misrepresentations in very pointed terms. My health is good, except a cold—from which I am recovering. I will write you again from *Savanah.*[4] I most sincerely hope that the Senatorial difficulty in Maury and Giles may be speedily settled.[5] See Dr. Hays & William[6] & tell them to see *Jonas E. Thomas* and have it settled. Whilst all things are going well, at a distance, it will effect me most disastrously, if the Senatorial divisions at home should not be healed. In haste.

AL, fragment. DLC–JKP. Addressed to Columbia.

1. See Sarah C. Polk to Polk, April 7, 1843.
2. Clipping of Polk's signature on the verso has occasioned the loss of several lines of text, probably descriptive of the campaign rally at Pleasant Exchange, Tennessee.
3. Perry County.
4. See Polk to Sarah C. Polk, April 14, 1843.
5. See William H. Polk to Polk, April 10, 1843, and Sarah C. Polk to Polk, April 17, 1843.
6. John B. Hays and William H. Polk. A Columbia physician, Hays was the husband of Ophelia Clarissa Polk, youngest sister of James K. and William H. Polk.

FROM WILLIAM H. POLK

Dear Brother   Columbia April 10th 1843

I returned home from Giles on Saturday evening last, having spent the week there attending Court. Col Wilks and Maj Campbell[1] were both at Pulaski on Monday last urging their claims for the Senate. The Whigs having on that day nominated Col. Cahal for the Senate and Mr. Goode for the House.[2] From this movement it was clear and important, in the absence of all knowledge, as to the course Cahal would persue, and fairly concluding that his *party* in Giles had some *authority* to nominate him—

that something *must* be speedily done to accommodate the difficulty between Campbell and Wilks, and secure entire harmony in our ranks, to avert the danger of defeat. Col Wilks, as you know, at no time anxious to run, solicited his friends in Giles, to persuade Campbell to agree that they should both decline in favor of some third *man*. This was accomplished without much difficulty, and Houston Thomas was agreed on as the candidate by our leading friends in that County, with the consent and approval of both *Campbell* and *Wilks*. The particulars of all this arrangement A. V. Brown can give you. When I arrived home I understood from the *women folks*, that from the account of Mr Walker, great disatisfaction prevailed in Maury County. Such though, you may *rest assured* is not the case. There are as far as I can learn but two or three men including Mr. Walker & Jack Johnson[3] who are disatisfied. This being monday, many persons were in *Town* from the different sections of the County. And I have made it my buisness to enquire & ascertain the true state of the case, and I repeat you need not be the *least uneasy*. Thomas is more than acceptable to the people, and will make a splendid run. Jonas E Thomas, Allen, Mumford Smith,[4] and many others of our leading friends say that Thomas[5] will do well, and be supported warmly, unless Jack Johnson & our *cousin* Bob Campbell who are very buisy in endeavouring to prijudice the people against him, should succeed to a great extent in their purpose. Bob Campbell is buisy now in advocating a Convention, in the hope that Mr. Walker's and Johnson influence will be cast for McKay Campbell, their disatisfaction being so great against Thomas. My own opinion is, that if they succeed in bringing about a *Convention*, that Nicholson will *scheme* himself into the *position* for the Senate. This I desire by all means to avoid, for with him, our party would be but little better off, than if a Whig represented the district. From all I can learn, the nomination of Thomas would have gone down with the people without a *murmer*, if Mr. Walker had not openly on the public street expressed his disapprobation in terms harsh and vindictive. This encouraged the *others* to raise the cry. He acted very imprudently for a man who pretends to have any interest for the safety of the party. It would be well for you to write to Dr. Hays. He has been very silent and will do what is right.

Since writing the above Bob Campbell has been here, and is very warm, harping on Mr Walker's opposition and influence, saying he will put the leading men on the North side of the river[6] in motion against Thomas. I could do nothing with him. It would not in my opinion be entirely safe for you to write to him on the subject; but in your letter to Dr. Hays, you might authorize him to show parts of it to *Bob*. Write me fully from Savanah. All [are] well.

WILLIAM H POLK

ALS. DLC–JKP. Addressed to Savannah.

1. Richard A. L. Wilkes and McKay W. Campbell.

2. Terry H. Cahal and John W. Goode. A Pulaski lawyer, Goode won election as a Whig to a single term in the Tennessee House, 1843–45.

3. James Walker and John B. Johnson. Johnson and Samuel P. Walker were proprietors of a general store in Columbia, styled "Johnson & Walker."

4. Jonas E. Thomas, Allen, and Mumford Smith. A successful lawyer and farmer, Thomas represented Maury County in the Tennessee House, 1835–41, and sat for Maury and Giles counties in the Senate, 1845–47. Mumford Smith was sheriff of Maury County, 1846–50 and 1854–56. Allen is not identified further.

5. James Houston Thomas.

6. Duck River.

FROM SARAH C. POLK

Dear Husband   Columbia April 11th 1843

I wrote you on last Friday by Mr. Walker,[1] who expected to meet you. Since then I have learned nothing of consequence. I received your letter from Jackson.[2] And your letter is all that we have heard from there, as there has been no notice in the papers as yet. But I suppose we shall have something to day. I have feared since I last wrote that my letter and Mr. Walker's views concerning Houston Thomas prospects would give you some uneasiness. William will write you all.[3] Since his return from Giles I learn, the objections are confined to the *kin, one family* & Jack Johnson,[4] which you knew all about before. There are no letters important to send you. One from the plantation.[5] All well, there. One from T. J. Read & Son,[6] giving an account of sales of 11 bales of cotton at 4 1/4¢, which is all that is worthy of notice. Every thing is quiet here and I think but little said on the subject of Politicks. At least I hear but little; you know that my opportunities are limited. All my fears are you can not stand the hard labour of the canvass. I am not patriotic enough to make sacrifices for my country. I love myself (*I mean my Husband*) better or more than my country. You have rather tantalized me in making appointments so near home and yet giving me no opportunity of seeing you.

                                                   Sarah Polk

ALS. DLC–JKP. Addressed to Savannah.

1. See Sarah C. Polk to Polk, April 7, 1843.

2. See Polk to Sarah C. Polk, April 4 and 7, 1843.

3. See William H. Polk to Polk, April 10, 1843.

4. James Walker, Robert Campbell, Jr., and John B. Johnson.

5. Letter not found.

6. A staunch Jacksonian, Thomas J. Read moved from Nashville to Louisville in 1835 and became a wealthy commission merchant. Read's letter has not been found.

TO SARAH C. POLK

My Dear Wife: Savanah April 14th 1843

I did not reach here until this morning, when I receivd your letter of the 11th and also one from William.[1] I saw Mr Walker and wrote you from Perryville.[2] I met good crowds at *Bath-Springs & Carrollville*,[3] & found the Democracy very firm & zealous & some gain, though in these Whig regions not so great, as in the other Counties through which I have passed.

It distresses me to hear from various sources, that the only trouble in the Giles & Maury Senatorial District, springs from two or three of my kin & one or two other friends. I am well satisfied, that the compromise by which *Campbell & Wilkes* withdrew & *Thomas* was announced is entirely satisfactory, to our *whole party* in Giles, and if my immediate friends at Columbia would yield their personal wishes for the good of the cause, all will be well. I wish you as soon as you receive this, to send for Dr. Hays, and urge him, for my sake and the sake of the party, to induce *Bob Campbell*, and the two or three others who are disatisfied to give up their objections, and whatever they may think of *Thomas* personally, to support him for the sake of principle. If they refuse to yield & are determined to persist, they will do infinite mischief—to me and the cause. Tell Dr. *Hays & William & Saml. Walker*,[4] that surely the trouble can be prevented.

My health continues good; I stand the canvass well; I will speak here to day & will leave this evening & speak at Purdy on tomorrow. You must write me as soon as you receive this, directed to *Memphis*.[5] I will write you again at Somerville.

JAMES K. POLK

P.S. *A. V. Brown* who is here, desires that notice be given that he & his competitor[6] will address the people at *Williamsport* on Thursday the 20th April, at *Mount Pleasant* on Friday the 21st & at Columbia on Saturday the 22nd April. See William & tell him to make these appointments made known. J.K.P.

ALS. DLC–JKP. Addressed to Columbia.
1. See William H. Polk to Polk, April 10, 1843.
2. See Polk to Sarah C. Polk, April 10, 1843.
3. Polk spoke at Bath Springs in Perry County on April 11, 1843, and at

Carrollsville in Wayne County on April 12, 1843.

4. John B. Hays, William H. Polk, and Samuel P. Walker.

5. See Sarah C. Polk to Polk, April 17, 1843.

6. Neill S. Brown, a Pulaski lawyer, represented Giles County in the Tennessee House, 1837–39; ran an unsuccessful race for Congress against Aaron V. Brown in 1843; and won election as a presidential elector on the Whig ticket in 1844. Brown served one term as governor of Tennessee 1847–49, and went to Russia as U.S. Minister from 1850 to 1853. Joining the Know-Nothing Party, he served one term as Speaker of the Tennessee House, 1855–57.

FROM WILLIAM FITZGERALD

Dear Sir   Paris April 16 1843

The paper[1] which I herewith enclose is one taken by my wife[2] who is & long has been a member of the Methodist church. I thought it quite probable that you did not view the paper and I send it to you on account of the pastoral address of the ministers of that church which you will find in its colums and because of what they say in relation to the Bankrupt Law.

You Know as well as I do that the Methodist church is numerous & powerful in Tennessee & that the members have much respect for the opinions of their ministers.

I wish you had seen this before your meeting with Milton Brown.[3] He is a member of that church. It would seem that he has disregarded the will of his constituents, the instructions of his Legislature and the admonition of his church. Instead of there being only the voice of a shylock against this Law it seems that the good & pious ministers of the church with the Bishop at their head are found warning their people against this Law. Some of the Baptist churches in this District have made rules to expell members who take benefit of this Law. Things go on well here.

WM. FITZGERALD

ALS. DLC–JKP. Addressed to Columbia.

1. Enclosure neither found nor identified further.
2. Elizabeth Wells Fitzgerald from Montgomery County.
3. See Polk to Sarah C. Polk, April 4, 1843.

FROM SARAH C. POLK

My Dear Husband   Columbia April 17th 1843

I received to day your letters from Perryville & Savannah.[1] And I am sorry to say that since I last wrote you, there has been nothing effected, among the friends in the Senatorial matter.[2] I sent for Jonas E. Thomas on saturday last and had a conversation on the subject, and urged him to have the matter settled. He said he had been and was doing all he could, but thinks there must be a convention now; it can not be avoided. Dissatisfaction has been sent out from this *town* to every part of the county towards *Houston Thomas*. I talked with Dr. Hays & Bob Campbell this evening. Bob is holding on to McKay Campbell. The truth is they are all at sea without a compass, no one to guide, all leaders, none with judgement and all controled by personal feelings or interest. So you may know that the result will be a matter of chance. And you need not be surprised to hear that Nicholson or Barkley Martin is the candidate. I expect this to be the result. Mr. Walker & Sam Walker are not at home. Knox & William[3] at Hickman court. So you may see that I have not much to opperate on and I doubt if any thing could be done if they were all here, as every one pulls his own way and according to his liking, *not principles*. Such is the state of things. You need not be surprised to hear any thing. I do not wish to make you uneasy, and I do not think you could do any good by writing *now*, to any one. Campbell[4] promised to come to see me in the morning, and I will try to get a talk with Jack Johnson tomorrow and I assure that if I can do any thing by urging them to union and harmony and getting our own sort of a man I will try. There is no excitement here on the subject of politicks. Only this jaring among our folks. I see from the Knoxville Argus most encouraging accounts from E. Ten. stating that the Democratic vote will be increased in every county, even in the strong Whig Counties. I beg and pray of you to take care of yourself. I can not feel happy and reconciled whilst you [are] undergoing so much fatigue at the risk of your health. Don't permit yourself to become to much excited.

Sarah Polk

ALS. DLC–JKP. Addressed to Memphis.
1. See Polk to Sarah C. Polk, April 10 and 14, 1843.
2. Reference is to the Democratic choice for the Tennessee Senate from Maury and Giles counties.
3. J. Knox Walker and William H. Polk.
4. Robert Campbell, Jr.

FROM JAMES M. HOWRY

My Dear Sir,   Oxford [Mississippi] 19 April '43
    I was in hope that I would be able to meet you at Memphis and hear the discussion but my health has been bad ever since I saw you in Novr. and my courts requiring my attention, I am denied the pleasure. I write

you a line to apprize you of the state of things in our state. We are *split* into *many* fragments and owing to the *nature* of the split, or cause I see no remedy to save us from general defeat in the fall. A sett of caucus candidates which are any thing but acceptable to the Northern Democracy. We have Union Bank[1] Bond repudiators, Planters Bank Bond repudiators & most of the first are for paying the latter bonds. We have *bond* paying Democrats, McNutt Democrats, Tucker *Dem*, Howard Dem & Dem against them all, but they will not unite on any one man or principle and from present appearances I anticipate a general defeat in Novr.[2] Our Leg Treasurer[3] will aid the Whigs too. If we could save the Legislature so as to secure a Senator and elect our Congressional Ticket, The State Govt. might go & do but little damage & it would have the tendency to cement us for the contest in 1844 which will be a bitter one. The *feeling* is growing too between VB[4] & Calhoun Democrats & the postponement of the Nat Convention until May 1844 will only increase the rivalry & not leave time to counteract it before Novr. especially if Mr VB should be the nominee.

I see Dick Johnson is to visit our state soon & has accepted invitations to Natchez, Jackson & *Pontotoc*, and what course your numerous friends will take towards him I do not know, nor do I know what they should do in the premise. But if any of his friends urge a meeting to invite him among us perhaps it would be best for your friends to unite, but it might be made capital of against you.

This Calhoun feeling here, will cause *that interest* to make a very great man out of the Hero of the Thames,[5] in our State, and I heard the other day that a high functionary in our neighborhood sneeringly remarked that "if VB was nominated *you would not be & he was surprised that you had not the sagacity to see it*"!! My opinion is that there is Juggling going on in our State and that some of our *great men* are determined to do every thing to defeat your nomination in their power.

I think it is highly probable that I will be in Hawkins as you pass through in July. Your friends are well pleased with the vigor & ability with which you prosecute the great task before you. They sympathise with you on account of the great labor you have to perform.

But we hope you will reestablish the principles of Jefferson & Jackson in the Hickory State, which will decide its political caste for many years.

J. M. Howry

ALS. DLC–JKP. Addressed to Memphis.

1. Chartered by the State of Mississippi in January 1837, the Mississippi Union Bank, located at Jackson, issued 50,000 shares of stock to the state in exchange for $5 million in state bonds that were subsequently sold by the bank.

2. Alexander G. McNutt, Tilghman M. Tucker, and probably Volney E.

Howard. A native Virginian, McNutt moved to Mississippi in 1824, held a seat in the state Senate in 1835, and by appealing to strong anti-bank sentiment won election as Democratic governor two years later. For two terms he opposed corruption in Mississippi's banking institutions. In his message of January 1840, McNutt detailed abuses in the banking system and recommended repeal of all bank charters. Howard, born in Maine, represented Scott County in the Mississippi House in 1836, served as reporter of the High Court of Errors and Appeals, and edited the Jackson *Mississippian*. He served in the U.S. House as a Democrat from Texas, 1849–53, and later moved to California.

3. Richard S. Graves, state treasurer, was arrested on an embezzlement charge in March 1843. During his trial he escaped to Canada. The amount of his defalcation totaled approximately $45 thousand.

4. Martin Van Buren.

5. Richard M. Johnson.

FROM SARAH C. POLK

My dear Husband   Columbia May 3rd 1843

Since I last wrote you there has nothing transpired but what was anticipated in the settlement of the Senatorial matter.[1] *Nicholson* is the candidate and every thing is quiet: your friends goin for him and there appears good feelings. I can not write you all that has been said and done on the subject; but will leave it open until you come home. The Whigs did not bring out candidates on Monday as was expected. There is a good feeling prevailing here. Cahal & Dave Looney[2] are all that talk much. The Whigs are dispirited. Genl. Pillow & Humphreys[3] has given such a fine account of things in the District[4] that the Democrats are in extacies. *Pillow* done nothing but talk on Saturday & Monday last, and it has had its effect. All I hear is good, but that does not reconcile me, to a seperation from you under such circumstances and I never wanted to see you more in my life than now. And as I hope to see you soon I will write no more.

SARAH POLK

ALS. DLC–JKP. Addressed to Camden.

1. See William H. Polk to Polk, April 10, 1843, and Sarah C. Polk to Polk, April 17, 1843.

2. Terry H. Cahal and David Looney. A son of Abraham Looney, David Looney owned part interest in an iron works in Wayne County. Looney moved to Memphis about 1844, where he practiced law.

3. Gideon J. Pillow and West H. Humphreys. A Columbia lawyer and general in the militia, Pillow played a key role at the 1844 Democratic National Convention. He served as a general officer in the Mexican War and commanded a Con-

federate brigade during the Civil War. Pillow's sister, Amanda Malvina Pillow, married West H. Humphreys in 1839.

4. Western District.

FROM GEORGE W. SMITH

Dr Sir, Memphis May 3rd 1843

You will perceive from the enclosed Eagle, that Gov Jones has answered the questions propounded to him & yourself through the Appeal.[1] He also answered those propounded in the Enquirer[2] before he left. They are in the Enquirer which I presume you have seen. The Whigs are talking about your not having answered &c. We think you had best forward your answer to the *Appeal* when you do answer them as that paper contained the interrogotories and our Editor[3] is a little sensative any way since the Democrats have started a paper[4] at Jackson. Matters are going well here & we have every thing to animate us in the approaching Canvass. We think you made a fine impression here. There are a good many Whigs who have declared their intention to vote for you since you left.

GEO. W. SMITH

ALS. DLC–JKP. Addressed to Camden.

1. Memphis *American Eagle* and *Memphis Appeal*. A Whig paper established in January 1842 and edited by Francis S. Latham, the *Eagle* carried Jones' answers to the Democratic interrogatories on May 2, 1843. The *Nashville Union* of May 2, 1843, reprinted the Democratic interrogatories that originally had appeared in the *Memphis Appeal*, the date of which has not been identified. For Polk's response, see Polk to George W. Smith et al., May 15, 1843, and Polk to Henry Van Pelt, May 15, 1843.

2. Jones' reply to the Whig interrogatories, which were first posed in the Memphis *Enquirer* of April 13, 1843, was published in the *Enquirer*, date not identified, and was reprinted in the *Nashville Union* on May 12, 1843. For Polk's response to the Whig interrogatories, see Polk to Wyatt Christian et al., May 15, 1843, and Polk to Henry Van Pelt, May 15, 1843.

3. Henry Van Pelt.

4. Reference is to the *Jackson Republican*, which began publication in March 1842.

FROM LEVIN H. COE

Dear Sir Somerville May 6. 1843

Your favors from Covington & Brownsville[1] are both to hand this week. I would have written you by the way but apprehended you might not receive my letter. I sent to Nashville by last Tuesdays mail a communication to be published over my own name.[2] The Mempis & Nashville Whig papers attempt to make *me* approve Jones acts.[3] This I have thought proper to notice & in a manner that I think will make them regret they named me at all.

Our candidates all met at Bolivar last Monday. I feel that our cause in this region is safe & that there will be a small gain in all the countys south of Hatchie River. Enough I hope in this County to elect Fisher.[4]

I recd. reliable news from McNairy Cty yesterday. You will reduce Jones majority 100 votes under his majority of 1841.

Judge Brown & myself & some others intend if circumstances call for it to take the field the 1st July and make speeches until the day of election. This we say to you in case a score of Deputy Governors turn out speech making under excuse of Jones sickness.[5] This however is a delicate game and we must if we start at all be sure it is advisable.

L. H. Coe

ALS. DLC–JKP. Addressed to Columbia.

1. Letters not found.

2. Coe's letter to the editor, dated May 2, 1843, appeared in the *Nashville Union* of May 12, 1843.

3. Memphis *Enquirer*, Memphis *American Eagle*, Nashville *Whig*, and Nashville *Republican Banner*. In the spring of 1842, while James C. Jones was visiting New Orleans, Tennessee's secretary of state, John S. Young, issued a reward proclamation for the recapture of six prisoners who had escaped from jail in Somerville. Subsequently Jones paid the reward when the fugitives were apprehended. The Democratic press argued that only the governor could issue proclamations of this nature and that the governor had abused his constitutional powers by making an improper delegation of authority to a "deputy" governor.

4. A farmer and merchant, George W. Fisher represented Fayette County for two terms in the Tennessee House, 1843–47, and served one term in the Senate, 1849–51, for Fayette, Hardeman, and Shelby counties.

5. The *Nashville Whig* of May 2, 1843, reported that Jones suffered from "a severe cold under which he had been laboring for several days" and that "he was extremely hoarse." See also Polk to Samuel H. Laughlin, May 8, 1843.

FROM WILLIAM M. LOWRY[1]

My Dear Sir   Greeneville Ten 6 May 1843

I presume you have a number of vigilant correspondents in E Ten, who keep you informd. from time to time of the state of the political atismophere in E Ten, but for fear they have been negligent of late, I embrace a leisure moment to address you a line. 1st you have seen that Col Johnson is the nomanee of the Democratic party for congress in this District,[2] and that our old friend Col. Aiken is also the Bank Democratic candidate. For fear that you may form some unfavourable opinion, as the result I have to say that I do not think Col Aikens running will effect anny thing. The Democrats will not touch him. Neither do I believe will a number of the Whigs. All seem distrustful of him. I entertain not the least fear, of the result between Johnson & Aiken. Johnsons majority will be large. I was fearful at one time the difficulty between B Campbell & Johnson[3] would injuriously effect Johnson, but that matter is now pretty well setled and reconciled. I was verry sorry of the split between Johnson & Campbell & not withstanding Campbell may have conceded too much to the Whigs in laying of[f] the Districts. Johnson was equally culpable in being so personal in his protest,[4] tho I am happy to inform you that I think this matter all setled & that we will hear no more of it. We are getting our Candidates for the Legislature all on the track and I hope our friends at a distance will feel easey in reference to the Block of counties in this quarter. They will do theire duty. You are doubtless aware that we have had some little difficulty, too manny great men, too manny aspireing for office. Still I think all things are working for the best. Our friends every where seem in high spirits in reference to the Canvass for Gov. & it is now reported in our part of the state that the Gov.[5] (to use a sportsmans phraze) has let down. Your friends are anxious to see you and to hear you & his Exc. discuss polatics in general. Some of the Whigs have become verry desperate on acct as they say of Tyler deserting them & appointing Democrats to office. The truth is they do seem to have a hard lot after doing all they could to elevate Tyler. Now that he is bestowing the patronage of the Gov. on those who Opposed his Election. Col Johnson soon Opens the canvass & will meet with you at Newport. In the mean time I should be pleased to hear from you frequently as also our friends what are prospects ahead.

Wm. M. Lowry

ALS. DLC–JKP. Addressed to McMinnville and forwarded to Columbia.

1. A business, personal, and political friend of Andrew Johnson, Lowry served as postmaster of Greeneville, 1843–50, and as U.S. marshal for the Eastern District of Tennessee during the years before the Civil War.

2. Tennessee's First Congressional District.

3. See E. G. Eastman to Polk, December 19, 1842.

4. Presented in writing to the Tennessee Senate and dated November 12, 1842, Johnson's protest against the reapportionment of the legislature was published in the *Senate Journal, 1842,* pp. 155–58. The sixth section of the protest alluded to Brookins Campbell in the following words: "The undersigned will not

be understood in the expression of his opinion, as charging that there was a political 'judas' on that committee from the upper counties in East Tennessee, who has brought seventeen hundred and seventy freemen into market from the counties of Greene, Hawkins, Sullivan, and Washington, and sold them as sheep in the shambles, for '*the thirty pieces of* silver.' "

5. James C. Jones.

TO SAMUEL H. LAUGHLIN

My Dear Sir: Camden May 8th 1843

I have [not] heard from your District[1] since I received your letter at *Savanah* on the 14th April.[2] Write me to Columbia where I will rest next week & let me know all about matters in your District, as they are now arranged. I have passed through 22 Counties. My prospects are better than they have ever been: better decidedly than they were in 1839. The Democracy every where are buoyant, confident of success and more active than I have ever known them. We have a gain in every County. I have not heard of the loss of a single man. The mass of the Whigs are dispirited, lukewarm & indifferent, & many of them will not vote at all. They cannot be *roused* by all the efforts of their leaders. *Jones* was out of the canvass & I was alone for 7 days until friday last; he joined me at *Christmasville* & is here, but is still complaining.[3] In great haste.

JAMES K. POLK

ALS. DLC–JKP. Addressed to McMinnville and marked "*Private.*" Published in *ETHSP*, XVIII, p. 163.

1. Tennessee's Fourth Congressional District.
2. Letter not found.
3. James C. Jones' complaint was that of a bad cold and accompanying hoarseness.

TO SARAH C. POLK

My Dear Wife: Camden May 8th 1843

I recd your letter of the 3rd here last night. My health continues very good & in less than a week I hope to be at home. *Jones* joined me again in the canvass at *Christmasville* & is here but is still complaining of bad health. My prospects continue to be good, better than they have ever been. Be sure to send the Buggy to Centerville. Let two come down in it, so that one can ride my horse & the other drive me. The moon will shine & in this way I think I can get home on Saturday night.

AL. DLC—JKP. Addressed to Columbia. Polk's signature has been clipped from the bottom third of the single-page manuscript.

FROM CAVE JOHNSON

Dear Sir   Clarksville 10th May 1843

I have intended to write you but have had nothing that would interest you. I have only been to Charlotte & made one Speech in this County.[1] There can be no doubt that you will gain on your old vote in the four counties[2] around me, more in Robertson than any other. Jones will loose more than you will gain. Many *White Whigs*[3] will not be *Clay Whigs* but from pride or something worse refuse to vote. We hope yet to bring them all in. So far I have not heard the loss of one vote to either of us. I am fearful that Jones giving out & our friends exulting over it will aid more than his Speeches. Our little paper[4] is doing us good service. Overton[5] has returned from Arkansas & will probably take charge of the editorial department. The Union is loosing ground here & should be edited with more spirit between now & the election.[6] We were compelled to run Willie & Dortch,[7] our strongest men unless so many of our family runing may injure one or more of us. I fear it will, but on whom it is to fall I cannot yet tell. I could bear it but neither of the others can. I think (under the circumstances) as we were all literaly forced out we may perhaps all be elected. Singly there would be no doubt of either. Willie Norflet (my wifes cousin)[8] is pressing Cheatham hardly & I have scarcely seen a man who does not believe that Cheatham will be defeated tho I cannot believe it. I leave to day for Paris & shall be absent ten days & shall be hereafter very active, if I can keep up. I have been very unwell with my old disease & am very fearful I shall not be able to keep up. If I keep well I think I can make my majority larger than ever before. Every Whig candidate in my old district[9] except Cheatham is an old Adams & Clay man & take up *the Bank* & a *protective Tariff*. The exchanges are working admirably for us. Every one returning from N. Orleans gives such accounts as adds to our cause. Clark M. Shelby[10] returns an *Anti Bank man* & will vote the first time for Polk & Johnson. Beaumont[11] the Pres. of the Planters Bank returns & openly expresses himself agt. a U.S. Bank such as Clays or Biddles.[12] He would like Jackson's old suggestion a Deposit Bank & selling Bills. Our old land lord Chilton[13] cant stand the Tariff & takes ground openly for the first time for Polk & Johnson. We strive here to make a distinction between White Whigs & Clay Whigs.

I will write you, on my return from Henry, to Knoxville. I omitted an appointment for you at Maysville. I thought you had too much on hand.

You may fairly calculate upon every member in my district[14] being democratic except Cheatham. Willie & Dortch are of course doubtful but the chances are for us.

C. JOHNSON

[P.S.] If you can spare time I should like to hear, tho do not put yourself to any unnecessary trouble.

ALS. DLC–JKP. Addressed to Columbia.
1. Montgomery County.
2. Stewart, Humphreys, Dickson, and Robertson counties.
3. Reference is to the followers of Hugh Lawson White.
4. The *Clarksville Jeffersonian*, a Democratic newspaper, began publication on March 18, 1843. Edited by Charles Faxon, the paper continued publication until 1862 under the editorship of Faxon and his three sons, Charles O., Leonard G., and Henry W. Faxon.
5. Probably William Overton, a lawyer and Democrat, who was former editor of the *Clarksville Chronicle*.
6. Reference is to the *Nashville Union*. See J. George Harris to Polk, January 16, 1843, and Robert Armstrong to Polk, March 31, 1843.
7. Willie B. Johnson and James N. Dortch. See Cave Johnson to Polk, January 4, 1843.
8. Willie L. Norfleet and Elizabeth Dortch Brunson Johnson.
9. Reference is to Tennessee's Eleventh Congressional District, which prior to 1842 included Robertson, Montgomery, Stewart, Dickson, Humphreys, and Hickman counties.
10. Shelby is not identified further.
11. A Clarksville commission merchant, minister, and civic leader, Henry F. Beaumont was president of the Clarksville branch of the Planters Bank of Tennessee for twenty years prior to the Civil War.
12. Henry Clay and Nicholas Biddle. Biddle was president of the Bank of the United States from 1822 until 1836.
13. Chilton is not identified further.
14. Tennessee's Ninth Congressional District.

FROM J. G. M. RAMSEY

My Dear Sir   Mecklenburg May 11. 1843

By this days mail I received yours of the 3rd inst[1] Post Marked Dresden. I hasten to reply to it. I could not satisfy myself that letters from here would certainly reach you at the offices off the Main lines of mail communication or you should have heard from me more frequently, & besides there was little that was really new or interesting to be communicated. Still I was desirous of keeping you informed of what we were doing in E.T. & a week or two back I wrote to Mr. Walker of Columbia, giving him a general outline of the condition of things here & requesting him to have its substance forwarded to you. As you are to be in Columbia on the 14th you will hear or see it. Since writing that I hear that Genl. Stone[2] is out for Congress in the 3rd Dist. & tho he will get but few votes it is believed that his running will make Blackwell's election certain. Late accounts from the Crescent (2nd.) Dist. say that the Democrats who generally were sympathising with Reneau & would have voted for him to beat an 11th hour Whig, Senter, are suddenly animated with a burning desire to defeat both of them & are going into the support of Wallace[3] with great spirit, & many of the Whigs disgusted at the mutual criminations & recriminations of their two candidates are also supporting Wallace. R. & S. are saving you a great deal of trouble. The former accuses S. of being an original Jackson man—against a Bank & all that & calls him a deserter of his party & of their principles. S. on the other hand calls R. a real old fashioned Federalist of the real Adams kind as far back as 1825 &c. &c. In this way their canvass was carried on till W. W. Wallace offered. Let their election terminate as it may I think it will operate against Jones & for you. Col. Blair writes me that Aiken will not carry off any considerable portion of the Democrats, is closely identified with the Whigs. Johnsons election is considered certain. For the Assembly[4] I believe I communicate nothing new, except that in this county[5] A. R. Crozier on last Saturday met his Whig competitors on the stump & made so favorable an impression that one by one in evidence of his devotion to the cause of Whiggery each competitor declared his willingness that moment to decline & let but one Whig run. They mentioned a Convention to be called the 5th June for that purpose (You may not recollect that an abortive Convention met for the same object in March & 17 set of delegates met then with 17 set of instructions & could not so far harmonise as to agree upon any nomination, broke up in confusion & five aspirants came out on their own hook.[6] But worse & worse for them the 2 Williamses[7] proposed Knoxville as the place of the meeting & the other three dissented—one for one place & one for another & if any thing definite has been arranged yet it has not transpired. The names of all of them are still in the Whig papers as candidates. This state of things is decidedly in our favor every way & if it continues Crozier will be elected. They cant decide who is their strongest man & the complexion of things is so discouraging that a man that is worth any thing or has future aspirations is afraid to offer. I expect however they will unite as a dernier resort upon (perhaps a new) some candidate & beat us, but just now Crozier would get 1000 votes. A good deal of interest is being felt in Jones denial of C's statement & we will make capital of that.[8] *Jones wont deny here for many Whigs heard his remarks.* I can give you names of his former friends. By the way will you allow some one to copy Croziers statement & the Post's reply to him, admitting substantially its correctness. C. wants it himself. Some of the 13 & others who are candidates have requested its republication for their own use on the stump & the No. we sent you is the only one in our reach.[9] Please have the copy forwarded immediately to me. This is a moment to use it here efficiently.

T. N. McCampell is Nelson's opponent & he is daily gaining upon him.[10] He is a strong Anti-Bankrupt Whig & as he that far helps us we will vote for him. Several of his Whig friends are going strong for you. There is a perfect apathy in the Whig masses & the leaders cannot remove it. Our friends are somewhat indifferent too but far exceed them in spirit & zeal. It is so above us & I have no doubt that changes in our favor are taking place, silently often & calmly but not the less surely. I am gladened by every letter I receive especially from the West. No wonder Jones is sick—some of his friends are sick of him. The masses care nothing for him. I will have the Argus[11] to meet you somewhere weekly. Eastman is doing well & his pen & his countenance show not only zeal but the assurance of success.

I got a letter last week from Smith at Memphis. It is already in the Argus as also one from Bolivar (E.P.).[12] The latter I have answered & will the other by this mail. Success to you in your arduous struggle for our cause. I feel scarcely less sanguine of your triumph than in 1839. The fight is hard but the victory not the less sure. May the reward be equal to your services.

J. G. M. RAMSEY

ALS. DLC–JKP. Addressed to Columbia.

1. Letter not found.

2. A hero of the War of 1812, William Stone served in the U.S. House from 1837 until 1839.

3. W. W. Wallace, a soft-money Democrat from Blount County, failed in his bid for election to Congress from Tennessee's Second Congressional District.

4. Tennessee General Assembly.

5. Knox County.

6. On March 25, 1843, Whigs in the seventeen civil districts of Knox County met to propose Whig legislative candidates to be considered at a convention in Knoxville on April 3, 1843.

7. James Williams and John Williams.

8. James C. Jones and Arthur R. Crozier. See Polk to E. G. Eastman, February 13, 1843, and J. G. M. Ramsey to Polk, March 27, 1843.

9. Reference is to the "immortal thirteen" Democrats in the Tennessee Senate, 1841–43.

10. Probably Thomas C. McCampbell and John R. Nelson. A Whig from Knox County, McCampbell served one term in the Tennessee House, 1845–47. A Knox County lawyer and attorney general for Tennessee's Fourth Judicial District, 1824–36, Nelson served two terms in the Tennessee House, 1823–25 and 1839–41, and three terms in the Tennessee Senate, 1841–45 and 1853–55.

11. Knoxville *Argus*.

12. Edwin F. Polk's letter to Ramsey is not identified further. On June 7, 1843, Edwin F. Polk wrote his nephew, James K. Polk, from Bolivar giving political news of the Western District and indicating that "all is right here." ALS. DLC–JKP.

FROM HENDERSON K. YOAKUM

Murfreesboro, Tennessee. May 11, 1843

Yoakum reports to Polk on politics across the state. John O. Cannon[1] of Athens foresees Whig victories in McMinn and Monroe; Reneau is gaining on Senter; and Blackwell may be defeated by Campbell. The Fifth Congressional District is divided and has not chosen a candidate. Jack Fletcher[2] is running against Ross for the Tennessee Senate in Franklin and Lincoln. From the West, Gaines[3] give a "cheering account" of Polk's visit. Hogan thinks the Democrats have a ten-thousand-vote majority and a "ten majority on joint ballot." Yoakum regrets the controversy between New York and South Carolina over the date for the National Democratic Convention and concludes that "every good democrat should agree to any time."

ALS. DLC–JKP. Addressed to Columbia.

1. A Madisonville lawyer, Cannon served a single term in the Tennessee House, 1837–39. Upon his election in 1844 as judge of the Third Judicial Circuit of Tennessee, he removed to Cleveland, Bradley County.

2. A farmer and Democrat, John D. Fletcher represented Rutherford County in the Tennessee House, 1839–43, and sat in the Senate for Franklin and Lincoln counties, 1845–47.

3. Pendleton G. Gaines, a lawyer and editor of the Memphis *Gazette* from 1834 until 1838, served a single term as a Democrat in the Tennessee House, 1839–41.

FROM HENRY STRANGE[1]

Dear Sir   Huntingdon May 12th 1843

Since my return from Camden accident threw me into the Company of several of our small village politicians by whom I was informed that their file leader Gov Jones held in reserve & would use on the first Suitable Occasion evidence with regard to your Course on abolition which they pretend will startle the public mind and throw you into shame and Confusion.

These disciples assert that some years since while you were a member of Congress a petition from some abolitionists residing in No[r]th Carolina was sent to Mr Shepherd[2] a Member of Congress from that State with a request that he would present it to Congress.[3] That amongst the prominent abolitionists who figured on that Occasion was the Celebrated Mr Mendenhall who was brought up to be slaughtered by Mr Clay some time since at a public meeting in Ohio.[4] That when Mr Shepherd received this petition he declined to present it, and that he handed it over to you with a request that you would present it, which you did. They also assert that Jones has in his possession the public records to prove these facts, and that there are now living witnesses by whom they Can be proven.

Upon inquiry I find that this matter has been talked of amongst the Whigs several weeks before your arrival at this place, and I have no doubt the Slanderous imputation of your Connection with the abolitionists has been secretly and insidiously circulated by Gov Jones throughout the Western District, with a view of having some influence in the pending election. The game has been to lie low and Keep dark while you were in this section of the State for fear of exposure, and in your absence to speak out and assume that bold front that is Charactoristic of many of the reckless of your political adversaries.

I have thought proper to advise you of the above facts to put you on your guard as to the Course which your *dignified* opponent is taking as well as to enable you to take such notice of the matter as you may think it deserves.

HENRY STRANGE

ALS. DLC–JKP. Addressed to Columbia.

1. A Democrat, Strange was clerk and master of Carroll County Chancery Court during the early 1840's.

2. Augustine H. Shepperd, a North Carolina Democrat, served numerous terms in the U.S. House, 1827–39, 1841–43, and 1847–51.

3. On February 14, 1837, Polk presented a memorial to the U.S. House for the North Carolina Society of Friends (Quakers), who urged the abolition of slavery in the District of Columbia and sought government aid for the American Colonization Society. The petition was signed by George Swain, Phineas Nixon, Jr., and Richard Mendenhall, a committee appointed by the yearly meeting of the Friends in North Carolina.

4. At a Whig meeting in Richmond, Indiana, on October 1, 1842, Richard Mendenhall presented Henry Clay a petition requesting that he emancipate his slaves. With great oratorical skill Clay argued that colonization accompanied by

gradual emancipation was the only practical remedy; his vigorous attack on aboli-
tionism won the admiration of the crowd as well as considerable notice in newspapers across the country.

FROM ROBERT ARMSTRONG

Govr.   Nashville May 15th 43
Kezer & Hogan will go out and I hope to do so by Thursday mornings
stage. Write me. I may not be able to go. I have every thing to do here.
Humphreys is become efficient and will do much good if you write him
and urge him on. My opinion is that Foster is alarmed and gives up the
Lower House. He is fighting for Davidson and our people will soon see
that the way to Aske a Democratic majority for a favour is to send
Democrats to power, not Whigs. Fosters *agencys* for the Banks give him
great power and influence. What of Nicholsons nomination?[1] What is
doing &c &c? I have letters from all the East Tenness. Counties and the
report is good, better than could be expected, wanting only for you to
Kindle up the fires &c &c.

My opinion is that Jones will not meet you at all your appointments
but fall in ocasionally. If so, you ought not to exert yourself too much.
Make short speeches and take care of yourself.

All that is necessary is for you to make the Trip, to go the rounds,
meet your friends and set them to working. Jones, Norvell, &c &c are
preparing a publication.[2] I hope to hear from you *tomorrow* night. It is
late. Excuse me. In haste.

R ARMSTRONG

ALS. DLC–JKP. Addressed to Columbia.
1. Reference is to A. O. P. Nicholson's selection as the compromise candidate
of Democrats in Maury and Giles counties for a seat in the Tennessee Senate.
2. By prior arrangement Jones and Polk agreed to publish their views on
government expenditures, public debts, tariffs, and a national bank. Jones'
Address to the People of Tennessee appeared in the *Nashville Whig* on May 20,
1843. For details of the publication agreement, see Sarah C. Polk to Polk, May
23, 1843.

FROM JOHN W. CHILDRESS

Dear Sir   MurfreesBoro. May 15 1843
Upon my return from the South a few days since I found my farm in
such condition, as to require my constant attention, for a while—and I

shall in consequence, not be able to meet you at Columbia this week as I had all along expected. I see from your appointments that you will be in Shelbyville about the 26th Inst. and I will be able to meet you there. My horse is in fine condition, and I will have him with me, and if you still want him, you can take him at Shelbyville, and I will send your horse home, or keep him for you as you may desire.[1] If yours has or will fail and you have one to buy, I believe you could not get one any where that would suit you as well. If you should want him earlier and will write immediately I can send him to you.

Our friends here think that the prospects are very fine for the election of Smith & Currin, and a majority for Crockett in this County,[2] and some say in the District.[3] From all I can learn I have no doubt of the success of the County ticket. Currin makes splendid speeches, and has acquired the reputation at home of being the most talented young man in the State. Smith is very effective on the stump.

JOHN W CHILDRESS

[P.S.] Write to me whether the arrangement about the horse will suit you—and your prospects of election.

ALS. DLC–JKP. Addressed to Columbia.
1. See John W. Childress to Polk, December 26, 1842.
2. Rutherford County.
3. Rutherford and Williamson counties.

TO WYATT CHRISTIAN ET AL.[1]

Gentlemen: Columbia, May 15, 1843

I have received through the Memphis *Enquirer* the communication of yourselves and other citizens of Shelby county addressed to Gov. Jones and myself,[2] propounding to each, certain interrogatories upon public subjects, to which I now proceed to reply.

Your first interrogatory is as follows, viz:

"1st. Are you in favor of a mixed currency of paper money and the precious metals?"

I answer, that I am in favor of such a currency—and for my views as expressed on the subject, I refer you to my Message to the General Assembly of this State, of the 22d of October 1839.[3] In that message you will find that after earnestly urging the propriety of an early resumption of specie payments by our Banks, I say:

Banks, and the use of Bank-paper and credits, have become from long habit interwoven and intimately connected with all our extensive commercial operations, and if it be conceded that their employment to a reasonable extent, in conducting our trade, has in the existing state of the currency, become conducive to our prosperity, it must also be allowed that no Banks or Bank issues should be tolerated which do not rest on a solid and substantial specie basis, and be required to meet the demands of trade.

The circulation which they issue should be based upon a solid metalic foundation, such as will ensure an ability at all times to meet their liabilities promptly, and its quantity should be kept as nearly as practicable at the same amount, varying as it necessarily must to a small extent, with the seasons of shipment of our produce to market, and the return of the proceeds; but this variation need not be such as to affect materially, the amount or value of their circulation.

To these views I now add, that in my opinion the precious metals should be the basis of whatever paper circulation may be authorised or tolerated by law. Like individual debtors, Banks should meet their liabilities honestly and promptly, and whenever they fail to do so, I hold it to be the duty of the Legislative power to take efficient means to compel them to do their duty.

To your second and third interrogatories, which are in the following words, to wit:

"*2d. If so, from what source should paper money emanate; from the State Governments or General Government?*

"*3d. If from the General Government, in what mode should the people receive it—through the agency of a Bank, or otherwise?*"

I answer that the States, having exercised the power of chartering Banks of issue, from an early period of the government, and with the general acquiescence of the people—and being in this respect beyond the power and control of the General Government—all must expect and concede that there must and will continue to be a State Bank paper circulation, whether a National Bank exists or not. There was a State Bank paper circulation during the whole period of the existence of the two Banks of the U. States—and if another National Bank were established, there would undoubtedly still continue to be such a circulation. Many of the State Banks have charters which have many years to run, and some of them I believe are perpetual. The establishment of a National Bank therefore, could not supercede them, but must, if established, issue a paper which would circulate with State Bank paper. The State Bank circulation would constitute much the largest amount of the aggregate paper circulation and the experience of the twenty years of the existence of the late Bank of the United States proves, that the paper of State Banks, used as it was by the great mass of the people in their daily transactions, was at much more ruinous rates of depreciation than it now is. The rates of exchange between different sections of the Union were higher and exchanges more difficult to be obtained than they now are, without a Bank of the United States. I am therefore in favor of a circulation to consist of the precious metals and the paper of specie paying State Banks, convertible on demand into specie—and should any such Bank suspend payment, or refuse to redeem its circulation in specie, I would adopt the most rigid means within the power of the Legislature, to compel such Bank to pay, and in the event of failure I would put it into a state of liquidation and wind it up. I will add further, that I would not yield my individual assent to the chartering of any future Bank by State authority, without making the Stockholders liable in their individual estates for the payment of the paper which they issue; I would place them upon the footing of other partnerships. Capitalists form partnerships and invest their money in merchandizing, manufacturing or other business, with a view to make profits, and are liable in their individual property for the payment of the debts of the firm, and I can see no good reason why capitalists who join together and invest their money in the business of Banking with a like view to make profit, should not in like manner be held liable to pay the joint debts of the Banking corporation or firm. I am opposed to the chartering by Congress, of a National incorporated Bank—I believe that Congress possesses no constitutional power to charter such a Bank, and if it did, it would in my opinion be inexpedient to exercise it. These opinions I have long held. The reasons for them have been often communicated to the public in writing, in printed speeches, and in public debate before many thousands of my fellow citizens of Tennessee, and I presume that it cannot be necessary that I should here repeat them.

To your fourth interrogatory, in the following words, viz:

"[*4th.*] *Are you in favor of the Sub Treasury system passed by Congress in 1840, and repealed in 1841?*"

I answer that I am; and for my views as given at some length on the subject, I refer you to my two published addresses to "the people of Tennessee," the one bearing date on the 3d of April,[4] and the other on the 25th of March, 1841.[5] In my address of 1839, I avowed myself to be "in favor of keeping the money of the people in the Treasury of the people under the care of officers elected by the people and responsible to them, where it can at all times be commanded for public purposes, and not in Banks, not elected by the people and not responsible to them, to be loaned out for private purposes."

In speaking of a fiscal agent of Government, I said in that address:

The Bank of the United States had been tried, and proved faithless. The State Banks had been tried and proved faithless. Was it not time to devise a system which should fulfil the requirements of the Constitution, and prevent any money from being "drawn from the Treasury but in consequence of appropriations made by law?" It has been the endeavor of the President and of the Republican party, for almost two years, to introduce such a system. They propose to establish an Independent Treasury—a Treasury independent of Banks—a Treasury in fact, and not in theory. They propose that the Government shall keep its own money in its own Treasury, where it can, at all times, in peace and in war, be commanded for the public uses. To a proposition so simple, and which, in earlier days of the Republic, would have struck every mind as self evident, many objections have been started, some of them plausible, but none of them substantial.

In my address of 1841, I said:

Another measure of the party in power is proclaimed to be the removal of the public money from the constitutional Treasury, where it is now kept, and where it has been kept safely under a financial system that has thus far worked well, and which will no doubt continue to work well, if it be preserved. Where it is proposed to place the public money, if the Independent Treasury law shall be repealed, has not been distinctly avowed. It was undoubtedly at one time, intended by many of the leading men of the party, to place it in the United States Bank of Pennsylvania,[6] and thus bolster up that rotten institution by furnishing to it the money of the public to Bank and to speculate upon. That Bank, which it will be remembered Mr. Biddle declared was stronger under the charter from Pennsylvania, than under that from the United States, and in reference to which Gen. Harrison in his letter to Sherrod Williams, dated "North Bend, May 1st, 1836," declared "Pennsylvania has wisely taken care to appropriate to herself the benefit of its large capital," [7] it has, however, recently gone down, and now lies a heap of ruin in a state of utter prostration, if not of insolvency.

The market price of its stock is down below $20 in the hundred. They cannot, therefore, place the public money in the bank. Where else will they put it? Most of the banks in the United States have suspended specie payments. Will they place it in their keeping, and if they do, will they receive and pay out to the Pensioners, the laborers on the public works, and other public creditors their depreciated paper? Do they mean that the taxes of the people, paid for the support of Government shall be furnished to these or any other banks, to be a part of their banking capital?

If it is not to be so kept and used, where is it to be kept? There is no National Bank, and if one was created it could not be put into operation in less than twelve or eighteen months so as to receive them. And yet it is manifest that the immediate repeal of the Independent Treasury System is one of the leading measures of the party in power.

It is not now my purpose to enter upon the argument of the policy of the Independent Treasury System, or of the necessity which led to its adoption. These have been often presented to my fellow citizens, and if necessary, will be again, in my personal intercourse with them. It has been sometimes urged by my political opponents that I, at one time, gave my support to the State Bank Deposite System. This was fully explained in my address to the people in 1839. In that address I stated that the late Bank of the United States had been tried and proved to be a faithless fiscal agent. For its long catalogue of crimes and misdemeanors, Gen. Jackson withdrew the public money from its keeping, and dismissed it as a fiscal agent of the Government. The State Banks were again employed. At that time they were generally in good credit. They paid specie for their notes, and it was believed they would continue to do so, and that as between their employment and that of the bank of the United States, they were to be preferred. It was believed that they would be faithful, and might be convenient fiscal agents. The Government was willing to try them; upon trial they proved to be unfaithful, and the State Bank System utterly failed.

It is unnecessary to enquire whether the failure of the State Bank Deposite System in 1837, happened from accident, an inherent defect in the system, from inevitable necessity, by design or by fraud. It is enough that it has once happened to put the Government on its guard against a recurrence for the future. After the Bank of the United States had been dismissed as the fiscal agent of the Government, and the public money had been placed in the State Banks, it was deemed to be proper to pass a law "regulating the deposite of the money of the United States in certain local banks." [8] A bill with that object was accordingly introduced at the session of Congress of 1834–5. It was violently opposed by all the friends of the Bank of the United States, and all those who were in favor of restoring the public money to the keeping of that institution. After a protracted discussion, and after the bill had been matured and was ready for the final action of the House, a proposition of amendment was made by a gentleman (Mr. Gordon)[9] who disapproved the removal of the deposites and was avowedly in favor of their restoration to the Bank of the United States—to dispense with the use of all Banks as fiscal agents. The proposition was presented in a crude and undigested form. It provided no vaults or other place in which the public money could be safely kept. It provided no punishment for the fraudulent or improper use of it—It contained none of the guards and checks of the present Independent Treasury law, by which the public money is so amply secured in the Treasury against peculation and fraud. It was a naked proposition without details, and had it been adopted would have been wholly impracticable. It was not brought forward in a manner, or und(e)r circumstances to attract the serious consideration of any considerable portion of either party in the House and the highest evidence that it was only intended to embarass the measure before the House consists in the fact that all who voted for it with a single exception, were the friends of the Bank of the United States, and in favor of restoring the public money to that institution. The fact that it was intended only to embarrass the measure before the House and to coerce the restoration of the deposites to the Bank of the United States, has been distinctly admitted by one of the friends of the Bank, who voted for it. (Mr. Wise, of Va.) in a letter addressed to his constituents on the 24th of March, 1840.[10] In that letter he says—"I am asked whether I voted for what is called Gordon's proposition in 1837, and for my explanation of that vote." And after making some explanation, he adds: "And I now declare that I would not have voted for either of these propositions if there had been the least prospect of its passage. This I expressly declared to General Gordon in relation to his amendment when he first named it to me."

The struggle at that Session [1835][11] was between the Bank of the United States on the one hand, and the regulation of the deposites by law in the State

Banks on the other. The friends of the Bank of the United States, insisted that the deposites should be restored to that institution. The opponents of the Bank insisted that so utterly faithless as a fiscal agent had that Bank proved itself to be, that they ought not to be restored, and that in the existing state of things it was proper to pass a law to regulate their safe keeping in the State Banks—calculating, doubtless, that if no law was passed that that system of deposite would soon get into confusion and the Government be compelled to return the public money to the Bank of the United States.

The condition of the State Banks at that time, and their condition after they suspended specie payments in 1837, was widely different. Whilst they paid specie and faithfully performed their duties as fiscal agents, it was considered that their employment was to be preferred to that of the Bank of the United States. When they ceased to pay specie, and faithfully to discharge their duties to the public they were dismissed. Whilst they paid specie the friends of the Bank of the United States objected to their employment, but when they failed to pay specie they became their apologists and advocates. On the other hand, whilst they paid specie the opponents of the Bank of the United States were willing to try them, but when they failed to do so, they were unwilling longer to continue the deposite of the public money with them. The Bank of the United States and the State Banks having both been tried, and both proved faithless, the Government learned wisdom from experience, and proposed to establish an Independent Treasury—a Treasury independent of Banks—a constitutional treasury in fact, and not in theory only. Such a treasury has been established, and I see no reason why it should be discontinued, and the Government resort back again to the Bank deposite system, either State or National.

I now only add, that I have seen no reasons to change my views as expressed in these addresses. The Constitution of the U.S. contemplates a public Treasury. It provides that "no money shall be drawn from the Treasury, but in consequence of appropriations made by law." [12] Such a Treasury is provided by the Independent Treasury Act,[13] called by you "the Sub Treasury System." It provided that the public money between the periods of collection and disbursement, should be kept in the vaults of the Treasury at Washington, and in strong boxes provided at the principal points of collection, that it should be under the lock and key of the Government—under the care of officers elected or chosen by the people according to the forms of the Constitution of the United States, that these officers should be placed under bonds with approved security, be under oaths, and be subject to ignominious punishment by long imprisonment in the common jail or penitentiary for a violation of their duty. The system had worked well, and was working well, when the party in power, at their extra session of Congress in 1841 repealed it.[14] It is error to attribute the defalcation of Swartwout[15] and others to this system. They occurred long before the Independent Treasury law was passed. *Swartwout's* defalcation commenced (though he was not detected until afterwards) during the period when the Bank of the U.S. was the fiscal agent depository of the public money. (The party in power repealed the Independent Treasury act, but have provided no substitute in its place.) They have been in power more than two years and where yet is the substitute which they have provided. They have left the public money to be kept under the act of 1789—which provides that it "shall be received and kept by the Treasurer of the United States." [16] They have left it to the discretion of their President Mr. Tyler to direct the place and manner in which it shall be kept. When the same thing occurred after the removal of the deposites from the late Bank of the United States by General Jackson, and before the act was passed regulating their keeping in the State Banks, the same party charged that there was a union of the purse and the sword in the hand of the President which was dangerous to liberty; and yet the moment they obtained possession of power, they did the same thing themselves. The charge that there was a union of purse and sword was false. They however made it, and if they still maintain its truth, they have themselves united them.

But the party in power may say, that they have attempted to furnish a substitute by passing Mr. *Clay's* Bank Bill "To incorporate *subscribers* to the Fiscal Bank of the United States," vetoed by Mr. Tyler.[17] That Bill proposed to make the Bank the fiscal agent and keeper of the monies of the United States. It provided that the "deposites of the money of the United States" should be made in that Bank, and that "all public monies in deposite in said Bank, or standing on its books to the credit of the Treasury, shall be taken and deemed to be in the Treasury of the United States." [18] This Bank then—by *Mr. Clay's* Bill was to be the Treasury of the United States. Mr. Clay's Bill provided that the United States was to subscribe for one third of the Capital Stock and other Stockholders for the remaining two thirds of the stock.—It provided that the Bank should be governed by *nine* Directors, *three* of whom were to be appointed by the United States, and *six* of whom by the other Stockholders. The public money was to be placed in its keeping; and when there, was declared to be considered in the Treasury of the United States. The Treasury of the United States was thus to be placed out of the power and control of the Government and in the keeping of six out of the nine Bank Directors not elected or appointed by the Government or people of the United States, owing no responsibility to either, under no bonds, no oaths, and subject to no punishment for an abuse of their trust. Such was the fiscal agency by Mr. *Clay's* Bank Bill. I fully submit to you, Gentlemen, whether such a treasury or plan of fiscal agency, is one which you can approve, or which you prefer to the Independent Treasury System, under which the Government kept control of its own money by placing it in a *Treasury* in fact, and not in theory only under the care and control of responsible agents, selected by the people according to the constitution and laws.

Your 5th and 6th Interrogatories in the following words to wit:

"*5th. Are you in favor of a tariff or direct taxes for the support of the General Government?*"

"*6th. If a tariff, do you approve of such a tariff as would give protection to home industry against foreign industry?*"

I answer that I am opposed to a system of direct taxation and am in favor of a moderate scale of duties, laid by a tariff on imported goods for the purpose of raising the revenue which may be needed for the economical administration of the Government. In fixing the rates of a tariff, my opinion is, that the object in view should be to raise the revenue needed by government leaving the interests engaged in manufactures, to enjoy the incidental advantage which the levy of such duties will afford to them. If by "giving protection to home industry," you mean to assert the distinct principle, that a tariff is to be laid solely or in any extent not for revenue, but for the protection of capitalists who have made their investments in manufacturing establishments, so as to compel the consumers of their articles, the agriculturists, mechanics, persons employed in commerce and all other pursuits to pay higher prices for them, then I say that I am opposed to such a principle, and to any tariff which recognises it. "Home industry," terms so often used by the advocates of the protective tariff system, are comprehensive in their meaning, and by a just legislation should be made to embrace the industry employed in agriculture, in the mechanic arts, in commerce and all other pursuits, as well as the industry employed in manufactures. I have at all times been opposed to prohibitory or high protective tariff laws, designed not for revenue, but to advance the interests of one portion of the people employed in manufactures, by taxing another and much the larger portion, thus making the many tributary to the increased wealth of the few. I am opposed to the tariff act of the late Congress,[19] considering it to be in many respects of this character—and, indeed so highly protective upon some articles as to prohibit their importation into the country, altogether. I am in favor of repealing that act, and restoring the compromise tariff act of March 2d, 1833;[20] believing as I do, that it would produce more revenue than the present law, and that the incidental protection afforded by the twenty per cent duty, especially when this would be paid in cash, and on the home valuation, will afford sufficient protection to the manufacturers and all that they ought to desire, or to which they are entitled.

Your last interrogatory is in the following words, to wit:

"*7th. Are you in favor of the election of U.S. Senators by joint ballot of both Houses of the Legislature? If not, by what mode should they be elected?*"

I answer, that by the Constitution of the United States it is provided that "The times, places, and manner of holding elections for Senators and

Representatives shall be *prescribed in each State by the Legislature thereof*, but that Congress may at any time by law, make or alter such regulations, except as to the places of choosing Senators." [21] The Legislature of this State have never *by law prescribed the times, places or manner* of electing Senators. Our practice has been to elect by joint ballot. In other States a different mode has been adopted, and in some of them the practice has been to choose by the concurrent vote of the two Houses—each House acting in its separate and distinct Legislative character, as it does in passing laws or performing any other Legislative act. Senators elected in each of these modes have been permitted to take their seats and serve as such—no constitutional question as to the *"manner"* of their election, so far as I know, having been raised. I think then, in the absence of any Legislative provision prescribing the *"manner,"* that it rests in the sound discretion of each House of the Legislature, to select the mode or manner, which in its judgment will best subserve the public interest. The mode by *concurrent vote* of each House is concededly constitutional, and if by insisting upon it as the preferable mode—that be the only means of effecting a great public good, or preventing a great public injury—such as preventing the election of persons to the Senate of the United States who conceal their opinons upon public subjects interesting to the people, and who refuse to make them known, or to say whether they admit or deny the right of instruction, when respectfully interrogated upon these points by any portion of the constituent body. In such cases, or similar, I hold that either branch of the Legislature would not only be justified in adhering, but it would be due to the rights of their constituents whose interests were to be deeply affected that they should adhere, to the *manner*, by which these rights would be protected and preserved. The chief, if not the only value of the right of suffrage consists in the fact, that it may be exercised *understandingly* by the constituent body. It is so, whether the immediate constituency consists of the Legislature, as in the case of the election of United States Senators, or of the people in their primary capacity, in the elections of their Executive or Legislative agents. In either case the constituent has a right to know the opinions of the candidate before he casts his vote.

I have now, gentlemen, answered your several interrogatories. I have also answered certain other interrogatories propounded through the public papers at Memphis, by a portion of your fellow citizens of Shelby County—and as the answer to each set of interrogatories, is, in some degree, connected with the answer to the other—some of the interrogatories in both being upon the same subjects—I shall forward both answers by the next mail which leaves for Memphis, that they may be published.

JAMES K. POLK

PL. Published in the *Nashville Union*, June 2, 1843. ALS, draft, not found, enclosed in Polk to Henry Van Pelt, May 15, 1843.

1. Addressed to Wyatt Christian, J. T. Leath and others. Christian, a physician, and Leath were both Whig operatives in Memphis.

2. See George W. Smith to Polk, May 3, 1843.

3. Published in the *House Journal, 1839*, pp. 53–68; in the *Senate Journal, 1839*, pp. 55–71; and in Robert H. White, ed., *Messages of the Governors of Tennessee* (8 vols.; Nashville: Tennessee Historical Commission, 1952–1972), III, pp. 279–99.

4. Printed at Columbia and dated April 3, 1839, Polk's twenty-eight page pamphlet presented a history of U.S. political parties and set forth his political principles on both national and state issues. Although published as a separate, the "Address of James K. Polk to the People of Tennessee" also appeared serially in the *Nashville Union* on April 10, 12, and 15, 1839.

5. Polk's "Address to the People of Tennessee," the first installment of which was published in the *Nashville Union* on March 29, 1841, sketched his public career and outlined his political philosophy. Forty pages in length, the pamphlet version was distributed throughout Tennessee during the 1841 gubernatorial campaign.

6. Upon the expiration of the Second Bank of the United States' federal charter in 1836, Nicholas Biddle secured a new charter from Pennsylvania and continued as president until 1839, two years before the Bank failed.

7. A lawyer from Kentucky, Sherrod Williams served in the Kentucky House, 1829–34 and 1846, and sat in the U.S. House as a Whig, 1835–41. William H. Harrison's letter to Williams appeared in *Niles' Weekly Register* on September 10, 1836.

8. Congress did not complete action on the deposit act until June 23, 1836. 5 *U.S. Stats.*, 52–56.

9. William F. Gordon, a Virginia lawyer, served in the Virginia House, 1818–29, and in the U.S. House, 1830–35. He offered his amendment on February 10, 1835.

10. Henry A. Wise's letter appeared in the *Richmond Whig* on March 31, 1840.

11. Brackets supplied by Polk.

12. United States Constitution, Article I, Section 9.

13. 5 *U.S. Stats.*, 385–92.

14. 5 *U.S. Stats.*, 439–40.

15. Customs collector for the port of New York City, Samuel Swartwout had stolen over a million dollars in Treasury funds and fled abroad.

16. Paraphrase of Section 4, Act of September 2, 1789. 1 *U.S. Stats.*, 65–67.

17. Henry Clay's bill was reported in the U.S. Senate on June 21, 1841, and was subsequently vetoed by Tyler on August 16, 1841.

18. For the text of Henry Clay's Fiscal Bank bill, see Senate Document No. 32, 27 Congress, 1 Session, pp. 7–20.

19. Reference is to the Tariff of 1842.

20. The Compromise Tariff of 1833 provided that advalorem duties gradually would be reduced to 20 percent and would be paid in coin or redeemable bank

notes; imported goods would be appraised at their domestic value as opposed to that of their place of manufacture.

21. United States Constitution, Article I, Section 4.

TO GEORGE W. SMITH ET AL.[1]

Gentlemen: [May 15, 1843][2]

My attention has been called to the interrogatories[3]—addressed by yourselves and others—to *Gov. Jones* and myself through the columns of the Memphis Appeal—and I respectfully submit to you and through you to the public, my response.

Your first interrogatory is as follows:

1st. Are you for or against the first Bank charter passed at the extra session of the late Congress commonly called *Clay's bill*—which was vetoed by Mr. Tyler.

I answer that I am "against the first bank charter passed at the extra session of the late Congress, commonly called *Clay's Bill*,[4] which was vetoed by Mr. Tyler." In a speech delivered at Pulaski on the 29th of September last, and which was afterwards published in some of the newspapers,[5] I stated the character of the bank which was proposed to be established by that Bill. I beg leave to refer you to the following extract from that speech, to wit:

The time was, and but a few years ago when the avowed bank party in this State was exceedingly small. All the prominent and leading men of the party who were now its advocates, including members of Congress, members of the Legislature, and others, were opposed to a National Bank. They supported with great unanimity General Jackson's Veto of the Bank bill in 1832. They supported Judge White and this same Mr. Tyler for the Presidency and Vice Presidency, in 1836, with their known and publicly avowed opinions against an incorporated National Bank of any kind. They had since that time changed their opinions. That, certainly they had a right to do; but it came with an ill grace from them to censure those who had not changed with them. One of the greatest difficulties which the opponents of a bank had had to encounter in this State, had been in meeting the vague generalities in which the bank advocates had dealt. They all, with perhaps rare exceptions, professed to condemn and oppose the bank of the United States, or any other bank organised on similar principles. They would say, we are opposed to the old bank, but we are in favor of a new bank, with suitable restrictions and modifications. What these modifications and restrictions were they would not specify. They talked of them in general and vague terms, but their plans of a bank they did not and would not give. Some, to be sure, had in their minds an uncertain and undefined notion of the plan of a bank with which they would be pleased, such as that there should be no private stockholders and that it should be owned by the General Government and the States. Many honest men had been made to think that a proper sort of bank might be framed that might be useful. He said he regarded it as fortunate in the future discussions of the subject that the party advocating a bank, in this State at least, had at length been driven from their vague generalities. They have brought in and passed a bank charter at the extra session of Congress. Mr. Clay was its author—President Tyler vetoed it, and because he had done so, they had denounced him as a traitor, and burnt and hung him in effigy. If President Tyler had signed that bill they said the whole scheme of Federal measures would have been complete. That bill, then, we must presume, contained their plan of a bank, and to get it they were now prepared to elect Henry Clay President of the United States.

Now, what was that bill, and what was the kind of bank which they promised by it to the country if they continued another Presidential term in power. A slight inspection of its provisions would show that it was an old fashioned incorporated Stock Bank, to be owned in part, and controlled by private stockholders, retaining all the bad features of the late bank, and embracing others that made it more objectionable than that bank, bad as it was. Its capital stock was to be thirty millions of dollars, with power reserved to increase it to fifty millions after the year 1850. One third of the capital stock, or Ten Millions of Dollars, was to be subscribed for by the United States, and two thirds or twenty millions of dollars, was to be subscribed by individuals, companies, corporations or States. The ten millions of dollars to be subscribed by the United States, was to be raised by borrowing the money. A public debt of ten millions of dollars was by the charter authorised to be created, and for that purpose a public stock of the United States was to be issued, bearing interest at the rate of five per centum, per annum, which was not to be paid until after the expiration of fifteen years. This loan must most probably, he might safely say, certainly have been made from foreigners. Thus presenting a nation of seventeen millions of freemen in the humiliating, if not degrading attitude of borrowing money on interest from foreigners to make a bank upon. The interest on the loan which was to be paid half yearly, was five hundred thousand dollars a year, and would have amounted for the fifteen years (sooner than the expiration of which it could not be redeemed) to seventeen millions five hundred thousand dollars. The bank was to be located at Washington City and was to be governed by nine directors, three of whom were to be appointed by the U. States and six by the private stockholders. All know that six would control three—so that the bank itself would in fact have been under the absolute control of the private stockholders. Indeed this seemed to have been designed by the charter itself—for it is provided that "not less than five directors shall constitute a board for the transaction of business, of whom the President shall always be one, and at least three of the five shall be of the directors elected by the stockholders." This provision made it absolutely impossible even in a thin board, for the three Government directors in any possible case, to constitute a majority. The principal board were empowered to appoint the directors or managers of the branches. The public money was directed to be deposited with the bank and as a considerable amount of it would necessarily be always on hand, it would be used and traded upon as banking capital. The taxes paid by the people for the support of Government would constitute a part of the banking capital, to be loaned out, and upon which the private stockholders would make profit. This was the outline of Mr. Clay's Bank Bill which President Tyler vetoed. He had searched in vain through its provisions for those restrictions and limitations which were so often and so vaguely spoken of, and which were to prevent it from running into all the corruptions and abuses of the late Bank of the United States. The United States was made by the charter to go into partnership with private stockholders, to place all the revenues in the concern, and was yet placed in a minority in the directory, and was therefore deprived of all power or control over them. Who would probably have become the private stockholders in such a bank? In the west and south, where there was but little surplus capital and where money bore high rates of interest, but little if any would have been taken. Scarcely a share of the stock in the late Bank of the United States was at any time owned in Tennessee. There could be no doubt that much the larger portion of it would have either been taken at first or been ultimately owned by the federalists of the northern and eastern sections of the Union, who were the largest capitalists of the country. This was the case with the old Bank. And though the stock could not be taken directly by foreigners, there was no doubt but that much of it would have been ultimately held by them under cover of secret trusts in the name of others. He could have no doubt that if it had been established it would have soon become an immense political engine, of deadly hostility to the purity of elections, and to the liberties of the people; and would have been wielded by a corrupt faction, as was the late Bank of the U. States, and for the worst of purposes. The thanks of the country, he had no hesitation in saying, were due to Mr. Tyler for having arrested it as he did by his Veto.

Was this the kind of Bank which the body of the party in this State wanted? He thought he could answer with certainty that it was not. And yet this was Mr. Clay's Bank, and to get it, they were not told by leading public men and newspapers, they must vote for him to be President of the United States. He did not deem it necessary, and if he did time would not allow him to enter upon the general discussion of the bank question and the currency on that occasion. He would only add that neither a National Bank nor any other Bank could prevent commercial revulsions or furnish a remedy against hard times. When we had a National Bank we had witnessed such times, and when we had none we had witnessed them.

Your second interrogatory is as follows, to wit:

2d. Are you in favor of restoring the principles of the Compromise Tariff Bill of 1833?

I answer that I am.

Your third interrogatory is as follows: to wit—

3d. Do you approbate the course of the Whig nominees for the Senate of the United States at the last regular session of the General Assembly, to wit: E. H. Foster and S. Jarnagin, in refusing to declare their opinions upon the subject of the Bankrupt Law, and other subjects, and the right of instruction when called upon by one branch of the elective power?

I answer that I cannot approve the "course of the Whig nominees for the Senate of the United States, at the last regular session of the General Assembly" or of any other aspirant or candidate for public station, in refusing to declare their opinions freely and without reserve, upon all public subjects, upon which they may be interrogated by a portion of the constituent body. The right of instruction by the constituent body to the Representative or public agent, and the duty of the latter to obey in good faith or resign, is one of the cardinal principles, held by the political party of which I am a member. Destroy this principle, or permit the candidate for office by his silence to evade it, and be thereby at liberty to act as he pleases, after he is elected, is to place the servant above his master. No man in my opinion who denies the right of instruction, or by his silence, refuses to admit it, ought to be intrusted with the care of the public interests.

Your fourth interrogatory is in the following words; to wit:

4th. Do you believe that, under the constitution of the United States, Senators in Congress may be elected by the separate actions of the two branches of the General Assembly?

I answer I do. Some of the States elect in that mode; and the constitutionality of such elections has never been denied or questioned.

Your fifth interrogatory is as follows; to wit:

5th. Did the proposition made by the Democrats in the last Legislature to elect one member of the Senate of the United States of the Whig party, and the other of the Democratic party meet your approbation, or did you approbate the refusal of the Whig members to accept such proposition?

I answer, that under the circumstances as they existed, the proposition of compromise, in the election of the United States Senators made by the Democratic party in the last Legislature, did meet my approbation. By the popular vote, it was apparent, that the political parties in the State, were very nearly equally divided. By the elections of members of the General Assembly, it appeared that one party had a majority of three in the popular branch, and the other of one in the Senate. There being three times as many Representatives as there are Senators, it follows, that one Senator represented precisely as many people as three Representatives, and that the majorities in the respective Houses, were precisely equal. I was desirous that the State should be represented in the Senate of the United States, and believed at the time the proposition of compromise was made, that it was fair and proper; and that if it had been acceded to, it would probably have been satisfactory to the moderate men of both parties. When the proposition of compromise was rejected my opinion was and is, that the majority of the Senate acted properly, in insisting upon a mode of election conceded to be constitutional, by which the rights of their constituents could be preserved, and the election of Senators be prevented who concealed their opinions on public subjects, and refused to avow them, when respectfully asked, by a portion of the constituent body to do so:

Your 6th and 7th Interrogatories are as follows; to wit:

6th Are you in favor of withdrawing the proceeds of the public lands from the support of the Federal Government and supplying the deficit occasioned thereby in the National Treasury by an increased Tariff—are you in favor of appropriating the proceeds aforesaid to meet the current expenses of the Government, and reducing to that amount the Tariff?

7th. If you are in favor of distributing the proceeds of the public lands among the States, are you of opinion that such distribution should be confined to the lands within the limits of the cessions of Virginia and other States to the United States—or are you in favor of distributing also the proceeds of the lands purchased by the United States from France, including Louisiana and the lands purchased by the United States from Spain, including the Floridas?

I answer that I am opposed to the policy of "withdrawing the proceeds of the public lands from the support of the Federal Government" and distributing them to the States—but would retain the moneys, derived from the sales of the lands in the Treasury, and apply them to the payment of the necessary expenses of the General Government. I would retain and thus apply the moneys derived from the sale of the lands, whether embraced in the cessions from the States, or the lands purchased by the U. States, from France and Spain. It has been sometimes assumed (erroneously as I think) that the lands, embraced in the cessions from the States, were conveyed in trust, and upon that ground it is said the moneys derived from them, may be distributed. I do not regard the acts of cession as containing such a trust; but if they did, the cost of extinguishing Indian title, of Indian wars, rendered necessary to get possession of them; of surveys, of salaries of officers, and other expenses of bringing them into market it will be found on examination, have cost more than the United States have ever received from the sale of lands— bringing the lands actually indebted to the Treasury. The lands purchased from *France* and *Spain*, it is not pretended constitute a trust fund, and it cannot be maintained that upon that ground the proceeds of their sale can be distributed. For my views more at large on this subject I refer you to my published address to "the people of Tennessee," bearing date on the 25th March, 1841. In that address I said:

The distribution of the proceeds of the sales of the public lands among the states, and the consequent increase of the Tariff to supply an amount of revenue equal to that which may be abstracted from the common treasury, will undoubtedly be among the measures of the new administration. This is not a new question. It has been repeatedly before Congress. It was brought up by Mr. Clay during the administration of Gen. Jackson, and was deliberately considered and settled at that time. At the Session of 1832–3, a Bill for that purpose passed both Houses of Congress, and was sent to the President for his approbation and signature on the last day of the Session. The President did not approve it, but not having time, before the adjournment, to prepare his reasons, withheld it until the opening of the next Session in December, following, when he communicated a message containing them, to the Senate of the United States.[6] The President placed his objections to the measure upon Constitutional grounds, as well as upon the grounds of its inexpediency. All the members of both Houses of Congress from this State, who were present at the vote, except one*[7] of the Representatives, voted against it. *Judge White* and *Judge Grundy* voted against it in the Senate; (see Senate Journal, 2d Session 22d Congress, p. 138). *John Blair, Wm. Hall, Jacob C. Isaacks, James Standifer* and myself voted against it in the House[8] (see Journal of the House of Representatives, 2d Session 22d Congress, p. 460). Three of our representatives were not present at the vote,[9] but it was well known at the time that they concurred in opinion with a majority of their colleagues, and would have voted against it if they been present. The veto of the President was every where approved by the Republican party, and by none was it more heartily or generally approved than by the people of Tennessee. The measure had been recently revived, was the subject of protracted discussion in the late Congress, and from the developements before us, will be pressed as an administration measure in the next.

The proposed distribution is in truth, but a branch of Mr. Clay's famed "American System"—a system embracing as its primary and leading objects, a high protective tariff, a profuse and wasteful expenditure of public money for objects of Internal Improvement, and high prices of the public lands; a system which operated so unjustly and oppressively upon the Southern and planting States, as to compel its advocates reluctantly to yield to the "Compromise Act" of 1833. Mr. Clay is the author of the measure, as he was of the "American System." The limits of this address will not allow me to enter upon an extended argument of the question. A few of the principal points of objection are all that can be here stated. If the receipts from the sales of the public lands amounting to several millions annually, shall be abstracted from the Treasury and given to the States, it follows that an equal amount must be raised by an increase of the tariff, or by a tax in some other form, to supply the deficiency; and if raised by an increase of the Tariff, it requires no argument to prove that the tax will be paid in unequal proportions by the people of the different sections of the Union—the Southern and planting States bearing much the greater part of the burden. To avoid this objection, and to conceal from the tax paying portion of the Union, the fact that the ultimate effect, if not the main object of the measure, will be to afford a plausible pretext for an increased protective tariff, it is said that the increased tax may be levied on Wines, Silks, and other luxuries. Still it will be a tax upon labor, and will naturally affect the value of our products given in exchange for them.

Must it not strike the advocates of distribution too, that the power of this argument is lost, when they reflect, that if luxuries are not sufficiently taxed, that the better plan would be to leave the monies arising from lands in the Treasury, to defray the public expenses, as far as they will go, and then to lighten the duties on necessaries and increase them on luxuries?

In another view, the proposed distribution is a tariff measure. If it prevail, Massachusetts, Vermont and other States, containing within their borders no portion of the public lands, will be immediately vested with a local pecuniary interest in them. The public lands will in effect be mortgaged to the several States, in proportion equal to their Federal representation in Congress, and they will have an interest in having them sold at the highest possible rates. They will have an interest in opposing the graduation or reduction of price, and in opposing the grant of pre-emptions at low rates to that hardy and enterprising race of pioneer occupants who have gone with their families to the West, built their "log cabins," opened their little farms and settled upon them, because they would apprehend that the amount of their respective dividends in the distribution would be thereby diminished. The manufacturing States would have a peculiar interest in resisting the reduction of price or the grant of pre-emption to settlers at a low rate, because to keep up the price of the lands, and withhold grants of pre-emption would be to check emigration, retain the laboring population at home, and thus reduce the wages of labor, and increase the profits of the capitalist engaged in manufactures. The manufacturing interests would be advanced by it for another reason. They would receive their federal proportion of the distribution, and would not contribute in the same ratio in the payment of the tax to supply the deficiency. They would in addition to this receive the bounties to their manufactures, which an increased tariff would afford, whilst these bounties would be paid by the South; in every view of the measure, it is an auxiliary to the protective policy. It is presented, it is true, in the seductive, but at the same time deceptive and disguised form, of giving money to the States out of the Federal Treasury, when it is in truth laying new burdens on the people. The manufacturing States so understand it, and hence the Legislatures of Vermont, Rhode Island, Connecticut, New York, Pennsylvania, Delaware and some other States, have during the past and present year, passed Legislative resolves instructing their Senators and requesting their Representatives in Congress to advocate the measure. The State of Connecticut, publicly declares that such is her object by passing Resolves, at the same time instructing her Senators and Representatives in Congress to "resist by all constitutional means every attempt to destroy or impair the protective policy," and to use their exertions to procure the passage of such laws as will effectually protect the labor of this country, "the manufacturing labor" of course is meant. The Legislature of Pennsylvania, in the month of January last, avowed in direct terms that an increase of the tariff was their object. They passed a Resolve instructing their Senators and Representatives to advocate and vote for the distribution, and passed a second Resolve in the following words viz:

Resolved. That our Senators be further instructed and our Representatives requested to vote for such remodification or adjustment of the tariff, as may increase the revenue derived from imports equal to the wants of the National Government, so that at no time hereafter, under any pretext whatever, shall any money, arising from the sales of the public lands be issued by the General Government.

All the Resolves referred to were passed by Legislatures, a majority of whose members were the political friends and supporters of the present National Administration. They have all been officially communicated to the Executive of this State, (as I presume they have been to the Executives of all the States,) with a request that the same may be laid before the next General Assembly of Tennessee. The States of Alabama and Mississippi have passed resolves responsive to the Resolves of Connecticut, in which they maintain the old ground of the South against the "protective policy." That this State will maintain similar ground with her southern sister States, when the Resolves of Connecticut come to be considered by her Legislature, I cannot doubt; in the face of this evidence before us, none can be so blind as not to see that the measure to "distribute" the proceeds of the sales of the public lands among the States, is but the pioneer step to the revival of a "protective tariff."

But there are other reasons which are conclusive against it. If the money derived from the public lands be taken from the use of the General Government to be distributed among the States, the States would receive it in sums diminished not only by the cost of distribution, but would be subjected to the additional cost necessarily incident to the collection of an equal sum by a tax in another form. In a more fiscal point of view, therefore, the policy of the measure cannot be justified. But there is still a higher and a weightier objection. The public lands are the common property of all the States, and when the money derived from them is collected and placed in the Treasury, it goes into the common fund of the nation, and is subject, as all other public monies collected from other sources are, to be applied to defray the necessary of expenses of Government—when in the Treasury, it cannot be distinguished from money collected by duties on imports, and the Government possesses the same power to distribute or give away money derived from the one source, as the other. What would be thought of a proposition to distribute or give to the States, as a mere donation, the money collected by duties on imports, thereby creating the necessity for a new tax, or increased tariff, to supply the deficiency, and yet there is the same constitutional power to do this, that there is to distribute the money derived from the lands. To distribute or give away to the States money in the Treasury derived from either source, would be in effect to make the Federal Government the tax gatherer for the States, a power not conferred upon that Government by the Constitution; and in this view the measure presents such insuperable objections to my mind that I cannot yield to it my support.

Should the policy of distribution prevail, another consequence which will follow will be the revival of that splendid and wasteful and corrupting system of Internal Improvements by federal authority, which was checked and arrested by the veto on the Maysville Road Bill.[10] Indeed a system of Federal Internal Improvements is the hand maid of a protective tariff, and furnishes the absorbent or spunge which is to suck up the revenues necessarily collected by a high protective tariff and whether prosecuted in the form of direct appropriations from the Treasury, or through the agency of the States, the effect is the same.

Your 8th Interrogatory is as follows, to wit:

8th. Are you in favor of restoring to General Jackson the fine imposed on him by Judge Hall at New Orleans, immediately after the siege of that city, and if so, are you in favor of doing so without condition or restriction—or would you impose as a condition of such restoration a provision in the act of approving the conduct of Judge Hall implying a censure of General Jackson.

I answer that I am in "favor of restoring to General Jackson the fine imposed on him by Judge Hall, immediately after the siege of New Orleans and I am in favor of restoring it, without condition or restriction. I would not in the act of restoration, approve the conduct of Judge Hall, and thereby imply a censure of General Jackson. I believe that the declaration of martial law by General Jackson was probably the only means of saving New Orleans. I believe that the act, which was charged against General Jackson to be a contempt of judical authority, was one which was necessary and proper for the continual safety of New Orleans. I believe that the conduct of Judge Hall was unpatriotic and vindictive, and the fine which General Jackson was required to pay under his sentence ought to be restored to him with interest from the date of its payment.

Your 9th Interrogatory is as follows, to wit:

9th. Are you in favor of the bill reported by a Whig Committee of the Senate of the United States in the last Congress, proposing to pay the heirs of General Hull his salary as Governor of Michigan, from the time he surrendered himself and the American army to the British commander during the last war, until he was exchanged for, tried by a Court Martial of American officers, sentenced by them to be shot, and pardoned by President Madison?[11]

I answer that I am opposed to "the Bill reported by a Whig Committee of the Senate of the United States in the last Congress, for the benefit of the Heirs of General Hull, not being able to perceive any principle of patriotism or of justice, which would entitle them to the donation which it proposed to make to them. In striking contrast with the proposition made for the benefit of the heirs of Hull, is the refusal of the same committee of the Senate to restore to General Jackson, the fine imposed on him at New Orleans, without accompanying it with a provision, acquitting Judge Hall of all improper conduct, thereby implying a censure on the conduct of General Jackson. The difference between the conduct of *General Hull* and *General Jackson* is; that the former commenced the war with disgrace to himself and the latter closed it with honor to himself and his country. The Whig committee of the Senate, proposed to reward the heirs of the former, and refused to do justice to the latter by restoring to him his own money, improperly taken from him, by a vindictive judge without accompanying it with a condition implying a censure, and thereby inflicting a wound upon his reputation.

Your 10th Interrogatory is as follows; to wit:

10th. Are you of opinion that it was constitutional or expedient to pass the act which was passed at the extra session of Congress donating to Mrs. Harrison, widow of the late President Harrison, almost twenty-three thousand dollars of the public money?[12]

I answer that in my opinion it was not constitutional or expedient to make the donation which was made by Congress to *Mrs. Harrison*, widow of the late President Harrison. Congress possesses no power to make *mere donations*, such as I regard this to be. The precedent if followed will lead to the worst of consequences. Upon the same principle, upon which the grant was made to *Mrs. Harrison*, similar grants may be made to the widows of our ministers abroad, of the members of Congress, of the Judges of our courts, and other civil officers, who may happen to die whilst in the public service. The precedent is a dangerous one, and if followed may lead to the establishment of an immense civil pension list, such as exists in the English monarchy. In the short debate which occurred in the Senate of the United States, whilst the Bill granting this donation to *Mrs. Harrison*, was pending before that body, a distinguished Senator declared that, "The aid of precedent is invoked in this case, but in vain. It has no precedent, but will form a dreadful one." [13] And again he said:

At the head of these cases so cited, stands the act for the benefit of Mrs. Brown, widow of General Brown,[14] which was passed by Congress, in the year 1828, and gave to her the remainder of her husband's pay for the year in which he died, that is to say about nine month's pay.

I was contemporary with this case—know all about it—acted a part in it—have its history in my mind, as well as in the debates of the day—and can show that it has no analogy to the present case, and was respectably opposed at the time as being without warrant from the Constitution—of evil example—and would be quoted in after times for even worse acts. I voted against it, and so did many others, and among them those who were usually found standing as a body guard around the Constitution. The vote against the bill was, Messrs. BELL, BENTON, BRANCH, CHANDLER, COBB, DICKINSON, ELLIS, FOOT, KING of Alabama, MACON, NOBLE, PARRIS, TAZWELL, TYLER, WHITE and WILLIAMS.[15] We were sixteen who stood together on that occasion—a number not large—but graced with some names which have weight with the country. This case of Mrs. Brown's is quoted as a precedent for Mrs. Harrison's bill, but most unjustly. It is a military, and not a civil case. Her husband died in the army, and the reporter of the bill (Gen. Harrison) produced the statements of the Surgeon General of the Army,

(Dr. Lovell) and of another physician, (Dr. Henderson)[16] to prove that Gen. Brown died in consequence of a disease contracted in the public service, and was to be classed with those who were killed in the line of their duty. *"It will be seen* (said Gen. Harrison) *that the Surgeon General asserts that if General Brown had lived, and retired from the army, he would have given him a certificate for a full pension under the existing laws of the country."* This was the argument of General Harrison, and in conformity to it, proposed a preamble to the bill in these words: *"Whereas the late Maj. Gen. Brown died in consequence of indisposition, contracted in the service of the United States,"* &c., and another member of the Senate, now a Senator (Mr. Berrien)[17] offered an amendment to the body of the bill, declaring the reasons for the grant in these words: *"Whose death is supposed to have been caused by disease, contracted while in the service of the United States on the Niagara frontier."* This preamble and this amendment were not adopted, for fear they would make precedents; and now the act becomes a far more dangerous precedent without these clauses than it would have been with them.

Such was the case of Mrs. Brown—a military case—coming within the equity, as the friends of the measure agreed, of the then existing pensions laws. And this case is to be made a precedent for Mrs. Harrison, whose case is a civil one, having nothing upon earth to do with pensions, and incapable of being assimilated in a solitary particular with the one to which it refers for justification. Such is precedent—such the folly—the danger of construeing our Constitution by precedents. The first instance is got upon one reason; the next upon another, and so on, until all good reasons are lost sight of; the Constitution itself is lost sight of—and the Legislature reigns supreme without a limit upon its power, or a guide to its acts!

The other precedents usually quoted, bear as little analogy to the case of *Mrs. Harrison,* as does that of *Mrs. Brown.* The grant to *La Fayette*[18] for example was based upon the ground of military services rendered in the War of the Revolution, for which he had never been adequately compensated. The case of *Mrs. Decatur,* and the officers and crew of the vessel commanded by her late husband, the gallant commander *Decatur,*[19] was not an application for a *donation,* such as was granted to *Mrs. Harrison,* but was a *claim* presented for prize-money, under the equity of the act of Congress, which grants prize money to the captors of vessels of war from a foreign enemy. *Decatur* and his officers and crew performed one of the most gallant deeds, of any age, by recapturing the Frigate Philadelphia under the walls and guns of Tripoli. By the order of the commander of the squadron before he set out on the expedition, he set fire to the vessel and burned her after she was recaptured, when, but for such orders, he could have brought her safely out. His widow after his death, and the brave officers and seamen, who were with him, claimed that they were equitably entitled to prize money. This is the case of *Mrs. Decatur,* sometimes referred to, and there are no points of analogy between it and the case of *Mrs. Harrison.* The one is a *claim:* the other is a *mere naked donation.* I cannot refer to the other precedents quoted, without swelling this answer to unreasonable length. I will only add that it is the principle involved in the grant to *Mrs. Harrison*, to which I object.

Your 11th Interrogatory is as follows, to wit,

11th. Are you in favor of the Tariff Act now in force passed by the last Congress?

I answer that I am not in "favor of the tariff act now in force, passed by the last Congress." It is in my opinion, in many of its provisions, highly *protective*, and not designed as a *revenue* measure. For my views as expressed at some length upon the subject, I refer you to a speech delivered by me at Pulaski on the 29th of September 1842; and also to one delivered by me at Jackson on the 3rd of April 1843; both of which have been published.[20]

Having now, gentlemen, answered your several interrogatories as I trust, satisfactorily, and having also answered certain other interrogatories, propounded by others of my fellow citizens of Shelby county—I shall forward both answers, by the next mail to Memphis, to the end that they may be published.

JAMES K. POLK

PL. Published in the *Nashville Union*, June 6, 1843. ALS, draft, not found, enclosed in Polk to Henry Van Pelt, May 15, 1843.

1. Addressed to "G. W. Smith, R. E. Titus, C. Stewart, and others." A Memphis mechanic, Charles Stewart was active in 1843 in an effort to eliminate the use of convict labor in the manufacture of mechanical products. Titus is not identified further.

2. Date identified through content analysis.

3. See George W. Smith to Polk, May 3, 1843.

4. Reference is to Henry Clay's Fiscal Bank Bill.

5. The "substance" of Polk's address was carried in the *Nashville Union* on October 8, 11, and 13, 1842.

6. Andrew Jackson's veto message, dated December 4, 1833, was received by the Senate the following day.

7. The name of Thomas D. Arnold was noted at the bottom of the newspaper column.

8. Originally from North Carolina, Hall sat in the Tennessee House, 1797–1805, and in the Senate, 1821–29. As Speaker of the Senate he succeeded to the governorship upon the resignation of Sam Houston in 1829 and served in that post for approximately five and a half months. Elected to the U.S. House, Hall served from 1831 until 1833. Standifer, a native of Virginia, served in the Tennessee Senate, 1815–23, and in the U.S. House, 1823–25 and 1829–37.

9. The other three members of Tennessee's congressional delegation to the Twenty-second Congress were John Bell, William Fitzgerald, and Cave Johnson.

10. Basing his decision on constitutional and fiscal considerations, Andrew Jackson vetoed the Maysville Road Bill on May 27, 1830. That measure would have provided federal financing for construction of a road between Maysville and Lexington, Kentucky.

11. The Senate Judiciary Committee recommended the payment to the heirs of General William Hull. Hull was appointed governor of Michigan Territory by Thomas Jefferson in 1805. In his military capacity as a brigadier general in the War of 1812, he surrendered Detroit to the British on August 16, 1812; he remained a prisoner of war until February 1813 and subsequently stood trial by court-martial for cowardice. Lewis Cass replaced him as governor in October 1813.

12. By Act of June 30, 1841, the U.S. Congress appropriated a sum of up to $25,000 to Anna Symmes Harrison, daughter of John Cleves Symmes.

13. Thomas Hart Benton spoke in the U.S. Senate on June 24, 1841.

14. Pamelia Williams Brown was the widow of Major General Jacob Jennings Brown, who served as commanding general of the U.S. Army from 1821 until his death in 1828.

15. Samuel Bell of New Hampshire, Thomas Hart Benton of Missouri, John Branch of North Carolina, John Chandler of Maine, Thomas W. Cobb of Georgia, Mahlon Dickerson of New Jersey, Powhatan Ellis of Mississippi, Samuel A. Foote of Connecticut, William Rufus King of Alabama, Nathaniel Macon of North Carolina, James Noble of Indiana, Albion K. Parris of Maine, Littleton W. Tazewell of Virginia, John Tyler of Virginia, Hugh Lawson White of Tennessee, and Thomas H. Williams of Mississippi.

16. Joseph Lovell, a native of Boston, served in that post from 1818–36. Henderson of Washington City is not identified further.

17. John M. Berrien of Georgia.

18. By Act of December 28, 1824, the U.S. Congress awarded the Marquis de Lafayette $200,000 and a township of land.

19. Susan Decatur, widow of Commodore Stephen Decatur, was the daughter of Luke Wheeler, a wealthy merchant and mayor of Norfolk, Virginia. A bill considered by the U.S. House on May 3, 1826, would have provided compensation to her and her husband's crew for their recapture of the *U.S. Frigate Philadelphia* on February 16, 1804, but the measure failed to pass.

20. The *Nashville Union* on May 5 and 19, 1843, carried lengthy extracts of Polk's speech, which was also published that year as a pamphlet addressed "To The People of Madison and Adjoining Counties." For the publication of the Pulaski speech, see above note 5.

TO HENRY VAN PELT

Sir: Columbia, May 15, 1843

At the earliest moment of leisure which I have had, since I received, through the Memphis papers, the two series of interrogatories[1] propounded to me by a portion of my fellow citizens of Shelby county, I have prepared my answers,[2] and herewith transmit them to you, that they may be published through the same papers which conveyed to me the interrogatories.

JAMES K. POLK

PL. Published in the *Nashville Union*, June 2, 1843.
1. See George W. Smith to Polk, May 3, 1843.
2. See Polk to Wyatt Christian et al., May 15, 1843, and Polk to George W. Smith et al., May 15, 1843.

FROM HENRY CLAY

Sir   Ashland 20th May 1843

I have received information, through so many concurring channels, public and private, that, although loth to believe, I am constrained to conclude, that you have made my conduct and motives, in the Presidential election by the House of Representatives of 1825, a frequent topic of discussion, in your public addresses to my fellow Citizens of Tennessee, during the political canvass now in progress in that State; reviving and propagating the charge, which originated against me at that epoch. Now, Sir, I recognize your clear and indisputable right to controvert any system of public policy which I ever supported, to animadvert upon any public measures which I may have sustained, or to question the correctness of any opinion on public affairs, which I ever expressed in any terms of language you may think proper to use; but I do not admit your right to assail my honor and probity, or the purity of my character, behind my back, and at a distance from me. And, if you choose to indulge in such a theme, I claim the right to be heard by the same tribunal before which you have arraigned me. I regret that it is impracticable for me to appear before every popular assembly which, I understand, you have addressed on the subject of my character and conduct, on the occasion alluded to. But I can present myself, upon the theatre which you have selected, to a portion, at least, of the People of Tennessee. My reputation is dear to me. After a long service in the public Councils, I have but little else to leave my descendants; and, according to the usual course of nature, I cannot expect to remain long with them.

The high offices which you have filled—member and Speaker of the H. of Representatives of the United States and Governor of the Commonwealth of Tennessee—and those to which you aspire, give to your charges a grave consideration, and demand a notice of them, to which, coming from any other source of less prominence, I should not deem them entitled.

I repose great confidence in the zeal and ability with which Governor Jones and other friends in Tennessee will, I am sure, defend me; but they have other objects to attend to, of far greater public importance than my vindication, and I have no right to impose on them entirely the burden of defending my character.

I have, therefore, to request that you will agree to meet me at such time and place in Tennessee, as may be mutually designated, and publicly discuss the charge which you have revived against me. I disclaim explicitly, all intention to interfere or influence, in the slightest degree, the approaching election in Tennessee. I have no such desire or purpose. My sole and exclusive object is, to repeal charges, deeply affecting my honor and the purity of my public conduct, which you have voluntarily renewed. And, whilst I may have this opportunity of self-vindication, before my neighbours of Tennessee, you will have an equal opportunity of sustaining your charges, without being longer liable to the reproach of seeking an advantage from the absence of a fellow Citizen, residing in another State.

With these views, and with that single purpose, on my part, I propose that we meet at Nashville, Knoxville, or the seat of Justice of the County of your residence,[1] at such time, during the month of June or July next, as you may deem most conformable to your own convenience, and publicly discuss the charge which you have revived against me, of improper conduct in the Presidential election of 1825. And, as I have full confidence in the intelligence, love of truth and justice of the great body of my fellow Citizens, of both political parties, in Tennessee, I further propose that twenty-four of them shall be selected, embracing twelve whigs and twelve democrats (you to choose the Whigs and I the Democrats) to whose final decision shall be submitted the question, whether you have or have not revived and propagated against me an exploded and groundless calumny, and whether you are—or are not bound to make any and what reparation.

Entertaining a just and confident hope that your sense of propriety and justice will prompt you cheerfully to accede to these proposals, through the same or a similar public channel to that which is the medium of this note, I remain, in the meantime, respectfully . . . .

H. CLAY

ALS. DLC–HC. Probably addressed to Columbia.
1. Columbia, seat of Maury County.

FROM ROBERT ARMSTRONG

Dear Sir   Nashville Monday night 22d [May 1843][1]

I will be at Shelbyville on Thursday night. Try and reach there your-self and write me a line if you will do so, and where I ought to Stop &c.

While at Fayetteville see Jones and arrange that Turney[2] be run in place of Long. It is better and puts all bad feeling down. Their is some and it had better be quieted. I hear that Genl. Moore and Nicks[3] &c. say they will go against the nomination. This may be for effect &c. Long could come to the House. Akin[4] will withdraw in the first district. Fentress is off and Staunton[5] in the field. In this County Fosters exertions are greater than ever they were. The party are dispirited and dissatisfied and will not hold togeather. Claiborne is at Home and in the field. We will do well and may succeed. Donelson is gaining daily. All we hear is *good* and looks well. As I told you Jones[6] will not follow you, be with you now & then. Make your task as easy as possible. Move as far as you can, but save yourself. Pay no attention to any striker he may send. My Impression is that Gentry, Carruthers[7] and all the great men of the party will be in the field. Write from every place or *have* it done, that we give the first Gun.

I assure all is safe and East Teness. only waits your comeing to sett every thing in motion. You will see as you advance, Whiggery flying in every direction. I can see the feeling, it is so. No news.

R. A.

ALI. DLC–JKP. Addressed to Fayetteville.

1. Month and year determined through content analysis.

2. George W. Jones and Henry Turney. A Lincoln County planter and farmer, Turney won election to two terms in the Tennessee House, 1843–47.

3. William Moore and A. T. Nicks. An early Lincoln County settler with large landholdings, Moore served two terms as a Democrat in the Tennessee House, 1825–29, and sat two terms in the Senate, 1833–37. He became state adjutant general in January 1840. Nicks was a Fayetteville merchant and Democrat.

4. John A. Aiken.

5. David Fentress and Frederick P. Stanton.

6. James C. Jones.

7. Meredith P. Gentry and Robert L. Caruthers.

FROM SARAH C. POLK

Dear Husband   Columbia May 23rd 1843

I received your letter to day from Pulaski.[1] I was pleased to find that you had time to play the *beaux* in receiving flowers from young ladies, for

I am sure that you did not *act* the *beaux* towards your wife when at home. There has nothing occure since you left worthy of remark. I have heard of none of *Jones* bragging whilst here. I do not think he had much to say, only that he would be here *on the day of the Election* and address the people. We have not had any Whig report from Lawrence[2] yet. All I know or have heard *Gordon* told me, who called at your request. I look out for another fiddling, bragging, stunt for *Jones* to bolster him up. Your address appeared in the Union[3] to day or a part of it. I send you a letter by the mail to morrow from Brownsville.

SARAH POLK

ALS. DLC–JKP. Addressed to Shelbyville via Nashville.
1. Letter not found.
2. Lawrence County.
3. On May 23 and 26, 1843, the *Nashville Union* printed Polk's Address to the People of Tennessee, which included his views on such subjects as government expenditures, public debts, tariffs, and a national bank. Having debated those issues without agreeing on basic facts, Polk and Jones agreed at Carrollsville on April 12, 1843, to publish in the press their respective positions. For Jones' Address, see Robert Armstrong to Polk, May 15, 1843.

FROM ROBERT ARMSTRONG

Dear Sir   Nashville May 25 43
    I find it impossible to leave at this moment. I was ready but had a Post office agent here and it is proper for me to remain. I will meet you some where before it is over.
    The efforts of the Whigs continue and the fight will be a hard one. They are Insolent and Overbearing, which shows that they expect defeat. Foster is bitter, more so I understand than usual. I *Know* & see that he is exerting himself.
    Now Govr let your whole aim be to reconcile conflicting claims &c to Keep our friends firm and togeather and excited, Confident. And urge and press on our friends Organization so that our full force may be turned out on the day of Election. Keep and make all smooth in the different Counties as you pass. It is all Important. I shall never feel again the same Interest in a State Election. If you have time write your friends before and behind you. All looks well, but still it is necessary to watch and some times pray.
    Moseley[1] made his first speech last night and made a fine Impression. We will soon be *warm* here. From other points our accounts are good; Stanton is out in place of Fentress. Our friends say that Akin[2] *will* be off. Laughlin will come to the Senate and I hope Turney may be nominated in

the Shelbyville District. He is True to you. Have it done if you can. Push Rice[3] in Marion &c. If he Keeps *sober* he will be Elected. The *same* with Lewis Sheppard. Of Waterhouse there is no danger. Have Sherrill[4] *Committed*. It is very easily done. He is inclined; and we ought to have a Candidate for the senate in Roane &c. Ross[5] is by no means strong. Tom Brown told me that he would go home and offer; Scarborough[6] of Anderson will be Elected. I Know him well. Let some friend *Commit* him; have a *particular* Conversation with him *yourself*.

We have nothing to fear if our party are only True to themselves. Exertion and a good understandg will insure success.

Your address on the Expenditures, Bank, Tariff &c[7] *Must be printed*—Your answer to Memphis[8]—and your *reply* to Jones's address &c which you tell Hogan you will prepare and send from Fayetteville. Conner and myself will try and effect this.[9] Publish say 10 thousand cops.

I send you some newspapers—last appeal[10] &c.

We will make a hard fight in Davidson. "May be Killed but never can be Whipt." [11] All well no news.

R. A.

[P.S.] Did you get my Letter by Doctr Bonner?[12] *Write me often.*

ALI. DLC–JKP. Addressed to Shelbyville.

1. A Democrat, Thomas D. Mosely sought election to the Tennessee House from Davidson County.

2. John A. Aiken.

3. Possibly George W. Rice, a Marion County landholder who served as deputy clerk of the county court from 1827 until 1830.

4. Cravens Sherrell.

5. An Anderson County merchant, manufacturer, and owner of Ross' Mills, James Ross served two terms in the Tennessee House, 1837–39 and 1841–43, and sat for one term in the Senate, 1843–45.

6. Scarborough is not identified further.

7. See Sarah C. Polk to Polk, May 23, 1843.

8. See Polk to Wyatt Christian et al., May 15, 1843.

9. Cornelius Connor. See Robert Armstrong to Polk, June 12, 1843.

10. *Memphis Appeal.*

11. Quotation not identified.

12. See Robert Armstrong to Polk, May 22, 1843. A wealthy and renowned Lincoln County surgeon and farmer, William Bonner was an ardent Democrat in politics.

TO SARAH C. POLK

My Dear Wife: Kingston, June 9th 1843

I receivd your two letters the one from Columbia and the other from Murfreesboro', by the mail of this evening.[1] I wrote you from *Cleveland*

and *Athens*,[2] but suppose you had not receivd them before you left home. It pains me that you write so despondingly. You must cheer up. It is now but 7 weeks until the election. The worst of the canvass is over. I am blessed with fine health, and am in good spirits. That I have gained considerably in the 8 counties[3] in East Tennessee through which I have passed there cannot be a doubt. My estimate is, that the gain in these 8 counties is from 600 to 800 votes. It may be much greater, by the failure of the dissatisfied Whigs to attend the polls, and by the fuller vote of the Democratic party. Our friends every-where are active & confident of success. The Whig leaders are using *desperate efforts* to rouse their party, but as far as I can judge, without success. My friends in middle Tennessee, I hope will be vigilant and active.

JAMES K. POLK

P.S. Write me to Knoxville, where I will be on Saturday next. If I shall have passed there it will be forwarded. *Greeneville* & Jonesborough are on this main stage route, & letters addressed to me at either place will come direct. J.K.P.

ALS. DLC–JKP. Addressed to Murfreesboro, care of William R. Rucker.

1. See Sarah C. Polk to Polk, May 23, 1843; letter from Murfreesboro not found.

2. Letters not found.

3. Polk had campaigned in the eight East Tennessee counties of Marion, Hamilton, Bradley, Polk, McMinn, Meigs, Rhea, and Roane.

FROM ROBERT ARMSTRONG

Dear Sir   Nashville June 12th 43

What are you doing, how goes every thing in East Tenss? I get nothing from you. Are you realy used up, or have you no time to give a line of prospects &c &c?

All is going on well here. Our Candidates by their Industry and boldness have alarmed the Whigs and every exertion is made to get up Meetings in the County, in the City & in the Wards. All will not do. They cannot get up an excitement. From every Quarter our friends write in spirit. Glenn[1] says that Stantons Election is now safe and sure. He is whipping Ashe badly.

Mathews[2] of Bedford says Dean[3] will be Elected and requests me to say to you that the Democrats are gaining and things look better. Huntsman writes in spirit, and has hopes of Madison and a great gain for you in that section. Settle as far as you can all the conflicting Interests and have no clashing with our friends. Smooth every thing down and let us succeed *this* time. Then second matters. I want to see you but it is Impossible. I cannot leave a moment and will not untill the Election is over. Our friends on the *stump* ought to show (where a Bank is urged) That the *old* notes or the issue of the *old* Bank are selling here and every where at 40 Cents on The Dollar.

Cave & Wilie Johnston[4] are both in high spirits. Some Doubt of Dortch. Norflit[5] will give Genl. Cheatham great Trouble if he does not beat him.

The Prospect for Donelson and Burford is good. Barry can effect nothing in Sumner. Crockett is howling in Rutherford & Williamson but to little purpose.

Give me all the news, our prospects &c &c. Tell Eastman and Crozier to write me freely including their views of East Tennessee. Tell them to make up a true case as our friends all want to Know what to do here.

Doctor McCall[6] will not go to night. Therefore I send the sack containing your Letters &c &c for Knoxville & *East* by the Stage *with this Letter.* I put them in a small sack marked Robert B. Reynolds Knoxville Ten. baggage freight paid from Nashville to Knoxville, on a Leather Labelled. A Mr. Suggert[7] will take charge of them to Sparta & will send them on to Knox. Enquire Immediately at the Stage Office. All for Middle and West Tennessee off.

If you succeed as you must and we carry the State we must then look to the Convention for Electing Delegates to nominate a Candidate for President & Vice President. These men must be of the true stripe. Their may be a clash between the friends of Van Buren & Calhoun that cannot be settled. Then your prospect as a compr[om]ise is best. The friends of V.B. &c are Democrats and could with great propriety agree upon you.

As you pass on look to such men as would be suitable. *Take care* of our friends settling on any particular person for *Senator.* Leave all open untill the Legislature meets. Any doubtfull men (Candidates)[8] should be made safe (if to be Elected) pledged for Senator, &c. Write me all the prospects. We will have out next week a Bank pamphlet.[9]

R ARMSTRONG

ALS. DLC–JKP. Addressed to Knoxville and marked *"Private."*

1. Philip B. Glenn, a Covington lawyer, served in the Tennessee House as a Democrat, 1837–41 and 1843–47.

2. Robert Mathews was an Irish-born Shelbyville merchant and Democrat.

3. A Bedford County farmer and owner of large tracts of land in the Flat Creek vicinity, Thomas Dean won election as a Democrat to the Tennessee House, 1835–39, 1851–53, and sat in the Senate, 1847–49 and 1855–57.

4. Cave Johnson and Willie B. Johnson.

5. P. T. Norfleet.

6. Possibly Alexander McCall, a doctor and resident of Washington County, Virginia.

7. Mr. Suggert is not identified further.

8. The word *Candidates* interlined; parentheses supplied.

9. On June 20, 1843, the *Nashville Union* announced publication of *The Expositor*, which would discuss "the frauds and corruption of the old National Bank, and the dangerous and corrupting tendencies of the new one as proposed by Clay, together with other useful and interesting matter." Scheduled for release from the Union Office on the day following, the eleven-page pamphlet would sell for two dollars per hundred copies.

FROM WILLIAM WALLACE

Maryville, Tennessee. June 16, 1843

Wallace relates that the "Bank question is the most important Lobby" of the Whigs in his county[1] and urges that Polk direct his "strongest artilery against it." Wallace argues that the old Bank[2] "did not regulate exchanges, nor the state Banks, and above all it needed regulating itself." Wallace further maintains that the electorate is being misled by those who say that relief would have come "but for Tylers veto." [3]

ALS. DLC–JKP. Addressed to Louisville.

1. Blount County.

2. Reference is to the Second Bank of the United States, headed by Nicholas Biddle.

3. Reference is to Tyler's Fiscal Bank Bill veto of August 16, 1841. See Aaron V. Brown to Polk, June 12 and August 8, 1841.

TO GEORGE W. MAYO ET AL.[1]

Gentlemen: Knox County June 17th 1843

Your communication of the 14th instant[2] enclosing the proceedings of a public "meeting of a large and respectable portion of the mechanics of the County of McMinn," was handed to me at Madisonville on the day it bears date.

My opinion is, that the convicts in the state Penitentiary should as far as practicable, be employed in such branches of labour, as will inflict upon them, the punishment designed by our criminal code, prevent the institution from becoming a charge upon the State Treasury, and at the same time avoid bringing the state into competition, with the labour of that large and respectable portion of our citizens who are engaged in mechanical pursuits—a portion of whom you represent. I concur with the mechanics of McMinn in the opinion expressed in their proceedings, that a "reasonable change in the present mode of prison labour" can and ought to be effected[3] and that such modification as is believed to be practicable, would prevent the degrading operation of the liberated convict, with the honest mechanic, of which the meeting you represent so justly complain. I will only add, that should I have the honour to fill, the office of Governor, it will give me sincere pleasure to recommend to the General Assembly, the adoption of all practicable measures, by which the desired change may be effected. That such change can to a great extent be effected, and that without prejudice to any public interest I do not doubt.

JAMES K. POLK

ALS, draft. DLC–JKP. Addressed to Athens and marked "*Copy.*"

1. Polk's letter is addressed to George W. Mayo, Edwin A. Atler, and Richard M. Fisher, members of the Mechanics' Committee, McMinn County.

2. In a letter of June 14, 1843, the McMinn County Mechanics' Committee requested Polk's views "in relation to the system of labor as at present conducted in our state penetentiary." In particular, was Polk "in favor of continuing the present system of employing the convicts in the Mechanical branches of labor?" ALS. DLC–JKP.

3. The remainder of this sentence written on a separate sheet and marked for insertion at this place.

TO SARAH C. POLK

My Dear Wife: Mecklenburg Knox County June 18th 1843

I receivd your letter of the 14th last evening.[1] You say that you have receivd no letter from me, since I left Winchester. I have written several times to you since that time, addressed to Columbia. I wrote you from *Kingston,* on the 12th to Murfreesboro'.[2] You continue to write despondingly, and it distresses me that you are in such low spirits. If I could be with you, you know I would be. It is however impossible for the next six weeks, and I hope you will endeavour to recover your former cheerfulness and good spirits. Since I wrote you at *Kingston* I have passed through *Monroe, Blount, & Knox,* in each of which there is a decided gain, though not a large one. The increase I think in these Counties cannot be less than 300, and my more sanguine friends think it will be double that number. The leading Whigs in this part of the State are making a desperate struggle. The Democrats are equally active, and as our canvass progresses, there are gradual & slow accessions to our ranks. I will be in *Sevier, Jefferson,* and *Cocke* on *Monday, Tuesday,* and Wednesday. Whiggerry has its strong hold in E. Tennessee in these Counties. I have favourable accounts from them, but will write you again when I get through them. I am still blessed with fine health & am in fine spirits. I shall be elected, as I think, but still the contest is becoming so *fierce,* that I hope my friends in the West will not relax their caution. Tell your brother[3] to write to me, to *Bean's Station,* where I will get his letter. Do write to me often.

JAMES K. POLK

P.S. I am at the Home of my friend *Dr. Ramsey.* The Doctor says he will write to you soon. J.K.P.

ALS. DLC–JKP. Addressed to Murfreesboro, care of William R. Rucker.
1. Letter not found.
2. Polk wrote Sarah from Kingston on June 9, 1843, not June 12, 1843.
3. John W. Childress.

TO SARAH C. POLK

My Dear Wife: Blountville Sullivan County June 29th 1843
    I am sure you cannot complain that I do not write to you often enough lately. I have been in Carter & this County, since I wrote you from Jonesboro'.[1] In Carter there was a very large crowd on yesterday, and although a strong Whig County, it was the most attentive assembly I have met in the state. My friends think a very decided impression was made and estimate that I will reduce Jones's majority in 1841—from 100 to 150 votes. This County (Sullivan) is still strongly Democratic. There has been & still continues to be some confusion here among the local candidates which is calculated, to prevent an increase, if not to weaken us a little. We have 5 Democratic candidates, and one Whig in disguise calling himself a Bank Democrat, running.[2] I hope some of them may yet be induced to withdraw. I continue to enjoy fine health, and will turn my course homeward on tomorrow morning—the next place of speaking being in Hawkins. Do write to me often.

JAMES K. POLK

P.S. The canvass is becoming very hot in this part of the state. The leading Whigs are becoming desperate & stop at nothing. J.K.P.

ALS. DLC–JKP. Addressed to Columbia.

1. Letter not found.

2. Not identified further. Jessee Cross, a Blountville farmer and Democrat, won election to three terms in the Tennessee House, 1839–41, 1843–45, and 1847–49.

FROM WILLIAM H. POLK

Dear Brother   Columbia July 12th 1843

I received your letter from Greenville,[1] but have been so busily engaged that it was not convenient to answer it according to request in time to reach you at Sparta. Sam Walker informed me last evening that he had written to you expressing the decided opinion that it would be better, if not derangeing your plans materialy, for you to meet Jones at this place on the day before the election. I have but little doubt, but what the friends of Jones here, made the *alteration* in his appointments, so as to throw him at Columbia the day before the election and at Lewisburg the day of the election. They discovered the runious effect of Jones being here the day of the election, concentrating all their opperating influential power at Columbia. It would have given us much advantage, therefore *the change.* I scearcely know how to give an opinion, as to your course, but from present indications am induced to believe, in view of the unsettled state of the public mind, (applicable alone to a portion of the Whig party), that it would be of much advantage, if you could be with him at this place, having the last speech. It would have the effect of sending our friends home, with renewed energy and feeling for the contest the next day. If you are not with him here, may not his friends raise the *hurrah*, and unballance many of the wavering, and succeed in casting a partial gloom over your prospects, thereby enlisting that wandering portion of the voters, who have no settled and fixed political opinions, but sheer off in all cases, with what they consider the strong party. It is better in any case to battle against argument, reason, and *principles*, than contend with the noisy, shout of triumph, which men are excited to raise, on the eve of an election. You know best what to do. I throw out these suggestions, in the full belief that your presence here the day before the election, would be of much advantage to you, and would greatly aid the Democratic county candidates.

The election of Devenport[2] in Lawrence is beyond all doubt. Buford of Giles will defeat his Whig opponent.[3] A. V. Brow[n] left his county on yesterday to fill appointments in Hickman. Every thing looks well. Boling Gordon will beat his opponent[4] beyond all doubt. Since you left for East

Tenn my clear impression is, that your prospects have been brightening in this section. The proper feeling pervades our ranks; our friends go into the battle with a full confidence of success, leaving no means unemployed to ensure victory. Write me.

WILLIAM H. POLK

ALS. DLC–JKP. Addressed to McMinnville.

1. Letter not found.

2. An early Giles County settler, Thomas D. Davenport moved in 1821 to Lawrenceburg in Lawrence County, where he engaged in farming, cotton manufacturing, and brickwork. An unsuccessful Democratic candidate for Congress in 1833, Davenport subsequently served two terms in the Tennessee House, 1835–37 and 1843–45.

3. James Buford's opponent was John W. Goode, a Pulaski lawyer and officer in the Columbia, Pulaski, Elkton, and Alabama Turnpike Company; Goode defeated Buford and served but that one term in the Tennessee House, 1843–45.

4. Gordon's opponent was Elijah Walker, a Hickman County lawyer and circuit court judge.

FROM THOMAS DAVIS[1]

Dr. Sir.   Shelbyville Ten July 16, 1843

I embrace the present moment to drop you a line mearly to Keep up your drooping Spirits. I expect they are quit languid about these times as you are in the midst of the coons. How are you geting a long in your campaign? I should like to hear from you, and Know your prospects through out the state moor particular the Eastern divition. I can assure you that you are loosing nothing in old Bedford but you must get an increase vote here. From the best calculation that I can make you will get some votes which you did not get in 41. Dean will beat old Barrenger.[2] I believe that is admitted but the Whigs will use every coertion that lies in their power eather fair or foul. They are trying to swap votes. They propose to the Democrats if they will vote for Barrenger they will vote for Long and go so far as to say they will not vote for Long unless they will vote for Barrenger,[3] but I hope & trust that the Democrats are wide awake on that score. I think our men are geting more firm than to be guled in that way. I think Warner & Black[4] both will be Elected. My prayer is for you & Dean in prefeanc to all others. I cannot say how the thing will be between Long & Jones. I had a line from Watterson by last mail. He is at Winchester Springs. He appears to be in fine Spirits about Long. His opinion is that Long is gaining in Franklin County very fast. I presume that will be a close run. He did not say anything relative to your vote in Franklin. I hope it will be an incresed one there and every where else. If you have it in your power drop me a line and give me the news. We are more active about your Election than we ever were before but you Know we were always glad at your success since 1825.

If any thing very particulare takes place I will drop you a line at Woodbury. I am afrade to write to many places for fear my letter might fall into the hands of our enemy.

THOS. DAVIS

ALS. DLC–JKP. Addressed to Gallatin.

1. A Democrat, Davis served as postmaster at Shelbyville during the 1830's.

2. Thomas Dean and Daniel L. Barringer. A lawyer from Raleigh, North Carolina, Barringer moved in 1836 to Bedford County, where he farmed and practiced law. Having served as a Democrat in the North Carolina Commons, 1813–14 and 1819–22, and in the U.S. House, 1826–35, Barringer lost his Tennessee bid for Congress in 1839 to Harvey M. Watterson. A Whig, he represented Bedford County for one term in the Tennessee House, 1843–45, and served in that session as House Speaker.

3. That is, the Whigs would support a local Democrat for the U.S. House, Medicus A. Long, if Bedford County Democrats would suport the Whig candidate for the Tennessee House, Daniel L. Barringer. Long ran against fellow Democrat, George W. Jones of Lincoln County; the Whig Party did not run a candidate in the congressional race.

4. Richard Warner and Thomas Black. A Bedford County farmer and Democrat, Black served four terms in the Tennessee House, 1839–47.

FROM AUSTIN MILLER

My Dear Sir   Bolivar July 18 1843

Your favor of the 9th[1] has been received. I am much pleased to learn that yr prospects are so flattering in E. Tennessee.

Things are working better here than we expected last spring. We see and hear of changes every day. Mr. Stanton is an able and efficient debater. He sustains the issues wherever he goes. Messrs. Turley and Williamson[2] are also doing there part well. Upon the subjects of the Bank & Tariff the Whig candidates take the Whig Banner[3] for their text Book. That paper has been of infinite advantage to us in this canvass; it has been the means of bringing out the Whig candidates in favour of a protective tariff. It has also Shewn to the people that the Whigs are in favour of protection and that to stick to that party they must submit to protection. We have recent inteligence from every county in this congressional

district.[4] They are all favourable and report gains. Mr. Sta[n]ton's majority will be about four hundred. He is much Ashe's superior as a public
debater and is gaining on him wherever they go. We set down the election of Williamson, Turley, Fisher, Glen,[5] and myself as certain. Banks of
Shelby[6] will be elected if Alexander does not get some of the democrats to
support him. He advocates so many of the democratic doctrines, and is
not altogether a strong Whig together with his personal popularity, may
enable him to save his election. There is no doubt, of Shelby County
giving a democratic majority. Judge Dunlap receivd a letter last night
from Mr. P. G. Gain's[7] in which he says that the whole Democratic ticket
will succeed in that county. There were some fifty odd Irish and Dutch
naturlized at the June term of the Circuit Court of Shelby, all Democrats
but three. The judges of the election at Memphis, are two Whigs and one
democrat. I am told that the Whig judges will decide that the votes of
these persons cannot be received because they have not been naturlized
six months previous to the election.

From the best information from Haywood, Taylors[8] majority will be
about fifty—and the democrats will carry the whole ticket by thirty or
thirty five votes. Col Meeks' chance to beat Mr. Trice in McNairy is
considered good.[9] Both Whigs and democrats consider the election in that
county doubtful. Your gain in McNary and Madison Counties will be more
than in any of the adjoining Counties to this—but the news from the
middle Counties are flattering but the information is not such as to be
relied on with the same certainty as from the adjoining counties. I shall
speak &[10] Burlen[11] tomorrow and at Slabtown on Saturday. Messrs
Stanton & Ashe will also speak at Burlen tomorrow and in La Grange on
Saturday. We will be completly organized before the election and every
thing in our power will be done. Never have I seen the democrats in
better spirits. We have fewer absent; all appear determined to remain at
home until after the election. I know of several who have business of
importance abroad but are determined to remain to vote before they
leave. On the other hand the Whigs are leaving daily. And some who have
been leaders in their neighbourhood declar they will not go to the polls.
From every thing we can learn and it is the opinion of every democrat I
have heard speak upon the subject, that your gain over the vote of 1841,
will be greater than it was over the vote of 1840. It certainly is so in this
part of the State—and should you do as well in the balance of the State
you will receive ten thousand votes more than at the last election.

AUSTIN MILLER

ALS. DLC–JKP. Addressed to Nashville.
1. Letter not found.

2. Thomas J. Turley and James M. Williamson. Turley, a lawyer, served as attorney general for Shelby County in 1836.

3. Nashville *Republican Banner*.

4. Tennessee's Tenth Congressional District included Dyer, Fayette, Hardeman, Haywood, Lauderdale, McNairy, and Shelby counties.

5. Philip B. Glenn.

6. Possibly Enoch Banks, a former director of the LaGrange and Memphis Railroad.

7. Pendleton G. Gaines.

8. Howell Taylor, a prominent Haywood County Democrat, had an extensive network of family connections in the Taylor neighborhood north of Brownsville.

9. Matthew A. Trice and probably John H. Meeks. Trice, a Whig, represented McNairy County for two terms in the Tennessee House, 1841–45. Meeks, a McNairy County farmer and Democrat, was a deputy U.S. Marshal in 1840. Subsequently, he won election to two terms in the Tennessee House, 1849–53.

10. Sentence structure requires the use of a preposition here in lieu of Miller's word choice.

11. Misspelling of "Berlin."

FROM A. W. GOODRICH[1]

Dear Col.   Holly Springs, July 20th 1843

In the political excitement of the times generally, you will not be surprized to hear, that in this state the interest manifested in regard to the Tennessee election for Governor is almost equal to that felt by your own Citizens.

Under this state of feeling much *bantering* & triumphant boasting by the Whigs are to be met with at every corner & in every part of the Town among that party. For the purpose of *cooling* them down, your friends desire to know your opinion *candidly* as to the result of the election, & when that is ascertained, let me assure you, a good account will be taken of their vain boasting & swaggering impudence.

Please let me hear from you immediately on the receipt of this, as delay would be *dangerous* to our purpose.[2]

A. W. GOODRICH

ALS. DLC–JKP. Addressed to Nashville; cancelled "July 19."

1. A longtime resident of Holly Springs, Goodrich also served as mayor of this northern Mississippi town.

2. Goodrich and his friends probably sought election advice for betting purposes.

FROM ROBERT B. REYNOLDS

Dear Governor   Knoxville July 20th 1843

I returned home on yesterday from Morgan County. Your speech made some impression upon the Whigs in that county, and I was informed that you would gain at least 20 votes upon Jones in that Co. Brown & Ross were there & made speeches & the vote will be close between them. Brown cannot electioneer well & if he is elected, it will be owing to the exertions of the Democrats.

Brown & Hembree both agree that you have gained considerably in Roane. I think Hembree will be elected. Brown's election is doubtful owing entirely to his want of tact. I saw the leading Democrats of Anderson & Morgan & they promise to go to work & beat Ross.

During the circuit court at Clinton, I managed to get Sharp off, & Scarborough & Cooper[1] are the Democratic candidates in Campbell & Anderson—result extremely doubtful. You have gained handsomely in Anderson, if our friends are not deceived. I learn from Cocke that you will certainly get 150 votes & perhaps 200. In Jefferson you will have a decided gain from the best information I can get. Anderson will be elected in McMinn & Blackwell's election is quite certain.

The news from Grainger continues good and our friends calculate upon a gain of at least 100 votes.

Gen Frazier & Hugh Graham[2] both write that we will have from 4 to 500 majty in Claiborne.

In this county[3] I set down our gain as 100 votes of the election of 1841, but our friends say 200. I think we may possibly give you 500 votes, but not more—though we are making great inroads upon the Whigs.

Crozier stands a good chance for success & is fighting the battle with energy. He has been utterly unable to get any certificates to sustain him in the issue drawn between himself & Jones.[4] Even those who heard Jim Williams say that Jones used the language attributed to him by Crozier have refused to give a statement. The statement of Jones should have been denied here in person, but it effects nothing against us here—that it would operate against Jones if properly made out, I have not a doubt. Crozier says he will yet fasten it upon him if possible. I shall urge Crozier to expose the Governor & brand him with falsehood as soon as the materials can be had.

To sum up our prospects in East Tenn. I set down Jones's majty at 1000. That we shall have two members to Congress and the Whigs one—that we shall have four senators certain, the Whigs 3, and one doubtful—

and that we shall have 12 representatives to 7 Whigs and 3 doubtful. Grainger, Anderson & Campbell, & Hamilton & Marion are doubtful districts. Gillespy & Hammill are both still on the track and I believe they will continue to run it out—either of whom could [be][5] elected.

Reneau is no longer in the field; hence Senter will be elected. Wallace will gain some on Senter, yet he cannot overcome the odds against him.

We Shall make every effort to improve our prospects in this division of the state that can be made. Judge Green[6] is full of political talk & harrangues the lawyers in repeated conversations upon the tariff & other federal measures. I suppose that they may go home & retail them out again. He ought to [be][7] remembered when the time comes &c.

I wish to hear from the result of the election in Middle Tennessee as soon as possible & will be obliged to you for early news from the counties adjoining Davidson.

R B Reynolds

ALS. DLC–JKP. Addressed to Nashville.

1. William D. Sharp, Scarborough, and Cooper. Cooper is not identified further.

2. Robert Frazier and Hugh Graham. Graham was a prominent Tazewell merchant and Democrat.

3. Knox County.

4. See Polk to E. G. Eastman, February 13, 1843.

5. One word obliterated by residue of wax seal.

6. Nathan Green served as chancellor for East Tennessee, 1827–31, and sat on the Tennessee Supreme Court from 1831 until 1853.

7. Word omitted by author.

FROM JAMES FULTON[1]

Dear Sir.   Fayetteville, 22nd July 1843

Your letter dated, Jacksboro, 6th inst.[2] postmarked 10th was received the 17th inst. when it was too late to address you at McMinnville.

Long has not been here since the 1st Monday in June, I know nothing of his movements. Geo. W. Jones set out for Bedford & Franklin about ten days ago, expected to be here today, but has not yet returned. I have delayed writing you, until 10 oclock Saturday night, hoping I might see Jones, and induce him to meet the Gov.[3] at Lewisburg. He will certainly be here in a day or two. Gov. Jones will effect nothing by a speech at Lewisburg on the day of election. The time will have arrived for voting, and the people, at 9 oclock, will rush to the polls. I have written to some friends in Marshall, and insisted that our friends should attend the polls in their respective districts, and deposite their votes in the ballot box as soon as possible. The contest between Jones & Long will in no way effect your election. Jones[4] will receive a majority of more than two thousand votes.

Your friends here are active and vigilant. The Democracy of this county[5] has been aroused to the *utmost,* and *every Democrat* will attend the polls. I think your majority in this county will be 1,650 votes; it cannot be less than 1,600, which will be a *gain* over your vote of *1839.* Your majority then was *1,843.* In 1841 it was 1,776. The Lincoln portion of Marshall votes 500, to 550 votes, where your majority was fully 300 votes. A majority of 1,550 votes in Lincoln as it now is, is equal to a majority of 1,843 as it was.

You are at head quarters,[6] and can, by this time, *guess* the result with some degree of certainty. *Upon receipt* of this, write me three lines, & say, what are your prospects. Without giving publicity to your letter, it may do you some service. It will inspire a few friends with renewed confidence, and renew their arms for the coming contest. *You must not omit to do this immediately.* I write in much haste.

JAMES FULTON

ALS. DLC–JKP. Addressed to Nashville.
1. A prominent Fayetteville lawyer, Fulton served one term as attorney general of Tennessee's Eighth Judicial District, 1824–27.
2. Letter not found.
3. James C. Jones.
4. George W. Jones.
5. Lincoln County.
6. Nashville, Tennessee.

FROM CAVE JOHNSON

Dear Sir   Clarksville 22nd July 1843
I am glad to learn that your labors are so near an end, that your health is good and your prospects of success so flattering.

I think our majority in my district[1] will not be far from 1000. The Whigs stick together better than I had expected. I fear W. B. Johnson will be beaten. Cheatham has gotten up a fever in Robertson that will probably unite the Whigs. It will be a close contest in this county[2]—and I fear the result—the chances I think for Dortch. Willy[3] will beat Marable.

Eubanks[4] now has substantially no opposition. Cherry is safe by as large a majority as ever. Frazier will be elected—none but himself & Edwards[5] running. I am glad to tell you that DeWitt[6] has declined & Gardner safe. Vhories[7] is beyond doubt. I have just finished a tour around my district & my health much improved. If I am in any danger I have been unable to find it out. Scarcely excitement enough in any county out of Robertson to bring out the voters. I shall spend the balance of my time in Robertson & Montgomery.

C. JOHNSON

ALS. DLC–JKP. Addressed to Gallatin. On the verso of this single-page letter Polk wrote extensive notes on James C. Jones' Gallatin speech of July 24, 1843.

1. Tennessee's Ninth Congressional District.
2. Montgomery County.
3. James Wyly.
4. John Eubank.
5. A Henry County farmer, Owen H. Edwards won election as a Democrat to a single term in the Tennessee House, 1843–45.
6. Probably Washington J. DeWitt, a practicing physician prominent in Paris political affairs. DeWitt later removed to Texas.
7. Jacob Voorhies.

FROM WILLIAM M. LOWRY

My Dear Sir   Greeneville Ten 22 July '43

I wrote you to Sparta[1] giving you the signs of the times. Since then things have been moving with us finely. The Democracy of this County[2] are united & determined. Our Bank Democrat Bell[3] has declined & is no longer a candidate. I am of the opinion we will increase your majority in this County from 1 to 200 votes. I feel well assured that in E Tenn. from every indication that we will cut down the Whig majority to 500 or at farthest to 1000. So that If you can retain your vote in the middle of the state or increase it a little all things will be well. Johnson will beat Aiken I think from a 1000 to 1500. Tell your friends that East Tennessee will do her duty and that we are all Organised and egar for the Contest. I would be pleased to have a line from you a day or two after the Election giving me the result of [it][4] so far as herd.

WM M LOWRY

ALS. DLC–JKP. Addressed to Lebanon. On the cover sheet of this letter Polk wrote extensive notes on James C. Jones' Lebanon speech of July 27, 1843.

1. Letter not found.
2. Greene County.
3. Probably Joseph E. Bell, a Greene County physician. Bell's son, Benjamin F. Bell, represented Blount, Cocke, Greene, and Sevier counties in the Tennessee Senate for one term, 1853–55.
4. Word omitted by the author.

FROM SARAH C. POLK

My dear Husband   Columbia July 23rd 1843
  I have not any thing of particular interest to write about since I wrote you last. The Democrats appear in good spirits and say that every thing is going on right. As far as I can learn the *Matlock* affair[1] has made no impression one way or the other. *Jones* appointment here for Wednesday has not been withdrawn by the Whigs and they say he will be here. Nicholson told me to day that I might write you he would be here whenever he[2] did speak and reply and that Brown would be here also. Your friends I believe generally think that you ought to come as they[3] boast so much that you tried to keep him from coming to Maury and now affraid to meet him here. All this is stuff, and my advice is to act according to your own judgement. *Yet I would like to know when you are coming home.*
  S. P. Walker will go to Nashville to meet you and can tell you more than I can write. All the object he has in going is to confer with you more fully than he could write. I will put in my letter a slip from the "Review" [4] on the subject of the Jones appointments and the Observer[5] had one of course simular to this—So that you can see what the papers say. I send you five shirts, socks, drawers and a white vest, which you can send back after wearing it at Nashville. There was no necessity for Elias to go, but I was affraid Samuel might loose your clothes—and the servant was so anxious to go—that I consented.

Sarah Polk

ALS. DLC–JKP. Addressed to Nashville. On the cover sheet of this letter Polk wrote extensive notes summarizing one of James C. Jones' campaign speeches, probably that given in Nashville on July 25, 1843.
  1. On July 20, 1843, Gideon C. Matlock of Carthage shot Jesse J. Bryan of Clarksville in a confrontation at the Nashville Inn. Matlock fled to Maury County, where he surrendered himself to local authorities. Robert Armstrong wrote Polk on July 22, 1843, that Bryan deliberately provoked the fight with Matlock for political purposes. ALS. DLC–JKP. Returned to Nashville, Matlock was arraigned in court on July 24 for examination and released on bail. Matlock had

published statements alleging that in 1839 James C. Jones had proposed making state bonds redeemable in sterling, a proposal that Jones denied and often accused Polk of having made.

2. James C. Jones.
3. The Whig partisans.
4. Probably the Franklin *Western Weekly Review*; enclosure not found.
5. *Columbia Observer.*

TO ROBERT ARMSTRONG

My Dear Sir: Columbia Augt. 7th 1843

I have received no further returns, since your letter of friday night[1] except from *Perry & Henderson.* A traveller reports the vote in these Counties to be:

In *Henderson* for *Jones*	1093	
Do	*Polk*	402 and one precinct giving a Democratic majority to be heard from
In *Perry* for *Jones*	726	
Do.	*Polk*	450

These returns show a gain over 1841 of 124 votes in these Counties.

This indicates the anticipated gain in the District. Still after the most unexpected giving-way in the middle Counties heard from, I have now no doubt but I have lost my election, and I fear the Legislative elections have gone the same way.

However discouraging this may be, it is no time to indulge in a desponding feeling. We have a great and a united party in the State, and though beaten I think it probable that my vote is larger than it has ever been. There must be an immediate and a bold rally of our friends through the Union.[2] Let them be urged to keep their armour on, and to fight on for principle. For myself so far from surrendering—my sword is still unsheathed & I am still ready to do battle for our principles. I shall write to Hogan if I have time before the mail leaves this morning. Shew him this letter and let a strong rallying article appear in tomorrow's Union. In haste.

JAMES K. POLK

ALS. DLC–JKP. Addressed to Nashville and marked *"Private."*
1. Letter not found.
2. *Nashville Union.*

TO MARTIN VAN BUREN

My Dear Sir: Columbia Tennessee Augt. 18th 1843

You have seen the result of our late election. It was as unexpected as it was unfortunate. Though temporarily defeated the Democracy of the State are neither conquered nor subdued, but are ready and willing to renew the contest as they will do in the Presidential canvass of 1844. Having laboriously canvassed the State for near five months, and made more than *ninety* speeches to popular assemblies of the people I think I can form a just opinion of the causes of the result. We were unfortunately greatly embarrassed and weakened by local causes, and questions of State policy. Upon these our opponents mainly relied, and by constantly urging them, they partially succeeded in drawing off the public mind, from the questions of federal policy as the exclusive tests. In addition [to]¹ this, great frauds were undoubtedly practiced. The vote polled was larger than was ever before given, not excepting the vote of 1840. My vote was upwards of 54,000—a number greater than Gov. Jones received when he was elected in 1841, or than I received when I was elected in 1839. Upon the naked questions of Federal policy, I have not a doubt. The Democracy are now in a clear and decided majority in the State, and this is the prevailing opinion with our best informed friends.

Measures are being taken for the call of a Democratic State convention, to assemble at Nashville early in October, for the purpose of adopting a more efficient organization than we have heretofore had, and for the purpose of appointing delegates to the Democratic National convention at Baltimore. The late indications are, that May 1844, is preferred to Nov. 1843, as the period of meeting of the National convention. The latter was the period proposed by Tennessee. Our convention will however, I have no doubt, yield that point as to the time for the sake of harmony in the party.

You must not give up Tennessee as lost to the Democracy. I have great confidence that when unembarrassed by the local & state causes which weakened us in the late election, she will yet do her duty, and fully redeem herself in 1844.

I was at Nashville two days ago, saw Majr *Donaldson*² from whom I learned that *Genl Jackson* was in his usual health.

JAMES K. POLK

ALS. DLC–MVB. Addressed to Kinderhook, New York.
1. Word omitted by the author.
2. Andrew Jackson Donelson.

TO JOHN H. BILLS[1]

Dear Sir: Columbia Sept. 14th 1843

As executors of S. W. Polk deceased, William[2] & myself have a small suit depending in the Circuit Court of Haywood County, against Wiley R. Powell[3] for the hire of *blacksmith Harry* for the year 1837. Notice has been given to take the deposition of *Majr Powers* (who lives at or near Walker's plantation in Hardeman)[4] at your counting room on the 22d instant. It may be that Majr Powers the witness has no notice of it. Will you do me the favour to have him notified to attend & give his deposition on that day. Request *Edwin Polk* to attend to the taking of it, & have it forwarded to the Clerk of the Haywood Circuit Court.[5] Genl Loving[6] who is the lawyer will forward a commission to take the deposition.

I have gone to my profession in earnest[7] & think I will *now* make some money. You must not conclude however that I have ceased to take my accustomed interest in politics. On the contrary I am if possible more than ever resolved to "fight on" for my principles. Though I be in the ranks I will not be the less zealous or active.

JAMES K. POLK

P.S. Has my old friend *Green Roper*[8] got in the notion yet of buying my land? I am anxious to sell it. J.K.P.

ALS. T. Addressed to Bolivar.

1. Bills, postmaster and merchant at Bolivar, was married to Polk's first cousin, Prudence Tate McNeal.

2. Samuel W. Polk and William H. Polk. Samuel W. Polk, the youngest brother of James K. Polk, died of tuberculosis on February 24, 1839, at twenty-one years of age.

3. No Haywood County Circuit Court records for 1843 have been found. Powell is not identified further.

4. Powers and Walker have not been identified.

5. Joseph W. Rutledge was Haywood County Circuit Court Clerk from 1840 until 1870.

6. William H. Loving, an early Haywood County settler and merchant, practiced law in the courts of that county.

7. On August 17, 1843, Polk and James Houston Thomas formed a law partnership, styled Polk & Thomas, to practice in the courts of Maury, Marshall, Giles, Lawrence, Hickman, and Bedford counties for a period of eighteen months from the date of agreement. ADS. DLC–JKP.

8. Polk received two letters from Ezekiel P. McNeal in 1842 concerning the sale of lands in Hardeman County to Green Roper. On February 18, McNeal wrote that Roper "Sometimes talks like buying the South half or that portion of

your land near this, that lies on this side of the Creek at $3.00 pr. at 1, 2 & 3 years from January last. I asked him 3.50 one third cash or $4.00 on three years, one third annually. . . . Shall I accept of Ropers offer of 3$ . . . ?" Polk's reply has not been found. However, on April 2 McNeal again wrote, "I have not as yet affected any Sale of land. Mr Roper is very fickel in his notions & is now off from the trade." ALsS. DLC–JKP.

FROM GEORGE W. RICE

My dear Sir,   Battle Creek Sept 22, 1843
    I have received Several letters within a few days from our democratic friends of this congressional district[1] on the subject of having a meeting in this county[2] to appoint delegates to attend the state democratic convention at Nashville in November next, all suggesting the propriety of appointing the delegates without committing them to the support of any particular person for the Presidency. And fearing the movement may be injurious to you, and perhaps deceived that you are to be benefited by that course, is the object I now have in writing to you, to apprise you of the movement and to know whether such course would be advantageous to your future prospects. I am well apprised my dear Sir of the delicacy of this request but when I assure you your interests and prospects with me is far above that of any other individual in the United States must be the apology, for no man in our country of the present day has laboured and effected more for the cause of democratic principles than yourself, and it is due from the great body of the party, that your late defeat in Tennessee should receive a rebuke by conferring upon you an office in which citizens of other states (beside your own) has by your talents and exertions in the cause been benefited. And who I doubt not would be anxious to aid your friends in this state to accomplish. I see in the Knoxville Argus and Athens Courier[3] that a preferance is expressed favorable to the election of Gen Cass for the Presidency. Whether this is intended to stimulate the friends of Mr. Van Buren in your behalf or as stated by them to aid the democratic cause by effecting the nomination of Gen. Cass, and you to be benefited thereby I know not, but one thing I freely declare to you that such a course to effect the object in your behalf if known will readily be acted on in this county by your political friends. We will have a meeting tomorrow two weeks. Genl. Stone will be a candidate for Senator in Congress. Petitions of instructions is now circulating instructing Anderson and Rawlings[4] but, my impressions, will be disregarded. I am told that perhaps Sherrill[5] will vote for him or as the Genl informed me he had so declared provided a respectable request

should be forwarded him. The Genl. bolted from supporting me on the ground of my refusing unconditionally to vote for him. Whether he had promises from Rawlings or not I am unable to say. If so capital could be made out of him. He is altogether for himself and as far as he can be benefited by a party so long he will remain with it but no longer. Write me and believe me as ever . . . .

GEO. W. RICE

ALS. DLC–JKP. Addressed to Columbia and marked "Private." Polk's AE on the cover states that he answered this letter on October 13, 1843; Polk's reply has not been found.

1. Tennessee's Third Congressional District.
2. Marion County.
3. The Athens *Courier*, established as a Democratic newspaper, was published from 1838 until 1849.
4. Pierce B. Anderson and Daniel R. Rawlings. A Marion County farmer, merchant, and tavern keeper, Rawlings won election as a Whig to a single term in the Tennessee House, 1843–45.
5. Cravens Sherrell.

FROM JULIUS W. BLACKWELL

Dear Sir,   Athens Ten. Octr. 5th 1843

No doubt you have read the articles in the Knoxville Argus on the subject of a candidate for the Presidency, and probably, you have also read two articles of the same kidney in the Athens Courier.[1] I have been mortified to see the dictatorial tone of both of these papers, and I believe they have been governed, and probably written by Gen. Anderson and his brother P. B.[2] Both of these Gentlemen are for Calhoun, as I have good reasons to believe, and are making a move for Cass, in order to get an oppertunity to abuse Van Buren, whom they hate. The fact is, they go for *self*, and if suffered to take the lead in E. Tennessee, they will *ruin* the Democratic cause. We, in this section, believe that we will have a heavy weight to carry if Mr. Van is the nominee of the Convention, and for that reason, would rather Cass should be nominated, but how indiscreet it is, either in Editors or aspirants to abuse Van Buren, even if they are honestly of opinion that Cass is our strongest man. If Van Buren is nominated, I am for him, if he has not another friend in this state. P. B. Anderson wishes to have things all his own way, and declared that "*we*"— mark the word we—will run Cass in Tennessee *any how*. Now as to Pearce, as he was for White when he suffered himself to be made a tool of in 1836, so he may *consistently* go for any other man who will suffer himself to be made a tool of in 1844, by suffering his name to be used against the nominee of a Democratic Convention. It might resuscitate us in Tennessee, but weaken us in the Union. We profess—as a party—to be opposed to an election by the H. of Rep. and shall we now throw away our strength on a candidate who is put up by a faction—for selfish interests—to divide and conquer in some shape or form? If they cannot conquer the Whigs, they will endeavour to conquer the Democrats by a division, and by starting up of new schemes and party's, in order to be the leaders themselves. These Andersons pretend to be your exclusive friends—or rather your warmest friends. I beseach you, my Dear Sir, to *watch*. I say *watch*.

You will see that the Whigs charge that it is by your orders that these Editors[3] have moved for Cass and to abuse Van Buren. I think I know better. I can never believe—untill I have it from your own lips or pen, that you encourage the abuse of Martin Van Buren. I feel fully assured that when the battle is fought that you and myself will be found on the same field, in the same cause. Without ever haveing heard a word from you, I am fully pursuaded that if our sentiments were fully made known, you and myself would not differ, materially, upon the subject of the Presidency. It is contrary to good policy—or good sense—to abuse Van Buren for I believe his chance for the nomination is the best among the Democratic States. If Cass could get the nomination, I think it would be better for us in Tennessee. But when the chances are so uncertain, it is the hight of foolishness to abuse Mr. Van Buren with whom we have fought and, *politically*, died.

It is with some delicacy that I approach the subject of your personal concerns. I say *personal*, but I mean political. All your friends—among whom I am proud to place myself—are extremely desirous that you should be the candidate for the Vice Presidency. Altho I am a weak and humble member of the Democratic party, I must, and always will, express my opinions on suitable occasions. It is my candid oppinion that should Van Buren or Cass be nominated, you will be put on the ticket for Vice President. I believe that the Democrat who goes furthest to abuse Van Buren, will do most to defeat your nomination. If I am rong, it is an honest error of the head. I write not, however, to give—but rather to receive advice from you. I am somewhat stubbourn in my opinions when I think I am right; but if I am wrong, there is no man, I assure you, could put me right sooner than yourself. I have full confidence in you, and if you and myself should differ and I could not be convinced of error, I should begin to doubt my own capacity for receiveing political truth.

The idea of forceing all the States to go into the election of Delagates to the Baltimore Convention, by the Congressional districts, is perfect stuff. I am in favour of elections by the districts if practicable, but wish every State to adopt its own play, if it is a fair one.

I would like to talk to you for about four hours, and would come as far as Nashville to do so, but, am too poor. I am here perfectly at leasure—nothing to do but await the meeting of Congress—and would like very much to spend a few days in Nashville. I have been extremely anxious to do so, but could not for the lack of means.

J. W. BLACKWELL

ALS. DLC–JKP. Addressed to Nashville, forwarded to Columbia, and marked "*Confidential.*" Polk's AE on the cover states that he answered this letter on October 12, 1843; Polk's reply has not been found.

1. No issues of the Knoxville *Argus* or the Athens *Courier* for that time frame have been found.

2. Alexander O. Anderson and Pierce B. Anderson.

3. E. G. Eastman edited the Knoxville *Argus*, and probably Jarvis Williams headed the Athens *Courier*. In late 1843 or early 1844 Williams sold his interest in the *Courier* to Robert Frazier, who previously had shared in the ownership of the newspaper.

FROM ARCHIBALD YELL

Dear Govr.   Little Rock 5th Octr. 1843

When I wrote you last from my residence in Washington Co. I promised you a letter on my return to this place. I now take pleasure in doing it, tho I am bearly able to walk about my roome from a slight attack of the fever, which caught me imediately on my return to the Seat of Governmt.

We are without news here, which could interest you. Our local concerns are rather *Muddy* at present, but we shall in the course of a few months right up last Winter. Our Democratic Editor[1] found himself in the clutches of the Banks which was managed by the Whigs and being himself a little easy of concience Sold us all out to the Whigs, Lock, stock & barrel. Since that time we have been without a Press until in the last few Weeks we have Started a thorough Democratic Paper the "Arkansas Banner." [2] The Whigs are making war upon it aided by a few Disaffected Bank Democrats and a Squad who have been disappointed in their calculations & are now considered a little *fishy*. The *Banner* however will in a short time drive them from their hideing places and make them throw off the garb of Democracy or ware it with more grace and good will. All such creatures are an incubas to any party & ultimately will join the enemy. We are now endeavoring for the first time to get up a State Convention[3] to Nominate Candidates for Govr. & Congress: an Electoral

Tickett, & to Send Delegates to the N. Convention; its a new thing and will require time and care to effect any good.

Heretofore I was Candid in expressing to you that I thought Col Johnson the favorite in this State for the Presidency. I now doubt it and if we should have a full and fare Convention, I shall not be supprised if there was to be [a] majority for Mr Van Buren for President, and yourself for Vice Presidnt. I am very sure you are the strongest man in this State that could be Selected and from that fact, I am inclined to believe that *your* friends know to whom you should be Connected—and besides Mr Van Buren has now and always has had numerous friends.

I am sure they Can not get up a Delegation who would prefer any one over you for the Vice Presidency. And if things are carried on in the old way, until the meeting of the Convention I shall not be surprised if Van Buren should receive the Nomination on the first Ballot. Should he fail in that a Combination may be formed by the Union of all the other aspirants to defeat his Nomination. And tho I am a strong states right man and an admirer of Mr. Calhoun I frankly confess that I greatly fear he is to give our Party much trouble & if he does not fly off, its a less matter? As things now stand I give Mr Van Buren Alabama, Tennessee, Mo, Ohio, probably Missi & Ark, Virginia, N Jersey, N York Conneticut, Vermont, N Hampshire, Maine & Massachusetts, which will give him enough on the first ballot to decide his fate in Convention. Besides he has a chance for Louisiana, Delaware, Maryland, and little *Rhoda*. And I presume Mr. Buchanan out of the way Pennsyla would go for him. But Sir, I have not of late kept up with the run of *intreague* and I may be miscalculating. My greatest fears are after the Convention. If that Can be but *Harmonious* we shall give the Whigs what they give us in 1840—a Waterloo defeat.

My own business as well as policy requires me to retire for a Season.[4] I leave my position with more Strength than when I took office so I am not driven from Pub life. Many others of our household are ambitious and restless and they will be gratified without weak[en]ing the Cause. Rotation in office is indispensable to pursue Harmoney and Strength.

Whether I shall ever enter public life again is perhaps depending upon the result of the *Die* in the politics of the State—in one or two more elections? We have lost our old & tried friend Wm Gilchrist. He was an honest & worthy man! Your old friend Wm. H Field[5] from Pulaski is here. He has as yet done but little. I have just appo[in]ted him to hold some special Courts.

I have just appt. Wm. K. Sabastion[6] Judge Supm. Court. He too is an old Tennessean. *Hickman Co.* They Say here (the Whigs) that I hunt up all the old broken down Ten. *hacks* & put them in office &c &c.

I am pleased to learn that Genl Macklin[7] is about to Settle here. I have not formed his acquaintance. He made a fine impression here & will no doubt do well. I shall endeavor to make him a friend. Present me to Mrs. Polk & believe me as ever . . . .

A. YELL

ALS. DLC–JKP. Addressed to Columbia. Polk's AE on the cover states that he answered this letter on October 14, 1843; Polk's reply has not been found.

1. William E. Woodruff founded the Little Rock *Arkansas Gazette* in 1819. In 1843 Woodruff sold the *Gazette* to Benjamin J. Borden, a Whig.

2. The Little Rock *Democratic Banner* was first published by the printing firm of Borland and Farley, with Solon Borland as its editor and E. H. English as associate editor on September 16, 1843. The *Banner* continued publication until 1853, when it became the *Arkansas True Democrat*, owned by Johnson and Yerkes and edited by Richard H. Johnson.

3. The Arkansas Democratic Convention met on December 4, 1843. It appointed three delegates to the Baltimore Convention and resolved to support Martin Van Buren as its first choice for nomination to the presidency and John C. Calhoun as a second choice.

4. Yell, first elected governor of Arkansas in 1840, resigned in 1844. Subsequently, he won election to a second term in the U.S. House where he sat in 1845 and 1846. He resigned his seat in the House in 1846 to serve in the Mexican War and was killed at the Battle of Buena Vista in 1847.

5. A Pulaski lawyer, Feild had removed to Arkansas.

6. William K. Sebastian, born and educated in Tennessee, removed to Arkansas in 1835. A Helena lawyer and planter, he served as circuit judge, 1840–43; associate justice of the Arkansas Supreme Court, 1843–45; and member and president of the Arkansas Senate, 1846–47. Sebastian sat in the U.S. Senate from 1848 until 1861.

7. Sackfield Maclin.

TO EDMUND BURKE

My Dear Sir   Columbia Tennessee October 8th 1843

The Democracy of this State, though defeated at the August election, are neither conquered nor dismayed. Unembarrassed by local causes and State questions (which contributed greatly to weaken us in that election) and upon the naked issues of Federal policy as the exclusive tests, we have no doubt we were then and are now in a decided majority in the State. We will hold a Democratic State Convention in November,[1] with a view to adopt the necessary measures, preparatory to the great contest of 1844, a contest into which our Democracy will enter with confidence of success.

The Democratic majority in the House of Representatives of the next Congress will be overwhelming, and it is deeply to be regretted that the result of the late election in Tennessee will prevent us from commanding a majority in the Senate also. The next Speaker of the House will of course be a Democrat. I know not who may be the aspirants to that Station, but am sure than none can present stronger claims upon his party than our friend *Cave Johnson* of this State. In the darkest hour of our trial in the State he was firm and unwavering. When *White & Bell* produced our present unfortunate divisions he was of the few who were faithful among the faithless. He has made many sacrafices in our cause. In the last canvass he was sincerely desirous to decline a re-election to Congress and had announced his determination to do so, but yielded to the wishes of his friends only because, it was believed that he was the only man in his District who could save it from the enemy. Though we are confident of success in 1844, it is not to be disguised that the contest will be a severe one, and his election to the Speakership would add greatly to our strength. I have thought it not improper to make the suggestion to you. I beg you to believe that I do so solely with the view to advance our cause & not with the slightest desire to interfere with the selection of any other who may have been thought of, if it be deemed best for the party. *Mr Johnson* is an exceedingly modest man and would not himself make known to his most intimate friend, any desire he might have upon the subject. I shall be pleased to hear from you when your leisure may permit.

JAMES K. POLK

NjP. Addressed to Newport, New Hampshire.
1. The Tennessee State Democratic Convention met at Nashville on November 23, 1843. Attended by approximately 230 delegates, the meeting elected delegates to represent the state at the Democratic National Convention in May 1844 and resolved to support the convention's choice for the presidential nomination.

FROM HENRY EWING[1]

Agency Merchants Ins & Tr Co. Nashville
Esteemed Sir.   Philadelphia October 12th 1843
Your favour of the 4th Inst is received.[2] I regret to say that it is not in my power to effect a loan here on the terms you propose. I have now on my table an authority to borrow $10,000 for an acquaintance at Nashville to be secured by mortgage on first rate real estate, and personal security

besides, at 7% per annum principal and interest payable here and another for $12,000 for which 8% per annum is offered & most undoubted security.The security you offer, I esteem perfectly undoubted and would recommend the loan with much pleasure. The difficulty is that neither our Banks or Capitalists will make such investments on any security or at any rate of interest. Several gentlemen from Tennessee are now in the city endeavouring to effect such loans, but without success. My attention has been repeatedly called to this subject and I have made every enquiry that my limited acquaintance would enable me. Money is very abundant here and rates of interest low from to 4% to 5 pr. annum, but it belongs chiefly to that class of persons who expect to engage in active business and are not willing to make any permanent investments. The rates on long mortgages in the city are about the same as in 1836 or 1840. It will afford me much pleasure to be able to serve you.

　　With the highest sentiments of respect.

HENRY EWING

ALS. DLC–JKP. Addressed to Columbia.

1. Henry Ewing, son of Nathan Ewing and grandson of Andrew Ewing of Nashville, served as Davidson County Court clerk, 1830–35. He was cashier of the Bank of Tennessee before removing to Philadelphia, where he was an agent for the Merchants Insurance & Trading Company of Nashville.

2. Letter not found.

FROM SAMUEL H. LAUGHLIN

Nashville, Tennessee. October 12, 1843

Laughlin relates that he has written to Gov. Yell, A. A. Kincannon, T. P. Moore,[1] H. Van Pelt, J. W. Ford, and others concerning the 1844 presidential ticket. Laughlin thinks that Polk should not attend the state convention in November, but requests that he draft the convention's public address. John J. Crittenden,[2] "Plenipotentiary of Harry of the slashes and mealbag," [3] is visiting Nashville, but Laughlin knows "nothing of the progress and character of his negociatons." Long has advised Nicholson to give Polk his wholehearted support; otherwise, Nicholson would never obtain Laughlin's support for anything.

ALS. DLC–JKP. Addressed to Columbia and marked "Private." Polk's AE on the cover states that he answered this letter on October 13, 1843; Polk's reply has not been found.

1. A Democrat from Mercer County, Kentucky, Thomas P. Moore sat three terms in the U.S. House, 1823–29; served as minister to Columbia, 1829–33; and ran unsuccessfully for Congress in 1833.

2. A Kentucky lawyer and prominent Whig politician, Crittenden held several governmental posts at the state and national levels during his public career, which spanned several decades. He served in the U.S. Senate, 1817–19, 1835–41, 1842–48, 1855–61; the U.S. House, 1861–63; the U.S. attorney generalship, 1841, 1850–53; and the governorship of Kentucky, 1848–50.

3. Reference is to Henry Clay.

FROM J. G. M. RAMSEY

My Dear Sir   Mecklenburg T. Oct. 12, 1843

Yours of the 9th inst[1] from Nashville is this moment received. I hasten to reply to it & also to add a word or two on other branches of the same subject.

I concur fully with those of our political friends who advise that Tennessee should remain as she now is—uncommitted by newspapers or other ways upon the Pres. question—& in the policy also of avowing our purpose to support the nominee at Baltimore & of abstaining from any abuse of either of the Dem. Candidates (with this exception however, if a V.B. or Calhoun editor does the least injustice to the pretensions of Tennessee we must retain the priviledge of rapping him across the knuckles). I also concur in the policy of the State Convention expressing no preference *direct or indirect* for either of the Pres. Candidates but directly & pointedly for the V.P.; nor should it give instructions to the Tenn. Delegates whom to support for P., but leave them responsible to their constituents—untrammelled & at liberty to do what *they will find next May to be necessary & best*. Now here comes the point—the mode of choosing delegates. The District system is the most democratic—it brings the Con. nearer to the people & is most [. . .][2] to all the candidates. [What] you have suggested comes very near [it] & if the people at the time of appointing their delegates to the State Convention understand that the members of their District will have the appointing of its delegate to Baltimore & select accordingly the District system is in fact acted upon & few I apprehend will object to it—especially if it is understood that the State Convention has no negative & [. . .][3] responsible to their own district we cant have any objections to it. It is virtually the District system. Could some one lay down this as a part of its organism in the Columbia Democrat, it would have an essential bearing in your favor out of Tennessee.

I suppose you see the S.C. papers that mention you as favorably & the Pa. (Cass) Journal[4] that almost comes out for you [. . .]. Your letters will reach me always here. I will not be at Nashville I presume & will be steadily at home. Please always present my best regards to your excellent Mrs. Polk & your good mother[5] & believe me to be . . . .

J. G. M. RAMSEY

ALS. DLC–JKP. Addressed to Columbia.
1. Letter not found.
2. Deterioration in the fold of the manuscript has obliterated at least two words on this line and on the verso of this page.
3. Ramsey has omitted a word or words here.
4. Possible reference to the *Philadelphia Evening Journal*, which began publication in the spring of 1842.
5. Jane Knox Polk.

TO H. A. COLE, DAVID HOWELL, ET AL.[1]

Gentlemen: Columbia Oct 16th 1843

I had the honour to receive some weeks ago your communication of the 9th ultimo,[2] inviting me to be present at a Democratic Convention of young men to be holden at Clarksville on the 9th of November next. I have delayed an answer until the present time, in the hope that it might be in my power to attend on the occasion, but have to regret that indispensible engagements which must occupy my attention will prevent it.

I am much gratified that the Democratic young men of Montgomry[3] have resolved to assemble themselves together in convention.

They are the first to "put this ball in motion" in the State, and I hope their example will be imitated in other Counties. Democratic associations and meetings of the young men of the several Counties would be powerful auxiliaries, in disseminating truth and sound political doctrine. My observation from an intimate acquaintance with the political opinions of the people of the State warrants the remark that whilst a large and decided majority of the old men—the men with gray heads—are Democratic in their principles, it is to be regretted that an undue proportion of the young men and especially of those residing in our towns and villages, are found in the ranks of the opponents of these principles. Though not less patriotic than their seniours, the cause of this may doubtless in many insantcis[4] be found in their associations and habits of life and the want of that careful examination of public subjects wich their importance demands. The Democratic convention of young men, which you propose to hold especially if it shall be followed by the organization of Democratic associations of the young men of each County will awaken a spirit of inquiry after political truth and will give an energy and force to the Democratic cause in the State, which it has never before possessed.

Public questions will be more carefully examined and instead of being hurried along with the current of opinion around them, as is but too often the case in our towns, we will very soon see the body of our young men enlisted with their fathers under the same banner & maintaining the same principles. Those associations should not be confined to the County towns, but should embrace the young men of each County.

Though the Democratic Party in this state were defeated at the August election, we have nothing to discourage us, but on the contrary every thing to animate us, to renew the contest with increased zeal and energy. It is well known that many local causes and state questions wholly unconnected with the issues of Federal policy contributed very largely to produce that result. Those have passed off with the occasion which gave rise to them, and cannot again be made to operate to the prejudice of the Democratic cause.

Let our young men throughout the State organize their whole strength as you propose to do. Let every Democrat keep his armor on, and our success in the next trial must be as certain as that "truth is mighty and will prevail." [5]

Regretting that I cannot be present to witness your proceedings on the 9th of November, I beg you to assure the Democratic young men of Montgomry, whom you represent, that they have my hearty good wishes in this noble exertion, to reclaim this Republic state from her present unnatural and false political position and to place her where she has always until recently been in the Republican ranks. So far as any humble exertions of mine may contribute to that result I will be found to be a faithful soldier at my post, doing service for the advancement of the great Democratic cause—a cause which it has been not only my duty—but my pride and my pleasure to sustain in past life.

With a tender of my acknowledgments for the honor done me by your invitation . . . .

JAMES K. POLK

Copy. DLC–JKP. Addressed to Clarksville and marked "*Copy.*"

1. Polk's letter is addressed to H. A. Cole and twenty-six other members of the Democratic Young Men of Montgomery County.

2. In their invitation of September 9, 1843, the young Democrats of Montgomery County declared that the purpose of the convention to which they were urging Polk's attendance was to "devise some means to produce a more thorough dissemination of our political principles." ALS. DLC–JKP.

3. Misspelling of "Montgomery."

4. Misspelling of "instances."

5. *Old Testament Apocrypha: II Esdras*, iv, 41.

FROM WILLIAM H. POLK

Dear Brother   Nashville Oct. 16th 1843

I received your letter[1] several days ago, but have defered answering it up to this time in the hope that some indication of the Whig purpose relative to senators would be discovered. They are still in great trouble, held meetings nearly every night during the past week without settleing the conflicting claims of the various aspirants from the Middle, East and West. They make a last effort to night, tomorrow being the day fixed on in the Resolution to elect.[2] What will be the result is very doubtful, as evident disatisfaction prevails. I will write you again by the next mail. I have seen Armstrong, Humphreys, Laughlin, Gardner & Powell and the Corresponding Committee[3] will organize tomorrow night and go vigorously to work. Maj Donelson was in the City to day and promised Armstrong and me to commence opperations immediately,[4] and from the feeling and interest he manifested I must believe he will do his duty. W. P. Martin[5] I think stands at this time a very fair chance to defeat Dillahunty.[6] My best impression is that he will beat him easily. When I write you tomorrow evening I can give you more particulars concerning all matters in which you are interested. Tell Mother[7] my Wife is *improving* but very slowly.[8]

Williams H. Polk

1. Polk's letter, probably written ca. October 12, 1843, has not been found.
2. On October 11, 1843, the Tennessee Senate concurred in a House Resolution to convene jointly on October 17, 1843, "to elect two Senators to the Congress of the United States, one for six years from the 4th of March 1841, and the other to serve out the unexpired term of the Honorable Felix Grundy, deceased."
3. Reference is to Polk's vice-presidential corresponding committee, which was organized at his behest to write political friends outside Tennessee who might be induced to support publicly a Van Buren-Polk ticket in 1844.
4. See Polk to Andrew J. Donelson, October 19, 1843.
5. A prominent Columbia lawyer, William P. Martin became judge of the Eighth Judicial District in 1851.
6. Edmund Dillahunty, also a prominent Columbia lawyer, served as Maury County solicitor, 1831–36, and as judge of the Eighth Judicial District, 1836–51.
7. Jane Knox Polk.
8. Belinda G. Dickinson Polk's illness is not identified further.

ALS. DLC–JKP. Addressed to Columbia.

FROM JOHN W. DAVIS[1]

My Dear Sir   Carlisle Ind Oct 17 1843
    Your esteemed favor of the 8th inst[2] reached me to day and I was
truly glad to hear that our prospects in your state are so flattering for
1844. I had almost dispaired of seeing Tennessee brought back to her high
place in the democratic ranks, after being defeated with you for a champion, but I have no doubt you are correct in saying that upon questions
strictly of a national character, she will be right side up. The star of
democracy seems to be in the ascendent almost every where. I have just
heard from Hamilton County, Ohio & Dunkin[3] is elected by a large majority. The late elections in our state were conducted throughout strictly
upon question of national policy. The line between federalism and democracy was closely drawn, no extrinsic or local question was agitated;
hence we conclude the politics of Indiana are now well settled.
    We have a democratic jubalee to come of in this county[4] on the 19th
inst. I heartily wish you could have been with us.
    In relation to our friend Cave Johnsons claim to the Speakership I can
assure you there is no one returned to Congress that I would rather see
elevated to that place than Mr. J. He shall have my voice most cheerfully.
I Shall be pleased to hear from you at Washington. Please present my
kind regard to Mrs. P.

                                                    JNO. W DAVIS

    ALS. DLC–JKP. Addressed to Columbia.
    1. A physician and resident of Carlisle, Indiana, Davis served several terms
in the Indiana House in the period between 1831 and 1857; he won election to four
terms in the U.S. House, 1835–37, 1839–41, and 1843–47; and he presided as
Speaker in the Twenty-ninth Congress.
    2. Letter not found.
    3. Alexander Duncan, a Cincinnati physician, sat for several terms in both the
Ohio House and Senate, 1828–34; he served three terms in the U.S. House,
1837–41 and 1843–45. Many Democrats celebrated Duncan's congressional
speeches for their forceful attacks on Whig principles.
    4. Sullivan County.

FROM WILLIAM H. POLK

Dear Brother   Nashville Oct 17th 1843
    The Convention has just ajourned after electing Foster & Jarnegan.[1]
By this election they have created much *disatisfaction* which must ulti-

mately work *great* advantage to our cause. I write merely to give the result of the election. The Democrats made no nomination, but scattered their votes on various prominent men of their party throughout the State. This I thought best, for the reason, that it would not do to place *your* name before the Convention, and thereby create the impression abroad, of a second defeat, nor would it do, in my opinion, to confer that distinction on any other, seeming to express a preference over *you*. This course I had adopted by the party, thinking it best.

I received your letter last evening & attended without delay to the contents.[2] I will write you again by the next mail. Belinda, tell Mother, is not so *well* to day.[3]

WILLIAM H. POLK

ALS. DLC–JKP. Addressed to Columbia.

1. On October 17, 1843, the Tennessee General Assembly, meeting in joint convention to fill the state's two vacant seats in the U.S. Senate, elected Ephraim H. Foster for the term ending March 3, 1845, and Spencer Jarnagin for the term ending March 3, 1847.

2. Polk's letter, probably written ca. October 15, 1843, has not been found.

3. Belinda Dickinson Polk and Jane Knox Polk.

TO ANDREW JACKSON DONELSON

My Dear Sir: Columbia Oct. 19th 1843

The result of the elections in Maryland and Georgia, the close vote and possible defeat in Ohio, are enough to rouse the Democracy, if not to a sense of their danger, to the fact now rendered certain that we are to have a hard contest in 1844. I am now anxious to hear from Pennsylvania. I have my fears that the recent defection of *Gov. Porter*,[1] may have produced some effect in that state. The indications are becoming stronger every day, that the Southern wing of our party are to give us trouble. It is most unfortunate that the period of meeting of the National Convention has been postponed so late as May. Should *Mr Calhoun* and his friends, refuse to abide by its decision, as I fear they may, the time will be so short, that it will require great energy and extraordinary exertions to rally the great body of the party on the nominee so as to avoid defeat. In this state of things what is the proper course to be pursued? In my judgment there is but one that is safe, and that is to denounce any such factious movement in advance, and for the Democracy at the North and East, to take open and decided ground at once in expressing their preference not only for the Presidency but for the Vice Presidency also. In regard to the former there will be but little division of opinion, & if there be faith in men, the public opinion in that section of the Union is settled in regard to the latter also. Why then the studied reserve and silence of the Democratic press in that section of the Union in regard to it? The question must be settled in May at furthest, and an expression of opinion *now*, would be much less likely to do mischief, than if delayed until that time. It is the same indecisive and cautious course, which I have always believed greatly weakened the party in 1839–40, and contributed largely to the defeat which followed. Had the convention at that time nominated *any-one* who was not positively objectionable, I have never doubted but that *Mr Van-Buren* would have carried the vote of *Pennslyvania, Maine* & perhaps states enough to have elected him; at all events his vote would have been much increased. The same error is now I fear from over-caution, and the apprehension of giving offence to some about to be committed. It may now I think be regarded as settled that *Mr Van-Buren* will be the nominee for the Presidency. Buchanan as Mr *Horn* writes me may get the vote of Pennsylvania as a matter of compliment on the first ballot. After that, it will be given to *Mr Van-Buren. Cass* has no embodied strength any-where, though he has scattering friends every-where. *Mr Calhoun's* strength is confined to less than half a dozen small states South of Virginia. *Col. Johnson* may get the vote of Kentucky & possibly of Arkansas in Convention. If then *Mr Van-Buren* is the nominee, the candidate for the Vice Presidency must come from the West, and from a slave-holding state, and especially as *Mr Clay* resides in a Western slave-holding state; and my own opinion is, that *Col. John-son* will ultimately yield his pretensions for the Presidency, and that he will be the only formidable competitor for the Vice Presidency. I am not conscious of any selfishness, and certainly of no unkind feeling towards *Col. Johnson*, when I say that if the party are mad enough again to force him upon us, it is my deliberate opinion that we must be again defeated.

Since I say you[2] I have received another letter from *Gov. Yell* of Arkansas, under date of 5 Oct. '43 in which among other things he says: "Heretofore I was candid in expressing that I thought *Col. Johnson* the favourite in this state for the Presidency. I now doubt it, and if we should have a full and fair Convention (state convention) I shall not be surprized if there was to be a majority for *Mr Van-Buren* & yourself for Vice President. I am very sure you are the strongest man in this state that could be selected and from *that fact* I am inclined to believe that *your* friends know to whom you should be connected, and besides *Mr Van-Buren* has now and always had numerous friends. I am sure they cannot get up a delegation who would prefer any one over you for the Vice-Presidency."

Have you written the letters of which we spoke when I last saw you? It is important I think that they should be written without delay. Our friends at the North and East, should understand the true state of things in this part of the Union, and take bolder ground before the public in reference to the Vice Presidency. By doing so they would concentrate public opinion, in reference to both stations before the meeting of the Convention, and thereby avoid much confusion and trouble. I do not understand *Blair's* course. I wrote Genl. *Armstrong* a letter on yesterday[3] in reference to it, which he will shew you. I do not think he is inclined to do me justice. Why I know not, unless it be that he has strong attachments for *Col. Johnson*, & looks to his *restoration* with *Mr Van-Buren*. But Genl. Armstrong will shew you my letter in which you will see the impressions I have and the suggestions I make. I have only one other remark to make to you, and that is that no one is now prominently presented for the Vice-Presidency, & that it is the opinion of *Gov Yell*, *T. P. Moore*, and others of my friends that the ground should be pre-occupied, before *Col J.* concludes to fall back upon it, as I think he will ultimately attempt to do. I will leave for my plantation in Mississippi on monday next & concluded to write you frankly & without reserve, what my views & impressions were. You will of course regard what I have said as *strictly confidential*. A letter addressed to me at *Somerville* Tennessee, any time within ten day or two weeks, will meet me on my way up.

JAMES K. POLK

P.S. I will be back before the meeting of the State Convention, and will be governed by the advice of my friends whether I will be at Nashville at that time or not. I must insist upon you to see *Laughlin* & *Humphreys* and have a proper address prepared before the convention meets. J.K.P.

ALS. DLC–AJD. Addressed to Nashville and marked *"Confidential."* Published in St. George L. Sioussat, ed., "Letters of James K. Polk to Andrew J. Donelson, 1843–1848," *Tennessee Historical Magazine*, III (1917), 53–54.

1. With his eyes on the vice-presidency, David R. Porter, governor of Pennsylvania, had used his influence and patronage to promote the political fortunes of President John Tyler. Porter's efforts in 1843 secured the nomination of his brother, James M. Porter, to be secretary of war; but the governor's advocacy of Tyler evoked strong opposition among regular Pennsylvania Democrats. In January 1844 the U.S. Senate rejected Tyler's nomination of James Porter.

2. Faulty word selection; context suggests that Polk intended to write the verb, "saw."

3. Letter not found.

FROM SAMUEL H. LAUGHLIN

at night

My dear Sir,   Nashville, Oct. 20, 1843

I have only time to inform you this evening, that in a consultation of Mr. Humphreys, Gen. Armstrong, W. H. Polk and myself, just concluded, it is agreed to meet at Judge A Miller's room in private—consulting Powell, Kinney, Gardner &c—on Monday night to agree on Delegates to National Convention for the State and several Congressional Districts, and to parcel out the work of preparing the Resolutions and Address for out[1] State Convention. The last is likely to fall on Mr. Humphreys and myself.

Who shall be Delegates? Coe & John Blair surely for state at large. A. Donelson if possible for this Congressional District, Gen. Pillow for yours, Dortch for C. Johnsons, &c. with the members for alternates where represented by a democrat.[2] Please before you leave, send me suggestions for others. I wish we could get Austin Miller to consent to serve for his District.[3] He is able to bear it.

I enclose you a letter[4] just received by me from Hon T. P. Moore. You will see his position. I think it is clear that he will go to the Convention with an *earnest* wish to get rid of Johnson.[5] Please enclose it back to me before you leave, as I wish to answer it.

I have received your last letter.[6] Moses Dawson[7] whom you mention as a proper person for Gen. Jackson and Donelson to write to in Ohio, is the most proper of all persons to be addressed. Donelson has promised A. V. Brown to write letters to several persons. I think to Mr. Wright among others—as I presume he will inform you on his way home from Nashville. I hope Donelson has and will write.

I have written all the letters we talked of, and several others. I think on Monday night we will appoint a Committee of correspondence.[8]

If I had time, and could spare means, I would willingly go to Tuscaloosa where the Alabama Legislature will be in session after we adjourn here, and to any point where personally or by writing I could cause our policy and position to be understood. If I had a fortune that would afford it, I would see, under proper credentials of introduction, the proper men at Tuscaloosa, Raleigh, Richmond, Albany &c. while the legislatures of Alabama, N. Carolina, Virginia and New York are in session during the approaching winter and spring, before the meeting of the National Convention. On political accounts, I never wished more for time, and power, and means than I now do in anticipation of next year's campaign which I intend and wish to be my last; but I only have the *will* while others blessed with time and means, lack the inclination. Although tied up in my sphere of action, I will be busy—busy to the end.

W. H. Polk desires me to say that he will write to you in a few days to Coffeeville.

Jonakin has gone home a Senator—and Ephe[9] is running about, grinning and jumping like a pleased monkey—with just about the dignity of one at least.

Let me hear from you before you leave—*sure*.

S. H. LAUGHLIN

ALS. DLC–JKP. Addressed to Columbia and marked "Private." Polk's AE on the cover states that he answered this letter on October 22, 1843; Polk's reply has not been found.

1. Miswriting of the possessive pronoun, "our."

2. References are to Tennessee's Sixth, Eighth, and Ninth congressional districts; in the 1843–44 session of Congress, Tennessee Democrats held six seats, having won races in the First, Third, Fourth, Fifth, Sixth, and Ninth districts.

3. Tennessee's Tenth Congressional District.

4. Enclosure not found.

5. Richard M. Johnson.

6. Letter not found.

7. Dawson, an ardent Irish nationalist, was forced to flee his native land; he worked in Philadelphia before moving to Cincinnati, where he edited the *Advertiser*, a Democratic newspaper.

8. See William H. Polk to Polk, October 16, 1843.

9. Spencer Jarnagin and Ephraim H. Foster.

TO SAMUEL H. LAUGHLIN

My Dear Sir: Columbia Oct. 20th 1843

I expect to leave home for my plantation[1] on monday morning next, the 23rd, & hope to hear from you by tomorrow's mail—what has been done & is doing in reference to the matter about which we have corresponded.[2] If you do not receive this letter in time to write by Saturday's mail, write me to *Bolivar* where I will get your letter on my way down. Letters addressed to me at *Somerville*, within the next ten days or two weeks I will receive on my way up. If I have good health, I will get home before the State Convention meets, but will be fatigued and you must not rely on me to prepare the address. Hoping to hear from you on tomorrow.

JAMES K. POLK

ALS. CSmH. Addressed to Nashville and marked *"Private."* Laughlin's AE on the cover states: "Rec'd Oct. 21st 1843. Wrote Gov. Polk last night 20th—before receiving."

1. Polk's plantation was in Yalobusha County, Mississippi.
2. See Laughlin to Polk, October 20, 1843.

FROM WILLIAM H. POLK

Dear Brother   Nashville Oct 22d 1843

I received your letter last evening,[1] and had intended in my last letter[2] to request you to rent my old office, for any price, until the 1st of January. If you have not time before leaving for Mississippi to attend to renting it, please authorize some one [to] rent it immediately.

The Committee,[3] which you recommended should be formed in your last letter,[4] have had one meeting, and have commenced working with energy and spirit. Powell and Dr Kinney have written to East Tennessee and to Western Virginia urging immediate action. Letters have also been written to Roger Barton and Judge Howry of Miss.[5] Humphreys promised to write to Barton and I presume he has done so. I will see him in the morning, and if he has not done so, I will urge him to write immediately. Cave Johnson left here this morning; whilst here, he had a full interview with your friends and has gone home to renew his labors to effect the desired purpose. Maj Donalson,[6] Genl Armstrong informs me has written many letters to the North. I will go to see Donalson on Wednesday, & stick to him until he does write. You may rest assured that every thing that can be done, shall be *done* to carry out your views. Tell Mother [that] Belinda has been improving for the last two days.[7] I will write you again to Somerville.

                                       WILLIAM H. POLK

ALS. DLC–JKP. Addressed to Columbia.
1. Polk's letter, probably written ca. October 20, 1843, has not been found.
2. See William H. Polk to Polk, October 17, 1843.
3. See Samuel H. Laughlin to Polk, October 20, 1843, and Polk to Andrew J. Donelson, October 19, 1843.
4. Probably a reference to a letter Polk wrote ca. October 12, 1843; see Polk to William H. Polk, October 16, 1843.
5. Roger Barton and James M. Howry. A lawyer, planter, and jurist, Barton was born in Knoxville and removed in 1827 to Bolivar, where he practiced law, won election to a single term in the Tennessee House, 1829–31, and held the post of attorney general for the Eleventh Judicial District from 1831 until 1836. In the latter year, he removed to Holly Springs, Mississippi, where he subsequently

won election to two terms in the Mississippi legislature.

6. Andrew J. Donelson.

7. Jane Knox Polk and Belinda Dickinson Polk.

TO SARAH C. POLK

My Dear Wife: Bolivar Oct. 26th 1843

We reached here to night, having had more or less rain on us every day for the last three days. The roads are becoming very muddy & bad & I am thinking of leaving the Buggy here and going down on horseback. *Sam P. Walker* is not here, but left a message that he would meet me at La Grange on tomorrow.[1] If he does so, I will get the notes & write from that place. My letter enclosing them will reach Columbia on wednesday next—which will be in time to send them to Nashville by thursday's mail. If you receive no letter from me on wednesday, get *Knox* to send the notes, which I left, to Nashville on thursday.

I saw *Lucius J. Polk*, the day I left home. He will start to North Carolina on tuesday next. See *Knox* & ask him to raise for me if he can $50 and give it to *Lucius* to bear little *Marshall's* expenses out.[2] *Lucius* says he will be hard run for money. Tell *Knox*[3] I will raise the money some-how on my return & repay it to him. *Mr James Armstrong* will go with me directly to my place,[4] & if he is pleased with it, I think it probable I will sell him half my land. *Genl. Pillow* goes from here to Memphis, & will be at my plantation on next Saturday or Sunday week unless he buys slaves. If I do not trade with Armstrong I think Pillow is strongly inclined to buy it.

Mr Armstrong requests that you will let *Wm.* Cooper know *where he is &c*, & request him to send word *to his wife*.[5]

Armstrong seems to have *special reasons* for being very affectionate towards his *young wife* just now. You will of course say nothing about the probabilities of my selling him half my land. I think the slaves on that I will sell to him. If I do I will retain the other half & still continue the farm. This I know will suit your views better than to sell the whole plantation.

JAMES K. POLK

ALS. DLC–JKP. Addressed to Columbia.

1. On October 27, 1843, Samuel P. Walker wrote from Memphis that he had intended to meet Polk at LaGrange, "but I found that nearly all the Planters of the Western District were sending their cotton off as fast as possible and most of them were coming with it to Memphis, to sell or get advances & ship." Further, Walker advised that if Polk could sell his plantation "for anything like a reasonable price," he should do so. ALS. DLC–JKP.

2. See Polk to William C. Tate, November 18, 1843.

3. Joseph Knox Walker, Polk's nephew.

4. Polk wished to sell part of his Yalobusha County, Mississippi, plantation to James Armstrong, probably a resident of the Zion Community of Maury County. Armstrong is not identified further.

5. William Cooper and Armstrong's wife are not identified further.

FROM EDMUND BURKE

My dear Sir,   Newport, N.H. Oct. 30th 1843

I had the honor of receiving your letter of the 8th inst. some days since, but my constant engagements in court, which was then in session in this place, have prevented me from replying more seasonably to it.

The intelligent members of our party in this section of the Union, were aware of the difficulties with which their brethern of Tennessee have had to contend, during the late canvass, and they were gratified with the result generally, although the victory was not complete. In the event of an election of the President by the House of Representatives, which from present appearances, is not impossible, Tennessee will be found acting with her democratic sisters.

With regard to the Speakership, I assure you, I have thought but little. I am yet pledged to no one, nor can I now say whose interests I shall favor when I arrive at Washington. I am, however, much obliged for the suggestions you have made in regard to our mutual friend, the *Hon Cave Johnson*. I know him well. I have been a member of the House with him during the 26th & 27th Congresses, and have seen him, and observed his conduct in the many difficult and trying emergencies in which the democratic portion of the House has been placed, and never has he failed to acquit himself with distinguished ability and with unwavering fidelity to his party. I know of no man more reliable than Mr Johnson in a critical emergency, and more faithful to the best interests of the country, at all times. Nor do I know any[one][1] whose elevation to the Speakership of the House would give me more pleasure than Mr Johnson's.

I shall go to Washington unpledged to any interest except the interest of the Democratic party of the Union; and if I shall be convinced after my arrival that the interest of our cause will be best consulted by the election of Mr Johnson to the Speakership, I shall give him my support with hearty good will. If his election would strengthen us in Tennessee, it would be a matter worthy of serious consideration, as that state must be one of the great battle grounds in the election of 1844.

Our prospects in this State are very encouraging. Gov. Hill,[2] although hostile to the democratic cause, cannot now injure us. He has, by his factious and treasonable conduct, utterly deprived himself of influence with our party,[3] and he has now no other recourse, but to surrender unconditionally, or go over to the Federal party. With great respect . . . . .

EDMUND BURKE

ALS. DLC–JKP. Addressed to Columbia.

1. An ink spot on the manuscript has blurred part of one word.

2. An ardent Democrat and longtime editor of the *New Hampshire Patriot*, Isaac Hill served as a member in both houses of the New Hampshire legislature; as second comptroller of the U.S. Treasury and member of Jackson's "Kitchen Cabinet," 1829–30; as U.S. Senator, 1831–36; as governor of New Hampshire, 1836–39; and as U.S. subtreasurer at Boston, 1840–41.

3. In June 1841, Isaac Hill tried unsuccessfully to block the state convention's nomination of Henry Hubbard for governor. Hill and conservative Democrats then backed John H. White in the gubernatorial election. During the winter of 1842, the party divided over state economic policies; Levi Woodbury, Hubbard, and their radical Democratic newspapers accused Hill of having united with the Whigs in representing banking and manufacturing interests. Even Franklin Pierce retired from the U.S. Senate in 1842 to support the radical Democratic cause in the state. Hubbard won the 1843 gubernatorial election and thereby ended Hill's influence in New Hampshire's Democratic party.

FROM ARCHIBALD YELL

Dear Govr   Little Rock 31st Octr 1843

Your friendly favor of the 14th Inst.[1] was received a few days since for which you will please accept my acknowledgements.

The recent elections in Georgia has settled the matter for Mr. Calhoun, and upon the whole I am glad of it. He has no doubt determined to set up for himself and to run at all hazards; therefore I pray God he may be defeated even at the risk of haveing Clay tacked upon us for four years. The Ohio & Pennsylvania elections will teach us that success alone depends upon "Union harmony & Concesion" but without Mr Van Buren [we] should loose N. York. He will Certainly receive the Nomination. In that event I look upon it as almost Certain that you will recieve the Nomination for Vice President. Without our party should feel disposed to run the old Tickett. In that event Johnson would Stand a good Chance for the Nomination, perhaps the best. But I have no idea he will desire the Vice Presidency. Tho you no doubt understand the views and wishes of our Party better than I can, I am Sattisfied now of one fact & that is that Mr Van Buren is the strong man in Arkansas. We are now arranging for a

State Convention[2] to come off the 1st Monday in Decr. at this place. We design to Nominate a Candidate for Govr & Congress & to appoint Delegates to the B. Convention[3] and from the Complection of the County meetings so fare I believe Van Buren will be Nominated. At all events he will or the members will be left free to do for the best.

Neither Judge Cross nor myself will be Candidates for reelection and that fact as well as a laudeble ambition has given us about a dozen Candidates or that many who will be before the convention. It is our first effort at a Convention, and I am not Certain that it will exactly do?

A few days since I received a letter from our old friend Sam Laughlin. He is your devoted friend and I wrote to him fully & freely on the subject of the next election.[4] What would you think if Laughlin was to become a Citizen of Arkansas. This is the very place for *Sam*. He would do a good business in his profession and he is a better Polititin than any we have and would soon become a leading man. I want him here to take Charge of [our] Paper the "Banner."[5] So what you would loose in Tennessee you would gain in Arkansas, and we are worth struggling for. Ten. is but a poor Concern at best and Cant be relyed on.

I begin to fear of late that if we suced at the next election it will be as much as a bargan. We have so many *scaly* Politutions in our ranks. I wish to god, it was *Unconstitutional* for a man to quit his party. I mean among the Politions & that they had to Suffer under the "2d Section."[6] I hope things are in a better condition than I now fear they are? Let me hear from you often & write me fully & freely.

Please Say to Madame Polk that I am Still a *Single young Gentleman*, that I am not disposed to quarul with old friends but that I Consider she has fed me on *hope* & expectations so long that I am not sure that I Can now marry at all. A *Widdow* is my choice and rather than be thought very fastidious, I will take the one that is left, but I ought to have had first Choice. Still Situated as I am in the matter I believe I prefer the one that is unmarried. She is a good *Democrat* & a fine splendid looking woman and about a proper age & I am as ever . . . .

                                                        A. YELL

ALS. DLC–JKP. Addressed to Columbia.

1. Letter not found.
2. See Archibald Yell to Polk, October 5, 1843.
3. National Democratic Convention at Baltimore.
4. See Samuel H. Laughlin to Polk, November 17, 1843.
5. Yell's reference is to the *Arkansas Democratic Banner*. See Yell to Polk, October 5, 1843.
6. Probably Yell refers to extradition rights detailed in Article IV, Section 2 of the U.S. Constitution.

FROM DAVID CRAIGHEAD

Dr Sir   Nashville [November 6][1] 43

The old leaven begins to work. A gentleman,[2] late U.S. now a state Senator is about to remove to Nashville. Preparatory thereto a political move is deemed necessary.

To night is selected for a democratic meeting.[3] The avowd object is the selection of delegates to the State Convention. A. Ewing is president of the meeting of to night. Senators Nicholson and Turney, Citizen Hollingsworth and others are to be the speakers. The design is to give the voice of this County directly for Governor Cass in the first instance for the presidency, subject however to the will of a majority. It is said that members from East Tennessee come readily into this measure and desire a proceeding here as a mould for their own at home. I need not waste my time nor yours in writing out at length the design of some who are engaged in this measure nor its inevitable tendency so far as it goes.

I can not be at the meeting to night. Genl. Armstrong and I have been in consultation and we will send a good many rank and file opposed to the proceedings but no leader. I start to Arkansas in a day or two with the design of being absent several months. I do not think I should help the cause of Democracy by making an effort at making a division or even at defeating their attempt and then leaving my views and opinions to the mercy of others unless there was some one on the spot able to understand and to sustain them. I have heretofore attempted to do some service in the cause of Democracy. I believe it to be the cause of our Country. I think I labored without the desire of reward and suffered without murmuring. At present I do not see any thing in my power that even promises to be useful. Indeed matters have come into a situation which I have long apprehended and have ineffectually struggled against. We have adopted the system of some of our older States of attempting to compromise. We have forgotten that their cement is money and that candidates pay for their districts and that many of the comon soldiers like other surfs fight only for pay. Here we have no money and most of our people are honest natives and are only induced by what they believe to be the Countrys good. What then is party organization in Tennessee but organized anarchy, an army commanded by Corporals and Seargeants but without a captain or Col much less a Genl. So long as the great mass of the people remain at home and are addressed in a mass none but the Strong and experienced and respected voices can reach them and they necessarily act in general concert. But when every County nay every cross road and every creek has its organization and its little local leaders and each acts upon local feeling, sensation, impression or the impulse of a casual orator the smartest or the Stupidest and most impudent of the neighbourhood, what is to be expected but the confusion of Babel and its consequent rout and dispersion.

I hardly know why I write you all this. It's dictated under a feeling of despondency to which my nature is almost a stranger but which the circumstances of the time have impressed upon me this feeling. I claim the privilege of writing for your own eye and I sincerely wish that it may be under this feeling alone that I add what is my firm conviction that if the measure to be proposed here to night should prevail through the state that in despite of the past you will find yourself occupying precisely that position in the democratic party which Mr. Bell holds amongst the Whigs, changing only Foster for Nicholson.

DAVID CRAIGHEAD

ALS. DLC–JKP. Addressed to Columbia.
1. Month and day identified through content analysis.
2. A. O. P. Nicholson.
3. The Davidson County Democratic Convention met on November 6, 1843, to nominate delegates to the Democratic State Convention, scheduled to convene on November 23, 1843. Chaired by James Overton, a Nashville physician, the meeting resolved to support the principles of the Democratic party and determined to support the candidates for president and vice-president nominated by the National Convention, "regardless of all personal preferences or sectional considerations."

FROM W. S. PICKETT[1]

New Orleans, Louisiana. November 6, 1843
Picket acknowledges receipt of Polk's letter of October 19[2] advising him of advances drawn in the amounts of $500 and $1000 on a forthcoming cotton shipment.

ALI. DLC–JKP. Addressed to Coffeeville, Mississippi and forwarded to Columbia, Tennessee.
1. Pickett, who remained Polk's cotton factor for several years, is not identified further.
2. Letter not found.

FROM CAVE JOHNSON

Dear Sir,   Clarksville 10th Nov. 1843
I recd your letter[1] a few days after it was written but delayed replying until the last moment, hoping to receive a reply from the North &

to have communicated it to you; but none such have arrived. I have been to Nashville but could spend but little time among the members as I am again sued as security in the Supreme Court for another 1000, which required much examination as it was very old case. P. B. Anderson is firm agt. Van Buren—for *Cass & you* (secretly for Calhoun). A few others I think have feelings for Cass as an available but not the hostility to Van, that is expressed by Anderson. Laughlin thought all right except Anderson. I doubt the policy of our convention being mute. An open & manly course is the best. Every indication at present is favorable to you so far as I can see. I shall spare no pains when I get to headquarters in ascertaining & informing you every thing of interest. I fear Kendall will oppose Blair for the public printing, & if so, it will give us much trouble if nothing worse. I wrote A. K.[2] strongly urging him to permit no such thing & it might be well, to intimate such a thing to Genl. Jackson, that he might if it can be properly done interpose and prevent if possible such collision. We are (our party) in a bad condition & I shall not be much surprised if we are as much distracted as the Whigs were in 1841.

Will you think at the State Convention of the propriety & the mode of getting the Whig districts supplied with documents? Ought not the county committees to supply funds & names to some of us? I can work hard but have no means to spare & I expect it is so with most of the democratic members. The county committees should get contributions. I was surprised to learn than Genl. Caruthers had said seriously to several of our friends that *he had written letters to his friends* urging them to elect me Speaker. I cant immagine what he means.

We are packed up & ready for the first boat going to Louisville. I shall expect to hear from you often during the winter.

C. Johnson

ALS. DLC–JKP. Addressed to Columbia. Polk's AE on the cover states that he answered this letter on November 17, 1843; Polk's reply has not been found.
1. Letter not found.
2. Reference is to Amos Kendall.

FROM SAMUEL H. LAUGHLIN

My dear Sir,   Nashville, Nov. 17, 1843
Your brother[1] has informed me to-day, that you are at home. I am so situated as to render it impossible for me to write at length, and as I hope you will come up here forthwith, it is, perhaps, not important for me to say much. I will say, that I think it all important that you should be here by Sunday evening, even if you should find it proper to go away before Wednesday.

We have had much trouble here in our own household, and possibly may have more. Pearce Anderson in the Assembly, and Andrew Ewing and a few others out of it, seem to be pursuing a course that lends to the ruin of our party. Attempts have been made to nominate Col. Cass in the democratic Association[2] here, but it has been defeated. Sam Turney, with whom Ewing seems to have become very intimate, aided in that attempt, and even Gardner was misled. Before the Convention sits, this must be put entirely down. In tomorrow's Union, will be an article on State Conventions, referring for example to the course pursued lately in Connecticut, which I wrote, hoping that it may have a tendency to produce some *sameness* and *uniformity* in the thinking of our delegates.[3] Hogan, however, is sick, and has been sick, and I have had to write every political editorial for the last fortnight. It is not known, nor do I wish it, for I have not time to write creditable articles.

I have just received a letter from A. A. Kincannon which I will show you, also a letter from Gov. Yell. In both Arkansas and Mississippi, *all's well*. But I fear the news from New York will grow worse instead of better. The damned Subteranean democrats, Calhounites and Tylerites, have divided our party and will ruin us I am affraid. All is not lost, however, which is in danger. Come up.

S. H. LAUGHLIN

ALS. DLC–JKP. Addressed to Columbia and marked "Private."

1. William H. Polk.

2. Formally organized in October 1843, the Young Men's Democratic Association of Nashville regularly met in a hall over Billings Bookstore on Union Street. Andrew Ewing served as president, and Timothy Kezer, as vice president. The Democratic State Convention, which met later in November, called for the creation of a Young Men's Association in each county of the state.

3. In an unsigned article in the *Nashville Union* of November 18, 1843, Laughlin proclaimed that the resolutions passed by the Connecticut Democratic State Convention on October 25, 1843, "embodied many of the cardinal principles and tenets of democracy." Connecticut Democrats had declared that the Democracy of each state maintained exclusive control over the process by which it would select delegates to the National Convention; however, in most instances the selection process would mirror that by which a state's presidential electors were chosen. Allocation of delegates would be the same as for that of electors in the Electoral College; state delegations would be allowed to adopt the unit rule in convention voting.

TO SAMUEL H. LAUGHLIN

My Dear Sir: Columbia Nov. 17th 1843

My brother has probably informed you that I reached home two days ago from Mississippi. I have heard nothing from Nashville except a short note[1] from him to day, in which he strongly urges me to be at Nashville, at furthest on Monday. He says it is the opinion of my friends that I should be there. *Coe* urged it, on my way up. My wife wishes to visit her friends in Rutherford & I have concluded to accompany her on Monday. We will be at the *Inn*[2] on Monday night, when I will determine whether to go on or remain until after the convention meets.[3] I hope you have the papers in a state of preperation. You must not fail to have them done by monday night, when we can examine them & compare opinions. The *Preamble, Resolutions & address* to the people should be carefully drawn. Our friend *Humphreys* is a safe counsellor & an able man, but is slow to be roused to action, and if you rely on him, the papers I fear will not be ready until the last hour. If the *whole writing* has not been *finished*, I hope you will devote yourself to it & have them done without fail by monday night. Leading friends as they come in from different Counties should have an opportunity to see & understand them before the Convention is in actual session.

JAMES K. POLK

ALS. MHi. Addressed to Nashville and marked *"confidential."*

1. On November 16, 1843, William H. Polk wrote Polk, "There are a fiew members . . . who are using every exertion to stir the Cass question, and your presence here would tend to check them." ALS. DLC–JKP. See also Samuel H. Laughlin to Polk, November 17, 1843.

2. The Nashville Inn.

3. The Democratic State Convention was scheduled to convene in Nashville on November 23, 1843.

TO WILLIAM C. TATE

Dear Sir: Columbia Tennessee Nov. 18th 1843

On my return home three days ago, after an absence of near a month, I received your letter of the 14th ultimo.[1] Before I left home on a visit of business to the State of Mississippi, where I have been, I made the arrangement with *Lucius J. Polk* to bring *Marshall* out with him in the event his mother and yourself yielded your assent.[2] I was not aware at the time, nor until I was informed of it in your letter, of his delicate state of health, or of the affliction to which you mention he is subject.[3] Upon receiving the information which you give me, I concur with you in opinion, that the route which I had proposed for him to travel might prove to be too severe for him to bear. I am much gratified to learn that his mother yields her consent for him to come as soon as a suitable and proper opportunity shall offer. The fall-season is now far advanced, and winter is almost at hand, or I would send a Buggy for him immediately as you suggest. I have concluded however that it will probably be most prudent to postpone it until next spring—when if no other suitable and safe opportunity offers, I will get my brother *William*[4] or some other safe and prudent man to go in, with a Buggy for him. I take great interest in him and his mother may be assured, that I will take all possible care of him, and adopt all possible means to enable him to outgrow his affliction. You advise me to procure a truss for him. I will certainly do so. I have known them used successfully with boys similarly affected in one or two instances, and it strikes me the earlier they are used the better. I anticipate great pleasure in having him with me and in superintending his education. I received one letter from him[5] & answered it[6] when on the eve of starting to Mississippi. Tell him, he must write to me again. Be pleased to present the kind regards of Mrs. Polk and myself to sister *Laura*,[7] and be assured that I am . . . .

JAMES K. POLK

ALS, draft. DLC–JKP. Addressed to Morganton, North Carolina.

1. On October 14, 1843, William C. Tate wrote Polk that "Mrs. Tate has given her consent for you to have Marshal." ALS. DLC–JKP.

2. See Polk to Sarah C. Polk, October 26, 1843.

3. In his letter of October 14, Tate wrote that Marshall had "laboured under *congenital hernia* all his life."

4. William H. Polk.

5. Marshall T. Polk, Jr., wrote to his uncle on September 29, 1843, expressing his wish to move to Tennessee. ALS. DLC–JKP.

6. Letter not found.

7. Tate's wife, Laura T. Wilson Polk Tate, was the widow of Polk's deceased brother, Marshall T. Polk.

FROM LUCIEN B. CHASE

Dear Sir   Clarksville Tennessee Nov 28 1843

I was deprived of the pleasure of being present at the state convention at Nashville. I had anticipated much pleasure, previous to the meeting of the convention in being present at an assemblage of warm, zealous, and talented Democrats from different portions of our state, but having made my arrangements to go to Nashville by water no boat came in time and my designs were thwarted. I was truly happy to learn that the meeting passed with perfect harmony, and that there was a degree of enthusiasm among the members which argues well for the success of our cause. It is manifestly the design of the Federal party to carry the election if possible in the same way they did in 1840. They are forming clay clubs, and are already taking steps to raise excitement. It might be advisable for our friends to pause, and reflect upon the proper course for us to pursue in the ensuing canvass. That no *reasonable* man, requires *excitement* to inducement him to discharge his duty does not admit of argument, but then that portion of our citizens who generally *decide* a political contest *are* evidently influenced by *enthusiasm.* And it may be a question how far it would be reprehensible to take the same course as that adopted by our opponents, to bring to our support men who cannot or will not be controlled by the dictates of reason. One thing is very certain that if our principles are established through their aid, no injury can result to *them.* Your experience in this matter will be of infinite advantage to us in deciding. I do not mean to be understood as asserting that we should reenact the disreputable scenes of 1840. For I believe that those scenes would bring contempt upon *any* party; but you are well aware that to produce *energetick action* there must be some *feeling,* that a powerful impulse may be communicated from one bosom to another. Now there ought to be an understanding among the democracy in what manner the canvass is to be conducted so that we can act in concert. I thought to day I would obtain an indication of the state of the publick mind, and as our circuit court is in session, I visited some dozen of our Democratick farmers from different part of our county[1] to meet me at my office. They came. I addressed them a few minutes and proposed that a committee of four or five in each civil district should be appointed to meet here on the 23 of next month to report the propriety of establishing *democratick clubs* in each civil district. The proposition took *admirably.* I have never witnessed more enthusiasm than was manifested by so small and assemblage. If we can once get the *people in motion* I entertain the most confident expectations of carrying the state.

I Start next Saturday for the Humphys[2] Court and in doing so I shall pass through Dickson County, and if possible I mean to start the ball in those counties before I return.

I would be much pleased to learn your views with regard to the course which ought to be pursued in the approaching canvass.

L. B. CHASE

ALS. DLC–JKP. Addressed to Columbia. Polk's AE on the cover states that he answered this letter on December 2, 1843; Polk's reply has not been found.

1. Montgomery County.
2. Humphreys County Court.

FROM CAVE JOHNSON

Washington City. November 28, 1843

Johnson acknowledges receipt of Polk's letter[1] and reports that Van Buren has written recently of his great "confidence in & friendship for" Polk.[2] Johnson also states that Van Buren expressed the view that in the August elections Tennessee Democrats "did not take sufficiently strong grounds, in opposition to the Banks."

ALS. DLC–JKP. Addressed to Columbia.
1. Letter not found.
2. Quotations here and below are from Johnson's account of Martin Van Buren's letter.

TO MARTIN VAN BUREN

My Dear Sir: Columbia Tennessee Novr. 30th 1843

Our State convention which convened on the 23rd Instant, as you will see from the published proceedings made no nomination for the Presidency, but appointed Delegates to represent the State, in the Democratic National Convention at Baltimore in May next. Shortly after our election in August, indications were given of an intention on the part of a few discontented members of our party, chiefly in the Eastern Division of the State to favour the nomination of *Genl. Cass*. Some imprudent and mischievous articles with that view appeared in the Knoxville Argus. Prompt measures were taken to check this movement & there was no reason to doubt, but that they had been successful. A few days before the meeting of the Convention, & during my absence to the State of Mississippi, an apparently concerted movement was made, by the friends of *Genl. Cass* to press his nomination upon the ground as they alledged, not of hostility to you, but of his (Genl. C's) superior availability. They brought forward their proposition to nominate him, at a meeting of *"The Democratic Association"* at Nashville, and anouncd their determina[tion][1] to press his nomination before the State Convention. This was promptly and successfully opposed by leading members of the Legislature and others, who having heard of the intended movement, attended the meeting of the *"Association."* The discussions however which took place, led unfortunately to some excitement and some division in our ranks, and though when the Convention met, our friends had no doubt of being able to carry your nomination, if it had been moved, yet thought it prudent under the circumstances, to abstain from the attempt, especially as the friends of *Genl. Cass*, agreed not to present him, if you were not brought forward, and expressed their entire willingness to support the nominee of the Baltimore Convention. It being ascertained, if any attempt was made to nominate, that there would be some division and probably an excited discussion, which it was feared would have a tendency to weaken us in the State, our friends of the Convention came to the conclusion that it was the more prudent course to appoint our Delegates to Baltimore, and leave them uninstructed. I was not present at the Convention but learn that these were the motives and reasons for the course which was adopted. Of the Delegates appointed, *ten certainly*, and I think *twelve* out of the *thirteen* will support your nomination. The two Delegates from the State at large[2] representing the Senatorial votes were appointed by the Convention, and will support your nomination. The seperate Delegations in attendance from each of the eleven Congressional Districts appointed one Delegate. *Genl. Anderson* who was a member of the U.S. Senate at the close of your administration, was without proper consideration on the part of the Delegates, chosen from the Knoxville District, and is favourable to the nomination of *Mr Calhoun*. Of the opinions of two other of the District Delegates, I am not certainly advised but think they will act with the body of the Delegation. *Anderson* too I think may possibly be unwilling to seperate from them. Your friend *Andrew J. Donaldson* should have been the *Delegate* instead of the *Alternate* from the Nashville District. The Delegate chosen[3] however is a true man, and I understand will probably decline going on, and request *Donaldson* to represent the District. Supposing it might not be uninteresting to you, I give you these particulars as I understand them. I have visited *Genl. Jackson* since the Convention adjourned, and though in common with the body of our Democratic friends, he would have preferred a nomination, he yet appreciates properly the motives of the Convention, and is satisfied that the course of our Delegates at Baltimore will be the one I have stated to you.

The course of our Whig Legislature[4] has added nothing to the strength of their party, but on the contrary, has greatly weakened them; and I repeat the opinion expressed in a former letter,[5] that now that we are unembarrassed by local causes and questions of State policy, we can and will carry the State in 1844. Nothing can prevent it, but the want of proper discretion and harmony in the action of the Baltimore Convention.

JAMES K. POLK

ALS. DLC–MVB. Addressed to Kinderhook, New York, and marked *"confidential."*

1. Part of one word was omitted at the end of a line.

2. Levin H. Coe and John Blair were elected to represent the state at-large at the Baltimore Convention. Frederick P. Stanton and Robert B. Reynolds were chosen as their respective alternates.

3. Samuel R. Anderson of Sumner County was chosen to represent the Eighth District at the Baltimore Convention. Donelson was to be his alternate.

4. Reference is to the election of Spencer Jarnagin and Ephraim H. Foster to the U.S. Senate by the Tennessee General Assembly on October 17, 1843.

5. See Polk to Martin Van Buren, August 18, 1843.

FROM J. GEORGE HARRIS

My Dear Sir,   Nashville Dec. 3, 1843

I have concluded to make the northern trip of which we conversed when you were last at Nashville; and shall probably leave home in all next week. I am well satisfied—the more I reflect upon our conversation—that it is important, nay, indispensable. I shall write you often.

I am pretty well acquainted with those with whom I wish to have a *judicious* conference, but I have thought that some two or three open letters from you, say to Benton, Wright and Allen of the Senate might be of use as strengthening my position when assuming to speak for the Southwestern democracy. It will be only necessary to state the position that I occupy, and the degree of confidence generally expressed in my paper by the democracy of the Miss. Valley. If you write these letters please enclose them to me by the earliest mail, if convenient.

Our committee[1] are at work to-day in preparing the manuscript circular letters spoken of, and I think they will have good effect.

J. GEO. HARRIS

ALS. DLC–JKP. Addressed to Columbia. AE states incorrectly that this letter was answered on "Jany. 4, 1843"; Polk's reply, presumably written in 1844, has not been found.

1. Reference is to Polk's vice-presidential corresponding committee of 1843–44.

TO SAMUEL H. LAUGHLIN

My dear Sir: Shelbyville Decr. 4th 1843

I have great anxiety about the forth-coming address to the people of the State.[1] At this juncture of time it will attract attention throughout the Union, and if it is ably drawn and is such a paper as the talents of our friends can make it, it will go far to settle the Vice Presidential nomination. It will go forth under the sanction of imposing names, with *Gov. Carroll* at their head. It will be understood abroad to embody the sentiment of the Democracy of this State, deliberately sent forth by their chosen organ, a committee appointed by their Convention. This being the case it should command the assistance in its preparation of the whole party. I wrote to *Humphreys* on the subject before I left home. *Nicholson* who came out in the stage to Columbia on saturday, informed me, that a meeting of a part of the committee had been held at *Gen. Carroll's* a night or two before he left, & that he had been requested to prepare it. I desire very much that you should be consulted and give your aid in its preparation. In regard to the general character of the paper, I believe I explained to you my views. It will be unnecessary to re-iterate, at any length at least, the general tenets of our political faith, for these have been so often & in so many forms presented to our people that they have become familiar with them. A concise history of the origin & progress of the existing parties in the State, with the causes of our divisions, accompanied with a bold and strong expression of confidence in our strength, will do much to inspire confidence in our success. The main objects of the address should be to impress our friends abroad that we have fair prospects of success, and that we will succeed, if the action of the Democratic Convention at Baltimore shall be judicious & harmonious. The address of course will carry out the views of the Convention & express no preference for the Presidency, but make an appeal to our friends to avoid all angry or excited discussion as to men, and to give their hearty and zealous support to the nominee of the Convention. It would be indelicate in me to say, what the paper should be touching the Vice Presidency. That I can safely leave to my friends. To *you* however I will say, that by turning to the *Weekly Union* of February 1840, you will find an article written immediately after our Convention of that year, entitled as well as I remember, *"A Voice from the South West,"* [2] which may aid you in the preparation of this part of the Address. I will return home on tomorrow or the next day, and if you advise me at Columbia that you will have the paper in a state of forwardness, I could be at Nashville on saturday or monday next. If I come I will revise the paper except so far as it may relate to myself.

There is another matter that I have thought much about since I saw you. There must be an able, a true and efficient editor of the Union, during the next year. I fear that occasional contributors would not make a uniformly good paper. It would be much better if we had some one to give his whole attention to it. I learned when at Nashville that $1500 could be readily raised in advance. If it were compatable with your intrest & inclination for you to undertake it, until the contest of 1844 is over, it is the very best arrangement which could be me.[3] I merely mention this now, that you may think of it, by the time I come to Nashville, when something definite must be settled in regard to it.

                                                            JAMES K. POLK

ALS. DLC–JKP. Addressed to Nashville and marked "*Confidential.*" Published in *ETHSP*, XVIII, pp. 163–64.

1. The Democratic State Convention, which convened at Nashville on November 23, 1843, appointed a committee of thirteen, one from each district and two from the state at large to prepare a statement of their views and opinions on current issues and the forthcoming national election. See Samuel H. Laughlin to Polk, December 18, 19, and 21, 1843, and William H. Polk to Polk, December 31, 1843.

2. Article not identified further.

3. Polk probably meant to write "made."

FROM SAMUEL H. LAUGHLIN

My dear Sir,   Nashville, Dec. 7, 1843

I would have answered your last[1] yesterday, but I expected to have an opportunity of writing by Mr. Jonas Thomas to-day, but find now that he will not leave before tomorrow morning. Besides this, I wished for some time to reflect upon the new suggestion contained in your letter concerning the condition and prospects of the Union newspaper. You know that a friend of ours,[2] more or less, proposed to have a supervising eye over its editorship and conduct during the approaching campaign, provided he should be excused from the performance of another service. I had never thought of any arrangement, upon any contingency, which would devolve the responsibility on me of which you speak. I am not vain enough to believe for a moment, that there are not others who can do the service in question better than myself. You are aware, that it might be improper for me, having a regard to the future, to undertake any duty that would deprive me of my local rights of *inhabitancy* in my district[3] in 1845. If we fail in all our other undertakings, and for which I am willing to labor day and night in any position, high or low, for the next twelve months, I can still fall back upon my claims to an election to Congress, from which Mr. Cullom nor no one else can drive me, unless I am willing. If my field of labor should be assigned me here, until after the election next fall, might it not affect my claims at home? My constituents, and the whole Mountain District, are jealous of, and hate Nashville. Could I undertake such a duty—although in behalf of the democratic [party] of the whole state—to be performed here—requiring a temporary sojourn and residence here—without becoming in a sense, detrimental to my interest at home, a citizen of Nashville, and identified with Nashville interests? These are things, personal to myself, which deserve my serious consideration, and the advice of friends. If I ever think of undertaking the temporary employment, it must not only be with the assent, but upon the solicitation of our leading democratic friends in my own district, and with the district understanding that my absence from home is temporary, transient, a *quasi* official absence, on public duty, and in no sense a change of permanent domicil. Think of these things, and I will think. I would not give the subject the consideration of a moment if it were not for the anxious solicitude I feel in the coming contest. To succeed in that I would willingly encounter any responsibility or drudgery, and forego my profession for the time, by which, even in my own circuit, I can make at least $2500 between this time and next December—and with moderate toil, and but little responsibility.

If I find it possible, and my friends think proper to confide in me so far as to intrust a post of such responsibility to me, two things I would suggest. One is a *sine qua non.* I must and will have nothing to do, in any form or manner, with the business concerns of the establishment; and the next would be, that before my absence in the Spring for a few weeks at Baltimore, if I go there, and soon as our Assembly adjourns, that I should make a flying excursion to Jefferson City, Springfield, Indianapolis and Columbus, while the legislatures of Missouri, Illinois, Indiana and Ohio are in session—or at least to Missouri and Illinois—with letters to friends, from proper persons, to see what arrangements and understandings it may be practicable to form before the Baltimore Convention sits. To be willing to encounter such a trip, in snow and ice, I hope will evince my zeal if not my discretion. My will and wish is, to leave no proper expedient for strengthening the prospect of success untried. In the legislatures of Missouri, Illinois and Indiana, I have some few respectable acquaintances, who are all democrats as far as I know. To Mississippi and Louisiana I would willingly make the same trip if deemed of any use. In regard to all these matters, I wish to see you, and shall hope to see you by Saturday, as that is the day you speak of being here.

I could never get a word written and put in the Union even in favor of Cave Johnson in time to let others see how he is esteemed at home, before the organization of Congress, until I wrote myself, and pressed in a short article the other day[4]—too late, however, for any purpose, but to show our friends at home and abroad what we think and wish about him.

I have written to Judge Catron, as per promise, to Frankfort, how our matters are. I have written again and again to Brown, Johnson and Cullom—confidentially to Johnson & Brown alone—how all our matters stand. I wrote to Yell, C. C. Clay, A. A. Kincannon &c. before you left here, and under an injunction of confidence; I have written, as solely from myself, to Moses Dawson.

I do not know how Mr. Nicholson *relishes* the editorial, as it appeared in the Union, speaking C. Johnsons claims to be Governor, or to have a seat in the Senate. I have written what I wish to form a portion of the Democratic Address.[5]

S. H. LAUGHLIN

P.S. I have made a speech on our tax bills, and proposition to withdraw $62000 of the annual School appropriation to pay interest &c. and have opposed the withdrawal.[6] Nicholson made a speech for it.[7] I am writing mine out for the press.[8]

ALS. DLC–JKP. Addressed to Columbia and marked "Private."

1. See Polk to Samuel H. Laughlin, December 4, 1843.

2. A. O. P. Nicholson.

3. Tennessee's Fourth Congressional District. Laughlin was from McMinnville, Warren County.

4. On December 5, 1843, the *Nashville Union* carried Laughlin's editorial on Johnson and the House Speakership; Laughlin concluded, "we shall be truly sorry when he retires from his present position unless it be to take a seat in the higher branch of the national Legislature, or to become the Governor of this, his native State."

5. See Polk to Laughlin, December 4, 1843.

6. Debate on a bill allocating the amount of profits of the Bank of Tennessee to be distributed to common schools and authorizing the county courts to assess a tax at their discretion for the support of common schools began in the Tennessee Senate on December 6, 1843.

7. An account of A. O. P. Nicholson's speech appeared in the *Nashville Union* of December 16, 1843.

8. Laughlin wrote his postscript in the left margin of his third page.

FROM AARON V. BROWN

Dear Sir   Washington Decr. 9th, 1843

You will have seen the Presidents message—all that he says about Texas.[1] *But this is not all.* I have reason to suppose it will soon be followed up with some definite and precise proposition. Some think a Treaty. The impression here among the whigs is, that this is all that he has to say on the subject & that he has brought it up only as a fire brand between the north & the South, hoping he may make profit to himself in the midst of the conflagration. In this view the subject may die away for a while both parties turning from it under the opinion that there are questions enough already to distract and divide them. This may be well enough for a time, but in the mean while the press (Whig & Democrat) in the S. & West must be kept in right position, neither committing themselves in the slightest degree against annexation. A special messenger is constantly expected with *authority* instantly to close a treaty. The convocation of the Texan Congress[2] may delay him a little.

Our organization was speedily & harmoniously made. How should our caucus nominations be made? We answerd by a majority of all the Democrats elect (not present). The Calhoun men add "by 2/3 of the Democrats present." Now the difference was so small we yielded; thereupon the nominations were all cheerfully acquiesced in & confirmed by the house. The relative strength is estimated as follows: Calhoun 24 or 25, Buchanan 11 or 12, Johnson 3 or 4, Cass none—not one I believe unless the Michigan men be counted for him. All the rest for Van Buren. As to the Vice the impression is gaining ground, that Colo. J.[3] has hung on so obstinately for the first office that he is not now entitled to the second if he should become willing to fall back on it. I have heard it confidently asserted that Benton & the Ohio men were all against him *and would be for you against him or any body.* I think it very probably so, & shall do every thing of course to encourage such a state of feeling.

Our good & sincere friend Langtry[4] is here for the post office. I could refuse him personally as a man but I fear the popular demonstrations are too strong in favor of Mr. Vorhies.[5] On this account I am endeavoring to get for him one of the $1500 clerkships of the house. It would suit him well if his business at home would allow him to accept of it, which is a little doubtful. If I can get it for him (being here) perhaps Vorhies might prefer exchanging positions presently, so as to enable L to attend better to his shattered affairs at home. This of course is only a suggestion for the convenience of both, as I would like to serve both. If this arrangement *can* be made it will be known Monday or Tuesday next.

The committees have not been announced yet & no one knows "the cast of characters in the play." I am indifferent about it, as I have but few political aspirations. Who on the Ways & means? I do not know. Wilkins wont do on act of the Tariff. I should as soon expect Rhett with Dromgoole his *alternate* as anybody else. Beardsley[6] as he is from *N. York* ought not to expect it.

You see I have missed my paging but you can make it out.[7] My messenger is waiting.

A V BROWN

ALS. DLC–JKP. Addressed to Columbia and marked "*Confidential.*" Polk's AE on the cover states that this letter was answered on December 20, 1843; Polk's reply has not been found.

1. President John Tyler delivered his message to Congress on December 5, 1843.

2. The Eighth Congress of Texas convened in the early part of December 1843.

3. Richard M. Johnson.

4. A Columbia merchant and director of the Bank of Tennessee's branch at Columbia, Hillary Langtry assumed postmastership of Columbia on January 9, 1844, and served in that post until June 1845.

5. One of the early settlers in Maury County, William Voorhies was a saddler by trade. His son, William, Jr., formed a law partnership with William H. Polk in 1844.

6. A lawyer and judge from Utica, New York, Samuel Beardsley won election to four terms in the U.S. House, 1831–36 and 1843–44.

7. Brown probably intended to write pages one and two on the front and back of one sheet and page three and cover on the front and back of a second sheet. He mispaged the letter by writing pages two and three on his second sheet.

FROM CAVE JOHNSON

Dear Sir,   Washington Dec 9th 1843

I should have replied to your letter[1] earlier but thought I had best delay until the organization of the House was completed. You will see by the papers what we have done—made a clean sweep except the P.M.[2] & he is suspended only a little while upon the prayers & tears of Holms.[3] We thought none should be permitted to remain in the Capitol who submitted to the plundering of the public by the whig Executive Committee in 1840. You see we acted with great unanimnity in all our movements so far as the public can see but we in truth had a good deal of excitement & much feeling. When I reached the city ten days before the meeting, I found Bryant (of the Post, the poet) under the patronage of Leonard,[4] backed by the Admn., a candidate for printer, & Wilkins arrived with me a candidate for Speaker. Very soon Shadrack Penn made his appearance, then Isaac Hill & Joel B. Sutherland & Gov. Porters Secretary.[5] Kendall also a candidate for printer. We soon had rumors of combinations between the Calhoun men, Buckhanan, Johnson & Cass men, first to elect Wilkins Speaker, then turn out the Globe & elect Kendall & then elect Sturges[6] of Georgia Clerk &c. We thought for a while the Globe in danger, which was of most importance. Those of us here went to work. Near two hundred members were in the City on Saturday night about 120 or 30

Democrats. The Calhoun men determined on Saturday morning not to go into caucus that evening. Genl Saunders arrived & changed their determination by promising to have a rule adopted that ⅔ should be necessary to a nomination. They came in, urged the rule, we adopted it & nominated Jones on the 1st ballot. Still the struggle for printer was to come on under the same rule. Kendall could get some democrats & the supposed combination would bring in others and defeat all nominations & of course the whigs would defeat Blair. Kendall placed his paper in the hands of every member in which he said after many professions of democracy, his fidelity &c "we shall find it necessary to form business & political connexions with another or others and having no committal to embarrass us, we shall be disposed as far as consistent with our duty to the public and ourself to conform to the wishes of those who support us." [7] I regarded it as an effort to bring in Penn, who dappled to control the Johnson & Cass men, & Bryant & his friends & Hill & his if he had any, by a division of the profits but then the use of the words "political connexions" looked like a bait for the whigs. I was apprehensive & I have but little doubt others so calculated that the ⅔ rule would defeat any nomination & of course it would be settled in the House by the whigs. We met in caucus, such apprehensions on my mind & not a little excited, I made a speech, shewing the consequences which I thought would result to our party from a defeat of the Globe & then expressed *"my regret"* at the appearance of such an article in the Expositor & was about commenting on severely when its reading was called for. It was read, & from the impression it seemed to make on every mind I made no comment further than a strong expression of *my regret*. Well we voted & ⅔ declared for the Globe. Since I have recd a long letter from Kendall, very kind & conciliatory hoping that I may say something to remove the suspicion cast on his "political integrity" as he calls it, which my course was calculated to make. I shall of course do no such thing because I am not yet satisfied that my impressions were erroneous. All soon became quiet & every thing since moves on harmoniously *because we have a dead majority of the whole House*—all odds & ends & whigs to boot. The Calhoun men wanted a chance to come in decently. Some of them declared that Calhoun had no chance & they would support the nominees & it is generally believed that Calhoun will be with drawn before May. We have now nothing to fear but the whigs. We have been occupied all day in the House & late at night in caucus, so that I have not even seen Silas Wright, and have had no conversation as yet with him or any others of our leaders as to the Vice presidency. Some of the Missouri members say Missouri will be certainly for you. McNair[8] of the Central Committee of Ky says the vote of Ky will be given you (he is a candidate for PM & may expect favors). Allen of Ohio & Weller intimated that they thought Ohio would go for you. In the course of a week or so, I shall fall in as if by accident with the leaders & bring up the subject & try what I can learn. I have recd no letter from Silas Wright. I have recd letters from Cheatham & Laughlin explaining the cause of no presidential nomination in such a way, that I think will be satisfactory to our Northern [friends]. It has a bad aspect on paper. It seems to say, that we hold ourselves in readiness to take part with the man who will take our Vice-president, and Ten. in such a minority cannot *excite fear*, and a nomination of both, if it could have been unanimous would have answered our purposes better (as I think). I will shew the letters to Wright & others. I think I informed you that the articles in the Enquirer[9] for Genl Cass was the production of Rives. Now it is said Rush[10] is the author.

We shall leave no clerk in the House except French, Gould & old man Frost.[11] I suppose the Senate will make Clarke their Secretary in the place of Dickins, if Capt Tyler does not make him Auditor of the post office in the place of Whitlesey.[12] Col Gardner wants a clerkship in the House. We have set our heads together, to claim a Clerkship for Tennessee & intend to give it to Langtry who visited me this evening. *I think we shall succeed.* I have not visited the Capt.[13] yet. My wife has not been out of her room until to day & perhaps tomorrow, if she is well enough we shall go. Almost every body is now democrats. Would you believe it? Even Harriman![14] Wanted me to recommend him for clerkship to the House, promising to write letters to the Union, *doing justice to we democrats* &c &c. I of course refused to have any thing to do with him. Genl Anderson & Clements are here & Berry Gillespie.[15] The latter I understand is very much out with me because I interposed last session & prevented a resolution of the House directing the awards of Eaton & Hubly[16] to be paid out of the Treasury, without being reviewed by the department or submitted to Congress. Jones acquits himself well. If we carry out the suggestions of our State Convention we cannot fail of success.[17] The Union should commence its weekly paper in some cheap form, so as to be ready in May. We shall do our business here & I hope adjourn in May.

C. JOHNSON

ALS. DLC–JKP. Addressed to Columbia and marked *"Private."* Polk's AE on the cover states that he answered this letter on December 19, 1843; Polk's reply has not been found.

1. Letter not found.
2. Postmaster of the House of Representatives.
3. Isaac E. Holmes.
4. William Cullen Bryant, New York *Evening Post*, and Moses G. Leonard. A

native of Stafford, Connecticut, Leonard moved to New York City and served as city alderman and judge, 1840–42, before winning election as a Democrat to one term in the U.S. House, 1843–45.

5. Shadrack Penn, Jr., Joel B. Sutherland, David R. Porter, and probably Anson V. Parsons. Penn was editor of the *Louisville Public Advertiser*, a partisan Democratic newspaper. A physician and lawyer in Philadelphia, Sutherland won election as a Democrat to five terms in the U.S. House, 1827–37. In 1836 he ran for reelection as a Whig and lost. Parsons served as secretary of the Commonwealth of Pennsylvania during Porter's second administration, 1842–45.

6. Possibly Joseph Sturgis, a lawyer and resident of Columbus, Georgia, who had served on the bench of the Superior Court of the Chattahoochee Circuit since December 1837.

7. Quotation in *Kendall's Expositor*, a bi-weekly journal published from 1841 until 1845, is not identified further.

8. D. R. McNair was an unsuccessful candidate for postmaster of the House of Representatives, a position won by John M. Johnson on January 5, 1844. In the late 1850's the U.S. Senate elected McNair its sergeant-at-arms and doorkeeper, a position he held until July 1861.

9. On October 30, 1843, the Washington *Globe* carried a reprint of a letter addressed to the editors of the *Richmond Enquirer*. The anonymous letter lauded Cass' abilities and proclaimed him highly qualified for the presidency.

10. A lawyer, diplomat, and writer, Richard Rush held several posts in the U.S. government during his long public career. He served as James Madison's attorney general, 1814–17; as acting secretary of state, 1817; as minister to Great Britain, 1817–25; as secretary of the Treasury, 1825–29; and as minister to France, 1847–49. An unsuccessful vice-presidential candidate on the John Q. Adams ticket in 1828, Rush moved into the Democratic ranks during the fight over rechartering the Second Bank of the United States. As the government's agent in England, 1836–38, to receive the bequest of James Smithson, Rush played a key role in the ultimate establishment of the Smithsonian Institute.

11. Benjamin B. French, Daniel Gold, and John T. Frost. A Democrat from New Hampshire, French served as clerk of the House of Representatives for several years prior to becoming treasurer of the national Democratic committee in 1848. Gold and Frost are not identified further.

12. Asbury Dickens, John Tyler, and Elisha Whittlesey. Dickens served as chief clerk of the Treasury Department and of the State Department before his tenure as secretary of the Senate, 1836–61. An Ohio lawyer and one of the founders of the Whig party, Whittlesey enjoyed a long career in public service: military aide to William H. Harrison during the War of 1812; member of the Ohio House, 1820–21; U.S. congressman, 1823–38; sixth auditor of the Treasury, 1841–43; and first comptroller of the Treasury, 1849–57 and 1861–63. On December 19, 1843, Matthew St. Clair Clarke replaced Whittlesey as sixth auditor of the Treasury.

13. John Tyler.

14. Not identified further.

15. A lawyer from Carroll County, Barry Gillespie sat two terms in the Tennessee House, 1827–31, representing Carroll, Dyer, Gibson, and Obion counties.
16. Not identified further.
17. See Polk to Edmund Burke, October 8, 1843.

FROM CAVE JOHNSON

Dear Sir,   Washington Dec 11th 1843

I gave you a slight sketch of our difficulties here in the organization.[1] The turn, I supposed, which things would take, is likely to be realised. All the fragments of our party seem likely to unite upon Van Buren, make his nomination unanimous & each party seek the succession by distinguished services in his behalf. The game for the succession is I think commenced. The friends of Calhoun are feeling to see how Mr. C. would go down for the Vice-presidency!! I heard S. W. Jr.[2] say to day, that would be *worse* than the old candidate.[3] Mr. C. & friends think he should be made the Vice or that he should return to the Senate in the spring. His wishes I presume are unknown & will depend upon what he thinks will most advance his interests for the succession. Either position will be unfavorable for us in the next election. In the former, I fear many of the old & true democrats will halt or loose their zeal upon his acct. & we shall have all his sins as well as those of Van[4] to answer for. In the latter we shall have a triangular war between him and B—ton & B—nan[5] & what influence that may have we cannot so readily guess. I was surprised to learn since that the pertinacity of the different branches of our party for Clerk, grew out of the supposed *preference* that the Van Buren men had, for the Bu—an or Ca—oun[6] interest or the B—ton interest. McNulty of Ohio was regarded for the latter. Sturges for C—oun and Burghler[7] for B—an. Most of us I am sure thought of no such thing, yet so deep an interest did one of the leaders feel, that he was accidently seen during the session of the caucus slipping about amidst the columns in the basement story, a very cold night wrapped in his cloak, waiting for the news no doubt of each voting. Mr Bu—an, his forces numbered 11. Sturges run well, on acct. of a proposition I made to divide out the petty offices among the friends of the other candidates. McNulty however finally prevailed, which I learn afforded some comfort to Mr. Bu—an that no preference had been shewn to the friend of C—oun over his. We get on most harmoniously & I think likely to continue so. We have sat every day almost until sun down. We will have a working House & we are trying to agree upon the 2nd monday in May for the Convention and adjournment. White is making a Jack of himself in making questions of order upon Jones. We sustain Jones admirably and he acquits himself well. The Senate have elected their old officers today.[8]

We are pressing Langtrys claim[9] with great earnestness and hope for success.

C. JOHNSON

ALS. DLC–JKP. Addressed to Columbia and marked *"Private."* Polk's AE on the cover states that he answered this letter on December 21, 1843; Polk's reply has not been found. Published in *THQ* XII, pp. 155–56.

1. Reference is to the organization of the U.S. House. See Cave Johnson to Polk, December 9, 1843.
2. Silas Wright, Jr.
3. Richard M. Johnson.
4. Martin Van Buren.
5. Thomas H. Benton and James Buchanan.
6. James Buchanan and John C. Calhoun.
7. Burghler is not identified further.
8. The U.S. Senate reelected Willie P. Mangum to be president pro tempore and Asbury Dickens to be secretary. Prior to his service as a Whig in the U.S. Senate, 1831–36 and 1840–52, Mangum won election to the North Carolina House, sat on the state's Superior Court, and completed two terms in the U.S. House, 1823–27.
9. See A. V. Brown to Polk, December 9, 1843, and Cave Johnson to Polk, December 9, 1843.

FROM CAVE JOHNSON

Dear Sir,   Washington Dec 15th 1843

Not knowing whether you take the Richmond Enquirer, I enclose you a letter[1] from Washington—this last editorial cut from the two last papers. Several of his[2] friends stated explicitly in caucus that he had no chance for the nomination or election (Payne & Belser[3] of Alabama) from whence inferences were drawn that he would balk, & some of *his* friends I know not which, have been certainly urging his selection for the vice in the highest quarters here. What his wishes are cannot be yet told. I think the Senate. He will have too much pride for the other especially knowing that it will be resisted by the friends of B—ton & Buc—an[4] & perhaps by yours & RMJ's[5] also. So Soon as the first *office is settled* as *I* think it *now* is, the second office will be the subject of discussion. Old Dick,[6] certainly sd. in the north that he *went alone for the first* & it is equally as certain when he left, after witnessing the organization of the House, that he went home determined to try for the second.

I think both the B's are afraid to yield to your nomination lest you should be in the way in 1848 & I fear may be inclined to throw their weight for Col. K.[7] of whom there is no danger. I thought I had satisfied Col B—ton that such would not be the case. I have spoken strongly on that subject today in a quarter from which he will hear it. And I am not satisfied but that his eyes are turned to V—a.[8] where his brother-in-law is Gov. & Ritchie & Stephenson[9] as thick as pick-pockets, out of which something may be made. This is a conjecture of my own without much data. I trust I shall know more before long.

I explained in proper quarters to day the cause of no nomination in Tenn. which not only gave satisfaction but was heartily approved of.

I think the feeling of the north is right & unless controlled by some political considerations not now known, the nomination will be given to you. I think the main point is to satisfy B—ton that you will not be in the way in 1848. For the reasons I mentioned I think K. the only dangerous competitor. I suspect, a bare suspicion, that Senator A.[10] of Ohio has been playing a little double with a view to our votes for the Clerkship.[11] I will find out.

I regretted to find our old friend Genl Thompson[12] here from Ohio, seeking employment—door keeper, deputy clerk or any thing. He has been broke up by securityships, old poor & needy. I regret we could give him nothing. I fear we have been doing too much in the way of removals for our popularity or the good of the service. I remonstrated as to the inferior offices but did no good. I think the Globe[13] is heartily for you.

C JOHNSON

ALS. DLC–JKP. Addressed to Columbia and marked *"private."* Polk's AE on the cover states that he wrote two letters in reply to Johnson, dated December 24 and 30, 1843; Polk's replies have not been found. Published in *THQ*, XII, pp. 156–57.

1. Enclosure not found.
2. Reference is to John C. Calhoun.
3. William W. Payne and James E. Belser. An Alabama planter and state legislator, Payne won election as a Democrat to three terms in the U.S. House, 1841–47. Belser, a Montgomery lawyer, served a single term as a Democrat in the U.S. House, 1843–45. He subsequently joined the Whig ranks and supported Zachary Taylor in 1848.
4. Thomas H. Benton and James Buchanan.
5. Richard M. Johnson.
6. Richard M. Johnson.
7. William R. King of Alabama.
8. Virginia.
9. James McDowell, Thomas Ritchie and Andrew Stevenson. McDowell, governor of Virginia, 1842–46, subsequently won election to the U.S. House where

he served from 1846 until 1851. Thomas H. Benton married McDowell's sister, Elizabeth McDowell.

10. William Allen.

11. See Cave Johnson to Polk, December 9 and 11, 1843.

12. Reference probably is to John Thomson, with whom Johnson and Polk served in the U.S. House from 1829 until 1837.

13. Washington *Globe.*

FROM SAMUEL H. LAUGHLIN

My dear Sir,   Nashville, Dec. 18, 1843

I have just received a few lines, written in haste, on the 5th inst. by Gov. Yell, in which he advises me, that on that day, the State Convention of Arkansas, being fully attended, had nominated Gen. Conway for Governor, Dr. Chapman for Congress,[1] and in performing their federal duties, had declared fully their preference for Mr. Van Buren and yourself for the Presidency and Vice Presidency.[2] Good.

I have just received letters of some length from Messrs. C. Johnson and A. V. Brown, in which they say *all* our matters at Washington wear a most favorable aspect. Old Shad Penn was present at Washington, interfering with matters—working for old Tecumseh[3]—causing matters to take such course as to produce an irreparable breach between Johnson and the Benton men of the North West. Brown says he is in correspondence with Gen. Howard[4] of Indiana; and that in all things they are on a strict look-out for any intrigue of Johnson or his friends with those who *must* be our friends to insure success.

Brown says expressly, that now, he knows of no man who looks to Gen. Cass as a first choice in the House[5]—and they both agree, that the warm friends of Mr. Van Buren double in number all the friends and factions and segments of opposition put together. Cave[6] says it is now certain that the war will be alone with the whigs, and that there will be no civil war among the different divisions of the democracy. This is all well.

I have seen Maj. Donelson to-day. I am sure that the old chief[7] is bestirring himself more in his correspondence with the proper parties than you are aware of.

To night the Address[8] is to be finally agreed on. After I returned all the papers to Nicholson after you left, and after he read the additions, he insisted I had made it too long—too much in detail—and when we met at Gen. Carroll's on Saturday night, he said nothing, but had, I am sure, filled the mouth of Ross and others with the like objections. B. Gordon came with him to the meeting; and he, though not of the Committee, made like objections, as did Stevenson,[9] who seems to have great faith in

Nicholson. After Nicholson's part of the paper was read, he went away—but Gordon, Ross and especially Stevenson (who has zeal but no knowledge) made the objections, praising the whole paper—all of them desiring the whole to be made up (that is the parts they proposed to omit) and published in another form. They professed to like it all, but said *all* your history and course in every thing was too extensively known to need re-iteration—but still they wanted it published, but that it would make the address so long it could not and would not be read by the people. Situated as I was, and not being of the committee, I said all I could and more I fear than delicacy rendered proper as I had written the paper, in favor of retaining the most of it. The whole was committed by order of the meeting to Nicholson, Carroll and Humphreys to revise, and fix up—with request that I should attend and assist. I made memorandum in a note to Carroll, of the special points of the paper which I wished to see retained in substance—and have left it to them. The main point, showing the *preference* of our Convention for Mr. V. Buren will be retained. I am most delicately situated, as in writing, I was a volunteer, and offered what I wrote at request and suggestion of Nicholson.

I have no idea what and whether any thing is [done][10] about the Union. Hogan, I think it possible, [could] be persuaded by Nicholson, that he will need no [assista]nce, or, that *he* will aid him. Hogan, I suppose, like others of his craft, thinks, if health permits,[11] that he is equal to anybody, and I fully believe Nicholson capable of misleading leading friends here, who do not know him, as to the assistance he will give, and by that means, he will slide imperceptably into the control of the paper. I suppose the Cass paper, which he and others lately contemplated, with Lewis[12] as the nominal editor, is now, of course, abandoned. As to the Union, I think it possible nothing will be done, and that it will go as above intimated—though, if it does, it will be against the wishes of Gen. Armstrong and your best friends here, who see below the surface of things. Possibly I may be mistaken, as to what may be the result, but I am not in a position to enquire—and shall let things take their course. I covet no position myself, and only hope and wish that whatever may be done, may be for the best.

S. H. LAUGHLIN

P.S. The Address will be out Thursday. Tomorrow's Union will contain result in Arkansas, and, as you perhaps know, will declare the majority of democracy in Tenn. are for Van buren &c.

ALS. DLC–JKP. Addressed to Columbia and marked "Private."

1. Elias N. Conway and Daniel J. Chapman. Born in Tennessee, Conway removed to Arkansas in 1833, served for many years as state auditor, 1835–49,

and became governor of Arkansas in 1852. The convention that nominated Conway and Chapman represented only sixteen of Arkansas' forty-six counties. As dissention grew over the nominations, Archibald Yell wrote Polk on January 10, 1844, "I am sorry to say that the Convention made Nominations for Gov & Congress that is not altogather acceptable to the party. Genl Conway has invited an other Convention as the last was not fully attended. He has taken the proper ground." ALS. DLC–JKP. A second convention was held in May 1844. Chapman was nominated for governor and Yell for Congress.

2. Archibald Yell also wrote Polk on December 5, 1843, informing him of the results of the Arkansas State Convention. ALS. DLC–JKP.

3. Richard M. Johnson.

4. Born in South Carolina, Tilghman A. Howard practiced law in Tennessee and won a single term in the Tennessee Senate, 1827–29. In 1830 he moved to Indiana and served as district attorney for Indiana from 1833 until 1837. He went to the U.S. House in 1839, but resigned his seat the following year to make what proved to be an unsuccessful bid for the Indiana governorship. Before his death in 1844 Howard served briefly as chargé d'affaires to the Republic of Texas.

5. Reference is to the Democratic caucus in the U.S. House.

6. Cave Johnson.

7. Andrew Jackson.

8. See Polk to Samuel H. Laughlin, December 4, 1843.

9. Vernon K. Stevenson, a Nashville merchant, became the first president of the Nashville and Chattanooga Railroad Company in 1848, a position that he held until the close of the Civil War.

10. A seal of the letter has obliterated words on three lines.

11. Thomas Hogan suffered from tuberculosis.

12. Micajah G. Lewis, a Columbia tavern keeper, had been Felix K. Zollicoffer's partner in publishing the *Columbia Observer* in 1834 and 1835.

FROM SAMUEL H. LAUGHLIN

Post Office—night
My dear Sir,   Nashville, Dec. 19, 1843

I am this moment from a Democratic meeting of Members, where the Address,[1] as prepared and agreed by the Com. last night,[2] has been read and finally ratified, and will be out in next Union.[3] It omits the important point of stating that majority of State Convention were for Mr. V. B. Carroll and others were cause of omission, after Nicholson had seemed to agree to it. Glenn[4] & others tried to save it, but Carroll's voice carried it. He and Nicholson, and one or two others, had been in private conference. Much of the matter I wrote is abridged, but still it would do very well if *that* had been in. My introduction &c. were retained. I wrote you yesterday evening, and have no news since. I think, I see, that things are *tending* as I stated to you.

Should our wishes succeed in the election, *as* we wish, those who, *in their hearts*, wish to see us defeated, will be foremost in their positions to claim credit and reward. N.[5] is evidently laying ground to obtain that kind of control which will place in[6] in position to creep and crawl into the candidacy for Governor. Let him get the extent of control he wishes to acquire here over the press and men, and over the soft part of the present and next Gen. Assembly, and he will have the fulcrum he wants to raise himself up to demand and expect what he pleases. Profound hypocracy is a most dangerous qualification. I am sick of witnessing its effects on many well meaning men; but cannot take any proper step to undeceive them. As to myself, I have neither good to hope or evil to fear. I am mad at the damned long-eared foolery of being cheated out of the most important point in the address.

Hogan told me on Saturday or Sunday that he would in to-day's paper—which he has not done—come out boldly with declaration, that the majority, a large majority of our democracy, are and were for Van Buren. I fear that the finger of the same influence is in this. I am, and have since Sunday, been so put out—in fact since the meeting at Carroll's on Saturday night, that I do not know what to say, think, or do. I am, come what may, as ever . . . .

S. H. LAUGHLIN

1. See Polk to Samuel H. Laughlin, December 4, 1843.
2. See Laughlin to Polk, December 18, 1843.
3. The Address of the Democratic State Convention has not been found. It was not published in the tri-weekly *Nashville Union* of December 21, 1843, as Laughlin had anticipated. On December 20, 1843, William H. Polk wrote that the Address would appear "in the Union of Saturday." The *Nashville Union* of December 23, 1843, has not been found. ALS. DLC–JKP.
4. Philip B. Glenn of Covington represented Tennessee's Tenth Congressional District on the committee.
5. A. O. P. Nicholson.
6. Laughlin probably meant to write the pronoun, "him."

ALS. DLC–JKP. Addressed to Columbia and marked "confidential."

TO ANDREW JACKSON DONELSON

My Dear Sir: Columbia Decr. 20th 1843

My letters received from *Brown* and *Johnson*[1] since I saw you, wear a more favourable aspect, than the one I read to you from *Brown* at

Nashville.[2] *Brown* writes under date of the 9th Inst. "The relative strength is estimated as follows, Calhoun 24 or 25; Buchanan 11 or 12; Johnson[3] 3 or 4: Cass none, not one I believe, unless the Michigan men be counted for him; All the rest for Van-Buren; As to the *Vice*, the impression is gaining ground, that Col. J. has hung on so obstinately for the first office, that he is not now entitled to the second, if he should become willing to fall back to it. I have heard it confidently asserted that *Benton* and the Ohio-men, were all against him, *and would be for you against him or any-body.* I think it very probably so." *Johnson* in a letter of the 11th confirms *Brown's* views and adds, "All the fragments of our party seem likely to unite upon Van-Buren, make his nomination unanimous, and each party seek the succession by distinguished services in his behalf: The game for the succession is I think commenced. The friends of Calhoun are feeling to see how Mr C. would go down for the Vice Presidency. I heard S. W. jr.[4] say to day, *that* would be worse than the old candidate. Mr C's friends think he should be made the *Vice*, or that he should return to the Senate in the Spring. His wishes I presume are unknown, and will depend upon what he thinks will most advance his interests for the succession." *Johnson* says further, "Every indication is decidedly favourable" to my nomination.

Col. R. M. J. I have every reason to believe is now struggling to secure the *Vice Presidential nomination.* The last account of him, he was at Columbus Ohio, on his way home.[5] The Democratic State Conventions in Ohio and Mississippi, will meet on the 8th of January next, and their action upon the subject, especially that of Ohio, whatever it may be, will go far to settle the question.[6] *Ohio* is in my judgment, at this moment, the point of most interest, though Mississippi is also important. The views of *Col. Benton, Allen* & *Tappan* will have a controlling influence in Ohio. Letters written to them by my friends here, presenting the views of the party in this State, would reach them in time for them to write to their friends in Ohio, before the 8th of January. *Mr Madison*[7] the Editor of the Ohio Statesman at Columbus, our old friend *Moses Dawson* of Cincinnati, and *Mr Medill* of the last Congress, are leading men and next to *Allen* & *Tappan*, give tone and direction to party movements in that State. It is very important that they should be written to, especially *Madison.* If no one here knows him personally, his public position, will authorize any member of the party to address a proper letter to him.[8] You know I cannot write, and it may seem immodest to make these suggestions even to *you.* I do so because I am satisfied of their great importance. If your judgement is, that it is proper to write, do so [with]out[9] delay.

From what I learn from *Laughlin* to day,[10] I fear [the] Committee has mutilated the forth-coming *address,* so as to make it of little value. I hope I may be mistaken.

Tell the *General*,[11] that I had an interview with both the Editors of the Union,[12] when I was at Nashville and both agreed to take decided and bold ground for *Van-Buren* in their paper. If they do not do so, in their next paper I will write to them and urge it upon them. The paper here[13] has done so. If you know any leading political friends at Jackson Mississippi, where the Legislature will be in Session on the 1st monday in January, write to him also. If you have any information of movements abroad other than what I have given to you, write to me.

James K. Polk

ALS. DLC–AJD. Addressed to Nashville and marked *"Confidential."* Published in *THM*, III, pp. 55–56.

1. See A. V. Brown to Polk, December 9, 1843, and Cave Johnson to Polk, December 11, 1843.

2. Syntax of sentence is garbled. On December 4, 1843, A. V. Brown wrote Polk from Washington about the presidential factions in Congress, but concluded that "On the whole we are all cheerd. with the hope that no serious disunion of our party is likely to happen." Of Richard M. Johnson's prospects, Brown wrote, "Nothing has transpired to shew whether the *Vice* would be accepted by him. That it will be *offerd.* to him in the way *compromise* I do not doubt. All our friends here think the thing will take that direction." ALS. DLC–JKP.

3. Richard M. Johnson.

4. Silas Wright, Jr.

5. Richard M. Johnson was from Kentucky.

6. The Ohio and Mississippi State Democratic conventions both resolved to support Martin Van Buren for the presidential nomination.

7. Polk probably intended to refer to Samuel Medary, who was editor of the Columbus *Ohio Statesman* and a major power in the Ohio Democracy.

8. See Polk to Samuel H. Laughlin, December 30, 1843.

9. A tear in the manuscript has obliterated part of one word on this line and the next.

10. See Samuel H. Laughlin to Polk, December 18 and 19, 1843.

11. Andrew Jackson.

12. John P. Heiss and Thomas Hogan were editors and publishers of the *Nashville Union*.

13. The Columbia *Tennessee Democrat*.

FROM JOHN P. HEISS

Union Office Wednesday night
Nashville Dec. [20][1] 1843

Dear Sir

The more I have considered on the subject we were conversing about a few days back the more I see the necessity of a change in the arrangement of the Union and on my part I will use every endeavor to accomplish the object or desires of our Democratic friends. Hogan is a first rate fellow and I like him, but I think he has too much confidence in his own abilities to give way to any other person. This is his only fault, and I cannot agree with him, that he is able to go into the coming contest and fight out the great battle of 1844 with the same health and strength that he now possesses.[2] In fact his health is declining daily, and I hardly believe he will live to see the commencement of it. I am as desirous of a change in the management of the Union as any other person, and in case I could purchase Hogan's interest in the Union, do you suppose the Democratic party would assist *me* personally, as they offered to a few days back to assist the firm jointly? All of my means is in the office and if I can purchase Hogans interest at a fair price I will give our Democratic friends the selection of the Editor; if they will contribute the amount you named a few days since, and will pay him a fair salary, say $1500 per year. If Hogan still continues to share a part of the proceeds of the establishment, it will not, with its present limited number of subscribers sustain the expense of employing an Editor. Hogan told me a few days ago that he would sell out his interest in the office. If he will and I can make arrangements to purchase the office myself I will do it. I will wait anxiously to have your advice on this subject.

I am using every exertion to stir up our young Democrats of Nashville to a party organization on the easteren plan, and I think the prospects so far, are exceedingly encouraging. I can assure you that we will be better organized in Nashville in 1844 than we have ever been before. Our Democratic Association, which I claim the honor of setting on foot, is going to have a good effect, and if the same kind of an organization is formed in the different counties throughout the state, our success is certain. You reccollect very well, in Massachusetts a few years back the Democratic vote was only little over 6000, and from the commencement of the organization of Young Mens Democratic Associations the vote of the Democratic Party began to increase, untill they Succeeded in carrying the state. It is the Same kind of management that causes the Democracy of the Easteren states to hold their own: look at the ward associations of the cities of New York, Philadelphia and Boston how well they regulate all their proceedings, and how successful they are in most cases in carrying out the wishes of a majority of their party. And another good effect it has towards strengthing the party, is that Young Men who are even below the age of twenty one are permitted to join the Young Mens Associations and share the benefits to be derived by visiting their Reading Rooms &c &c. And when you once have a young man's name to the constitution of an organization of that kind, he stands committed to a set of principles which he will most generally support in life. We have no news stiring worthy of notice. The Address[3] is out, ready for publication, and will be published in pamphlet form in a few days.

                                                          JOHN P. HEISS

ALS. DLC–JKP. Addressed to Columbia. Polk's AE on the cover states that he answered this letter on December 21, 1843.
1. Heiss clearly wrote, "Dec. 19"; however, in 1843 that date fell on Tuesday rather than Wednesday. In his reply to this letter, Polk wrote, "I have received your letter of yesterday."
2. Hogan suffered from tuberculosis.
3. See Polk to Samuel H. Laughlin, December 4, 1843.

FROM ROBERT ARMSTRONG

Sir,   Nashville 21 Decemr. 43
    I am at a loss to understand what these people are at and fear that Hogan is more to be feared than Heiss. I have had Cheatham[1] at work all day, but Humphreys this evening seems to think that Nicholson should have the paper,[2] and that he would take it for $7,000. We have allways suffered by keeping men in our ranks to make them strong, then turn and injure us. Lewis, Cheatham informs me, says that you cannot get the nomination at Baltimore and Van Buren will be badly beaten, &c &c. To put such a man into the Union "looks like Treason."
    See the enclosed.[3] I have looked over it. You had better come in. Put these things to rest and have them settled. Now is the time to do most. And if we act now I do not think we have much to fear. In haste . . . .
                                                          R ARMSTRONG

ALS. DLC–JKP. Addressed to Columbia.
1. A Nashville lawyer and prominent Democrat, Leonard P. Cheatham was president of the Democratic State Convention that assembled at Nashville on November 23, 1843.
2. The *Nashville Union*.
3. Enclosure not found.

TO JOHN P. HEISS

My Dear Sir: Columbia Decr. 21st 1843
    I have received your letter of yesterday.[1] I am very anxious for the reasons assigned to Mr *Hogan* and yourself, that the Union should be

made a more vigorous and efficient paper, than I fear Mr Hogan's present State of health will enable him to make it. If Mr H. desires to sell his interest and you should become the purchaser, you ask my opinion whether the Democratic party would assist you personally as they proposed a few days ago to assist the firm jointly. I have good reason to believe that they would. I have no reason to believe that they would not. As a member of the party, I can say, that the change if made, by the mutual assent of Mr *Hogan* and yourself will be entirely satisfactory to me, and especially as you propose—to leave to your Democratic friends, the selection of the Editor, if they will contribute the amout named a few days ago, and that you will pay him a fair salary. I would much prefer this arrangement, to see *Mr H.* sell his interest to a third person whose future course in conducting the establishment, might be uncertain, and indeed such as to injure the cause. The Editor who is to be preferred above all others, for the coming contest, is our friend *Laughlin.* He has talents and experience, is perfectly familiar with the politics of the State and the Union, and is extensively known as a *sound democrat.* In his hands, I doubt not the patronage of the paper would be greatly inceased and the cause advanced. What we want is a sound, and able Democratic paper, as a reliable organ of the party in the State. He would make it so, whilst some others into whose hands it might pass, might not. It is a matter of importance, that whatever arrangement is made should be speedily made. The public need know nothing of what is contemplated, until it is consummated, and announced by the parties. In whatever is done I must urge, that *Laughlin's* services be secured during the canvass of the next year.

After closing this letter, I will envelope it to *Genl. Armstrong*, that it may go directly into your hands, and not run the risk of falling into the general package for your office and run the risk of being opened by your clerk. I will mention to *Armstrong* its general purport, of course *confidentially*, and desire that you will have an early interview with him. Any arrangement agreed upon between you and Him, with *Hogan's* assent will be agreeable to me as a member of the party.

You see our paper here[2] has taken ground for *V. Buren.* I mentioned to *Hogan* and yourself the propriety of the Union's doing the same thing, to which I understood you both to assent. Since my return home, I am the more confirmed in the views then expressed. *A. V. Brown* writes under date of the 9th Inst.[3] "The relative strength is estimated as follows— *Calhoun* 24 or 25, *Buchanan* 11 or 12: *Johnson* 3 or 4: *Cass* none, *not one* I believe unless the Michigan men be counted for him: All the rest for *Van-Buren.*" *Cave Johnson*, writes under date of the 11th,[4] "All the fragments of our party seem likely to unite upon *Van-Buren*, make his nomination *Unanimous*, and each party seek the succession—by distinguished services in his behalf." You can if you choose shew this letter to Mr *Hogan*, who is my friend, and I would do, or advise nothing that would be prejudiced to his interests. I sincerely regret his feeble state of health. Shew it to no one else unless it be to *Hogan* or *Armstrong*, and that in the same confidence, that it is written to you.

JAMES K. POLK

P.S. I have said to *Armstrong* that you would shew him this letter.

ALS. T–JPH. Addressed to Nashville and marked "*Confidential*." Published in *THM*, II, pp. 140–41.
1. See John P. Heiss to Polk, December 20, 1843.
2. The Columbia *Tennessee Democrat*.
3. See Aaron V. Brown to Polk, December 9, 1843.
4. See Cave Johnson to Polk, December 11, 1843.

FROM SAMUEL H. LAUGHLIN

My dear Sir,   Nashville, Dec. 21, 1843
I have just received yours of the 19th inst.[1] I wrote you twice[2] since you left. When I wrote last, I felt sure that the Address would be in the Union[3] of this morning. Mr. Nicholson, Dr. Kenney and Mr. Glenn were the publication Committee. I went to the office again and again to see if it was in progress—but on applying to Mr. Nicholson who had the manuscript this morning, he said that he could not get it in time for to-day. I have been again at the office, and understand it is now in hand for Saturday's paper. I hope it will be out. One great object of the paper will be lost if it is not published, as suggested by you. It has all along been my wish that it should reach Columbus[4] and other places, where State Conventions are to sit on or before the 8th of January, *prox*. If it comes out on Saturday, it will be in time.

I have just seen Mr. Cheatham who informs me that there are several counter and thwarting projects on hand in regard to the Union.[5] He says he had it from Lewis (Nicholson's creature from Columbia) that he has come here expecting to be Editor. If so, the scheme is, that he is to be *sub* and Nicholson is to be *master*. I think they have been in negociation with Hogan about it. Hogan, I suppose, is ready for any arrangement for his own relief and profit: and Heiss has no feelings but those of interest. I have no doubt they will conclude something soon. Gen. Armstrong you know is confined to his office—besides he is in the delicate position of holding office. I, of course, can say not a word to any one—nor can I disabuse our real friends as to the faithless course of those who have the division and destruction of the party at heart. In such case, what can be done? I have no doubt of Johnson, Brown, and Cullom agreeing with you, in pressing the service upon me, and that they prefer me to any other. But the question *now* arises, requiring some distinct prospective arrangement to be made *instanter*. If something express—something binding—is not forthwith arranged, Nicholson and his friends, nearly all of them friends because they do not know him, will have the whole control of our party affairs, and the leading press, in their own hands, or under their unconditional control. When this is accomplished, you, Johnson, Brown and others, to say nothing of such small fry as myself and others, will have to look for friends, as far as the press is concerned, where we can find them. Even the old chief,[6] for justice, and future defence; and Gen. Armstrong, and the entire old set and family of the old fashioned democracy, will have to be more or less dependant on the press thus placed under *newlight* control. The time has been when the democracy could not have been exposed to such dangers. It is possible, however, that these latter day Saints in our church, will carry everything their own way.

You mentioned to me something about the precise terms upon which I thought I could undertake the work, if I could do it at all. You and Gen. Armstrong had both mentioned to me the sum of $1500, as the sum which could be raised for service until after the Presidential election next December. I stated to you that if I could do it at all, I was willing to do it for what our friends could give; I stated that in next year, and during the same term of time, I could make $2000 or $2500 with less labor by my profession, and that if it were not for my poverty, and the helpless persons dependent on me, and owing some money, I would be proud to do the service gratuitously and for the good of the cause. This, you said, could not be expected.

I will now say, that if you were here, I am sure an arrangement can and shall be made. I will have no possible connexion with the business of the paper. Let the proprietors pay in some way, or at some time, what they may prove themselves willing to pay. Leave it to their own discretion. In addition, let true friends here, pay *reasonably*, in moderate contributions, what they will agree to pay without being hard on them, according to their means, but promptly. If this falls short of what my confidential friends may think I ought to have and shall deserve and earn, I will depend for the deficit on the means we hope to raise abroad. If we are successful in raising money, I can be paid all I would accept, and if not, I will loose the balance of my labor and time as I have often done. If final success crowns our efforts, I shall consider *that* compensation enough for all [. . .][7] in pay. If you were here, I say again, all can be fixed. I once thought I never would touch such a thing, and I now consent, because I see that the self preservation of myself and friends who never deceived me, demands it. Weak as I know myself to be, I see that the cause demands of me to act, because another better qualified cannot be had, and because, if I do not, the power and influence of the press, at this central point, will pass into the hands of the enemy.

If you were here, I could show you the state of my wants, and the line of action I propose for myself, with the approval of friends, right off. Nothing however to be announced or known till the proper time. Can you come? I have asked Gen. Armstrong, to whom I have shown this letter, to write to you. I will look to the printing of the address so as to see it is correctly done.

S. H. LAUGHLIN

ALS. DLC–JKP. Addressed to Columbia and marked "Confidential."
1. Letter not found.
2. See Samuel H. Laughlin to Polk, December 18 and 19, 1843.
3. For plans to publish the Address of the Democratic State Convention in the *Nashville Union*, see Laughlin to Polk, December 19, 1843.
4. The Ohio Democratic State Convention met at Columbus on January 8, 1844, and resolved to support Martin Van Buren as the Democratic candidate for the presidency.
5. See Robert Armstrong to Polk, December 21, 1843.
6. Andrew Jackson.
7. Word or words illegible.

FROM ROBERT ARMSTRONG

Govr.,   Nashville 22 Decr. [1843][1]

I have settled Humphreys in a Chat, of two hours in my room up stairs. He now understands what N.[2] & Carroll are at. He wrote you by to nights mail. Cheatham also, who I found it necessary to call in to my aid.

I feel satisfied that Hesse[3] will do nothing but what the friends and our party wish him to do in relation to the paper.[4] I can manage him.

Donelson will be down in the morning. We will have the letters written to Ohio & Miss. Send in any names you recollect.

My Impression is that you should go to the north. Visit Pennsyl. New York Virginia &c. &c. They are all working for themselves and you should do so too. Genl. Jackson perhaps never would have been Presidt. if he had not been sent to the Senate by his friends against his will. Mail closing. In haste . . . .

R. ARMSTRONG

ALS. DLC–JKP. Addressed to Columbia.
1. Year determined through content analysis.
2. A. O. P. Nicholson.
3. John P. Heiss.
4. The *Nashville Union*.

FROM LEONARD P. CHEATHAM

Dr. Sir: Nashville, December 22nd 1843

I have read your letter to Armstrong,[1] & before its reception we had ascertained the substance of all your allusions & were at work.[2] Hogan is still slow in deciding whether he will sell out, or still retain his interest & permit us to select our own *Editor*; either course will do, & we are pressing a decision as strong as prudense dictates. We have burnt your letter as a prudent course in our opinion, & of course as that fact is here communicated, you can burn this if you choose. We have conversed with but few friends, but all say for fear of some accident you had best come in without delay & that with a view of delaying longer than you did before. Such seems to be the *fate* of *War*.

L. P. CHEATHAM

P.S. Heiss pledges himself that no man shall come in as joint partner with him unless with our assent,[3] & further that he is willing we shall elect the Editor & that he will attend to all the business & let Hogan still remain joint partner, or that if Hogan prefers selling, he will buy, by geting some aid & in the latter event we would forthwith have the controul. The matter has been pressed on Hogan this evening, now nearly sun down. We are compelled to have patience & wait for the moving of the waters. L.P.C.

ALS. DLC–JKP. Addressed to Columbia.
1. Letter not found.
2. See Robert Armstrong to Polk, December 21, 1843.
3. See John P. Heiss to Polk, December 20, 1843.

FROM JOHN P. HEISS

Friday evening
Dear Sir [Nashville] Union Office Dec. [22][1] 1843

I have taken the liberty to again freely address you on the subject of my last communication.[2] There has been a report in circulation to day at this place, which has given our friends some alarm, and the subject of it, was that Mr Lewis was about purchasing an interest in the Union.[3] In the first place neither myself or Hogan has any acquaintance with Lewis, and in the second place our friends need not be under any apprehensions of a change unless their will is consulted on the subject. But to the point. I have conversed with Hogan since I last wrote you on the subject of your proposal when in Nashville, and I think he will accede before long to the proposition without any other change you contemplated. Hogan thinks with myself that it will be more than we possibly can do, to add an expense of $750 per year to our now heavy outlay; but my dear sir I am for one willing to make the venture and depend upon our Democratic bretheren to sustain us by an increase of patronage. We are you [see][4] progressing with our buisiness at present on a true foundation and to add to our expenses without any return, it would perhaps be the means of bringing us into difficulties we could not encounter. We are both poor and on our own exertions, are we dependant for the support of our families.

With your exertions in our favour I know we shall be repaid and I would request you to write to Hogan on this matter, but not at once urge it too strongly, as he is a good hearted fellow, but a person whose constitution is feeble requires some forbearance. You may rest assured my dear sir that all in my power necessary to carry out your desires, shall be freely tendered towards the advancement of Democratic Principles, and the elevation of my respected friend James K. Polk.

JOHN P. HEISS

ALS. DLC–JKP. Addressed to Columbia.
1. Heiss clearly wrote, "Dec. 20"; however, in 1843 that date fell on Wednesday rather than Friday.
2. See John P. Heiss to Polk, December 20, 1843.
3. *Nashville Union*.
4. Heiss dropped a word or words at this place in his sentence.

TO ANDREW JACKSON

My Dear Genl: Nashville Decr 25th 1843
I would call to see you, but am compelled to return home on tomorrow. The information I have from Washington is, that all the fragments of our party are likely to unite on *Mr Van-Buren*, nominate him *unanimously*, and each of the leading aspirants for the succession, seek favour with the party by distinguished services in his behalf. The Vice Presidency is not so well settled. My friends write to me that all the indications

from the North are decidedly favourable. They give me at the same time an account of the movements, upon that subject, which are being made. *Cave Johnson* writes that some of the leading friends of *Calhoun*, are pressing him in high quarters for the Vice Presidency, on Mr Van-Buren's ticket.[1] He thinks, it meets with no favour from the leading members of the party. He states further that Col. J.[2] left Washington. He has no doubt determined if he could not get the first, to seek the nomination for the second office. The last account I have seen of the *Colonel*, he was at Columbus Ohio, on his way home. The State conventions of Ohio, and Mississippi will meet on the 8th of January next, and their action on the Vice Presidential nomination will have great influence in settling that question. Ohio is the great State in the West, and when she speaks her voice will be listened to, throughout the Union, and will have great influence. Both *Johnson & Brown* incline to the opinion that Col. B.[3] and the Ohio gentlemen are favourable to my nomination, but they can learn nothing definite and distinct on that point. Next to Mr Senator Allen & Tappan, the man who commands most influence and power in the Democratic party in Ohio, is *Col. Samuel Medary* of Columbus, who is a gentleman of high intelligence and character, and the Editor of the "Ohio Statesman." What his views or opinions are I am not informed. *Ohio* I regard to be the *pivot*, upon which the question of the Vice Presidential nomination will turn.

   Genl. Armstrong, will inform you, of the arrangements which have been made to make the *Union* a more efficient organ in the State. I saw both the Editors[4] to day, and they have agreed to take bold and unequivocal ground *for Van-Buren*. The Columbia paper[5] you see[6]

AL. DLC–AJ. Addressed to the Hermitage and marked *"Private."*
1. See Cave Johnson to Polk, December 11, 1843.
2. Richard M. Johnson.
3. Thomas H. Benton.
4. John P. Heiss and Thomas Hogan. See John P. Heiss to Polk, December 20 and 22, 1843, and Polk to John P. Heiss, December 21, 1843.
5. The Columbia *Tennessee Democrat*.
6. The end of the final sentence, closing, and signature of Polk's letter have been torn from the last page.

FROM SAMUEL H. LAUGHLIN

Sir,   [Nashville] Evening Dec. 25, 1843
   I am writing letters, but will see you again this evening at Gen. Armstrong's after supper. In meantime, think of the following things:

1. Mr. Hogan, I know feels sensitive about any name *supplanting* his, or seeming to do it. My wish will be, as my connexion is to be temporary, that my name shall not go in the paper[1] as Editor; though the first publication will show my connexion under my own hand. I shall prefer this. It is so of most our leading papers, the Pennsylvanian[2] &c.

2. As Kezer is my connexion, and will otherwise, as he always has done, contribute through the Davidson Dem. Association,[3] and as a member of the Big State Committee of five at Nashville,[4] his full quota of all moneys for paying for the cause, I would rather he were not asked to sign the paper—and would rather he should pay his tax in any other way. I ask this not to relieve or release him, but because I do not wish it to appear that he had any agency in inducing me to come here and embark in the engagement. It is the effect it would, and possibly might have on me *at home* I wish to avoid, and which I understand better than I have time here to explain.

3. I am clear, upon reflection, that the arrangements ought to be secret now—but I will to-night, have an agreement for H & Heiss[5] and myself to sign.

4. I am also satisfied, that the Central Committee here (Kezer's name being left out) ought to address me a request to assist in conducting the paper to be called the Star Spangled Banner[6]—and that their request should say I can do it, as a service to the party, temporarily, and without changing my residence. If they were to do so now, I could take it under advisement, and answer after I get letters from Washington. I will talk with you about this. I *think* Nicholson has poisoned Stevenson—but he is not one of the Central Committee. That committee is:

> Felix Robertson
> A. J. Donelson
> Willo: Williams
> J. J. B. Southall[7] &
> T. Kezer.

These would sign such note as you would dictate and leave to be copied with Gen. Armstrong.

On a line from you, Huntsman would forthwith send such a request to me from the Jackson Committee—which is,

> A. Huntsman
> J. Caruthers[8]
> A. O. W. Totten[9]
> Thomas Ewell
> Geo. Snider.[10]

Think of these things until I see you. In haste . . . .

S. H. L.

P.S. I *must* show my folks at home that I have had a *call* that I cannot, as a true democrat, resist.

ALI. DLC–JKP. Addressed to No. 71, Nashville Inn.
1. *Nashville Union.*
2. The Philadelphia *Pennsylvanian*, a democratic newspaper that began publication in 1832.
3. Young Men's Democratic Association of Nashville.
4. The Democratic State Convention of November 1843 resolved that the president of the convention, Leonard P. Cheatham, should appoint three central committees, one each at Nashville, Knoxville, and Jackson, to consist of five members each. Each central committee would organize party affairs in its grand division of the state, including the creation of corresponding committees and Democratic Young Men's Associations in each county.
5. Thomas Hogan and John P. Heiss.
6. A Democratic campaign newspaper, the *Star Spangled Banner*, was published by John P. Heiss and edited by Samuel H. Laughlin between May and October 1844.
7. A Nashville Democrat, Southall considered running for a seat in the Tennessee House in 1841, but declined the race. He is not identified further.
8. An early Madison County settler, James Caruthers became president of the Jackson Branch of the Union Bank upon its creation in 1832; he also served a term as president of the trustees for West Tennessee College, 1843–44.
9. A successful West Tennessee lawyer, Archibald W. O. Totten sat on the Tennessee Supreme Court from 1850 until 1855.
10. George Snider was an early resident and physician at Jackson.

FROM MARTIN VAN BUREN

My dear Sir   Lindenwald Decr. 27th 1843

I thank you kindly for your friendly letter.[1] No explanations were necessary to satisfy me of the goodness of the motives of my friends in Tenn. & being on the spot they were the best judges & I am you know, not one of the complaining sort, but am on the contrary always willing to let such matters take their own course. This I have done in respect to the Presidential question to an extent which many of my warmest friends would hardly credit. You know what my course was at Columbia. Such it was also every where else & by the thousands & tens of thousands I saw in the course of that five months journey there is not a man who can with truth say that I made a single effort to give a direction to the nomination. In all this part of the Union we have the best feeling, & there is not the slightest doubt of a cordial support of the nominee of the Convention whoever he may be.

It is as mortifying, as it is incomprehensible, that Tennessee, which in time past knew not Federalism, should have been proof agt. the feelings & convictions which have within the last two or three years brought all the rest of the old Democratic States into their former, & true positions. You must, & I doubt not will, in good time, seek out the cause and apply the remedy. It is not to be endured that the Old Chief should go out of the world with his favourite Tenn. in Whig Hands.

Remember me very kindly to Mrs. Polk, & to my sweetest friend Mrs. Lucius Polk,[2] & believe me to be . . . .

M VAN BUREN

ALS. DLC–JKP. Addressed to Columbia.
1. See Polk to Martin Van Buren, November 30, 1843.
2. Mary Eastin Polk, a niece of Rachel Jackson, married Lucius J. Polk of Columbia in 1832.

FROM SAMUEL H. LAUGHLIN

Friday Evening

My dear Sir, Nashville, Tenn. Dec. 29, 1843

Our friend Mr. H. L. Turney has just arrived here, earlier than the time indicated in his letter to you,[1] and requests me to write you forthwith to come up here as soon as you receive this.

I have no news. I have been writing letters, and watching things generally. Howard's speech,[2] and things out of my control, kept the article which I wrote out of the Union on yesterday. It will be *in* in the morning.[3] It is short, but plainly to the point.

All, I hope, now wanting, is to get our plenipotentiaries off to Columbus.[4] I do not know the result of Gen. Armstrong's trip to the Hermitage. In haste . . . .

S. H. LAUGHLIN

N.B. We do not know yet whether Maj. Donelson can go[5]—and then, the propriety of *his* going, is still an undecided question. I think he ought to go. But, as Mr. Turney is here ready, we all agree, that if Maj. D. cant go, or ought not to go, that Gen. Pillow *must if possible.*[6] We intreat him to lay down the law, and all other personal considerations in the present great emergency. I have seen yours to Gen. Armstrong,[7] and write this to be communicated to Pillow in the event he has not left Columbia. Come yourself, & bring him by our order.

P.S.[8] Maj. Donelson will be here tomorrow, and letters will be here from the Old Cock.[9]

ALS. DLC–JKP. Addressed to Columbia. Polk's AE on the cover states that he answered this letter on December 30, 1843.

1. On December 26, 1843, Turney wrote Polk that he would meet him in Nashville on the first of January, "that being the earlyest possible day for me." In a postscript the following day, Turney doubted that he could meet Polk in Nashville at all. ALS. DLC–JKP.

2. The *Nashville Union* of December 28, 1843, carried an extract of a speech delivered by Tilghman A. Howard at an assembly honoring him at Sullivan County, Indiana, in October 1843. Howard stressed that free trade, free industry, and freedom of thought and action were basic principles of true Democracy.

3. Laughlin's editorial in the *Nashville Union* of December 30, 1843, entitled "Posture of Affairs—Position of Tennessee," claimed that harmony and union continued within Democratic ranks at the national and state levels, even in the face of numerous presidential aspirants. In Tennessee, harmony prevailed with the resolve of the State Convention to support the nominees of the national convention, even though Van Buren "was and is" the choice of "an overwhelming majority of the Democracy of the States," and "notwithstanding the ardent and earnest wishes of the friends" of Polk for the Vice Presidency.

4. Reference is to Columbus, Ohio, where the State Democratic Convention was to convene on January 8, 1844. See Robert Armstrong to Polk, December 22, 1843.

5. On December 31, 1843, Robert Armstrong wrote Polk that Andrew J. Donelson could not go to Columbus. Turney and Laughlin were at the Hermitage getting letters of introduction from Andrew Jackson and Donelson. Leonard P. Cheatham could not make the trip, but Turney would leave "on Tuesday morning." ALS. DLC–JKP.

6. Gideon J. Pillow wrote Polk on December 30, 1843, that the illness of two of his children would prevent his traveling to Nashville with Polk or going on to Ohio. ALS. DLC–JKP.

7. Letter not found.

8. Laughlin's postscript is written in the left margin of the first page of the letter.

9. Andrew Jackson.

TO SAMUEL H. LAUGHLIN

My Dear Sir: Columbia Decr. 29th 1843

Genl. Pillow informs me that it will be impossible for him to go to Columbus, as I had hoped he would.[1] He concurs with us, that it is vastly

important, that some one or two discreet friends should go. He attaches
even more importance to it, than we did. He thinks the result of the
contest of 1844, as well as my own political destiny in future life, may
depend upon it. If *Turney* come to Nashville on tomorrow I am sure he
will go, if it is possibly in his power. If he and Donaldson[2] would go, *all
would be safe*. If *Donaldson* cannot do so, prevail on *Cheatham* to accompany him. I hope *Armstrong, Humphreys, Donaldson, Cheatham, Turney, my brother*[3] and *yourself* will hold your consultation on tomorrow,
and see that some two friends go without fail. I have written the letter
which you suggested to *Huntsman*,[4] and make no doubt you will hear
from his committee[5] soon. I will prepare the letter for the Nashville
committee[6] and enclose to *Armstrong* by tomorrow's mail, to be copied &
signed by them. The article of agreement between Hogan & Heiss and
yourself I hope has been signed. I see the *Van-Buren* article is not in the
Union of yesterday, as was agreed upon.[7] It ought to appear soon. I hope
you will put into the form of *Editorial* or *communications*, the substance
of your manuscript for the address,[8] which was not incorporated in the
published paper. That part of it which relates to the causes of our defeat
in August & to organization would have a decidedly good effect, if put
into the form of a letter & signed by the State Committee of *five* at
Nashville—and I advise that it be made to assume that form. Let them
sign it, & publish it in the Union, as an appeal to the party in the State to
organize. Let me hear from you on tomorrow and on monday.

JAMES K. POLK

ALS. NjMoHP–L. W. Smith Collection. Addressed to Nashville and marked
"Confidential."
1. See Samuel H. Laughlin to Polk, December 29, 1843.
2. Andrew J. Donelson.
3. William H. Polk.
4. Polk's letter not found. See Samuel H. Laughlin to Polk, December 25,
1843.
5. Jackson Democratic Central Committee.
6. Nashville Democratic Central Committee.
7. See Laughlin to Polk, December 29, 1843.
8. Address of the Democratic State Convention.

FROM LEVIN H. COE

Dear Sir   Somerville Decr. 30 1843
Your favor was to hand two days ago.[1] I have written to my friend
Col. Jos. S. Watkins,[2] an old acquaintance of Medary & who is in constant

correspondence with him. He recd a letter a few days ago from him speaking most despondingly of the prospects of the Dem. party in that State.[3] I have also written the letters you suggest. I start to H. Springs[4] to the Chy Court[5] to morrow, and if I possibly can will leave there about the middle of the week in the stage. I will see our friends at that Court from all north Missi. & rouse them up to an active effort. I entertain no fear of *Dick*[6] getting the nomination there. The only danger is a throwing off upon Walker. The vanity of the little stuffed frog is so inordinate that he would be willing to risque the fate of the party in the Nation to get for himself even a State nomination.

L. H. Coe

ALS. DLC–JKP. Addressed to Columbia.
1. Letter not found.
2. A resident of Goochland County, Virginia, Watkins served numerous terms in the state legislature, 1820–28 and 1832–37.
3. Reference is to the state of Ohio.
4. Holly Springs, Mississippi.
5. Chancery Court.
6. Richard M. Johnson.

FROM CAVE JOHNSON

Dear Sir,   Washington Dec. 30th 1843

I recd. two letters[1] today from you. I should have written you before if I could have learned any agreeable intelligence to have written you. It is difficult to learn the various considerations operating upon our distinguished men. I am now regarded here (particularly since the election of Blair & Rives)[2] as a thorough reliable democrat, so much so, that some of the Southerners call me a northern democrat & our leaders talk of course more freely to me than ever. I think there is nothing yet setled as to the Vice-presidency, but suspect there is a good deal of billing & cooing. Buckhanan[3] has withdrawn. Of course King has no prospect on his ticket & is looking with much anxiety to the movement of T.H.B.'s[4] friends in the West & from the considerations I mentioned in my last,[5] I fear with good grounds to hope for success. There has been recently much said as to the position of Ten. & greatly I fear to your injury. They talk of Tennessee, Jackson's State, having hauled down her flag—standing in a position to go on either side—that a new spirit has sprung up among our people since Jackson's day &c &c, and the current now sets strongly toward King. Many indeed speak of your having lost the nomination by it.

I had a long talk with Senator A.[6] on yesterday. He regretted the position of Tenn. & thought it would injure you with Ohio. I explained all that I could & he promised me to send the letter of Cheatham to their convention on the 8th, but I could nothing on either side from him & therefore I suspected him to be agt. us. I saw Senator B—ton,[7] a day or two since & had a good deal of conversation on that & other subjects. He regretted the position of Ten. It injured the State. The Spirit of Jackson was gone & *feared* it would loose you the nomination & seemed full of wrath that *Jacksons State* should have taken such a course. I have had several such conversations with him at one of which Senator K.[8] was present & he took much apparent pride in shewing the position of Alabama & contrasting it with that of Ten. I took great pains in shewing, how nearly balanced our State was & the great necessity of caution in our movement, so as to secure harmony, that by going for the nominee we kept down any dissentions & mentioned that Senator Anderson from our state had started the movement for Cass & it was supposed that Mr. N—son[9] secretly favored the movement (Foster has stated the fact to be so several times). Senator B—ton said with a good deal of emphasis—Is he not Polk's right hand man? I stated the true condition existing between you & him, which seemed to surprise him. I can learn nothing further from him than the expression of *his fears*. I have had conversations with S.W.Jr.[10] & several others of NY, who approve the course of Tennessee. They act with great reserve lest Van[11] might be affected. My impression is that they would favor you in preference to any other but think they would like to follow the great body of the Democrats instead of taking the lead. It is probable your fate will be sealed at Columbus on the 8th of Jany.[12] I shall write Medary & Medill. I should fear to write Genl. Thompson,[13] who is broke & poor and has been here, wanting, sargeant at arms, door keeper, deputy clerk or anything & we could give him nothing & I fear he thinks hard of me. I saw Brown since I recd yours & he will write Medill immediately. I dont exactly know how Brown stands. He speaks very favorably of Cass & seemed inclined to favor him for a while. He seems decided for Van, yet hates Benton and Benton regards him as a Calhoun man.

There is but little doubt I think, that the friends of Calhoun will try & so arrange it, that he be the Vice, with a view to the succession. That cannot be, whatever they may attempt. Lynn Boyd & Steenrod[14] both your friends think the current running strongly agt. you at this time & in favor of King for the reasons I mentioned. I do not yet despair however. Senator K. voted for *the old U.S. Bank*—that we'll have it brought particularly before the convention. My opinion yet is that the contest will be between you & K. I do not know but that I am acting wrong in stating the conversations with other members, which perhaps they might not expect to be communicated particularly to you & yet I could not without it, give you proper data upon which to form an opinion for yourself. You will see the grounds from which I form my conclusion.

Mark it certain that the Pres. & his influence will go for Clay because we elected Blair & Reeves,[15] which they effect to consider an *endorsement* of the Globe slanders of Tyler. There is understood to be secret negotiations on hand for the confirmation of Wise's appointment to France[16] & the appointment of John Sargeant in the place of Judge Thompson & thus opening the way for Jno Davis—honest John![17] It is thought that Spencer or Sargeant will get the place.

I think that we shall have the 21st Rule[18] repealed & then be flooded with abolition petitions & the annexation of Texas & these with the Tariff will be used now to injure Van if possible. Wise returns from *the battle* with that view. Dick Davis,[19] declared in his place today, that he was agt. emancipation in the South by the action of the free States or *even the Southern States themselves* & if the South *voluntarily emancipated* he should go for a dissolution of the Union, because the northern states would be flooded with free blacks, paupers, rogues, vagabonds, the laboring people of the north be broke down, ruined by the introduction of pauper labor etc. The proceedings of the Ten. & Arkansas Convention appeared in the Globe[20] & as far as I can learn Blair seems disposed to do you full justice but I expect he is watching the movements of others here. I expect Col Benton thinks harshly of Woodbury. Why I know not.

I will not fail to give you any information of anything interesting. Nicholson wrote Allen a letter urging your nomination for the Vice presidency as I learned by accident which gave occasion to Allen to make some harsh remarks about our Convention.

C JOHNSON

[P.S.] I have had more of my old disease[21] today than I have had for several months. I shall not be surprised, if I am soon laid up.

ALS. DLC–JKP. Addressed to Columbia and marked *"private."*
1. Letters not found.
2. See Cave Johnson to Polk, December 9, 1843.
3. James Buchanan.
4. Thomas H. Benton.
5. See Cave Johnson to Polk, December 15, 1843.
6. William Allen of Ohio.
7. Thomas H. Benton.
8. William R. King of Alabama.
9. A. O. P. Nicholson.
10. Silas Wright, Jr.

11. Martin Van Buren.

12. See Samuel H. Laughlin to Polk, December 21, 1843.

13. John Thomson.

14. Linn Boyd and Lewis Steenrod. Steenrod, a Democrat and lawyer from Wheeling, Virginia, won election to three terms in the U.S. House, 1839–45.

15. Francis P. Blair and John C. Rives.

16. John Tyler placed the name of Henry A. Wise before the U.S. Senate to be minister to France, in place of Lewis Cass. First nominated on February 27, 1843, Wise was rejected by the Senate on March 3, 1843. Tyler reappointed Wise a second and third time on March 3, 1843; Wise was twice more rejected. On January 18, 1844, Tyler nominated Wise to be minister to Brazil; Wise's nomination received Senate approval on February 9, 1844.

17. John Sergeant, Smith Thompson, and John Davis. A Philadelphia lawyer, Sergeant served seven terms in the U.S. House, 1815–23, 1827–29, and 1837–41, as a Federalist, a National Republican, and a Whig, successively. He served as chief legal and political adviser to Nicholas Biddle, president of the Second Bank of the United States. Thompson, a lawyer from New York, was U.S. secretary of the navy, 1819–23, and associate justice of the Supreme Court, 1823–43. Thompson died on December 18, 1843. A Massachusetts lawyer, Davis served as a National Republican in the U.S. House, 1824–32; as governor of Massachusetts, 1833–34 and 1840–41; and as a Whig in the U.S. Senate, 1835–40 and 1845–53. Nicknamed "Honest John," Davis sought the Whig vice-presidential nomination in 1844, as did John Sergeant. Thompson's death occasioned a prolonged contest between Tyler and the U.S. Senate. Tyler offered the seat on the Supreme Court to Martin Van Buren, who declined. Tyler then nominated John C. Spencer on January 8, 1844. Ardently opposed by the Clay Whigs, the Senate rejected Spencer's appointment on January 31, 1844. Subsequently, Tyler offered the appointment to John Sergeant, Horace Binney of Philadelphia, and Silas Wright, Jr., each of whom rejected the offer.

18. Following the precedent of previous Congresses, the House had passed a "gag resolution" on December 4, 1843.

19. Richard D. Davis, a lawyer from New York, served two terms as a Democrat in the U.S. House, 1841–45.

20. Washington *Globe*, December 13 and 27, 1843.

21. Johnson suffered from neuralgia.

TO SAMUEL H. LAUGHLIN

My Dear Sir   Columbia, Saturday night Decr. 30th 1843

I received your letter of yesterday, at noon today. *Genl. Pillow* is himself unwell, has three sick children, and cannot possibly leave home. This I regret exceedingly. But for the indisposition of himself and his family, he had I think made up his mind to lay down every thing, and go not only to Nashville, but if necessary to Columbus. I would myself go forthwith to Nashville, but have strong impressions that there would be an impropriety in it. Should the step contemplated get into the Whig newspapers, as it is possible it may, it would be attributed to my personal agency, especially if I were at Nashville at this time. I am satisfied too, that I could not promote, the object in view, by going, further than I have done. Yourself and my other *confidential friends*, are already fully in possession of all my views, and of the importance I attach to the movement. My friends I know are already as zealous in the matter, and as anxious to have it effected as I can be. All that I could do, if I were present, would be to urge it, and this perhaps I have already done, as far as a proper regard for my friends and their convenience would make it proper for me to do. I will write to Turney to night, and inclose my letter under cover to *Genl. Armstrong*, hoping to meet with a private opportunity to forward, both letters on tomorrow. No mail leaves here for Nashville until Monday. *Turney* can effect more than any man in the State, unless it be *Donaldson*.[1] The two I am satisfied could accomplish the object. *Cheatham* having been twice *President* of our State Convention is known abroad, and would have great weight. They will both I know, do anything in their power, & will go, if they possibly can.[2] I think it best under all the circumstances, to leave whatever is done to my friends, and shall be perfectly satisfied with whatever they do. Write me at the earliest moment what is done.

JAMES K. POLK

ALS. DLC–JKP. Addressed to Nashville and marked *"confidential."* Laughlin's AE on the cover states that he answered this letter on January 1, 1844, informing Polk that Hopkins L. Turney and he had visited the Hermitage the previous day to obtain letters from Jackson to Medary, Dawson, and Burke and that he would try to find someone to accompany Turney to Columbus. Published in *ETHSP*, XVIII, pp. 164–66. A strong Jacksonian, William Burke served as postmaster of Cincinnati from 1832 until 1841.

1. Andrew J. Donelson.

2. Robert Armstrong wrote on January 7, 1844, that Turney did not visit Columbus. On January 9, 1844, Polk wrote Laughlin and supposed that Turney's decision had been "unavoidable." Two days later, on January 11, 1844. Laughlin replied that Turney had "declined under the advice of others, his own impressions, and against my urgent advice." ALsS. DLC–JKP.

FROM WILLIAM H. POLK

Dear Brother Nashville Dec. 31st 1843

The *address* of the Democratic Convention has been sent to every portion of the Union according to your direction. Col. Turney has been in the City several days. He is, I believe, entirely willing to go to *Ohio*. Donalson[1] says he cannot go. Cheatham[2] would go, probably, if he had the means. We will get some suitable person to accompany Turney if possible.[3] *Laughlin & Turney* went this morning to the Hermitage, to have the proper letters *written* to the right quarter. Laughlin said they would not leave the *old General*,[4] until they obtained their object—got possession of the letters, and *mailed them*.

Every exertion will be made to carry out your views. I will write you by the next mail, and inform you of the result of his visit.

Tell Mother[5] my wife[6] is improving and much better.

WILLIAM H. POLK

ALS. DLC–JKP. Addressed to Columbia.
1. Andrew J. Donelson.
2. Leonard P. Cheatham.
3. See Samuel H. Laughlin to Polk, December 30, 1843.
4. Andrew Jackson.
5. Jane Knox Polk.
6. Belinda Dickinson Polk.

CALENDAR

N.B. Items entered in *italic* type have been published or briefed
in the Correspondence Series.

1816

14 July   From William Leetch. ALS. Pvt. Ms. of W. R. Ewing, Cleveland, Tennessee. Sends personal and family news to Polk, who attends the University of North Carolina.

1817

8 July   *From Samuel Thomas Hauser.*

9 July   From William Polk. ALS. Pvt. Ms. of W. R. Ewing, Cleveland, Tennessee. Encloses $150 as requested in Polk's letter of July 8.

4 Aug   *From William Hooper.*

3 Oct [1817]   From William H. Haywood, Jr. ALS. Pvt. Ms. of W. R. Ewing, Cleveland, Tennessee. Sends copy of John H. Eaton's *Life of Andrew Jackson.*

12 Nov   *From [Hardy L. Holmes.]*

1818

8 Jan   From anonymous writer. L. Pvt. Ms. of W. R. Ewing, Cleveland, Tennessee. Wishes to know whether Polk desires to invest in lotteries sponsored by Whitworth & Yancey of Raleigh, North Carolina.

30 April   *From Joseph Delaplaine.*

3 May   To William Polk. ALS. Polk Ancestral Home, Columbia, Tennessee. Reports that although he has been ill, he is improving and will complete his studies on schedule.

18 Aug   From Samuel Polk. ALS. Pvt. Ms. of W. R. Ewing, Cleveland, Tennessee. Directs Polk to purchase a horse and advises him of the death of Jethro Brown.

1820

June   *From Jesse W. Egnew.*

27 Sept   *To Samuel Houston.*

30 Dec   *From John S. Williamson.*

1821

17 Feb   *From William Polk.*

1822

2 March	From John S. Williamson.
15 March	To Samuel H. Laughlin.
25 March	From John S. Williamson.
5 May	From Samuel R. Rucker.
24 Sept	To William Polk.
4 Nov	To Henry Charles Carey and Isaac Lea.

1823

11 Aug	From William F. Brown.
18 Aug	From Pleasant M. Miller.
25 Nov	From Isham G. Searcy.

1824

10 July	From Archibald Yell. ALS. T–JKP. Urges large vote in Tennessee legislative elections.
18 July	To Felix Grundy. ALS. NcU. Requests legal assistance in Nashville for a client.
2 Sept	From Henry Crabb.

1825

22 Jan	From William Davidson.
6 Aug	From Anderson Childress.
2 Dec	From John McLean.
3 Dec	From [William M. Stewart].
3 Dec	From Thomas L. McKenney.
10 Dec	From Thomas L. McKenney.
20 Dec	From Aaron McWhorter.
21 Dec	From Peter Hagner.
21 Dec	From Peter Hagner.

1826

18 Jan	From Peter Hagner.
20 Jan	From Robert H. McEwen.
22 Jan	From Thomas Washington.
26 Jan	To James Barbour.
2 Feb	From Thomas L. McKenney.
16 Feb	To James L. Edwards.
23 Feb	From [Peter Hagner].
27 Feb	From John McLean.
2 March	From Francis Porterfield.
13 March	To [Postmaster General].
3 April	To Andrew Jackson.
14 April	To James Barbour.
3 May	From Andrew Jackson.
16 June	From Peter Hagner.
18 July	From Williamson Smith.

17 Aug	*From Peter Hagner.*
19 Aug	*From Peter Hagner.*
18 Sept	*From William Davidson.*
25 Sept	*To Robert L. Caruthers.*
17 Oct	From J. Hamilton. ALS. Maury County Court Records, Columbia, Tenn. Requests legal assistance.
23 Oct	*From Thomas Kercheval.*
6 Nov	*From Charles Boyles.*
1 Dec	*From Charles W. Webber.*
2 Dec	*From Robert H. McEwen.*
4 Dec	*To Andrew Jackson.*
7 Dec	*From James L. Edwards.*
8 Dec	*From Thomas L. McKenney.*
9 Dec	*From Peter Hagner.*
9 Dec	*From Peter Hagner.*
11 Dec	*From Charles Worthington.*
13 Dec	*To Samuel L. Southard.*
14 Dec	*To William Polk.*
15 Dec	*From Samuel L. Southard.*
15 Dec	*From James Walker.*
19 Dec	*From Peter Hagner.*
19 Dec	*From Robert A. Taylor & Co.*
20 Dec	*From George Graham.*
[24] Dec	*From Andrew Jackson.*
27 Dec	*From John C. Wormeley.*
30 Dec	*From Thomas Washington.*
30 Dec	*From James R. White.*

1827

6 Jan	*From James Walker.*
6 Jan	*From Joel Walker.*
8 Jan	*From John McLean.*
9 Jan	*From James R. White.*
15 Jan	*From James Walker.*
23 Jan	*From Charles W. Webber.*
25 Jan	*To Samuel L. Southard.*
27 Jan	*From Peter Hagner.*
27 Jan	*From N. S. Hartin.*
27 Jan	*From James E. Heath.*
27 Jan	*From Samuel L. Southard.*
31 Jan	*To Alfred Flournoy.*
31 Jan	*From Peter Hagner.*
4 Feb	*. From William Davidson.*
4 Feb	*From James Houston.*
4 Feb	*From Henry Robertson.*
5 Feb	*To James Caruthers.*
7 Feb	*From David Love.*
8 Feb	*From James R. White.*
10 Feb	*From Peter Hagner.*

10 Feb	*From Alfred M. Harris.*
11 Feb	*From Collin S. Tarpley.*
15 Feb	*From Peter Hagner.*
15 Feb	*To Samuel L. Southard.*
16 Feb	*From Samuel L. Southard.*
17 Feb	*To James L. Edwards.*
21 Feb	*From Peter Hagner.*
22 Feb	*To James L. Edwards.*
1 March	*From George Graham.*
20 March	*To Alfred Flournoy.*
24 April	*From Peter Hagner.*
25 May	*From John McLean.*
27 May	*From Peter Hagner.*
16 Aug	*From George Lovell.*
30 Aug	*From William Davidson.*
5 Sept	*To Henry Clay.*
6 Sept	*To Samuel L. Southard.*
25 Sept	*From Navy Department.*
11 Oct	*To Alfred Flournoy.*
17 Oct	*From James Caruthers.*
21 Nov	*From James Walker.*
6 Dec	*To Alfred Flournoy.*
7 Dec	*To [Henry Clay].*
7 Dec	*From James Walker.*
8 Dec	*To [Department of War].*
10 Dec	*To [Department of War].*
10 Dec	*To [Pension Office]. ALS. NN. Encloses pension application for constituent.*
11 Dec	*To James Walker.*
12 Dec	*From Franklin E. Polk.*
13 Dec	*From William Dunlap.*
14 Dec	*From Peter Hagner.*
14 Dec	*From Peter Hagner.*
14 Dec	*From Peter Hagner.*
14 Dec	*From Peter Hagner.*
17 Dec	*From James L. Edwards.*
17 Dec	*From John McLean.*
20 Dec	*From Peter Hagner.*
22 Dec	*From William D. Beall, Jr.*
26 Dec	*From Peter Hagner.*
27 Dec	*From Green Pryor.*
31 Dec	*From James L. Edwards.*

1828

1 Jan	*To James Walker.*
3 Jan	*To Peter B. Porter.*
5 Jan	*From Jane Polk.*
11 Jan	*From Peter Hagner.*
11 Jan	*From John Lowry.*

12 [Jan]	*From John McLean.*
20 Jan	*From Archibald Yell.*
23 Jan	*From William C. Cross.*
24 Jan	*From Phineas Bradley.*
25 Jan	*From Edmund Dillahunty.*
26 Jan	*From Adam R. Alexander.*
1 Feb	*From Joseph Greer.*
1 Feb	*From Joseph Greer.*
6 Feb	*From Phineas Bradley.*
6 Feb	*From Jeremiah Cherry.*
8 Feb	*From Nathaniel Laird.*
9 Feb	*From Lester Morris.*
10 Feb	*From Jonathan Webster.*
10 Feb	*From Archibald Yell.*
11 Feb	*To James L. Edwards.*
11 Feb	*From James Williams.*
13 Feb	*From James N. Smith.*
14 Feb	*From Leroy Hammons.*
15 Feb	*From William P. Smith.*
20 Feb	*From William Henry.*
20 Feb	*From Marshall T. Polk.*
21 Feb	*From Jesse W. Egnew.*
21 Feb	*From James L. Walker.*
25 Feb	*From Charles Becket and William P. Martin.*
[26 Feb]	*From James Rainey.*
27 Feb	*From Robert Harris.*
29 Feb	*From Benjamin W. Wilson.*
29 Feb	*From Peter Hagner.*
2 March	*From Nathaniel Steele.*
2 March	*From Archibald Yell.*
3 March	*From John Abernathy.*
5 March	*From George W. Terrell.*
6 March	*From Archibald Yell.*
7 March	*From Ezekiel P. McNeal.*
9 March	*From Adlai O. Harris.*
12 March	*From Darrel N. Sansom.*
13 March	*From Peter Hagner.*
15 March	*From R. E. C. Dougherty.*
15 March	*From William Fitzgerald.*
23 March	*From Andrew Jackson.*
27 March	*From Fielding Lucas, Jr.*
28 March	*From Joseph H. Wallace and William P. Martin.*
29 March	*From Samuel L. Southard.*
1 April	*To Henry Clay.*
13 April	*To Andrew Jackson.*
15 April	*From Henry Clay.*
15 April	To Andrew Jackson. ALS. DLC–AJ. Advises against publishing a personal rejoinder to James B. Ray's attacks.
21 April	*To Henry Clay.*
25 April	*From James L. Edwards.*

28 April	*From Henry Clay.*
3 May	*From Andrew Jackson.*
20 May	*From James L. Edwards.*
21 May	*From William Davidson.*
29 June	*To Andrew Jackson.*
12 July	*From Joseph Watson.*
21 July	From William Wirt. Copy. DNA–RG 60. Rejects request for copy of an opinion written for James Monroe in January 1824.
22 July	*From Daniel Brent.*
29 July	*From Phineas Bradley.*
1 Aug	*To [Andrew Jackson].*
10 Aug	*To [Department of War].*
16 Aug	*To Daniel Brent.*
19 Aug	*From William Davidson.*
26 Aug	*From John T. Brown.*
26 Aug	*From William Davidson.*
26 Aug	*From David Jarrett.*
26 Aug	*From William R. Rucker.*
31 Aug	*From John H. Camp.*
4 Sept	*To William R. Rucker.*
8 Sept	*To Andrew Jackson.*
8 Sept	*From Ezekiel P. McNeal.*
12 Sept	*From Daniel Brent.*
14 Sept	*From Charles Beckett.*
16 Sept	*From Andrew Jackson.*
20 Sept	*From Joel Pinson.*
24 Sept	*From Joseph B. Porter.*
[Oct 1828]	From Samuel P. Ashe. ALS. DLC–JKP. Discusses division and sale of a tract of Samuel Polk's lands in Haywood County.
20 Oct	*From James Brown.*
22 Oct	*From Sidney J. Harris.*
22 Oct	*From Ezekiel P. McNeal.*
4 Nov	*From John W. Childress.*
6 Nov	*From William B. Sutton.*
15 Nov	*To Andrew A. Kincannon.*
20 Nov	*From John M. Daniel.*
21 Nov	*From Benjamin R. Harris.*
24 Nov	*From Matthew Wood.*
28 Nov	*From Lester Morris.*
1 Dec	*To Andrew Jackson.*
5 Dec	*To Andrew Jackson.*
7 Dec	*From William Davis.*
11 Dec	*From George Graham.*
12 Dec	*From Peter Hagner.*
15 Dec	*From Peter Hagner.*
23 Dec	*From Lunsford M. Bramlett.*
25 Dec	*From Samuel Ragsdale.*
27 Dec	*From Lester Morris.*

27 Dec	*To Samuel L. Southard.*
28 Dec	*From John W. Childress.*

1829

4 Jan	From Marshall T. Polk. ALS. T–JKP. Advises that he has been offered half interest in the court clerkship of Mecklenburg County, North Carolina.
5 Jan	*From George Graham.*
5 Jan	*From Peter Hagner.*
5 Jan	*From Samuel L. Southard.*
8 Jan	*From William R. Rucker.*
10 Jan	*To John Campbell.*
15 Jan	*From George W. Barnett.*
15 Jan	*To James L. Edwards.*
15 Jan	*From Langford Fitzgerald.*
16 Jan	*To Davison McMillen.*
24 Jan	*To Benjamin F. Currey.*
27 Jan	*From William R. Rucker.*
31 Jan	*From Matthew Rhea.*
9 Feb	*From Nash Legrand.*
10 Feb	*To Andrew A. Kincannon.*
14 Feb	*From Archibald Yell.*
16 Feb	*From Burd S. Hurt.*
16 Feb	*From Fielding Lucas, Jr.*
17 Feb	*To Pryor Lea.*
20 Feb	*From Jonathan Webster.*
21 Feb	*From Peter Hagner.*
21 Feb	*From Peter Hagner.*
23 Feb	*From David C. Mitchell.*
28 Feb	*From Samuel D. Sansom.*
4 March	*From Susan Decatur.*
6 March	*From James L. Edwards.*
6 March	*To John McLean.*
13 March	*From Thomas J. Hodson.*
14 March	*From James L. Edwards.*
26 March	From Marshall T. Polk. ALS. T–JKP. Reports that his legal practice is paying his expenses.
31 March	*From Peter Hagner.*
22 April	*To Andrew Jackson.*
[25 April]	*From Adam R. Alexander.*
1 May	*To Adam R. Alexander.*
13 May	*From Joel Pinson.*
10 June	*From Peter Hagner.*
12 June	*To William Davidson.*
12 June	*To Daniel Graham.*
24 June	*To William R. Rucker.*
9 July	*From William Martin.*
30 July	*From James Leetch.*
23 Aug	*From William Davidson.*

27 Aug	*From Phineas Bradley.*
6 Sept	*From Joel Henry Dyer.*
9 Sept	*From Thomas Gore.*
9 Sept	*From Archibald Yell.*
10 Sept	*From Charles K. Gardner.*
19 Sept	*From Lester Morris.*
23 Sept	*From Arthur Nelson.*
30 Sept	*From Robert P. Harrison.*
3 Oct	*From Robert P. Harrison.*
3 Oct	*From David Jarrett.*
3 Oct	*From Ezekiel P. McNeal.*
22 Oct	*From Jonathan Currin.*
23 Oct	*From A. Y. Partee.*
5 Nov	*From Archibald Yell.*
30 Nov	*From Elisha Forrest.*
10 Dec	*From Henry Goodnight.*
12 Dec	*From James L. Edwards.*
12 Dec	*From Peter Hagner.*
12 Dec	*From Thomas White.*
15 Dec	*From Peter Hagner.*
15 Dec	*From Peter Hagner.*
16 Dec	*To Peter Hagner.*
18 Dec	*From Charles Gratiot.*
26 Dec	To [Pension Office]. ALS. TU. Forwards documents supporting a constituent's pension application.
29 Dec	*From John R. Vickers.*
31 Dec	*From William Gordon.*

1830

[1830?]	*From James Sikes.*
[Jan 1830?]	*From John E. Kirt.*
7 Jan	*From Charles T. Reese.*
8 Jan	*From Selah R. Hobbie.*
11 Jan	*From Robert T. Richey.*
12 Jan	*From James L. Edwards.*
12 Jan	*From Selah R. Hobbie.*
16 Jan	*From Peter Hagner.*
18 Jan	*From James Davis.*
21 Jan	*From George Graham.*
23 Jan	*To William T. Barry.*
26 Jan	*From Charles Gratiot.*
27 Jan	*From Patrick Maguire.*
29 Jan	*From Joseph McMurry.*
1 Feb	*From James L. Edwards.*
6 Feb	*From Benjamin Clements.*
6 Feb	From James L. Edwards. LS. DLC–JKP. Returns certificates in behalf of a constituent's pension claim.
8 Feb	*From William Gordon.*
16 Feb	*From Selah R. Hobbie.*
17 Feb	*From Peter Hagner.*

17 Feb	From Robert C. Thompson.
19 Feb	To Asbury Dickens.
25 Feb	From Henry Conway.
26 Feb	From George Graham.
27 Feb	From Archibald Yell.
1 March	From Joseph Greer.
2 March	From Obadiah B. Brown.
4 March	From John M. Bowyer.
5 March	From Linneus Smith.
7 March	From James L. Edwards.
7 March	To James L. Edwards.
7 March	From Thomas Kercheval.
8 March	To [Charles Gratiot?].
8 March	From Selah R. Hobbie.
10 March	From Rebecca Bregance.
16 March	From Charles C. Abernathy.
16 March	From Selah R. Hobbie.
17 March	From John H. Eaton.
30 March	From Peter Hagner.
1 April	From Alexander McDonald.
3 April	From Selah R. Hobbie.
10 April	From Ebenezer Hill and John H. Laird.
17 April	To William Gordon.
17 April	From James Walker.
19 April	From Peter Hagner.
20 April	From William F. Smith.
21 April	From John H. Rivers.
22 April	From Jane Maria Walker.
23 April	From James Eakin.
24 April	From Samuel Baker.
27 April	From George Graham.
30 April	From George Graham.
1 May	To [William Polk].
5 May	From [Thomas L. McKenney].
7 May	From Peter Hagner.
7 May	From William B. Lewis.
24 May	From Obadiah B. Brown.
25 May	From [Selah R. Hobbie?]
18 June	From Jackson Calhoun Blackburn.
23 June	From Charles K. Gardner.
29 June	From Samuel Gwin.
20 July	From David Jarrett.
31 July	From D. W. Wood.
[Aug 1830]	From William Polk.
2 Aug	From David Jarrett
13 Aug	From Benjamin Reynolds. ALS. Pvt. Ms. of W. R. Ewing, Cleveland, Tennessee. Acknowledges receipt of Polk's letter of August 6; states that he will conduct twenty Indian chiefs to Franklin, Tennessee, to meet with the president on the subject of land exchange; and expects to meet Polk at Columbia en route from the Chickasaw Agency to Franklin.

14 Aug	*To Andrew Jackson.*
15 Aug	*From Andrew Jackson.*
15 Aug	*From Collin S. Tarpley.*
16 Aug	*From Samuel D. Ingham.*
21 Aug	*From James L. Edwards.*
24 Aug	*From Ezekiel P. McNeal.*
24 Aug	*From Hugh Lawson White.*
27 Aug	*From David Jarrett.*
31 Aug	*From Andrew Jackson.*
31 Aug	*To Andrew Jackson.*
1 Sept	From Marshall T. Polk. ALS. T–JKP. Reports that he has been urged to run for the clerkship of the North Carolina House of Commons.
3 Sept	*From Alfred Balch.*
8 Sept	*From William B. Ross.*
14 Sept	*From Matthew St. Clair Clarke.*
27 Sept	*From Cave Johnson.*
29 Sept	*From James Bright.*
30 Sept	*From James Brown.*
1 Oct	From Marshall T. Polk. ALS. T–JKP. Inquires about an appointment to a consular post for himself.
11 Oct	*From Cave Johnson.*
16 Oct	*From George W. Lane.*
23 Oct	*From John H. Rivers.*
28 Oct	*From James Brown.*
10 Nov	*From George W. Lane.*
10 Nov	*From Samuel G. Smith.*
13 Nov	*From John W. Saunders.*
16 Nov	*From Archibald Yell.*
22 Nov	*From Peter Swanson.*
24 Nov	*From John H. Maney.*
24 Nov	*From Archibald Yell.*
25 Nov	*From Peter Swanson and Richard H. Allen.*
26 Nov	*From John W. Perry.*
27 Nov	*From John Edgar.*
1 Dec	*From William D. Moseley.*
1 Dec	*From Archibald Yell.*
5 Dec	*From James Walker.*
5 Dec	*From Joshua Williams.*
6 Dec	*From Marshall T. Polk.*
6 Dec	*From Gerard Van Buren.*
7 Dec	*From Jared S. Allen.*
8 Dec	*From Arnold Zellner.*
11 Dec	*From Robert Hill.*
11 Dec	*From Lester Morris.*
12 Dec	*From John A. Marrs.*
12 Dec	*From William L. Williford.*
13 Dec	*From Joseph Brown.*
13 Dec	*From John P. Smith.*
14 Dec	*From James H. Piper.*

15 Dec	*From Adam R. Alexander.*
15 Dec	*From William Gordon.*
15 Dec	*From Peter Hagner.*
15 Dec	*From Elijah Hayward.*
16 Dec	*From Arnold Zellner.*
19 Dec	*From Marshall T. Polk.*
20 Dec	*From James L. Edwards.*
20 Dec	*From Peter Hagner.*
20 Dec	*From John C. Hamilton.*
20 Dec	*From Ebenezer Hill.*
21 Dec	*From Archibald Yell.*
22 Dec	*From James L. Edwards.*
22 Dec	*From Elisha Whittlesey.*
23 Dec	*From James A. Craig.*
23 Dec	*To Peter Hagner.*
27 Dec	*From William Hill.*
27 Dec	*To Elisha Whittlesey.*
28 Dec	*From Peter Hagner.*
31 Dec	*From Marshall T. Polk.*

1831

2 Jan	*To John H. Eaton.*
2 Jan	*To Lester Morris.*
2 Jan	*From Archibald Yell.*
3 Jan	*From Peter Hagner.*
3 Jan	*From Peter Hagner.*
6 Jan	*From Alfred Balch.*
6 Jan	*From Obadiah B. Brown.*
8 Jan	*From Obadiah B. Brown.*
9 Jan [1831]	*From Owen Holmes.*
10 Jan	*From James Bright.*
10 Jan	*From Obadiah B. Brown.*
10 Jan	*From Archibald Yell.*
11 Jan	*From Jesse W. Egnew.*
12 Jan	*To William Newsum.*
14 Jan	*From James L. Edwards.*
14 Jan	*From Samuel D. Ingham.*
20 Jan	*To Martin Van Buren.*
22 Jan	To David Barton. ALS. DNA–RG 46. Recommends Stokely D. Hays for an appointment in the land office.
22 Jan	*From William C. Flournoy.*
29 Jan	*From John Blair and Peter Parsons.*
31 Jan	*From Terry H. Cahal.*
31 Jan	*From Joseph McBride.*
1 Feb	*From William Monroe.*
4 Feb	*From John P. Smith.*
4 Feb	*From William Coventry H. Waddell.*
5 Feb	*From Selah R. Hobbie.*
7 Feb	*From William Coventry H. Waddell.*

9 Feb	*From George W. Netherland.*
12 Feb	*From John K. Yerger.*
13 Feb	*From William Coventry H. Waddell.*
15 Feb	*From Joseph Greer.*
17 Feb	*From William H. Haywood, Jr.*
26 Feb	*From William Newsum.*
2 March	*From James L. Edwards.*
2 March	*From Peter Hagner.*
2 March	*To Sarah Polk.*
4 March	*From William D. Orr.*
8 March	*From William Davidson.*
12 March	*From Obadiah B. Brown.*
13 March	*From Archibald Yell.*
23 March	*From James Walker.*
28 March	*To Andrew Jackson.*
2 April	*From William B. Ross.*
6 April	*From George Lovell.*
18 April	*From A. M. M. Upshaw.*
19 April	*From Charles Veazie.*
5 May	To Hugh Lawson White. PL. Published in Nancy N. Scott, ed., *A Memoir of Hugh Lawson White* (Philadelphia: J. B. Lippincott & Co., 1856), 247–48. Urges White to accept a place in Jackson's cabinet, should the offer be made.
23 May	*From Joel M. Smith.*
26 May	*From Powhatan Ellis.*
10 June	*From Edward Ward.*
22 June	*From Hardin Perkins.*
23 June	*From James Brown.*
8 July	*To Hugh B. Porter.*
9 July	*From Matthew St. Clair Clarke.*
23 July	*From Moses Green.*
6 [Aug]	*From Lucius W. Stockton.*
9 Aug	*From Patton Anderson.*
10 Aug	*From James R. White.*
17 Aug	*From Cave Johnson.*
23 Aug	*From James R. White.*
1 Sept	*From Isham Robertson.*
4 Sept	*From John H. Rivers.*
4 Sept	*From Archibald Yell.*
17 Sept	From John H. Eaton. ALS. DLC–JKP. Encloses tabulated statistics on Indiana's population.
17 Sept	*From John H. Eaton.*
22 Sept	*From Andrew Derryberry.*
Oct	*From James Wilkins.*
2 Oct	*To John Coffee.*
17 Oct	*From Clement C. Clay.*
17 Oct	*From George G. Skipwith.*
25 Nov	*From Allen B. McElhany.*
8 Dec	*From Thomas N. McClain.*
13 Dec	*From Elijah Hayward.*

14 Dec	*To James L. Edwards.*
16 Dec	*From William Green.*
[16 Dec 1831]	*From William Green et al.*
16 Dec	*From Peter Hagner.*
17 Dec	*From William Gordon.*
17 Dec	*From Edward Stubbs.*
18 Dec	*From William and Sarah Logan.*
22 Dec	*From Bernard M. Patterson.*
23 Dec	*From Thomas B. Coleman.*
24 [Dec]	*From Charles A. Wickliffe.*
26 Dec	*From William Gordon.*
27 Dec	*From Hampton C. Williams.*
29 Dec	*To William A. Thompson.*
31 Dec	*From Charles Gratiot.*

1832

[1832?]	*From Benjamin Clearwaters.*
3 Jan	*From William B. Lewis.*
[4 Jan 1832]	*From P. Odlin et al.*
5 Jan	*From Selah R. Hobbie.*
9 Jan	*From Peter Hagner.*
14 Jan	*From John Medearis and Washington D. Medearis.*
15 Jan	*From Samuel Baker.*
21 Jan	*From Peter Hagner.*
21 Jan	*From Charles A. Wickliffe.*
29 Jan	*From Charles A. Wickliffe.*
31 Jan	*To Charles A. Wickliffe.*
4 Feb	*From Andrew M. D. Jackson.*
4 Feb	*From Thomas Wortham.*
27 Feb	*From Thomas Smith.*
2 March	*To Edward Livingston.*
4 March	*From Hall Hudson.*
5 March	*From Micheal Tipps.*
8 March	*From Amos Kendall.*
10 March	*From Peter Hagner.*
13 March	*From James L. Edwards.*
13 March	*From William Green.*
14 March	*To Isaac J. Thomas.*
17 March	*From Lewis Cass.*
19 March	*To Peter Hagner.*
20 March	*From Elbert Herring.*
21 March	*From William Green.*
22 March	*From William A. Thompson.*
23 March	*From Peter Hagner.*
4 April	*From John Medearis.*
11 April	*From William Brown.*
16 April	*From Thomas Harney.*
17 April	*From William C. Flournoy.*
17 April	*From Andrew C. Hays.*

18 April	*From Charles C. Mayson.*
19 April	*From Charles Boyles.*
22 April [1832]	*From A. Patterson.*
22 April	*From D. S. Shields.*
25 April	*From Jonathan Webster.*
26 April	*From [Grand Jury of Maury County].*
27 April	*To Jared Sparks.*
2 May	*From Thomas C. Whiteside.*
3 May	*From Jonathan Webster.*
4 May	*From Terry H. Cahal.*
5 May	*From James L. Edwards.*
6 May	*To James L. Edwards.*
6 May	*To Levi Woodbury.*
8 May	*From Levi Woodbury.*
11 May	*From William Hill.*
13 May	*From William D. Sims.*
15 May	*To Jared Sparks.*
19 May	*From Charles C. Mayson.*
31 May	*From Selah R. Hobbie.*
2 June	*From William Gordon.*
4 June	*From William B. Lewis.*
7 June	*From Obadiah B. Brown.*
11 June	*To Lewis Cass.*
12 June	*From John Robb.*
16 June	*From Charles Alexander.*
20 June	*From Selah R. Hobbie.*
21 June	*From Peter Hagner.*
25 June	*From Peter Hagner.*
4 July	*To Levi Woodbury.*
7 July	*From Jesse W. Egnew.*
10 July	*From Jesse W. Egnew.*
14 July	*From Talbot Jones & Company.*
15 July	*From Jeremiah Dial.*
15 July	*From Henry R. Taylor.*
22 July	*From Thomas Hartley Crawford.*
7 Aug	*From Henry Horn.*
8 Aug	*From Archibald Yell.*
11 Aug	*From William Rutledge.*
15 Aug	*To Andrew A. Kincannon.*
16 Aug	*From John W. Childress.*
24 Aug	*From David Gillespie.*
2 Sept	*From James Bates.*
3 Sept	*From Charles Cassedy.*
5 Sept	*From John H. Bills.*
11 Sept	From Selah R. Hobbie. N. DLC–JKP. Advises appointment of Homer Rainey as postmaster at Richland in Giles County.
12 Sept	*To William D. Sims.*
18 Sept	*From Matthew St. Clair Clarke.*
16 Oct	*To William R. Rucker.*
18 Oct	*From John Vickers.*

19 Oct	*To Lucius J. Polk.*
20 Oct	*From Archibald Yell.*
24 Oct	*To John Coffee.*
2 Nov	*From Samuel Bigham.*
2 Nov	*To [William Polk].*
15 Nov	*From John H. Bills.*
18 Nov	*From William Gilchrist.*
19 Nov	*From Kenneth L. Anderson.*
20 Nov	*From William J. Bingham.*
20 Nov	*From James McKisick.*
20 Nov	*From James Walker.*
21 Nov	*From Erwin J. Frierson.*
21 Nov	*From William M. Inge.*
21 Nov	*From William H. Polk.*
22 Nov	*From William E. Butler.*
23 Nov	*From Herbert Biles.*
23 Nov	*From John C. Brooke.*
23 Nov	*From Aaron V. Brown.*
25 Nov	*From Archibald Yell.*
26 Nov	*From Andrew A. Kincannon.*
26 Nov	*From A. M. M. Upshaw.*
27 Nov	*From William T. Barry.*
27 Nov	*To John Coffee.*
27 Nov	*From William S. Moore.*
27 Nov	*From Isaac Southworth.*
28 Nov	*To [William Polk].*
28 Nov	*From Thomas Smith.*
28 Nov	*To Harvey M. Watterson and John H. Laird.*
29 Nov	*From McKay W. Campbell.*
29 Nov	*From William D. Moseley.*
2 Dec	*From William H. Waide.*
3 Dec	*From Charles C. Mayson.*
3 Dec	*From James Walker.*
5 Dec	*From William H. Polk.*
6 Dec	*From Joseph Brown.*
6 Dec	*From Thomas Harney.*
6 Dec	*From William Polk.*
[6 Dec 1832]	*From Jonathan Webster.*
7 Dec	*From Elisha S. Campbell.*
7 Dec	*From John Rayburn.*
8 Dec	*From William L. S. Dearing.*
9 Dec	*From Henry C. Lester.*
11 Dec	*From John O. Cooke and William B. Cooke.*
11 Dec	*From Adlai O. Harris.*
11 Dec	*From James Walker.*
11 Dec	*From James L. Walker.*
12 Dec	*From James A. Craig.*
12 Dec	*From Peter Luna.*
12 Dec	*From John C. Wormeley.*
13 Dec	*To William Polk.*

13 Dec	From Samuel H. Williams.
14 Dec	To James L. Edwards.
14 Dec	From Alfred Flournoy.
14 Dec	From James Meriwether.
15 Dec	From Peter Hagner.
15 Dec	From John P. Smith.
15 Dec	From William J. Whitthorne.
16 Dec	From Andrew Jackson.
16 Dec	From David R. Mitchell.
16 Dec	From Archibald Yell.
18 Dec	From Blackman Coleman.
18 Dec	From James E. Heath.
18 Dec	From Charles C. Mayson.
18 Dec	From Isaac J. Thomas.
19 Dec	From Adlai O. Harris.
20 Dec	From Joel Henry Dyer.
20 Dec	From Thomas Martin.
20 Dec	From Gilbert D. Taylor.
22 Dec	From Owen Holmes.
23 Dec	From Thomas J. Porter.
24 Dec	From Joseph N. Johnson.
24 Dec	From Isaac J. Thomas.
25 Dec	From Samuel C. Mabson.
26 Dec	From William Polk.
26 Dec	From John C. Wormeley.
27 Dec	From Archibald Yell.
29 Dec	From William J. Alexander.
29 Dec	From Lewis Cass.
30 Dec	From John W. Childress.
31 Dec	From John W. Yeats.

1833

1833	From Louis McLane. ALS. DLC–JKP. Requests a meeting with Polk.
[1833?]	From [Reuben M. Whitney].
1 Jan	From Samuel Baker. ALS. DLC–JKP. Requests Polk's assistance in obtaining a land warrant.
3 Jan	From McKay W. Campbell.
3 Jan	From Charles C. Mayson.
3 Jan	From William S. Moore.
3 Jan	From Roger B. Taney.
4 Jan	From Ebenezer J. Shields.
5 Jan	From Frederick E. Becton, Jr.
5 Jan [1833]	From Samuel Bigham.
5 Jan	From Benjamin Clements.
6 Jan	From Gideon J. Pillow.
8 Jan	From Samuel H. Laughlin.
9 Jan	From John W. Childress.
9 Jan	From Ezekiel P. McNeal.

9 Jan	*From John Rayburn.*
11 Jan	*From Benjamin Clements.*
11 Jan	*From James W. Wyly.*
13 Jan	*From William P. Bradburn.*
13 Jan	*From Marshall P. Pinkard.*
13 Jan	*From William H. Polk.*
14 Jan	*From Joseph Brown.*
15 Jan	*From William R. Rucker.*
15 Jan	*From Jonathan Webster.*
16 Jan	*From A. W. Bills.*
16 Jan	*From Thomas Collin.*
16 Jan	*From Archibald Yell.*
17 Jan	*From Herbert Biles.*
18 Jan	From William Barnett. ALS. DLC–JKP. Requests information concerning his application for a pension.
18 Jan	*From Daniel Leatherman.*
18 Jan	*From Spivey McKissick.*
19 Jan	*From Samuel Bigham.*
19 Jan	From A. M. Hughes. ALS. DLC–JKP. Cancels subscription to the Washington *Globe*.
19 Jan	*From Daniel Stephens.*
20 Jan	*From Aaron V. Brown.*
21 Jan	*From Isaac Southworth.*
22 Jan	*From Isaac J. Thomas.*
22 Jan	*From John A. Thomas.*
23 Jan	*From Samuel P. Black.*
23 Jan	*From Samuel W. Polk.*
23 Jan	*From John C. Wormeley.*
24 Jan	*From Elisha S. Campbell.*
24 Jan	*From Joseph Cotton.*
24 Jan	*From Lincoln County Citizens.*
24 Jan	*From James Walker.*
24 Jan	*From Russell M. Williamson.*
25 Jan	*From John H. Anderson.*
25 Jan	*From Hiram Holt.*
25 Jan	*From Collin S. Tarpley.*
26 Jan	*From Lincoln County Citizens.*
26 Jan	*From Barkly Martin.*
26 Jan	From John W. Norton. ALS. DLC–JKP. Requests Polk's assistance in obtaining a pension for Hezekiah Jordan of Lincoln County.
[26 Jan 1833]	From William L. Williford. ALS. DLC–JKP. Believes that James Walker's absence is the reason why his name is not on the enclosed petition. (Enclosure not found.)
27 Jan	*From John Eliot.*
27 Jan	*From Henry Robertson.*
27 Jan	*From Samuel G. Smith.*
27 Jan [1833]	*From Reuben M. Whitney.*
28 Jan	*From Charles C. Mayson.*
29 Jan	*From William H. Polk.*

Feb	*From Shadrack Penn.*
1 Feb	*From Isaac Southworth.*
1 Feb	*From A. M. M. Upshaw.*
1 Feb	*From John K. Yerger.*
2 Feb	*From John W. Childress.*
2 Feb	*From Benjamin Clements.*
3 Feb	*From Louis McLane.*
3 Feb	*From Andrew Matthews.*
3 Feb	*From Joseph Knox Walker.*
4 Feb	*From Louis McLane.*
6 Feb	*From Lewis Cass.*
6 Feb	*From Jonathan Webster and Moses Hart.*
7 Feb	*From William Dearing.*
7 Feb	*From Jonathan S. Hunt.*
7 Feb [1833]	*From A. O. P. Nicholson.*
7 Feb	*From Matthew Rhea.*
8 Feb [1833]	*From Louis McLane.*
9 Feb [1833]	*From Louis McLane.*
9 Feb	*From Reuben M. Whitney.*
11 Feb	*From Noah's Fork Citizens.*
11 Feb	*From Reuben M. Whitney.*
12 Feb	From Henry C. Martin. ALS. DLC–JKP. Requests Polk's assistance in obtaining pensions for three neighbors.
13 Feb	*From Adlai O. Harris.*
15 Feb	*From Herbert Biles.*
15 Feb	*From Benjamin Carter.*
17 Feb	*From William H. Polk.*
18 Feb	*From Samuel G. Smith.*
19 Feb	*From Elijah Hayward.*
26 Feb	*From James Robert Donaldson.*
27 Feb	From George Beltzhoover. LS. DLC–JKP. Responds to Polk's request concerning transportation arrangements from Baltimore to Pittsburgh.
2 March	*From Louis McLane.*
4 March	*To James L. Edwards.*
9 March	*From William Davidson.*
25 March	*To Clement C. Clay.*
25 March	*From Isaac S. Lyon.*
24 April	*To Cave Johnson.*
8 May	*To James L. Edwards.*
16 May	*To Levi Woodbury.*
22 May	From James L. Edwards. ALS. DLC–JKP. Advises Polk concerning disposition of various pension claims.
30 May	*From Andrew Jackson Donelson.*
11 June	To James L. Edwards. ALS. DNA–RG 15. Forwards pension request for Isaiah Reed.
11 June	*To James L. Edwards.*
12 June	*From Ebenezer Rice.*
[16] June	*From Thomas B. Coleman.*
20 June	*To Cave Johnson.*

24 June	*From Edwin A. Keeble.*
24 June	*To Louis McLane.*
25 June	*From Cave Johnson.*
26 June	*From John Blair.*
29 June	*From John Robb.*
2 July	*From Clement C. Clay.*
3 July	*From William T. Fitzgerald.*
10 July	*From Archibald Yell.*
13 July	From John S. Waddle. ALS. DLC–JKP. Requests action concerning legal matters.
8 Aug	*To Francis P. Blair.*
10 Aug	*From Lewis Cass.*
13 Aug	*To William B. Lewis.*
19 Aug	*From Clement C. Clay.*
26 Aug	*From Humphrey H. Leavitt.*
28 Aug	*From William M. Inge.*
29 Aug	*From Cave Johnson.*
31 Aug	*From Andrew Jackson.*
1 Sept	*To James L. Edwards.*
4 Sept	*To James L. Edwards.*
[7 Sept 1833]	*From Joseph W. Chinn.*
7 Sept	*To Cave Johnson.*
18 Sept	*From John Turney.*
26 Sept	*To Cave Johnson.*
26 Sept	*To William B. Lewis.*
5 Oct	*From Henry Horn.*
8 Oct	*From Terry H. Cahal.*
8 Oct	*From James L. Edwards.*
16 [Oct]	*From Ephraim Beanland.*
19 Oct	*From Benjamin Clearwaters.*
20 Oct	*From John W. Childress.*
20 Oct	*From James Walker.*
21 Oct	*From Felix Grundy.*
22 Oct	*From William Polk.*
22 Oct	*From James Walker.*
27 Oct	*From Andrew A. Kincannon.*
28 Oct	*From William L. S. Dearing.*
28 Oct	*From Nathan Green.*
30 [Oct]	*From Ephraim Beanland.*
30 Oct	*From James Campbell.*
30 Oct	From Robert Neelly. ALS. DLC–JKP. Requests information concerning possible land purchases.
31 Oct	*From Adlai O. Harris.*
3 Nov	*From Robert L. Caruthers.*
4 Nov	*From Adlai O. Harris.*
5 Nov	*From Thomas P. Moore.*
7 Nov	From Thomas B. Coleman. ALS. DLC–JKP. Requests prompt action on his claim.
7 Nov	*From William L. Neal.*
7 Nov	*From James Walker.*

8 Nov	*From John F. Goneke.*
9 Nov	*From Adlai O. Harris.*
12 Nov	*From William R. Rucker.*
13 Nov	*From Samuel P. Walker.*
14 Nov	*From William L. S. Dearing.*
16 Nov	*From Adlai O. Harris.*
20 Nov	*From Elliott Hickman.*
20 Nov	*From James C. O'Reilly.*
21 Nov	*From John Beck.*
21 Nov	*From Adlai O. Harris.*
22 Nov	*From Benjamin Clements.*
22 Nov	From William Davis. ALS. DLC–JKP. Requests attention to several pension claims.
23 Nov	*From Jacob Bletcher.*
23 Nov	*From McKay W. Campbell.*
24 Nov	From John Turney. ALS. DLC–JKP. Introduces William Campbell.
25 Nov	*From Peter R. Booker.*
25 Nov	From William E. Butler. ALS. DLC–JKP. Recommends Harper Shepherd for appointment in the Navy.
25 Nov	*From McKay W. Campbell.*
25 Nov	*From William H. Polk.*
26 Nov	*From Henry Horn.*
[27 Nov 1833]	From Samuel G. Smith. ALS. DLC–JKP. Encloses duplicate certificate of Polk's reelection to Congress; orders subscription to the Washington *Congressional Globe.* (Enclosure not found.)
28 Nov	*From Samuel G. Smith.*
29 Nov	*From Jonathan Webster.*
29 Nov	*From James C. Wilson.*
30 Nov	*From James H. Thomas.*
[Dec 1833?]	From George Johnson. LS. DLC–JKP. Recommends an increase in the salary of government clerks.
[Dec 1833]	*From Roger B. Taney.*
[Dec 1833]	*From Roger B. Taney.*
1 Dec	*From Ephraim Beanland.*
1 Dec	*From James M. Wayne.*
1 Dec	*From Archibald Yell.*
2 Dec	*From Henry Horn.*
3 Dec	*From Samuel Burch.*
3 Dec	*From Benjamin F. McKie.*
3 Dec	*From John F. McWhirter.*
3 Dec	*From James N. Smith.*
3 Dec	*From Roger B. Taney.*
4 Dec	*From John A. Allen.*
4 Dec	*From Richard Long.*
4 Dec	From Nathaniel Simmons. ALS. DLC–JKP. Requests information concerning disposition of pension claim.
5 Dec	*From William P. Bradburn.*
5 Dec	*From George W. Campbell.*

5 Dec	*From Nash Legrand.*
[5 Dec 1833]	*From Thomas P. Moore.*
5 Dec [1833]	*From A. O. P. Nicholson.*
[8 Dec 1833?]	From John M. Brodhead. ALS. DLC–JKP. Extends regards of his father, John Brodhead, now residing in East Salisbury, Massachusetts.
8 Dec	*From John W. Childress.*
9 Dec	*From Thomas Hartley Crawford.*
9 Dec	*From Thomas J. Lacy.*
9 Dec	*From William Minter.*
9 Dec	From John Stone. ALS. DLC–JKP. Submits pension claim.
10 Dec	*From John T. Sullivan.*
11 Dec	*From William S. Fulton.*
11 Dec	From Joseph Rosson. ALS. DLC–JKP. Requests inquiry concerning a pension claim.
12 Dec	*From Levin H. Coe.*
12 Dec	*From Joel R. Smith.*
13 Dec	From Lewis Cass. Copy. DNA–RG 107. Transmits a request from the commissioner of pensions for an additional appropriation of $5,000 for clerk hire.
13 Dec	*To Roger B. Taney.*
13 Dec	*From James Walker.*
13 Dec	*From William L. Williford.*
14 Dec	From Samuel Burch. ALS. DLC–JKP. Requests return of memorial from the directors of the Bank of the United States.
[14 Dec 1833]	*From Ophelia C. Hays.*
14 Dec	*From James Walker.*
14 Dec	*From James Walker.*
16 Dec	*From Joel Henry Dyer.*
16 Dec	*To James L. Edwards.*
16 Dec	*From James Walker.*
17 Dec	*From Adlai O. Harris.*
17 Dec	*From Richard H. Mosby.*
17 Dec	*From Samuel P. Walker, Jr.*
18 Dec	*From Gerrard T. Greenfield.*
18 Dec	*From Andrew Jackson.*
18 Dec	*From James Walker.*
19 Dec	*From John Barney.*
19 Dec	From Lewis Cass. Copy. DNA–RG 107. Transmits request for an early appropriation for the corps of engineers. (Enclosure not found.)
19 Dec	From Louis McLane. Copy. DNA–RG 59. Requests that four items be appended to the State Department budget estimate for 1834.
19 Dec [1833]	*From Gideon J. Pillow.*
19 Dec	*From John Wurts.*
20 Dec	*From John Campbell.*
20 Dec	*From James Walker.*
20 Dec	*From John K. Yerger.*

21 Dec	*From Matthew Rhea.*
22 Dec	*From Ephraim Beanland.*
22 Dec	*From Aaron V. Brown.*
22 Dec	*From Charles Dayan.*
22 Dec	*From William T. Fitzgerald.*
23 Dec	From Lewis Cass. Copy. DNA–RG 107. Responds to an application that Polk made on behalf of Bostick's claim.
23 Dec	*From John Conrad.*
[23 Dec 1833]	*From Andrew Jackson.*
23 Dec	*To Andrew Jackson.*
24 Dec	*From Lewis Cass.*
24 Dec	*From William Moore.*
26 Dec	From Samuel McCall. ALS. DLC–JKP. Requests assistance with debt collection.
26 Dec	*From William H. Polk.*
27 Dec	*From anonymous writer.*
27 Dec	*From John Welsh, Jr.*
28 Dec	*From Lemuel Prewett.*
28 [Dec]	*To James Walker.*
30 Dec	*From Adlai O. Harris.*
31 Dec	*From Louis McLane.*

1834

[1834?]	*From Benjamin F. Currey.*
1 Jan	*From Erwin J. Frierson.*
2 Jan	*From Terry H. Cahal.*
2 Jan	*From Caruthers, Harris & Company.*
2 Jan	From Lewis Cass. Copy. DNA–RG 107. Encloses copy of letter requesting pay increases for watchmen of the War Department building. (Enclosure not found.)
2 Jan [1834]	*From William H. Polk.*
3 Jan	*From McKay W. Campbell.*
3 Jan	*From Adlai O. Harris.*
3 Jan	*From Robert P. Harrison.*
3 Jan	*From William Jenkins.*
4 Jan	*From Silas M. Caldwell.*
5 Jan	*To William Polk.*
7 Jan	*From McKay W. Campbell.*
7 Jan	*From George W. Haywood.*
7 Jan	*From John A. Moore.*
7 Jan	*From James C. Wilson.*
7 Jan	*From Joel Yancey.*
8 Jan	*From William G. Angel.*
8 Jan	*From Jesse D. Elliott.*
8 Jan	*From Gales & Seaton.*
8 Jan	*From Adlai O. Harris.*
8 Jan	From [Roger B. Taney]. Copy. DNA–RG 56. Advises that the Union Bank of New Orleans has purchased recently a considerable amount of domestic bills.

8 Jan	*From Isaac J. Thomas.*
8 Jan	*From John W. Yeats.*
9 Jan	*From Gerrard T. Greenfield.*
9 Jan	From Stoaks and Springer. LS. DLC–JKP. Requests Polk's assistance in obtaining payment for mail deliveries.
9 Jan	From [Roger B. Taney]. Copy. DNA–RG 56. Requests that an appropriation item for printing the records of the Supreme Court be added to the statement of estimates for the support of government.
9 Jan	*From James Walker.*
9 Jan	*From James Walker.*
10 Jan	From Lewis Cass. Copy. DNA–RG 107. Encloses a special estimate for additional appropriations for the Ordnance Department. (Enclosure not found.)
10 Jan	From Lewis Cass. Copy. DNA–RG 107. Encloses a letter from the commissioner of Indian Affairs requesting an appropriation. (Enclosure not found.)
10 Jan	*From John Ewing.*
10 Jan	*From Andrew C. Hays.*
10 Jan	*From Charles D. McLean.*
10 Jan	*From A. M. M. Upshaw.*
11 Jan	From Lewis Cass. Copy. DNA–RG 107. Transmits from the chief engineer an additional estimate for funds. (Enclosure not found.)
11 Jan	From Lewis Cass. Copy. DNA–RG 107. Transmits a copy from the commissary general of the estimate of purchases for that department. (Enclosure not found.)
11 Jan	*From David R. Mitchell.*
11 Jan	*From James Walker.*
12 Jan	*From Walker F. Leak.*
13 Jan	*From William L. Storrs.*
13 Jan	*From Roger B. Taney.*
13 Jan	*From Roger B. Taney.*
13 Jan	*From Roger B. Taney.*
14 Jan	*From W. F. Boyakin.*
14 Jan	*From Gideon Riggs.*
14 Jan	From Roger B. Taney. Copy. DNA–RG 56. Requests appropriations for several specified items.
15 Jan	From Noah T. George. ALS. DLC–JKP. Requests a copy of Polk's speech to the House on withdrawal of public deposits from the BUS.
16 Jan	From Lewis Cass. Copy. DNA–RG 107. Transmits letters pertaining to the removal of the raft on the Red River. (Enclosures not found.)
16 Jan	*From William H. Polk.*
17 Jan	*From Benjamin E. Carpenter.*
17 Jan	*From James Walker.*
18 Jan	*From Granville H. Frazer.*
18 Jan	*From John Medearis.*
18 Jan	*From William H. Stephens.*

20 Jan	*From Samuel C. Allen.*
20 Jan	*From Adlai O. Harris.*
20 Jan	*From Isaac J. Thomas.*
20 Jan	*From William M. Townsend.*
20 Jan	*From James Walker.*
20 Jan	*From William L. Williams.*
21 Jan	*From William Davidson.*
21 Jan	*From John H. Dew.*
21 Jan	*From Henry Hill.*
21 Jan	From N. T. C. Rosseter. ALS. DLC–JKP. Requests assistance in obtaining an appointment as a midshipman in the Navy.
21 Jan	*From Joel R. Smith.*
21 Jan	From Nathan Towson. Copy. DNA–RG 99. Returns appropriation bills, altered as requested.
21 Jan	*From Samuel P. Walker.*
22 Jan	From George Bomford. Copy. DNA–RG 156. Transmits a condensation of the special estimate of the Ordnance Department. (Enclosure not found.)
22 Jan	*From Silas M. Caldwell.*
22 Jan	*From William J. Crans.*
22 Jan	From Peter Hagner. Copy. DNA–RG 217. Responds to request for information on the War Department estimate for paying arrearages prior to July 1, 1815.
22 Jan [1834]	*From Gaspard Richard.*
22 Jan	*From James Walker.*
23 Jan	*From William Carroll.*
23 Jan	*From Edward W. Dale.*
23 Jan	*From George M. Dallas.*
23 Jan	From Wade Griffin. ALS. DLC–JKP. Requests Polk's intercession with the Treasury Department.
23 Jan	*From Archibald Yell.*
24 Jan	From J. Snow. ALS. DLC–JKP. Requests copy of Polk's speech to the House on withdrawal of public deposits from the BUS.
24 Jan	From Charles C. Tyler. ALS. DLC–JKP. Requests copy of Polk's speech to the House on withdrawal of public deposits from the BUS.
25 Jan	From George William Crump. LS. DLC–JKP. Discusses items from the appropriation request for the pension office.
25 Jan	*From William P. Martin.*
26 Jan	*From William J. Alexander.*
26 Jan	*From John H. Kain.*
27 Jan	*From Burd S. Hurt.*
27 Jan	*From Robert Mack.*
27 Jan	From John F. Marion. ALS. DLC–JKP. Expresses gratitude for aid in obtaining pension.
27 Jan	*From Gideon J. Pillow.*
28 Jan	From Nathaniel Steele. ALS. DLC–JKP. Introduces William D. Ferguson of Arkansas.

29 Jan	*From Joseph Brown.*
30 Jan	*From Washington Barrow.*
30 Jan	To Henry Clay. ALS. DLC–JKP. Forwards document addressed to Clay.
31 Jan	*From J. A. W. Andrews.*
31 Jan	*From Elijah H. Burritt.*
31 Jan	*From Henry Horn.*
1 Feb	*From Ephraim Beanland.*
1 Feb	*From William L. S. Dearing.*
1 Feb	*From Hillary Langtry.*
1 Feb	*From William B. Turley.*
1 Feb	*From John Wallace.*
2 Feb	From Cyrus P. Bradley. ALS. DLC–JKP. Requests copy of Polk's speech to the House on withdrawal of public deposits from the BUS.
2 Feb	*From Arthur T. Isom.*
2 Feb	From Edward Nunnelee. ALS. DLC–JKP. Requests information concerning pension claim of Nathan Sunderland.
2 Feb	*From Isham G. Searcy.*
2 Feb	*From Joseph Ury.*
3 Feb	From Daniel Kurtz. Copy. DNA–RG 107. Encloses explanations of expenditure requests. (Enclosure not found.)
3 Feb	*From Louis McLane.*
3 Feb	*From William H. Polk.*
3 Feb	*From Gaspard Richard.*
4 Feb	*From Richard H. Mosby.*
4 Feb	*From Nathaniel Smith.*
4 Feb	*From William F. Smith.*
4 Feb	From Roger B. Taney. Copy. DNA–RG 56. Discusses appropriations concerning the purchase of land and erection of custom houses in several cities.
4 Feb	From Roger B. Taney. Copy. DNA–RG 56. Requests correction of clerical error in letter of January 14, 1834.
4 Feb	*From Roger B. Taney.*
5 Feb	*From Alfred Balch.*
5 Feb	*From Thomas J. Lacy.*
6 Feb	From Lewis Cass. Copy. DNA–RG 107. Transmits a report from the commissioner of pensions. (Enclosure not found.)
6 Feb	*To Lewis Cass.*
6 Feb	*From Anne Newport Royall.*
6 Feb	*From James H. Thomas.*
7 Feb	From William T. Barry. Copy. DNA–RG 28. Discusses errors in a report of October 1, 1833, regarding employment of clerks in the Post Office Department.
7 Feb	*From William T. Barry.*
7 Feb	*From William J. Whitthorne.*
8 Feb	*From Caruthers, Harris & Company.*
8 Feb	*From Adlai O. Harris.*
8 Feb	*From Samuel G. Smith.*
9 Feb	*From Josephus C. Guild.*

9 Feb	*From Andrew C. Hays.*
10 Feb	*From James H. Piper.*
10 Feb	*From Roger B. Taney.*
10 Feb	*From Archibald Yell.*
10 Feb	*From Zach B. Ziegler.*
11 Feb	*From Samuel Bigham.*
11 Feb	From Lewis Cass. Copy. DNA–RG 107. Transmits a report from the chief engineer regarding the continuation of a road in Alabama. (Enclosure not found.)
11 Feb	*From Laurence Loller.*
11 Feb	*From John G. Mosby.*
11 Feb	*From Archibald Yell.*
12 Feb	*From Nathan Gaither.*
13 Feb	*From Ephraim Beanland.*
13 Feb	From Lewis Cass. Copy. DNA–RG 107. Transmits a letter from the commissioner of Indian Affairs regarding the necessity of a further appropriation to complete the surveys under the treaty of Prairie du Chien. (Enclosure not found.)
13 Feb	From Lewis Cass. Copy. DNA–RG 107. Transmits a communication from the commissioner of Indian Affairs requesting funds to effect the 4th Article of the treaty with the Appalachicola Indians in Florida. (Enclosure not found.)
13 Feb	From Lewis Cass. Copy. DNA–RG 107. Transmits a letter from the second auditor requesting an appropriation to pay Indian claims now due. (Enclosure not found.)
13 Feb	*From Peter Hagner.*
13 Feb	*From Archibald Yell.*
14 Feb	*From Joseph Brown.*
14 Feb	*From Samuel W. Polk.*
14 Feb	*From James Walker.*
16 Feb	*From Horatio Coop.*
16 Feb	*From Ephraim D. Dickson.*
16 Feb	*From George W. Haywood.*
17 Feb	From Lewis Cass. Copy. DNA–RG 107. Transmits a report from the chief engineer regarding improvement of the Savannah River. (Enclosure not found.)
[17 Feb 1834]	From Robert Coleman. ALS. DLC–JKP. Requests assistance in obtaining receipts from S. D. Frierson.
17 Feb	*From Moses Dawson.*
18 Feb	*From Kenneth L. Anderson.*
18 Feb	*From McKay W. Campbell.*
18 Feb	*From Ebenezer J. Shields.*
18 Feb	*From Samuel G. Smith.*
18 Feb	From [Roger B. Taney]. Copy. DNA–RG 56. Transmits a letter from the second comptroller requesting additional clerks. (Enclosure not found.)
18 Feb	*From James Walker.*
18 Feb	*From James Walker.*
19 Feb	*From James M. Long.*
19 Feb	From Roger B. Taney. Copy. DNA–RG 56. Requests addi-

	tional appropriation for the members of the legislative council of Florida for the year 1833.
19 Feb	*From James Walker.*
20 Feb	*From Spencer Clark Gist.*
20 Feb	*From Thomas Watson.*
21 Feb	*From Elijah Hayward.*
22 Feb	*From Samuel Bigham.*
22 Feb	*From William Carroll.*
22 Feb	*From John Chisholm.*
22 Feb	*From Powhatan Gordon.*
23 Feb	*From James Walker.*
24 Feb	From Lewis Cass. Copy. DNA–RG 107. Transmits report from the chief engineer regarding obstructions in the Savannah River. (Enclosure not found.)
24 Feb	From Lewis Cass. Copy. DNA–RG 107. Transmits report from the commissary general regarding the costs for removal of the Cherokees to the West. (Enclosure not found.)
24 Feb	From John Clark. ALS. DLC–JKP. Requests a copy of Polk's speech to the House on withdrawal of public deposits from the BUS.
24 Feb	*From James Walker.*
25 Feb	From John Gordon. ALS. DLC–JKP. Introduces his brother, William Gordon.
26 Feb	From Lewis Cass. Copy. DNA–RG 107. Transmits a report from the quartermaster general regarding an additional appropriation for road construction in Arkansas. (Enclosure not found.)
26 Feb	*From James Walker.*
27 Feb	*From David T. Caldwell.*
27 Feb	*From William H. Polk.*
27 Feb	*To Levi Woodbury.*
28 Feb	*To Lewis Cass.*
28 Feb	From Roger B. Taney. Copy. DNA–RG 56. Transmits a copy of a letter from Peter Hagner. (Enclosure not found.)
1 March	*From A. W. Bills.*
1 March	From Addison Lea et al. LS. DLC–JKP. Inform Polk of his election as an honorary member of the Literary Society of Randolph Macon College.
1 March	*From John G. Mosby.*
1 March	*From James Walker.*
4 March	*From S. Morris Waln.*
5 March	From William Barnett. ALS. DLC–JKP. Requests Polk's aid in securing pension.
5 March	From Lewis Cass. Copy. DNA–RG 107. Transmits estimate of claims for the buildings at Harper's Ferry. (Enclosure not found.)
5 March	From Thomas B. Coleman. ALS. DLC–JKP. Requests action concerning his claim.
5 March	*From Andrew Hays.*
5 March	*From James Walker.*

6 March	*From Samuel H. Laughlin.*
7 March	*From Ephraim Beanland.*
7 March	*From Elbert Herring.*
7 March	*From James McKisick.*
7 March	From Hampton C. Williams. ALS. DLC–JKP. Requests copy of Polk's speech to the House on withdrawal of public deposits from the BUS, and the counter report by Horace Binney.
8 March	*From William D. Quin.*
10 March	*From Orange H Dibble.*
10 March	From Roger B. Taney. Copy. DNA–RG 56. Requests an appropriation for payment of legal fees.
10 March	*From George W. Terrell.*
10 March	*From Joel Webster.*
11 March	From Samuel D. Frierson. ALS. DLC–JKP. Discusses legal matters.
11 March	From Louis McLane. Copy. DNA–RG 59. Requests an appropriation for an additional payment for the statue of Washington.
11 March	*From J. M. Neely.*
11 March	*From Nathaniel Smith.*
11 March	*From Roger B. Taney.*
12 March	*From Kenneth L. Anderson.*
[12 March 1834]	From William L. S. Dearing. ALS. DLC–JKP. Requests that Polk present the enclosed (not found) to the commissioner of the General Land Office.
12 March	*From William Hogan.*
13 March	From Roger B. Taney. Copy. DNA–RG 56. Requests additional appropriation for the legislative council of Michigan Territory.
13 March	*From John A. Thomas.*
14 March	*From Allen Brown.*
14 March	*From Elijah H. Burritt.*
14 March	From Roger B. Taney. Copy. DNA–RG 56. Responds to inquiry concerning the estimate of appropriation for balance due Lucius Lyon.
14 March	From John T. Wait. ALS. DLC–JKP. Requests a copy of Polk's speech to the House on withdrawal of public deposits from the BUS.
15 March	*From Charles Caldwell.*
15 March	*From Isaac Edwards.*
16 March	*From Moses Dawson.*
17 March	*From William H. Polk.*
17 March	From Peter Swanson. ALS. DLC–JKP. Requests assistance in obtaining better postal service.
17 March	*From Peter Wager.*
18 March	*From Silas M. Caldwell.*
18 March	From Lewis Cass. Copy. DNA–RG 107. Returns letters requesting appropriation for surveying Indian reservations. (Enclosures not found.)

18 March	From Louis McLane. Copy. DNA–RG 59. Discusses the justification for supporting the claims agents in London and Paris.
19 March	*From Samuel A. Gillespie.*
19 March	From Louis McLane. Copy. DNA–RG 59. Transmits copies of the correspondence containing the terms of the agreement for the execution of the statue of Washington. (Enclosures not found.)
19 March	*From David R. Mitchell.*
20 March	*From McKay W. Campbell.*
21 March	*From John W. M. Breazeale.*
21 March	*From Thomas P. Moore.*
21 March	From Roger B. Taney. Copy. DNA–RG 56. Transmits an audit on the sale of government property in New Orleans.
22 March	*From James Brown.*
23 March	*From John W. Jones.*
23 March	*From John G. Mosby.*
23 March	*From James Osburn.*
23 March	*From John A. Thomas.*
24 March	*From Stephen Adams.*
26 March	*From William P. Duval.*
26 March	*From Seaborn Jones.*
28 March	*From Seaborn Jones.*
28 March	From Louis McLane. Copy. DNA–RG 59. Requests appropriation for the pavement of the passages on the lower floor of the North East Executive Building.
29 March	From Lewis Cass. Copy. DNA–RG 107. Recommends purchase of land as a site for quarters for the engineers and laborers employed in the erection of the fort in Pensacola harbor, Florida.
29 March	*From Louis McLane.*
1 April	*From Ephraim Beanland.*
1 April	*To Roger B. Taney.*
7 April	From M. R. Talbot. ALS. DLC–JKP. Solicits position as clerk of one of the House committees.
8 April	From Thomas Chapman. ALS. DLC–JKP. Encloses a memorial to Congress.
8 April	*From James H. Thomas.*
9 April	From Louis McLane. Copy. DNA–RG 59. Forwards a note on the balances credited to the diplomatic service and explains some of the accounts outstanding.
10 April	*To a Philadelphia Committee.*
11 April	*From Silas M. Caldwell.*
11 April	*From William B. Lewis.*
11 April	From John Maxwell. ALS. DLC–JKP. Requests information regarding pension law.
12 April	*From Eleazar Early.*
12 April	*From Robert Mack.*
15 April	*From Roger B. Taney.*
15 April	*From Roger B. Taney.*

15 April	*From Abraham Whinnery.*
16 April	*From Jeremiah Cherry.*
16 April	*From Jesse D. Elliott.*
16 April	*To William H. Polk.*
17 April	*From Lewis Cass.*
17 April	*From Matthew St. Clair Clarke.*
17 April	*From Isaac K. Hanson.*
[18 April 1834]	*From Isaac K. Hanson.*
18 April	From Isaac S. Lyon. ALS. DLC–JKP. Requests copy of Polk's speech to the House on withdrawal of public deposits from the BUS.
19 April	From Lewis Cass. Copy. DNA–RG 107. Encloses request for additional appropriation to complete the road from Detroit to Fort Gratiot. (Enclosure not found.)
20 April	*From James Walker.*
21 April	*From Samuel G. Smith.*
21 April	*From Roger B. Taney.*
23 April	From Lewis Cass. Copy. DNA–RG 107. Requests an appropriation for the removal of Creek Indians.
24 April	From Lewis Cass. Copy. DNA–RG 107. Transmits a statement from the chief engineer justifying the necessity of changes in the estimate of funds required to cover arrearages due several agents. (Enclosure not found.)
24 April	*From Lewis Cass.*
24 April	*From Benjamin Phillips.*
27 April	*To James L. Edwards.*
27 April	*From John McKenzie.*
28 April	*From Micajah Bullock.*
28 April	*From Boling Gordon.*
28 April	From Louis McLane. Copy. DNA–RG 59. Transmits a statement of appropriations and expenditures on account of intercourse with the Mediterranean powers for the last five years.
30 April	From Lewis Cass. Copy. DNA–RG 107. Transmits papers showing the situation of the works at Fort Calhoun. (Enclosures not found.)
30 April	From Roger B. Taney. Copy. DNA–RG 56. Requests an appropriation to compensate collectors, surveyors, and other employees whose income has suffered due to a reduction in tariffs.
[May 1834]	*From Lewis Cass.*
1 May	*From Ephraim Beanland.*
1 May	*From [Barry] Gillespie.*
1 May	*From Roger B. Taney.*
2 May	*From James Walker.*
2 May	*From James L. Walker.*
3 May	*From Marshall P. Pinkard.*
3 May	*From William H. Polk.*
3 May	From Richard Taylor, Jr. ALS. DLC–JKP. Responds to an inquiry about a land warrant in the name of James Upshaw.

5 May	*From Robert Mack.*
5 May	*From Louis McLane.*
5 May	*From John Y. Mason.*
7 May	*From Richard C. Allen.*
7 May	From Louis McLane. Copy. DNA–RG 59. Returns letter of Isaac T. Smith and copies of the census for 1790 and 1800.
7 May	*From Robert Mills.*
8 May	*From Lewis Cass.*
8 May	*From Jeremiah Cherry.*
9 May	From William Newsum. ALS. DLC–JKP. Requests a duplicate of his pension authorization.
10 May	*From Spencer Clark Gist.*
10 May	*From James L. Guest.*
10 May	*From John Y. Mason.*
12 May	*To Lewis Cass.*
12 May	*From Powhatan Ellis.*
[12 May 1834]	*From George W. Haywood.*
[14 May 1834]	From Peter Swanson. ALS. DLC–JKP. Requests information concerning congressional action.
15 May	From anonymous writer. L. DLC–JKP. Comments on the current political scene.
15 May	From Lewis Cass. ALS. DLC–JKP. Requests that Polk return the letter and enclosure relating to the road in Arkansas.
15 May	*From Lewis Cass.*
15 May	*From David Jarrett.*
15 May	*From James Walker.*
16 May	From Lewis Cass. Copy. DNA–RG 107. Transmits a duplicate of the estimate for the construction of certain roads. (Enclosure not found.)
16 May	From Lewis Cass. Copy. DNA–RG 107. Transmits estimates of the costs of surveys. (Enclosure not found.)
16 May	From Thomas Greer. ALS. DLC–JKP. Encloses two notes (not found) on Hesekiah J. Balch.
[16 May 1834]	*From Thomas P. Moore.*
17 May	From Thomas B. Coleman. ALS. DLC–JKP. Requests information on his claim.
18 May	*From Andrew Jackson.*
19 May	From Lewis Cass. Copy. DNA–RG 107. Transmits reduced estimate for the number of rifles required for the emigrating Creek Indians. (Enclosure not found.)
21 May	*From James Bright.*
21 May	*From William H. Polk.*
21 May	From Roger B. Taney. Copy. DNA–RG 56. Requests a bill for the relief of legal expenses incurred by Willaim C. H. Waddell, U.S. marshal.
23 May	*From Powhatan Ellis.*
24 May	From anonymous writer. L. DLC–JKP. Discusses the character of the U.S. Senate.
24 May	From James Blair. ALS. DLC–JKP. Requests that his let-

ter, denouncing Congress as a tool of the Anti-Christ, be read before the House.

26 May   *From McKay W. Campbell.*

27 May   From Talbot Jones & Co. LS. DLC–JKP. Acknowledges receipt of letters and packages and explains disposition of packages.

28 May   From J. B. Lowe. ALS. DLC–JKP. Requests pension for Thomas Stewart.

29 May   *From James Walker.*

1 June   *From Ephraim Beanland.*

1 June   *From William E. Gillespie.*

3 June   *From Elliot H. Fletcher.*

3 June   *From William H. Polk.*

4 June   From Lewis Cass. Copy. DNA–RG 107. Transmits a request from the Ordnance Department. (Enclosure not found.)

4 June   *From Gaspard Richard.*

4 June   *From Archibald Yell.*

5 June   From J. Wallace Griffith. ALS. DLC–JKP. Requests copies of Polk's speeches on the removal of deposits from the BUS.

9 June   From Lewis Cass. Copy. DNA–RG 107. Requests appropriations for the second auditor's office to cover arrearages prior to 1817 and to cover half-pay pensions.

11 June   *From Joseph M. Nourse.*

12 June   From Edward Nunnelee. ALS. DLC–JKP. Requests information concerning claim application for Nathan Sunderland.

15 June   From Conway D. Whittle. ALS. DLC–JKP. Requests information about a tract of land reserved for certain veterans.

16 June   *From William J. Alexander.*

18 June   From Lewis Cass. Copy. DNA–RG 107. Transmits draft of an appropriations bill for Indian treaties ratified since commencement of the present session of Congress. (Enclosure not found.)

20 June   *From George A. Waggaman.*

21 June   *From William G. Childress.*

21 June   *From James A. Craig.*

21 June   *From Richard Peters.*

21 June   From Joseph Taylor & Son. LS. DLC–JKP. Advises that a package has been forwarded to Polk at Washington; encloses charge to cover the handling expenses.

24 June   *From Benjamin F. Butler.*

24 June   *From Roger B. Taney.*

24 June   *From Roger B. Taney.*

24 June   *From James Walker.*

25 June   *From Lewis Cass.*

25 June   *From Robert Mills.*

28 June   *From [Andrew C. Hays].*

30 June   *From James Walker.*

1 July	From Frederick Konig. ALS. DLC–JKP. Polk to recommend a lawyer in Columbia who could assist in collecting outstanding debts.
1 July	*From William W. Topp.*
8 July	*From Thomas Martin and George W. Martin.*
11 July	*From John W. Fowler.*
15 July	*From Cave Johnson.*
21 July	From Andrew Murdock. ALS. DLC–JKP. Advises that for shares purchased in the Columbia Railroad Co., the first installment of $1.00 per share is due on or before August 15.
22 July	*From Albert M. Lea.*
26 July	*From William C. Dunlap.*
27 July	From Thomas B. Coleman. ALS. DLC–JKP. Requests response to letters of November 7, 1833, and March 5, 1834.
28 July	*From James Forgey.*
29 July	From Gideon J. Pillow. ALS. DLC–JKP. Orders twelve barrels of corn to be delivered to James Walker's store.
31 July	*To James L. Edwards.*
2 Aug [1834]	*From Ephraim Beanland.*
2 Aug	*From John W. Childress.*
4 Aug	From B. M. Berry (for W. S. Franklin). ALS. DLC–JKP. Sends the Register of Debates; advises that Polk's books have arrived.
4 Aug	From Samuel King. ALS. DLC–JKP. Requests payment of $4.87 toward his travel expenses.
6 Aug	*From William Barnett.*
[9] Aug	*From William G. Childress.*
11 Aug	*From James L. Edwards.*
13 Aug	*From John McKinley.*
14 Aug	*From Samuel Burch.*
15 Aug	*From Abraham H. Quincy.*
18 Aug	*From Archibald Yell.*
19 Aug	*From John W. Childress.*
19 Aug	*From John F. Goneke.*
20 Aug	*From William P. Bradburn.*
20 Aug	*From Elliott Hickman.*
20 Aug	*From Robert J. Nelson.*
22 Aug	*From Willie Blount.*
23 Aug	*To Andrew Jackson.*
24 Aug	*From Ephraim Beanland.*
24 Aug [1834]	*From John W. Childress.*
25 Aug	*From James Standifer.*
27 Aug	*From Robert M. Burton.*
28 Aug	From John Hopkins. ALS. DLC–JKP. Offers statement supporting Andrew Jackson.
31 Aug	*From Andrew Beaumont.*
1 Sept	*To Andrew Jackson.*
1 Sept	*From Cave Johnson.*
1 Sept	*From James Parker.*
2 [Sept]	*From Ephraim Beanland.*

2 Sept	*To Hugh Lawson White.*
3 Sept	*From John D. Goneke.*
4 Sept	*To James L. Edwards.*
4 Sept	From Alston B. Estes. ALS. DLC–JKP. Submits statement of charges for subscription to the Pulaski *Tennessee Beacon.*
4 Sept	*From Samuel H. Laughlin.*
6 Sept	*From Samuel H. Laughlin.*
6 Sept	*From Samuel G. Smith.*
6 Sept	From James Thompson. Copy. DNA–RG 217. Acknowledges receipt of letter supporting the Nathan Sunderland claim.
8 Sept	*From Charles K. Gardner.*
8 Sept	*From Alvin Q. Nicks.*
9 Sept	*From Williamson Haggard.*
9 Sept	*From Samuel H. Laughlin.*
10 Sept	*From Seaborn Jones.*
10 Sept	*From Edward Kavanagh.*
11 Sept	*From Leonard Jarvis.*
12 Sept [1834]	*From Cave Johnson.*
13 Sept	*From Clement C. Clay.*
13 Sept	*From Cave Johnson.*
14 Sept	*From Benedict J. Semmes.*
15 Sept	*From Edward Kavanagh.*
16 Sept	*To James L. Edwards.*
16 Sept	*From Samuel Jackson Hays.*
16 Sept	*From John T. Stoddert.*
16 Sept	*From Archibald Yell.*
18 Sept	*From John W. Childress.*
18 Sept	From Thomas B. Coleman. ALS. DLC–JKP. Requests response to previous letters of November 7, 1833; March 5, 1834; and July 27, 1834.
18 Sept	*From Joseph Thompson.*
19 Sept	*From William Garrett.*
19 Sept	*From John Thomson.*
20 Sept	*From Samuel G. Smith.*
22 Sept	*From Joseph Hall.*
22 Sept	From James L. Edwards. LS. DLC–JKP. Responds to inquiry concerning claim.
22 Sept	*From James Walker.*
23 Sept	*From Clement C. Clay.*
23 Sept	*From Clement C. Clay.*
23 Sept	*From Archibald Yell.*
24 Sept	*From Samuel King.*
24 Sept	*From George W. Terrell.*
25 Sept	From James Sloan, Sr. ALS. DLC–JKP. Requests aid in obtaining a plot of land in the military district of Illinois.
25 Sept	*From Archibald Yell.*
26 Sept	*From Charles Cassedy.*
26 Sept	*To Sarah Polk.*
26 Sept	*From D. C. Topp.*
28 Sept	*From William C. Dunlap.*

28 Sept	*From Ebenezer J. Shields.*
29 Sept	*From James Standifer.*
30 Sept	*From Alfred Flournoy.*
2 Oct [1834]	*From Cave Johnson.*
4 Oct	*From Ephraim Beanland.*
4 Oct	*From Samuel King.*
4 Oct	*From Samuel W. Mardis.*
7 Oct	*From John W. Childress.*
8 Oct	*From Henry D. Hatton.*
9 Oct	*From Thomas J. Lacy.*
10 Oct	*From Ephraim Beanland.*
12 Oct	*From John H. Bills.*
12 Oct	From Claudius C. Jones. ALS. DLC–JKP. Discusses a land purchase.
12 Oct	*From William R. Rucker.*
13 Oct	*From Ephraim Beanland.*
13 Oct	*From Ephraim Beanland.*
[13] Oct	*From William Brady.*
14 Oct	*From Ephraim Beanland.*
14 Oct	*From John B. Johnson.*
16 Oct	*From Joseph B. Boyd.*
16 Oct	*To William R. Rucker.*
17 Oct	*From Andrew Beaumont.*
18 Oct	From Thomas L. Hamer. ALS. DLC–JKP. Gives results of elections in Ohio's Fifth Congressional District.
18 Oct	*From Archibald Yell.*
19 Oct	From Benoni Adams. ALS. DLC–JKP. Discusses the Nathan Sunderland claim.
20 Oct	*From Samuel H. Laughlin.*
21 Oct	*From John H. Dunlap.*
21 Oct	*From Archibald Yell.*
23 Oct	*From Ephraim Beanland.*
26 Oct	*From Ephraim Beanland.*
28 Oct	*From Stockly Donelson.*
29 Oct	From Edward Nunnelee. ALS. DLC–JKP. Discusses the Nathan Sunderland claim.
30 Oct	From Robert Armstrong. ALS. DLC–JKP. Discusses stagecoach schedule from Nashville via Gallatin, Harrodsburg, and Lexington to Maysville, Kentucky.
30 Oct	From William L. Burney. ALS. DLC–JKP. Requests establishment of a post office in Carroll County, Mississippi.
30 Oct	*From Archibald Yell.*
1 Nov	*From Ephraim Beanland.*
2 Nov	*From William K. Hill.*
2 Nov	*From Sherman Page.*
3 Nov	*From William Gilchrist.*
[3 Nov 1834?]	From Cave Johnson. ALS. DLC–JKP. Advises that if his health permits he will meet Polk in Bowling Green and travel with him to Washington City; if unable to do so, he will resign his seat in Congress.
4 Nov	*From James Brown.*

7 Nov	*From Adlai O. Harris.*
8 Nov	*From Micajah Bullock.*
10 Nov	From Joel Pinson. ALS. DLC–JKP. Requests a deed for William Woodward.
10 Nov	From John Turney. ALS. DLC–JKP. Expresses gratitude for recommendation for the land office; requests delivery of enclosed letter to William Campbell.
10 Nov	*From Archibald Yell.*
11 Nov	*From Stephen Adams.*
11 Nov	*From John H. Dunlap.*
11 Nov	From George W. Haywood. ALS. DLC–JKP. Requests assistance in obtaining claims for two veterans.
11 Nov	*From Joseph Thompson.*
15 Nov	*From Adlai O. Harris.*
15 Nov	*From Albert M. Lea.*
15 Nov	*From Henderson White.*
18 Nov [1834]	*From Joseph Thompson.*
20 Nov	*From William Brady.*
20 Nov	*From Samuel G. Smith.*
21 Nov	*From Caruthers, Harris & Company.*
22 Nov	From James H. Thomas. ALS. DLC–JKP. Requests assistance in obtaining a pension for a friend.
25 Nov	*From Silas M. Caldwell.*
25 Nov	*From Benjamin F. Currey.*
29 Nov	*From William Brady.*
29 Nov	From Meredith Buzby. ALS. DLC–JKP. Requests information regarding a claim.
29 Nov	*From Harvey M. Watterson.*
1 Dec	From Benjamin F. Butler. Copy. DNA–RG 60. Transmits budget estimate for the attorney general's office. (Enclosure not found.)
1 Dec	From John McC. Hill. ALS. DLC–JKP. Requests autograph for his collection.
1 Dec	*From James Walker.*
2 Dec	*From James Walker.*
2 Dec	*From James Hays Walker.*
4 Dec	From Thomas B. Coleman. ALS. DLC–JKP. Requests a reply to his previous inquiries.
4 Dec	*From Thomas J. Lacy.*
[4 Dec 1834]	*From Joseph W. McKean.*
5 Dec	From Levi Woodbury. Copy. DNA–RG 56. Requests that the estimate for one budget item be increased.
6 Dec	*From Caruthers, Harris & Company.*
6 Dec	*From Archibald Yell.*
7 Dec	From Richard Cochran. ALS. DLC–JKP. Requests that a trunk entrusted to Polk's care be given to Dangerfield Fauntleroy.
8 Dec	*From Preston Frazer.*
10 Dec	From William B. Lewis. LS. DLC–JKP. Discusses the James Brown claim.

10 Dec	*From Alexander Martin.*
10 Dec	*To Levi Woodbury.*
11 Dec	*From David T. Caldwell.*
11 Dec	From Peter Hagner. Copy. DNA–RG 217. Discusses the Nathan Sunderland claim.
11 Dec	From Peter Hagner. Copy. DNA–RG 217. Discusses the Abraham Shook claim.
11 Dec	*To Levi Woodbury.*
12 Dec	*From William Garrett.*
12 Dec	*From Robert Mack.*
12 Dec	*To Levi Woodbury.*
13 Dec	From Mahlon Dickerson. Copy. DNA–RG 45. Encloses drafts of the general naval appropriation bill. (Enclosures not found.)
13 Dec	*From James Walker.*
14 Dec	*From James Walker.*
15 Dec	*From Jonathan Bostick.*
16 Dec	*From William H. Ellis.*
17 Dec	From John McKenzie. ALS. DLC–JKP. Introduces E. B. Clemson, who is assisting with a claim prosecution.
18 Dec	*From Alexander Delaunay.*
18 Dec	From Mahlon Dickerson. Copy. DNA–RG 45. Submits letters justifying increased expenditures for the Navy and Marines. (Enclosures not found.)
18 Dec	*From Samuel G. Smith.*
19 Dec	*From William Carroll.*
20 Dec	*From William J. Alexander.*
20 Dec	*From John W. Childress.*
20 Dec	*To Mahlon Dickerson.*
21 Dec	*From James Brown.*
22 Dec	*From Thomas Barbour.*
22 Dec	*From James A. Craig.*
22 Dec	*From Thomas W. Dyott.*
22 Dec	From Peter Hagner. Copy. DNA–RG 217. Returns papers relating to a claim of John W. Yeats. (Enclosures not found.)
23 Dec	From Thomas P. Plaster. ALS. DLC–JKP. Requests opinion regarding the validity of a land warrant.
23 Dec	*From William L. Williford.*
23 Dec	From [Levi Woodbury]. Copy. DNA–RG 56. Transmits communications regarding budget requests from the attorney general, first auditor, treasurer, and commissioner of the General Land Office. (Enclosures not found.)
23 Dec	*From Levi Woodbury.*
23 Dec	*To Levi Woodbury.*
24 Dec	From Mahlon Dickerson. Copy. DNA–RG 45. Requests appropriation to meet arrearage claims for 1830.
24 Dec	*From Andrew C. Hays.*
24 Dec	*From Samuel King.*
24 Dec	*To James Walker.*
25 Dec	*From Joseph Brown.*

25 Dec	*From James Y. Green.*
25 Dec	*From Henry Horn.*
25 Dec	*To James Walker.*
26 Dec	*From William Brady.*
26 Dec	*From Samuel W. Polk.*
26 Dec	From Levi Woodbury. Copy. DNA–RG 56. Discusses the annual report of the Treasury Department.
28 Dec	From H. C. Armstrong. ALS. DLC–JKP. Introduces his nephew, P. M. Armstrong.
28 Dec	*From Spivey McKissick.*
28 Dec	*From Samuel G. Smith.*
29 Dec	*From James P. Grundy.*
29 Dec	*From Adlai O. Harris.*
29 Dec	*From Hillary Langtry.*
29 Dec	From Isaac Rainey. ALS. DLC–JKP. Requests information concerning his pension application.
29 Dec	*From Joseph Royall.*
29 Dec	*From Thomas Smith.*
29 Dec	From [Levi Woodbury]. Copy. DNA–RG 56. Requests appropriation for pay owed the superintendent of the South East Executive Building.
29 Dec	From [Levi Woodbury]. Copy DNA–RG 56. Transmits communications from the secretary of war, fifth auditor, and comptroller of the General Land Office. (Enclosures not found.)
29 Dec	From [Levi Woodbury]. Copy. DNA–RG 56. Encloses copy of a bill that he supports. (Enclosure not found.)
30 Dec	*From William P. Bradburn.*
30 Dec	*To Mahlon Dickerson.*
30 Dec	*From S. Jones.*
30 Dec	*From Charles W. Morgan.*
30 Dec	*From Joseph Thompson.*
31 Dec	*From William J. Alexander.*
31 Dec	From Lewis Cass. Copy. DNA–RG 107. Transmits documents regarding the erection of a house for public worship at Fort Monroe. (Enclosures not found.)
31 Dec	From Mahlon Dickerson. Copy. DNA–RG 45. Submits additional explanatory documents from the commandant of the Marine Corps. (Enclosures not found.)
31 Dec	From Mahlon Dickerson. Copy. DNA–RG 45. Submits documents from the navy commissioners explaining items questioned by the Ways and Means Committee. (Enclosures not found.)
31 Dec	From [Levi Woodbury]. Copy. DNA–RG 56. Transmits letter from the register of the Treasury. (Enclosure not found.)

1835

[1835]	From John H. Eaton. ALS. DLC–JKP. Encloses estimate of appropriations for the Florida Territory.

[1835]	From Adam Huntsman. ALS. DLC–JKP. Discusses travel schedule.
1 Jan	*From Adam Huntsman.*
1 Jan	*From Francis Slaughter.*
1 Jan	From [Levi Woodbury]. Copy. DNA–RG 56. Transmits estimates of appropriations for the Florida Territory.
1 Jan	From Levi Woodbury. Copy. DNA–RG 56. Sends statement (not found) showing rates of domestic exchange charged by state banks in different parts of the union and rates charged by the BUS and its branches.
2 Jan	*From Silas M. Caldwell.*
2 Jan	*From Daniel Graham.*
2 Jan	*From George W. Terrell.*
2 Jan	*From Levi Woodbury.*
3 Jan	*From Vincent L. Bradford et al.*
3 Jan	*From William K. Bradshaw et al.*
4 Jan	*From Archibald Yell.*
5 Jan	*From William R. Rucker.*
6 Jan	*From William P. Bradburn.*
[6] Jan	*To Vincent L. Bradford et al.*
6 Jan	*To William K. Bradshaw et al.*
6 Jan	To Lewis Cass. ALS. DNA–RG 107. Sends copy of the army appropriation bill. (Enclosure not found.)
6 Jan	From Mahlon Dickerson. Copy. DNA–RG 45. Requests appropriation for rebuilding the *Java* and *Cyane.*
[6] Jan	*To James Goodman et al.*
6 Jan	*From James P. Grundy.*
6 Jan	*From Samuel G. Smith.*
6 Jan	*From Levi Woodbury.*
7 Jan	*From James C. Alderson.*
7 Jan	*From Mahlon Dickerson.*
7 Jan	*From Jesse D. Elliott.*
7 Jan	*To Cave Johnson.*
7 Jan	*From Hugh Waddell.*
7 Jan	*From James Walker.*
8 Jan	From [Levi Woodbury]. Copy. DNA–RG 56. Advises that the Union Bank of New Orleans has recently purchased a large amount of domestic bills.
9 Jan	*From James Forgey.*
10 Jan	From John Forsyth. Copy. DNA–RG 59. Requests appropriation for an outfit for a chargé d'affaires to Portugal.
10 Jan	From [Levi Woodbury]. Copy. DNA–RG 56. Encloses copy of a letter from the Bank of Virginia regarding current rates of exchange. (Enclosure not found.)
11 Jan	*To James L. Edwards.*
11 Jan	*To Richard Long.*
12 Jan	From Robert Glass. ALS. DLC–JKP. Requests aid in expediting the claim of his father, Samuel Glass.
12 Jan	*From Hugh Smith.*
12 Jan	*From James Walker.*

12 Jan	*To Levi Woodbury.*
13 Jan	From Levin H. Coe. ALS. DLC–JKP. Solicits support for his appointment as surveyor of public lands south of the Tennessee River.
13 Jan	*From John Forsyth.*
13 Jan	*From John McCrory.*
13 Jan	*From Hezekiah Ward.*
14 Jan	*To Lewis Cass.*
14 Jan	*From Simpson Shaw.*
14 Jan	From [Levi Woodbury]. Copy. DNA–RG 56. Transmits explanatory statements regarding the Treasury Department appropriation bill. (Enclosure not found.)
14 Jan	From Levi Woodbury. Copy. DNA–RG 56. States that allowances to the law agent, assistant counsel, and district attorney in Florida do not exceed normal appropriations.
15 Jan	*From Aaron V. Brown.*
15 Jan	From John Forsyth. Copy. DNA–RG 59. Requests an appropriation for an outfit for a new minister at Madrid.
15 Jan	*From James Walker.*
15 Jan	From Levi Woodbury. Copy. DNA–RG 56. Transmits report explaining some of the items in the appropriation bill. (Enclosure not found.)
16 Jan	*From George W. Haywood.*
16 Jan	*From Kenderton Smith.*
17 Jan	*From Thomas McCleland.*
17 Jan	*From Daniel McKissick.*
17 Jan	*From James Walker.*
17 Jan	From Levi Woodbury. Copy. DNA–RG 56. Submits report on the U.S. Mint.
18 Jan	*To James Walker.*
19 Jan	*To John Blair.*
19 Jan	*From Joseph B. Boyd.*
19 Jan	From [Levi Woodbury]. Copy. DNA–RG 56. Transmits communication from the General Land Office. (Enclosure not found.)
19 Jan	From [Levi Woodbury]. Copy. DNA–RG 56. Transmits request for an additional appropriation to pay the expenses of an extra session of the Michigan Legislative Council. (Enclosure not found.)
20 Jan	*To John Blair et al.*
20 Jan	*From Aaron Boyd.*
20 Jan	*From David Jarrett.*
21 Jan	*To Lewis Cass.*
21 Jan	*To Lewis Cass.*
21 Jan	*To Mahlon Dickerson.*
21 Jan	*To Mahlon Dickerson.*
21 Jan	*To John Forsyth.*
21 Jan	From [Levi Woodbury]. Copy. DNA–RG 56. Transmits copy of a communication on private land claims in Florida. (Enclosure not found.)
21 Jan	*To Levi Woodbury.*

21 Jan	*To Levi Woodbury.*
22 Jan	*From William F. Coplan.*
22 Jan	From [Levi Woodbury]. Copy. DNA–RG 56. Sends communication from the U.S. Mint.
23 Jan	*From John W. Childress.*
23 Jan	*From Adlai O. Harris.*
23 Jan	From Thomas Underwood. ALS. DLC–JKP. Requests assistance in obtaining a pension.
24 Jan	*From William T. Barry.*
24 Jan	*From John M. Bass.*
24 Jan	*From Laurence Loller.*
24 Jan	*From Samuel Moore.*
24 Jan	*From Benjamin Reynolds.*
24 Jan	*From Samuel G. Smith.*
26 Jan	*To Felix Grundy.*
26 Jan	*From Samuel G. Smith.*
27 Jan	From Mahlon Dickerson. Copy. DNA–RG 45. States that he perceives no need for a change in the number or arrangement of clerks in the Navy Department.
27 Jan	*From Samuel G. Smith.*
27 Jan	*From James C. Wilson.*
27 Jan	From Levi Woodbury. Copy. DNA–RG 56. Requests an additional appropriation for the erection of a public warehouse in Baltimore.
28 Jan	*To Andrew Jackson.*
29 Jan	*From Daniel Graham.*
29 Jan	*From Sutherland S. Mayfield.*
29 Jan	From [Levi Woodbury]. Copy. DNA–RG 56. Submits copy of a communication from the U.S. Mint. (Enclosure not found.)
29 Jan	From Levi Woodbury. Copy. DNA–RG 56. Discusses state banks employed by the BUS as commissioners of loans and available funds reserved for payment of the public debt.
30 Jan	*From Samuel G. Smith.*
30 Jan	From Levi Woodbury. Copy. DNA–RG 56. Submits reports from the Treasury regarding clerks and clerk hire. (Enclosures not found.)
31 Jan	*From John C. McLemore.*
31 Jan	From George A. Miller. ALS. DLC–JKP. Requests Polk's autograph.
Feb [1835]	*From Joel H. Haden.*
2 Feb	From T. L. D. W. Shaw. ALS. DLC–JKP. Asks Polk to make inquiries about replacing lost land certificates.
3 Feb	From James L. Childress. ALS. DLC–JKP. Requests Polk's opinion regarding Texas and its future.
3 Feb	From Henry D. Hatton. ALS. DLC–JKP. Requests assistance in obtaining news of Mary Hatton Weems, the wife of William L. Weems.
3 Feb	From Ralph I. Ingersoll. ALS. DLC–JKP. Introduces J. H. Jacocks.
3 Feb	*From Samuel G. Smith.*

4 Feb	*From Richard C. Allen.*
4 Feb	*From Samuel King.*
4 Feb [1835]	*To Levi Woodbury.*
5 Feb	From Mahlon Dickerson. Copy. DNA–RG 45. Sends information regarding per diem and extra allowances to persons in the offices of the navy secretary and navy commissioners. (Enclosures not found.)
5 Feb	From John F. Lewis. ALS. DLC–JKP. Requests assistance in getting a bill passed "for the remission of duty."
5 Feb	*From George R. Powel.*
6 Feb	*From George W. Long.*
6 Feb	*From Elizabeth Nunn.*
6 Feb	*From Benjamin Utley.*
7 Feb	*To James Walker.*
8 Feb	*From James Walker.*
9 Feb	*From Samuel H. Laughlin.*
10 Feb	*From Cave Johnson.*
11 Feb	*From Silas M. Caldwell.*
11 Feb	*From Zalmon Wildman.*
12 Feb	*From John Catron.*
12 Feb	*From James H. Thomas.*
12 Feb	*From James Walker.*
12 Feb	*From William Whitson.*
13 Feb	*From Silas M. Caldwell.*
13 Feb	*From Samuel G. Smith.*
14 Feb	*From William G. Childress.*
14 Feb	*From James L. Edwards.*
14 Feb	*From David C. Gibson.*
14 Feb	*From James Walker.*
15 Feb	From Samuel Winn. ALS. DLC–JKP. Discusses the possible purchase and sale of a tract of land in East Tennessee.
16 Feb	*From David C. Gibson.*
16 Feb	From Moses Long. ALS. DLC–JKP. Sends a circular describing his "patent bridge."
16 Feb	From S. H. Long. ALS. DLC–JKP. Advises that he has forwarded a favorable report to the loan department regarding construction of a railroad.
16 Feb	*From Leonidas Polk.*
17 Feb	*From John Forsyth.*
17 Feb	From John B. Saunders. ALS. DLC–JKP. Explains that he is late in carrying out a contract to provide pine masts for the navy; requests Polk's support for an extension.
[18 Feb 1835]	To John Forsyth. LS. DNA–RG 59. Requests employment for Robert Clements.
18 Feb	From William Jackson. ALS. DLC–JKP. Requests aid in securing bounty land.
19 Feb	From Thomas B. Johnson. ALS. DLC–JKP. Argues against plans to abolish his office as collector of the port of St. Marys; requests that if the change occurs he be given the new position of surveyor.

19 Feb	*To Samuel Jones.*
19 Feb	*From Stockton and Stokes Stage Line.*
20 Feb	*To Lewis Cass.*
[20] Feb	From Thomas B. Coleman. ALS. DLC–JKP. Requests an answer to his several letters.
20 Feb	*From Archibald Yell.*
21 Feb	From S. B. Barrell. ALS. DLC–JKP. Requests assistance in bringing to a vote a bill that would exempt certain merchandise from import duties.
21 Feb	From Lewis Cass. LS. DLC–JKP. Copy in DNA–RG 94. Acknowledges receipt of a recommendation to the U.S. Military Academy for Joseph B. Boyd.
21 Feb	*To John Forsyth.*
21 Feb	*From Elijah Hayward.*
22 Feb	From Hamilton Smith. ALS. DLC–JKP. Requests copy of a report on the deposit banks.
23 Feb	*From Stockton and Stokes Stage Line.*
23 Feb	From George Templeman. ALS. DLC–JKP. Discusses book sales.
24 Feb	From Lewis Cass. Copy. DNA–RG 75. Encloses report from Indian Affairs regarding the claim of Amelia Shehemunga. (Enclosure not found.)
24 Feb	From Granville H. Frazer. ALS. DLC–JKP. Suggests that Polk recommend no further Indian land transfers in Mississippi until fraud allegations have been investigated.
24 Feb	*From James Walker.*
24 Feb	*From Hugh L. White.*
25 Feb	From James E. Heath. ALS. DLC–JKP. Sends a draft to cover arrears of pension for Frederick Fisher.
25 Feb	*To George Templeman.*
[25 Feb 1835]	*From Hugh L. White.*
25 Feb [1835]	To Hugh L. White. LS, draft, penned and signed as a joint communication by Cave Johnson. Respond to Hugh L. White's letter of February 24, 1835.
25 Feb	*To Hugh L. White.*
26 Feb	*From Hugh L. White.*
26 Feb	*To Hugh L. White.*
26 Feb	From [Levi Woodbury]. L. DLC–JKP. Discusses arrangements for a meeting at Polk's request regarding the Deposit bill.
27 Feb	From Lewis Cass. Copy. DNA–RG 75. Transmits a report from Indian Affairs on the subject of the letter of Samuel Mitchell. (Enclosure not found.)
27 Feb	*To Levi Woodbury.*
28 Feb	*From James Walker.*
28 Feb	*From Levi Woodbury.*
2 March	To Lewis Cass. ALS. DNA–RG 107. Wishes information on the treaties to which the amendments of the Senate Indian annuity bill refer.
2 March	*To Lewis Cass.*

2 March [1835]	*From John B. Forester.*
3 March	*From Thomas Callen.*
4 March [1835]	From S. B. Barrell. ALS. DLC–JKP. Urges prompt action on his bill at the next session.
5 March	From Levi Woodbury. LS. DLC–JKP. Discusses a claim from the heirs of John Medearis.
6 March	*From Henry Horn.*
6 March	*From William Wilson Polk.*
10 March	*From William Whitson.*
13 March	From Peter Hagner. Copy. DNA–RG 217. Discusses the case of Nathan Sunderland.
16 March	*From Henry Hubbard.*
23 March	*From Joseph B. Boyd.*
24 March	*From Cave Johnson.*
26 March	To [Cave Johnson]. AL, draft. DLC–JKP. Discusses the Tennessee delegation, party divisions, and the question of presidential succession.
28 March	*From Clement C. Clay.*
28 March	*To Cave Johnson.*
28 March	*From William H. Polk.*
29 March	*From Gerrard T. Greenfield.*
30 March	*To Cave Johnson.*
[30 March 1835]	*From Harvey M. Watterson.*
31 March	*To Cave Johnson.*
31 March	*From John McKinley.*
1 April	From John James Abert. Copy. DNA–RG 77. Advises that W. B. Guion has been ordered to superintend the survey applied for by Leonidas Polk and others.
1 April	*From William Carroll.*
1 April	From Henry D. Hatton. ALS. DLC–JKP. Requests assistance in obtaining news of Mary Hatton Weems, the wife of William L. Weems.
2 April	*From Jesse Meek, Jr.*
3 April [1835]	*From Cave Johnson.*
4 April	*From Alfred Balch.*
6 April	*To Lewis Cass.*
9 April	*From Ralph I. Ingersoll.*
13 April	*To Mahlon Dickerson.*
13 April	*To Cave Johnson.*
16 April	From John Dunlap. ALS. DLC–JKP. Requests receipt for a business transaction.
16 April	*To Cave Johnson.*
17 April	*From Kenneth L. Anderson.*
17 April	*To Cave Johnson.*
17 April	*From Samuel H. Laughlin.*
[17 April 1835]	From Joseph Thompson. ALS. DLC–JKP. Requests advice on obtaining the postmastership at Livingston, Alabama.
18 April	*From Andrew Beaumont.*
19 April	*To Cave Johnson.*
20 April	*From Lewis Cass.*

20 April	*From Portland J. Curle.*
21 April	*From Samuel H. Laughlin.*
27 April	From Mahlon Dickerson. Copy. DNA–RG 45. Acknowledges receipt of recommendation of Isaac J. Thomas, Jr., for appointment as midshipman.
27 April	*From William R. Rucker.*
28 April	*To Andrew Jackson Donelson.*
28 April	*To Samuel H. Laughlin.*
29 April	*To Andrew Jackson Donelson.*
29 April	*To Andrew Jackson.*
1 May	*To Andrew Beaumont.*
1 May [1835]	*From Cave Johnson.*
3 May	*From Andrew Jackson.*
4 May	*From Samuel A. Gillespie.*
7 May	*From Ephraim D. Dickson.*
7 May	*To Cave Johnson.*
11 May	*From Felix Grundy.*
12 May	*To Lewis Cass.*
12 May	*From Andrew Jackson.*
14 May	From William Garrett. ALS. DLC–JKP. Requests information about his claim.
15 May	*To Andrew Jackson.*
16 May	*To Lewis Cass.*
16 May	*To Andrew Jackson.*
18 May	*To Samuel H. Laughlin.*
19 May	*From John H. Bills.*
20 May	From B. M. Berry. ALS. DLC–JKP. Encloses copies (not found) of information relative to a constitutional amendment.
21 May [1835]	From Cave Johnson. ALS. DLC–JKP. Advises that he is sending by the same mail "five or six sheets of my answers" in the dispute with the White–Bell faction. Asks Polk to "amend or correct in any way & send it back"; Johnson then will show it to Felix Grundy.
22 May	*From Cave Johnson.*
25 May	*To Cave Johnson.*
25 May	*To Cave Johnson.*
25 May [1835]	From Felix K. Zollicoffer. ALS. DLC–JKP. Wishes to borrow several U.S. Senate journals.
26 May	*To Cave Johnson.*
27 May	*To Andrew Jackson.*
27 May	*To Cave Johnson.*
28 May	*From Felix Grundy.*
29 May	*From Samuel H. Laughlin.*
30 May	*From Joseph B. Boyd.*
30 May	*From Samuel H. Laughlin.*
1 June	*From Thomas Harney.*
1 June	*From Carey A. Harris.*
1 June	*From Andrew A. Kincannon.*
2 June	*To James L. Edwards.*

[2] June	*To Andrew A. Kincannon.*
5 June	*From Felix Grundy.*
6 June	*To Cave Johnson.*
7 June	*From Felix Grundy.*
8 June	*From James W. Breedlove.*
8 June	*From James Leetch.*
8 June	*From Robert Mitchell.*
9 June	*From Felix Grundy.*
10 June	*From Gerrard T. Greenfield.*
10 June [1835]	*From Cave Johnson.*
10 June	From John Rheiner, Jr. et al. LS. DLC–JKP. Invite Polk to a dinner on July 4, 1835.
15 June	*From Cave Johnson.*
15 June	From McClintock Young. Copy. DNA–RG 56. Advises that Polk's letter of June 2 has been received and referred to the Pension Office.
17 June	*From Samuel H. Laughlin.*
18 June	*From Felix Grundy.*
21 June	*From Alfred Flournoy.*
21 June	*From Felix Grundy.*
24 June	From George William Crump. ALS. DLC–JKP. Advises that Polk's letter of June 2 has been received in the Pension Office; the information requested has been communicated to W. D. Medearis.
24 June	*From William C. Dunlap.*
25 June	*From Felix Grundy.*
26 June	*From Robert Armstrong.*
26 June	From W. C. Blake. ALS. DLC–JKP. Wishes to know if Polk received a transcript of the records in the suit of W. M. Blake *vs.* James Erwin.
26 June	From William Gordon. ALS. DLC–JKP. Discusses the case of Josiah Laws.
26 June	*From Felix Grundy.*
26 June	*From James Osburn.*
27 June [1835]	From Cave Johnson. ALS. DLC–JKP. States opposition to all corporations for banking purposes, federal or state; and advises that in a few days he will send a circular on the subject.
28 June	*From William C. Dunlap.*
29 June	*From Archibald Yell.*
[30 June 1835]	To Francis P. Blair. ALS, fragment. NjP. Discusses the probable state of parties in the next U.S. House.
1 July	From John Nelson. ALS. DLC–JKP. Requests employment for an acquaintance.
1 July	*From George Washington Pollard.*
1 July	*From Valerius P. Winchester.*
2 July	From Richard Harvey. ALS. DLC–JKP. Wishes to know the circumstances surrounding the failure of the Tennessee land bill, especially regarding David Crockett's reversal of position.

4 July	*From Andrew Jackson Donelson.*
4 July	From Henry D. Hatton. ALS. DLC–JKP. Thanks Polk for informing him of the death of Mary Hatton Weems, his sister.
5 July	*From Samuel H. Laughlin.*
6 July	*To William C. Dunlap.*
6 July	*From Israel Fonville.*
6 July	To Samuel H. Laughlin. ALS. KyLoF. Details his knowledge of a controversy arising over publication of a letter from John Bell to Charles Cassedy.
7 July	*To Samuel H. Laughlin.*
7 July	From Robert Lucas. LS. DLC–JKP. Sends copy (not found) of his message of June 8 to the Ohio General Assembly, together with other documents (not found) relating to boundary controversies.
8 July	*To James L. Edwards.*
9 July	*From Memucan H. Howard.*
9 July	*To Campbell P. White.*
10 July	From Thomas B. Coleman. ALS. DLC–JKP. Requests an answer to his previous letters.
12 July	*From Archibald Yell.*
14 July	*From John F. H. Claiborne.*
14 July [1835]	From Cave Johnson. ALS. DLC–JKP. Advises that his health has improved and that he is campaigning again; his prospects for victory are improving steadily.
16 July [1835]	*From Cave Johnson.*
20 July	*From James L. Edwards.*
21 July	*From Andrew A. Kincannon.*
24 July	*From Kenneth L. Anderson.*
25 July	From West H. Humphreys. ALS. DLC–JKP. Requests the return of his unanswered letter.
31 July	*From Richard Warner.*
3 Aug	*From Andrew Jackson.*
5 Aug	*From Joel Yancey.*
6 Aug	*From Samuel H. Laughlin.*
7 Aug	*From Kenneth L. Anderson.*
7 Aug	*From William J. Whitthorne.*
8 Aug [1835]	From Cave Johnson. ALS. DLC–JKP. Gives election results in his district insofar as they are available.
9 Aug	*From Joel R. Smith.*
11 Aug [1835]	From Cave Johnson. ALS. DLC–JKP. Reports on his victory and other election results.
14 Aug	*To Andrew Jackson.*
14 Aug	*From James Walker.*
16 Aug [1835]	*From Cave Johnson.*
17 Aug	*From Henry W. Connor.*
20 Aug	*From W. H. Y. Jones.*
20 Aug	From Abraham B. Lindsley. ALS. DLC–JKP. Wishes aid in obtaining the position of sergeant at arms in the U.S. House.

21 Aug	*From Samuel H. Laughlin.*
22 Aug	*From William Moore.*
24 Aug	*From James Brown.*
24 Aug	From Robert Glass. ALS. DLC–JKP. Inquires about estate business.
26 Aug	*From Alfred Flournoy.*
27 Aug	*From Aaron V. Brown.*
28 Aug	*From Andrew Jackson Donelson.*
30 Aug	*From Samuel H. Laughlin.*
31 Aug	*From John F. Gillespy.*
2 Sept	From William E. Butler. ALS. DLC–JKP. Advocates the reappointment of Alexander B. Bradford as solicitor general.
4 Sept	*From Andrew A. Kincannon.*
5 Sept	*From Andrew Beaumont.*
6 Sept	*To Samuel H. Laughlin.*
7 Sept	*From William Armour.*
8 Sept	From Mrs. A. L. Clements. ALS. DLC–JKP. Discusses a boarding house she has recently acquired.
8 Sept	*From Jacob Greer.*
10 Sept	*From Alfred Flournoy.*
10 Sept	*To Andrew Jackson.*
10 Sept	From George W. Martin. ALS. DLC–JKP. Supports Turner F. Jack for postmaster at Clinton, Mississippi.
11 Sept	*From Felix Grundy.*
11 Sept [1835]	*From Cave Johnson.*
12 Sept	*To Aaron Vanderpoel.*
14 Sept [1835]	*From Henry L. Ellsworth.*
14 Sept	*To Alfred Flournoy.*
14 Sept	*From Bromfield L. Ridley.*
15 Sept	*From Andrew Jackson.*
16 Sept	*From Silas M. Caldwell.*
16 Sept	From William Gann. ALS. DLC–JKP. Requests information on his petition to exchange his pension for land.
16 Sept [1835]	*From Cave Johnson.*
17 Sept	*To Samuel H. Laughlin.*
22 Sept	*To Andrew Jackson Donelson.*
23 Sept	From J. Green. ALS. DLC–JKP. Discusses legal affairs.
24 Sept	*From Andrew Jackson Donelson.*
24 Sept	From Henry Fry. ALS. DLC–JKP. Sends pamphlet (not found) and requests advocacy of his claim.
26 Sept	*From Thomas L. Hamer.*
26 Sept [1835]	*From Cave Johnson.*
26 Sept	*To Felix Robertson et al.*
28 Sept	From S. B. Alexander. ALS. DLC–JKP. Wishes to purchase some land, the sale of which Polk would administer.
29 Sept	*From Andrew Jackson Donelson.*
1 Oct	From Caruthers, Harris & Co. LS. DLC–JKP. Reviews prospects for cotton growers.
2 Oct	*From Charles D. McLean.*

3 Oct	*To Francis P. Blair.*
[4] Oct	From William Robinson. ALS. DLC–JKP. Applies for the position of sergeant at arms of the U.S. House.
[4 Oct 1835]	From Reuben M. Whitney. ALS. DLC–JKP. Endorses William Robinson for the position of sergeant at arms of the U.S. House.
6 Oct	From Carey A. Harris. ALS. DLC–JKP. Recommends William Robinson for the position of sergeant at arms of the U.S. House.
8 Oct	*From Franklin Pierce.*
10 Oct	*To Andrew Jackson.*
10 Oct	*To Andrew Jackson.*
10 Oct	*From Francis O. J. Smith.*
11 Oct	*From Russell M. Williamson.*
13 Oct	*From Alfred Balch.*
13 Oct	*From John F. Gillespy.*
13 Oct	*From William E. Kennedy et al.*
14 Oct	From John H. Bills. ALS. DLC–JKP. Advises that Polk may be asked to give a character reference for James G. Bell.
14 Oct	*To William E. Kennedy et al.*
15 Oct	*From William J. Polk.*
16 Oct [1835]	*From Greenville Cook.*
16 Oct	*From George W. Jones.*
17 Oct	*From Cave Johnson.*
18 Oct	*To Andrew Jackson Donelson.*
18 Oct	*From William Moore.*
[19 Oct 1835]	*From Felix Grundy.*
19 Oct	*To Samuel W. Kilpatrick et al.*
19 Oct	From James K. Murrah. ALS. DLC–JKP. Asks if Polk would like to travel to Washington City with Joshua L. Martin.
20 Oct	*From William G. Childress.*
20 Oct	*From Andrew Jackson Donelson.*
20 Oct	*From Andrew Jackson.*
21 Oct	From John P. Burgett. ALS. DLC–JKP. Requests copies of speeches "in favour of the cause of the Democracy."
21 Oct	*From Robert M. Cooper et al.*
21 Oct	*From Samuel H. Laughlin.*
23 Oct	*To Robert M. Cooper et al.*
23 Oct	*From John Vincent et al.*
24 Oct [1835]	From Joab H. Banton et al. LS. DLC–JKP. Request a meeting on October 26.
24 Oct	*To Alfred Flournoy et al.*
25 Oct	From William Grayham. L. DLC–JKP. Requests assistance in expediting a claim.
28 Oct	*To A. O. P. Nicholson.*
29 Oct	*From John McKinley.*
2 Nov	*From John W. Childress.*
2 Nov	*From Clement C. Clay.*

2 Nov	*From Clement C. Clay.*
2 Nov	From Robert Glass. ALS. DLC–JKP. Recommends Marcus W. Cage as postmaster at LaGrange.
3 Nov	*From Dutee J. Pearce.*
3 Nov	*To James Walker.*
4 Nov	From John H. Dunlap. ALS. DLC–JKP. Advises that he has sold some of Polk's land to John H. Warren.
4 Nov	*From Samuel H. Laughlin.*
[4] Nov	*To James McKisick.*
5 Nov	From John H. Warren. ALS. DLC–JKP. Requests that Polk arrange with the General Land Office details of a transaction in which he is interested.
10 Nov	From anonymous writer. L. DLC–JKP. Requests a copy of the *"Horn Book* of Polaticks."
10 Nov	From Andrew C. Hays. ALS. DLC–JKP. Requests on behalf of Buford Turner a subscription to the Washington *Globe.*
11 Nov	From anonymous writer. L. DLC–JKP. Requests a copy of the *"Horn Book* of polaticks."
13 Nov	*From James Walker.*
15 Nov	*From Felix Grundy.*
16 Nov	From Peter Stubblefield. ALS. DLC–JKP. Asks Polk to see if funds have been deposited for him at the Washington branch of the BUS.
17 Nov	*From Adlai O. Harris.*
18 Nov	From Adlai O. Harris. ALS. DLC–JKP. Advises Polk of the death of James Simpson Walker.
18 Nov	*From Joseph C. Herndon.*
18 Nov	*From Samuel H. Laughlin.*
20 Nov	*From John H. Rivers.*
20 Nov	*From William R. Rucker.*
21 Nov	*From Edward Everett.*
21 Nov	*From Andrew C. Hays.*
22 Nov	*From John W. Childress.*
22 Nov	*From George Gammon.*
25 Nov	*From William Martin.*
25 Nov	*From Campbell P. White.*
26 Nov	*From James M. Wayne.*
27 Nov	*From Silas M. Caldwell.*
28 Nov	From Andrew C. Hays. ALS. DLC–JKP. Submits a list of Maury County residents who wish to subscribe to the Washington *Extra Globe.*
28 Nov	From Joel M. Smith. ALS. DLC–JKP. Requests that Polk support legislation to increase Smith's salary as the collector of customs at Nashville.
29 Nov	From Thomas J. Kennedy. ALS. DLC–JKP. Asks Polk's assistance in transacting some business at the General Land Office.
30 Nov	From Andrew C. Hays. ALS. DLC–JKP. Submits a list of new subscribers to the Washington *Globe.*

30 Nov	*From Benjamin C. Howard.*
30 Nov	*From Campbell P. White.*
[Dec 1835]	*From John McKeon.*
[Dec 1835]	*From David D. Wagener.*
1 Dec	From Eleazar Early. ALS. DLC–JKP. Requests support of his application as the agent to supply soda water to the Capitol.
1 Dec	*From Samuel H. Laughlin.*
2 Dec	From John Turney. ALS. DLC–JKP. Requests assistance in behalf of John Dowling.
3 Dec	*From Edward Everett.*
3 Dec	From J. H. Linebaugh. ALS. DLC–JKP. Requests copies of forthcoming biographies of Martin Van Buren and Richard M. Johnson.
4 Dec	From Davis Eastland. ALS. DLC–JKP. Submits application (not found) for a pension in behalf of John Evans.
7 Dec	*From Jacob Greer.*
7 Dec	*From Andrew C. Hays.*
7 Dec	*From Henry Hubbard.*
8 Dec [1835]	From John Davis. ALS. DLC–JKP. Forwards an enclosure (not found).
[8 Dec 1835]	*From Henry L. Ellsworth.*
8 Dec	From Peter Hagner. Copy. DNA–RG 217. Submits statement of the accounts of three government contractors involved in the War of 1812.
8 Dec	*From Joseph Henderson.*
8 Dec	*From Jacob Miller.*
8 Dec	From Joe D. Riggs. ALS. DLC–JKP. Requests assistance in obtaining an appointment as cadet at West Point.
9 Dec	*From Henry Horn.*
9 Dec	*From Joseph N. Johnson.*
9 Dec	From C. Macalister. ALS. DLC–JKP. Congratulates Polk on his election as Speaker of the U.S. House.
9 Dec	From Hampton C. Williams. ALS. DLC–JKP. Requests aid in obtaining appointment for E. W. Smallwood as a House messenger.
10 Dec	From William Brent. ALS. DLC–JKP. Recommends E. W. Smallwood for employment.
10 Dec	*From James S. Cannon.*
10 Dec [1835]	*From Henry L. Ellsworth.*
10 Dec	*From Ralph I. Ingersoll.*
11 Dec	*From John M. Bass.*
11 Dec	*From Frederick W. Hatch.*
11 Dec	From Andrew C. Hays. ALS. DLC–JKP. Submits a list of Maury County residents who wish to subscribe to the Washington *Extra Globe*.
11 Dec	*From Benjamin C. Howard.*
11 Dec	*From John A. Thomas.*
12 Dec	*From Caleb Cushing.*
12 Dec	From Mahlon Dickerson. ALS. DLC–JKP. Advises that

"Mr. J. will be gratified with the place which you propose to offer to dine."

23 Dec	*From Andrew C. Hays.*
23 Dec	*From Henry B. Kelsey.*
23 Dec	*From James McKisick.*
25 Dec	*From Isaac J. Thomas.*
26 Dec	From anonymous writer. L. DLC–JKP. Requests permission to play the bagpipes for members of Congress.
27 Dec [1835]	*From Henry L. Ellsworth.*
27 Dec	*From Joel R. Smith.*
28 Dec	*From Archibald Yell.*
29 Dec	*From Hartwell H. Brown.*
30 Dec	*From Joel Yancey.*
31 Dec	*From John Anderson.*
31 Dec	From Thomas Hord. ALS. DLC–JKP. Seeks information concerning ownership of a tract of land surveyed by Polk's father, Samuel Polk.
31 Dec	From Henry Tripple. ALS. DLC–JKP. Asks Polk's influence in obtaining a change in the route between Springfield, Ohio, and Richmond, Indiana; wishes the mail service to include Dayton.
[1835–39]	From B. M. Berry. ALS. DLC–JKP. Reports that a mailing of documents from the office of the U.S. House clerk is only partially completed.
[1835–39]	From Robert Wyman. ALS. DLC–JKP. Solicits autograph.

1836

[1836]	From J. F. H. Claiborne. ALS. DLC–JKP. Requests for Sutherland S. Southworth a reporter's seat in the U.S. House.
[1836]	From Richard M. Johnson. ALS. DLC–JKP. Requests a wage increase for William Emmons and a job for his brother, John.
[1836]	From John C. Mullay. ALS. DLC–JKP. Requests a reporter's seat in the U.S. House. Endorsed by John Chambers.
1 Jan	*From Benjamin F. Allen.*
1 Jan	*From Greenville Cook.*
1 Jan	From George M. Dallas et al. PL. DLC–JKP. Invite Polk to a public dinner on January 8.
2 Jan	*From Isaac J. Thomas.*
4 Jan	From John Forsyth. Copy. DNA–RG 59. Transmits a copy of the register of all officers and agents in the service of the United States. (Enclosure not found.)
4 Jan	From John Forsyth. Copy. DNA–RG 59. Transmits a report on clerks employed during 1835 in the State Department.
4 Jan	*From Samuel H. Laughlin.*
5 Jan [1836]	*From William J. Polk.*
6 Jan	From Mahlon Dickerson. Copy. DNA–RG 45. Submits reports on clerks employed during 1835 in the Navy Department and the commissioner's office.
6 Jan	From Mahlon Dickerson. Copy. DNA–RG 45. Transmits

	copies of the Naval Register for the year 1836. (Enclosures not found.)
6 Jan	From Thomas Hurdle. ALS. DLC–JKP. Applies for a position as messenger for the U.S. House.
6 Jan	*From William Montgomery.*
6 Jan	*From William Moore.*
7 Jan	*From Joseph B. Boyd.*
7 Jan	*From James McKisick.*
8 Jan [1836]	*From John Catron.*
8 Jan [1836]	*To Samuel H. Laughlin.*
8 Jan	From E. W. Smallwood. ALS. DLC–JKP. Requests the position of messenger for the U.S. House during the present session.
9 Jan	*From Samuel H. Laughlin.*
11 Jan [1836]	*From Orpha Conant.*
12 Jan	From Robert J. Nelson. ALS. DLC–JKP. Suggests that the election of Robert J. Walker to the U.S. Senate has damaged anti-administration forces in Mississippi; advises that it is an opportune time to sell property.
12 Jan	From William S. Woods. ALS. DLC–JKP. Congratulates Polk on his election as House Speaker and requests that on occasion he be sent public documents.
13 Jan	*From Denison Olmsted.*
13 Jan	*From Archibald Yell.*
14 Jan	From Overton Carr. ALS. DLC–JKP. Advises that the seats assigned in the U.S. House to reporters are now filled.
14 Jan	From W. G. Nye. ALS. DLC–JKP. Requests that Sterling H. Lester be considered for the position of land office register, should a vacancy occur.
15 Jan	*From Portland J. Curle.*
16 Jan	*From Silas M. Caldwell.*
16 Jan	From Thomas Wright III. ALS. DLC–JKP. Requests that Polk forward the papers that establish Aaron V. Brown's claim to a portion of the estate of John Beard.
17 Jan	From Benoni Adams. ALS. DLC–JKP. Discusses depositions relative to the claim of Nathan Sunderland's heirs.
17 Jan	*From William G. Childress.*
17 Jan	*To Samuel H. Laughlin.*
17 Jan	*From Ezekiel P. McNeal.*
17 Jan	*From William R. Rucker.*
18 Jan	*From Jacob Miller.*
18 Jan	From William R. Rucker. ALS. DLC–JKP. Discusses the effect of Polk's election as Speaker of the U.S. House, Hugh Lawson White's political prospects, and local issues. Encloses names (not found) of persons wishing to subscribe to the Washington *Globe*.
18 Jan	*From James Walker.*
19 Jan	*From Joab H. Banton.*
19 Jan	*From John H. Rivers.*
20 Jan	*From George R. Fall.*

21 [Jan 1836]   From Amos Kendall. Copy. DNA–RG 28. Transmits report on clerks employed in the Post Office Department during the past year. (Enclosure not found.)

22 Jan   *To Samuel H. Laughlin.*

22 Jan   *From A. O. P. Nicholson.*

23 Jan   *From Ephraim Beanland.*

23 Jan   From Mahlon Dickerson. Copy. DNA–RG 45. Submits statements detailing current government pensions; explains apparent discrepancies; and lists sources of income for the navy pension fund. (Enclosures not found.)

23 Jan   From West Harris. ALS. DLC–JKP. Requests consideration of Samuel Vaught to be postmaster of Randolph, Tennessee.

24 Jan   *From Thomas Dean.*

24 Jan   From Denison Olmsted. ALS. DLC–JKP. Acknowledges receipt of a check for Samuel W. Polk.

25 Jan   *From William S. Fulton.*

25 Jan   From Edward Postlethwayt Page. ALS. DLC–JKP. Sends 196 copies of his picture for the members of the U.S. House; also sends two copies of No. 16 of "Elements of Astrology."

26 Jan   *From Granville S. Crockett.*

27 Jan   From Lewis Cass. Copy. DNA–RG 107. Duplicate copy in DNA–RG 75. Acknowledges receipt of Polk's letter of January 8; submits copy of a letter to the General Land Office showing the directions the president has given on the sale of certain public lands. (Enclosure not found.)

27 Jan [1836]   *From John W. Childress.*

27 Jan   *From Edwin A. Keeble.*

27 Jan   From V. Maxcy. ALS. DLC–JKP. Requests the use of the hall of the U.S. House for a meeting of the American Historical Society.

27 Jan   *From Williamson Smith.*

28 Jan   *From George Gammon.*

28 Jan   From Nathan Green. ALS. DLC–JKP. Requests an endorsement of a memorial sent by the residents of Winchester seeking improvement in mail service.

29 Jan   From Joel M. Smith. ALS. DLC–JKP. Requests that Polk hand the enclosed communication to Blair and Rives. (Enclosure not found.)

29 Jan   *From John A. Thomas.*

30 Jan   *From Robert W. Brahan.*

[30 Jan 1836]   From Andrew Jackson Donelson. ALS. DLC–JKP. Requests that Polk show the enclosed invitation to Elijah Hayward. (Enclosure not found.)

30 Jan   From William Karr. ALS. DLC–JKP. Requests that Polk determine the disposition of the claim of James Miller.

30 Jan   *To Samuel H. Laughlin.*

30 Jan   From John B. Perkins. ALS. DLC–JKP. Seeks aid in obtaining a position as surveyor of the Cherokee lands.

31 Jan   *From Silas M. Caldwell.*

31 Jan   *From William C. Campbell.*
31 Jan   *From Medicus A. Long.*
31 Jan   *From A. O. P. Nicholson.*
[Feb 1836]   From Amos Lane. ALS. DLC–JKP. Requests appointment
                      to a select committee considering the possibility of extend-
                      ing provisions of the pension law of 1832.
1 Feb   From Lewis Cass. Copy. DNA–RG 94. Transmits abstracts
                      of the general returns of the militia of the U.S. and of their
                      arms, accoutrements, and ammunition for the year 1835.
                      (Enclosures not found.)
1 Feb   From John W. Nelson. ALS. DLC–JKP. Asks Polk to send
                      congressional documents that may be of interest; requests
                      Polk's support of the revival or extension of the preemption
                      law.
2 Feb   From Jesse B. Clements. ALS. DLC–JKP. Asks Polk to
                      assist in the passage of legislation to relieve claimants who
                      sustained losses in the survey of Spanish claims in Florida.
2 Feb   *From Francis A. Owen.*
2 Feb   *From Samuel W. Polk.*
2 Feb   *From Archibald Yell.*
3 Feb   From Lewis Cass. Copy. DNA–RG 94. Transmits a com-
                      munication from the adjutant general, with 250 copies of the
                      official army register.
3 Feb   From Mahlon Dickerson. Copy. DNA–RG 45. Transmits a
                      statement of the appropriations for the naval service for the
                      year 1835. (Enclosure not found.)
6 Feb   From Edmund L. Williams. ALS. DLC–JKP. Requests
                      help in obtaining better mail service for Moscow, Tennessee.
7 Feb   *From Silas M. Caldwell.*
7 Feb   *From A. O. P. Nicholson.*
7 Feb   *From A. O. P. Nicholson.*
8 Feb   From James L. Edwards. ALS. DNA–RG 15. Advises that
                      James Miller is not eligible for a pension.
8 Feb   From William Frazier. ALS. DLC–JKP. Sends thirty dol-
                      lars and requests that it be given to Rufus K. Polk in pay-
                      ment of a loan.
8 Feb   From Nathaniel Smith. ALS. DLC–JKP. Introduces
                      Lieutenant M. W. Bateman.
8 Feb   *From Levi Woodbury.*
9 [Feb 1836]   *From Alfred Balch.*
9 Feb   From Frederick Freeman. ALS. DLC–JKP. Requests
                      Polk's autograph.
10 Feb   *From John McKinley.*
11 Feb   From William Gordon. ALS. DLC–JKP. Returns the re-
                      quest of William Jackson for compensation due him by Vir-
                      ginia for service during the Revolutionary War; the claim
                      must be made to the individual state. (Enclosure not found.)
11 Feb   *From David R. Mitchell.*
12 Feb   *From Adlai O. Harris.*
12 Feb   *From David W. McRee.*
12 Feb   From William S. Woods. ALS. DLC–JKP. Asks if preemp-

	tion will be extended and requests Polk to forward copies of previous legislation on this subject.
13 Feb	*From Angel Calderon de la Barca.*
13 Feb	From E. Blocker. ALS. DLC–JKP. Requests aid in expediting Thomas P. Winn's claim.
13 Feb	From Mahlon Dickerson. Copy. DNA–RG 45. Sends papers in the claims case of Margaret E. Shaw; and explains the difficulty arising from existing statutes. (Enclosure not found.)
13 Feb	From Peter Hagner. Copy. DNA–RG 217. Advises that he has approved the claim filed by the heirs of Nathan Sunderland.
[14 Feb 1836]	*To Angel Calderon de la Barca.*
14 Feb	*From A. O. P. Nicholson.*
14 Feb	*From James Walker.*
15 Feb	*From John W. McCrabb.*
15 Feb	*From Bromfield L. Ridley.*
15 Feb	*From Henry Turney.*
16 Feb	*From Medicus A. Long.*
16 Feb	*From John S. Young.*
17 Feb	From Andrew C. Hays. ALS. DLC–JKP. Requests subscription to the Washington *Globe* for Nathaniel Willis.
17 Feb	*From Abraham McClellan.*
18 Feb [1836]	From John O. Bradford. ALS. DLC–JKP. Requests assistance in obtaining a position as chaplain in the navy.
19 Feb	*From William S. Fulton.*
19 Feb	*From William W. Gant.*
20 Feb	*From Edwin H. Durrell.*
20 Feb	To Ohio's First Congressional District Committee. AL, draft. DLC–Misc. Coll., Moses Dawson Papers. Fragment (4 pages). Declines invitation to a public celebration to be held on March 4, the date that BUS charter expires.
21 Feb	*From Jonathan Webster.*
22 Feb	*From Silas M. Caldwell.*
22 Feb	*From Thomas G. Polk.*
22 Feb	*From James C. Record.*
22 Feb	*To William R. Rucker.*
23 Feb	From Ashton Garrett. ALS. DLC–JKP. Solicits a small loan with which to keep his newspaper, the Rockville *Maryland Free Press*, from financial collapse.
23 Feb	*From James Walker.*
24 Feb	*From David Gillespie.*
25 Feb	*From Archibald Yell.*
26 Feb	*From William J. Polk.*
28 Feb	*From Angel Calderon de la Barca.*
1 March	*From Daniel Graham.*
1 March	*From Robert Mack.*
2 March	From Peter Hagner. Copy. DNA–RG 217. Specifies further information that is necessary before Nathan Sunderland's widow can be compensated.
2 March	*From Gideon J. Pillow.*

2 March	*From Thomas Whaley.*
3 March	*From James Walker.*
4 March	From Mahlon Dickerson. Copy. DNA–RG 45. Transmits a statement of the contracts made by the navy commissioners during the year 1835. (Enclosure not found.)
4 March	*From Josephus C. Guild.*
4 March	*To Andrew Jackson.*
4 March	*From Gideon J. Pillow.*
4 March	*From James Walker.*
5 March	From William Callender. ALS. DLC–JKP. Wishes to know the disposition of his petition.
5 March	*From Daniel Graham.*
7 March	From C. K. Gardner. ALS. DLC–JKP. Discusses candidates for the postmastership at Mt. Pleasant.
7 March	*From Samuel P. Walker.*
8 March	*From John H. Bills.*
9 March	*From William J. Alexander.*
10 March	From James I. McKay. ALS. DLC–JKP. Calls attention to probable violations of the statutes providing travel expenses to members of Congress.
10 March	From V. P. McLemore. ALS. DLC–JKP. Writes that in Lebanon, Tennessee, he finds strong support for Hugh L. White and little backing for Martin Van Buren.
12 March	*From James Walker.*
12 March	*From William J. Whitthorne.*
13 March	From James Perry. ALS. DLC–JKP. Recommends a clergyman, Daniel Comfort, to a position in the land office in Clinton, Mississippi.
14 March	*From James Walker.*
14 March	*From James Walker.*
17 March	From Joel Henry Dyer. ALS. DLC–JKP. Requests assistance in obtaining appointment as the federal district attorney for Mississippi.
18 March	From Kenneth L. Anderson. ALS. DLC–JKP. Encloses money for the purchase of lottery tickets.
18 March	*From James Walker.*
19 March	*From Kenneth L. Anderson.*
19 March	From Thomas Davis. ALS. DLC–JKP. Encloses money for the purchase of lottery tickets.
19 March	From N. T. Rosseter. ALS. DLC–JKP. Seeks advice on what section of the country would offer good career prospects for a young lawyer.
21 March	*From Jonathan Bostick.*
22 March	From William Carr. ALS. DLC–JKP. Expresses thanks on behalf of a friend who is now receiving a government pension.
22 March	*From James Walker.*
23 March	*From Silas M. Caldwell.*
24 March	From William Garrett. ALS. DLC–JKP. Wishes to know the disposition of his claim.

24 March	*From David C. Mitchell.*
24 March	From Charles T. Stewart. ALS. DLC–JKP. Requests Polk's autograph.
25 March	*From Richard H. Allen.*
25 March	*From David J. Craig.*
25 March	*From Chiles McGee.*
25 March	*From William Martin.*
25 March	*From Samuel Stockard.*
26 March	*From Kenneth L. Anderson.*
26 March	*From Joseph Mason.*
27 March	*From Richard Stockard.*
28 March	*From James Walker.*
28 March	*From John S. Young.*
29 March	*From William R. Rucker.*
30 March	*From William Gilchrist.*
30 March	*From Samuel A. Gillespie.*
30 March	From Mark R. Roberts. ALS. DLC–JKP. Asks Polk to use his influence with the postmaster general to obtain mail service to Miller County, Arkansas.
30 March	*To Richard D. Spaight, Jr.*
31 March	*From Thomas J. Hardeman.*
31 March	*From John McKinley.*
1 April	*From James Walker.*
2 April	From George W. Niles. ALS. DLC–JKP. Requests Polk's autograph.
3 April	From Robert P. Harrison. ALS. DLC–JKP. Writes from Shelbyville, Tennessee, that Van Buren forces are gaining.
5 April	*From James Walker.*
6 April	From Isaac Moore. ALS. DLC–JKP. Writes on behalf of Mrs. H. Black to urge prompt disposition of her claim.
6 April	*From Bromfield L. Ridley.*
6 April	*From Archibald Yell.*
7 April	From McKay W. Campbell. ALS. DLC–JKP. Introduces A. B. Morton of Lexington, Kentucky.
8 April	*From Kenneth L. Anderson.*
8 April	From Virgil David. ALS. DLC–JKP. Thanks Polk for sending several books to the lyceum at Lawrenceville, Pennsylvania.
10 April	*From James Walker.*
12 April	*To Charlotte Baynton.*
12 April	*From John W. Ford.*
12 April	*From Samuel H. Laughlin.*
12 April	From John Wurts. ALS. DLC–JKP. Introduces Arthur Stout of New York.
13 April	From John H. Anderson. ALS. DLC–JKP. Asks Polk to inquire at the War Department concerning the status of claims by Shadrack Holt and James Milton.
13 April	*From Mahlon Dickerson.*
13 April	*From Adlai O. Harris.*
13 April [1836]	*From Francis O. J. Smith.*

13 April	*From Williamson Smith.*
15 April	From Peter Hagner. Copy. DNA–RG 217. Encloses list of clerks employed in the third auditor's office. (Enclosure not found.)
15 April	From Hardy L. Holmes. ALS. DLC–JKP. Introduces his brother, Theophilus H. Holmes; asks help in obtaining a military promotion for him.
15 April	*To Andrew Jackson.*
15 April	*From Levi Woodbury.*
16 April	From Jacob Greer. ALS. DLC–JKP. Discusses the slavery issue in general and opposes in particular the introduction of abolition petitions before Congress.
16 April	*From Jacob Greer.*
16 April	From James Wilson. ALS. DLC–JKP. Requests that his son be appointed as a waiter or messenger to the U.S. House.
19 April	From John McKeon. ALS. DLC–JKP. Forwards an application for a seat in the reporters' gallery. (Enclosure not found.)
19 April	*From James H. Piper.*
20 April	*From James Walker.*
20 April	*From James Walker.*
21 April	*From Robert Fenner.*
21 April	*From James Walker.*
22 April	From Mahlon Dickerson. Copy. DNA–RG 45. Transmits information pertaining to clerks employed in the Navy Department. (Enclosure not found.)
22 April	From Mahlon Dickerson. Copy. DNA–RG 45. Transmits information pertaining to naval oficers' compensation, allowances, and travel. (Enclosure not found.)
22 [April 1836]	From Amos Kendall. Copy. DNA–RG 28. Submits a list of clerks in the Post Office Department. (Enclosure not found.)
[22 April 1836]	From A. O. P. Nicholson. ALS. DLC–JKP. Discusses political affairs in Columbia and his speech denouncing John Bell and Hugh L. White.
22 April	*From James Walker.*
23 April	*From Thomas J. Lacy.*
23 April	*From A. O. P. Nicholson.*
25 April	*From William D. Moseley.*
26 April	From Samuel P. Carson. ALS. DLC–JKP. Hopes in a few days to deliver personally a letter from T. J. Hardeman to Polk.
[26 April 1836]	*From John Catron.*
26 April	*From Andrew C. Hays.*
26 April	*From James H. Piper.*
27 April	*From Thomas Davis.*
28 April	*From Silas M. Caldwell.*
28 April	*From A. O. P. Nicholson.*
29 April	*From James Walker.*
30 April	From Powhatan Gordon. ALS. DLC–JKP. Wishes to know

if a mail route from Franklin to Williamsport is likely to be established.

2 May — From Benoni Adams. ALS. DLC–JKP. Wishes to know if Polk received his two previous letters, one containing a deposition.

2 May — From Ethan A. Brown. ALS. DLC–JKP. Copy in DNA–RG 49. Advises that Daniel Graham was not compensated for his services to the General Land Office because he never submitted an account of estimated costs; should Polk wish to fix an amount, Brown will submit it to the secretary of the Treasury for a final decision.

3 May — From William Gordon. ALS. DLC–JKP. Introduces [Jesse?] Bean and asks Polk's aid in settling Bean's claims.

3 May — From Peter Hagner. Copy. DNA–RG 217. Advises that he can find no record of service in the case of George Black.

3 May — From Davison Smith. ALS. DLC–JKP. Asks Polk's assistance in regard to a claim.

4 May — From Thomas B. Jones. ALS. DLC–JKP. Solicits the position of postmaster at Courtland, Alabama, should John McMahon not wish the appointment.

4 May — *From Denison Olmsted.*

5 May — *From Daniel Graham.*

6 May — From Samuel Craig. ALS. DLC–JKP. Applies for the job of postmaster at Pontotoc, Mississippi.

6 May — *From James Walker.*

13 May — *From John B. Hays.*

13 May — To Andrew Jackson. LS. DLC–GW. Endorses the application of Thomas Eastin to be navy agent at Pensacola.

14 May — From C. K. Gardner. ALS. DLC–JKP. Advises that a new post office has been established at Rich Valley in Bedford County, Tennessee; Jordan S. Holt is its postmaster.

14 May — *From Thomas J. Lacy.*

16 May [1836] — From anonymous writer. L. DLC–JKP. Suggests that Polk should take action to prevent reporters from using the stationery of the U.S. House.

16 May — From Mahlon Dickerson. Copy. DNA–RG 45. Submits a special account of naval appropriations transferred and their application during the present session of Congress. (Enclosure not found.)

17 May — From Nathan Green. ALS. DLC–JKP. Renews request for better mail service between Winchester and Shelbyville.

17 May — From Williamson Smith. ALS. DLC–JKP. Forwards names of subscribers to the Washington *Extra Globe.*

19 May — From Moses Lynch. ALS. DLC–JKP. Wishes to be kept informed on political matters in Washington City.

20 May — *From James Walker.*

21 May — *From John H. Bills.*

21 May — From Milton Giles. ALS. DLC–JKP. Approves of Polk's political actions as Speaker; hopes he will run again for Congress rather than seek an office in the executive branch.

22 May	From Thomas B. Jones. ALS. DLC–JKP. Requests that Polk submit to John McMahon his recollections of conversations with Jones relating to the appointment of postmaster at Courtland, Alabama.
22 May	From [John J. McMahon]. AL, fragment. DLC–JKP. Wishes to know details surrounding the appointment of Thomas B. Jones as postmaster at Courtland, Alabama.
23 May	*From Erwin J. Frierson.*
23 May	*From Richard Warner.*
24 May	*From Greenville Cook.*
24 May	*From Denison Olmsted.*
24 May	From James N. Smith. ALS. DLC–JKP. Requests support for the position of postmaster at Covington; discusses political affairs in Tipton County.
25 May	*From George Gammon.*
25 May	*From Joseph C. Herndon.*
25 May	*From Samuel H. Laughlin.*
25 May	*From James Walker.*
26 May	From Jacob Miller. ALS. DLC–JKP. Acknowledges receipt of the Washington *Extra Globe*; gives opinions on the political climate in East Tennessee.
26 May	*From George R. Powel.*
28 May	From Andrew C. Hays. ALS. DLC–JKP. Submits additional subscriptions to the Washington *Extra Globe*.
30 May	*From William J. Alexander.*
30 May	*From Joab H. Banton and Wesley Nixon.*
30 May	From Wilson H. McKisick. ALS. DLC–JKP. Requests help in obtaining the appointment of surgeon in the volunteers.
30 May	*From A. O. P. Nicholson.*
31 May	*From William Bobbitt.*
31 May	From C. K. Gardner. ALS. DLC–JKP. Requests information regarding the situation in the post office at Richmond in Bedford County, Tennessee.
31 May	*From Henry A. Miller.*
31 May	*From Gideon J. Pillow.*
31 May	*From James Walker.*
1 June	From Caruthers, Harris & Co. LS. DLC–JKP. Submits invoice with letter advising of shipment of one sulky and harness.
3 June	*From James H. Thomas.*
5 June	*From Williamson Smith.*
6 June	*From William Gammon.*
6 June	*From William M. Green.*
6 June	*From James Walker.*
6 June	*From Richard A. L. Wilkes.*
7 June	From Benjamin B. Coffey. ALS. DLC–JKP. Asks aid in obtaining the appointment of register of the new land office in northeast Alabama.
7 June	From Andrew C. Hays. ALS. DLC–JKP. Submits list (not found) of new subscribers to the Washington *Extra Globe*.
7 June	*From George W. Jones.*

7 June	From Sutherland S. Southworth. ALS. DLC–JKP. Complains of rude conduct by pages of the U.S. House.
10 June	*From John W. Childress.*
10 June	*From James Walker.*
12 June [1836]	From J. L. Murray. ALS. DLC–JKP. Recommends Mr. Sebastian to be proprietor of the U.S. House refectory.
13 June	From Joseph Trotter. ALS. DLC–JKP. Recommends William H. Whitaker as commissioner to settle Indian claims to land in the Choctaw Nation.
15 June	*From Samuel Burch.*
15 June	*From Walter S. Franklin.*
15 June	*To John J. McMahon.*
15 June	*From William R. Rucker.*
16 June	From Nathaniel P. [Causin?]. ALS. DLC–JKP. Requests Polk's signature on an appeal for clemency.
18 June	From Lawson Gifford and James L. Sparks. LS. DLC–JKP. Enclose a prospectus for the Jonesboro *Tennessee Sentinel* and request aid in promoting its circulation. (Enclosure not found.)
18 June	From Thomas S. Holmes. ALS. DLC–JKP. Expresses thanks for help in receiving an appointment in the army.
19 June	*From William Davis.*
19 June	*From Samuel W. Polk.*
20 June	From Henry B. Coffey. ALS. DLC–JKP. Recommends Benjamin B. Coffey as register of the land office in the Cherokee country.
20 June	From Virgil David. ALS. DLC–JKP. Acknowledges with gratitude receipt of presents to the lyceum at Lawrenceville, Pennsylvania.
20 June	From Lunsford L. Dilliard. ALS. DLC–JKP. Requests aid in expediting a claim for George Yocom.
20 June	*From James Walker.*
20 June	From Archibald Yell. ALS. DLC–JKP. Recommends Benjamin B. Coffey as register of the land office in the Cherokee country.
22 June	*To James B. Thornton.*
23 June	From Joseph Thompson. ALS. DLC–JKP. Recommends J. B. [Handcock] of Livingston, Alabama, to be commissioner for the Choctaw nation to investigate land claims.
24 June	*From George W. Campbell.*
25 June	*From John McKinley.*
25 June	From C. Wilson. ALS. DLC–JKP. Requests Polk's intervention in a dispute involving her son.
26 June	*From Archibald Yell.*
29 June	*From Henry Horn.*
4 July	From James K. Murrah. ALS. DLC–JKP. Seeks aid in preventing a change in the mail route serving Athens, Alabama.
5 July	From T. J. Kennedy. ALS. DLC–JKP. Wishes to know if any action has been taken on his claim.
5 July	*To L. Knowles and Company.*

6 July	*To Walter S. Franklin.*
6 July	From William H. Haywood, Jr. ALS. DLC–JKP. Asks Polk to forward his mail; mourns loss of his son, who died during his visit to Washington.
6 July	From George Wolf. ALS. DLC–JKP. Discusses payments due U.S. House members for mileage and attendance.
7 July	*To Mahlon Dickerson.*
7 July	*From David R. Mitchell.*
14 July	From C. E. Haynes. ALS. DLC–JKP. Requests a copy of the Journal of the Tennessee Convention of 1834.
16 July	*From James Walker.*
17 July	*From Charles Cassedy.*
17 July	From William H. McClelan, Jr. ALS. DLC–JKP. Requests aid in obtaining an appointment as an assistant surveyor of public lands.
18 July	*To John W. Childress.*
22 July	From Charlotte Baynton. ALS. DLC–JKP. Asks assistance for her claim.
26 July	From J. B. Boyd. ALS. DLC–JKP. Asks Polk to persuade the president to intercede at the U.S. Military Academy so that Rowley S. Jennings may be allowed to graduate on schedule.
26 July	From J. C. Temple. ALS. DLC–JKP. Advises of a pair of match horses for sale which Polk may wish to buy.
30 July	*From John C. Wormeley et al.*
[Aug 1836]	*To Bigbyville Citizens.*
1 Aug	*To James L. Edwards.*
1 Aug	*From John C. Whitsitt.*
[2 Aug 1836]	From Alfred Balch. ALS. DLC–JKP. Requests help in a business matter.
2 Aug [1836]	*From Cave Johnson.*
3 Aug	*From Samuel H. Laughlin.*
3 Aug	*From Samuel H. Laughlin.*
4 Aug	*From John S. Young.*
5 Aug	*From Samuel H. Laughlin.*
5 Aug	*To Samuel H. Laughlin.*
7 Aug	*From W. Bowling Guion.*
[8] Aug	From William Bobbitt. ALS. DLC–JKP. Wishes to know if John P. King is still visiting Polk; Bobbitt would like to invite him to a dinner honoring Polk.
8 Aug	*To James L. Edwards.*
8 Aug	*From Samuel H. Laughlin.*
9 Aug	*To Andrew Jackson Donelson.*
9 Aug	*To Samuel H. Laughlin.*
10 Aug	From Alfred Balch. ALS. DLC–JKP. Asks for a copy of Samuel Polk's will in order to settle a claim.
11 Aug	*From Madison Caruthers.*
11 Aug	*From Ransom H. Gillet.*
11 Aug	*From John S. Young.*
13 Aug	From James L. Edwards. ALS. DLC–JKP. Advises that he

cannot transfer the pension of Isaiah Reed from the agency at Nashville to that at Jackson until Reed has submitted certain affidavits.

14 Aug *From Albert G. Harrison.*

15 Aug *From James M. Howry et al.*

15 Aug [1836] From Andrew Jackson Donelson. ALS. DLC–JKP. Accepts on behalf of Andrew Jackson an invitation by the citizens of Maury County; Jackson's reply to the committee will give the exact date of his arrival.

15 Aug *From Abraham Whinnery.*

16 Aug From George Grennell, Jr. ALS. DLC–JKP. Advises that he has visited the carriage factory and construction of the coach Polk ordered is proceeding well; however, the cost may be more than anticipated.

18 Aug *From Richard Warner.*

19 Aug From L. Knowles & Co. LS. DLC–JKP. Advises that Polk's carriage is nearing completion and asks his preferences regarding finishing details.

19 Aug From [M. G. Raines?]. ALS. DLC–JKP. Advises that he must work late into the evening and cannot keep his appointment.

19 Aug *From Sutherland S. Southworth.*

21 Aug *From John P. King.*

21 Aug *From Medicus A. Long.*

22 Aug From Calvin Jones. ALS. DLC–JKP. Offers to pay Polk a small sum originally due Polk's father, Samuel Polk.

23 Aug *From Archibald Yell.*

24 Aug *From Denison Olmsted.*

26 Aug *From Boling Gordon.*

27 Aug *To James M. Howry et al.*

29 Aug *From Henry W. Connor.*

29 Aug From James Gwin. ALS. DLC–JKP. Introduces Mr. Bradford of Lexington, Kentucky.

29 Aug *From Richard Warner et al.*

30 Aug From David McClure. ALS. DLC–JKP. Sends pamphlet (not found) on a system of education and asks Polk's views on it.

3 Sept From Jared S. Allen. ALS. DLC–JKP. States that he has listed a tract of land in Perry County held in the name of Samuel Polk at the highest tax rate.

3 Sept From Thomas Durham. ALS. DLC–JKP. Asks for the deed to some land he bought from Polk but for which he has not completed payment; notes that he has resold the land and is being sued for a clear title.

3 Sept *To Andrew Jackson Donelson.*

4 Sept *From Ransom H. Gillet.*

5 Sept From Sutherland S. Southworth. ALS. DLC–JKP. Wishes to know who will be the correspondent for the *Nashville Union* during the upcoming session of Congress.

6 Sept [1836] *From John Catron.*

7 Sept	*From W. Bowling Guion.*
7 Sept	From Daniel B. Turner. ALS. DLC–JKP. Requests endorsement for the position of postmaster of Huntsville, Alabama.
7 Sept	*From James Walker.*
8 Sept	*From Samuel H. Laughlin.*
9 Sept [1836]	*From Cave Johnson.*
10 Sept [1836]	*From Jacob Greer.*
10 Sept	From Robert J. Nelson. ALS. DLC–JKP. Asks Polk to investigate a claim on behalf of the estate of his father, John Nelson.
11 Sept	*From Felix Grundy.*
12 Sept	*From George Gammon.*
[12 Sept 1836]	*From Cave Johnson.*
12 Sept	*From James McKisick.*
[13 Sept 1836]	*From George C. Conrad et al.*
15 Sept	*From William G. Childress.*
15 Sept	*From Samuel H. Laughlin.*
17 Sept [1836]	From John Catron. ALS. DLC–JKP. Reports on efforts to get campaign literature printed and circulated.
17 Sept	*From William C. Dunlap.*
17 Sept	*From Samuel H. Laughlin.*
17 Sept	From William S. Mayfield. ALS. DLC–JKP. Wishes to apply for the job of postmaster at Lewisburg.
17 Sept	*From Austin Miller et al.*
19 Sept	*From John H. Bills.*
19 Sept	*From Isaac E. Crary.*
21 Sept	From Jesse M. Wilkes. ALS. DLC–JKP. Asks Polk to make a political appearance soon in Bedford County; requests copies of the journals of Congress.
22 Sept	*From William C. Dunlap.*
23 Sept	*From Erwin J. Frierson.*
25 Sept	From William N. Warner et al. LS. DLC–JKP. Invite Polk to attend a public dinner to be held at Somerville in his honor.
26 Sept	*From Lyman Knowles.*
26 Sept	From T. P. Moore. ALS. DLC–JKP. Discusses personal business affairs.
26 Sept	*From John C. Mullay.*
27 Sept	*From Samuel H. Laughlin.*
27 Sept	*From Gideon Lee.*
27 Sept	From Samuel Mitchell et al. LS. DLC–JKP. Invite Polk to a public dinner in his honor to be held in Shelbyville on October 8, 1836.
27 Sept	*To Denison Olmsted.*
28 Sept	*To Samuel H. Laughlin.*
28 Sept	*To Francis Thomas.*
29 Sept	*To George C. Conrad et al.*
30 Sept	*From John Catron.*
30 Sept	From Erwin J. Frierson. ALS. DLC–JKP. Advises of a

public dinner in Polk's honor to be held in Shelbyville on October 8; the committee will call on Polk, probably at Lewisburg.

30 Sept	*From Samuel Mitchell.*
1 Oct	*From Thomas L. Hamer.*
3 Oct	From Blair & Rives. L. DLC–JKP. Requests the returns of the 1836 presidential election in Maury and adjacent counties as soon as they become available.
3 Oct	*From West H. Humphreys.*
3 Oct	*From Silas Wright, Jr.*
4 Oct	*From Felix Grundy.*
4 Oct	*From Thomas J. Lacy.*
8 Oct	*From Denison Olmsted.*
[8 Oct 1836]	*From Samuel W. Polk.*
8 Oct	*From Sidney C. Posey.*
9 Oct	*To Joel L. Jones et al.*
10 Oct	*To John H. Bills.*
10 Oct	*From John W. Childress.*
10 Oct	*To Austin Miller et al.*
11 Oct	From William K. Hill. ALS. DLC–JKP. Advises that the presence of house guests will prevent his accompanying Polk to Bedford County.
11 Oct	*From William R. Rucker.*
12 Oct	*From Walter S. Franklin.*
12 Oct	*From Jesse Miller.*
13 Oct	*From Cave Johnson.*
13 Oct	From Denison Olmsted. ALS. DLC–JKP. Acknowledges receipt of a check, which is placed to the credit of Polk's brother, Samuel Washington Polk.
13 Oct	*From Henry Welsh.*
14 Oct	*From Francis Thomas.*
15 Oct	From Edward B. Hubley. ALS. DLC–JKP. Reports results of congressional elections in eastern Pennsylvania.
18 Oct	From Joel L. Jones. ALS. DLC–JKP. Advises that absence from home has prevented an earlier reception of Polk's letter of October 9; states that he has not heard from Felix Grundy or Cave Johnson, but that the dinner at Somerville is scheduled for October 25.
19 Oct	To William C. Dunlap. ALS. DLC–JKP. Requests a statement from Dunlap regarding his attendance at a meeting of the Tennessee delegation held in Washington City about January 1, 1835, and his recollections as to what transpired at the meeting.
19 Oct	From Thomas McKnight. ALS. DLC–JKP. Requests support for his petition to receive the appointment of postmaster at Lewisburg.
19 Oct	*From Archibald Yell.*
21 Oct	*From Williamson Smith.*
22 Oct	*From Henry Horn.*
24 Oct	From James L. Edwards. LS. DLC–JKP. Advises that the

	bill extending the provisions of the Act of June 7, 1832, passed the U.S. House but not the U.S. Senate and did not become law.
25 Oct	From Charles Fitzhugh. ALS. DLC–JKP. Reports that while traveling the previous day he was given by mistake Polk's saddle bags rather than his own; promises to forward Polk's bags as soon as possible.
25 Oct	From John M. Patrick et al. LS. DLC–JKP. Invite Polk to a public dinner to be held in his honor at Cornersville.
26 Oct [1836]	From Lawson Gifford. ALS. DLC–JKP. Requests a loan in order to sustain the Jonesboro *Tennessee Sentinel*.
27 Oct	*From James Walker.*
[28 Oct 1836]	From Joseph Coe. ALS. DLC–JKP. Requests subscriptions to the *Nashville Union* and to the Washington *Globe*.
29 Oct	*From William F. McRee.*
29 Oct	*From George W. Owens.*
30 Oct	From John H. Bills. ALS. DLC–JKP. Requests copy of a toast given by Polk at a dinner the previous week.
31 Oct	*From Alvin Cullom.*
2 Nov	*From Greenville Cook.*
2 Nov	*From Thomas Davis.*
3 Nov	From W. C. Newsom. ALS. DLC–JKP. Recommends Benjamin E. Roper to be postmaster of Vernon, Mississippi.
3 Nov	*To A. O. P. Nicholson.*
4 Nov	*From John H. Bills.*
4 Nov [1836]	*From Cave Johnson.*
8 Nov	From Benjamin P. Jett. ALS. DLC–JKP. Requests assistance in obtaining the appointment as register for the Red River land district.
8 Nov	*From Samuel Mitchell.*
9 Nov	From Thomas Davis. ALS. DLC–JKP. Gives the Bedford County election results.
9 Nov	From Thomas Dean. ALS. DLC–JKP. Encloses election results for Bedford County.
9 Nov	*From William Gammon.*
10 Nov	*From Ezekiel P. McNeal.*
11 Nov	*From Silas M. Caldwell.*
11 Nov	*From George Gammon.*
12 Nov	*From Thomas Davis.*
13 Nov	From James R. McMeans. ALS. DLC–JKP. Recommends Barryman T. Hamilton for appointment to the U.S. Military Academy.
14 Nov	*To Samuel H. Laughlin.*
15 Nov	*To Samuel H. Laughlin.*
16 Nov	*From William Gilchrist.*
17 Nov	From Hezekiah Bradbury. ALS. DLC–JKP. Seeks the appointment of postmaster at Lexington, Tennessee.
17 Nov	From H. B. Kelsey. ALS. DLC–JKP. Reports that he has heard from 31 counties and that Hugh L. White is about 2,500 votes ahead.

20 Nov	From Caruthers, Harris & Co. LS. DLC–JKP. Authorizes Polk to discount up to $5,000 in bank notes falling due in the four month period beginning April 1, 1837.
20 Nov	From Spencer Clark Gist. ALS. DLC–JKP. Requests that his claim be given early consideration.
20 Nov	*From Zadock Motlow.*
20 Nov	From W. W. Woods. ALS. DLC–JKP. Asks support for the claim of William Warden.
21 Nov	*From John H. Bills.*
21 Nov	From Hugh W. Wormsley. ALS. DLC–JKP. Recommends James Gholson for promotion to lieutenant in the army.
22 Nov	From Erwin J. Frierson. ALS. DLC–JKP. Requests on behalf of A. H. Coffey a subscription to the Washington *Globe.*
22 Nov	*From Adlai O. Harris.*
22 Nov	*From Richard Warner.*
23 Nov	From Hugh W. Wormeley. ALS. DLC–JKP. Recommends Richard A. McCree to be postmaster of Lexington, Tennessee.
24 Nov	*From John Catron.*
27 Nov	From John S. Young. ALS. DLC–JKP. Requests assistance in expediting claim of David Caldwell.
28 Nov	*From William Martin.*
29 Nov	*From Samuel P. Walker.*
30 Nov	*From William Bobbitt.*
30 Nov	From Robert Woods. ALS. DLC–JKP. Requests support for a petition for relief on behalf of Germanicus Kent.
[Dec]	*From Jacob Greer.*
1 Dec	*From William Armour.*
2 Dec	*From William H. Haywood.*
2 Dec	*From Denison Olmsted.*
3 Dec	*From Jacob Greer.*
3 Dec	*From Jesse Speight.*
[4 Dec 1836]	From James Walker. L, fragment. DLC–JKP. Discusses the presidential election of 1836.
7 Dec	From Mahlon Dickerson. Copy. DNA–RG 45. Transmits accounts of contingent expenses of the offices of the secretary of the navy and navy commissioners. (Enclosures not found.)
7 Dec	From John Forsyth. Copy. DNA–RG 59. Submits statements of expenditures for incidental and contingent expenses of the Department of State. (Enclosure not found.)
8 Dec	From [Susan Dougherty]. ALS. DLC–JKP. Requests assistance in a business matter.
8 Dec	*From H. W. K. Myrick.*
10 Dec	From Mahlon Dickerson. Copy. DNA–RG 45. Submits reports pertaining to the practicability of establishing certain navy yards. (Enclosures not found.)
10 Dec	From Susan Page. ALS. DLC–JKP. Requests on behalf of the heirs of Thomas Nelson aid in expediting their petition.

10 Dec	*From Joseph H. Talbot.*
13 Dec	From Caleb Cushing. ALS. DLC–JKP. Asks Polk to accept the accompanying books.
16 Dec	*To Caleb Cushing.*
17 Dec	*From Samuel W. Polk.*
17 Dec	*From William H. Polk.*
19 Dec	*From Denison Olmsted.*
20 Dec	*To James L. Edwards.*
23 Dec	*From James L. Edwards.*
23 Dec	*From George R. Powel.*
25 Dec	*From John H. Dew.*
25 Dec	*From George R. Fall.*
26 Dec	*To William R. Rucker.*
26 Dec	From Joel M. Smith. ALS. DLC–JKP. Asks that his memorial for an increase in pay be laid before Congress during the current session.
27 Dec	*From Nathan Gaither.*
27 Dec	From Amos Kendall. Copy. DNA–RG 28. Submits an estimate of expenditures for the Post Office Department for the year beginning July 1, 1837.
28 Dec [1836]	*From John W. Childress.*
28 Dec	*From George Gammon.*
28 Dec	*From John C. Whitsitt.*
29 Dec	From Mahlon Dickerson. Copy. DNA–RG 45. Submits copies of papers pertinent to the naval commission's examination of the navy yard at Pensacola. (Enclosures not found.)
29 Dec	From Peter Hagner. Copy. DNA–RG 217. Advises that Alexander Nelson is not entitled to commutation pay and that John Nelson has already received pay; returns the depositions to Polk. (Enclosures not found.)
29 Dec	*From John C. Mullay.*
29 Dec	From Joel Yancey. ALS. DLC–JKP. Requests aid in obtaining a promotion to a better position.
30 Dec	From Mahlon Dickerson. Copy. DNA–RG 45. Submits the plan of the navy yard at Pensacola. (Enclosure not found.)
31 Dec	From Mahlon Dickerson. Copy. DNA–RG 45. Transmits a statement of expenditures made from the contingent fund for the navy for the year ending September 30, 1836. (Enclosure not found.)

1837

[1837]	From A. S. Abell. ALS. DLC–JKP. Requests a seat in the U.S. House gallery as a reporter.
[1837]	From Richard M. Johnson. ALS. DLC–JKP. Expresses support for Polk's actions.
[1837?]	From John Stuart Skinner. ALS. DLC–JKP. Invites Polk to dinner.
1 Jan [1837]	*From John C. Mullay.*

2 Jan [1837]   From D. Callihan. ALS. DLC–JKP. Submits two letters supporting his application for an appointment. (Enclosures not found.)

2 Jan   From Mahlon Dickerson. Copy. DNA–RG 45. Transmits for members of the House copies of the "Naval Register" for 1837.

2 Jan   *From William R. Rucker.*

3 Jan   From Mahlon Dickerson. Copy. DNA–RG 45. Discusses the claim of the heirs of Robert Fulton.

4 Jan   From Mahlon Dickerson. Copy. DNA–RG 45. Submits a report on clerks employed during the previous year.

4 Jan   From John Forsyth. Copy. DNA–RG 59. Submits a report on clerks employed during the previous year in the Department of State.

4 Jan   From Peter Hagner. Copy. DNA–RG 217. Refers Polk to Thomas Hart Benton for information regarding the claim of the heirs of Roger B. Sappington.

4 Jan   *From Hopkins L. Turney.*

4 Jan   From Levi Woodbury. Copy. DNA–RG 56. Transmits a report on the relief of certain insolvent debtors of the United States. (Enclosure not found.)

4 Jan   From Levi Woodbury. Copy. DNA–RG 56. Transmits report of the register and receiver of the land office for the Southeastern District of Louisiana and a communication from the General Land Office vouching for the validity of the claims. (Enclosures not found.)

5 Jan   *From Carey A. Harris.*

5 Jan   *From Samuel H. Laughlin.*

6 Jan   From Charlotte Baynton. ALS. DLC–JKP. Requests aid in expediting her claim.

8 Jan   *From Daniel Graham.*

9 Jan   *From John Blair.*

9 Jan   *From John H. Dew.*

10 Jan   *From William G. Childress.*

10 Jan   *From George Moore.*

11 Jan   From William S. Anderson. ALS. DLC–JKP. Requests help in obtaining a patent.

11 Jan   From Joseph R. Brittain. ALS. DLC–JKP. Wishes to suspend for a season his subscription to the Washington *Globe*.

11 Jan   *From Humphrey H. Leavitt.*

11 Jan   *From John Y. Mason.*

12 Jan   *From Daniel Graham.*

13 Jan   From William L. Brent. ALS. DLC–JKP. Introduces Mr. Tolson and recommends him for a job in the land office.

13 Jan   From N. S. Harlin. ALS. DLC–JKP. Supports extension of the preemption law.

13 Jan   From James E. Heath. ALS. DLC–JKP. Encloses a draft (not found) for the pension due F. Fisher, a Virginia pensioner residing in Tennessee.

13 Jan   *From William J. Whitthorne.*

14 Jan   *From Joseph Brown.*
14 Jan   From Mahlon Dickerson. Copy. DNA–RG 45. Submits the
                 names of naval officers who received during the previous
                 year orders for service and asked to be excused, together
                 with the reasons offered.
15 Jan   From William Davis. ALS. DLC–JKP. Expresses concern
                 over Whig influence in the postmastership at Benton and
                 other towns in southeastern Tennessee.
15 Jan   From George L. Leonard and Joel Yowell. LS. DLC–JKP.
                 Support the petition to change the stage route from Shelby-
                 ville to Fayetteville via Lynchburg to that via Petersburg.
16 Jan   From A. A. [Finney?]. ALS. DLC–JKP. Requests Polk's
                 autograph.
16 Jan   *To Boling Gordon.*
16 Jan   *To Samuel H. Laughlin.*
16 Jan   From James Whitcomb. Copy. DNA–RG 49. Requests the
                 address of James McKisick, recent appointee to the land
                 office at Fayetteville, Arkansas.
17 Jan [1837]   *From John W. Childress.*
17 Jan   *From Greenville Cook.*
17 Jan   *From William D. Moseley.*
18 Jan   From J. W. [Brest]. ALS. DLC–JKP. Offers to sell the
                 U.S. government a collection of paintings "at a sum by no
                 means comparative with their value—and would at once
                 place the object in competition with the most celebrated
                 galleries of Europe."
19 Jan   *From William Yancey.*
20 Jan   *From Joseph W. Chinn.*
20 Jan   *From William R. Rucker.*
20 Jan   From Levi Woodbury. Copy. DNA–RG 56. Submits a state-
                 ment showing the gross revenue receivable on each article of
                 foreign imports for the last four years, distinguishing the
                 amount received in each year, together with the amount of
                 drawback in each year. (Enclosure not found.)
22 Jan   *From A. O. P. Nicholson.*
23 Jan   From Thomas Chapman. ALS. DLC–JKP. Requests favor-
                 able consideration of his memorial.
23 Jan   From William Morriss. ALS. DLC–JKP. Writes of distant
                 family ties with Polk.
24 Jan [1837]   *From Andrew C. Hays.*
24 Jan   *From Richard Warner.*
24 Jan   *From John S. Young.*
25 Jan   *From Samuel Mitchell.*
26 Jan   From L. Knowles & Co. LS. DLC–JKP. In accordance with
                 Polk's request, the company agrees to make a coach for
                 James Walker "as good and well finished and on as good
                 terms as yours."
27 Jan   From Richard C. Allen. ALS. DLC–JKP. Introduces
                 Samuel H. DuVal and recommends his appointment as mar-
                 shal of the Middle District of Florida.

27 Jan   From William Armstrong. ALS. DLC–JKP. Introduces Lt. A. Harris.

30 Jan   From Peter Hagner. Copy. DNA–RG 217. Approves the claim of the heirs of Nathan Sunderland.

30 Jan   From John Kincaid. ALS. DLC–JKP. Requests that his son, William G., be given appointment to the U.S. Military Academy.

1 Feb   From Mahlon Dickerson. Copy. DNA–RG 45. Transmits a statement of the appropriations for the naval service for the year 1836. (Enclosure not found.)

1 Feb   *From Nicholas Fain.*

1 Feb   From Sterling H. Lester. ALS. DLC–JKP. Wishes to acquire appointment to the registers office at Chulahoma, Mississippi.

2 Feb   *To James L. Edwards.*

2 Feb   *From Alfred Emerson.*

2 Feb   From Henry L. Pinckney. ALS. DLC–JKP. Offers to move that Reuben Chapman's memorial be referred to the Judiciary Committee.

2 Feb   *From John A. Thomas.*

3 Feb   From Mahlon Dickerson. Copy. DNA–RG 45. Advises that he can find no record that the Navy Department ever received direction to survey the coast from the Rigolets to Mobile Point.

4 Feb   From John Anderson. ALS. DLC–JKP. Introduces Henry Massey.

4 Feb   From Adlai O. Harris. ALS. DLC–JKP. Requests Polk's signature on a receipt necessary for settling the estate of John Lee Polk.

4 Feb   From Ralph I. Ingersoll. ALS. DLC–JKP. Introduces H. Augur.

4 Feb   *From Denison Olmsted.*

4 Feb   *From John Innes Pocock.*

4 Feb   From James Whitcomb. Copy. DNA–RG 49. Transmits a copy of his communication to the secretary of the Treasury respecting the compensation claimed by Daniel Graham. (Enclosure not found.)

5 Feb   *From John W. Ford.*

[5 Feb 1837]   From James P. Peters. ALS. DLC–JKP. Recommends George W. May to be postmaster at Chulahoma, Mississippi.

6 Feb   *From Jabez Jackson.*

7 Feb   From Benjamin F. Butler. Copy. DNA–RG 75. Transmits names and salaries of persons employed in the Bureau of Indian Affairs during 1836. (Enclosure not found.)

8 Feb   *From Andrew C. Hays.*

8 Feb   *From Denison Olmsted.*

9 Feb   From Peter Hagner. ALS. DLC–JKP. States the amounts due the widow and daughter of Nathan Sunderland.

9 Feb   From Thomas H. R. Jett. ALS. DLC–JKP. Expresses concern over Whig strength in Maury County; wishes to know if

	the rumor is true that Polk is about to receive an executive appointment.
10 Feb [1837]	From R. E. Huntington. ALS. DLC–JKP. Requests Polk's autograph.
11 Feb	From James Walker. ALS. DLC–JKP. Asks to be considered for an appointment in the land office.
12 Feb	From Augustus H. White. ALS. DLC–JKP. Submits petition (not found) requesting the establishment of a post office at Davis' Mills.
13 Feb	*From George R. Powel.*
14 Feb	From Robert J. Nelson. ALS. DLC–JKP. Requests an answer to his inquiry regarding claims on behalf of his father, John Nelson; also requests the appointment of Mrs. Francis Hurlbert as postmistress of his area of Arkansas, between Marion and Helena.
14 Feb	*From Richard Warner.*
15 Feb	*From Samuel H. Laughlin.*
15 Feb	*From William H. Polk.*
16 Feb	From Granville H. Frazer. ALS. DLC–JKP. Asks for the appointment of marshal of Arkansas or that of Indian agent.
16 Feb	From W. J. Frierson. ALS. DLC–JKP. Requests information about submitting a claim for compensation for a servant lost during the Florida campaign.
17 Feb	From Benjamin F. Butler. Copy. DNA–RG 107. Answers Polk's inquiry of February 14 regarding John C. Mubay.
17 Feb	From Benjamin F. Butler. Copy. DNA–RG 107. Advises that it is not within his power to comply with the House resolution requiring charts of the harbors of Provincetown, Nantucket, Great Point, and Holmes' Hole.
17 Feb	*From John W. Childress.*
17 Feb	*From George W. Churchwell.*
17 Feb	*From James Walker.*
20 Feb	From John Blair. ALS. DLC–JKP. Requests that Polk negotiate a banking transaction for him.
20 Feb	From James Gillespy. ALS. DLC–JKP. Argues against the removal of the postmaster at Canonsburg, Pennsylvania.
21 Feb	From Benoni Adams. ALS. DLC–JKP. Regarding the claim of his wife, the daughter of Nathan Sunderland, Adams advises that her Christian name is Elizabeth.
21 Feb	*From Samuel H. Laughlin.*
22 Feb [1837]	*From John Catron.*
23 Feb	From E. J. Shields. ALS. DLC–JKP. Requests advice on a business matter.
25 Feb	*To Andrew Jackson.*
[25 Feb 1837]	*To Andrew Jackson, Jr.*
26 Feb	From J. A W. Andrews. ALS. DLC–JKP. Requests advice on how to get a road built and a post office established in his part of McNairy County.
27 Feb	From J. A. Thomas. ALS. DLC–JKP. Requests assistance in obtaining a military promotion.
1 March	From John H. Hall. ALS. DLC–JKP. Wishes advice on where a prospective law graduate might locate.

1 March	*From Jabez Jackson.*
3 March	*To Andrew Jackson.*
3 [March 1837]	From Amos Kendall. Copy. DNA–RG 28. Submits report from the auditor showing the balances due from late postmasters. (Enclosure not found.)
[4 March 1837]	*From Andrew Jackson Donelson.*
5 March	From James Bright. ALS. DLC–JKP. Recommends Matthew Martin to fill the vacancy in the position of postmaster at Fayetteville.
7 March	*From Walter S. Franklin.*
8 March	*To Mahlon Dickerson.*
8 March	From Roderick Dorsey. ALS. DLC–JKP. Submits statement of accounts charged to Polk as Speaker for the second session of the Twenty-fourth Congress.
8 March	From George Henry Moore. ALS. DLC–JKP. Requests Polk's autograph.
8 March	From George Wolf. LS. DLC–JKP. Advises that Polk's account (as agent for paying the members of the U.S. House for mileage and attendance at the second session of the Twenty-fourth Congress) has been adjusted and will be closed on the books.
10 March	*From Walter S. Franklin.*
11 March	*From Samuel W. Polk.*
13 March [1837]	*From John Catron.*
13 March	From Walter S. Franklin. ALS. DLC–JKP. Advises that he is sending a copy of the journal of the last day of the second session, Twenty-fourth Congress, and wishes to know if Polk has any changes to suggest.
[18 March 1837]	*From Andrew Jackson Donelson.*
20 March	From J. B. Bland et al. PL. Published in the *Nashville Union*, April 4, 1837. Invite Polk to a public dinner during his visit to Louisville, Kentucky.
20 March	To J. B. Bland et al. PL. Published in the *Nashville Union*, April 4, 1837. Declines invitation to a public dinner because his stay in Louisville, Kentucky, is too brief.
[24 March 1837]	*From Samuel H. Laughlin.*
25 March	*From Jared S. Allen.*
25 March	*From Kenneth L. Anderson.*
27 March	From Andrew A. Kincannon. ALS. DLC–JKP. Wishes assistance on behalf of his brother to become a provision contractor for the Cherokee Indians removing West.
27 March	*From William J. Whitthorne.*
29 March	*From Samuel H. Laughlin.*
29 March	*To Samuel H. Laughlin.*
1 April	*From Cave Johnson.*
4 April	From A. M. M. Upshaw. ALS. DLC–JKP. Submits claim (not found) and asks Polk to forward it to Joel R. Poinsett.
9 April	From William H. Ellis. ALS. DLC–JKP. Discusses election results in Connecticut.
10 April	*From Samuel Powel.*
11 April [1837]	From James L. Williams. ALS. DLC–JKP. Advises that he has no evidence that Major Muller was connected with the

Continental army; asks Polk if he can find any evidence to support the claim from Muller's heir.

12 April	*From David Fentress.*
14 April	From Jonathan Elliot. ALS. DLC–JKP. Advises that one of Polk's books was left in Washington and one of Elliot's packed in its place; Elliot will make the exchange at Polk's convenience.
14 April	From Landon A. Kincannon. ALS. DLC–JKP. Seeks recommendation as a provision contractor for the Cherokee Indians removing west.
16 April	*From John Catron.*
17 April	From William R. Brown. ALS. DLC–JKP. Requests Polk's opinion regarding certain provisions in the distribution bill.
17 April	*From Samuel Mitchell.*
19 April	*To William Trousdale.*
19 April	From Levi Woodbury. LS. DLC–JKP. Acknowledges receipt of recommendation for Sterling H. Lester to be register of land office at Chulahoma, Mississippi; advises that the place was filled a month previously.
21 April	*From Joseph H. Talbot.*
22 April	*From John Catron.*
22 April [1837]	From Cave Johnson. ALS. DLC–JKP. Discusses suit against William Warwick for nonpayment of debt.
22 April [1837]	*From Cave Johnson.*
22 April	*From William R. Rucker.*
24 April	From John H. Dunlap. ALS. DLC–JKP. Acknowledges receipt of a power of attorney and advises that he will collect the debt owed by John M. Warner.
24 April	*From Alfred Flournoy.*
25 April	*From Felix Grundy.*
25 April	From John L. Horner. ALS. DLC–JKP. Encloses pamphlets (not found) containing the laws passed at the first session of the first legislature of the Wisconsin Territory.
25 April	*From Ezekiel P. McNeal.*
25 April	From James Rawlings. ALS. DLC–JKP. Discusses suit against William Warwick for nonpayment of debt.
27 April	*From William Trousdale.*
28 April	*From James McKisick.*
28 April	*From William B. Turley.*
30 April	From John H. Dunlap. ALS. DLC–JKP. Forwards amount received from John M. Warner, less expenses.
1 May	*From John H. Bills.*
2 May	*From Samuel W. Polk.*
3 May	*From George Moore.*
4 May	*From Silas M. Caldwell.*
4 May	*From Samuel H. Laughlin.*
4 May	*From Ezekiel P. McNeal.*
4 May	From Vernon K. Stevenson. ALS. DLC–JKP. Discusses shipment and transport of several chairs belonging to Polk.
5 May	*From John F. Gillespy.*

5 May	*From John McKinley.*
8 May	*From John Catron.*
9 May	*From Rufus P. Neely.*
11 May	From H. B. Cenas. LS. DLC–JKP. Issues notice that John B. Hays' draft in Polk's favor for $1,492.70 has not been paid by Caruthers, Harris & Co.
13 May	*From George W. Bratton.*
14 May	*From David Fentress.*
15 May	*From Silas M. Caldwell.*
16 May	*From William C. Dunlap.*
19 May	*To Andrew Jackson.*
20 May	*To Mahlon Dickerson.*
22 May	*From Andrew Jackson.*
22 May	*From Samuel H. Laughlin.*
24 May	*From Samuel H. Laughlin.*
25 May	From Frederick E. Becton. ALS. DLC–JKP. Requests aid in obtaining the chair of surgery at the medical school to be established in Louisville, Kentucky.
25 May	*From Daniel Graham.*
28 May [1837]	From Cave Johnson. ALS. DLC–JKP. Reports on the progress of his congressional campaign and outlines his itinerary for the next month.
28 May	*From Medicus A. Long.*
29 May	*To Andrew Jackson.*
29 May	*To Martin Van Buren.*
30 May	*From William Moore.*
2 June	From Mahlon Dickerson. Copy. DNA–RG 45. Acknowledges receipt of the recommendation of John O. Bradford for appointment as a chaplain.
2 June	*From James Walker.*
7 [June 1837]	*From West H. Humphreys.*
7 June	*From Samuel W. Polk.*
8 June	*From James Walker.*
9 June	*From William M. Warner.*
10 June	From A. M. M. Upshaw. ALS. DLC–JKP. Submits a copy of his letter to Peter Hagner regarding his claim.
11 June	*From Levin H. Coe.*
12 June	From Lewis J. Cist. ALS. DLC–JKP. Requests Polk's autograph.
13 June	From Ephraim Hunter. ALS. DLC–JKP. Announces a rally in Farmington on June 23; urges Polk to attend and speak.
14 June	*To Andrew Jackson.*
14 June	*From Samuel Mitchell.*
15 June	*From Andrew Jackson.*
15 June	*To William R. Rucker.*
16 June	*From Robert Armstrong.*
16 June	*To Andrew Jackson.*
17 June	*From John Catron.*
17 June	*From John F. H. Claiborne.*
17 June	*From Daniel Graham.*

18 June	*From Felix Grundy.*
19 June	*To William M. Warner.*
20 June	*From Sidney C. Posey.*
21 June	From Blair & Rives. LS. DLC–JKP. Confirm that they have sent the semi-weekly Washington *Globe* to those who wished subscriptions.
21 June	*To Andrew Jackson.*
22 June	*To Andrew Jackson.*
23 June	*From Andrew Jackson Donelson.*
24 June	*From John H. Bills.*
25 June	*From John C. McLemore.*
26 June	*To John F. H. Claiborne.*
27 June [1837]	From Lawson Gifford. ALS. DLC–JKP. Wants his paper, the Jonesboro *Tennessee Sentinel*, to print the laws of Congress; solicits Polk's endorsement.
27 June	*From John C. McLemore.*
27 June	*From Denison Olmsted.*
28 June	*From John H. Dew.*
29 June [1837]	From Robert Armstrong. ALS. DLC–JKP. Reports on arrangements for John Catron to meet with Polk; suggests that the *Nashville Union* would be placed on solid footing with a capital of $3,500.
30 June	*From William R. Rucker.*
2 July	*From Hopkins L. Turney.*
[3?] July	From William Grayham. ALS. DLC–JKP. Wishes assistance regarding his claim.
5 July	*From Jabez Jackson.*
6 July	*From Gorham Parks.*
7 July	*From John Catron.*
7 July	*From John F. Gillespy.*
8 July [1837]	*From John O. Bradford.*
10 July	From Gorham Parks. ALS. DLC–JKP. Introduces Thomas Davee, congressman from Maine.
11 July	*From John W. Childress.*
11 July	*From Josephus C. Guild.*
11 July	From Andrew A. Kincannon. ALS. DLC–JKP. Requests copies of the journals of the U.S. House for the two previous sessions.
12 July	*To Andrew Jackson Donelson.*
13 July	*From Nathaniel Smith.*
15 July	*From Alfred Flournoy.*
15 July	From Ransom H. Gillet. ALS. DLC–JKP. Introduces his successor in Congress, James B. Spencer.
16 July	*From J. A. W. Andrews.*
16 July	*From Robert Armstrong.*
18 July	*From Aaron V. Brown.*
18 July	*From George R. Powel.*
19 July	*From Daniel Graham.*
19 July	*From William Moore.*
20 July	*From Andrew Jackson Donelson.*
21 July	From Robert B. Reynolds. ALS. DLC–JKP. Reports that

Robert Armstrong is making progress in East Tennessee in his race for the governorship.

22 [July 1837]	*From John O. Bradford.*
23 July	*From John H. Bills.*
23 July [1837]	From Cave Johnson. ALS. DLC–JKP. Anticipates electoral majorities in various counties.
23 July	*From William R. Rucker.*
26 July	From John F. H. Claiborne. ALS. DLC–JKP. Reports that he and Samuel J. Gholson have won decisive victories in the Mississippi special election.
26 July [1837]	*From Lawson Gifford.*
26 July	*From John F. Gillespy.*
26 July	*From James N. Smith.*
30 July [1837]	*From Cave Johnson.*
31 July	*From Clement C. Clay.*
1 Aug	From Ira E. Douthit. ALS. DLC–JKP. Asks Polk to recommend to the U.S. House a petition in Douthit's favor.
3 Aug	From H. B. Macomb. AES. DLC–JKP. Encloses copies of letters from Henry St. George Tucker recommending Septemus Tuston as chaplain to Congress; requests that Polk show these letters to his friends.
[4 Aug 1837]	From William G. Dickinson. ALS. DLC–JKP. Wishes copy of his payroll and information regarding payments in behalf of certain lieutenants in the First Regiment of Tennessee Volunteers.
4 Aug	*From Felix Grundy.*
4 Aug	*From William R. Rucker.*
5 Aug	*From John H. Bills.*
5 [Aug]	*From George R. Powel.*
6 Aug	*To Andrew Jackson Donelson.*
6 Aug	*From Andrew Jackson.*
7 Aug	*From William C. Dunlap.*
7 Aug	*From Abram L. Gammon.*
7 Aug	*From Cave Johnson.*
8 Aug	*From Levin H. Coe.*
8 Aug	*From Sidney C. Posey.*
9 Aug	From Blair & Rives. LS. DLC–JKP. Warns that the Whigs have written their membership in the U.S. House to be punctual in attending the opening of the Extra Session in hopes that they may have a majority in attendance and thereby control the organization of the House.
9 Aug	*From William C. Flournoy.*
9 Aug	*From Robert B. Reynolds.*
12 Aug	From Robert Campbell, Jr. ALS. DLC–JKP. Submits a list of names of the most prominent men in Maury County's Nineteenth Civil District.
14 Aug	From William H. Feild. ALS. DLC–JKP. Recommends James M. McKissack to be postmaster at LaGrange.
14 Aug	*From Cave Johnson.*
16 Aug	*To Francis P. Blair.*
17 Aug	From Daniel Graham. ALS. DLC–JKP. Gives the majori-

ties for the persons from Tennessee elected to the Twenty-fifth Congress.

17 Aug — From Aaron Vanderpoel. ALS. DLC–JKP. Introduces new member of the New York delegation, Zadock Pratt.

18 Aug — From Edward Kavanaugh. ALS. DLC–JKP. Writes from Lisbon, Portugal, regarding the political situation there; also discusses his views of the political situation in the United States.

18 Aug — From Abbott Lawrence. ALS. DLC–JKP. Introduces his successor in Congress, Richard Fletcher.

18 Aug — From Gorham Parks. ALS. DLC–JKP. Requests that Hugh J. Anderson be assigned to the Commerce Committee or to the Committee on Naval Affairs.

18 Aug — From Aaron Vanderpoel. ALS. DLC–JKP. Introduces new member of the New York delegation, Robert McClellan.

19 Aug — *From James Walker.*

20 Aug [1837] — From Lawson Gifford. ALS. DLC–JKP. Asks help in getting the printing of the laws of Congress transferred from the *Knoxville Register* to the Jonesboro *Tennessee Sentinel*.

20 Aug [1837] — *From Cave Johnson.*

20 Aug — From Richard Warner. ALS. DLC–JKP. Supports petition for a mail stage route from Nashville to Fayetteville, but observes that the offices off the main road should be kept up by a horse mail.

21 Aug — From Preston Frazer. ALS. DLC–JKP. Asks Polk's assistance in obtaining compensation for two horses lost during the Florida campaign.

23 Aug — From Richard C. Allen. ALS. DNA–RG 59. Recommends Samuel H. Duval to be marshal of the Middle District of Florida.

23 Aug — From John Frazier. PL. DLC–JKP. Encloses map of the new railroad line from Philadelphia to Baltimore via Wilmington.

23 Aug — *From Frederick P. Stanton.*

24 Aug — From Jacob Greer. ALS. DLC–JKP. Urges action on his petition.

25 Aug — From John Adams. ALS. DLC–JKP. Introduces his successor in Congress, Zadock Pratt.

25 Aug — From William W. Woods. ALS. DLC–JKP. Asks assistance in a business matter in behalf of W. B. Jenkins.

25 Aug — From Eli Neelly. ALS. DLC–JKP. Asks to be recommended for a mail contract.

26 Aug — From William Armour. ALS. DLC–JKP. Urges adoption of a paper currency independent of national and state banks.

26 Aug — From A. M. M. Upshaw. ALS. DLC–JKP. Requests assistance in obtaining the appointment of agent for the Chickasaws.

27 Aug — From Ransom H. Gillet. ALS. DLC–JKP. Congratulates Polk on his reelection; recommends that James B. Spencer be named to the Commerce Committee.

27 Aug	From William Patterson. ALS. DLC–JKP. Introduces his successor in Congress, William H. Hunter.
27 Aug	*From James Walker.*
27 Aug	From Moses Woolson. ALS. DLC–JKP. Requests Polk's autograph.
29 Aug	From Joseph Herndon. ALS. DLC–JKP. Wishes to rent Polk's office in Columbia, if it is available.
30 Aug	*From John H. Bills.*
30 Aug	*From John F. H. Claiborne.*
30 Aug	*From John Field.*
30 Aug	From Robert Tinnin. ALS. DLC–JKP. Recommends Samuel Weakly to be postmaster at Florence, Alabama.
31 Aug	*From Isaac H. Haley.*
31 Aug	From Gideon Lee. ALS. DLC–JKP. Introduces Zadock Pratt of New York.
31 Aug	From S. W. Skinken. ALS. DLC–JKP. Recommends that John Taliaferro be named to the Committee on Military Claims.
[Sept 1837]	From D. M. Wilson. ALS. DLC–JKP. Requests a salary increase for himself and the assistant Capitol watchmen.
[Sept 1837?]	From John Fairfield. ALS. DLC–JKP. Recommends Hugh J. Anderson for the Commerce Committee.
1 Sept	From Matthias J. Bovee. ALS. DLC–JKP. Requests ruling on franking privileges allowed former members of Congress.
1 Sept	From Joseph B. Boyd. ALS. DLC–JKP. Requests Polk's autograph.
1 Sept	*From Richard Stanton.*
2 Sept	From James Armstrong. ALS. DLC–JKP. Requests assistance in settling a claim.
2 Sept [1837]	*From John O. Bradford.*
2 Sept	From J. C. Brasfield. ALS. DLC–JKP. Advises that he has become connected with a newspaper in Athens, Alabama; wishes to receive the Washington *Extra Globe* on an exchange basis.
2 Sept	*From John Catron.*
2 Sept	*From Dutee J. Pearce.*
4 Sept	From John O'Neal. ALS. DLC–JKP. Submits information (not found) necessary to obtain a pension for Thomas Buchanan; wishes to be advised when a decision has been made on the petition.
4 Sept	From J. M. Parrish. ALS. DLC–JKP. Solicits an appointment to see Polk.
5 Sept	From William Slade. ALS. DLC–JKP. Requests that he be removed from the Committee on Claims.
6 Sept	From Abraham B. Lindsley. ALS. DLC–JKP. Solicits a position for his son in the U.S. House.
7 Sept	From Thomas M. East. ALS. DLC–JKP. Supports a stage route from Mt. Pleasant or Pulaski to Savannah, via Waynesboro.
7 Sept	*From Jacob Fry, Jr.*

7 Sept	From Robert Johnston. LS. DLC–JKP. Reports public support for moving the post office at Thompson's Creek in Bedford County to Rowesville with James S. Fowler as the new postmaster.
7 Sept	From Richard Long. ALS. DNA–RG 15. Requests aid in getting his pension paid.
7 Sept	*From John Y. Mason.*
7 Sept	*From Ann M. Polk.*
7 Sept	*From James Walker.*
8 Sept	From Samuel Burch. ALS. DLC–JKP. Recommends Joseph Johnson for the Committee on Revolutionary Pensions.
8 Sept	From Preston Frazer. ALS. DLC–JKP. Asks Polk to intercede with the third auditor's office in an effort to expedite his claim.
9 Sept	From Cave J. Couts. ALS. DLC–JKP. Asks Polk to obtain for him an arithmetic book that he has not been able to find elsewhere.
9 Sept	From Leonard Rainey. ALS. DLC–JKP. Requests in behalf of his mother assistance in obtaining the pension due his late father.
10 Sept	*From John Catron.*
10 Sept [1837]	*From Jabez Jackson.*
10 Sept	*From Samuel W. Polk.*
10 Sept	*From James Walker.*
[11 Sept 1837]	From [William Plummer Bradburn]. AL, fragment. DLC–JKP. Applies for appointment in the revenue service.
11 Sept	From O. C. Comstock. ALS. DLC–JKP. Wishes to be appointed chaplain of the U.S. House.
11 Sept	From A. G. Ewing. ALS. DLC–JKP. Gives character reference for Thomas Sorrell, a physician.
11 Sept [1837]	*From Cave Johnson.*
11 Sept	From Sackfield Maclin. ALS. DLC–JKP. Recommends Campbell Stewart to be postmaster at LaGrange, in place of Samuel McMannus, resigned.
11 Sept	From Rufus P. Neely. ALS. DLC–JKP. Recommends Campbell P. Stewart for postmaster at LaGrange.
11 Sept	From J. M. Parrish. ALS. DLC–JKP. Expresses gratitude for Polk's interest in his behalf.
12 Sept	From Bennet G. Rainey. ALS. DLC–JKP. Opposes proposed stage mail route from Nashville to Fayetteville via Chapel Hill; supports instead the route through Franklin and Lewisburg.
13 Sept	From Thomas Durham. ALS. DLC–JKP. Requests assistance in obtaining a government contract.
13 Sept	*To John Forsyth.*
13 Sept	*From James C. Mitchell.*
13 Sept	*From Joel Yancey.*
14 Sept [1837]	*From John O. Bradford.*
14 Sept	To James L. Edwards. ALS. DNA–RG 15. Encloses dec-

laration of Thomas Buchanan, a pension applicant. (Enclosure not found.)

14 Sept   From Joel R. Poinsett. Copy. DNA–RG 94. Duplicate copy in DNA–RG 107. Encloses a report from Charles Gratiot respecting the application of Cave J. Couts for appointment to the U.S. Military Academy; the vacancy named in the report will be kept open for Couts. (Enclosure not found.)

14 Sept   From D. M. Wilson. ALS. DLC–JKP. Explains reasons for seeking a permanent affixment of the pay of the police of the Capitol.

15 Sept   From John Forsyth. Copy. DNA–RG 59. Acknowledges receipt of letter and enclosure recommending Samuel H. Duval for the appointment of marshal for the Middle District of Florida.

15 Sept   From Isaac Turner. ALS. DLC–JKP. Requests a letter from Polk.

16 Sept   From James L. Edwards. LS. DNA–RG 15. Advises that the declaration of Thomas Buchanan has been examined and filed with suspended cases.

16 Sept   From George Loyall. ALS. DLC–JKP. Congratulates Polk on his election as House Speaker and introduces Navy Lieutenant John L. Saunders.

17 Sept   *From William G. Childress.*

17 Sept   From Blackman Coleman. ALS. DLC–JKP. Solicits the position of surveyor general for lands recently acquired from the Chippewa Indians in the Wisconsin Territory.

17 Sept   *From Alfred Flournoy.*

17 Sept   From C. E. Haynes. ALS. DLC–JKP. Recommends friend as a messenger to the U.S. House.

17 Sept   From Egbert Haywood. ALS. DLC–JKP. Recommends Blackman Coleman to be surveyor general for lands recently acquired by treaty with the Chippewa Indians.

17 Sept   *From Charles D. McLean.*

18 Sept   *To James L. Edwards.*

18 Sept   From William Turner. ALS. DLC–JKP. Requests, as a reporter, access to the floor of the U.S. House.

19 Sept   From George A. Blanchard. ALS. DLC–JKP. Requests Polk's autograph.

19 Sept   *From Andrew J. Henry.*

[19 Sept 1837]   From West H. Humphreys. ALS. DLC–JKP. Recommends Campbell Stewart for postmastership at LaGrange.

19 Sept   From Robert Johnston. LS. DLC–JKP. Requests an opinion on the recommendation of Isaac Moore for postmastership at Bigbyville in Maury County.

19 Sept   *From Joel M. Smith.*

20 Sept   From J. H. Lewis. ALS. DLC–JKP. Requests a letter of introduction to Sam Houston.

20 Sept   From Mayes and Frierson. LS. DLC–JKP. Inquires about firm's subscription to the Washington *Extra Globe.*

20 Sept   *From William R. Rucker.*

20 Sept	*From James Walker.*
21 Sept	From J. M. Carthel. ALS. DLC–JKP. Requests that Willis Jones be given the mail contract from Huntington to Trenton.
21 Sept	From William Hunter. ALS. DLC–JKP. Requests a recommendation to the position of chief clerk in the comptroller's office.
21 Sept	From D. M. Noyes. ALS. DLC–JKP. Requests Polk's autograph.
22 Sept	From James Elliot. ALS. DLC–JKP. Opposes the current policy of land distribution; suggests that a portion of each new state be reserved for sale to actual settlers.
22 Sept	*From Samuel W. Polk.*
22 Sept	From H. B. Robertson. ALS. DLC–JKP. Applies for the position of House messenger.
22 Sept	From Sutherland S. Southworth. ALS. DLC–JKP. Forwards note from a temperance organization in Philadelphia. (Enclosure not found.)
23 Sept	From Henry L. Ellsworth. ALS. DLC–JKP. Acknowledges receipt of "John C. Yates' specification & sketch of an improvement in the Saw Mill."
23 Sept	*From William S. Hatch.*
23 Sept	From Selah R. Hobbie. LS. DLC–JKP. Acknowledges receipt of Polk's letter and accompanying memorial regarding changes in mail routes.
23 Sept	*From J. Knox Walker.*
23 Sept	*From Archibald Yell.*
24 Sept	*From Abijah Mann, Jr.*
25 Sept	To William G. Childress. ALS. MHi. Praises the first issue of the Franklin *Weekly Record.*
25 Sept	*From David B. Molloy.*
25 Sept	From John Richey. ALS. DLC–JKP. Requests Polk's aid in expediting his claim.
25 Sept	From John C. Rives. ALS. DLC–JKP. Recommends Benedict Milburn for employment by the U.S. House.
25 Sept	From Isaac Turner. ALS. DLC–JKP. Congratulates Polk on his election as House Speaker; encourages him not to alter his political course.
26 Sept	From Ira E. Douthit. ALS. DLC–JKP. Requests assistance regarding his claim.
26 Sept	*From Samuel W. Polk.*
26 Sept	From Nathan Towson. Copy. DNA–RG 99. Advises that A. H. Brown has been paid in full for his services in the Tennessee Brigade, but as the accounts are now in the second auditor's office, the matter has been referred there.
26 Sept	From War Department Pension Office. L. DNA–RG 15. Approves the claim of Thomas Buchanan, provided the applicant gives under oath a satisfactory reason for not having made an earlier application.
27 Sept	*From John Catron.*

27 Sept	From Thomas Wheet. ALS. DLC–JKP. Requests Polk's autograph.
28 Sept	From William S. Anderson. ALS. DLC–JKP. Expresses concern that he has had no word from the patent office; requests that Polk investigate the matter.
28 Sept	From William Emmons. ALS. DLC–JKP. Requests Polk's intercession with the General Land Office.
28 Sept	From Joel R. Poinsett. Copy. DNA–RG 107. Acknowledges recommendation of [Abraham?] Whinnery to be named sub-agent for the Osage Indians.
28 Sept	*From Leonidas Polk.*
29 Sept	*From Moses Dawson.*
29 Sept	From Joseph A. French. ALS. DLC–JKP. Requests Polk's autograph.
29 Sept	From William Noland. Copy. DNA–RG 42. Submits report and accompanying papers showing the design and other information regarding the new Treasury building. (Enclosures not found.)
[Oct 1837?]	From William K. Clowney. ALS. DLC–JKP. States that his poor health will not permit him to serve on the Committee on Privilege, should such a committee be ordered.
1 Oct	From John Davis. ALS. DLC–JKP. Requests recommendation for his son as sub-doorkeeper or sub-messenger in the U.S. House.
2 Oct	From William H. Haywood, Jr. ALS. DLC–JKP. Introduces Levi Silliman Ives, Episcopal Bishop of North Carolina.
2 Oct	From Andrew Kinnard. ALS. DLC–JKP. Solicits assistance in obtaining appointment as secretary to the Austrian mission.
2 Oct	To D. M. Noyes. ALS. NN–Emmett Collection. Gives Noyes his autograph.
2 [Oct]	From James P. Smith. ALS. DLC–JKP. Submits claim and requests aid in expediting it. (Enclosure not found.)
3 Oct	From John Forsyth. Copy. DNA–RG 59. Acknowledges receipt of letter recommending that the laws be published in the Memphis *Gazette*.
3 Oct	From Joseph Mason. ALS. DLC–JKP. Requests assistance in obtaining a mail contract in Alabama.
3 Oct	*From George W. Terrell.*
4 Oct	From L. Lawler. ALS. DLC–JKP. Sends two letters which he requests that Polk forward for him.
5 Oct	From William Hogan. ALS. DLC–JKP. Requests help in obtaining a clear title to some land in Alabama.
6 Oct	From John W. Harrison. ALS. DLC–JKP. Requests assistance in obtaining employment.
[8 Oct 1837]	From Francis W. Pickens. ALS. DLC–JKP. Urges Polk to devote all efforts toward passage of the Independent Treasury bill.
[8 Oct 1837]	*From Francis W. Pickens.*

9 Oct
From Leonard Jones. ALS. DLC–JKP. Congratulates Polk on his election as House Speaker; urges him to be fair and impartial.

9 Oct
To A. O. P. Nicholson.

10 Oct
From Adam Dale. ALS. DLC–JKP. Asks Polk to subscribe for him to the Washington *Globe*.

10 Oct
From Joel R. Poinsett. Copy. DNA–RG 107. Transmits reports of the pay and quartermasters general, regarding the claim of William G. Dickinson. (Enclosures not found.)

11 Oct
From Peter Hagner. ALS. DNA–RG 217. Acknowledges receipt of letter regarding claim of William Hood and advises that he has referred it to the Pension Office.

12 Oct
From John Davis. ALS. DLC–JKP. Wishes to know if there is any prospect of his son's receiving the appointment of assistant messenger in the U.S. House.

12 Oct
From Mahlon Dickerson. Copy. DNA–RG 45. Reports on the causes of the detention of the South Sea Squadron and on the expenditures occasioned thereby.

12 Oct
From Ezekiel P. McNeal. ALS. DLC–JKP. Requests assistance in obtaining subscriptions to various publications.

13 Oct
From John Davis. ALS. DLC–JKP. Expresses gratitude for Polk's kindness in behalf of Davis' son, who seeks employment in the U.S. House.

14 Oct
From James L. Edwards. LS. DLC–JKP. Explains procedure William Hood should follow in his efforts to obtain a pension.

16 Oct
To Mahlon Dickerson.

16 Oct
From William Gordon. ALS. DLC–JKP. Explains why William Hood's claim for bounty land was rejected.

16 Oct
From Michael Hill. ALS. DLC–JKP. Requests Polk's intercession in a matter in which he feels he has been wronged.

17 Oct
From Felix Grundy.

18 Oct
From Mahlon Dickerson. LS. DLC–JKP. Copy in DNA–RG 45. Acknowledges receipt of letter and enclosure in behalf of Joseph Dwyer, who seeks the appointment of purser in the navy.

18 Oct
From Amos Kendall. Copy. DNA–RG 28. Submits statement of accounts for the Post Office Department and estimates of receipts and expenditures for the remainder of the current year.

25 Oct
From W. Bowling Guion.

25 Oct
From Jesse Miller. LS. DLC–JKP. Encloses certificate of the comptroller showing Polk's account is closed on the books of the Treasury. (Enclosure not found.)

25 Oct
From Aaron B. Quinby. ALS. DLC–JKP. Encloses plans "proposed to Congress last winter for preventing explosions in the boilers of steam engines," and asks Polk's help in getting a bill through Congress to appropriate funds for testing.

25 Oct
From Williamson Smith.

26 Oct	From John F. Gillespy. ALS. DLC–JKP. Recommends Pleasant J. R. Edwards to the position of assistant surgeon in the army.
27 Oct	From Alvin Q. Nicks. ALS. DLC–JKP. Asks Polk to consult War Department records to see if Francis Mitchell, administrator of the estate of a Creek Indian, is entitled to sell the chief's land.
28 Oct	From Felix Robertson et al. LS. DLC–JKP. Request copies of speeches delivered that day at the Nashville Inn.
29 Oct	*From Andrew Jackson.*
30 Oct	From Erasmus McDowell. ALS. DLC–JKP. Recommends D. W. Parrish for the office of general surveyor of the Chickasaw country.
1 Nov	From Edney A. McCoy. ALS. DLC–JKP. Wishes information concerning a possible land grant in Arkansas for his father.
1 Nov	From M. B. Winchester. ALS. DLC–JKP. Submits statement of Polk's account showing the current balance due.
2 Nov	From John H. Prentiss. ALS. DLC–JKP. Indicates that Samuel B. Beach is eager to assume the editorship of the *Nashville Union*, provided the situation will afford sufficient income.
2 Nov	*From John H. Prentiss.*
2 Nov	From William C. Swanson. ALS. DLC–JKP. Encloses petition (not found) to the postmaster general requesting establishment of a post office at Sinking Creek in Bedford County.
7 Nov	*From Francis Thomas.*
9 Nov	*To A. O. P. Nicholson.*
10 Nov	*To Andrew Jackson Donelson.*
16 Nov	*From John S. Young.*
17 Nov	From Sam R. Anderson. ALS. DLC–JKP. Requests endorsement for the position of postmaster at Gallatin.
18 Nov [1837]	*From Albert G. Harrison.*
19 Nov	From William G. Childress. ALS. DLC–JKP. Advises that he has sent a list of names of persons in Williamson County to whom public documents should be mailed.
20 Nov	*From Joseph Ficklin.*
20 Nov	From C. Lewis. ALS. DLC–JKP. Recommends J. R. A. Tomkins for the position of postmaster at Gallatin.
20 Nov	*From Henry A. Miller.*
20 Nov	*From Joel M. Smith.*
21 Nov	*From William Trousdale.*
22 Nov	From Levi W. Fowler. ALS. DLC–JKP. Wishes to purchase a tract of land near Wolf's Ferry.
22 Nov	From Leonard Jones. ALS. DLC–JKP. Exhorts Democrats to be humble and fair in their legislation.
22 Nov	From W. W. Jossey. ALS. DLC–JKP. Submits list of persons who live in the vicinity of "Mackmurrys Store" in Columbia.
23 Nov	*From Josephus C. Guild.*

25 Nov	*From Granville S. Crockett.*
25 Nov	From John H. Dew. ALS. DLC–JKP. Encloses letter renewing subscription to the Washington *Globe* and requests that Polk handle the matter for him.
25 Nov	*From Ransom H. Gillet.*
25 Nov	From Samuel Neill. ALS. DLC–JKP. Recommends William B. Dameron to be marshal for Mississippi.
26 Nov	*From Daniel Graham.*
27 Nov	From David J. Craig. ALS. DLC–JKP. Requests endorsement for the position of postmaster at Mt. Pleasant.
27 Nov	From John Forsyth. ALS. DLC–JKP. Recommends Thomas Chaney for employment.
27 Nov	From John M. McCreary. ALS. DLC–JKP. Requests that a copy of the president's message be sent by express mail.
27 Nov	*From Robert Mathews.*
28 Nov	*From Cave Johnson.*
28 Nov	From William Ledbetter. ALS. DLC–JKP. Introduces Henry Y. Rains.
28 Nov	From A. O. P. Nicholson. ALS. DLC–JKP. Introduces Henry Y. Rains.
29 Nov	From Walter W. Coleman. ALS. DLC–JKP. Requests that Polk give prompt attention to Samuel Newsom's claim.
29 Nov	*From Robert P. Harrison.*
30 Nov	From William Allen. ALS. DLC–JKP. Introduces his friend Mr. Ferguson.
[Dec 1837]	From Richard M. Johnson. ALS. DLC–JKP. Introduces William Gunton, president of the Bank of Washington; recommends that this bank be used by the U.S. House for payment of its members.
1 Dec	From anonymous writer. L. DLC–JKP. Recommends that Josiah O. Hoffman or Francis Mallory be named to the Naval Committee.
1 Dec	*From John I. DeGraff.*
1 Dec	From John W. Hunter. ALS. DLC–JKP. Recommends that the same number of pages and messengers be employed in the Twenty-fifth Congress as in the Twenty-fourth.
2 Dec	From Richard M. Johnson. ALS. DLC–JKP. Recommends Mr. McPeak for the position of messenger in the U.S. House.
2 Dec	*From William H. Polk.*
4 Dec	From James B. Amway. ALS. DLC–JKP. Introduces Edward C. Crary.
4 Dec	From G. M. Briggs. ALS. DLC–JKP. Requests that Mr. Wheeler be given a reporter's access to the U.S. House floor.
4 Dec	*To Mahlon Dickerson.*
4 Dec	From Richard Fletcher. ALS. DLC–JKP. Requests that [Eswald] MacLeod, reporter for the *New York Commercial List*, be given access to the U.S. House floor.

4 Dec	From Richard Fletcher. ALS. DLC–JKP. Requests that a reporter for *Niles' National Register* be given access to the U.S. House floor.
4 Dec	From Ann Gordon. ALS. DLC–JKP. Requests Polk's influence in order to obtain for her son a position as U.S. House messenger.
4 Dec	From Jacob Greer. ALS. DLC–JKP. Requests assistance in expediting his claim.
4 Dec [1837]	From William Cost Johnson. ALS. DLC–JKP. Requests that William Ogden Niles, editor of *Niles' National Register*, be admitted as a reporter in the U.S. House.
4 Dec	From John O'Neal. ALS. DLC–JKP. Requests that Polk check with the pension office to see if the affidavit for Thomas Buchanan was received.
4 Dec	From David Russell. ALS. DLC–JKP. Requests that William MacLeod be admitted to the U.S. House floor as a reporter.
4 Dec	From Sutherland S. Southworth. ALS. DLC–JKP. Files notice that he is a representative for the *Philadelphia Inquirer* and the Philadelphia *American Saturday Courier*.
5 Dec [1837]	*From John Catron.*
5 Dec	From Robert Johnston. LS. DLC–JKP. Requests an opinion on the applications of Henry A. Miller and Isaac A. Duncan for the position of postmaster at Mount Pleasant.
5 Dec	From James Perry. ALS. DLC–JKP. Requests employment as marshal, should a vacancy occur.
5 Dec	From Rebecca Stoddart. ALS. DLC–JKP. Requests assistance in expediting a claim.
6 Dec	From Mahlon Dickerson. Copy. DNA–RG 45. Acknowledges receipt of letter and enclosures in behalf of Joseph Dwyer for the appointment of purser in the navy.
7 Dec	From George W. Featherstonhaugh. ALS. DLC–JKP. Introduces Mr. Langendorffer, a painter who wishes the use of one of the rooms at the Capitol assigned to artists.
7 Dec	From John Forsyth. LS. DNA–RG 59. Submits statement of expenditures for the Department of State from the contingency fund. (Enclosure not found.)
7 Dec	From T. A. Howard. ALS. DLC–JKP. Recommends Amos Lane, an applicant for a mission to one of the South American states.
7 Dec	From German Lester. ALS. DLC–JKP. Requests assistance in obtaining a stage route through portions of Tennessee, Alabama, and Mississippi.
7 Dec	*From James Walker.*
8 Dec	From Thomas Eastin. ALS. DNA–RG 59. Introduces Levin Gayle.
9 Dec	From Hiram Gray. ALS. DLC–JKP. Advises of his arrival in Washington City.
9 Dec	From Amos Kendall. Copy. DNA–RG 28. Submits a state-

ment of expenditures of the Post Office Department from the contingency fund for the year 1837. (Enclosure not found.)

10 Dec   From Joseph B. Boyd. ALS. DLC–JKP. Requests a second autograph, as the first arrived in a mutilated condition.

11 Dec   From W. A. Deitrick. ALS. DLC–JKP. Requests assistance in collecting a debt.

11 Dec   *From Josephus C. Guild.*

11 Dec   *From Amos Lane.*

11 Dec   *From James C. Mitchell.*

11 Dec   From Joel R. Poinsett. Copy. DNA–RG 75. Duplicate copy in DNA–RG 107. Advises that the information Alvin Q. Nicks requests is contained in the report of the commissioner of Indian Affairs.

12 Dec   From A. H. Coffey. ALS. DLC–JKP. Recommends Solomon Kimzey for the office of register of Missouri.

12 Dec   From Mahlon Dickerson. Copy. DNA–RG 45. Transmits abstract of expenditures for the year ending September 30, 1837, under the head of contingent expenses of the naval establishment. (Enclosure not found.)

12 Dec   *To Andrew Jackson Donelson.*

12 Dec   From Robert Johnston. LS. DLC–JKP. Requests an opinion on the applications of Henry A. Miller and Isaac A. Duncan for the position of postmaster at Mount Pleasant.

12 Dec   *From Samuel Martin.*

12 Dec   *From J. Knox Walker.*

13 Dec   From Abraham Fulgham and Joshua Dickson. LS. DLC–JKP. Advise Polk of his election as an honorary member of a secret literary society.

13 Dec   From George W. Terrell. ALS. DLC–JKP. Requests that his application for marshal be given fair consideration; defends his friendship with Charles Lynch; and affirms his loyalty to the party.

15 Dec   *From Richard H. Alexander.*

15 Dec   From Mahlon Dickerson. Copy. DNA–RG 45. Transmits petition of Cornelius Tiers, with accompanying papers and depositions. (Enclosures not found.)

15 Dec   *To Robert Johnston.*

15 Dec   From Wilson C. Newsum. ALS. DLC–JKP. Recommends Miles Cary to be marshal of North Mississippi.

16 Dec   *From John Bragg.*

16 Dec   To James L. Edwards. ALS. DNA–RG 15. Requests information regarding any action taken in the case of Thomas Buchanan's claim.

17 Dec   *From Samuel W. Polk.*

18 Dec   *From Andrew Beaumont.*

18 Dec [1837]   *From John O. Bradford.*

18 Dec   From James J. Deavenport. ALS. DLC–JKP. Recommends William B. Dameron to be marshal of North Mississippi.

18 Dec   *To Andrew Jackson Donelson.*

18 Dec	*From Samuel Martin.*
19 Dec	From Mahlon Dickerson. Copy. DNA–RG 45. Submits reports (not found) pertaining to various locations in New York that might be suitable for construction of dry docks.
19 Dec	*From William H. Haywood, Jr.*
19 Dec	From Archibald Wright. ALS. DLC–JKP. Recommends Albert M. Anderson for appointment to the U.S. Military Academy at West Point.
20 Dec	*From Joseph Brown.*
20 Dec [1837]	*From John W. Childress.*
20 Dec	*From Elihu C. Crisp.*
20 Dec	From David Gallaher. ALS. DLC–JKP. Advises that William Stanfield and S. J. Alexander have contracted to carry the mail from Shelbyville to Waynesboro.
21 Dec	From Mahlon Dickerson. Copy. DNA–RG 45. Transmits report (not found) of the Navy Board.
21 Dec	From Joseph Dwyer. ALS. DLC–JKP. Expresses gratitude for Polk's support of his application for purser; asks that Polk renew efforts to obtain the appointment for him.
21 Dec	*From Samuel A. Gillespie.*
21 Dec	From War Department Pension Office. L. DNA–RG 15. Advises that the claim of Thomas Buchanan has been approved.
22 Dec	*From Joel Pinson.*
22 Dec	From William H. Tuck. ALS. DLC–JKP. Requests the name of an attorney "in the neighbourhood of Mr. Wm. L. Weems of your State."
23 Dec	*From Joel M. Smith.*
25 Dec	From Simeon Marsh. ALS. DLC–JKP. Requests assistance in finding prospective land investors whom he might serve as an agent in locating suitable lands in Arkansas; expresses concern over the possibility of the passage of a preemption act.
26 Dec	From Taswell S. Alderson. ALS. DLC–JKP. Encloses a petition (not found); requests that Polk send speeches to several persons in Mississippi.
26 Dec	From Mahlon Dickerson. DNA–RG 45. Gives information pertaining to the advisability of establishing a navy yard at Charleston, South Carolina.
26 Dec [1837]	*From Charles G. Greene.*
26 Dec	From Thomas Martin et al. LS. DLC–JKP. Recommend James Perry to be marshal of North Mississippi.
28 Dec	From William B. Anderson. ALS. DLC–JKP. Submits an estimate of "*necessary* expenses and *probable* profits" for the Shelbyville *Western Star*, indicating that without additional support the newspaper will be discontinued.
28 Dec	From Charlotte Baynton. ALS. DLC–JKP. Advises that documents requisite for Congress have been dispatched; reaffirms her determination never to give up her claim.
28 Dec	*From Andrew Jackson Donelson.*

28 Dec [1837]	From George W. Eubank. ALS. DLC–JKP. Submits copy of his New Year's address. (Enclosure not found.)
28 Dec	*From Ezekiel P. McNeal.*
30 Dec	From Archibald Henderson. ALS. DLC–JKP. Introduces James Rhodes and recommends him for employment by the U.S. House.
30 Dec	From Selah R. Hobbie. LS. DLC–JKP. States distance from Washington City to Columbia, Tennessee, by the most direct stage routes.
31 Dec	*From James Walker.*

1838

[1838]	From L. Henry Cutts. ALS. DLC–JKP. Requests that her son not be removed from his position as U.S. House attendant.
[1838]	From William J. Graves. ALS. DLC–JKP. Reports on mileage and per diem and wishes to know the balance due him.
[1838]	From Felix Grundy. ALS. DLC–JKP. Forwards 200 copies of his address for distribution in Polk's district.
[1838]	From William H. Haywood, Jr. ALI. DLC–JKP. Gives permission for Polk to communicate verbally to Robert J. Walker "what I reported to you."
[1838]	From Michael Hill. ALS. DLC–JKP. Requests Polk's intercession in a matter in which he feels he has been wronged.
[1838]	From Jabez Jackson. ALS. DLC–JKP. Explains that ill health prevented his attending Polk's party the previous Monday.
[1838]	From William Cost Johnson. ALS. DLC–JKP. Requests that a friend be appointed to fill a vacant position as U.S. House messenger.
[1838]	From J. W. Latham. ALS. DLC–JKP. Advises that he has printed two packs of calling cards "with 'Mrs' added."
[1838]	From Luke Lea. ALS. DLC–JKP. Requests that Polk support Spencer C. Gist's petition to the Committee on Naval Affairs.
[1838]	From Anne Royall. ALS. DLC–JKP. Requests financial assistance.
[1838]	From Aaron Vanderpoel. ALS. DLC–JKP. Advises that an afternoon engagement will prevent his joining Polk as early as planned.
1 Jan	From Joel Henry Dyer. ALS. DLC–JKP. Requests assistance in learning what disposition has been made of his claim.
1 Jan	*From Adam Huntsman.*
1 Jan	From Joel Pinson. ALS. DLC–JKP. Recommends Thomas H. Williams to be United States marshal of Mississippi, should a vacancy arise.
2 Jan	From Amos Kendall. Copy. DNA–RG 28. Transmits list giving the names and the salaries of clerks employed in the Post Office Department during the previous year.

2 Jan	*From Samuel Mitchell.*
3 Jan	From J. A. W. Andrews. ALS. DLC–JKP. Advises that he has forwarded to his congressman a memorial supporting the establishment of a local post office in McNairy County, but that the congressman may oppose Andrews' appointment as postmaster of the new office.
3 Jan	*To Andrew Jackson Donelson.*
3 Jan	From Peter Hagner. LS. DLC–JKP. Responds to an inquiry of January 1 regarding the disposition of several claims.
3 Jan	*From Thomas J. Hall.*
4 Jan	*From Andrew Jackson Donelson.*
4 Jan	From John Forsyth. LS. DNA–RG 59. Transmits list giving names and salaries of clerks employed in the State Department during the previous year.
4 Jan	*To Edward J. Roberts et al.*
5 Jan	*From Jeremiah Day.*
5 Jan	From John Lowry. ALS. DLC–JKP. Requests assistance in obtaining additional compensation for his claim.
5 Jan	From Carey A. Harris. Copy. DNA–RG 75. Responds to an inquiry of January 1 regarding a claim.
6 Jan	*From Levin H. Coe.*
6 Jan	*To James Page et al.*
7 Jan	From Preston Frazer. ALS. DLC–JKP. Requests that Polk inquire of the Treasury Department what disposition has been made of John A. Jenkins' claim.
[7 Jan 1838]	*To Andrew Jackson.*
7 Jan	*To Andrew Jackson.*
7 Jan	*From A. O. P. Nicholson.*
8 Jan	*To Jeremiah Day.*
8 Jan	From Joel R. Poinsett. Copy. DNA–RG 75. Responds to a House resolution requesting information on the removal of the Cherokee Indians.
9 Jan	From Benjamin F. Allen. ALS. DLC–JKP. Requests public documents that will assist him in assessing the merits of the 1835 treaty between the Cherokees and the U.S. government.
9 Jan	From Joel R. Poinsett. Copy. DNA–RG 107. Transmits report showing that the claim of Curtis Ivey has been satisfied. (Enclosure not found.)
9 Jan	From Milton Webb. ALS. DLC–JKP. Requests information on the disposition of his claim.
10 Jan	*To William C. Dawson.*
10 Jan	From Carey A. Harris. Copy. DNA–RG 75. Responds to an inquiry regarding Jesse B. Mitchell's claim.
10 Jan	*From Charles G. Greene.*
10 Jan	*From Williamson Smith.*
10 Jan	From John P. Van Ness. ALS. DLC–JKP. Advises that the board of directors of the Bank of the Metropolis has not received a report from its special committee appointed to

	investigate the bank's differences with Roderick R. Dorsey, sergeant at arms.
10 Jan	From Augustus H. White. ALS. DLC–JKP. Requests assistance in establishing a post office in Bedford County and in sustaining the present postal route.
11 Jan	From Mahlon Dickerson. Copy. DNA–RG 45. Transmits list giving the names and salaries of clerks employed during the previous year in the offices of the navy secretary and navy commissioners. (Enclosure not found.)
12 Jan [1838]	From L. A. Godey (for Nat R. Menee). ALS. DLC–JKP. Acknowledges receipt of $9.00, which sum has been credited.
12 Jan	From Joel R. Poinsett. Copy. DNA–RG 75. Transmits report from the commissioner of Indian Affairs explaining the causes that have prevented a compliance with a House Resolution of February 21, 1837, in relation to alleged frauds upon the Indians. (Enclosure not found.)
12 Jan	From George Thomas. ALS. DLC–JKP. Advises that in paying Treasury notes to members of Congress the Bank of the Metropolis will continue to pay specie change when required.
13 Jan	From John Forsyth. LS. DNA–RG 59. Reports on the amount of postage expended by the Department of State for express mail.
13 Jan	*From Samuel A. Gillespie.*
13 Jan	*To A. O. P. Nicholson.*
14 Jan	*From John W. Childress.*
14 Jan	From James C. Wilson. ALS. DLC–JKP. Requests that his son, James Balch Wilson, be recommended to a vacant clerkship.
15 Jan	From Mahlon Dickerson. Copy. DNA–RG 45. Reports on the amount of postage paid by the Navy Department for express mail.
16 Jan	From James C. Wilson. ALS. DLC–JKP. Expresses gratitude for Polk's aid in obtaining the clerk's appointment for Wilson's son, James Balch Wilson.
17 Jan	From L. A. Godey (for Nat R. Menee). ALS. DLC–JKP. Acknowledges receipt of $9.00, which sum has been credited.
17 Jan [1838]	*From Cave Johnson.*
17 Jan	From Leonidas Polk. ALS. DLC–JKP. Introduces John C. Yeates, who is attempting to secure a patent on a machine designed to improve sawmills.
17 Jan	From B. S. Russ. ALS. DLC–JKP. Requests assistance in expediting his claim.
18 Jan	From Susannah Dougherty. ALS. DLC–JKP. Requests that Polk try to locate papers pertaining to her claim and present them to Congress.
18 Jan	*From Charles G. Greene.*
18 Jan	From Carey A. Harris. Copy. DNA–RG 75. Advises that

	the claim of Jesse B. Mitchell has been approved and the amount ($810) will be remitted.
18 Jan	*To Andrew Jackson.*
19 Jan	From Joel R. Poinsett. Copy. DNA–RG 107. Advises that Polk's district has its full complement of cadets at the U.S. Military Academy.
21 Jan	From Preston Frazer. ALS. DLC–JKP. Submits affidavit supporting his claim and requests Polk's assistance in expediting it.
21 Jan	*From Richard Warner.*
[22] Jan	*From Samuel W. Polk.*
23 Jan	*From Jesse F. Cleveland.*
23 Jan	From James P. Deams. ALS. DLC–JKP. Requests appointment as attendant surgeon during the Cherokee removal, should such a position be available.
23 Jan	From Mahlon Dickerson. Copy. DNA–RG 45. Transmits statement showing appropriations and expenditures for the Navy Department during the previous year. (Enclosure not found.)
23 Jan	To John Forsyth. ALS. DNA–RG 59. Forwards letters from T. A. Howard and J. L. Holman.
23 Jan	From Charles G. Greene. ALS. DLC–JKP. Introduces Seth L. Thomas, who is delivering a package from Greene to Polk.
23 Jan	*From Charles G. Greene.*
24 Jan	From Blackman Coleman. ALS. DLC–JKP. Solicits appointment as judge or surveyor in the Wisconsin Territory.
24 Jan	*From Andrew Jackson Donelson.*
24 Jan	*From George Thomas.*
25 Jan	From John Forsyth. LS. DLC–JKP. Copy in DNA–RG 59. Acknowledges receipt of recommendation for Amos Lane to be appointed chargé d'affaires to one of the South American republics.
25 Jan	*From James Walker.*
26 Jan	From Mahlon Dickerson. Copy. DNA–RG 45. Transmits statements of expenditures of the contingent fund by the offices of the navy secretary and navy commissioners.
26 Jan	From Alvin Q. Nicks. ALS. DLC–JKP. Wishes advice on how to obtain a clear land title and compensation for the heirs of the property.
27 Jan	*From John A. Thomas.*
28 Jan	*From Samuel W. Polk.*
28 Jan	From Robert H. Rose. ALS. DLC–JKP. Requests that Polk sign the enclosed letter to John Nelson of Baltimore. (Enclosure not found.)
28 Jan	From William C. Swanson. ALS. DLC–JKP. Requests that his subscription to the Washington *Globe* be addressed to the new post office at Sinking Creek.
28 Jan	*From Moses Wood.*

29 Jan   From Samuel D. Frierson. ALS. DLC–JKP. Wishes to
                      know whether a bond for a Mr. Emmerson is in Polk's
                      possession.
29 Jan   From Daniel Kenney. ALS. DLC–JKP. Submits list of "the
                      best men of Greene County" to whom public documents
                      should be sent.
29 Jan   *From Daniel Kenney.*
29 Jan [1838]   From William F. McRee. ALS. DLC–JKP. Discusses poli-
                      tical climate at the theological seminary at Princeton, New
                      Jersey; introduces Abner Cruser.
30 Jan   From William R. Caswell. ALS. DLC–JKP. Requests aid in
                      obtaining a post office for Russellville, Tennessee.
30 Jan   From Joseph Dwyer. ALS. DLC–JKP. Urges Polk to inter-
                      cede with Mahlon Dickerson in behalf of his application for a
                      purser's appointment.
30 Jan   *From Aaron Finch.*
30 Jan   From Preston Frazer. ALS. DLC–JKP. Wishes appoint-
                      ment as sales agent between the U.S. government and
                      Texas.
1 Feb   From Mahlon Dickerson. Copy. DNA–RG 45. Transmits
                      statement of the contracts made by the Navy commissioners
                      during 1837. (Enclosure not found.)
1 Feb   From Thomas J. Dye. ALS. DLC–JKP. Recommends John
                      Milam to be postmaster of Chulahoma, Mississippi.
1 Feb   *From Andrew Jackson.*
2 Feb   *To James L. Edwards.*
2 Feb   From Peter Hagner. LS. DLC–JKP. Acknowledges receipt
                      of letter and papers pertaining to the claim of James M.
                      Chilton.
2 Feb   From Peter Hagner. LS. DLC–JKP. Returns Polk's letter
                      and Preston Frazer's deposition with explanation why
                      Frazer's claim cannot be authorized. (Enclosures not found.)
2 Feb   *From Andrew Jackson.*
3 Feb   From James N. Brown. ALS. DLC–JKP. Recommends
                      George W. Ury to be postmaster of Chulahoma, Mississippi.
3 Feb   *From Robert Campbell, Jr.*
3 Feb   From Mahlon Dickerson. Copy. DNA–RG 45. Transmits
                      copy (not found) of a survey report.
3 Feb   From Francis Jackson. ALS. DLC–JKP. Sends several res-
                      olutions passed on January 25, 1838, by the Massachusetts
                      Anti-Slavery Society.
3 Feb   From John A. Thomas. ALS. DLC–JKP. Discusses military
                      bills presently before the Congress.
4 Feb   From Joseph B. Boyd. ALS. DLC–JKP. Requests Polk's
                      autograph.
4 Feb   *To Andrew Jackson Donelson.*
4 Feb   From Joseph Kincaid. ALS. DLC–JKP. Wishes to know if
                      Polk has received his petition in behalf of James Kincaid, his
                      father; discusses national bank question; and requests that

	Polk send him a Washington newspaper and any public documents of interest.
5 Feb	*From James M. Howry.*
5 Feb	*From William H. Polk.*
5 Feb	*To Levi Woodbury.*
6 Feb	From anonymous writer. L. DLC–JKP. Recommends Andrew G. Edmondson to the vacant position of receiver in the land office at Pontotoc, Mississippi.
6 Feb	From Charles A. Beares. ALS. DLC–JKP. Advises that Polk has been elected as an honorary member of the Franklin Literary Institute, which is located in Pittsburgh, Pennsylvania.
6 Feb [1838?]	From Cornelia Campbell. ALS. DLC–JKP. Details the history of her father's war service and requests compensation, either in money or land.
6 Feb	*From Matthew D. Cooper.*
6 Feb	*From Lawson Gifford.*
6 Feb	From William Gunton. ALS. DLC–JKP. Solicits for the Bank of Washington Polk's account as Speaker of the House.
6 Feb	*To Alexander G. McNutt.*
7 Feb	*From John Golder.*
7 Feb	*From Andrew C. Hays.*
7 Feb	From William Patterson. ALS. DLC–JKP. Solicits for his brother, John Patterson, the appointment of marshal of Ohio.
7 Feb	*From James Walker.*
8 Feb	From William Gunton. ALS. DLC–JKP. Advises that eight of the directors of the Bank of Washington have signed the bond "and two more will do so in the morning when it shall be promptly forwarded to you."
8 Feb	From Joel R. Poinsett. Copy. DNA–RG 75. Transmits a report from the commissioner of Indian Affairs pertaining to the Indian boundary in Missouri.
8 Feb	From Albert S. White. ALS. DLC–JKP. Requests that Jacob Bigelow be admitted to the floor of the U.S. House as a reporter for the *Michigan City Gazette* (Indiana).
9 Feb	From Louis D. Henry. ALS. DLC–JKP. Introduces William Faherty and recommends him for the position of messenger to the U.S. House.
9 Feb	From T. J. Kennedy. ALS. DLC–JKP. Requests assistance and information regarding his land claims.
10 Feb	From Peter Hagner. ALS. DLC–JKP. Advises that the claims of Samuel B. Newsom and Milton Webb have been approved.
11 Feb	From John Lynch. ALS. DLC–JKP. Wishes Polk's assistance in obtaining a position in the U.S. House.
12 Feb	To Joseph B. Boyd. ALS. Ia–HA. Gives Boyd his autograph.
12 Feb	From Daniel Campbell. ALS. DLC–JKP. Solicits Polk's aid

	in obtaining an appointment to one of the proposed new land offices.
12 Feb	From Henry K. Middleton. ALS. DLC–JKP. Writes that he has quit the Democratic Party because of Polk's support of the Gag Rule.
12 Feb	From William Radcliff. ALS. DLC–JKP. Urges formation of a select committee of the U.S. House to consider a memorial on the subject of a navigable route between the Atlantic and Pacific oceans.
13 Feb	*From Alexander H. Coffey.*
13 Feb	From Virgil David. ALS. DLC–JKP. Requests copy of the National Calendar.
14 Feb	From John F. H. Claiborne. ALS. DLC–JKP. Advises that he is preparing an address to the people and needs the yeas and nays in recent voting on the Gag Rule, with the Whigs marked in italics.
14 Feb	*To John Forsyth.*
14 Feb	*From A. M. M. Upshaw.*
15 Feb [1838]	*From Robert Armstrong.*
15 Feb	From Mahlon Dickerson. Copy. DNA–RG 45. Transmits for members of the U.S. House copies of the *Naval Register for 1838.*
15 Feb	*From Andrew Jackson Donelson.*
15 Feb	From Robert P. Dunlap. ALS. DLC–JKP. Encloses invitations to the Georgetown Ball. (Enclosures not found.)
15 Feb	From Adam Fergusson. ALS. DLC–JKP. Explains that John Newman's claim for bounty land has been denied on a technicality and requests that Polk introduce a bill for Newman's relief.
15 Feb	From Milton Webb. ALS. DLC–JKP. Urges that this claim be expedited.
16 Feb	*From Joseph H. Talbot.*
17 Feb	*From William Carroll.*
18 Feb	From J. C. Brasfield. ALS. DLC–JKP. Recommends a Dr. Cowan to be receiver of the land office at Pontotoc, Mississippi.
19 Feb	From William E. Butler. ALS. DLC–JKP. Recommends R. J. Chester for marshal of the Western District of Tennessee.
19 Feb	From Levi Woodbury. LS. DLC–JKP. Acknowledges receipt of letter recommending Andrew G. Edmondson for the office of receiver of public moneys at Pontotoc, Mississippi.
20 Feb [1838]	*From John O. Bradford.*
20 Feb	From William M. Byrd et al. LS. DLC–JKP. Request that Polk address the Dialectical and La Fayette societies of LaGrange College.
20 Feb	*From Clement C. Clay.*
20 Feb	From Benjamin B. Coffey. ALS. DLC–JKP. Solicits appointment as register of the land office in the Cherokee country.
20 Feb	From John Ross. ALS. DLC–JKP. Wishes to know if he is eligible for any kind of government pension.

20 Feb	From Horatio Woodman. ALS. DLC–JKP. Requests Polk's autograph.
21 Feb	From A. G. McNutt. ALS. DLC–JKP. Acknowledges receipt of letter of February 6, with the accompanying resolutions.
22 Feb	From anonymous writer. L. DLC–JKP. Denounces Polk, Andrew Jackson, and Martin Van Buren.
22 Feb	*To Mahlon Dickerson.*
23 Feb	*From John H. Dew.*
23 Feb	From Mahlon Dickerson. Copy. DNA–RG 45. Transmits report from the navy commissioners relating to a survey of St. Helena Bar in South Carolina. (Enclosure not found.)
23 Feb	From Mahlon Dickerson. ALS. DLC–JKP. Copy in DNA–RG 45. Acknowledges receipt of letter recommending John F. Young for appointment of lieutenant of marines.
23 Feb	From Joseph H. Talbot. ALS. DLC–JKP. Requests aid in obtaining clear title to land that he has purchased.
23 Feb	From Levi Woodbury. LS. DLC–JKP. Encloses statement showing the dividends declared on the capital stock of the BUS from its incorporation through 1833.
25 Feb	*From Joseph N. Johnson.*
25 Feb	From Levi Lincoln. ALS. DLC–JKP. Declines to serve on committee to superintend the interment of Jonathan Cilley of Maine.
26 Feb	From G. W. Davis. ALS. DLC–JKP. Wishes to know the approximate time when the present session of Congress will close.
26 Feb	From Antonio Knight. ALS. DLC–JKP. Requests permission to address Congress in order to present his plan for a sound currency.
26 Feb	To Horatio Woodman. ALS. WHi–Horatio Woodman Autograph Collection. Gives Woodman his autograph.
27 Feb	From A. J. Cotton and Peggy Cotton. LS. DLC–JKP. Urge passage of a bill providing for the sufferers by French spoliations prior to September 30, 1800.
27 Feb	From Cave J. Couts. ALS. DLC–JKP. Discusses plans to visit his home during the spring and his eagerness to learn of his appointment to the U.S. Military Academy.
27 Feb	*From James Walker.*
1 March	*From Daniel Graham.*
2 March	From anonymous writer. L. DLC–JKP. Protests the U.S. House's refusal to seat Mississippi's congressional delegation.
2 March [1838]	From E. G. Eastman. ALS. DLC–JKP. Requests that Polk deliver a letter for him.
2 March	From Abner Houston. ALS. DLC–JKP. Requests Polk's intercession to obtain a change in the mail route from Shelbyville to Mount Pleasant; wishes the route to include the town of Lewisburg.
2 March	From Joel R. Poinsett. Copy. DNA–RG 107. Returns papers relating to Albert Muller and reports showing why Muller is not entitled to compensation.

3 March	*From Richard C. Hancock.*
3 March	From A. O. P. Nicholson. ALS. DLC–JKP. Encloses paper relating to B. S. Russ' claim. (Enclosure not found.)
3 March	From Joel R. Poinsett. Copy. DNA–RG 107. Advises that when the Chickasaw agency is vacant, Polk's recommendation of A. M. M. Upshaw will be "respectfully considered."
4 March	From Jeremiah Cherry. ALS. DLC–JKP. Wishes position of entry taker or receiver for Crittenden County, Arkansas.
4 March [1838]	*From West H. Humphreys.*
5 March [1838]	*From John O. Bradford.*
5 March	From Mahlon Dickerson. Copy. DNA–RG 45. Transmits report containing estimates of the cost of proposed improvements of the navy yard at Pensacola. (Enclosure not found.)
5 March	*To Joseph Gales, Sr.*
5 March	From Albert A. Muller. ALS. DLC–JKP. Requests information on the disposition of his claim.
5 March	*From William J. Whitthorne.*
6 March [1838]	*From John O. Bradford.*
6 March	From A. C. Cazenove. ALS. DLC–JKP. Acknowledges receipt of check covering bill owed by Andrew Jackson.
6 March	From Joseph Gales. ALS. DLC–JKP. Acknowledges receipt of an order on the Bank of Washington as payment from the Rock Creek Colonization Society.
6 March	*To Martin Van Buren.*
7 March	From J. S. Buckingham. ALS. DLC–JKP. Encloses paper on dueling. (Enclosure not found.)
7 March	*To Mahlon Dickerson.*
7 March	*To John Forsyth.*
7 March	From John W. Harrison. ALS. DLC–JKP. Renews his request for aid in obtaining employment in Washington City.
7 March	*To Andrew Jackson.*
7 March	From Joseph Kincaid. ALS. DLC–JKP. Wishes to know if Polk has received his letter of February 4 concerning his petition in behalf of James Kincaid, his father.
7 March	From Vestal Marsh. ALS. DLC–JKP. Wishes to receive a Washington newspaper and any documents favorable to the present administration.
8 March	*From Andrew Jackson Donelson.*
8 March	From John Forsyth. Copy. DNA–RG 59. Acknowledges receipt of letter recommending John O. Bradford for a consulate.
8 March	From J. D. Hand. ALS. DLC–JKP. Advises that Polk has been elected an honorary member of the literary society of Rutgers College.
9 March	*To Blair & Rives.*
9 March	From Robert Mitchell. ALS. DLC–JKP. Requests that Peter A. Rodgers' claim be expedited.
9 March	*From J. Knox Walker.*
9 March	From R. M. Williamson. ALS. DLC–JKP. Introduces John S. Gooch of Mississippi.

10 March	*To William M. Byrd et al.*
10 March	*From Charles Douglas.*
10 March	From Jacob Greer. ALS. DLC–JKP. Wishes to know the disposition of his petition and discusses his opposition to the Sub-Treasury bill.
10 March	*From William H. Haywood, Jr.*
10 March	From Coleman Jackson. ALS. DLC–JKP. Submits list of persons wishing to subscribe to the Washington *Extra Globe.*
10 March	*From Joel M. Smith.*
[11 March 1838]	*From Isaac J. Thomas.*
12 March	From Mahlon Dickerson. Copy. DNA–RG 45. Transmits report and letter pertaining to proposed improvements in the navy yard at Pensacola. (Enclosures not found.)
12 March	From Susan Dougherty. ALS. DLC–JKP. Acknowledges receipt of Polk's letter of January 24 and lists the names of those whose depositions should be on record.
12 March [1838?]	From T. L. Hamner. ALS. DLC–JKP. Advises that he expects to return to Charleston in a few days "& to have another interview with my young friends. It would delight them not a little if I shd. have a communication to make to them from you."
12 March	From Oliver B. Hays. ALS. DLC–JKP. Reports from Philadelphia that prospects for selling Tennessee's state bonds are "gloomy if not hopeless."
12 March	From Henry A. P. Muhlenberg. ALS. DLC–JKP. Introduces his successor, George May Keim.
13 March	From Samuel Dunlap. ALS. DLC–JKP. Acknowledges receipt of two issues of the Washington *Extra Globe*; requests copies of speeches on the Sub-Treasury bill and other information that may be of interest.
13 March [1838?]	From West H. Humphreys. ALS. DLC–JKP. Writes in support of David Blalock's petition for a pension.
13 March	From Jabez Jackson. ALS. DLC–JKP. Declines to serve on the House committee for the revision of the naturalization laws.
13 March	From Leonard Jones. ALS. DLC–JKP. Discusses Henry Clay's speech on the Sub-Treasury bill; solicits employment.
13 March	From J. A. Willard. ALS. DLC–JKP. Requests Polk's autograph.
14 March	From Mahlon Dickerson. Copy. DNA–RG 45. Acknowledges receipt of recommendation for John O. Bradford to a pursership in the navy; states that because Joseph Dwyer has just been appointed, Dickerson cannot "with propriety give another to that state immediately."
14 March	From Warren W. Huntington. ALS. DLC–JKP. Requests Polk's autograph.
14 March	From J. B. Mitchell. ALS. DLC–JKP. Encloses certificate of the second auditor for $810, receipted as directed. (Enclosure not found.)

16 March   From A. H. Buckner. ALS. DLC–JKP. Urges speedy disposition of claims made by Samuel H. Garner and James R. Williams.

16 March   From Mahlon Dickerson. Copy. DNA–RG 45. Reports on the vessels, crews, and costs surrounding the proposed exploring expedition to the South Seas.

16 March   *To Martin Van Buren.*

17 March   *From Caruthers, Harris & Company.*

18 March   From Susan Dougherty. ALS. DLC–JKP. Requests that Polk obtain from the office of James Clark a deposition submitted by Sarah Caruthers.

18 March   From Mahlon Dickerson. ALS. DLC–JKP. Suggests that the navy "might make two or three appointments of midshipmen for Tennessee—if proper persons should be recommended."

18 March   From Anderson Landers. ALS. DLC–JKP. Requests subscription to the Washington *Extra Globe*.

18 March   From Richard Henry Stanton. ALS. DLC–JKP. Solicits aid in procuring government printing patronage for the *Maysville Monitor* (Kentucky).

18 March   *From James Walker.*

18 March   From Richard Warner. ALS. DLC–JKP. Reports on local politics and voices favor for the Sub-Treasury bill.

19 March   *From George W. Jones.*

19 March   From David W. McRee. ALS. DLC–JKP. Requests that Polk forward him political information that may be of interest.

19 March   *From Anne Royall.*

20 March   From Langtree & O'Sullivan. LS. DLC–JKP. Enclose copies of the *United States Magazine and Democratic Review*. (Enclosures not found.)

20 March   From Albert A. Muller. ALS. DLC–JKP. Acknowledges receipt of Polk's letter and asks him to intercede with the members of the Committee of Revolutionary War Claims.

21 March   From Joel R. Poinsett. Copy. DNA–RG 107. Copy also in DNA–RG 75. Returns letters of James P. Deams; advises that Nathaniel Smith, superintendent of the Cherokee emigration, administers applications for appointment as physician to the Cherokees. (Enclosure not found.)

21 March   *From Jonas E. Thomas.*

22 March   *From Powhatan Gordon.*

22 March   From Samuel Hamilton. ALS. DLC–JKP. Solicits position of assistant doorkeeper of the U.S. House, should John W. Hunter be promoted.

22 March   From Selah R. Hobbie. LS. DLC–JKP. Advises that the application for increased mail service on route No. 3486, McMinnville to Shelbyville, Tennessee, has been denied.

22 March   From Selah R. Hobbie. LS. DLC–JKP. Advises that the application for mail to be carried in stages on routes No. 3686 and No. 3493 (rather than by horse service) has been denied.

22 March	From J. L. Martin. ALS. DLC–JKP. Solicits an appointment for John Addison.
22 March	From Mary A. Pierce. ALS. DLC–JKP. Solicits in behalf of Joseph Follansbee the position of doorkeeper to the U.S. House.
22 March	From Joel R. Poinsett. Copy. DNA–RG 75. Transmits report and papers on Creek Indian affairs. (Enclosures not found.)
23 March	*From Joshua Cunningham.*
23 March	*From Andrew Jackson.*
23 March	*From William Patterson.*
23 March	From Perry Smith. ALS. DLC–JKP. Requests character reference for E. Hill of Fayetteville.
24 March	From John B. Bond. ALS. DLC–JKP. Requests aid in expediting a claim by the estate of Allen H. Powel.
24 March	From Mahlon Dickerson. ALS. DLC–JKP. Regrets error in stating that there are vacancies in the Corps of Midshipment.
24 March	From A. C. Hays. ALS. DLC–JKP. Submits names of persons wishing to subscribe to the Washington *Extra Globe.*
24 March	From David Petrikin. ALS. DLC–JKP. Asks Polk to investigate "tricks played by some of the people in the folding room" whereby packages were incorrectly labeled.
24 March	From Joel R. Poinsett. Copy. DNA–RG 107. Acknowledges receipt of recommendation by Colonel Pierce in favor of Lieutenant John R. Irwin for promotion in the army.
24 March	From Moses W. Weld. ALS. DLC–JKP. Requests Polk's autograph.
25 March	*From Levin H. Coe.*
25 March	From Cave J. Couts. ALS. DLC–JKP. Advises that he has decided not to go home for a visit before entering the U.S. Military Academy at West Point.
25 March	*From Cave Johnson.*
25 March	From Samuel Martin. ALS. DLC–JKP. Requests aid in expediting claim of his late father, Nathaniel Martin.
25 March	From Thomas N. Ross. ALS. DLC–JKP. Thanks Polk for helping him to obtain a pension; asks help in making arrangements to draw his pay in Jackson rather than in Nashville.
26 March	From Charles A. Davison. ALS. DLC–JKP. Requests Polk's autograph.
26 March	*To Andrew Jackson Donelson.*
27 March	*From John Y. Mason.*
27 March	*From Samuel P. Walker.*
27 March	From Hugh W. Wormsley. ALS. DLC–JKP. Requests assistance regarding claim by Mrs. Williamson, daughter of Captain Rains Cook.
28 March	From Robert Johnston. LS. DLC–JKP. Requests opinion on the recommendation of J. M. Calvert to fill the vacancy of postmaster at Mooresville, Tennessee.
28 March	From Alvin Q. Nicks. ALS. DLC–JKP. Requests informa-

tion regarding the proposed disposition of certain Indian lands.

28 March   *From William R. Rucker.*

29 March   *To John Forsyth.*

29 March   From Preston Frazer. ALS. DLC–JKP. Wishes appointment of surgeon to the Cherokees and Creeks, if the compensation is adequate.

29 March   *To Amos Kendall.*

29 March   From M. A. Mount. ALS. DLC–JKP. Solicits for her husband the appointment of doorkeeper to the U.S. House.

30 March   From Luther H. Sheldon. ALS. DLC–JKP. Wishes to be advised "in what year Mr. John H. Eaton was Secretary of War, if he is living Still, and if So, at what place he resides."

30 March   From Edward D. Tippett. ALS. DLC–JKP. Requests the use of the Congress Hall for a lecture on safety in steam power.

31 March   *From James M. Howry.*

31 March   *From Samuel B. Marshall.*

31 March   *From James Walker.*

1 April   From William Montgomery. ALS. DLC–JKP. Forwards letter that he has just received (Enclosure not found.)

2 April   From William W. Curran. ALS. DLC–JKP. Requests transfer to a different seat on the U.S. House floor.

2 April   *From Alfred Flournoy.*

2 April   From Hampton C. Williams. ALS. DLC–JKP. Solicits position as doorkeeper; cites influential family connections; and details how he thinks various House members will vote.

3 April   From Charles F. Chace. ALS. DLC–JKP. Urges indemnity of French spoliations prior to September 30, 1800.

3 April   From Samuel Hart. ALS. DLC–JKP. Solicits appointment as postmaster for Carrollton, Mississippi.

3 April   From John Hatchett. ALS. DLC–JKP. Requests subscription to the Washington *Extra Globe.*

3 April   *To Andrew Jackson.*

4 April   From Sam Reid. ALS. DLC–JKP. Solicits appointment as receiver of public moneys at Tallahassee, Florida.

5 April   From Frederick P. Stanton. ALS. DLC–JKP. Requests information on provisions and possible passage of a preemption bill; requests copies of speeches on the Sub-Treasury by John C. Calhoun, Henry Clay, Daniel Webster, Thomas H. Benton, and others.

5 April   *From Richard M. Woods.*

6 April   From William Alexander. ALS. DLC–JKP. Submits petition to Congress. (Enclosure not found.)

6 April   *From Aaron V. Brown.*

6 April   From George A. Miller. ALS. DLC–JKP. Wishes verification of enclosed autograph of Jonathan Trumbull, former Speaker of the House.

8 April   From Joel Henry Dyer. ALS. DLC–JKP. Asks Polk to inquire regarding the disposition of his claim.

8 April   *From Daniel Graham.*

9 April	From James N. Barker. ALS. DLC–JKP. Encloses bond. (Enclosure not found.)
9 April	*From John W. Childress.*
9 April	From Henry Turney. ALS. DLC–JKP. Requests information concerning benefits due widows of Revolutionary War veterans.
10 April	From Joseph Brown. ALS. DLC–JKP. Requests on behalf of his sister compensation for property lost to the Indians on May 9, 1787.
10 April	*From Andrew Jackson Donelson.*
10 April	*From James Walker.*
13 April	*From Daniel Kenney.*
14 April	*From Andrew Jackson Donelson.*
14 April	From John Johnson. ALS. DLC–JKP. Wishes to know "what there has been in my conduct that I was dismised."
14 April	From John Kirk. ALS. DLC–JKP. Wishes to purchase some of Polk's land that adjoins his own.
16 April	From Claiborne Cooke. ALS. DLC–JKP. Asks Polk's help in establishing a post office at Williamsborough, Tennessee.
16 April	From Richard H. Smith and Micajah Saratt. LS. DLC–JKP. Advise Polk of his election as an honorary member of the Union Literary Society of Miami University, Oxford, Ohio.
17 April	From William S. Anderson. ALS. DLC–JKP. Requests that Polk have some drawings executed in Washington City "from the model and transmit them to me so as I can amend my papers here and then send them to you for the Patent office . . . ."
17 April	From Littleberry R. Starkes. ALS. DLC–JKP. Solicits employment as a clerk in the Treasury Department.
18 April	From Samuel Cooper. Copy. DNA–RG 75. Submits report of the commissioner of Indian Affairs, "shewing that there is no information in this Department in respect to the destruction of property of the late Genl. Nathaniel Taylor by the Chickasaw Indians." (Enclosure not found.)
19 April	From Mahlon Dickerson. Copy. DNA–RG 45. Reports on the progress of a surveying expedition, which has not been completed on schedule.
19 April	*To Andrew Stevenson.*
20 April	*From Philo White.*
21 April	From Robert Campbell Jr. ALS. DLC–JKP. Submits affidavits (not found) relative to a claim by the heirs of William Stubens.
21 April [1838]	*From Isaac J. Thomas.*
22 April	*From John H. Bills.*
22 April	*To Andrew Jackson Donelson.*
23 April	From Mahlon Dickerson. Copy. DNA–RG 45. Corrects information in a previous report relative to the date of appointment of members of the scientific corps of the exploring expedition.
[23 April 1838]	*From West H. Humphreys.*

24 April	*From John B. Hays.*
24 April	From R. J. Powell. ALS. DLC–JKP. Solicits clerkship in one of the executive departments.
25 April	*From William H. Feild.*
26 April	From Preston Frazer. ALS. DLC–JKP. Solicits appointment as emigration agent for the Cherokees.
26 April	*From David B. Molloy.*
27 April	From William Hawley. ALS. DLC–JKP. Asks Polk's interpretation of a House rule respecting privileges for ex-chaplains.
28 April [1838]	*From John Catron.*
28 April	*From Israel Fonville.*
29 April	*From Cave Johnson.*
30 April	From John Forsyth. Copy. DNA–RG 59. Encloses certificate of the election of John P. Kennedy to fill the vacancy created by the death of Isaac McKim. (Enclosure not found.)
1 May	From William Yerger. ALS. DLC–JKP. Encloses his affidavit (not found) relating to a claim by Preston Frazer.
2 May	*From James Walker.*
4 May	*From Willie B. Johnson.*
5 May	From John [Billimas?]. ALS. DLC–JKP. Requests Polk's autograph.
5 May	*From Gideon J. Pillow.*
7 May	From Roger [Barton]. ALS. DLC–JKP. Recommends James Murray as a member of a board of commissioners to hear private claims against the government, should such a board be established.
7 May	*From John Gardiner.*
7 May	From Frederick Hussey. ALS. DLC–JKP. Requests Polk's autograph.
8 May	From William H. Caruthers. ALS. DLC–JKP. Introduces John W. Jordan; requests copies of political speeches that are favorable to the present administration.
8 May	From Samuel Cooper. Copy. DNA–RG 75. Transmits report and documents from the commissioner of Indian Affairs relative to the payment of the annuity due the Seneca Indians for 1837. (Enclosure not found.)
8 May	*To Andrew Jackson Donelson.*
8 May	*From Samuel P. Walker.*
8 May	From [W. L. Williams]. ALS. DLC–JKP. Requests help in obtaining release from a bond supporting Samuel Burton's mail contract bid.
9 May	*From William Scott Haynes.*
9 May	From Albert A. Muller. ALS. DLC–JKP. Requests aid in expediting his claim.
10 May	*To Arthur P. Bagby.*
10 May	From James Walker. ALS. DLC–JKP. Requests that the vacant postmastership at Fairfield be filled by a Republican.
10 May	*From James Walker.*
10 May	From James Whitcomb. ALS. DLC–JKP. Transmits patent

	(not found) for a section of land and requests that Polk acknowledge receipt of the same.
11 May	From anonymous writer. L. DLC–JKP. Attacks Polk's character.
12 May	From anonymous writer. L, fragment. DLC–JKP. Urges Polk to speak in Knoxville during his travels through East Tennessee.
12 May	*From Amos Kendall.*
14 May	*From Silas M. Caldwell.*
15 May [1838]	*From John O. Bradford.*
15 May	From William Gowans. ALS. DLC–JKP. Requests copy of the dueling report "about to be printed by order of the House."
15 May	*From James Walker.*
16 May	*From John H. Dew.*
16 May	From Robert J. McElhaney. ALS. DLC–JKP. Requests copies of speeches and other news of congressional activity.
16 May	*From Jacob L. Martin.*
16 May	From James Whitcomb. ALS. DLC–JKP. Transmits patent (not found) in favor of William H. Polk; requests that Polk acknowledge receipt of the patent and send the General Land Office the duplicate receipt.
17 May	*From Cave J. Couts.*
18 May [1838]	*From John W. Childress.*
18 May	From Mahlon Dickerson. Copy. DNA–RG 45. Offers to provide John O. Bradford passage on a ship from New York to Pensacola, but not to Puerto Rico; suggests that it would be preferable for him to complete his voyage on a merchant vessel.
18 May	*To Andrew Jackson Donelson.*
18 May	From Robert Johnston. LS. DLC–JKP. Advises of petition recommending John W. Ragsdale for postmastership at Davis' Mill in Bedford County and requests Polk's comments on the recommendation.
19 May	From Samuel Cooper. Copy. DNA–RG 107. Returns claim of Dr. Cheairs with a report explaining why the claim cannot be paid. (Enclosure not found.)
19 May	From William H. Haywood, Jr. ALS. DLC–JKP. Introduces John Roberts and Asa Jones.
19 May	From J. B. Knowlton. ALS. DLC–JKP. Requests Polk's autograph.
19 May	*From James Walker.*
20 May	From John H. Jacocks. ALS. DLC–JKP. Submits petition for a claim and requests that it be read before the U.S. House.
20 May	*To A. O. P. Nicholson.*
21 May [1838]	*From John O. Bradford.*
21 May	*From Andrew Jackson.*
21 May	From George Smith, Sr. ALS. DLC–JKP. Requests that his attorney be authorized to collect his pension for him and

	that Polk intercede with the Nashville office in arranging the matter.
21 May	From J. P. Van Tyne and Samuel Raub, Jr. LS. DLC–JKP. Complain about the manner in which the refectory in the Capitol basement is being operated by Michael Hill.
22 May	From John H. Jacocks. ALS. DLC–JKP. Urges that his claim be expedited; argues that he has been wronged by unethical government officials.
24 May	From A. P. Bagby. ALS. DLC–JKP. Acknowledges receipt of official notification of vacancy created by the death of Joab Lawler.
24 May	*To Mahlon Dickerson.*
24 May	*To Jonathan Webster.*
25 May [1838]	*From John O. Bradford.*
25 May	From James O. Buswell. ALS. DLC–JKP. Requests Polk's autograph.
25 May	*From A. O. P. Nicholson.*
25 May	From Joel R. Poinsett. Copy. DNA–RG 75. Submits statement estimating the expenses involved in the Cherokee removal.
25 May	*From William H. Polk.*
25 May	From Archibald Wright. ALS. DLC–JKP. Requests copy of the land grant or grants issued to the heirs of Cuthbert Harrison.
26 May	*From Edwin Croswell.*
26 May	*From Adam Huntsman.*
26 May	From Joseph Lancaster. ALS. DLC–JKP. Acknowledges receipt of Polk's letter and subscription; encloses a letter to P. P. Barbour and asks Polk to forward it. (Enclosure not found.)
27 May	From F. W. Pickens. ALS. DLC–JKP. Advises that he will call on Polk tomorrow.
28 May	From Robert Johnston. LS. DLC–JKP. Advises of the recommendation of William Collier to be postmaster at Unionville, Tennessee, and requests Polk's comments on the matter.
28 May	From T. J. Matthews. ALS. DLC–JKP. Requests copies of several political speeches, especially Henry Clay's speech on the occupant question.
29 May	From John M. Brodhead. ALS. DLC–JKP. Introduces Harriet Livermore.
29 May	*To Andrew Jackson Donelson.*
29 May	*From James Walker.*
31 May	From T. Boulanger. ALS. DLC–JKP. Solicits refreshment concession in the Capitol basement.
31 May	From George M. Keim. ALS. DLC–JKP. Recommends T. Boulanger to superintend the refectory in the Capitol basement.
31 May	*To Andrew Stevenson.*
1 June	*From Cave Johnson.*

1 June	From Joel R. Poinsett. Copy. DNA–RG 75. Transmits report from the commissioner of Indian Affairs relative to the valuation of improvements, and the amounts paid therein, under the Cherokee Treaty of 1835. (Enclosure not found.)
2 June	From John W. Davis. ALS. DLC–JKP. Solicits appointment as receiver of public money.
2 June	From Joseph Kincaid. ALS. DLC–JKP. Encloses memorial requesting reconsideration of claim of James Kincaid. (Enclosure not found.)
2 June	*From Joseph H. Talbot.*
2 June	*From Hopkins L. Turney.*
2 June	*To Hopkins L. Turney.*
5 June	*From Lucius J. Polk.*
5 June	From George W. Terrell. ALS. DLC–JKP. Recommends Isaac N. McCampbell for the appointment of attorney for the proposed Northern District of Mississippi; requests for himself the position of marshal of the Northern District.
6 June	From Benjamin B. French. ALS. DLC–JKP. Recommends Simon Brown for permanent employment in the document room of the U.S. House.
7 June	From John I. DeGraff. ALS. DLC–JKP. Requests recommendation for Eliphlet Cramer, who is seeking the office of surveyor general in Wisconsin.
7 June	From A. Y. Van Kluck. ALS. DLC–JKP. Wishes to know the probable time when Congress will close its present session.
8 June	*From Caruthers, Harris & Company.*
8 June	From John Cramer. ALS. DLC–JKP. Requests for his son a recommendation to be named surveyor general of Wisconsin.
[9 June 1838]	From F. W. Coleman. ALS. DLC–JKP. Encloses advertisement of the Concord Academy, of which he is the president; solicits Polk's patronage.
9 June	From Mahlon Dickerson. Copy. DNA–RG 45. Transmits copies of documents pertaining to the construction and equipping of the *U.S.S. Fulton.* (Enclosures not found.)
9 June	From Mahlon Dickerson. Copy. DNA–RG 45. Encloses report of a board of officers relative to proposed alterations in the *U.S.S. Fulton.* (Enclosure not found.)
9 June	From Charles Douglas. ALS. DLC–JKP. Solicits aid in obtaining the appointment of chargé d'affaires to one of the South American republics.
10 June	From Joseph Dwyer. ALS. DLC–JKP. Requests help in getting reinstated in the position of navy purser.
11 June	From William S. Anderson. ALS. DLC–JKP. Thanks Polk for help in obtaining a patent and advises he will soon reimburse Polk for money paid to the draftsman.
11 June	*From Joseph C. Herndon.*
11 June	*To Andrew Jackson.*
12 June	*From William E. Butler.*

12 June   From John M. Jackson. ALS. DLC–JKP. Recommends David M. Hunter to be receiver of the land office "said to be in contemplation in the Cherokee nation."

12 June   From John Ray. ALS. DLC–JKP. Requests on behalf of a daughter of Captain William Gilbreath an inquiry concerning the fate of the vessels and cargo owned at the time of his death.

13 June   From Mahlon Dickerson. Copy. DNA–RG 45. Lists names of persons employed and amounts paid by the navy for architectural plans and drawings since July 4, 1836.

13 June   From E. Dyer. ALS. DLC–JKP. Recommends John Foy to superintend the refectory in the Capitol basement.

13 June   From Frederic Perley. ALS. DLC–JKP. Requests Polk's autograph.

13 June   *From Philo White.*

14 June   From James Gallagher. ALS. DLC–JKP. Recommends David M. Hunter to be receiver of the land office "to be established in that part of the Cherokee country lying within the limits of Alabama."

14 June   From David M. Hunter. ALS. DLC–JKP. Wishes to be appointed receiver of the public moneys, should a new district be created to handle the sale of lands in Alabama ceded by the Cherokees.

14 June   From Albert Miller Lea. ALS. DLC–JKP. Wishes recommendation for the appointment of U.S. commissioner to survey the southern boundary of Iowa Territory.

15 June   *From Alfred Balch.*

15 June   From Joel Henry Dyer. ALS. DLC–JKP. Wishes to be appointed attorney general of the Western District of Tennessee.

15 June   From David M. Hunter. ALS. DLC–JKP. Recommends William J. McCord for the position of register in the land office, should one be created in the Cherokee lands of Alabama.

15 June   *From Albert T. McNeal.*

15 June   From B. W. Williamson. ALS. DLC–JKP. Requests on behalf of Dr. Isaac Edmonds payment for medical services rendered during the time that Polk owned a plantation in Fayette County, Tennessee.

16 June   *From Edwin Croswell.*

16 June   From James Maguire. ALS. DLC–JKP. Wishes Polk to advise his friends in Washington City that he is not the James Maguire (a clerk to Thomas S. Jessup) who has been acting against the administration.

16 June   From J. B. Morgan & Co. LS. DLC–JKP. Answers question raised about an account rendered on September 12.

17 June   *From John B. Hays.*

17 June   *From William H. Polk.*

21 June   From Leonard Jones. ALS. DLC–JKP. Submits memorial

(not found) and requests that it be presented to the U.S. House.

21 June	*To Franklin Pierce.*
21 June	From Major Andrew Price. ALS. DLC–JKP. Introduces William L. S. Dearing.
22 June	*From Levin H. Coe.*
22 June	*From Susan McWhorter.*
22 June	*From James Walker.*
23 June	From Samuel A. Gillespie. ALS. DLC–JKP. Wishes aid in obtaining authority to establish a mercantile house in the Chickasaw and Choctaw nations in the West.
24 June	*From Silas M. Caldwell.*
24 June	*From Robert J. Chester.*
24 June	*From Edwin Croswell.*
25 June	From John B. Hays. ALS. DLC–JKP. Requests renewal of the enclosed note. (Enclosure not found.)
25 June	From William McCabe. ALS. DLC–JKP. Requests help in obtaining an appointment in the army.
25 June	*To William H. Polk.*
26 June	From John Nelson. ALS. DLC–JKP. Requests aid in obtaining the appointment of marshal of the Northern District of Mississippi.
27 June	From John H. Bills. ALS. DLC–JKP. Asks Polk to "answer the Enclosed, as I have no information to give Esq. Robinson." (Enclosure not found.)
28 June	*From Alfred Flournoy.*
28 June [1838]	From B. F. Hallett. ALS. DLC–JKP. Requests consideration of the bill for relief of Thomas L. Winthrop.
29 June	*From Stephen C. Pavatt.*
29 June	From Joel R. Poinsett. ALS. DLC–JKP. Also copy in DNA–RG 107. Advises that there is no vacancy at the Military Academy that can be filled from Polk's district.
29 June	From William F. Sellers. ALS. DLC–JKP. Requests Polk's autograph.
29 June	*From James Walker.*
30 June	From Robert P. Harrison. ALS. DLC–JKP. Requests on behalf of John Ross information on how to proceed in order to submit a claim for a pension.
30 June	*From Adam Huntsman.*
1 July	*From Ransom H. Gillet.*
2 July	*From Caruthers, Harris & Company.*
2 July	*To Joel R. Poinsett.*
2 July	*From Joel M. Smith.*
3 July	From Joel R. Poinsett. Copy. DNA–RG 75. Transmits copies (not found) of correspondence between the War Department and Winfield Scott in relation to the removal of the Cherokees.
4 July	From Benjamin Clements. ALS. DLC–JKP. Solicits appointment of surveyor of the U.S.–Texas boundary.

4 July	*From Major Andrew Price.*
4 July	*From Moses Wood.*
5 July	*From Isaac Hill.*
6 July	*From Edwin Croswell.*
6 July	*From Jabez Jackson.*
[7 July 1838?]	From A. J. Blakemore. ALS. DLC–JKP. Urges Polk to make a speech at the town of X Plains, on his route from Springfield to Gallatin.
7 July	*To Martin Van Buren.*
10 July	*From James M. Howry.*
10 July [1838]	From Robert Mills. ALS. DLC–JKP. Requests that he be retained to supervise the House chamber renovation.
10 July	*From E. B. Robinson.*
12 July	From James N. Barker. ALS. DLC–JKP. Advises that Polk's account for the pay and mileage of members at the Second Session of the Twenty-fifth Congress has been closed on the books of the Treasury.
12 July	*From Henry Hubbard.*
12 July	To James K. Paulding. ALS. DLC–JKP. Recommends Henry Elliott for appointment as midshipman in the navy.
14 July	*To Henry Horn et al.*
14 July	*From Jabez Jackson.*
14 July	*From Ralph Metcalf.*
14 July	From William V. Pettit et al. LS. DLC–JKP. Invite Polk to meet with "republican friends in the City and County of Philadelphia" during his visit there.
17 July	From Robert J. Nelson. ALS. DLC–JKP. Requests that his neighborhood in Arkansas be given a post office, to be called Whites Post Office, and filled by Americus White.
20 July	*To John W. Childress.*
20 July	*From Henry Toland.*
21 July	From Moses Ridley et al. LS. DLC–JKP. Invite Polk to a public dinner in his honor, to be held in Murfreesboro at a time in August to be arranged.
21 July	From Henderson K. Yoakum. ALS. DLC–JKP. Urges Polk to accept the invitation to a public dinner in Murfreesboro.
24 July	From Henry B. Kelsey. ALS. DLC–JKP. Advises that the date for the dinner at Lewisburg has been set for August 4.
24 July	From James Osburn et al. LS. DLC–JKP. Invite Polk to a public dinner to be held in Lewisburg to honor Polk and Hopkins L. Turney.
26 July	*From William Scott Haynes.*
26 July	*From William V. Pettit.*
27 July [1838]	*From John J. Gilchrist.*
30 July	From Thomas Dodson. ALS. DLC–JKP. Wishes to close the sale of some of Polk's lands and to receive the commission thereon.
30 July [1838]	*From Adam Huntsman.*
30 July	*From Hopkins L. Turney.*

1 Aug	*From John H. Bills.*
1 Aug	*From Albert T. McNeal.*
3 Aug	From Hudson A. Kidd et al. LS. DLC–JKP. Advise Polk of his election as an honorary member of the Erosophian Society of Nashville University.
4 Aug	*From John J. Gilchrist.*
5 Aug [1838]	From John W. Childress. ALS. DLC–JKP. Urges Polk to give an early reply to the Rutherford County dinner invitation.
5 Aug	*To Moses Ridley et al.*
6 Aug	From Andrew Jackson Donelson. ALS. DLC–JKP. Encloses letter from Andrew Jackson to the dinner committee at Lewisburg. (Enclosure not found.)
6 Aug	From Henry Van Pelt. ALS. DLC–JKP. Wishes to know when certain persons were appointed to office.
7 Aug	*From Edmund Burke.*
7 Aug	*To Andrew Jackson.*
8 Aug	*From James Page.*
8 Aug	*To Martin Van Buren.*
9 Aug	From Moses Ridley et al. LS. DLC–JKP. Acknowledge receipt of Polk's acceptance of their invitation, and advise that they have designated August 30 as the date for the public dinner.
9 Aug	*From William R. Rucker.*
12 Aug	*From Charles G. Olmsted.*
14 Aug	*From Joseph H. Talbot.*
15 Aug	*From Albert G. Harrison.*
18 Aug	*To Edmund Burke.*
20 Aug	From George W. Jones et al. LS. DLC–JKP. Invite Polk to a public dinner in his honor to be held in Fayetteville on September 7.
21 Aug	From Bennel Bicknell. ALS. DLC–JKP. Asserts that New York Democrats are confident of carrying their state in the coming elections; wishes to know about the party's prospects in Tennessee.
21 Aug	From George Shafer. LS. DLC–JKP. Urges Polk to subscribe to a lottery sponsored by Funkstown, Maryland.
21 Aug	*To Martin Van Buren.*
22 Aug	*To Edmund Burke.*
22 Aug	From Thomas J. Read & Son. LS. DLC–JKP. Acknowledges receipt of Polk's order, which will be filled and delivered as soon as possible.
25 Aug	*From John H. Bills.*
27 Aug	From Jesse B. Clements. ALS. DLC–JKP. Repeats invitation to a public dinner in Fayetteville on September 7; cites uncertainty in the mail delivery as his reason for duplicating the invitation.
27 Aug	From George W. Jones. ALS. DLC–JKP. Sends copy of his letter of August 20 inviting Polk to a public dinner; requests

a prompt answer; and advises that the committee is proceeding with arrangements on the assumption that Polk will attend.

29 Aug   From Albert A. Muller. ALS. DLC–JKP. Wishes to know if any action has been taken on his claim, or if he needs to submit additional information.

30 Aug   From John H. Dunlap. ALS. DLC–JKP. States that he will deposit in one of the Nashville banks the notes that Polk sent.

30 Aug   From John J. Gilchrist. ALS. DLC–JKP. Advises that he has received Polk's letter to Edmund Burke of August 18 and that he has forwarded the same to Burke as requested.

1 Sept   *From Samuel H. Laughlin.*

[2] Sept   *To Andrew Jackson.*

3 Sept   *From James P. Grundy.*

4 Sept [1838]   *From Robert Armstrong.*

6 Sept   From Robert Johnston. LS. DLC–JKP. Advises that Charles T. Philpot has been recommended as postmaster at Flat Creek, Bedford County, Tennessee, and requests Polk's comments on the matter.

7 Sept   *From George W. Bratton.*

7 Sept   *From Joel M. Smith.*

8 Sept   *From Hampton C. Williams.*

10 Sept   *From John H. Bills.*

10 Sept   From Thomas H. Bradley et al. LS. DLC–JKP. Invite Polk to a public dinner in Franklin during the month of September.

10 Sept   *From Edmund Burke.*

10 Sept   *From Samuel H. Laughlin.*

11 Sept   *From John H. Bills.*

11 Sept [1838]   *From John W. Childress.*

11 Sept   *From Jesse Leigh.*

11 Sept   From Philander Priestley. ALS. DLC–JKP. Urges Polk to stop in Dover during his tour of the Western District and invites Polk to be his guest should he come.

11 Sept   From Philander Priestley. ALS. DLC–JKP. Duplicates letter of same date with the notation that he is writing also to Jackson in the event that Polk may have left Columbia before receiving this letter.

12 Sept   From Samuel Cushman. ALS. DLC–JKP. Reports on Democratic victories in Maine and Vermont.

12 Sept   *From Claiborne Kyle.*

12 Sept   From John Lauderdale et al. LS. DLC–JKP. Invite Polk to a public dinner in his honor to be held in Hartsville, Sumner County, at such time as might be convenient.

12 Sept   From Henry E. Riell. ALS. DLC–JKP. Reports on election results in Maine and Vermont.

12 Sept   *From A. M. M. Upshaw.*

13 Sept   From William L. Berry. ALS. DLC–JKP. Bills Polk for subscriptions to the Fayetteville *Independent Yeoman* and the Lincoln County *Standard of the Union*.

13 Sept	*From George W. Bratton.*
13 Sept	*From Sutherland S. Southworth.*
13 Sept	From Reuel Williams. ALS. DLC–JKP. Reports on Democratic victories in Maine.
14 Sept [1838]	From Robert Armstrong. ALS. DLC–JKP. Introduces Joseph Dwyer, who is seeking reappointment as navy purser.
14 Sept	From Adam Deck et al. LS. DLC–JKP. Invite Polk to a public dinner honoring Polk and Hopkins L. Turney, to be held near Livingston on October 30.
14 Sept	From Henry E. Riell. ALS. DLC–JKP. Encloses news of the Democratic victory in Maine. (Enclosure not found.)
15 Sept	*From Greenville Cook.*
15 Sept	From John H. Dunlap. ALS. DLC–JKP. Advises that he will forward Polk's money to Jackson "if a safe opportunity offers."
15 Sept	From Archibald Wright et al. LS. DLC–JKP. Invite Polk to speak in Pulaski, preferably on September 25.
16 Sept	*From William R. Rucker.*
17 Sept	*From Aaron V. Brown.*
[17] Sept	*From John W. Childress.*
17 Sept	From James M. Howry. ALS. DLC–JKP. Invites Polk to a public dinner in his honor to be held in Oxford, Mississippi, at a time to be arranged.
17 Sept [1838]	*From West H. Humphreys.*
18 Sept	From David Gallaher. ALS. DLC–JKP. Invites Polk to speak in Waynesboro on October 12.
18 Sept	*From Henry Mabry.*
18 Sept	*To Samuel Mitchell.*
19 Sept	From Peter Stubblefield. ALS. DLC–JKP. Requests that Polk transact some business for him with David H. Allen, an attorney in Virginia.
19 Sept	From M. B. Winchester and James P. Davis. LS. DLC–JKP. Advise of receipt in Memphis of items shipped from Louisville "which are in Store and will await your instructions."
20 Sept	*From Joseph H. Talbot.*
22 Sept [1838]	*From Robert Armstrong.*
22 Sept	*To Adam Deck et al.*
22 Sept	From Michael Hill. ALS. DLC–JKP. Requests that Polk forward some personal documents believed to be in Polk's possession.
22 Sept	From James M. Howry. ALS. DLC–JKP. Reiterates invitation to a public dinner in Oxford, Mississippi; explains that the original letter was sent to Columbia.
22 Sept	From Robert N. Johnson. ALS. DLC–JKP. Informs Polk of the death of Walter S. Franklin, clerk of the U.S. House, on September 20.
22 Sept	From R. M. Newlin. ALS. DLC–JKP. Advises that business prevents his meeting Polk; expresses support for Polk's gubernatorial bid.

23 Sept	From Daniel Gold. ALS. DLC–JKP. Reports that he has recovered his health and will be able to continue serving as a clerk in the U.S. House.
23 Sept	From Jonathan P. Hardwicke. ALS. DLC–JKP. Invites Polk to a public dinner in his honor to be held in Dickson County at such time as may suit his convenience.
23 Sept	*To Andrew Jackson.*
23 Sept	*To John Lauderdale et al.*
24 Sept	From John Blair et al. LS. DLC–JKP. Invite Polk to visit Jonesboro during his travels through East Tennessee en route to Washington City.
26 Sept	*From Levin H. Coe.*
26 Sept	*From Joseph Drake.*
26 Sept	*From Abraham McClellan.*
27 Sept	*From P. C. Caldwell.*
27 Sept	*From Samuel H. Laughlin.*
27 Sept	*From James R. McMeans.*
28 Sept	*From Samuel H. Laughlin.*
29 Sept	*From John H. Bills.*
29 Sept	*From Edmund Burke.*
30 Sept	From J. Holland (for Blair & Rives). ALS. DLC–JKP. Reports from the Washington *Globe* office on subscriptions and charges.
30 Sept	*From Ezekiel P. McNeal.*
1 Oct	*From John P. Campbell.*
1 Oct	*From Matthew St. Clair Clarke.*
1 Oct	From John Smither et al. LS. DLC–JKP. Invite Polk to a public dinner in his honor to be held in Huntingdon at his convenience.
2 Oct	*From John H. Bills.*
3 Oct	From James Davis et al. LS. DLC–JKP. Invite Polk to attend a public meeting in his honor to be held in Holly Springs, Mississippi, during his pending visit to that state.
3 Oct	From Arnold Nandain. LS. DLC–JKP. Announces candidacy for the office of clerk of the U.S. House.
4 Oct	*From Isaac Fletcher.*
4 Oct	*From Ezekiel P. McNeal.*
6 Oct	From Samuel Beardsley. ALS. DLC–JKP. Recommends Edward Livingston of Albany, New York, to be clerk of the U.S. House.
6 Oct	*From Alvin W. Bills.*
6 Oct	*From Andrew Jackson Donelson.*
6 Oct	*From Jacob Fry, Jr.*
6 Oct	From Thomas Mumford. ALS. DLC–JKP. Requests Polk's autograph.
8 Oct	From M. B. Winchester. ALS. DLC–JKP. Encloses receipt for Polk's account. (Enclosure not found.)
9 Oct	From Amos Kirkpatrick. ALS. DLC–JKP. Urges Polk to make a public speech at Gainesboro.
10 Oct	From Joel R. Poinsett. Copy. DNA–RG 107. Also copy in

	DNA–RG 75. Acknowledges recommendation of Andrew A. Kincannon as special agent to adjudicate Indian claims to replace Aaron V. Brown, resigned; advises that if a successor is necessary, Kincannon will receive the appointment.
10 Oct	From John Thomson. ALS. DLC–JKP. Reports on election results in Ohio.
11 Oct	*From John H. Bills.*
11 Oct	*From Samuel Burch.*
[11 Oct 1838]	From Jonas R. McClintock. ALS. DLC–JKP. Reports on the governor's race and other election results in Pennsylvania.
11 Oct	From Stephen C. Pavatt. ALS. DLC–JKP. Expresses pleasure that Polk will visit Huntingdon on October 23 and suggests that he will win support on his internal improvements policy.
11 Oct	From Luther Reily. ALS. DLC–JKP. Reports on the election of David R. Porter as governor of Pennsylvania.
11 Oct	From Samuel P. Walker. ALS. DLC–JKP. Advises that he has heard nothing from John C. McLemore; adds that he has given William H. Polk and A. O. P. Nicholson the business papers as instructed.
12 Oct	From John A. Gardner. ALS. DLC–JKP. Invites Polk to a dinner to be given in Dresden on October 25 or 26.
12 Oct	From James M. Howry. ALS. DLC–JKP. Encloses letter (not found) containing subscriptions to the *United States Magazine and Democratic Review*; regrets that he was unable to see Polk in Oxford, Mississippi.
12 Oct	*From William V. Pettit.*
12 Oct	*From Daniel Sheffer.*
13 Oct	From Samuel Hughes. ALS. DLC–JKP. Reports on election results in Pennsylvania.
13 Oct	*From James R. McMeans.*
13 Oct	*From William N. Porter.*
13 Oct	*From Collin S. Tarpley.*
13 Oct	*From Henderson K. Yoakum.*
[15 Oct 1838]	From Robert Armstrong. ALS. DLC–JKP. Reports on elections in Ohio, Maryland, and Pennsylvania.
15 Oct	From John H. Dunlap et al. LS. DLC–JKP. Invite Polk to a public dinner in his honor to be held in Paris on October 24.
15 Oct	From George W. Terrell. ALS. DLC–JKP. Recommends Henry A. Garrett to be federal judge of the Southern District of Mississippi.
15 Oct	*From James Walker.*
15 Oct	From M. B. Winchester. ALS. DLC–JKP. Advises that the supplies for Polk's plantation were forwarded to Mississippi and a receipt for the payment was forwarded to Columbia.
16 Oct	*From Austin Miller.*
17 Oct	From Maclin Cross. ALS. DLC–JKP. Reports that notices have been posted in McNairy County announcing Polk's speech there on October 20; expects a good attendance.

17 Oct [1838?]   From David M. Hunter. ALS. DLC–JKP. Solicits appoint-
                    ment as receiver of public moneys for Cherokee lands in
                    Alabama.
17 Oct   From Henry Mabry. ALS. DLC–JKP. Submits bill of $6.00
                    for Polk's subscription to the Murfreesboro *Weekly Times.*
17 Oct   From Philander Priestley. ALS. DLC–JKP. Expects Polk
                    to speak in Dover on October 26; says that he has advertised
                    this appointment throughout Stewart County.
17 Oct   From David Shaver, Jr. ALS. DLC–JKP. Urges Polk to
                    give a speech in Sullivan County on his way to Washington
                    City; comments on election results in other states and gives
                    his opinion on Polk's prospects in several counties in East
                    Tennessee.
18 Oct   *From James G. M. Ramsey.*
18 Oct   *From Moses G. Reeves.*
19 Oct   From Emerson Etheridge et al. LS. DLC–JKP. Invite Polk
                    to a public dinner in his honor to be held in Dresden on
                    October 25.
20 Oct   From B. L. Bogan. ALS. DLC–JKP. Solicits appointment
                    as senior doorkeeper of the U.S. House.
20 Oct   *From James Walker.*
21 Oct   From Stephen C. Pavatt. ALS. DLC–JKP. Advises that
                    urgent business at the Humphreys County court requires
                    his attendance on October 22 and prevents his being in
                    Huntingdon on the 23rd, when Polk will arrive; adds that he
                    will try to meet Polk in Paris.
22 Oct [1838]   *From West H. Humphreys.*
24 Oct   From Joel R. Poinsett. Copy. DNA–RG 107. Also copy in
                    DNA–RG 75. Encloses appointment of Andrew A.
                    Kincannon to succeed Aaron V. Brown as special agent to
                    adjudicate Indian claims; requests that the commission be
                    forwarded to Kincannon. (Enclosure not found.)
25 Oct   From Lycurgus Winchester. ALS. DLC–JKP. Encloses list
                    of persons in West Tennessee who are interested in receiv-
                    ing public documents.
26 Oct   *From Samuel Mitchell.*
27 Oct [1838]   *From John Catron.*
29 Oct   *To Robert Armstrong.*
29 Oct   *From George W. Hopkins.*
29 Oct   From William Wallace. ALS. DLC–JKP. Introduces him-
                    self to Polk, endorses Polk's candidacy for governor, and
                    urges establishment of a newspaper in the Knoxville area.
1 Nov   *From Aaron V. Brown.*
1 Nov   *From Jonathan Elliot.*
1 Nov   *From Ezekiel P. McNeal.*
2 Nov   *To Aaron V. Brown.*
2 Nov   *From William G. Childress.*
2 Nov   *From Cave Johnson.*
4 Nov   From William Moore. ALS. DLC–JKP. Regrets that heavy
                    rains have prevented his traveling to Nashville to see Polk;

	adds that he thinks Lincoln County is safely in the Democratic fold.
5 Nov	*From Samuel Mitchell.*
5 Nov	From John Nelson. ALS. DLC–JKP. Introduces M. D. Haynes of Lexington.
5 Nov	From Joseph Sherman. ALS. DLC–JKP. Solicits recommendation in behalf of Carver D. King, applicant to the U.S. Military Academy at West Point.
[6 Nov 1838]	From Alfred Balch. ALS. DLC–JKP. Wants to talk with Polk about "the 5000 acre tract located by your Father in Hardeman County."
6 Nov	*From Andrew A. Kincannon.*
6 Nov	*From Charles G. Olmsted.*
6 Nov	From Ray S. Orton. ALS. DLC–JKP. Bills Polk again for his $50 subscription.
8 Nov [1838]	From Robert Armstrong. ALS. DLC–JKP. Reports rumors that Hugh Lawson White has resigned his seat in the U.S. Senate; thinks that White will run for governor.
8 Nov	*From A. M. M. Upshaw.*
[9 Nov 1838]	From Robert Armstrong. ALS. DLC–JKP. Reports that he has learned from Josephus Guild that "every thing went off well at Hartsville"; asks Polk to write from Blountsville "what you think of the state of feeling in East Tennessee."
10 Nov	From Russell Houston. ALS. DLC–JKP. Advises that he has been requested to write Polk on the subject of the claim for a horse lost by Reuben F. White; wants Polk to learn from the auditor what further proof is necessary "to have the claim authenticated & settled."
10 Nov	From Thomas J. Read & Son. LS. DLC–JKP. States that Polk's order will be filled provided the river is navigable for shipment.
12 Nov	From R. G. Kelsey. ALS. DLC–JKP. Wishes to know the settlement pertaining to the guardianship of Cornelia Kelley.
12 Nov	*From Abraham McClellan.*
13 Nov	*From John H. Dew.*
15 Nov	From Joel M. Smith. ALS. DLC–JKP. Requests that Polk present to John Forsyth the enclosed application.
15 Nov	From Joel M. Smith. ALS. DLC–JKP. Requests support for certain land claims, soon to be presented to Congress.
15 Nov	From John Wattemelen. ALS. DLC–JKP. Sends personal greetings.
16 Nov	*From Samuel McRoberts.*
16 Nov	From David Shaver, Jr. et al. LS. DLC–JKP. Report that the people of Sullivan County eagerly anticipate Polk's visit, advise that of the two public houses in Blountsville, the eastern one is patronized by Van Buren supporters.
17 Nov	*From William M. Lowry.*
19 Nov	*From Henry Ewing.*
20 Nov	From William L. S. Dearing. ALS. DLC–JKP. Requests

	Polk's help in bringing some claims to the attention of Congress.
20 Nov	From Lewis Turner. ALS. DLC–JKP. Comments on the pension laws, which he believes are unfair because they give no compensation to war veterans who served less than six months.
20 Nov [1838]	From Joseph L. Williams. ALS. DLC–JKP. Reports that illness prevents his departure that day for Washington City; regrets that he will not be able to accompany the Polks on the journey.
21 Nov	*From Thomas Love.*
21 Nov	*From Robert B. Reynolds.*
22 Nov	From Abraham B. Lindsley. ALS. DLC–JKP. Solicits in behalf of his son a patronage position in the U.S. House.
22 Nov	From Elizabeth D. Love. ALS. DLC–JKP. Solicits in behalf of her brother an appointment in the navy.
22 Nov	*From James Walker.*
23 Nov	From Thomas B. Jones. ALS. DLC–JKP. Requests speedy House action on a private bill.
24 Nov	*From George W. Bratton.*
24 Nov	From Azariah C. Flagg et al. LS. DLC–JKP. Recommend Edward Livingston of Albany, New York, to be clerk of the U.S. House.
24 Nov	*From Joseph H. Talbot.*
25 Nov	*From William H. Polk.*
26 Nov	*From Richard H. Allen.*
26 Nov	From David Gallaher. ALS. DLC–JKP. Lists the names of several neighbors; requests that public documents be sent them. Also requests help in the establishment of a post office near his home in Wayne County.
27 Nov	*From Elisha Whittlesey.*
[28 Nov 1838?]	From Robert Armstrong. ALS. DLC–JKP. Reports that Alexander Duncan of Ohio has won his congressional race and that William Grason has been elected governor of Maryland.
28 Nov	*From Robert Armstrong.*
28 Nov	From Arthur R. Crozier. ALS. DLC–JKP. Lists names of persons in his area who wish to receive public documents.
28 Nov	From Russell Jarvis. ALS. DLC–JKP. Solicits position as a clerk in the U.S. House.
28 Nov	*From Absalom Johnson.*
28 Nov	From Humphrey H. Leavitt. ALS. DLC–JKP. Introduces Henry Swearingen, new member of the U.S. House.
28 Nov	From John G. [Park?]. ALS. DLC–JKP. Lists names of citizens in Smith County "who are gentlemen of respectability and firm Republicans."
28 Nov	From Levi R. Reese. ALS. DLC–JKP. Solicits position of chaplain to the U.S. House.
28 Nov	*To William R. Rucker.*
29 Nov	From Joel Henry Dyer. ALS. DLC–JKP. States that he has

	sent a memorial to Congress to solicit passage of a private act allowing him his claim for indemnity against the War Department; requests Polk's aid in getting this legislation passed.
29 Nov	From George Thomas. ALS. DLC–JKP. Offers his services as cashier of the Bank of the Metropolis in making the Speaker's payments to "members of Congress as heretofore through the agency of this Institution."
30 Nov	From B. L. Bogan. ALS. DLC–JKP. Solicits position of senior doorkeeper in the U.S. House.
30 Nov	*From Aaron V. Brown.*
30 Nov	*From William Carroll.*
30 Nov	*From Lyman Knowles.*
1 Dec	From James D. Doty. ALS. DLC–JKP. Reviews federal legislation governing the election of territorial delegates to Congress and argues that he, rather than George W. Jones, is entitled to represent Wisconsin Territory in the third session of the Twenty-fifth Congress.
1 Dec	From William Frederic McRee. ALS. DLC–JKP. Urges that the Washington *Globe* be sent to the Princeton Theological Seminary in order "to dispel *false doctrine* in politics."
3 Dec	From Susan Dougherty. ALS. DLC–JKP. Urges Polk to press her claim.
3 Dec	From John Forsyth. LS. DNA–RG 59. Submits accounting of contingent expenses by the Department of State for the year ending November 30, 1838.
3 Dec	From John Kennedy. ALS. DLC–JKP. Requests assistance in expediting his claim.
3 Dec	*From Samuel Martin.*
4 Dec	From James Gillespy. ALS. DLC–JKP. Encloses letter to the editors of the Washington *Globe*. Wishes Polk success in the coming elections. (Enclosure not found.)
4 Dec	*From John B. Hays.*
4 Dec	From Abraham B. Lindsley. ALS. DLC–JKP. Requests that his son be named a page in the U.S. House.
4 Dec	*From Lewis P. Roberts.*
4 Dec	From Nathaniel Smith. ALS. DLC–JKP. Encloses draft (not found) from the postmaster general and asks Polk to present it for payment.
5 Dec	*From Sackfield Maclin.*
5 Dec	From Ray S. Orton. L. DLC–JKP. Encloses Samuel P. Walker's answer to his letter; requests that Polk deposit the proper sum of money in one of the Washington Banks. (Enclosure not found.)
5 Dec	From Hampton C. Williams. ALS. DLC–JKP. Encloses his "Congreve Rocket"; suggests that he has "endeavored to put it in a coarse strong and plain hand. It will need a careful revision." (Enclosure not found.)
6 Dec	To Joshua Cunningham. ALS. DLC–JKP. Responds to charges made against him by Ephraim H. Foster in a letter

to the Memphis *Enquirer* and reprinted in the *Nashville Whig* and other newspapers.

6 Dec   *From Amos Kirkpatrick.*

6 Dec   *From Lyman Knowles.*

6 Dec   From James K. Paulding. Copy. DNA–RG 45. Transmits abstract of contingent expenditures by the Navy Department for the past year. (Enclosure not found.)

6 Dec   From James K. Paulding. Copy. DNA–RG 45. Transmits statements of contingent expenses by the offices of the navy secretary and the navy commissioners for the past year. (Enclosures not found.)

7 Dec   From Joseph Brown. ALS. DLC–JKP. Asks Polk to assist in expediting his sister's claim.

7 Dec   From Francis Rayron. ALS. DLC–JKP. Solicits government employment.

7 Dec   *From Samuel P. Walker.*

7 Dec   *From John S. Young.*

8 Dec [1838]   *From Robert Armstrong.*

8 Dec   From Benjamin C. Card. ALS. DLC–JKP. Requests documents pertaining to legislation on preemption.

8 Dec   *From John Catron.*

8 Dec   From Joel L. Jones. ALS. DLC–JKP. Reports that he has complied with Polk's request and has paid to B. W. Williamson the medical charges owed to Dr. Isaac Edmonds.

[8 Dec 1838?]   From Langtree & O'Sullivan. LS. DLC–JKP. Request assistance in obtaining a printing contract.

8 Dec   *From James M. Lassiter.*

8 Dec   *From Joseph H. Talbot.*

9 Dec   From William B. Martin. ALS. DLC–JKP. Solicits assistance in getting his brother Henry appointed receiver of public moneys, should a new land district be established in Alabama.

9 Dec   From Sampson Williams. ALS. DLC–JKP. Requests assistance in expediting certain claims; urges the appointment of Alexander Montgomery to the postmastership at Gainesboro, should that position become vacant.

10 Dec   *From Robert J. Chester.*

10 Dec   From M. D. Cooper & Co. LS. DLC–JKP. Advise that none of Polk's crop has been received; promises that when the shipment arrives, "strict attention shall be paid to your letter of instructions."

10 Dec   *From Thomas Dean.*

10 Dec   *From Cave Johnson.*

10 Dec   From Philander Priestley. ALS. DLC–JKP. Encloses letter to the General Land Office; urges reinstatement of tri-weekly mail service through Dover. (Enclosure not found.)

10 Dec   *From Joel M. Smith.*

10 Dec   *From James Walker.*

11 Dec   From James K. Paulding. Copy. DNA–RG 45. Reports on the appointment of extra clerks in the Navy Department during the late session of Congress.

12 Dec	From James Caruthers. ALS. DLC–JKP. Urges establishment of mail routes from Columbia to Jackson and from Jackson to Ashport.
12 Dec	*From John W. Childress.*
12 Dec	*From William Conner.*
12 Dec	From Thomas Love. ALS. DLC–JKP. Asks Polk to send public documents bearing upon many of the major issues of the day.
12 Dec	*To Joseph H. Talbot.*
13 Dec	From John Langtry. ALS. DLC–JKP. Asks Polk to inquire of Edward Cross whether he collected Middleton H. Hill's debt.
14 Dec	From Simon Brown. ALS. DLC–JKP. Requests assistance in obtaining employment in the U.S. House as a clerk.
14 Dec	*From John B. Fonville.*
14 Dec	From James Edmonston. ALS. DLC–JKP. Advises that "the within specified Claims have been transmitted to Washington through S. S. Prentiss."
14 Dec	*From Hopkins L. Turney.*
14 Dec	*From Samuel P. Walker.*
15 Dec	From A. L. Burris. ALS. DLC–JKP. Expresses desire to see Polk elected to the governship; requests that Polk send him copies of the Washington *Congressional Globe* for the present session.
15 Dec	*From William C. Campbell.*
15 Dec	*From Abraham McClellan.*
15 Dec	From Campbell P. White. ALS. DLC–JKP. Introduces A. Bullir.
15 Dec	From Thomas Whiteside. ALS. DLC–JKP. Encloses petition for establishment of a post office at Bean's Station. (Enclosure not found.)
15 Dec	From John Woodfine. ALS. DLC–JKP. Encloses power of attorney from the administrator of George L. Kinnard's estate, authorizing collection of Kinnard's congressional expenses; requests on behalf of the heirs of Samuel Kennedy assistance regarding their claim. (Enclosures not found.)
16 Dec	*From Adam Huntsman.*
17 Dec	From Thomas Brown. ALS. DKC–JKP. Lists names of persons in East Tennessee who are interested in receiving political documents.
17 Dec	*From Thomas H. Fletcher.*
17 Dec	From Thomas King. ALS. DLC–JKP. Reminds Polk of an offer to assist him in procuring a pension; advises that he hopes soon to place his application before Congress.
17 Dec	From Charles G. Olmsted. ALS. DLC–JKP. Solicits advice on whether or not to make an application for the appointment of minister to Mexico.
17 Dec	From Joel R. Poinsett. Copy. DNA–RG 107. Advises that the commissioner of Indian Affairs acted correctly with regard to William H. Carroll's pay.
17 Dec	From Sampson Williams. ALS. DLC–JKP. Sends list of

persons who wish subscriptions to the Washington *Congressional Globe* and *Appendix*. (Enclosure not found.)

18 Dec   From N. A. Davis and James M. Scott. LS. DLC–JKP. Solicits appointments to the U.S. Military Academy at West Point.

[18 Dec 1838]   *To Samuel Martin.*
18 Dec   From Porter & Partee. LS. DNA–RG 92. Submit claim in behalf of Andrew Pauley and request that Polk present it to the proper authorities for payment. (Enclosure not found.)

18 Dec   *From Joseph H. Talbot.*
18 Dec   *From John A. Thomas.*
20 Dec   From Kemp S. Holland. ALS. DLC–JKP. Introduces N. A. Bryant.

20 Dec   *From William R. Rucker.*
[20 Dec 1838?]   From William Wilkins et al. LS. DLC–JKP. Invite Polk to a public dinner to be given in Pittsburgh, Pennsylvania, on the anniversary of the Battle of New Orleans.

21 Dec   From James A. Hamilton. ALS. DLC–JKP. Asks to be allowed general access to the lobby of the U.S. House.

21 Dec   From Robert Johnston. LS. DLC–JKP. Requests Polk's advice on the recommendation of Charles T. Philpot to be postmaster at Flat Creek, Bedford County, Tennessee.

21 Dec   From William P. Purdy. ALS. DLC–JKP. Asks Polk's help in obtaining for P. B. Cobb the position of postmaster at Mifflin, Tennessee, to replace John Purdy, deceased.

22 Dec   From George H. Bullard. ALS. DLC–JKP. Requests Polk's autograph.

22 Dec   From James A. Craig. ALS. DLC–JKP. Seeks information regarding the army's pension program for invalid veterans.

22 Dec   *From George W. L. Marr.*
24 Dec   *From George W. Bratton.*
24 Dec   From Sackfield Maclin. ALS. DLC–JKP. Recommends P. B. Cobb to be postmaster at Mifflin, Tennessee, to replace John Purdy, deceased.

24 Dec   From Isaac McPherson. ALS. DLC–JKP. Requests assistance in obtaining better mail service through East Tennessee.

25 Dec   From Benjamin B. French. ALS. DLC–JKP. Urges Polk to use his influence to obtain for a Mr. Brown a clerkship in the U.S. House.

25 Dec   *From Herndon Haralson.*
25 Dec   From Thomas B. Jones. ALS. DLC–JKP. Applies for an appointment in the federal government that does not involve foreign travel and that pays from one to two thousand dollars a year.

25 Dec   From George A. Miller. ALS. DLC–JKP. Requests Polk's autograph.

26 Dec [1838]   *From Robert Armstrong.*
[26?] Dec   From P. Anderson. ALS. DLC–JKP. Encloses statement to be used in an application to the Treasury Department for

remission of a fine; asks Polk to present the papers, "obtaining a speedy determination of the matter," and advise of the result. (Enclosure not found.)

27 Dec   From William Armour. ALS. DLC–JKP. Urges Polk to abandon support for hard money policies; argues that a metallic circulating medium cannot be maintained in the face of recurring unfavorable trade balances with foreign nations; and concludes that the South must industrialize and develop an internal commercial system if it wishes to retain the productivity of its labor force and to sustain its position in the Union.

27 Dec   From T. Boulanger. ALS. DLC–JKP. Advises that unless the refectory is allowed to sell beverages other than malt liquor and wine, he will be unable to realize a profit and maintain his contract.

27 Dec   From J. B. Clements. ALS. DLC–JKP. Introduces his brother, Ruben E. Clements, and requests aid for him in pressing his claim.

27 Dec   *To Jeremiah G. Harris.*

27 Dec   From A. E. McClure. ALS. DLC–JKP. Recommends William F. McGregor to be postmaster at Lewisburg, Tennessee.

27 Dec   From Robert G. Simonton. ALS. DLC–JKP. Encloses petitions for a mail route from Jackson to Columbia. (Enclosures not found.)

27 Dec   *From Joel M. Smith.*

27 Dec   *To Joseph H. Talbot.*

28 Dec   *From E. S. Davis.*

28 Dec   From C. K. Gillespie. ALS. DLC–JKP. Requests support in securing appointment as receiver or register of the new land office in Alabama.

29 Dec   From James Y. Grayson. ALS. DLC–JKP. Submits memorial protesting the proposed recognition of Haiti.

29 Dec   *To William Noland.*

30 Dec [1838]   From B. S. Russ. ALS. DLC–JKP. Requests financial assistance so that he can complete his medical studies.

31 Dec   From Thomas Hartley Crawford. LS. DLC–JKP. Also copy in DNA–RG 75. Acknowledges receipt of Polk's letter of December 29, enclosing one from Aaron V. Brown, respecting the appointment of Brown's successor and the condition of the business on which he has been engaged; advises that Andrew A. Kincannon has accepted the appointment and that Brown will be notified accordingly.

31 Dec   From Amos Kendall. Copy. DNA–RG 28. Submits proposed budget for the Post Office Department for the year beginning July 1, 1839.

31 Dec   *From Daniel Kenney.*

1839

[1839]	From David Craighead. ALS. DLC–JKP. Wishes to see Polk that evening or the following morning.
[Jan 1839]	From Jabez Jackson. ALS. DLC–JKP. Asks help in obtaining pay for the last sixteen days of the previous session of Congress, the period of his illness.
Jan	From Levi Woodbury. Copy. DLC–LW. Submits reports on defalcations by receivers and collectors since October 1, 1837.
1 Jan	From Amos Kendall. Copy. DNA–RG 28. Submits report on the names and salaries of clerks employed in the Post Office during the previous year.
2 Jan	From Elisha Forrest. ALS. DLC–JKP. Requests from Congress a pension for his military service.
2 Jan	From John Johnson. ALS. DLC–JKP. Requests that Polk use his influence to have Johnson reinstated as a carpenter in the U.S. House.
2 Jan	*From William H. Polk.*
3 Jan	From D. H. Allen. ALS. DLC–JKP. Acknowledges receipt of Polk's letter of December 25, 1838, "relative to the business of Peter Stubblefield of Tennessee"; expects to be in Washington City soon and will adjust this matter then.
3 Jan	*From Alfred Balch.*
3 Jan	*To Andrew Jackson Donelson.*
3 Jan	From Lyman C. Draper. ALS. DLC–JKP. Requests Polk's autograph.
3 Jan	From John Forsyth. LS. DNA–RG 59. Submits report on the names and salaries of clerks employed in the State Department during the previous year.
4 Jan	From William B. Jones. ALS. DLC–JKP. Acknowledges with thanks receipt of a copy of the president's message.
5 Jan	From S. J. Gholson. ALS. DLC–JKP. Recommends George Wightman of Aberdeen, Mississippi, to be locating agent for the Choctaw Indians.
5 Jan	*From J. G. M. Ramsey.*
5 Jan	*From Joel M. Smith.*
5 Jan	From Sutherland S. Southworth. ALS. DLC–JKP. Warns that Polk is about to be attacked in several newspapers; disclaims authorship of any of the articles.
6 Jan	*From James W. Hale.*
6 Jan	*From Samuel A. Warner.*
7 Jan [1839]	*From M. D. Cooper & Co.*
7 Jan	From P. J. Curle. ALS. DLC–JKP. Asks assistance in expediting a claim submitted by George C. Harris.
7 Jan	To Joel R. Poinsett. ALS. DNA–RG 92. Submits a claim by Andrew Pauley for services performed as a waggoner during the Florida campaign of 1836; asks to be advised when the claim is settled.

8 Jan   From John McNeil. ALS. DLC–JKP. Asks Polk to give the enclosed letter to J. George Harris.

8 Jan   From [Joel R. Poinsett]. L. DNA–RG 92. Also copy in DNA–RG 107. Advises that Polk's letter of January 7 regarding Andrew Pauley's claim has been referred to the proper officer for settlement.

9 Jan   From Joel Henry Dyer. ALS. DLC–JKP. Acknowledges receipt of Polk's letter of December 19; thanks Polk for promising to support his claim.

[9 Jan 1839]   *From John B. Hays.*

10 Jan   *From William C. Dunlap.*

10 Jan   *From Pendleton G. Gaines.*

10 Jan   From Jesse Leigh. LS. DLC–JKP. Requests that Polk send the Dresden *Tennessee Patriot* copies of speeches and public documents that may be available.

11 Jan [1839]   *From Robert Armstrong.*

11 Jan   From Joseph Ballew. ALS. DLC–JKP. Sends documents supporting an increase in his pension; asks Polk's aid in expediting his claim.

11 Jan   *From Solon Borland.*

11 Jan   *From Philip B. Glenn.*

11 Jan   *From John B. Hays.*

11 Jan   From Langtree & O'Sullivan. LS. DLC–JKP. Requests that Polk forward the enclosed letter addressed to James M. Howry.

11 Jan   *From Samuel H. Laughlin.*

11 Jan   From Levi Woodbury. LS. DLC–JKP. Acknowledges receipt of Polk's letter of January 9, enclosing the petition of Alexander Badger; advises that he has no authority to remit penalties or forfeitures and returns the papers to Polk.

12 Jan   From William Davis. ALS. DLC–JKP. States that although William Williams and William McGregor have been suggested as candidates to fill the vacancy of postmaster at Benton, Marshall County, he recommends neither; suggests that he himself be appointed temporarily until a suitable replacement can be found.

12 Jan   *From Jabez Jackson.*

12 Jan   *From Thomas P. Moore.*

[12 Jan 1839]   From Major Andrew Price. ALS. DLC–JKP. Writes from Marion County, Alabama, that Joel Hughes has resigned as postmaster; recommends Charles Tennant as a replacement; and expresses concern that he has not heard from Andrew Stevenson.

12 Jan   From John Thorp. ALS. DLC–JKP. Requests assistance in obtaining a pension.

13 Jan [1839]   From Joseph B. Boyd. ALS. DLC–JKP. Reports that Cave J. Couts has passed his examinations at the U.S. Military Academy at West Point; expresses confidence that Polk will win the governorship in the coming elections.

13 Jan   From E. W. Gilbert. ALS. DLC–JKP. Offers his political support for Polk's gubernatorial bid.

13 Jan [1839]	*From John B. Hays.*
13 Jan	*From Ezekiel P. McNeal.*
14 Jan	From William Aldridge. ALS. DLC–JKP. Requests an alteration in the mail route between Franklin and Cornersville.
14 Jan	From B. B. Coffey. ALS. DLC–JKP. Solicits position as register, should a new land office be established in the Cherokee country of Alabama.
14 Jan	From Robert Johnston. LS. DLC–JKP. Requests advice on the petition recommending James M. Johnston for appointment as postmaster at Rowesville in Bedford County.
14 Jan	From Robert Johnston. LS. DLC–JKP. Requests opinion on the several applicants recommended to fill the vacant postmastership at Trenton.
14 Jan	From James K. Paulding. Copy. DNA–RG 45. Submits surveyor's report (not found).
[14] Jan	From Hugh W. Wormsley. ALS. DLC–JKP. Requests that Lucy Williamson's petition be reconsidered.
15 Jan	From O. F. Bledsoe. ALS. DLC–JKP. Asks to be recommended for the office of district attorney of the Southern District of Alabama, should a vacancy occur.
15 Jan	From Cyrus A. Kennedy. ALS. DLC–JKP. Requests assistance in obtaining an appointment to the U.S. Military Academy at West Point.
15 Jan	From Mordecai Lincoln. ALS. DLC–JKP. Urges Polk to visit Greeneville and other towns in East Tennessee on his return trip from Washington City.
15 Jan	*From Lewis P. Roberts.*
16 Jan	From [Joel R. Poinsett]. Copy. DNA–RG 92. Also copy in DNA–RG 107. Returns papers sent on January 7, with the acting quartermaster general's remarks showing the objections to the claim of Andrew Pauley. (Enclosures not found.)
16 Jan	From J. M. Wilks. ALS. DLC–JKP. Submits list of persons in Wayne County and requests that Polk send them public documents.
17 Jan	From James K. Paulding. Copy. DNA–RG 45. Transmits report from the fourth auditor regarding claims submitted to the Navy Department.
17 Jan	From William Smith, Jr. ALS. DLC–JKP. Asks to receive public documents sympathetic to the Democratic point of view.
18 Jan	From William Fitzgerald. ALS. Pvt Ms of J. Carroll Peak, Redlands, California. Advises that the costs of hiring a replacement and supporting his family have put him in financial difficulty; wishes to obtain a loan at the time of his army discharge.
19 Jan	From Blair & Rives. LS. DLC–JKP. Requests that the bearer of this letter be admitted to the U.S. House as a reporter for the Washington *Globe*.
19 Jan	From James K. Paulding. Copy. DNA–RG 45. Advises that

	the chart of Newark Bay and vicinity is in the possession of the Treasury Department.
19 Jan	*From Joseph H. Talbot.*
20 Jan	From John T. Brown. ALS. DLC–JKP. Requests receipt for money sent Polk the previous October; asks Polk to intercede with the Post Office Department to obtain mail delivery at Middleton, Mississippi.
20 Jan	*From William S. Haynes.*
21 Jan	From John A. Buckingham. ALS. DLC–JKP. Requests access to the U.S. House as a reporter for the *Boston Courier*.
21 Jan	*From M. D. Cooper & Co.*
22 Jan	From Rufus Dawes. ALS. DLC–JKP. Requests seat in the reporters' gallery as a reporter for the *New York Daily Whig*.
22 Jan	From James K. Paulding. Copy. DNA–RG 45. Submits statement of contracts made by the navy commissioners during the year 1838. (Enclosure not found.)
22 Jan	*From Thomas J. Read & Son.*
22 Jan	From James E. Root. ALS. DLC–JKP. Requests Polk's autograph.
22 Jan	From James M. Saunders. ALS. DLC–JKP. Advises that he has a package which he wishes to send to Tennessee; requests that Polk transport it for him to Nashville and leave it in the care of someone there.
23 Jan	From James K. Paulding. Copy. DNA–RG 45. Transmits for House members 275 copies of the *Naval Register* for the year 1839.
23 Jan	From R. J. Powell. ALS. DLC–JKP. Requests recommendation for a position in the patent office.
24 Jan	From Josephus C. Guild. ALS. DLC–JKP. Recommends Oscar F. Bledsoe for the position of district attorney for the Southern District of Alabama.
24 Jan	From Amos Kendall. Copy. DNA–RG 28. Reports that the Post Office Department will not need additional funding for the year; explains why the South and Southwest experienced more retrenchment of service than other parts of the country.
24 Jan	*From Hillary Langtry.*
24 Jan	From James K. Paulding. Copy. DNA–RG 45. Transmits copies of the proceedings of two courts martial. (Enclosures not found.)
24 Jan	*From David A. Street.*
[25 Jan 1839]	From George W. Bratton. ALS. DLC–JKP. Acknowledges receipt of Polk's letter; reports on the cotton crop and other plantation business.
25 Jan	*From J. George Harris.*
[25 Jan 1839]	From Isaac Turner. ALS. DLC–JKP. Praises Polk for his speech at Bolivar and seeks news from Washington.
26 Jan	*From Alfred Balch.*
26 Jan	*From William H. Polk.*

27 Jan [1839]	*From John W. Childress.*
28 Jan	From John W. Campbell. ALS. DLC–JKP. Urges establishment of a stage line from Ashport to Jackson.
28 Jan	From Henry Hubbard. ALS. DLC–JKP. Encloses newspaper article relating New Hampshire politics and the anti-slavery question. (Enclosure not found.)
28 Jan	From Joseph Kidder. ALS. DLC–JKP. Requests Polk's autograph.
28 Jan	From George Chesley Peavey. ALS. DLC–JKP. Requests Polk's autograph.
28 Jan	From Sampson Williams. ALS. DLC–JKP. Asks Polk to assist in expediting his claim.
28 Jan	*From Richard M. Woods.*
29 Jan	From Peter Hagner. Copy. DNA–RG 217. Acknowledges receipt of Polk's letter of January 26; advises that Polk will receive from another branch of the office a letter concerning Joel Dyer's claim.
29 Jan	*From William E. Owen.*
30 Jan	From Joseph Follansbee. ALS. DLC–JKP. Nominates replacement for Samuel Goldsmith, former messenger of the U.S. House.
30 Jan	From R. A. Glenn. ALS. DLC–JKP. Encloses claim by the widow of Nathaniel Laird; asks Polk's attention to the matter. (Enclosure not found.)
[30 Jan 1839]	*From Jabez Jackson.*
[30] Jan [1839]	*From Samuel W. Polk.*
31 Jan	To the Postmaster at Jamestown, North Carolina. Copy. DLC–JKP. Returns package of petitions, which were addressed to Polk without instructions.
31 Jan	From George W. Jones et al. LS. DLC–JKP. Recommend Samuel W. Carmack to be federal judge in Florida.
31 Jan	From George W. Jones et al. LS. DLC–JKP. Recommend Samuel W. Carmack to be judge of the Apalachicola district in Florida.
31 Jan	*To Amos Kendall.*
31 Jan	From Albert A. Muller. ALS. DLC–JKP. Recommends John Wills of Russellville, Kentucky, for appointment to the U.S. Military Academy at West Point.
31 Jan	From James K. Paulding. Copy. DNA–RG 45. Transmits annual statement of appropriations for the naval service for the year 1838.
1 Feb	*From Erwin J. Frierson.*
[1 Feb 1839]	From Joel H. Root. ALS. DLC–JKP. Requests Polk's autograph.
1 Feb	From Littleton W. Tazewell. ALS. DLC–JKP. Advises that he is enclosing a letter "with a request that you will give it such a direction as will insure its reception by the gentleman for whom it is intended." (Enclosure not found.)
1 Feb	To Levi Woodbury. ALS. DLC–LW. Transmits letter from John L. Murray of Kentucky to Woodbury; concurs with

	Murray's request for information from the Treasury secretary.
2 Feb	From M. D. Cooper & Co. LS. DLC–JKP. Advise of the receipt of 34 bales of Polk's cotton; expect to send sales account and proceeds in a few days.
2 Feb	From Amos Kendall. Copy. DNA–RG 28. States that no additional clerks were employed by the Post Office Department in order to respond to information calls by the U.S. House.
2 Feb	From Ezekiel P. McNeal. ALS. DLC–JKP. Advises that collections for rents and purchases totaled $255; will purchase a check on an eastern bank and will remit funds through the Bank of Tennessee, Nashville.
3 Feb	From William G. Childress. ALS. DLC–JKP. Wishes names of the Constitutional Convention members who opposed the first BUS; discusses political prospects for his election to Congress.
4 Feb	From Richard H. Allen. ALS. DLC–JKP. Asks Polk to introduce a bill to Congress providing compensation to Revolutionary War veterans who served less than six months.
4 Feb	*From Lawson Gifford.*
4 Feb	From Amos Kendall. Copy. DNA–RG 28. Submits reports concerning the number and causes of mail failures to and from New Orleans during the previous six months. (Enclosures not found.)
4 Feb	From James M. Saunders. ALS. DLC–JKP. Reports that the box which Polk has agreed to deliver to Nashville "has been forwarded to Mr. Enoch Tucker of Washington City, with instructions to complete the package & deliver it to you."
4 Feb	*From John Thomson.*
5 Feb	To Ephraim H. Foster. ALS. DLC–JKP. Declines to write a recommendation to the U.S. Military Academy at West Point for Mr. Caldwell.
5 Feb	From David B. Molloy. ALS. DLC–JKP. Expresses confidence in Polk's election; hopes Polk will visit Murfreesboro in the spring to campaign; and asks Polk to arrange a subscription to the Washington *Globe* for D. L. Burrus.
5 Feb	To Joel R. Poinsett. ALS. NNC. Asks that Poinsett make no recommendation to the U.S. Military Academy at West Point from Polk's district until Polk has had a chance to talk personally with him.
5 Feb	From Felix Robertson. ALS. DLC–JKP. Asks Polk's aid in obtaining for Abraham Litton the appointment of visitor to the U.S. Military Academy at West Point.
6 Feb [1839]	*From Robert Armstrong.*
6 Feb	*To Benjamin F. Butler.*
6 Feb	From William H. Cobbs. ALS. DLC–JKP. Requests Polk's autograph.
6 Feb	From Selah R. Hobbie. LS. DLC–JKP. Advises that Polk's

	letter of February 4 enclosing an application for a post office in Wayne County, Tennessee, has been referred to Robert Johnston.
6 Feb	From Abraham Morrill. ALS. DLC–JKP. Encloses petition to Congress for compensation of goods supplied during the war and asks Polk to read it to the Congress.
7 Feb	From J. M. Burt. ALS. DLC–JKP. Advises that he is sending Polk papers on the abolition question, as connected with the politics of New York State.
7 Feb	*To Azariah C. Flagg.*
7 Feb	*From John B. Hays.*
7 Feb	*To Andrew Jackson.*
7 Feb	*From Ezekiel P. McNeal.*
7 Feb	To the Postmaster at Jamestown, North Carolina. ALS, copy. DLC–JKP. Encloses a package of petitions, with the request that they be returned to the petitioners.
7 Feb	From Joel M. Smith. ALS. DLC–JKP. Reports that J. George Harris has arrived to edit the *Nashville Union* and has been favorably received; plans to enlarge the paper to a tri-weekly and seeks funding assistance from the Democratic party.
7 Feb	From Frank Williams. ALS. DLC–JKP. Encloses check for $250, which he is forwarding from E. P. McNeal. (Enclosure not found.)
8 Feb	*From William Carroll.*
8 Feb	From Amos David. ALS. DLC–JKP. Opposes internal improvements involving "reckless accumulation of Debt."
9 Feb	*From J. George Harris.*
9 Feb	From James E. Root. ALS. DLC–JKP. Requests Polk's autograph.
9 Feb	From Enoch Tucker. ALS. DLC–JKP. Forwards package from James M. Saunders of Virginia.
10 Feb	From _____ Egbert. ALS. DLC–JKP. Solicits contribution to the German Evangelical Church in Washington City.
11 Feb	From J. Carroll. ALS. DLC–JKP. Solicits money to enable him to continue his journey north to his home.
11 Feb	*From Jesse B. Clements.*
11 Feb	From John H. Dew. ALS. DLC–JKP. Recommends George S. Golladay to be postmaster at Grenada, Mississippi; encloses petition concurring in his recommendation. (Enclosure not found.)
11 Feb	*From Lawson Gifford.*
11 Feb	*From Andrew Jackson.*
11 Feb	From John Morgan Jones. ALS. DLC–JKP. Solicits appointment in the Marine Corps.
11 Feb	From Daniel Kenney. ALS. DLC–JKP. Reports on political climate in East Tennessee and opposition attacks against Polk.
11 Feb	From Joel R. Poinsett. LS. DLC–JKP. Also copy in DNA–

RG 107. Advises that he will not fill the vacancy at the U.S. Military Academy from Polk's district, until after Polk's return to Tennessee.

11 Feb   *From George R. Powel.*

11 Feb   From D. W. Stone. ALS. DLC–JKP. Asks Polk to recommend a lawyer in Memphis.

12 Feb   *From M. D. Cooper & Co.*

12 Feb   From Selah R. Hobbie. LS. DLC–JKP. Advises that the postmaster general has denied applications for a tri-weekly mail in four-horse post coaches from McMinnville to Columbia, and in stages from Mount Pleasant to Jackson.

12 Feb   *From Nathaniel Smith.*

13 Feb   From Frederick S. Heiskell. ALS. DLC–JKP. Recommends Henry Talbot Cox to be postmaster at Louisville in Blount County.

13 Feb   From James H. Thompson. ALS. DLC–JKP. Encloses letter to James Walker and asks Polk to forward it. (Enclosure not found.)

13 Feb   *From John S. Young.*

14 Feb   From Daniel Graham. ALS. DLC–JKP. Advises that he has been traveling in East Tennessee; reports on Polk's election prospects in that area.

14 Feb   From James K. Paulding. Copy. DNA–RG 45. Answers questions contained in a House resolution pertaining to the South Seas exploring expedition.

15 Feb   From George H. Bullard. ALS. DLC–JKP. Requests Polk's autograph.

15 Feb   *From Samuel H. Laughlin.*

15 Feb   From William F. McRee. ALS. DLC–JKP. Thanks Polk for sending the Washington *Globe* to Princeton; requests advice or assistance in obtaining an appointment as chaplain in the navy.

15 Feb   From David B. Molloy. ALS. DLC–JKP. Reports criticisms of the express-mail service from Nashville to Montgomery, Alabama.

15 Feb   From James K. Paulding. Copy. DNA–RG 45. Transmits copies of information pertaining to the court martial proceedings in the case of Lieutenant C. G. Hunter. (Enclosure not found.)

15 Feb   From Frederic Perley. ALS. DLC–JKP. Requests Polk's autograph.

16 Feb   From Edward Stanly. ALS. DLC–JKP. Refers to several abolition petitions presented by Caleb Cushing and asks if they have been received officially.

16 Feb   *From James H. Thompson.*

16 Feb   *From William Wallace.*

16 Feb   *From Richard Warner.*

17 Feb   *From J. George Harris.*

17 Feb   *From William H. Polk.*

17 Feb	*From Philander Priestley.*
17 Feb	From John S. Young. ALS. DLC–JKP. Requests 100 copies of Alexander Duncan's speech.
18 Feb	*From William L. S. Dearing.*
18 Feb	*From William V. Pettit.*
18 Feb	From Henry L. Pinckney. ALS. DLC–JKP. Introduces Maurice S. [Lewis], who is seeking appointment as a midshipman in the navy.
18 Feb	From Charles Polk. ALS. DLC–JKP. Wishes to know whether they might be related; asks to be informed "from what state your father or grandfather emigrated and at what period."
18 Feb	*From William H. Polk.*
18 Feb	*From Robert B. Reynolds.*
18 Feb	From Margaret E. Shaw. ALS. DLC–JKP. Requests assistance in expediting her claim.
19 Feb	From John M. Bass. ALS. DLC–JKP. Advises that the Union Bank of Tennessee has agreed to discount Polk's note on or after the first of March.
19 Feb	From Porter & Partee. LS. DLC–JKP. Encloses note on Felix Grundy and asks Polk's assistance with its collection.
19 Feb	*From J. G. M. Ramsey.*
19 Feb	From Hugh Waddell. ALS. DLC–JKP. Asks Polk to intercede with the Treasury Department to prevent collection of a debt from his father's estate; asserts his confidence that his brother will repay the debt within the year.
19 Feb	From Henderson K. Yoakum. ALS. DLC–JKP. Reports information received from East Tennessee regarding Polk's election prospects in that section.
20 Feb	To James L. Edwards. ALS. DNA–RG 15. Submits claim by the widow of Nathaniel Laird; requests decision before the close of the present session of Congress.
21 Feb	*From Alfred Balch.*
21 Feb	*From Nathan Gammon.*
21 Feb	*From William H. Polk.*
21 Feb	*From Robert B. Reynolds.*
22 Feb	From James L. Edwards. LS. DLC–JKP. Advises that the papers in the case of Hugh Suckey have been referred to the third auditor.
22 Feb	From Campbell P. White. ALS. DLC–JKP. Introduces William Brown of Liverpool, England.
23 Feb	*To Edward Stanly.*
24 Feb	*From William H. Polk.*
[24 Feb 1839]	*From J. Knox Walker.*
27 Feb	From Susan Dougherty. ALS. DLC–JKP. Wishes to know what action has been taken regarding her claim.
27 Feb	From James Gillespy. ALS. DLC–JKP. Requests that Polk deliver the enclosed letter and bill to Blair & Rives; expresses his desire to see Polk elected governor; but urges him not to become overly confident.

27 Feb	From J. George Harris. ALS. DLC–JKP. Encloses circular of Newton Cannon's; asks Polk's advice about responding to it; reports on congressional election prospects. (Enclosure not found.)
28 Feb	*From M. D. Cooper & Co.*
28 Feb	From Robert Johnston. LS. DLC–JKP. Requests Polk's advice concerning recommendation of Alfred Campbell to be appointed postmaster at Flat Creek in Bedford County.
28 Feb	From Albert Miller Lea. ALS. DLC–JKP. Solicits appointment as agent for public works on the Cumberland River.
28 Feb	From Joel R. Poinsett. Copy. DNA–RG 75. Encloses reports pertaining to the execution of the treaties of 1832 and 1834 with the Chickasaw Indians and the treaty of 1830 with the Choctaw Indians. (Enclosures not found.)
[March 1839]	From Felix Robertson et al. LS. DLC–JKP. Extend invitation to a public dinner to be held in Nashville at a time convenient to all.
[March 1839]	From Joseph L. Williams. ALI. DLC–JKP. Discusses postmastership at Louisville, Tennessee.
1 March	*From James Brown.*
1 March	From Talbot Jones & Co. LS. DLC–JKP. Encloses statement of moneys sent to pay charges on goods to be forwarded.
1 March	From Henry A. Wise. ALS. DLC–JKP. Wishes to know what disposition will be made of a portrait that he presented to Congress.
[3 March]	*From Sutherland S. Southworth.*
4 March	From C. Lillybridge. ALS. DLC–JKP. Requests introductions to Jesse F. Cleveland and William C. Dawson.
4 March	From John A. McCurdy. ALS. DLC–JKP. Solicits employment in the office of the commissioner of Indian Affairs.
5 March	From anonymous writer. L. DLC–JKP. Expresses respect for Polk and good wishes for his future.
6 March	*From James N. Barker.*
7 March	*From George & Robert Blackburn & Co.*
7 March	From Benjamin S. Russ. ALS. DLC–JKP. Asks Polk's aid in promoting his claim.
11 March	*From M. D. Cooper & Co.*
11 March	From Sutherland S. Southworth. ALS. DLC–JKP. Advises that he has written articles critical of John Bell and others; mentions that he has published a letter wishing Polk success in his gubernatorial campaign.
12 March	From Talbot Jones & Co. LS. DLC–JKP. Advise that they have forwarded two boxes to Hopkins L. Turney and that the balance due Polk has been, as requested, applied toward the payment of charges on the boxes.
13 March	*From George W. Bratton.*
13 March	*From Samuel Cushman.*
14 March	*From Joseph Coe.*
14 March	From Medicus A. Long et al. LS. DLC–JKP. Extend invi-

tation to a public dinner in Polk's honor to be held in Shelbyville on the earliest day in April that will suit his convenience.

15 March [1839]   *From Aaron V. Brown.*

15 March   *From Daniel Kenney.*

16 March   *From Charles G. Atherton.*

19 March   *From Samuel H. Laughlin.*

19 March   From Philander Priestley. ALS. DLC–JKP. Invites Polk to attend the battalion muster in Dover on April 5.

23 March   *To Medicus A. Long et al.*

23 March   From John S. Young. ALS. DLC–JKP. Requests confirmation that he has been given an appointment in the office of Indian Affairs.

[24 March 1839]   *From Robert Armstrong.*

24 March   *From Robert M. Burton.*

24 March [1839]   *From John W. Childress.*

24 March   From Ransom H. Gillet. ALS. DLC–JKP. Encloses political documents and news. (Enclosures not found.)

25 March   From William G. Childress. ALS. DLC–JKP. Advises that the battalion muster in Franklin will be held on April 13; expects Polk to attend.

25 March   *From William Conner.*

25 March   From Thomas Hartley Crawford. Copy. DNA–RG 75. Encloses copy of the attorney general's opinion in reference to several claims for damages growing out of the execution of the treaty of 1835, with a special view to the liability of the Cherokee fund for them. (Enclosure not found.)

25 March [1839]   From E. S. Haines. ALS. DLC–JKP. Encloses article from Charles Hammond. (Enclosure not found.)

25 March   From J. George Harris. ALS. DLC–JKP. Reports that he has not completed his campaign pamphlet; asks Polk to supply public documents unavailable in Nashville.

[26 March 1839]   From J. George Harris. ALS. DLC–JKP. Advises that work on the pamphlet continues slowly because of lack of information.

27 March   *From Samuel H. Laughlin.*

27 March   From John W. Weeks. ALS. DLC–JKP. Commends acquaintance of Harry Hibbard, should he decide to move to Tennessee.

28 March   From Medicus A. Long. ALS. DLC–JKP. Advises that Polk's acceptance of a public dinner arrived too late for an April 1 appointment; relates that the dinner has been rescheduled for April 6.

28 March   From Henry Turney. ALS. DLC–JKP. Reports that he has just returned home to find his wife very ill and that he cannot leave home again at the time discussed with Polk; suggests that Polk try to find someone to take his place.

29 March   From J. A. W. Andrews. ALS. DLC–JKP. Urges Polk to visit McNairy County in the spring; discusses political situation in that county.

29 March	*From Aaron V. Brown.*
29 March	From Edward Cage. ALS. DLC–JKP. Urges Polk to visit Clarksville during the campaign.
29 March	From Joel Henry Dyer. ALS. DLC–JKP. Requests loan of $100, which he will repay by January 1, 1840.
29 March	*To Samuel H. Laughlin.*
29 March	*From Denison Olmsted.*
30 March [1839]	*From Robert Armstrong.*
30 March	From Hugh Francis. ALS. DLC–JKP. Advises that Samuel H. Laughlin is urging Polk's visit to the Fifth Congressional District during the month of April and that Hopkins L. Turney will be available to travel with Polk.
30 March	*To J. G. M. Ramsey.*
30 March	From Joel M. Smith. ALS. DLC–JKP. Advises that "Burton has consented to run for Congress, Craighead for the Senate, and Col. Robt Weakly and L. P. Cheatham for the House in the next Legislature."
31 March	From John S. Young. ALS. DLC–JKP. Wishes to know if he received any appointment before Polk left Washington City.
1 April	From David M. Hunter. ALS. DLC–JKP. Asks if he received the appointment of receiver of public moneys at the land office to be located in that part of the Cherokee nation within the limits of Alabama.
1 April	*From Joseph H. Talbot.*
1 April	From Marcus B. Winchester. ALS. DLC–JKP. Recommends Lewellyn Cassels Rembert for an appointment to the U.S. Military Academy at West Point.
2 April	*From John H. Bills.*
2 April	*From J. George Harris.*
2 April	From James Rembert. ALS. DLC–JKP. Requests for his son, Lewellyn Cassels Rembert, an appointment to the U.S. Military Academy at West Point.
3 April	*From William G. Childress.*
3 April	From Thomas Y. Ramsey. ALS. DLC–JKP. Advises Polk of his election as an honorary member of a literary society at the University of Alabama.
3 April	*To Robert B. Reynolds.*
4 April	*From Robert M. Burton.*
4 April	From Samuel Seay. ALS. DLC–JKP. Advises that when Polk's boxes arrive, "they shall be forwarded as you have requested."
4 April	From Joel M. Smith. ALS. DLC–JKP. Requests a meeting with Polk for himself and Robert Armstrong.
6 April	*From William Allen.*
8 April	*To Sarah C. Polk.*
13 April	From William V. Pettit. ALS. DLC–JKP. Advises that he has forwarded a copy of the *Olive Branch* to Polk.
14 April	*To Sarah C. Polk.*
17 April	*To Sarah C. Polk.*

20 April	*To Sarah C. Polk.*
22 April	*From M. D. Cooper & Co.*
22 April	From Calvin Hubbell. ALS. DLC–JKP. Requests payment of $22 for the purchase of a dictionary.
22 April	*To Sarah C. Polk.*
22 April	From Peter Stubblefield. ALS. DLC–JKP. Asks to be informed "what you have done with my business with David H. Allen of Virginia intrusted to your charge."
23 April	From Amanda P. Craig. ALS. DLC–JKP. Asks Polk to inquire concerning rent collections on her sons' land; needs advice on the best disposition of the land when her sons are of age.
24 April	From Jacob Forsyth & Co. LS. DLC–JKP. Submits bill of expenses on a box shipped to Nashville in the care of Samuel Seay.
28 April	*To Sarah C. Polk.*
30 April	From J. C. Brasfield. ALS. DLC–JKP. Urges removal of William W. Tyus as postmaster at Athens, Alabama; solicits appointment in Tyus' place.
30 April	*From Samuel H. Laughlin.*
30 April	From Joel R. Poinsett. Copy. DNA–RG 75. Also copy in DNA–RG 107. Acknowledges receipt of recommendation for John S. Young; explains that because Congress failed to provide for disbursing agents for the Indian service, the War Department has no power to make such appointments and must make its disbursements through the Indian agencies.
30 April	*To Sarah C. Polk.*
30 April	*From George W. Rice.*
1 May	From Isaac Golladay. ALS. DLC–JKP. Writes from Lebanon, Tennessee, about the political situation there.
2 May	*To Sarah C. Polk.*
3 May	*From George W. Bratton.*
5 May	*To Sarah C. Polk.*
8 May	*To Sarah C. Polk.*
10 May	*From Albert G. Harrison.*
10 May	From Jordan Reece. ALS. DLC–JKP. Asks Polk if he thinks he will win the gubernatorial election.
10 May	From W. P. Sayle. ALS. DLC–JKP. Notifies Polk of his appointment to meet John Bell at Lebanon on June 12.
10 May	From W. P. Sayle. ALS. DLC–JKP. Advises that John Bell has designated June 12 as the date for meeting Polk in Lebanon; urges Polk to be there.
12 May	*To Sarah C. Polk.*
13 May	*To Sarah C. Polk.*
13 May	*To Levi Woodbury.*
16 May	From W. P. Sayle. ALS. DLC–JKP. Acknowledges that prior commitments will make it difficult for Polk to be in Lebanon on June 12; states that he has asked John Bell to agree to a one-day postponement.

17 May	From B. F. Liddon. ALS. DLC–JKP. Indicates his support for Polk; requests public documents illustrating the Democratic position, which he will defend in his bid for a seat in the Mississippi legislature.
18 May	*From John W. Childress.*
18 May	*To Sarah C. Polk.*
19 May	*From Robert M. Burton.*
19 May	*From James Vaughn and John F. Gillespy.*
21 May	From Thomas J. Turley et al. LS. DLC–JKP. Extend invitation to a barbecue to be held near Raleigh in Shelby County on July 12.
22 May	From Daniel Gold. ALS. DLC–JKP. Advises that the clerk's office of the U.S. House has sent the requested documents to Joseph Powell.
22 May	*To Sarah C. Polk.*
23 May	*From M. D. Cooper & Co.*
23 May	From Joseph Hickey. ALS. DLC–JKP. Assesses status of the Democratic party and candidates in several counties in the southeast portion of the state.
23 May	From Levi Woodbury. ALS. DLC–JKP. Submits informal report on losses sustained under each administration from defaulting debtors and defaulting officers. (Enclosure not found.)
24 May	*To Sarah C. Polk.*
24 May	*From George M. Porter.*
25 May	From John Laird et al. LS. DLC–JKP. Extends invitation to visit Lynnville in Giles County at the earliest possible date.
25 May	*From James Walker.*
28 May	From C. Cowan. ALS. DLC–JKP. Reports that Polk's speech in Sevierville swayed many voters to his cause.
28 May	*To Sarah C. Polk*
29 May	From E. B. Mason. ALS. DLC–JKP. Invites Polk to visit Mason's Grove in Madison County, preferably at the same time that Newton Cannon is there.
30 May	*From James Gillespy.*
[June 1839]	From Roderick McIver. ALS. DLC–JKP. Urges settlement of a claim by the estate of Lewis Jones against the estates of Samuel Polk and Joseph B. Porter.
1 June	From Nathan B. Ives. ALS. DLC–JKP. Presents bill in the amount of $4.00 against the estate of Samuel W. Polk for medical attendance.
1 June	*From Ezekiel P. McNeal.*
2 June	*To Sarah C. Polk.*
4 June [1839]	*From Robert Armstrong.*
4 June	From B. L. Nicks. ALS. DLC–JKP. Urges Polk to visit Fayetteville in Lincoln County before the end of July.
4 June	*To Sarah C. Polk.*
5 June	*From Robert M. Burton.*
5 June	From M. D. Cooper & Co. LS. DLC–JKP. Submits an

	accounting of the sale of four bales of cotton.
5 June	From Andrew Hays. ALS. DLC–JKP. Writes from Jackson, Mississippi, requesting information on the election campaigns in Tennessee.
5 June [1839]	*From Cave Johnson.*
6 June	From Cleon Moore. ALS. DLC–JKP. Writes that the Whigs are giving Newton Cannon a dinner at Greeneville on June 28; thinks that the Whigs will lose in spite of their renewed efforts.
8 June	*From John P. Chester.*
8 June	From George R. Powel. ALS. DLC–JKP. Predicts that Polk will carry Hawkins County with a thousand-vote majority.
11 June	*From George W. Bratton.*
[11 June 1839]	From Daniel Kenney. ALS, fragment. DLC–JKP. Reports that he expects to see Polk in Knoxville on July 4.
12 June	From Adam Huntsman. ALS. DLC–JKP. Suggests that Polk add Denmark and McLemoresville to his itinerary.
[12 June 1839]	*From J. G. M. Ramsey.*
16 June [1839]	*From Lawson Gifford.*
16 June	*From George M. Porter.*
17 June	From W. C. Henry. ALS. DLC–JKP. Requests clarification of some statements that Polk reportedly made to George W. Crabb.
17 June	*From Daniel Kenney.*
17 June	From Samuel D. Langtree. ALS. DLC–JKP. Sends copy of an article on the New Jersey election and suggests that it be published in Democratic newspapers and distributed in pamphlet form. (Enclosure not found.)
18 June	*From Sackfield Maclin.*
18 June	From Moses Wood. ALS. DLC–JKP. Urges Polk to speak at Denmark on his way to Brownsville.
20 June	*From John T. Macon.*
20 June	From J. J. Polk. ALS. DLC–JKP. Urges Polk to visit again in Hardeman, Fayette, and Shelby counties before the election.
20 June	From Peter Stubblefield. ALS. DLC–JKP. Requests return of business papers in Polk's possession.
21 June	*From Robert B. Reynolds.*
21 June	*From Hopkins L. Turney.*
22 June	From John Vineyard. ALS. DLC–JKP. Requests address of James G. Beatty and information regarding the administration of the estate of John Beal.
23 June	From Henry Talbot Cox. ALS. DLC–JKP. Reports efforts by Polk's friends in Louisville, Tennessee.
23 June	*From Andrew A. Kincannon.*
23 June	From James Lafferty. ALS. DLC–JKP. Believes Polk will get a majority in Grainger County; reports on other campaigns in the area.

24 June	From Ezekiel P. McNeal. ALS. DLC–JKP. Advises that he has added McLemoresville to Polk's itinerary.
25 June	*From Sarah C. Polk.*
28 June	*From J. G. M. Ramsey.*
28 June	*From Robert B. Reynolds.*
28 June	From Robert B. Reynolds. ALS. DLC–JKP. Lists several appointments scheduled by Newton B. Cannon in East Tennessee and urges Polk to join Cannon at those meetings.
29 June	*From Alexander O. Anderson.*
29 June	From Granville S. Crockett. ALS. DLC–JKP. Urges Polk to visit Middleton and Jefferson before the election.
30 June	*From Joseph Powell.*
1 July	*From John F. Gillespy.*
1 July	*To Sarah C. Polk.*
1 July	From Richard M. Woods et al. LS. DLC–JKP. Urge Polk to spend as much time as possible campaigning in East Tennessee and suggest a schedule of appointments for him.
2 July	*From James Cowan.*
[2] July [1839]	From Lawson Gifford. ALS. DLC–JKP. Submits list of Newton Cannon's appointments for East Tennessee and advises that "Your friends expect you to come on him at some one of the places." (Enclosure not found.)
4 July	From William M. Stokely. ALS. DLC–JKP. Urges Polk to accompany Newton Cannon on his campaign tour of East Tennessee.
6 July	From John Kennedy. ALS. DLC–JKP. Encloses notice of Newton Cannon's intended visit to East Tennessee. (Enclosure not found.)
6 July	*To Robert B. Reynolds.*
7 July	*From S. Bell.*
7 July	*To Sarah C. Polk.*
8 July	From William Gammon et al. LS. DLC–JKP. List Newton Cannon's East Tennessee speaking appointments and urge Polk to meet him at some of the places; express confidence that William B. Carter and John A. McKinney will be defeated in their congressional races.
8 July	From William Mosely et al. LS. DLC–JKP. Extend invitation to a public dinner honoring Samuel L. Barringer, to be held at Big Spring on July 26.
[9 July 1839]	From George R. Powel. ALS. DLC–JKP. Expresses views regarding election prospects for Polk and other candidates in East Tennessee.
9 July	From Philander Priestly. ALS. DLC–JKP. Advises that a barbecue has been planned at Dover on July 19 to coincide with Polk's speaking engagement there; adds that Newton Cannon and others also have been invited.
9 July	*From James Walker.*
10 July	*From Alexander O. Anderson.*
11 July	From John B. Fonville. ALS. DLC–JKP. Urges Polk to

	speak to the people at Christmasville in Carroll County on the day following his appointment at Trenton.
12 July	From James Cowan. ALS. DLC–JKP. Advises of the death of George W. Bratton and urges Polk to find a new overseer as soon as possible.
12 July	From C. W. Hall. ALS. DLC–JKP. Gives opinions concerning Democratic prospects in East Tennessee.
12 July	*From James Walker.*
15 July	*To Cave Johnson et al.*
18 July	From C. F. Cole. ALS. DLC–JKP. Asks Polk about employment prospects "of an Attorney, Clerk, or common school teacher . . . in your highly favoured section of the union."
19 July	From Jeremiah Tranum. ALS. DLC–JKP. Reports that he has visited Polk's plantation and was favorably impressed by the temporary overseer and the condition of the crops and the slaves.
20 July	From Thomas Dodson. ALS. DLC–JKP. Encloses description of the boundaries of a 45-acre tract of land located in Fayette County.
24 July	*From George R. Powel.*
25 July	*From N. G. Frazier.*
27 July	*From John F. Rhoton.*
28 July	*From William M. Lowry.*
28 July	*To Robert B. Reynolds.*
28 July	*From John S. Young.*
29 July	From William M. Alexander et al. LS. DLC–JKP. Advise that the speaking arrangements for the day will not be altered.
29 July	From Y. P. King. ALS. DLC–JKP. Asks Polk's opinion on what effect the alcoholic license law has had on the state.
29 July	From S. D. Mitchell et al. LS. DLC–JKP. Extend invitation to a barbecue honoring Newton Cannon to be held at Rogersville on July 29.
30 July [1839]	*From Robert B. Reynolds.*
30 July	*From Lewis P. Roberts.*
[Aug 1839]	From Robert Armstrong. ALS. DLC–JKP. Reports on Tennessee election results.
2 Aug	From John T. Alford. ALS. DLC–JKP. Sends voting results for Humphreys and Benton counties.
2 Aug	From Maclin Cross. ALS. DLC–JKP. Gives voting results for McNairy County.
2 Aug	From William Fitzgerald. ALS. DLC–JKP. Sends voting results for Henry County.
2 Aug	*From Nathan Gammon.*
2 Aug	From John A. Gardner. ALS. DLC–JKP. Reports voting results in Weakley County.
2 Aug	From W. S. Scott. ALS. DLC–JKP. Gives voting results in Weakley County.
2 Aug	From James H. Talbot. ALS. DLC–JKP. Gives partial election returns from Madison and Hardeman counties.

3 Aug	From David Armour. ALS. DLC–JKP. Reports majorities for Cannon and Polk in the several counties of West Tennessee.
3 Aug	From William M. Lowry. ALS. DLC–JKP. Gives voting results in Greene County.
3 Aug	From James R. McMeans. ALS. DLC–JKP. Gives complete returns for Henry County.
3 Aug	From James Sevier. ALS. DLC–JKP. Gives election results for Greene and Washington counties.
4 Aug	From Alexander O. Anderson. ALS. DLC–JKP. Reports what he has heard regarding voting results in East Tennessee.
4 Aug	From E. M. Anderson. ALS. DLC–JKP. Reports from Memphis that the people there expect a victory for Polk.
4 Aug	From A. T. Nicks. ALS. DLC–JKP. Recommends William Moore to be inspector general of Tennessee, a gubernatorial appointment.
5 Aug	*From Julius W. Blackwell.*
5 Aug [1839]	*From Adam Huntsman.*
5 Aug	From W. F. Mason. ALS. DLC–JKP. Gives available information on the gubernatorial election results in East Tennessee.
5 Aug [1839]	*From Robert B. Reynolds and Lewis P. Roberts.*
6 Aug	*From Alexander O. Anderson.*
6 Aug	From Alexander O. Anderson. ALS. DLC–JKP. Gives unofficial returns from all of East Tennessee except Marion and Hamilton counties.
7 Aug	*From Aaron V. Brown.*
7 Aug	*From Abraham McClellan.*
7 Aug	From John Smither. ALS. DLC–JKP. Thinks Polk will win the state, although he has lost the Sixth Congressional District.
8 Aug	From James Conn. ALS. DLC–JKP. Expresses confidence that Polk will be elected and asks help in obtaining the appointment of census taker.
9 Aug	*From Robert B. Reynolds.*
9 Aug	*From John S. Young.*
10 Aug [1839]	From Robert Armstrong. ALS. DLC–JKP. Recommends John McGavock of Williamson County to Polk's military staff.
10 Aug	*From Leonard P. Cheatham.*
10 Aug	From James P. Grundy. ALS. DLC–JKP. Recommends John McGavock to Polk's military staff.
10 Aug	*From Samuel H. Laughlin.*
10 Aug	From Sackfield Maclin. ALS. DLC–JKP. Expresses satisfaction with the overall results of the party's races in the state, although he has lost his bid for a seat in the legislature.
[10 Aug 1839]	From Gideon J. Pillow. ALS. DLC–JKP. Suggests that he host the meeting with Sam Houston and Clement C. Clay, for their coming to town might attract unwanted attention.

10 Aug   From Joel M. Smith. ALS. DLC–JKP. Recommends John McGavock to Polk's military staff.

12 Aug   From E. Ames. ALS. DLC–JKP. Advises that he desires to go to France and asks Polk for a letter of introduction to Lewis Cass, U.S. minister to France.

12 Aug   *From Felix Grundy.*

12 Aug   *To Andrew Jackson.*

12 Aug   From Samuel Roberts. ALS. DLC–JKP. Congratulates Polk on his election victory.

13 Aug   *From Andrew Jackson.*

13 Aug   *From John T. Leigh.*

13 Aug   *From Henry Mabry.*

13 Aug   From James S. Smith. ALS. DLC–JKP. Congratulates Polk on his victory.

14 Aug   From John Blair et al. LS. DLC–JKP. Congratulate Polk on his election as governor and thank him for his efforts to restore the Democratic party to greater strength.

14 Aug   From Archibald Yell. ALS. DLC–JKP. Requests deed to property that he has sold for Polk; reports that he has heard no news on the gubernatorial election and is anxious for Polk's success.

15 Aug   *From William G. Childress.*

15 Aug   *To Andrew Jackson.*

15 Aug   *From Joseph Powell.*

15 Aug   *From Joel M. Smith.*

16 Aug   From H. J. Anderson. ALS. DLC–JKP. Congratulates Polk on his election.

16 Aug   From John Blair and Daniel Kenney. LS. DLC–JKP. Enclose letter congratulating Polk on his election.

16 Aug   From Ira McKinney. ALS. DLC–JKP. Advises that a committee of Madison County, Alabama, citizens will meet soon to arrange a public dinner honoring Polk.

16 Aug   From Levi R. Reese. ALS. DLC–JKP. Requests payment for some trees that Polk purchased from him.

16 Aug   From William M. Warner. ALS. DLC–JKP. Congratulates Polk on his victory; urges him not to run for the vice presidency, but rather to serve his full term as governor and then go to the U.S. Senate.

17 Aug   From William Fitzgerald. ALS. DLC–JKP. Urges Polk to take control of the banks in the state away from the Whigs.

17 Aug   From Philander Priestly. ALS. DLC–JKP. Advises that he intends to seek the position of secretary of state.

17 Aug   *From Robert H. Watkins et al.*

18 Aug   *From John Cramer.*

18 [Aug]   From William Moore. ALS. DLC–JKP. Advises that he is aware that friends have recommended him for a staff appointment and wishes to know confidentially Polk's views on the subject.

18 Aug   *From John H. Prentiss.*

19 [Aug]   From John A. Aiken. ALS. DLC–JKP. Congratulates Polk

	on his victory and solicits an appointment on his military staff.
19 Aug	From Willie B. Johnson. ALS. DLC–JKP. Congratulates Polk on his election victory and recommends Philander Priestly, applicant for secretary of state.
19 Aug	From Thomas J. Read. ALS. DLC–JKP. Congratulates Polk on his victory and suggests Thomas H. Fletcher of Nashville as a possible successor to Ephraim H. Foster in the U.S. Senate.
19 Aug	From William Rice et al. LS. DLC–JKP. Extend invitation to a public dinner in Jasper honoring Polk and Julius W. Blackwell; set the date of September 5 for the meeting.
20 Aug	*From Isaac H. Bronson.*
20 Aug	From William Scott Haynes et al. LS. DLC–JKP. Congratulate Polk on his victory and request that they be given an opportunity to honor him in Shelbyville on a day suitable to Polk's convenience.
20 Aug	*From Samuel H. Laughlin.*
20 Aug	*From Franklin Pierce.*
20 Aug	*From J. G. M. Ramsey.*
20 Aug	*From David A. Street.*
21 Aug	*From Kenneth L. Anderson.*
21 Aug	From Pierce B. Anderson. ALS. DLC–JKP. Congratulates Polk on his election and his part in bringing the state back into the Democratic ranks; expresses confidence that Martin Van Buren will be elected president in 1840.
21 Aug	*From John W. Childress.*
21 Aug	From James M. Jetton. ALS. DLC–JKP. Solicits appointment as assistant surgeon in the army.
21 Aug	*From Robert Barnwell Rhett.*
21 Aug	From George W. Terrell. ALS. DLC–JKP. Requests that Polk send public documents dealing with national politics that may be useful in campaigning against the Whigs in Mississippi.
21 Aug	*From John S. Young.*
22 Aug	*From Alexander O. Anderson.*
22 Aug	From anonymous writer. L. DLC–JKP. Denounces Polk's election to the governorship.
22 Aug	*From Randolph D. Casey.*
22 Aug	From Calvin Hubbell. ALS. DLC–JKP. Wishes to know if Polk has received a copy of *Richardson's English Dictionary*; requests payment of $22.
23 Aug	From Alexander Gray et al. LS. DLC–JKP. Invite Polk to a public dinner in his honor to be held at Parham's Spring in Hickman County on September 4.
24 Aug	*From George W. Meek.*
24 Aug	*From John E. Wheeler.*
25 Aug	*From Ezekiel P. McNeal.*
25 Aug	*From John S. Young.*
26 Aug	*From Moses Dawson.*

26 Aug	*To Boling Gordon.*
26 Aug	*To Alexander Gray et al.*
26 Aug	From Absalom Johnson. ALS. DLC–JKP. Solicits appointment as clerk of the Tennessee Senate.
26 Aug	From William Kee. ALS. DLC–JKP. Asks Polk for money to be used in the presidential campaign.
26 Aug	From Lucius J. Polk. ALS. DLC–JKP. Thinks that his excess rope and bagging has been sold and that Polk should look elsewhere for such supplies.
26 Aug	*To William Rice et al.*
27 Aug	*From John Catron.*
27 Aug	*To John N. Esselman.*
27 Aug	*To William S. Haynes et al.*
27 Aug	*From Thomas Maxwell.*
28 Aug	From Benjamin B. French. ALS. DLC–JKP. Congratulates Polk on his election and suggests that it is the greatest Democratic victory in the country.
28 Aug	From Philip B. Glenn. ALS. DLC–JKP. Congratulates Polk on his election; suggests A. O. P. Nicholson for the U.S. Senate to replace Ephraim H. Foster.
28 Aug	From John Kennedy. ALS. DLC–JKP. Suggests George W. Rowles of Cleveland to be secretary of state; wishes to know Polk's views on the subject.
28 Aug	From Isaac Turner. ALS. DLC–JKP. Congratulates Polk on his election as governor.
28 Aug	*To Robert H. Watkins et al.*
28 Aug	*To Silas Wright.*
29 Aug	*From J. George Harris.*
29 Aug	From John Jett. ALS. DLC–JKP. Solicits aid in obtaining a state job.
29 Aug	*From William Smith et al.*
31 Aug	*To Andrew Jackson.*
31 Aug [1839]	From John Kirk. ALS. DLC–JKP. Advises that he has found someone who can furnish supplies for Polk's plantation in Mississippi and requests instructions regarding quantity and shipping procedures.
31 Aug	*From Joel M. Smith.*
31 Aug	*To William Smith et al.*
1 Sept [1839]	*From John Catron.*
1 Sept	*From Archibald Yell.*
1 Sept	*From John S. Young.*
2 Sept	From J. C. Brasfield. ALS. DLC–JKP. Asks help in obtaining the position of postmaster at Athens, Alabama.
2 Sept	From Aaron V. Brown. ALS. DLC–JKP. Declines invitation to the dinner in Hickman County and encloses a reply to the committee. (Enclosure not found.)
2 Sept	From Samuel Denby. ALS. DLC–JKP. Requests help in obtaining the position of doorkeeper in the Tennessee Senate.

2 Sept	From Marcus B. Winchester. ALS. DLC–JKP. Acknowledges receipt of order for bale rope and bagging; advises that the order will be shipped as soon as possible.
3 Sept	*From Alfred Balch.*
3 Sept	From B. S. Brooks. ALS. DLC–JKP. Wishes to know whether adjoining lands belong to Polk or to his brother; asks if it is for sale.
3 Sept	*From David Craighead.*
3 Sept	From E. S. Davis. ALS. DLC–JKP. Announces his candidacy for the position of secretary of state.
4 Sept [1839]	*From Robert Armstrong.*
4 Sept	From Aaron V. Brown. ALS. DLC–JKP. Reports that he is leaving for Mississippi; hopes to meet Polk on September 17 at the Courtland dinner and to go with him to the Madison dinner.
4 Sept	From Robert J. Chester. ALS. DLC–JKP. Solicits position on Polk's military staff.
4 Sept	*From Isaac Fletcher.*
4 Sept	*From Robert H. Watkins.*
5 Sept	From Julius W. Blackwell. ALS. DLC–JKP. Discusses financial difficulties; comments on the lack of Democratic leadership in McMinn County; and recommends G. W. Rowles of Cleveland, who wishes to become secretary of state.
5 Sept	From Thomas J. Dye. ALS. DLC–JKP. Requests help in establishing a post office near Fayetteville.
5 Sept	*From Nathan Gammon et al.*
6 Sept	From Nathan Gammon. ALS. DLC–JKP. Congratulates Polk on his election.
6 Sept	*From Samuel H. Laughlin.*
6 Sept	From Lewis S. Thomas. ALS. DLC–JKP. Advises Polk of his election as an honorary member of the Philomathic Society at the University of Alabama.
6 Sept	From Richard Waterhouse. ALS. DLC–JKP. Requests aid in obtaining permission for Tennessee to furnish a regiment of mounted volunteers for service in Florida.
7 Sept	From Richard Nelson. ALS. DLC–JKP. Hopes that Polk will not interfere in local elections, such as that of land register in the Mountain District.
7 Sept	*From Archibald Yell.*
[8 Sept 1839]	From Robert Armstrong. ALS. DLC–JKP. Advises that Rhode Island has gone Whig; states that he will go to the Hermitage on Tuesday and write Polk of "the Genl's determination about the Alabama visit."
8 Sept	*From Clement C. Clay.*
8 Sept	From James C. Record. ALS. DLC–JKP. Asks to be recommended for the position of census taker in Marshall County.
9 Sept	*From Julius W. Blackwell.*
9 Sept	*From John W. Childress.*

9 Sept	*From Abraham McClellan.*
9 Sept	From J. G. M. Ramsey. ALS. DLC–JKP. Recommends Arthur R. Crozier to a position on Polk's staff.
9 Sept	From Levi R. Reese. ALS. DLC–JKP. Acknowledges receipt of Polk's letter of August 25; advises that he has received a check from Samuel P. Walker for $325, but that this amount does not include interest from April 1 to September 1.
9 Sept	*From Turner Saunders.*
10 Sept	From Henry W. Anderson. ALS. DLC–JKP. Suggests that it would be politically unpopular should Polk resign the governorship to run for the vice-presidency.
10 Sept	*From John J. Garner.*
10 Sept	From John W. McManus. ALS. DLC–JKP. Urges appointment of a Democrat as circuit judge, rather than Thomas Maney, who was recommended by the Whig majority of the bar association.
10 Sept	*From Harvey M. Watterson.*
12 Sept	From William Moore. ALS. DLC–JKP. Reports from Nashville on political activities, speculation over Ephraim H. Foster's successor in the U.S. Senate, and rumors that Polk will try to move the seat of government to Columbia.
12 Sept	From C. G. Olmsted. ALS. DLC–JKP. Requests copies of government documents dealing with the bank question.
13 Sept	*From Thomas Von Albade Anderson.*
13 Sept	From Samuel Cooper. Copy. DNA–RG 107. Also copy in DNA–RG 75. Acknowledges recommendation of John S. Young to an agency or clerkship in the Indian Department; advises that at the present time there is no vacancy.
13 Sept	From J. Dickson et al. LS. DLC–JKP. Recommend William M. Lowry of Greeneville to Polk's military staff.
13 Sept	From William Gammon. ALS. DLC–JKP. Advises that Abraham McClellan received the check for $100, but "left home without acknowledging the receipt of it"; urges special attention to Jessee Cross to insure his party loyalty.
13 Sept	*To Samuel H. Laughlin.*
15 Sept	From Charles Fenderich. ALS. DLC–JKP. Wishes to know the name of someone in Nashville who could act as an agent for him.
15 Sept	From Andrew A. Kincannon. ALS. DLC–JKP. Requests help in obtaining for Alexander F. Young the appointment of attorney general of the Northern District of Mississippi, should a vacancy occur.
15 Sept	*From Archibald Yell.*
16 Sept	*From William Wallace.*
17 Sept	From anonymous writer. L. DLC–JKP. Advocates abolition of the law providing for imprisonment of debtors, or at least exempting physicians and clergy from this law.
17 Sept	From Rufus P. Neely. ALS. DLC–JKP. Advises that he will be detained in Bolivar longer than expected and will not

pass through Columbia at the time originally scheduled; states that he will try to get to Nashville a few days before the legislature meets.

17 Sept   From C. W. Rozele et al. LS. DLC–JKP. Invite Polk to address two literary societies at La Grange College on June 6, the day preceding their annual commencement.

18 Sept   From Benjamin F. Butler. ALS. DLC–JKP. Introduces John A. Stemmler, who is visiting Tennessee for the purpose of making arrangements for the establishment of German emigrants in the state.

18 Sept   From Thomas Dean et al. LS. DLC–JKP. Invite Polk to a public dinner in his honor on October 1 in Shelbyville.

18 Sept   *From Felix Grundy.*

18 Sept   *From Jonathan P. Hardwicke.*

20 Sept   *From William M. Lowry.*

21 Sept   From Silas M. Caldwell. ALS. DLC–JKP. Recommends John Edwin Taliaferro to Polk's military staff.

23 Sept   From E. S. Davis. ALS. DLC–JKP. Advises that business commitments in Mississippi will keep him from being in Nashville at the time of elections for state officers; states that he would like to remain a candidate for secretary of state.

23 Sept   From Lyman Knowles. ALS. DLC–JKP. Requests payment of $41.25, the amount of discount on Polk's draft sent as payment for his carriage.

23 Sept   From D. B. Turner. ALS. DLC–JKP. Encloses "the letter Sent to my care from our mutual friend Genl Armstrong." (Enclosure not found.)

24 Sept   *To Thomas Dean et al.*

24 Sept   *From J. George Harris.*

24 Sept   From William E. Owen. L. DLC–JKP. Recommends John Edwin Taliaferro as inspector general on Polk's staff.

24 Sept   *From Joel M. Smith.*

24 Sept   *From John S. Young.*

25 Sept   From David Hubbard. ALS. DLC–JKP. Recommends David M. Hunter to be receiver of public moneys in the Cherokee country of Alabama; asks Polk to use his influence in the matter.

25 Sept [1839]   *From West H. Humphreys.*

26 Sept   From James P. H. Porter. ALS. DLC–JKP. Solicits in behalf of his son, Thomas, a clerkship in the legislature, preferably that of engrossing clerk to the Senate.

26 Sept   *From J. G. M. Ramsey.*

26 Sept   *From John S. Young.*

27 Sept   *From Robert Armstrong.*

27 Sept   From Henry Mabry. ALS. DLC–JKP. Advises that he is a candidate for engrossing clerk in the Tennessee House; states that if successful, he will make arrangements to have his newspaper, the Winchester *Highlander*, published during his absence.

27 Sept	From William Wallace. ALS. DLC–JKP. Introduces Thomas P. H. Porter and recommends him as engrossing clerk to the Tennessee Senate.
28 Sept	From Sanford C. Blanton. ALS. DLC–JKP. Seeks advice on his education; asks if he should study languages before reading law; and inquires in whose office he might apply for a legal apprenticeship.
28 Sept [1839]	*From Cave Johnson.*
29 Sept [1839]	*From Robert Armstrong.*
29 Sept	From Richard Warner. ALS. DLC–JKP. Advises that he will be unable to visit Columbia before leaving for Nashville; assures Polk that he will vote with the party "on all important subjects in that way that may be most conducive to the interest of the Country and the advancement of Democratic principles."
30 Sept	From David Gallaher. ALS. DLC–JKP. Requests assistance in obtaining a loan; lobbies for passage of legislation in which he has a personal interest.
30 Sept	From James H. Gallaher. ALS. DLC–JKP. Asks for $2 toward the cost of a barrel of cider that he provided on election day.
30 Sept [1839]	*From Samuel H. Laughlin.*
[Oct 1839]	From Bates Cooke. ACS. T–GP. Asks that enclosed questions about state stock be delivered to the proper officer for reply.
[Oct 1839]	From Julian Frazier. ALS. DLC–JKP. Advises that John A. Aiken of Washington County wishes a post on Polk's military staff.
Oct 1839	From Benjamin B. French. CS. T–GP. Transmits three copies of the *House Journal* for the Second Session of the Twenty-fifth Congress.
1 Oct	*To Samuel H. Laughlin and Robert Armstrong.*
1 Oct	From Aaron H. Palmer. C. T–GP. Expresses willingness to handle financial matters in Europe.
2 Oct	*From Barkly Martin and Samuel H. Laughlin.*
2 Oct	From Thomas J. Matthews. ALS. DLC–JKP. Asks help in obtaining the position of census taker in Lawrence County.
4 Oct	From Jesse Lewis. ALS. DLC–JKP. Recommends George W. Churchwell to Polk's military staff.
[5 Oct 1839]	From William P. Martin. ALS. DLC–JKP. Expresses regret that he did not get to visit before Polk left Nashville.
5 Oct	From William Moore. ALS. DLC–JKP. Advises that serious family illnesses prevent his coming to Nashville; discusses resolutions that he would like to see passed by the legislature.
7 Oct	From William Lyon. ALS. DLC–JKP. Solicits for his son, Thomas C. Lyon, the appointment of attorney general for the Eastern District.
7 Oct	From John Stephens. ALS. DLC–JKP. Seeks advice on what procedure he should follow to obtain clear title to lands that were formerly in Indian territory.

8 Oct	From Coplestone C. Hodges. ALS. DLC–JKP. Asks if he might place a box at the Nashville Theatre at Polk's disposal for the following evening.
8 Oct	From James C. Record. ALS. DLC–JKP. Advises that contrary to rumor, he has not removed his name as applicant for census taker of Marshall County.
10 Oct	From Charles Cassedy. ALS. DLC–JKP. Encloses a memorial on the subject of popular education. (Enclosure not found.)
10 Oct	From Isaac J. Thomas, Sr. ALS. DLC–JKP. Introduces his son, Isaac J. Thomas, Jr., who is seeking a place on Polk's staff.
10 Oct	From William J. Whitthorne. ALS. DLC–JKP. Explains that when he told Polk that James C. Record no longer sought the position of census taker for Marshall County, he thought his information was reliable; adds that he had no ulterior motive.
11 Oct	From Lewis P. Roberts. ALS. DLC–JKP. Reports on a Whig meeting in Knoxville and recommends George W. Churchwell to Polk's military staff.
12 Oct	From John H. Bills. ALS. DLC–JKP. Recommends John R. Fentress of Bolivar for appointment to Polk's staff.
13 Oct	From Abram Caruthers. ANS. T–GP. Notifies Polk that he will be unable to hold the court for Fentress and Overton counties during the current term and requests that a substitute be named.
14 Oct	*From George W. Churchwell.*
15 Oct	From William D. Johnson. ALS. DLC–JKP. Solicits appointment as quartermaster general.
[15 Oct 1839]	From Malinda Moore McGinnis. ALS. DLC–JKP. Asks for a legislative act to have her son released from prison.
15 Oct	*From James Walker.*
17 Oct	*From Felix Grundy.*
17 Oct	*From Amos Kirkpatrick.*
18 Oct	From William Moore. ALS. DLC–JKP. Advises that "If in filling your Genl Staff my name may be attached or included, it will be a source of the highest grattification to have a line from you seting forth some of the reasons for that appointment."
19 Oct	From James R. McMeans. ALS. DLC–JKP. Asks help in obtaining the appointment of chancellor for the Western District.
19 Oct	From Benjamin S. Russ. ALS. DLC–JKP. Encloses note and asks Polk to assign it as security.
20 Oct	*From William Allen.*
20 Oct	*From Julius W. Blackwell.*
20 Oct	From Lilburn W. Boggs. C. T–GP. Transmits copy of a series of resolutions passed by the General Assembly of Missouri on the subject of slavery.
20 Oct	From Joel Henry Dyer. ALS. DLC–JKP. Renews his request for a loan of $100.

20 Oct	*From James Walker.*
20 Oct	*From Levi Woodbury.*
21 Oct	From Frederick R. Smith. ALS. T–RG 5. Encloses certification of the board of directors of the Big Hatchie Turnpike & Bridge Company pursuant to obtaining state bonds.
21 Oct	*From Hampton C. Williams.*
22 Oct	From Charles Cassedy. ALS. DLC–JKP. Wishes appointment in order to discuss the manuscript of a book.
22 Oct	From James Gamble. ALS. DLC–JKP. Suggests George W. Churchwell for appointment to Polk's staff.
23 Oct	*From David Hubbard.*
23 Oct	From Bromfield L. Ridley. ALS. T–GP. Accepts commission to hold the upcoming terms of the Overton and Fentress courts.
24 Oct	From Graham H. Chapin. ALS. DLC–JKP. Introduces Thomas E. Hastings, who is moving from Rochester, New York, to Tennessee.
25 Oct	From Nathaniel H. Allen. ALS. T–GP. Resigns as attorney general of the Seventh District.
26 Oct	*From E. G. Eastman.*
26 Oct	To Calvin Hubbell. ALS. DLC–JKP. Advises that he has received *Richardson's English Dictionary* and encloses a check for $23 to cover the subscription and postage.
26 Oct	From John B. Johnson. ALS. DLC–JKP. Returns Polk's bill of exchange with endorsers' signatures.
26 Oct	From Stephen Mitchel. ALS. DLC–JKP. Offers his personal views on the state's economic and political affairs.
26 Oct	*From J. G. M. Ramsey.*
28 Oct	*From William H. Polk.*
28 Oct	*From Joseph H. Talbot.*
28 Oct	From Sampson Williams. ALS. DLC–JKP. Sends payment for subscriptions to the Washington *Congressional Globe* and *Appendix.*
29 Oct	From Joseph N. Johnson. ALS. DLC–JKP. Asks Polk's influence in helping Johnson to obtain the appointment of attorney general for Arkansas.
29 Oct	*From Hopkins L. Turney.*
30 Oct	From W. Winthrop Sifford. ALS. DLC–JKP. Asks for the reports of the geological surveys made in Tennessee.
30 Oct	From James Walker. ALS. DLC–JKP. Suggests that all public officials should be made to swear allegiance to the Constitution; maintains that if found supporting anything not specifically sanctioned in the Constitution (such as a national bank), said officials should be removed.
30 Oct	From J. Knox Walker. ALS. DLC–JKP. Reports that he is sending Polk's trunk by tomorrow's stage and asks to be notified if the trunk does not arrive.
1 Nov	From Charles G. Greene. ALS. DLC–JKP. Introduces John T. Ward of Boston, Massachusetts.
1 Nov	From William Gunton. ALS. DLC–JKP. Requests the re-

	turn of a bond that was given Polk as Speaker of the U.S. House.
1 Nov	*From J. G. M. Ramsey.*
1 Nov	From Hugh W. Wormsley. ALS. DLC–JKP. Requests help in obtaining the appointment of postmaster at Lexington, Tennessee.
2 Nov	*From Joshua L. Martin.*
3 Nov	*From Alexander O. Anderson.*
3 Nov	*From John J. Garner.*
4 Nov	To R. G. Douglass. Copy. T–GP. Assures Douglass that state bonds will be issued as soon as all information required by law is received from the Gallatin & Cumberland Turnpike Company.
4 Nov	To James S. W. Hawkins. Copy. T–GP. Explains militia act of 1825 and assures Hawkins that arms will be delivered to him when the provisions of the act are met.
4 Nov	From Samuel Martin. ALS. DLC–JKP. Offers advice on internal improvements.
4 Nov	From John C. Mullay. ALS. DLC–JKP. Asks assistance in obtaining a position with the Bureau of Indian Affairs.
4 Nov	From Sutherland S. Southworth. ALS. DLC–JKP. Congratulates Polk on his election and on his inaugural address.
5 Nov	From H. J. Anderson. ALS. T–GP. Recommends that prison sentences of Thomas Hudson and Lewis D. St. Leger be commuted.
5 Nov [1839]	*From John Catron.*
5 Nov	From George W. Gibbs. ALS. T–GP. Resigns post as chancellor of the Western Division of Tennessee.
6 Nov	From John W. Ford. ALS. DLC–JKP. Recommends Landon A. Kincannon to be a director of the Bank of Tennessee.
6 Nov	To Frederick R. Smith. Copy. T–GP. Advises that state bonds totaling $8,000 will be issued on behalf of the Big Hatchie Turnpike & Bridge Company.
6 Nov	From James W. Williamson. ALS. T–GP. Requests certification that Valentine D. Barry is a circuit court judge of Tennessee.
7 Nov	*From John Blair.*
7 Nov	From Boling Gordon. ALS. DLC–JKP. Advises that there is doubt about the passage of instructing resolutions in support of the Sub-Treasury bill; expresses concern over the matter.
8 Nov	From John W. Yeats. ALS. DLC–JKP. Asks Polk to write to Christopher H. Williams in behalf of his claim, which is now before the Congress.
9 Nov	From Return J. Meigs. ALS. T–GP. Resigns position as attorney general.
9 Nov	From William Trousdale. ALS. DLC–JKP. Introduces John Claiborne of Smith County.
9 Nov	*From Hopkins L. Turney.*

9 Nov	*From John S. Young.*
[10] Nov	From Elisha Adair. ALS. DLC–JKP. Requests advice regarding a petition on behalf of the estate of Joseph Adair.
10 Nov	*From Alexander O. Anderson.*
10 Nov	From Aaron V. Brown. ALS. DLC–JKP. Advises that he is sending a servant, Sophia, to Nashville; asks Polk to arrange transportation for her to Pulaski.
10 Nov	From James Cason. ALS. DLC–JKP. Recounts history of a Madison County debt owed by the estates of Samuel Polk and Joseph B. Porter to the estate of Lewis Jones.
10 Nov [1839]	*From Cave Johnson.*
11 Nov	From Robert Blain, Jr. ALS. DLC–JKP. Advises Polk that he has been elected an honorary member of the Chi Delta Society of East Tennessee College.
11 Nov	From Lewis P. Roberts. ALS. DLC–JKP. Reports on gathering in Knoxville at which John Bell and Hugh Lawson White were the principal speakers.
11 Nov	*To Martin Van Buren.*
12 Nov	From Milner Echols. ALS. DLC–JKP. Wishes to know if the orphaned daughter of Mary Sansom Childress and Anderson Childress is being reared by Sarah Childress Polk.
12 Nov	From John B. Johnson. ALS. DLC–JKP. Reports that he has received from James Mitchell, a tenant, 28 barrels and 1 bushel of corn and has credited Polk's account with $35.25; states that Mitchell wants to send his bond to Polk, but that it might be better to send it to William H. Polk.
12 Nov	To the President and Directors of the Clarksville & Russellville Turnpike Company. ALS, draft. T–GP. States that as soon as they comply with the provisions of the 1838 internal improvements act, the state will issue bonds in the amount of $10,000.
13 Nov	*From Alexander O. Anderson.*
13 Nov	From Anthony Jones et al. NS. T–RG 5. Discuss capitalization of the Nashville & Kentucky Turnpike Company and request issuance of state bonds for the company.
14 Nov	To H. J. Anderson. ALS, draft. T–GP. States that he will consider commuting the sentence of Lewis D. St. Leger if Anderson will supply the documentation required by the law of 1835.
14 Nov	From William James Lauderdale. ANS. T–GP. Reports delivery of Alexander Webb, charged with murder, by William D. Winston and George W. Moore.
14 Nov	*From Joel R. Poinsett.*
15 Nov	From Levin H. Coe. ALS. DLC–JKP. Thanks Polk for offering him an appointment; declines because a friend of his is seeking the same appointment; and states that at the end of the present session of the legislature he intends to withdraw entirely from public life.
15 Nov	From George Talcott. ALS. T–GP. Requests arms requirement for Tennessee militia in 1840.

15 Nov [1839]	From C. M. Wilcox. ALS. DLC–JKP. Wishes to know the result of his earlier request for an appointment either as midshipman in the navy or as cadet at West Point.
16 Nov	*From Alexander O. Anderson.*
16 Nov	From B. S. Brooks. ALS. DLC–JKP. Wishes to know whether a tract of land previously discussed belongs to Polk or to Polk's brother; inquires whether the land is for sale and if so, at what price.
16 Nov	From Andrew Johnston. ALS. DLC–JKP. Asks to be recommended for the appointment of census taker for Hickman and Perry counties.
16 Nov	From William Wallace. ALS. DLC–JKP. Asks Polk to consider a pardon or a reduced sentence for Thomas Davis.
17 Nov	From Bromfield L. Ridley. ALS. DLC–JKP. Expresses confidence that Polk will be the vice-presidential nominee in 1840; recommends Landon A. Kincannon and Timothy Kezer as directors of the Bank of Tennessee.
18 Nov	From J. Watson Andrew. ALS. DLC–JKP. Requests Polk's autograph.
18 Nov	*From Edward S. Dwight*
18 Nov	From Albert Miller Lea. ALS. DLC–JKP. Asks for a legislative act to refund him money for a draft that was protested for non-payment.
19 Nov	From H. J. Anderson. ALS. T–GP. Recommends commutation of the prison sentence of Lewis D. St. Leger, convicted on an assault charge.
19 Nov [1839]	*From John Catron.*
19 Nov [1839]	*From Cave Johnson.*
19 [Nov]	From James K. Paulding. ALS. DLC–JKP. Thanks Polk for sending a copy of his address to the Tennessee legislature; asks for names of two or three persons who might be good candidates for midshipmen appointments.
19 Nov	From George A. Wylie. ALS. T–RG 5. Encloses certification of the board of directors of the Nashville & Kentucky Turnpike Company.
20 Nov	From Gideon J. Pillow. ALS. T–GP. Asks Polk to appoint three persons to make a report to the governor regarding the condition of the road being constructed by the Columbia Central Turnpike Company.
20 Nov	*From George F. Strother.*
21 Nov	From M. C. Bowles. ALS. DLC–JKP. Requests that the Trenton branch of the Bank of Tennessee be moved to Paris.
21 Nov	From Aaron Vail, Jr. CS. T–GP. Requests that Polk acknowledge receipt of three sets of the documents of the Second Session of the Twenty-fifth Congress.
22 Nov	*From Alexander O. Anderson.*
22 Nov	From anonymous writer. L. DLC–JKP. Supports a national ticket in 1840 of Martin Van Buren and Polk.
22 Nov	From Robert A. Baker. ALS. DLC–JKP. Requests information on public education in Tennessee, including the superintendent's annual report to the legislature.

22 Nov   *From Henry Horn.*
22 Nov   From Thomas G. Polk. ALS. DLC–JKP. Advises that he is enclosing "the Deed and certificate of Monney. You will please have the seal of the State and your Testimonial appended & send by the return mail."
22 Nov   From Phinehas Pomeroy. ALS. T–GP. Applies for job as an engineer.
23 Nov   From William Fitzgerald. ALS. T–GP. Encloses petition asking for a pardon for Simpson W. Alexander.
23 Nov   From Benjamin B. French. CS. T–GP. Transmits three copies of the *House Journal* for the Third Session of the Twenty-fifth Congress.
23 Nov   *From John J. Garner.*
23 Nov [1839]   From William H. Polk. ALS. DLC–JKP. Advises that Polk owes $30 to Jeremiah Tranum for transporting goods and slaves to Mississippi.
23 Nov   To George A. Wylie. ALS, draft. T–GP. Informs Wylie that state bonds totaling $9,000 for the benefit of the Nashville & Kentucky Turnpike Company have been issued.
24 Nov   From Lunsford M. Bramlett. ALS. DLC–JKP. Urges salary increases for the judges of the Supreme Court and for the chancellors; argues that the work load for the chancellor of the Middle District is too great and the district should be divided.
25 Nov   From Arthur R. Crozier. ALS. DLC–JKP. Advises that soon he will forward to Julius W. Blackwell a mailing list for public documents to be sent to voters in Knox and other counties in the Third Congressional District of Tennessee.
25 Nov   From John R. Nelson et al. LS. T–GP. Request pardon and commutation of the prison sentence for Addison Leath, convicted of stabbing Hugh Lawson White.
26 Nov   *From Joshua L. Martin.*
26 Nov   To Gideon J. Pillow. Copy. T–GP. Notifies Pillow that he will appoint directors of the Columbia Central Turnpike Company when documentation required by law is received.
26 Nov   To Joel R. Poinsett. ALS, draft. T–GP. Assures Poinsett that the interest on $250,000 in Tennessee state bonds, held by the government of the U.S., will be paid.
27 Nov   *From Robert B. Reynolds.*
27 Nov   From Marcus B. Winchester. ALS. DLC–JKP. Introduces J. Fowlks, a physician.
28 Nov   From H. J. Anderson. ALS. T–GP. Reports on the conduct of Addison Leath, a prisoner from Anderson County.
28 Nov   To John Forsyth. ALS. DNA–RG 59. Recommends Matthew Figures for a consulate position at Tampico, Mexico.
28 Nov [1839]   *From Cave Johnson.*
28 Nov   From William Smith. ALS. DLC–JKP. Congratulates Polk on his inaugural address and advises that he is sending copies of two speeches opposing the BUS.

28 Nov	From Hampton C. Williams. ALS. DLC–JKP. Discusses Felix Grundy's eligibility for election to the U.S. Senate and candidates for Speaker of the U.S. House.
29 Nov	*To Robert A. Baker.*
29 Nov	To R. G. Douglass. ALS, draft. T–GP. Informs Douglass that under the law of 1838 no additional state bonds can be issued to the Gallatin & Cumberland Turnpike Company.
29 Nov	From David McKamy. ALS. DLC–JKP. Recommends John A. Aiken of Washington County for appointment to Polk's staff.
29 Nov	From Winfield S. Rainey. ALS. DLC–JKP. Advises Polk that he has been elected an honorary member of a literary society at Jackson College, Columbia.
29 Nov	*From Harvey M. Watterson.*
30 Nov	To Robert Blain, Jr. ALS, draft. DLC–JKP. Expresses thanks for being elected an honorary member of the Chi Delta Society of East Tennessee College.
30 Nov	From Gideon J. Pillow. ALS. T–GP. Reports that seven miles of the Columbia Central Turnpike Road have been completed and asks Polk to appoint commissioners to examine the road.
1 Dec	*From Felix Grundy.*
1 Dec [1839]	*From Cave Johnson.*
1 Dec	*From Harvey M. Watterson.*
2 Dec [1839]	From David Hubbard. ALS. DLC–JKP. Advises that the U.S. House is debating the question "whether New Jersey shall be represented by either party in the Election of speaker"; discusses candidates for Speaker and their prospects.
2 Dec [1839]	From Cave Johnson. ALS. DLC–JKP. Discusses the debate on seating the New Jersey delegation.
3 Dec	From James D. Eads. ALS. DLC–JKP. Wishes to know what effect the "quart law" has had on the morals of the people of Tennessee.
3 Dec	*From Harvey M. Watterson.*
4 Dec	*From Alexander O. Anderson.*
4 Dec	From Abram Caruthers. ALS. T–GP. Notifies Polk of his illness and requests him to appoint a special judge to hold the Carthage Court.
[4 Dec 1839]	From Nathan Green, William B. Reese, and William B. Turley. LS. T–GP. Certify cases in which Reese has recused himself.
4 Dec [1839]	*From Cave Johnson.*
4 Dec	*From Cave Johnson.*
4 Dec	From Aaron H. Palmer. ALS. T–GP. Requests appointment as agent to handle sale of Tennessee bonds in Europe.
4 Dec	To William Smith. ALS, draft. DLC–JKP. Thanks Smith for sending copies of two speeches opposing the BUS; discusses the bank question.
5 Dec	*From Thomas Hart Benton.*

5 Dec	From Joel R. Poinsett. LS. DLC–JKP. Also copy in DNA–RG 107. Acknowledges receipt of Polk's letter recommending Joel M. Smith for pension agent and advises that Smith will be appointed.
5 Dec	From Hopkins L. Turney. ALS. DLC–JKP. Laments lack of legislative action in the U.S. House.
[6 Dec 1839]	From Nathan Green and William B. Turley. LS. T–GP. Certify case in the Sixth Circuit Court in which Green has recused himself.
[6 Dec 1839]	From Cave Johnson. ALS. DLC–JKP. Writes that the U.S. House "decided that the N. Jersey men shall not vote"; anticipates long debate on the election of Speaker.
6 Dec	To James K. Paulding. ALS. DNA–RG 45. Discusses case of H. P. Robertson, a midshipman in the navy; asks that Robertson be given the rank that he would have achieved had he been able to stand his examinations at the regular time.
7 Dec	*From Aaron V. Brown.*
7 Dec	From David M. Hunter. ALS. DLC–JKP. Advises that he is still an applicant "for the appointment of receiver in the Cherokee nation Should an office be established there."
7 Dec [1839]	*From Cave Johnson.*
7 Dec	To the *New York Observer.* ALS. DLC–JKP. Encloses check for $9 to pay for Jane Polk's subscription; requests discontinuance of the newspaper at the end of 1839.
7 Dec	From Robert Wilson et al. NS. T–RG 5. Report results of their examination of the Columbia Central Turnpike Road.
8 Dec [1839]	*From Cave Johnson.*
8 Dec [1839]	From Cave Johnson. ALS. DLC–JKP. Reports that the Whigs have nominated William H. Harrison for president.
8 Dec	*From David A. Street.*
9 Dec	From Thomas Dodson. ALS. DLC–JKP. Wishes information concerning ownership and possible purchase of a tract of land situated near his own acreage.
9 Dec	From David Gallaher. ALS. DLC–JKP. Advises that he has reversed his opinion of William Stanfield and thinks Stanfield is an adequate census taker.
9 Dec	From John T. Hill. ALS. DLC–JKP. Advises that he has sent Polk "an Ink Stand of E. Tennessee Marble Near Rogersville made by me . . . ."
9 Dec	From [Thomas Summers]. L, fragment. DLC–JKP. Asks Polk to check the land office in Nashville concerning ownership of a piece of land near Knoxville.
9 Dec	From Charles C. Trabue. ALS. T–GP. Requests use of arms presently held in the Nashville arsenal.
10 Dec	To Thomas W. Barksdale. ALS, draft. T–GP. Tells Barksdale that he has issued state bonds in the amount of $10,000 for the benefit of the Clarksville & Russellville Turnpike Company.
10 Dec	From Charles Cassedy. ALS. DLC–JKP. Discusses issue of public education.

10 Dec	From Seth Ford. ALS. DLC–JKP. Thinks he can locate a gold mine on top of Cumberland Mountain; will give the locality, provided he can have half of the gold after it is coined.
10 Dec	From W. Thad Plummer. ALS. DLC–JKP. Advises Polk that he has been elected an honorary member of a literary society at Jackson College, Columbia; asks for a donation for the library.
10 Dec	To the President and Directors of the Nashville & Charlotte Turnpike Company. ALS, draft. T–GP. Informs them that the documents they have submitted do not comply with the requirements of the 1838 internal improvements act and that no additional state bonds can be issued to their company.
10 Dec	To Charles C. Trabue. ALS, draft. T–GP. Refuses to distribute a portion of the state's public arms to the Corporation of Nashville; cites lack of legal authority.
10 Dec	From William Trousdale. ALS. DLC–JKP. Supports application for the release of R. M. Boyers of Gallatin from a prison sentence in the Davidson County jail.
11 Dec	From Preston Frazer. ALS. DLC–JKP. Suggests William Gray as a director of the Bank of Tennessee.
11 Dec	From Joseph Hickey. ALS. DLC–JKP. Advises that "In the event that the present legislature should elect an other senator I wish you to write to him on the subject of my appointment"; names Samuel H. Laughlin as the best replacement, should Hugh Lawson White resign.
11 Dec	*From Kenedy Lonergan.*
11 Dec	From Marcus B. Winchester. ALS. DLC–JKP. Requests Polk's support for legislative amendment of state's 1831 emancipation act.
12 Dec	From Julius W. Blackwell. ALS. DLC–JKP. Discusses delays in the election of Speaker of the U.S. House; urges support for Robert Frazier in his bid to get money to sustain the Athens *Courier*.
12 Dec [1839]	*From Cave Johnson.*
12 Dec	*From Archibald Yell.*
[13 Dec 1839]	From Cave Johnson. ALS. DLC–JKP. Writes of the actions taken that day by the U.S. House.
14 Dec	*From John H. Bills.*
14 Dec [1839]	From Cave Johnson. ALS. DLC–JKP. Gives vote counts on the six ballots for Speaker of the U.S. House taken that day.
14 Dec	From Samuel Martin. ALS. DLC–JKP. Expresses opposition to proposed internal improvements and banking measures before the Tennessee legislature.
14 Dec	*From Hopkins L. Turney.*
14 Dec	From Harvey M. Watterson. ALS. DLC–JKP. Sends results of the first six ballots for Speaker of the U.S. House.
15 Dec	From Samuel C. Dunlap. ALS. T–GP. Asks release of Simpson W. Alexander from the penitentiary.

15 Dec [1839]   From Cave Johnson. ALS. DLC–JKP. Discusses events surrounding the balloting for Speaker of the U.S. House.

16 Dec [1839]   *From Cave Johnson.*

16 Dec   From Harvey M. Watterson. ALS. DLC–JKP. Gives balloting results that day for Speaker of the U.S. House.

17 Dec   *From David Hubbard.*

17 Dec [1839]   From Cave Johnson. ALS. DLC–JKP. Reports that the day has been spent debating the question of seating the New Jersey delegation.

17 Dec   From Jonathan Pope. ALS. DLC–JKP. Argues against the state's offering a reward for the capture of his son, Leroy Pope, who is accused of killing Plesant Thomas, son of Elisha Thomas.

18 Dec   *From J. G. M. Ramsey.*

18 Dec   From Moses G. Reeves. ALS. DLC–JKP. Reports that the people of Murfreesboro are skeptical that William H. Harrison will be the Whig candidate for president.

[20 Dec 1839]   From John McKenzie. ALS. DLC–JKP. Requests that Polk handle his Revolutionary War claim.

21 Dec   *From Alexander O. Anderson.*

21 Dec   From Thomas L. Bransford and Samuel Turney. NS. T–GP. Request commutation of the remainder of the sentence of John Cummins of Jackson County.

21 Dec   *From Cave Johnson.*

[23 Dec 1839]   From William B. Turley, William B. Reese, and Nathan Green. LS. T–GP. Certify cases in the Eighth Circuit Chancery Court in which Green and Reese have recused themselves.

24 Dec   From E. S. Davis. ALS. DLC–JKP. Solicits appointment to the directorship of the LaGrange & Memphis Railroad Company.

24 Dec   From William Hightower et al. LS. T–GP. Request release of Thomas J. Davis from the penitentiary.

24 Dec   From Charles J. McDonald. ALS. T–GP. Assures Polk that the Georgia legislature will complete the proposed railroad to the Tennessee River.

25 Dec   *From John J. Garner.*

27 Dec   From Philip Lindsley. ALS. DLC–JKP. Solicits appointment to the directorship of the Union Bank of Tennessee.

27 Dec   From Samuel Martin. ALS. DLC–JKP. Expresses approval of legislative efforts to require resumption of specie payments by the state banks and registers complaint against further expenditures in support of the Hiwassee Railroad Company.

27 Dec   From Richard M. Woods. ALS. DLC–JKP. Urges that the postmaster of Elizabethton, Hiram Daily, be discharged and replaced by Joseph Powell; states that Daily is too closely aligned to William G. Brownlow, editor of the Elizabethton *Tennessee Whig.*

28 Dec   To John T. Hill. ALS, draft. DLC–JKP. Thanks Hill for the ink stand made of East Tennessee marble.

28 Dec	From W. E. Watkins et al. LS. T–RG 5. Report on the capital calls of the Nashville & Charlotte Turnpike Company.
29 Dec	From Thomas Fielding Scott. ALS. DLC–JKP. Urges support for a state loan to Columbia's Jackson College, which is troubled financially.
30 Dec	*From Julius W. Blackwell.*
30 Dec	From James Caruthers. ALS. DLC–JKP. Recommends appointment of his brother–in–law, George K. Morton of Grenada, Mississippi, to be U.S. district attorney for Northern Mississippi.
30 Dec	*To David Hubbard.*
30 Dec	*From William H. Polk.*
30 Dec	*From James Walker.*
31 Dec	*From John J. Garner.*
31 Dec	From Thomas B. Jones. ALS. DLC–JKP. Solicits appointment as receiver or register of the federal office to be established for the sale of Cherokee lands in the Hiwassee District.
[1839–41]	From S. W. Fitzpatrick. ANS. T–GP. Certifies that Maury County volunteer company of militia is in full uniform and entitled to arms.

1840

1840	From James Black et al. NS. T–RG 5. Discuss state bonds for the Franklin & Columbia Turnpike Company.
[1840?]	From Thomas Clarkson. ACS. T–GP. Attacks slavery and the slave trade.
[1840]	From Gideon J. Pillow. ALS. DLC–JKP. Says that he is too ill to come to town this day.
[Jan 1840]	From E. B. Alexander et al. LS. T–GP. Request pardon for Jesse Williams of Lincoln County.
1 Jan	From E. A. Cartwright et al. NS. T–GP. Recommend Edward A. White of Lebanon to replace William W. Masterson as director of the Union Bank of Tennessee at Nashville.
1 Jan	*From Cave Johnson.*
1 Jan	From Samuel Martin. ALS. DLC–JKP. Proposes creation of a state bank at Campbell's Station and suggests restriction of its operations to loans, deposits, and exchanges.
1 Jan	*To William Moore.*
1 Jan	From Marman Spence. ALS. T–GP. Reminds Polk that he must appoint one-third of the directors of the Nashville, Murfreesboro & Shelbyville Turnpike Company.
1 Jan	From Virgil A. Stewart. ALS. T–GP. Requests that his enclosed petition be delivered to the Tennessee General Assembly.
3 Jan	From Ebenezer Alexander. ALS. T–GP. Resigns as attorney general of the Second Judicial District.
3 Jan	*From John Catron.*

3 Jan   From Levin H. Coe. ALS. T–GP. Recommends appointment of E. S. Davis and David Jernigan, residents of Fayette County, to be directors of the LaGrange & Memphis Railroad Company to replace Epps Moody and George H. Wyatt, who have moved to Mississippi.

3 Jan   *From Ezekiel P. McNeal.*

3 Jan   *From William H. Polk.*

3 Jan   From James Walker. ALS. DLC–JKP. Offers to take the slave Ruben on a "for hire" basis; expresses consternation that the Democratic majority in the legislature has not united behind a common internal improvements plan.

4 Jan [1840]   From Joseph W. Clay. ALS. T–RG 5. Reports progress of the Lebanon & Nashville Turnpike Company.

4 Jan   From M. D. Thompson and A. R. Cartwright. NS. T–RG 5. Report on the progress of the Franklin & Columbia Turnpike Company.

4 Jan   *From James Walker.*

5 Jan [1840]   *From Mary S. Childress.*

5 Jan   From John Dupont. ALS. DLC–JKP. Solicits relief for his family fortunes, which were ruined in the Mobile fire.

6 Jan   From H. J. Anderson. ALS. T–GP. Recommends commutation of the prison sentence of Gilford Cook.

6 Jan   To the President and Directors of the Nashville & Charlotte Turnpike Company. ALS, draft. T–GP. Notifies them that the sum of $6,000 in state bonds has been issued for their company.

7 Jan   From Asbury Dickens. CS. T–GP. Asks Polk to send any available reports on Tennessee's geology and mineralogy to the Congressional Library.

7 Jan   *From Samuel P. Walker.*

8 Jan   *To Andrew Jackson Donelson.*

8 Jan   From N. G. Hearn et al. LS. T–GP. Request release of Curtis Manly from the state penitentiary.

10 Jan   From Gideon J. Pillow. ALS. T–GP. Asks Polk to examine papers relating to the possible issuance of state bonds for the Columbia Central Turnpike Company and to inform him of his views on the matter.

10 Jan   From William C. Smartt. ALS. DLC–JKP. Recommends Landon A. Kincannon to be a director of the Bank of Tennessee.

11 Jan   From Alexander O. Anderson. ALS. DLC–JKP. Recommends Robert Frazier to be chosen Democratic elector for 1840 presidential contest.

11 Jan   From M. D. Thompson and A. R. Cartwright. NS. T–RG 5. Request issuance of $49,000 in state bonds for the benefit of the Franklin & Columbia Turnpike Company.

11 Jan   From Edmund Wayman. ALS. T–GP. Requests that a reward be offered for the capture of Patrick Thurman, accused murderer of Aden G. Wimpey.

13 Jan	*From Felix Grundy.*
13 Jan	From Cave Johnson. ALS. DLC–JKP. Relates that Hugh Lawson White read to the U.S. Senate his written answer to the legislature's instructions.
13 Jan	From L. P. Sims. ALS. T–GP. Discusses murder of William Coltart by Zebulon Payne.
14 Jan	From H. Tookman. ALS. T–GP. Discusses case of Caleb Holly, convicted of stealing.
15 Jan	*From Albert T. McNeal.*
15 Jan	To James K. Paulding. ALS. DLC–JKP. Confirms earlier nomination of Nathaniel F. Carr to be a midshipman in the navy.
15 Jan	From William T. Ross. ALS. T–GP. Writes on behalf of Jesse Williams, a prisoner in the state penitentiary.
15 Jan	From J. B. White. ALS. T–GP. Discusses case of Jesse Williams.
16 Jan	From James Black et al. LS. T–RG 5. Report on the progress of the Franklin & Columbia Turnpike Company.
16 Jan	From James Black et al. NS. T–RG 5. Request $49,000 in state bonds for the Franklin & Columbia Turnpike Company.
16 Jan	From Henry Brown. ALS. DLC–JKP. Gives details of debt owed him by Samuel Polk; argues that there was an "over plus" of acreage in the tract sold to Polk's father.
16 Jan	From James D. McClellan. ALS. T–GP. Encloses petition in behalf of John D. Robinson of Madison County.
17 Jan	From Robert Clark. ALS. DLC–JKP. Requests that his name be removed as a nominee for director of the Bank of Tennessee; suggests A. H. White in his stead.
17 Jan	To Gideon J. Pillow. ALS, draft. T–GP. Reports to Pillow that the certificate from the board of the Columbia Central Turnpike Company regarding payments by the stockholders cannot be located in the office of secretary of state.
18 Jan	From John R. Dabbs and W. D. Pufoss. LS. T–RG 5. Report results of their examination of the Lebanon & Nashville Turnpike.
18 Jan	From Granville H. Frazer. ALS. DLC–JKP. Recommends James Walker of Bedford County to be director of the Bank of Tennessee.
18 Jan	From Preston Frazer. ALS. DLC–JKP. Recommends James Walker of Bedford County to be director of the Bank of Tennessee.
18 Jan	From James Gamble. LS. DLC–JKP. Advises that inclement weather has prevented his traveling to Nashville to lobby the legislature for internal improvements.
20 Jan	From John Autry. ALS. T–GP. Requests that Polk intervene in the case of Curtis Manly.
20 Jan	To the President and Directors of the Gallatin Turnpike Company. ALS, draft. T–GP. Informs them that he will

take no further action on their request for the issuance of $9,000 in additional state bonds until they submit the documentation required by law.

21 Jan   From Pleasant M. Miller. ALS. DLC–JKP. Warns that the Union Bank cannot resume specie payments and survive.

22 Jan   From Andrew M. Ballentine et al. LS. T–RG 5. Request issuance of $14,000 of state bonds for the benefit of the Columbia, Pulaski, Elkton, & Alabama Turnpike Company.

[23 Jan]   From Nathan Green, William B. Turley, and William B. Reese. LS. T–GP. Certify that Reese has recused himself in the case of John C. McLemore *vs.* Peter G. Rives and Wife, a case coming to the Sixth Circuit Chancery Court.

25 Jan   From H. J. Anderson. ALS. T–GP. Recommends commuting the prison sentence of James H. Brown.

25 Jan   From Newton Cannon. ALS. T–GP. Transmits papers to be filed by the secretary of state.

25 Jan   From Patrick Noble. CS. T–GP. Transmits report and resolutions adopted by the legislature of South Carolina regarding a controversy between Georgia and Maine over the removal of a slave from Georgia by citizens of Maine.

25 Jan   From Gideon J. Pillow. ALS. T–GP. Transmits documents relating to the Columbia Central Turnpike Company and a communication from Newton Cannon related thereto; asks Polk to act quickly on them.

26 Jan   *From Adam Huntsman.*

28 Jan   *From Julius W. Blackwell.*

28 Jan   From Egbert Haywood. ALS. DLC–JKP. Recommends William Conner of Haywood County to be inspector general in the place of John Edwin Taliaferro, resigned.

28 Jan   From Frank McGavock and Joseph B. Southall. LS. T–GP. Request that a reward be offered for the capture of Samuel Earthman, charged with the murder of James McGavock.

28 Jan   From William E. Owen. ALS. DLC–JKP. Recommends William Conner to be inspector general in the place of John Edwin Taliaferro, resigned.

29 Jan   From C. E. McEwen and John Cowles. LS. T–GP. Report on their examination of seven miles of the Franklin & Columbia Turnpike.

[30] Jan   From Julius W. Blackwell. ALS. DLC–JKP. Reports that the firm of Blair & Rives has been elected printers to the U.S. House.

30 Jan   From Harvey M. Watterson. ALS. DLC–JKP. Reports that the firm of Blair & Rives has been elected printers to the U.S. House.

31 Jan   From Hays Blackman et al. LS. T–RG 5. Report on the capitalization of the Nolensville Turnpike Company.

[Feb 1840]   From John F. Gillespy et al. LS. T–GP. Recommend state directors for the Hiwassee Railroad Company.

3 Feb   *From Felix Grundy et al.*

3 Feb   *From Samuel P. Walker.*

4 Feb	*From Alexander O. Anderson.*
4 Feb	*From Aaron V. Brown.*
4 Feb	*To John W. Childress.*
4 Feb	From Moses H. Henry. ALS. T–GP. Requests that a reward be offered for the capture of Richard Gillespie, charged with the murder of Ira Strother.
6 Feb	From A. R. Cartwright. ALS. T–RG 5. Suggests individuals to examine the progress of the Franklin & Columbia Turnpike Company.
6 Feb	To Moses H. Henry. Copy. T–GP. States that he will have to have additional evidence before he can consider offering a reward for Richard Gillespie, charged with murder.
6 Feb	*From Samuel H. Laughlin.*
7 Feb	*To David Hubbard.*
8 Feb [1840]	*From A. O. P. Nicholson.*
9 Feb	*From Felix Grundy.*
10 Feb	*From Alexander O. Anderson.*
10 Feb	From M. D. Thompson et al. LS. T–RG 5. Report progress of the Franklin & Columbia Turnpike Company.
10 Feb	From Archibald Wright. ALS. DLC–JKP. Refuses to be a candidate for presidential elector in Tennessee's Tenth Congressional District and recommends George W. Jones instead.
13 Feb	From Eastin Morris. ALS. T–GP. Discusses appointment of the state's directors to the board of the LaGrange & Memphis Railroad Company.
13 Feb	From Gideon J. Pillow. ALS. T–GP. Requests that $45,000 in state bonds be issued for the benefit of the Columbia Central Turnpike Company.
14 Feb	From Stephen C. Pavatt. ALS. T–GP. Requests appointment as attorney general of the Tenth Judicial District.
14 Feb	From Stephen H. Turner. ALS. T–RG 5. Discusses election of directors of the Nashville & Kentucky Turnpike Company.
15 Feb	To Moses H. Henry. ALS, draft. T–GP. States that he has issued a reward of $200 for the capture of Richard Gillespie.
17 Feb	From Stephen A. Douglas et al. CS. DLC–JKP. Enclose copy of letter by S. Dewitt Bloodgood, who discusses the background of William H. Harrison's recent nomination for president by the Whig party.
18 Feb	From Charles A. Wickliffe. CS. T–GP. Encloses copy of resolutions passed by the General Assembly of Kentucky concerning legislation on public lands.
19 Feb	To James K. Paulding. ALS. T–JPH. Recommends John P. Heiss for appointment of navy purser.
19 Feb	To the President and Directors of the LaGrange & Memphis Railroad Company. ALS, copy. T–GP. Encloses certificate for subscription by the state for 1,250 shares of stock in the company; states that the state will appoint nine directors.
20 Feb	From Richard Hall et al. NS. T–GP. Request that a reward

be offered for Richard M. Hall, charged with the murder of his mother.

20 Feb   To Gideon J. Pillow. ALS, copy. T–GP. Declines to issue $45,000 in state bonds for the benefit of the Columbia Central Turnpike Company.

21 Feb   *From Theophilus Fisk.*

23 Feb   *From David Hubbard.*

24 Feb   From Jacob Critz and Allen Raimey. LS. T–RG 5. Discuss their examination of the Franklin & Columbia Turnpike.

24 Feb   From John F. Gillespy et al. LS. T–GP. Suggest that Polk appoint Adam H. Tenor of Bradley County to replace Avery Hannah of Meigs County as a commissioner in the Ocoee District.

24 Feb   From John W. Goode. ALS. T–RG 5. Discusses appointment of state directors to the Columbia, Pulaski, Elkton, & Alabama Turnpike Company.

24 Feb   *From Cave Johnson.*

24 Feb   From James K. Paulding. LS. DLC–JKP. Also copy in DNA–RG 45. Discusses Polk's previous nominations for appointment as midshipmen in the navy.

24 Feb   From David Wallace. CS. T–GP. Forwards resolution of the General Assembly of Indiana concerning the Northeastern boundary disputes.

[24 Feb 1840]   From John S. Young. ALS. DLC–JKP. Requests return of documents submitted to the legislature on the Bank of Tennessee; states that one of the bank clerks took the reports without authorization.

27 Feb [1840]   *From Cave Johnson.*

27 Feb   From George Talcott. ALS. T–GP. Requests answer to his earlier inquiry regarding arms required for the Tennessee militia.

27 Feb   From Jonas E. Thomas. ALS. DLC–JKP. Offers to go to Nashville and search for the manuscript reports to the Tennessee House from the committees on banking, education, and Robert H. McEwen's defalcation; expresses determination to see that the House Journal and Appendices are properly printed.

28 Feb   To John W. Goode. ALS, copy. T–GP. Sends commissions for Edward D. James and Andrew Gordon to act as commissioners to examine the work of the Columbia, Pulaski, Elkton & Alabama Turnpike Company.

29 Feb   From William Lee. ALS. T–GP. Requests reward be offered for the capture of George Finley, wanted for murder.

29 Feb   From George W. Thompson. ALS. T–RG 5. Discusses Pelham & Jasper Turnpike Company.

[March 1840?]   From Burchett Douglass. ALS. T–GP. Recommends Phineas T. Scruggs for judge of the Eleventh Judicial District.

[March 1840]   From Ephraim W. M. King, Austin Miller et al. NS. T–GP.

	Recommend appointment of William C. Dunlap as judge of the Eleventh Judicial District.
[March 1840?]	From James E. Manford. ALS. T–GP. Recommends Thomas J. Turley to the judgeship of Valentine D. Barry, resigned.
[March 1840?]	From James F. Ruffin et al. LS. T–GP. Recommend Phineas T. Scruggs to succeed Valentine D. Barry as judge of the Eleventh Judicial District.
2 March	*From Alexander O. Anderson.*
2 March	To Henry Brown. Copy. DLC–JKP. Assures Brown that his claim against the estate of Samuel Polk will be honored.
2 March	*From John J. Garner.*
2 March	*From Felix Grundy.*
3 March	From Samuel Mitchell. ALS. DLC–JKP. Regrets that he cannot accept Polk's financial proposition, for there is no available money in Shelbyville.
4 March	*From Andrew Jackson Donelson.*
4 March	From William Fitzgerald. ALS. T–GP. Solicits pardon for Simpson W. Alexander.
4 March	From Jarmon Koonce. ALS. T–RG 30. Discusses commission of George W. Wilkerson as notary public for Fayette County.
5 March	From Valentine D. Barry. ALS. T–GP. Resigns as judge of the Eleventh Judicial District due to inadequate compensation.
5 March	From O. G. Finley. ALS. T–RG 5. Resigns as state director of the Lebanon & Nashville Turnpike Company.
6 March	*From Thomas P. Moore.*
8 March	From J. George Harris. ALS. DLC–JKP. Discusses political activities in the North and recommends William H. Stevens as U.S. attorney for the West Tennessee District.
9 March	*From Alexander O. Anderson.*
9 March	From John W. Coe. ALS. T–GP. Certifies election of justices of the peace in the proposed county of Powell.
9 March	From Solomon Cosslinger. ALS. T–RG 5. Resigns as state director of the Lebanon & Sparta Turnpike Company.
9 March	From Eastin Morris. ALS. T–GP. Asks Polk to suspend any further action in regard to appointing the state's directors of the LaGrange & Memphis Railroad Company until a special committee of the board makes its report on the subject.
10 March	From Jeptha Gardner. ALS. T–GP. Poses legal question regarding the election of the clerk of the county court.
10 March	From John Hearn et al. LS. T–RG 5. Applies for state bonds for the benefit of the Lebanon & Sparta Turnpike Company.
10 March	*From Cave Johnson.*
12 March	*From Cave Johnson.*
14 March	From John Bell. ALS. T–GP. Notifies Polk of the escape of three prisoners from the Coffee County jail.

14 March   From George W. Thompson. ALS. T–RG. Discusses
                  Pelham & Jasper Turnpike Company.
18 March   From Phineas T. Scruggs. ALS. T–GP. Withdraws applica-
                  tion to be judge of the Eleventh Judicial District; recom-
                  mends William C. Dunlap for that post.
18 March   From Levi Woodbury. ALS. T–GP. Requests that Polk in-
                  itiate action to insure payment of interest due on $66,666 of
                  Tennessee state bonds issued on behalf of the Nashville,
                  Murfreesboro & Shelbyville Turnpike Company.
20 March   From James C. O'Reilly. ALS. DLC–JKP. Requests letters
                  of introduction.
21 March   From E. Spriggs. ALS. T–GP. Recommends Adam
                  Huntsman Teaner to be land appraiser for the school sec-
                  tions in Ocoee district.
21 March   From M. D. Thompson et al. LS. T–RG. Report progress of
                  the Franklin & Columbia Turnpike Company.
22 March [1840]   From William C. Campbell. ALS. DLC–JKP. Requests rec-
                  ommendation for appointment to the position of receiver for
                  a public land office in western Missouri.
23 March   From anonymous writer. L, fragment. T–GP. Requests
                  that a reward be offered for the capture of Josiah Massy and
                  John Voils, who are charged with theft.
23 March   *From Levin H. Coe.*
23 March   From Samuel Martin. ALS. DLC–JKP. Urges that the Ten-
                  nessee banks be required to redeem their note issues.
23 March   *From James Walker.*
24 March   From E. N. Drury. ALS. DLC–JKP. Requests Polk's auto-
                  graph.
26 March   From Eastin Morris. ALS. T–GP. Argues that the governor
                  should be allowed to appoint only three additional directors
                  to the board of the LaGrange & Memphis Railroad Company
                  and that these appointees should be stockholders.
26 March   *To Joseph H. Talbot.*
27 March   To Cave Johnson. ALS, draft. DLC–JKP. Discusses vice–
                  presidential question and forthcoming national convention
                  in Baltimore. Polk's AE on the cover indicates that the let-
                  ter was not sent, but was modified and rewritten.
[27] March   *From Williamson Smith.*
27 March   To Levi Woodbury. ALS, copy. T–GP. States that the
                  $1,750 semi-annual interest payment on state bonds, issued
                  in behalf of the Nashville, Murfreesboro & Shelbyville Turn-
                  pike Company, has been paid in specie to the U.S. Treasury
                  account at the Union Bank in Nashville.
28 March   To John Bell. ALS, copy. T–GP. States that additional in-
                  formation about the Coffee County fugitives is required be-
                  fore a reward can be posted.
28 March   To William Fitzgerald. ALS, copy. T–GP. Refuses to par-
                  don Simpson W. Alexander.
28 March   To Richard Hall. ALS, copy. T–GP. Requests additonal in-

formation in the case of Richard M. Hall before deciding if a reward should be posted for his capture.

28 March	From Alexander Johnson et al. LS. T–RG 5. Discuss their examination of the Columbia, Pulaski, Elkton & Alabama Turnpike Company.
29 March	From George C. Hatch. ALS. DLC–JKP. Requests assistance in obtaining the certificate to a land claim that he has purchased.
29 March	From Benjamin F. Weakley. ALS. T–GP. Resigns as director of the Nolensville Turnpike Company.
30 March	To Anderson B. Carr and Buckley Kimbrough. ALS, copy. T–GP. Discusses their request that he demand the return of felons who have fled to Louisiana.
30 March	From Jacob Critz and C. E. McEwen. LS. T–RG 5. Discuss their examination of the Franklin & Columbia Turnpike Company road.
30 March	From Thomas Durham. ALS. DLC–JKP. Requests deed to land he has purchased from Polk, along with a statement that the full price has been paid.
30 March	*To Cave Johnson.*
30 March	To George W. Thompson. ALS, copy. T–GP. Forwards copy of a law relating to internal improvement companies and discusses its applicability to the Pelham & Jasper Turnpike Company.
31 March	From John Fairfield. CS. T–GP. Transmits resolutions adopted by the legislature of Maine regarding the northeastern boundary.
31 March	To George Talcott. ALS, copy. T–GP. Discusses arms allotment for the Tennessee militia.
31 March	From William Wyne et al. LS. DLC–JKP. Invite Polk to attend the anniversary celebration of the Nashville Typographical Society.
[April 1840?]	From John C. Stockton et al. LS. T–GP. Ask for the release of William Clarke from the state penitentiary.
[1] April	From Joseph G. Barclift. ALS. DLC–JKP. Advises that the deed he has received from William H. Polk conveys the wrong piece of land and requests a correction.
1 April	*To Samuel H. Laughlin.*
2 April	*To Samuel H. Laughlin.*
2 April	From John Edwin Taliaferro. ALS. DLC–JKP. Opposes appointment of W. B. Grove, applicant for the position of attorney general in the West Tennessee District.
3 April	From Levin H. Coe. ALS. DLC–JKP. Reports that Phineas T. Scruggs cannot attend the Democratic National Convention in Baltimore.
4 April	*To William R. Rucker.*
5 April	*To David Hubbard.*
6 April	*To Arthur R. Crozier.*
6 April	From John Hearn. ALS. T–RG 5. Discusses appointment of

	commissioners to the Lebanon & Sparta Turnpike Company.
6 April	From R. K. Hicks et al. LS. DLC–JKP. Invite Polk to a public dinner in his honor to be held at Springfield during the month of May.
6 April	From Levi Woodbury. ALS. DLC–JKP. Explains that the draft sent to Joel M. Smith, pension agent at Nashville, was lost in the mails and that another draft has been sent to him.
[7] April	From E. S. Davis. ALS. DLC–JKP. Asks Polk to recommend Grant Stevens for appointment as midshipman in the navy.
7 April	From John Hearn. ALS. T–RG 5. Discusses affairs of the Lebanon & Sparta Turnpike Company.
8 April	From George W. Allen. ALS. DLC–JKP. Advises that he will come to Nashville and arrange the legislative reports and journals for the printers; denies that he is responsible for the publication delays.
8 April	*From Samuel H. Laughlin.*
9 April	*From Daniel Graham.*
9 April	*From Josephus C. Guild.*
9 April	From Elijah W. Headrick. ALS. T–GP. Inquires about commissions for the justices of the peace for the proposed county of Powell.
9 April	To John Hearn. ALS, copy. T–GP. Appoints Thomas Durham to act as a commissioner to examine the Lebanon & Sparta Turnpike.
9 April	*From William H. Polk.*
9 April	From Jonas E. Thomas. ALS. DLC–JKP. Advises of a change in his scheduled arrival date in Nashville, where he will join other delegates with whom he will travel to the Democratic National Convention at Baltimore.
10 April	From William G. Childress. ALS. DLC–JKP. Apologizes for not having returned a book he had borrowed; plans to visit Nashville the following day, if health permits.
10 April	To Joel R. Poinsett. ALS. DNA–RG 99. Recommends A. Harris for appointment of paymaster in the army.
10 April	From William B. Reese and William B. Turley. NS. T–GP. Certify cases in which Turley has recused himself.
10 April	*From William R. Rucker.*
11 April	From George C. Conrad. ALS. DLC–JKP. Invites Polk to a public dinner in his honor to be held at Springfield on May 2, or a subsequent date to be designated by Polk.
13 April	From James H. Reagan. ALS. T–GP. Asks Polk to commission Allen McRoy a captain and Edmond R. Hinley a lieutenant in the Tennessee militia.
14 April	From Alexander O. Anderson. ALS. DLC–JKP. Writes of political maneuvers prior to the Democratic National Convention and Polk's prospects for the vice-presidential nomination.
14 April	*From Alexander O. Anderson.*
14 April	*From M. D. Cooper & Co.*

15 April	*From Felix Grundy.*
15 April	From Asa Young. ALS. DLC–JKP. Explains that he is a former Tennessean now living in Iowa and requests copies of newspapers "or something in the shape of News."
16 April	From H. J. Anderson. ALS. T–GP. Recommends commuting the prison sentence of John Rhea.
16 April	From John W. Goode. ALS. T–RG 5. Discusses issuance of state bonds for the benefit of the Columbia, Pulaski, Elkton & Alabama Turnpike Company.
16 April	To Elijah W. Headrick. ALS, draft. T–GP. Discusses commissions for the justices of the peace elected in the proposed county of Powell.
16 April	To R. K. Hicks et al. ALS, copy. DLC–JKP. Accepts invitation to a public dinner at Springfield on May 2.
17 April	From Sackfield Maclin. ALS. DLC–JKP. Advises that E. S. Davis has agreed to be a delegate to the Democratic National Convention, if his appointment can be approved in time.
18 April	To John W. Goode. ALS, draft. T–GP. Discusses report of the commissioners appointed to examine the Columbia, Pulaski, Elkton & Alabama Turnpike.
18 April	From John Reed. ALS. T–GP. Certifies that William Miller, attorney general of the Tenth Judicial District, resides in Mississippi.
18 April	From Stephen H. Turner. ALS. T–RG 5. Discusses capitalization of the Nashville & Kentucky Turnpike Company.
18 April	From Josiah Watton et al. LS. T–RG 5. Suggest possible commissioners to be appointed to examine the progress of the Nashville & Kentucky Turnpike Company.
20 April	To John Reed. ALS, copy. T–GP. Discusses appointment of an attorney general for the Tenth Judicial District.
21 April	From Aaron V. Brown. ALS. DLC–JKP. Discusses U.S. House proceedings and upcoming national convention at Baltimore.
21 April	From A. R. Cartwright. ALS. T–RG 5. Names directors elected by the stockholders of the Franklin & Columbia Turnpike Company; suggests persons suitable for appointment as state directors.
22 April [1840]	From John W. Childress. ALS. DLC–JKP. Requests that Polk contact Robert M. Burton about arrangements for having his carriage in Nashville on Friday for purposes of making a trade.
23 April	From Nicholas Fain. ALS. DLC–JKP. Sends copy of his nominations for the board of directors of the Bank of Tennessee at Rogersville.
23 April	*From Felix Grundy.*
23 April	From James K. Paulding. Copy. DNA–RG 45. Acknowledges receipt of information pertinent to midshipmen applicants, C. M. Wilcox and S. D. Williams; requests further information regarding character and educational background of Williams.

24 April	To the President and Directors of the Columbia, Pulaski, Elkton & Alabama Turnpike Company. ALS, copy. T–GP. Notifies them that additional state bonds cannot be issued to their company until documents required by law are submitted.
24 April	To the President and Directors of the Franklin & Columbia Turnpike Company. ALS, copy. T–GP. Advises them that their company is entitled to $49,000 in additional state bonds.
24 April	To the President and Directors of the Nolensville Turnpike Company. ALS, copy. T–GP. Advises them that their company is entitled to $14,000 in additional state bonds.
28 April	From Richard Warner. ALS. DLC–JKP. Submits names of persons suggested for the board of directors of the Bank of Tennessee at Shelbyville, and asks Polk's advice.
29 April	From John W. Childress. ALS. DLC–JKP. Has found a buyer for his cotton and wishes to know if Polk has arranged a prior sale.
29 April	*From Samuel H. Laughlin.*
29 April	*From Samuel H. Laughlin.*
29 April	From J. H. J. Wynn. ALS. DLC–JKP. Requests documentation to support the claim by William H. Harrison's opponents that Harrison resigned his commission before the close of the War of 1812.
[May 1840?]	From Abigail Freeland. ANS. T–GP. Asks for a pardon for her son, Joseph Freeland, who was convicted of horse stealing.
2 May	*From Aaron V. Brown.*
2 May	From Oliver Gorman. ALS. DLC–JKP. Advises that Pleasant C. Watson, who is believed to be a fugitive from Tennessee, is living in Washington County, Texas.
2 May	*From Samuel H. Laughlin.*
[3 May 1840]	*From Aaron V. Brown.*
3 May	*From John J. Garner.*
3 May	*From Samuel H. Laughlin.*
3 May	*From A. O. P. Nicholson.*
4 May	From William H. Seward. CS. T–GP. Transmits resolutions on the public lands passed by the New York legislature.
5 May	From Joseph Gibson et al. LS. T–GP. Testify to the character of Abigail Freeland and her son, Joseph.
6 May	*From Pierce B. Anderson.*
6 May	From William C. Hazen. ALS. DLC–JKP. Suggests ways to counter Whig arguments blaming the Democrats for hard times.
6 May	*From Samuel H. Laughlin.*
6 May	From Stokely D. Rowan et al. LS. DLC–JKP. Invite Polk to a public dinner at Beersheba Springs.
7 May	*To Matthew D. Cooper.*
7 May	*From David Hubbard.*
7 May	*From Hopkins L. Turney.*

8 May	*From Aaron V. Brown.*
8 May	To A. R. Cartwright. ALS. T–JKP. Also copy in T–GP. Advises that the stockholders of the Franklin & Columbia Turnpike Company are entitled to elect seven, rather than nine, directors.
8 May	To William Doherty. Copy. T–GP. Discusses bond that must be executed before arms can be issued to the militia company that he commands in Bradley County.
8 May	To R. G. Douglass. ALS, copy. T–GP. Discusses capitalization of the Gallatin & Cumberland Turnpike Company.
8 May	From Boling Gordon. ALS. DLC–JKP. Relates plans for his part in the presidential canvass in Tennessee's Eleventh Congressional District.
8 May	*From Thomas P. Moore.*
8 May	To Eastin Morris. ALS, copy. T–GP. Discusses composition of the board of directors of the LaGrange & Memphis Railroad Company.
9 May	*From Aaron V. Brown.*
9 May	*From Andrew Jackson.*
9 May	From James Whitcomb. LS. DLC–JKP. Reports that he has instructed the land register at Fayetteville, Arkansas, to amend his records as requested in Polk's letter of April 29,1840.
10 May	From Cave Johnson. ALS. DLC–JKP. Suggests that Polk and the *Nashville Union* temporarily refrain from commenting on the proceedings of the Democratic National Convention at Baltimore, or on what course of action Polk might take.
11 May	*From James Walker.*
12 May	*From Erwin J. Frierson.*
14 May	From Daniel S. Donelson et al. LS. T–GP. Discuss attempted rape by Charles, a slave belonging to Priestly Bradford.
14 May	From Sackfield Maclin. ALS. DLC–JKP. Accepts appointment of inspector general of the Tennessee militia.
14 May	From J. G. M. Ramsey et al. LS. DLC–JKP. Invite Polk to a public dinner in Knoxville on July 4.
14 May	*From Hopkins L. Turney.*
14 May	From James Walker. ALS. DLC–JKP. Advises Polk of the death of Andrew C. Hays.
15 May	*From Andrew Jackson.*
15 May	*From A. O. P. Nicholson.*
15 May	*From William Wallace.*
16 May	From William P. Bryan. ALS. T–GP. Certifies that P. F. Foster has organized a volunteer militia company in Nashville.
16 May	From A. H. Judkins. ALS. DLC–JKP. Lists appointments for Boling Gordon in Tennessee's Eleventh Congressional District.
16 May	*From Robert B. Reynolds.*

17 May [1840]	*From West H. Humphreys.*
18 May	To Buckley Kimbrough. ALS, copy. T–GP. Encloses letter addressed to the governor of Louisiana concerning the return of fugitives from justice.
18 May	From William L. Marcy. ALS. DLC–JKP. Introduces Ezekiel Brown and Samuel Brown.
18 May	From A. O. P. Nicholson. ALS. DLC–JKP. Reports presidential campaign activities in Maury County.
18 May	From J. P. H. Porter, Jr. ALS. DLC–JKP. Requests that Polk write a rejoinder to Whig charges and submit it for adoption by the Democrats, who are to convene at Knoxville on July 4.
18 May	From Willford Reynolds. ALS. DLC–JKP. Requests campaign money.
18 May	*From James Walker.*
18 May	From James Walker. ALS. DLC–JKP. Reports that the *Senate Journal* has been completed and discusses related financial affairs.
19 May	From John Hearn. ALS. T–RG 5. Discusses issuance of state bonds for the benefit of the Lebanon & Sparta Turnpike Company.
19 May	From John Webb. ALS. DLC–JKP. Recommends Andrew McClain to be a director of the Shelbyville branch of the Bank of Tennessee.
20 May	From Amos Kendall. ALS. DLC–JKP. Asks Polk to solicit subscriptions to the Washington *Extra Globe.*
21 May	From Hardy M. Cryer et al. LS. DLC–JKP. Advise Polk of housing arrangements made for him during his visit to Gallatin to attend a public dinner.
21 May	From A. H. Judkins. ALS. DLC–JKP. Advises that James C. Jones will speak in Robertson County on June 1 and asks that the Democrats designate someone to speak in rebuttal.
22 May	*From Alexander O. Anderson.*
22 May	To John Hearn. ALS, copy. T–GP. Discusses state bonds for the Lebanon & Sparta Turnpike Company.
22 May	To the President and Directors of the Gallatin & Cumberland Turnpike Company. ALS, copy. T–GP. Agrees to the reduction of the company's capital stock.
23 May	From W. R. Burditt. ALS. DLC–JKP. Discusses persons suggested for the board of directors for the Bank of Tennessee's Shelbyville branch.
23 May	From Boling Gordon. ALS. DLC–JKP. Discusses scheduling of his campaign appointments.
23 May [1840]	*From West H. Humphreys.*
[23 May 1840]	From James Walker. ALS. DLC–JKP. Discusses financial matters related to the printing of the *Senate Journal.*
23 May	From John E. Wheeler. ALS. DLC–JKP. Reports on the presidential canvass in Grainger and Anderson counties.
24 May	*From Cave Johnson.*

24 May	*From Miner K. Kellogg.*
24 May	From Archibald W. O. Totten. ALS. DLC–JKP. Reports on the presidential canvass in the Western District.
25 May	From P. J. R. Edwards and James Walker LS. DLC–JKP. Recommend Joel K. Brown as a director of the Bank of Tennessee's Athens branch.
25 May	From Boling Gordon. ALS. DLC–JKP. Discusses changes in his campaign appointments.
25 May	To James S. W. Hawkins. ALS, copy. T–GP. Discusses issuance of public arms to the cavalry unit under Hawkins' command.
25 May	*From Adam Huntsman.*
25 May	*To Robert B. Reynolds.*
25 May	From Clinton Roosevelt. ALS. DLC–JKP. Reports that rumors in New York City tell of Tennessee's selling state lands at a discount to purchasers who pay their taxes promptly.
25 May	*From James Walker.*
26 May	From Willie B. Johnson. ALS. DLC–JKP. Discusses results of a campaign rally at Clarksville.
26 May	From E. J. Lanier. ALS. DLC–JKP. Requests appointment with Polk.
26 May	*From Ezekiel P. McNeal.*
26 May	*From James Walker.*
27 May	From Henry Brown. ALS. DLC–JKP. Urges response to his claim against the estate of Samuel Polk.
27 May	*To Felix Grundy.*
27 May [1840]	From Cave Johnson. AL, fragment. DLC–JKP. Reports that Samuel P. Walker has been appointed postmaster at Columbia.
27 May	From Thomas J. Matthews et al. LS. DLC–JKP. Urge Polk to include Lawrence County in his canvass.
27 May	From J. G. M. Ramsey. ALS. DLC–JKP. Discusses possible campaign appointments in East Tennessee.
28 May	From Newton Clark. ALS. DLC–JKP. Discusses appointment of directors for the Bank of Tennessee's Shelbyville branch.
28 May	*From William Fitzgerald.*
28 May	From D. C. Humphreys. ALS. DLC–JKP. Requests information on current political topics.
28 May	From Thomas J. Kelly. ALS. DLC–JKP. Invites Polk to address the citizens of Dickson County at Charlotte.
28 May	From James R. McMeans. ALS. DLC–JKP. Discusses candidates for the board of directors for the Bank of Tennessee's Trenton branch.
28 May	*To A. O. P. Nicholson.*
29 May	From Thomas J. Matthews. ALS. DLC–JKP. Invites Polk to a public dinner at Lawrenceburg.
29 May	*From A. O. P. Nicholson.*

29 May	From James Osburn. AL. DLC–JKP. Withdraws recommendation of Thomas Ross to be a director of the Shelbyville branch of the Bank of Tennessee.
30 May	From Levin H. Coe. ALS. DLC–JKP. Quotes at length speech given at Somerville by Pleasant M. Miller in favor of William H. Harrison.
30 May	*From Levin H. Coe.*
30 May	From Samuel Wheatly. ALS. DLC–JKP. Urges Polk to call a special session of the legislature to consider new relief measures.
31 May	From Jeremiah Hall et al. LS. DLC–JKP. Recommend Andrew McClain to be appointed a director of the Shelbyville branch of the Bank of Tennessee.
1 June	From H. J. Anderson. ALS. T–GP. Recommends commuting the prison sentence of Craven C. Butts.
1 June	From Levin H. Coe. ALS. DLC–JKP. Discusses local campaign work.
1 June	*From John J. Garner.*
1 June	*From Felix Grundy.*
1 June	From Samuel Martin. ALS. DLC–JKP. Discusses Polk's campaign tour and asks Polk to speak at Campbell's Station.
1 June	To the President and Directors of the Clarksville & Russellville Turnpike Company. ALS, copy. T–GP. Discusses issuance of state bonds to the company.
1 June	From W. P. Rowles. ALS. DLC–JKP. Asks for extracts of Polk's speech at Gallatin relating to Martin Van Buren's support of the War of 1812; wishes to include the speech in a proposed publication, "Facts for the People."
2 June	From William P. Bryan. ANS. T–GP. Reports that William H. Carroll requests arms for his militia company, the Nashville Blues.
2 June	From Thomas J. Buchanan. ALS. DLC–JKP. Advises that he has sent Polk a copy of the Ohio *Senate Journal* that contains William H. Harrison's "white slavery" votes.
2 June	From Robert P. Harrison. ALS. DLC–JKP. Gives account of a speech by A. O. P. Nicholson at Shelbyville.
2 June	From Robert Mathews. ALS. DLC–JKP. Discusses selection of officers for the Bank of Tennessee at Shelbyville.
[2 June 1840]	From Blake Sageby. ALS. DLC–JKP. Requests appointment as a director for the Bank of Tennessee at Shelbyville.
3 June	*From Levin H. Coe.*
3 June	From Benjamin R. Harris. ALS. DLC–JKP. Recommends Samuel Stockard as director for the Bank of Tennessee at Columbia.
3 June	*From William R. Harris.*
3 June	From Abraham Johnston et al. LS. DLC–JKP. Extends invitation to a public dinner honoring Polk, Andrew Jackson, and William Carroll.
3 June [1840]	*From A. O. P. Nicholson.*
3 June	*From Robert B. Reynolds.*

3 June	From William A. Tennille et al. L. DLC–JKP. Invite Polk to a celebration on July 4 at Milledgeville, Georgia.
4 June	From A. R. Cartwright. ALS. T–RG 5. States that John Miller, one of the state directors of the Franklin & Columbia Turnpike Company, has refused to serve and that another person must be appointed to replace him.
4 June	From Samuel Martin. ALS. DLC–JKP. Asks that Polk speak at Campbell's Station on his way to Knoxville.
5 June	To A. R. Cartwright. ALS, copy. T–GP. Discusses appointment of a state director to the Franklin & Columbia Turnpike Company to replace John Miller.
5 June	From James K. Paulding. Copy. DNA–RG 45. Acknowledges receipt of testimonials in behalf of S. D. Williams; advises that there are at present no vacancies in the corps of midshipmen.
6 June	*From Alexander O. Anderson.*
6 June	From James K. Paulding. Copy. DNA–RG 45. Acknowledges receipt of testimonials in behalf of Charles P. McCrohan; advises that at present there are no vacancies in the corps of midshipmen.
6 June	*To J. G. M. Ramsey et al.*
7 June	*From John J. Garner.*
7 June	From Samuel H. Laughlin. ALS. DLC–JKP. Relates results of campaign rallies at Sparta.
8 June	From Joseph F. Gibson et al. LS. DLC–JKP. Invite Polk to a celebration on June 24 given by Nashville's Cumberland Lodge No. 8 of the Masonic Order.
8 June	From Joel R. Poinsett. Copy. DNA–RG 107. Advises that John Williamson is not entitled to a Revolutionary War bounty claim.
9 June	From Cornelius Connor. ALS. T–GP. Resigns as a director of the Union Bank of Tennessee.
9 June	From Joel Dickinson. ALS. DLC–JKP. Seeks to determine the validity of some figures purporting to have been reported from the Treasury during Polk's tenure as Speaker of the U.S. House.
10 June	From Thomas Glascock. ALS. DLC–JKP. Wishes to know whether Martin Van Buren will carry Tennessee; expresses confidence that Van Buren will have a large majority in Georgia.
10 June	*From J. G. M. Ramsey.*
10 June	From Bromfield L. Ridley. ALS. DLC–JKP. Reports on his trip to East Tennessee and on political maneuverings there.
10 June	From John A. Stemmler. ALS. DLC–JKP. Solicits appointment as bond commissioner for Tennessee in and for the City and State of New York.
11 June	*From Levin H. Coe.*
12 June	*From Henry Trott, Jr.*
12 June	*From William Wallace.*
13 June	*From J. G. M. Ramsey.*

14 June   From Thomas Black. ALS. DLC–JKP. Discusses appointment of directors for the Bank of Tennessee at Shelbyville.

14 June   From Gabriel Blackwell and Joseph Thompson. LS. T–GP. Ask Polk to offer a reward for Zebulon Payne, who murdered and robbed William Coltart.

14 June   From Thomas Ross. ALS. DLC–JKP. Requests that his name be withdrawn from consideration as director of the Bank of Tennessee at Shelbyville; urges that James C. Record be appointed.

14 June   From Charles C. Trabue et al. NS. T–GP. Ask that a large reward be offered for the capture of Zebulon Payne, charged with the murder of William Coltart.

15 June   From James Gamble. ALS. DLC–JKP. Invites Polk to speak at Kingston on July 1.

15 June   From Lewis W. Jordan. ALS. DLC–JKP. Recommends that W. L. McEwen, a moderate Whig from Roane County, be appointed a director of the Athens branch of the Bank of Tennessee.

15 June   *From A. O. P. Nicholson.*

15 June   From James Osburn. ALS. DLC–JKP. Discusses candidates for director to represent Marshall County in the Bank of Tennessee at Shelbyville.

15 June   From Robert B. Reynolds. ALS. DLC–JKP. Urges Polk to speak at Campbell's Station on July 2; discusses preparations for Polk's visit to that area.

15 June   *To Stokely D. Rowan et al.*

16 June   From Samuel Martin. ALS. DLC–JKP. Asks help in pressing war claims in behalf of his father's estate.

17 June   From Thomas J. Caldwell et al. LS. DLC–JKP. Invite Polk to a public dinner at Madisonville.

17 June   From Orvis Nichols. ALS. DLC–JKP. Writes from New York to ask Polk's opinion on whether the Democrats will carry Tennessee in the upcoming election.

17 June   From Porter & Partee. LS. DLC–JKP. Requests information on claim made to the quartermaster general's office in behalf of Andrew Pauley.

17 June   From William T. Willis. ALS. DLC–JKP. Urges that Martin Van Buren's speeches supporting the War of 1812 be published in the *Nashville Union*.

18 June   From Pierce B. Anderson. ALS. DLC–JKP. Discusses candidates for the directorship of the Bank of Tennessee at Athens.

18 June   *To John H. Bills.*

18 June   From James M. Scantland. ALS. DLC–JKP. Solicits aid in obtaining employment.

19 [June]   *From Thomas Von Albade Anderson and Pierce B. Anderson.*

19 June   From Nathaniel Borum. ALS. DLC–JKP. Requests assistance in expediting a pension case on behalf of Ambrose Cayce.

19 June   From William P. Bryan. ALS. T–GP. Reports that a volun-

teer militia company entitled the "Nashville Cadets" has been formed.

19 June   *From Levin H. Coe.*

19 June   To the President and Directors of the Gallatin & Cumberland Turnpike Company. ALS, copy. T–GP. Informs them that their company is entitled to $3,000 in additional state bonds.

19 June   To the President and Directors of the Lebanon & Sparta Turnpike Company. ALS, copy. T–GP. Informs them that additional state bonds cannot be issued to their company until proper documents are received.

19 June   *From Lewis P. Roberts.*

20 June   From N. E. Benson et al. LS. DLC–JKP. Invite Polk to attend a Democratic convention in Montgomery, Alabama, on July 16.

20 June   From Robert B. Currey. ALS. T–GP. Encloses copy of the judge's report in the case of Joseph Freeland and calls attention to some mitigating circumstances in the case.

20 June   To the President and Directors of the Nashville & Kentucky Turnpike Company. ALS, copy. T–GP. Informs them that their company will receive $4,000 in additional state bonds.

20 June   *From James Walker.*

21 June   *From Samuel H. Laughlin.*

21 June   From J. A. Minnis. ALS. DLC–JKP. Writes from Gainesboro concerning political activities there.

22 June   *From Issac Cooper et al.*

22 June   From Henry Liggett et al. LS. DLC–JKP. Invite Polk to speak at Kingston on June 29 or July 1.

22 June   To the President and Directors of the Columbia, Pulaski, Elkton & Alabama Turnpike Company. ALS, copy. T–GP. Informs them that $34,000 in additional state bonds will be issued to their company.

22 [June]   From Samuel P. Walker. ALS. DLC–JKP. Reviews political prospects in Maury County.

23 June   From William R. Burditt. ALS. DLC–JKP. Asks that he be defended against Whig charges that he opposed George Davidson.

23 June   *To Samuel H. Laughlin.*

24 June   To the President and Directors of the Columbia, Pulaski, Elkton & Alabama Turnpike Company. ALS, copy. T–GP. Notifies them that he has issued $34,000 in state bonds for the use of their company.

24 June   To the President and Directors of the Franklin & Columbia Turnpike Company. ALS, copy. T–GP. Informs them that he has issued $49,000 in state bonds for the use of their company.

24 June   To the President and Directors of the Gallatin & Cumberland Turnpike Company. ALS, copy. T–GP. Informs them that he has issued $3,000 in state bonds for the use of their company.

24 June   To the President and Directors of the Nashville & Kentucky

Turnpike Company. ALS, copy. T–GP. Notifies them that $4,000 in state bonds have been issued for the use of their company.

24 June   To the President and Directors of the Nolensville Turnpike Company. ALS, copy. T–GP. Tells them he has issued $14,000 in state bonds for the use of their company.

25 June   From Harrison Locke et al. LS. DLC–JKP. Invite Polk to speak at a public meeting near LaGrange.

[25 June 1840]   From George W. Rice et al. LS. DLC–JKP. Invite Polk to a public dinner at Jasper.

26 June   From Benjamin R. Harris. ALS. DLC–JKP. Recommends Richard H. Allen as director of the Bank of Tennessee at Columbia in place of William Davis.

26 June   *From J. G. M. Ramsey.*

26 June   From Thomas Shirly et al. LS. DLC–JKP. Invite Polk to a public barbecue in Danville on July 11.

27 June   From Gideon J. Pillow. ALS. T–GP. Discusses issuance of $29,000 of additional state bonds for the benefit of the Columbia Central Turnpike Company.

27 June   From J. G. M. Ramsey. ALS. DLC–JKP. Discusses plans for Polk's visit to East Tennessee.

27 June   From Robert B. Reynolds. ALS. DLC–JKP. Advises that he goes to Knoxville to prepare for Polk's reception there; suggests that Polk reach Knoxville on the evening of July 2.

28 June   *From Alexander O. Anderson.*

28 June   From Adam Huntsman. ALS. DLC–JKP. Discusses campaign strategy in Tennessee's Twelfth Congressional District.

28 June   From William Lyon. ALS. DLC–JKP. Invites Polk to stay with him at Union Mills on July 2.

29 June   From John B. Johnson. ALS. DLC–JKP. Requests recommendation in behalf of Marcus L. Pillow, candidate for army captain.

30 June   From John B. Hays. ALS. DLC–JKP. Requests recommendation in behalf of Marcus L. Pillow, candidate for army captain.

30 June   *From Miner K. Kellogg.*

30 June   From J. G. M. Ramsey. ALS. DLC–JKP. Advises that a delegation will meet Polk outside Knoxville on the evening of July 2 and will ride with him into town.

1 July   *From Robert Armstrong.*

1 July   From Jesse Rodgers. ALS. DLC–JKP. Solicits financial assistance.

1 July   From John D. Traynor et al. LS. DLC–JKP. Invite Polk to speak in Bradley County.

2 July   From William Lyon. ALS. DLC–JKP. Invites Polk and his travel companions to stay at his home for the night.

2 July   From Robert McNeilley et al. LS. DLC–JKP. Invite Polk to a public dinner in Dickson County on August 5.

2 July   From E. L. W. Schmidt. ANS. DLC–JKP. Invites Polk to attend a reception in Knoxville.

2 July	From Lewis Shepherd et al. LS. DLC–JKP. Invite Polk to a public dinner at Vanville on July 11.
4 July	From Robert M. Burton. ALS. DLC–JKP. Recommends several men of standing to be directors of the Lebanon & Nashville Turnpike Company.
5 July	*From John J. Garner.*
5 July	*From Samuel H. Laughlin.*
6 July	From Nathan Green and William B. Reese. NS. T–GP. Certify cases in Knoxville in which Reese has recused himself.
6 July	From A. V. S. Lindsley. ALS. T–RG 5. Reports names of the directors elected by the stockholders of the Lebanon & Nashville Turnpike Company.
7 [July]	From J. A. Minnis. ALS. DLC–JKP. Invites Polk to speak at a public dinner honoring Andrew Jackson; states that the celebration will be held in Gainesboro on July 21.
8 July	From Robert A. Dabney. ALS. DLC–JKP. Denounces gag bill and those in power who use force over reason.
8 July	From Jonathan Pope et al. LS. DLC–JKP. Invite Polk to a public dinner in Bledsoe County.
8 July	From Robert Sellers. ALS. DLC–JKP. Suggests that the $200 reward for Charles J. Sowel is insufficient to warrant his apprehension and extradition from Texas to Tennessee; urges Polk to increase the bounty.
9 July	From James L. Minor. ALS. T–GP. Acknowledges receipt of the act of the General Assembly of Tennessee for 1839–40.
11 July	From Simeon Dammeron. ALS. T–GP. Requests pardon for Thomas R. Henson.
11 July	From Alexander Montgomery. ALS. DLC–JKP. Invites Polk to a public dinner in Gainesboro on July 21.
11 July	From William Montgomery. ALS. T–GP. Asks favorable consideration for Joseph Freeland, imprisoned for horse stealing.
11 July	*From Sarah C. Polk.*
12 July	From John C. Haley. ALS. DLC–JKP. Seeks information concerning a state bond that was to be issued to him.
13 July	From Jethro Bass et al. LS. DLC–JKP. Invite Polk to a public dinner in Stewart County.
14 July	From L. Conklin et al. LS. DLC–JKP. Notify Polk of his election as an honorary member of the Union Society of Hamilton College, located in Clinton, New York; request that he signify acceptance by sending his autograph so written that it may be framed.
15 July	From Isaac H. Haley. ALS. DLC–JKP. Explains that he has paid a small debt to Polk through Silas M. Caldwell.
16 July	From Thomas H. Duncan et al. LS. DLC–JKP. Invite Polk to a public dinner in DeKalb County.
17 July	From Alexander Montgomery. ALS. DLC–JKP. Acknowledges receipt of Polk's acceptance to a public dinner in Gainesboro on July 21; expresses hope that Andrew Jackson will attend also.

18 July	*From John H. Bills.*
20 July	From William Fitzgerald et al. LS. DLC–JKP. Invite Polk to a public dinner at Paris on August 27.
21 July	*From Adam Huntsman.*
22 July	From John F. Linton. ALS. DLC–JKP. Encloses letter to Andrew Jackson soliciting financial assistance. (Enclosure not found.)
23 July	*From James Walker.*
23 July	From Henderson K. Yoakum. ALS. DLC–JKP. Reminds Polk of an earlier promise to visit Jefferson.
24 July	*From Samuel H. Laughlin.*
25 July	*From William Fitzgerald.*
25 July	From A. W. O. Totten. ALS. DLC–JKP. Discusses Democratic campaign and urges Polk to accept invitations to speak in Gibson and Dyer counties.
26 July	*From Levin H. Coe.*
27 July	From Jonathan P. Hardwicke. ALS. DLC–JKP. Urges Polk to speak at Charlotte and if possible to have Andrew Jackson and William Carroll present as well.
27 July	To Benjamin I. Hinton. ALS, copy. T–GP. Transmits authorization to receive arms for the Independent Guards of the 91st regiment of Tennessee militia.
27 July	To Ira McKinney. ALS, copy. T–GP. Discusses issuance of arms to the militia company commanded by John Wood.
27 July	*From A. O. P. Nicholson.*
27 July	To John M. Patrick. ALS, copy. T–GP. Discusses disposition of public arms in his possession.
27 July	To Gideon J. Pillow. ALS, copy. T–GP. Discusses issuance of additional state bonds for the benefit of the Columbia Central Turnpike Company.
27 July	From Samuel P. Walker. ALS. DLC–JKP. Asks Polk to recommend Marcus L. Pillow for an army captaincy.
27 July	To Milton Webb. ALS, copy. T–GP. Discusses return of arms issued to the militia company under his command.
28 July	*From A. O. P. Nicholson.*
28 July	To the President and Directors of the LaGrange & Memphis Railroad Company. ALS, copy. T–GP. Denies their request for $50,000 in state bonds.
28 July	From Philander Priestly et al. LS. DLC–JKP. Invite Polk to a public dinner at Clarksville.
28 July	*From Archibald Yell.*
29 July	From John Hearn. ALS. T–RG 5. Discusses commissions for the directors of the Lebanon & Sparta Turnpike Company.
29 July	*From Moses G. Reeves.*
29 July	From David Shaver. ALS. DLC–JKP. Regrets that the arrangements committee for the Knoxville meeting failed to send invitations to the Democratic members of the Tennessee congressional delegation.
29 July	From William Wright. ALS. DLC–JKP. Solicits personal loan.

31 July From William Y. Chapman. ALS. DLC–JKP. Sends political circular and asks its return after Polk has used it in his campaign.

31 July From Jonas E. Thomas. ALS. DLC–JKP. Requests copy of the Ohio *Senate Journal* containing William H. Harrison's votes on the Missouri Compromise.

[Aug 1840] From Frederick Bradford. ALS. T–GP. Requests that a reward be offered for the apprehension of Jacob, a slave accused of murdering Robert Bradford.

[Aug 1840?] From William Griffin et al. LS. T–GP. Request release of James Grooms from the state penitentiary.

[Aug 1840] From James C. Record et al. NS. T–GP. Request that Lewis Parham be excused from paying the bail on Alexander Pruett, who failed to appear in court.

1 Aug *From John J. Garner.*

1 Aug From Thomas Glascock et al. LS. DLC–JKP. Invite Polk to a public dinner at Indian Springs, Georgia.

1 Aug From George W. Jones. ALS. T–GP. Resigns seat in the Tennessee Senate.

[1 Aug 1840] *From George W. Jones.*

[1 Aug 1840] From Thomas Scott et al. LS. DLC–JKP. Invite Polk to a public dinner on September 1 at Samuel Atkinson's place on the Harpeth River.

1 Aug From Richard Sharp, Sr., et al. LS. DLC–JKP. Invite Polk to a public dinner at Winchester.

1 Aug From Robert L. Weakley et al. LS. DLC–JKP. Urge Polk to speak at Jefferson, as soon as convenient.

2 Aug *To Samuel H. Laughlin.*

2 Aug From John H. Thomas. ALS. T–GP. Requests that a reward be offered for Will Bird, charged with the murder of William Carlile.

3 Aug From H. J. Anderson. ALS. T–GP. Recommends commuting the prison sentence of Larkin Tims, alias James Davis.

3 Aug From James Couper. ACS. T–GP. Offers to supply Tennessee with a standard set of weights.

3 Aug From Johoyle Fugate. ALS. T–GP. Certifies that the Claiborne Blues, a volunteer cavalry company in Tennessee's 17th regiment of militia, is fully equipped.

3 Aug *From Samuel H. Laughlin.*

3 Aug To the President and Directors of the Gallatin Turnpike Company. ALS, copy. T–GP. Notifies them that he has issued $11,000 in state bonds for use by their company.

4 Aug From H. Addison, Samuel McKenney, and W. Redin. CS. T–GP. Transmit resolution of the citizens of Georgetown, District of Columbia, asking that their district be retroceded to Maryland.

4 Aug From John H. Bills. ALS. DLC–JKP. Discusses arrangements for placing two persons from Hardeman County in the Tennessee Lunatic Asylum at Nashville.

4 Aug *From Levin H. Coe.*

4 Aug *From Adam Huntsman.*

4 Aug	From William Moore et al. LS. DLC–JKP. Invite Polk to a public dinner at Trenton.
4 Aug	From Henderson K. Yoakum. ALS. DLC–JKP. Requests that someone be designated to speak in Williamson County during his absence; promises to canvass the county fully after his return from East Tennessee.
5 Aug	From William Fitzgerald. ALS. DLC–JKP. Advises that Polk has not acknowledged an invitation to attend a Democratic rally at Paris on August 27; urges Polk to accept the appointment.
5 Aug	*From William S. Haynes.*
5 Aug	From John M. Patrick et al. LS. DLC–JKP. Invite Polk to a public dinner at Cornersville.
5 Aug	From J. C. Spencer. ACS. T–GP. Notifies Polk that three copies of the laws of New York passed at the last session of the legislature have been mailed and asks him to send the laws of Tennessee if he has not already done so.
6 Aug	From H. J. Anderson. ALS. T–GP. Recommends commuting the prison sentence of Thomas Ely.
6 Aug	From Cornelius McLean. CS. T–GP. Notifies Polk that three sets of laws passed in 1839 and one set of the *Maryland Reports* have been mailed.
6 Aug	From George W. Meek. ALS. DLC–JKP. Offers to manage Polk's farm in Yalobusha County, Mississippi, for the coming year.
7 Aug	To H. L. Douglass et al. ALS, copy. T–GP. Grants authorization to use a piece of artillery.
7 Aug	From R. S. Graves et al. LS. DLC–JKP. Invite Polk to a public dinner in Choctaw County, Mississippi.
7 Aug	From Solomon D. Jacobs. ALS. T–GP. Informs Polk that the Hiwassee Railroad Company expects to apply for an additional issuance of state bonds; asks his position on the issuance of such bonds to internal improvement companies.
7 Aug	*From Samuel H. Laughlin.*
7 Aug	From Medicus A. Long. ALS. DLC–JKP. Advises that the proposed public dinner in Bedford County has been postponed until a time shortly before the election.
8 Aug	From John P. Chester. ALS. DLC–JKP. Encloses copy of campaign pamphlet on William H. Harrison's "nine lives."
8 Aug	From Eastin Morris. ALS. T–GP. Tells Polk that the majority of the directors of the LaGrange & Memphis Railroad Company believe that the company is entitled to receive $125,000 in bonds immediately.
9 Aug	*From James M. Howry.*
9 Aug	*To Samuel H. Laughlin.*
10 Aug	From David Craighead. ALS. DLC–JKP. Agrees to attend a meeting of the campaign committee, although his efforts must be occasional.
10 Aug	From David Dobbins et al. LS. DLC–JKP. Invite Polk to a public dinner at Columbia.

10 Aug	From Enoch Ensley. ANS. T–RG 5. Recommends several persons as directors of the Nolensville Turnpike Company.
10 Aug	From Green Pryor. ALS. DLC–JKP. Requests information that might prove useful in his defense in a civil suit arising from a debt for which he was co-signer.
11 Aug	*From Samuel H. Laughlin.*
11 Aug	To the President and Directors of the Clarksville & Russellville Turnpike Company. ALS, copy. T–GP. Notifies them that he has issued $8,000 in state bonds for the use of their company.
12 Aug	From Thomas J. Matthews. ALS. DLC–JKP. Advises that there will be no public dinner in Lawrenceburg, but rather a general meeting at which Polk is urged to speak. ·
12 Aug	From Benjamin Reeves et al. LS. T–GP. Request pardon for Isham Walker of Maury County.
14 Aug	From William Brent, Jr. LS. DLC–JKP. Submits questions dealing with constitutional interpretations; requests that Polk, a possible candidate for national office, answer these questions.
14 Aug	*From Harvey M. Watterson.*
14 Aug	From Cynthia Williams. ALS. T–GP. Asks if Polk received a petition in behalf of Jesse Williams, a prisoner in the state penitentiary.
15 Aug [1840]	From J. Anthony. ALS. DLC–JKP. Asks if moneys owed for land purchases in Missouri may be paid in Nashville.
15 Aug	From William Fitzgerald. ALS. DLC–JKP. Acknowledges receipt of Polk's acceptance to attend a rally at Paris on August 27; wishes to know precisely when he will cross the Tennessee River, so that they may provide an escort into town.
15 Aug	From James Goodner. ALS. T–RG 5. Encloses report by the commissioners appointed to examine the Lebanon & Sparta Turnpike and discusses issuance of state bonds.
15 Aug	*To Samuel H. Laughlin.*
16 Aug	*To Alexander O. Anderson.*
16 Aug	From James Bright et al. LS. DLC–JKP. Invite Polk to a public dinner at Fayetteville.
17 Aug	From John Ashley et al. LS. DLC–JKP. Invite Polk to a public dinner at Talladega, Alabama.
17 Aug	*From Samuel H. Laughlin.*
17 Aug	From E. M. Patterson et al. LS. DLC–JKP. Invite Polk to a public dinner in Davidson County.
17 Aug	From Henry Trott, Jr., et al. LS. DLC–JKP. Invite Polk to a public dinner at Woodbury.
18 Aug	To William Fitzgerald et al. ALS, draft. DLC–JKP. Communicates formal acceptance of their invitation to attend a Democratic festival at Paris on August 27.
18 Aug	From Moses G. Reeves. ALS. DLC–JKP. Discusses campaign strategy in East Tennessee.
19 Aug	From R. H. Campbell and E. H. Lewing. NS. T–GP. Re-

	quest that a reward be offered for the capture of Jacob, a slave accused of murdering his master, Robert Bradford.
19 Aug	From Benjamin Y. Dill et al. LS. DLC–JKP. Invite Polk to a public dinner in Hernando, Mississippi, on October 13.
19 Aug	From Joseph H. Robinson et al. LS. DLC–JKP. Invite Polk to a public dinner at Chapel Hill, Tennessee, on August 29.
19 Aug	*From James Walker.*
20 Aug	From H. J. Anderson. ALS. T–GP. Encloses statement of the judge who presided in the case of James Grooms, convicted of larceny.
20 Aug	*To Robert M. Burton.*
20 Aug	From Adam Huntsman. ALS. DLC–JKP. Discusses his travel itinerary for the coming week.
20 Aug	From Robert L. Weakley et al. LS. DLC–JKP. Invite Polk to a public dinner in Rutherford County.
21 Aug	To Hezekiah Bradbury. ALS, copy. T–GP. Explains proper manner of resigning his command of the 20th brigade in the Tennessee militia.
21 Aug	To John Hearn. ALS, copy. T–GP. Informs him that $31,000 in state bonds will be issued for the benefit of the Lebanon & Sparta Turnpike Company.
21 Aug	To Solomon D. Jacobs. ALS, copy. T–GP. Discusses law regulating the issuance of state bonds to internal improvement companies.
21 Aug	From David B. Molloy. ALS. DLC–JKP. Reiterates invitation to a public dinner in Rutherford County and requests an early response.
21 Aug [1840]	From Lewis P. Roberts. ALS. DLC–JKP. Gives account of a campaign rally that he attended; discusses Democratic prospects in East Tennessee.
21 Aug	From Henderson K. Yoakum. ALS. DLC–JKP. Describes travels in East Tennessee and impression of Democratic prospects in that area.
22 Aug	From James Alexander. ALS. DLC–JKP. Asks Polk to predict what the popular vote for the presidency will be in Tennessee.
22 Aug	From Reddick Dishough. ALS. DLC–JKP. Expresses hope that Polk one day will be elected president.
22 Aug	From Joseph Donohoo. ALS. DLC–JKP. Invites Polk to a dinner at Cleveland.
22 Aug	To Wheeler Jasper. ALS, copy. T–GP. Discusses Zebulon Payne, for whose apprehension Polk has offered a reward.
22 Aug	To L. P. Lines. ALS, copy. T–GP. Discusses case of Zebulon Payne.
22 Aug	From William McNeill. ALS. T–GP. Resigns as director of the Union Bank of Nashville.
22 Aug	From Samuel P. Walker. ALS. DLC–JKP. Reports that the public dinner to be held in Columbia will be a general county

	affair; discusses campaign speeches made in Columbia the previous week.
23 Aug	From Arthur R. Crozier. ALS. DLC–JKP. Gives impressions of Democratic prospects in various parts of East Tennessee; urges Felix Grundy's visit to several counties.
23 Aug	From J. D. Traynor. ALS. T–GP. Discusses murder of A. J. Hodge by Calvin Wrinkle.
24 Aug	*From Pierce B. Anderson.*
24 Aug	From Cyrus Barton et al. L. DLC–JKP. Invite Polk to a meeting in Concord, New Hampshire, celebrating the passage of the Independent Treasury bill.
24 Aug	From John Crawford et al. LS. DLC–JKP. Invite Polk to a public dinner at Athens.
24 Aug	From Barkly Martin. ALS. DLC–JKP. Says that family commitments prevent his leaving home to campaign in other counties.
24 Aug	To Eastin Morris. ALS, copy. T–GP. Refuses to issue state bonds for the benefit of the LaGrange & Memphis Railroad Company until all provisions of the law have been met.
24 Aug	*From William H. Polk.*
26 Aug	From Jessey B. Gant et al. LS. DLC–JKP. Invite Polk to speak at Savannah, Tennessee.
26 Aug	From Francis Markoe, Jr. LS. DLC–JKP. Advises Polk of his election as a corresponding member of the National Institution for the Promotion of Science.
26 Aug	From John Norvell et al. L. DLC–JKP. Invite Polk to a dinner to be held on September 28 in Detroit, Michigan, in honor of Richard M. Johnson.
26 Aug	*From Robert B. Reynolds.*
26 Aug	From S. Stafford et al. LS. DLC–JKP. Invite Polk to a public dinner in Vicksburg, Mississippi, on September 29.
27 Aug	From A. O. P. Nicholson. AL, fragment. DLC–JKP. Gives details of his campaign tour with Andrew Johnson through East Tennessee.
27 Aug	From John M. Patrick. ALS. DLC–JKP. Acknowledges receipt of Polk's acceptance of the invitation to speak at Cornersville on September 7; urges him to bring Felix Grundy also.
27 Aug	*From Edwin Polk.*
27 Aug	From Henderson K. Yoakum. ALS. DLC–JKP. Gives account of the meeting in Tazewell on this date when he and John Bell were the speakers.
28 Aug	From James Bright. ALS. DLC–JKP. Acknowledges Polk's acceptance of an invitation to visit Fayetteville; suggests September 25 as a desirable date.
28 Aug	From Enoch P. Connell. ALS. T–RG 5. Recommends several persons for state-appointed directors of the Nashville & Kentucky Turnpike Company.

28 Aug   From Andrew A. Kincannon. ALS. DLC–JKP. Expresses concern that Tennessee may vote Whig in the coming election; asks Polk's opinion on the subject.

28 Aug   From James Park et al. LS. DLC–JKP. Invite Polk to a public dinner in Franklin on September 12.

29 Aug   From Grant Allen et al. LS. DLC–JKP. Invite Polk to a public dinner at Dixon's Springs in Smith County.

29 Aug   From H. J. Anderson. ALS. T–GP. Recommends commuting the prison sentence of Joseph Hullett.

29 Aug   From James Bright et al. LS. DLC–JKP. Acknowledge receipt of Polk's acceptance to attend a public dinner in Fayetteville; suggest September 26 as a suitable date.

29 Aug   From A. T. Moore et al. LS. DLC–JKP. Invite Polk to a public dinner in Canton, Mississippi, on September 30.

29 Aug   From John M. Patrick et al. LS. DLC–JKP. Advise that the barbecue planned for September 7 has been canceled, but that the public speaking will be held as scheduled.

29 Aug   From William H. Polk. ALS. DLC–JKP. Advises that the Cornersville appointment will be held as scheduled.

30 Aug   From A. W. O. Totten. ALS. DLC–JKP. Advises that illness has forced him to interrupt his campaigning.

30 Aug   From John S. Young. ALS. DLC–JKP. Discusses problems arising in the distribution of copies of the acts and journals of the last session of the Tennessee General Assembly.

31 Aug   From Francis Duffy. ALS. DLC–JKP. Asks Polk to assist Robert Armstrong in making arrangements to visit Hartsville.

31 Aug   *From Albert T. McNeal.*

31 Aug   From Ezekiel P. McNeal. ALS. DLC–JKP. Urges that Felix Grundy be detailed to campaign in the Western District, where he enjoys his greatest measure of popularity.

31 Aug   To Eastin Morris. ALS, copy. T–GP. Refuses application for the issuance of state bonds for the benefit of the LaGrange & Memphis Railroad Company.

31 Aug   *To Thomas Scott et al.*

31 Aug   *From Samuel P. Walker.*

31 Aug   From Prosper M. Wetmore et al. L. DLC–JKP. Invite Polk to speak at a convention in Poughkeepsie, New York, on September 16; explains that the meeting will celebrate passage of the Independent Treasury bill.

1 Sept   *From Arthur P. Bagby.*

1 Sept   From Levin H. Coe. ALS. DLC–JKP. Advises that family illness has prevented his keeping some of his campaign appointments; requests journals of the last four sessions of Congress.

1 Sept   From L. Devault et al. L. DLC–JKP. Invite Polk to a celebration in Lafayette, Indiana, on October 5; explain that they wish to commemorate the Battle of the Thames and to honor Richard M. Johnson.

1 Sept	From Benjamin Gambell et al. LS. DLC–JKP. Invite Polk to a public dinner at Shelbyville.
1 Sept	From John Sharp. ALS. DLC–JKP. Requests that Polk explain to the pension agent that illness has prevented his coming to Nashville to collect his pension.
1 Sept	From Larkin Stowe et al. L. DLC–JKP. Invite Polk to a celebration at Lincolnton, North Carolina, on October 7; explain that they wish to commemorate the Battle of King's Mountain.
2 Sept	From John M. Bass. ALS. DLC–JKP. Submits list of all of Polk's notes held by the Union Bank of Nashville.
2 Sept	From William C. Demoss et al. L. DLC–JKP. Invite Polk to a public dinner in Hinds County, Mississippi, on September 24.
2 Sept	From Cave Johnson. ALS. DLC–JKP. Suggests October 3 as a good date for speaking in Clarksville; urges a prompt reply; and expresses concern that his illness will prevent him from being an effective campaigner.
2 Sept	From A. Kennedy. ALS. DLC–JKP. Requests that Polk stay in Spring Hill on his way to Columbia.
4 Sept	From William Lamb. ALS. DLC–JKP. Urges Polk to stop the rumor that he has conceded Tennessee to the Whigs in the coming election.
4 Sept	From Joseph H. Talbot et al. LS. DLC–JKP. Invite Polk to a public dinner honoring Andrew Jackson, to be held in Jackson, Tennessee, on October 8.
5 Sept	From Samuel H. Laughlin. ALS. DLC–JKP. Gives account of his campaigning in Haywood County; expresses confidence that the county will be carried by the Democrats.
5 Sept	From Thomas R. Richardson et al. LS. DLC–JKP. Extends invitation from the Whigs of Rutherford County to attend a public dinner at Jefferson on September 16.
7 Sept	*From Robert M. Burton.*
9 Sept	From Pierce B. Anderson et al. LS. DLC–JKP. Renew invitation to a public dinner in McMinn County.
10 Sept	From A. M. Caldwell et al. LS. DLC–JKP. Invite Polk to a public dinner in Carroll County on October 3.
10 Sept	From John Forsyth. CS. T–GP. Advises that 468 copies of the *Acts of Congress* of the First Session of the Twenty-sixth Congress are being sent to Tennessee.
10 Sept	From William D. Mitchell et al. LS. DLC–JKP. Invite Polk to a celebration commemorating the Battle of the Thames; states that the festival is to be held on October 5 in Oldham County, Kentucky.
10 Sept	From L. R. Stewart et al. LS. DLC–JKP. Invite Polk to a celebration in Grenada, Mississippi, on October 5, commemorating the Battle of the Thames.
11 Sept	From Samuel Anderson. ALS. T–GP. Reports illness and asks that Edwin A. Keeble take his place until he recovers.

12 Sept	From David Burford et al. LS. DLC–JKP. Invite Polk to a public dinner in Hartsville honoring Felix Grundy.
[12 Sept 1840]	From Francis Duffy. ALS. DLC–JKP. Discusses preparations surrounding the proposed dinner to be given in Hartsville.
12 Sept	From William C. Dunlap. ALS. T–GP. Advises Polk that due to physical disability he will be unable to hold the upcoming courts in the Eleventh Judicial District and suggests appointment of a special judge to take his place.
12 Sept	*From Samuel Wallace.*
13 Sept	From Francis R. Shunk. CS. T–GP. States that he has sent Polk three copies of the laws passed by the Pennsylvania General Assembly during 1840.
14 Sept	From H. J. Anderson. ALS. T–GP. Recommends commuting the prison sentence of Jonas Brown.
14 Sept	From John Blair et al. LS. DLC–JKP. Invite Polk to a public dinner at Jonesboro.
14 Sept	From William J. Brown et al. L. DLC–JKP. Invite Polk to a meeting in Indianapolis, Indiana, on October 14, honoring Richard M. Johnson.
14 Sept	*To C. W. Nance et al.*
15 Sept	From James Land. ALS. DLC–JKP. Urges denial of a petition requesting that Edward Land be released from the penitentiary.
15 Sept	From Austin Miller et al. LS. T–GP. Recommend Sylvester Baily to fill the office of special judge in the Eleventh Judicial District.
15 Sept	From J. M. Withers et al. L. DLC–JKP. Invite Polk to a state convention in Tuscaloosa, Alabama.
16 Sept	*From Alexander O. Anderson.*
17 Sept	From Joel R. Poinsett. ALS. DLC–JKP. Expresses hope that Polk will accept the appointment of corresponding member of the National Institution for the Promotion of Science and will provide copies of reports on Tennessee agriculture and science, together with "any specimens of Natural History that can be spared."
[17 Sept 1840]	From Hampton C. Williams. ALS. DLC–JKP. Asks Polk to send copies of several publications to the National Institution for the Promotion of Science; requests for his own use for a short time a copy of Matthew S. Dixon's paper, which was given "before the Medical Society at Nashville upon the Milk sickness."
18 Sept	From Samuel Anderson. ALS. DLC–JKP. Advises that illness prevents his holding court in Cannon and Wilson counties; requests that Edwin A. Keeble be commissioned in his place.
18 Sept	To William Conner. Copy. T–GP. Discusses application for state bonds to benefit the Ashport Turnpike Company.
18 Sept	From William M. S. Ridley. ALS. DLC–JKP. Requests letter of recommendation for an appointment in the navy.

19 Sept	From William M. S. Ridley. ALS. DLC–JKP. Requests letter of recommendation for an appointment in the navy and urges that the letter be written immediately.
19 Sept	From Samuel R. Rucker. ALS. DLC–JKP. Wishes to know if Polk could arrange to attend a public dinner in Murfreesboro in late October.
20 Sept	From W. Jones. ACS. T–GP. Asks Polk to communicate to the Tennessee legislature a remonstrance against the exercise of power by the present Congress over the District of Columbia.
23 Sept	From C. A. Bradford. ALS. DLC–JKP. Invites Polk to a public dinner in Pontotoc County, Mississippi, on October 9.
23 Sept	From David B. Molloy. ALS. DLC–JKP. Requests that Robert A. Lawing, rather than John Jones, be appointed as a director of the Cumberland & Stones River Turnpike Company.
24 Sept	From William Moore et al. LS. DLC–JKP. Invite Polk to a public dinner in Trenton.
25 Sept	From Robert Weakley et al. L. DLC–JKP. Invite Polk to a public dinner at the Island Spring near Nashville on September 30.
26 Sept	From P. W. Davis et al. LS. DLC–JKP. Extend invitation from the Whigs of Sumner County to a public dinner on October 13.
28 Sept	From H. J. Anderson. ALS. T–GP. Recommends commuting the prison sentence of William P. Jacobs.
28 Sept	From James C. Labreskie. ALS. DLC–JKP. Expresses confidence that New Jersey will vote Democratic; wishes to know about the party's prospects in Tennessee.
28 Sept	From Wesley W. Pepper et al. LS. DLC–JKP. Extend invitation from the Whigs of Robertson County to a public dinner in Springfield on October 16.
28 Sept	From Joseph Philips et al. LS. DLC–JKP. Invite Polk to a public dinner in Rutherford County on October 23.
29 Sept	*From Alexander O. Anderson.*
29 Sept	From J. A. Battle et al. LS. DLC–JKP. Extend invitation from the Whigs of Davidson County to a public dinner on October 10.
[Oct 1840?]	From Williamson Bonner. LS. T–GP. Requests release from the penitentiary of William L. James, convicted of grand larceny in Shelby County.
[Oct 1840?]	From William C. Douglass et al. LS. T–GP. Request pardon for William Summerville.
[Oct. 1840]	From J. H. Drake et al. LS. T–GP. Request pardon for William Summerville.
[Oct 1840]	From John J. Potts et al. LS. T–GP. Request pardon for Thomas Wilson, convicted of larceny and sentenced to the penitentiary.
1 Oct	*From Nicholas Fain.*
1 Oct	From Joseph Herndon. ALS. DLC–JKP. Advises that John

	H. Dew is attending court at Lebanon and cannot at this time accept the appointment of special judge.
1 Oct	From Joel L. Jones et al. LS. DLC–JKP. Invite Polk to a public dinner at Somerville on October 14.
2 Oct	From John H. Dew. ALS. DLC–JKP. Resigns as special judge for Wayne and Lawrence counties.
2 Oct	*To Seth M. Gates.*
2 Oct	From John Hearn. ALS. T–RG 5. Requests appointment of commissioners to examine the progress of the Lebanon & Sparta Turnpike Company pursuant to obtaining state bonds.
2 Oct	*To Samuel H. Laughlin.*
2 Oct	From Robert J. Nelson. ALS. DLC–JKP. Wishes to know Polk's opinion as to the outcome of the presidential election.
2 Oct	*From Hopkins L. Turney.*
3 Oct	From Mrs. George B. Coleman et al. LS. DLC–JKP. Invite Polk to a public supper at Brownsville on October 10.
3 Oct	From Charles Harrington et al. LS. DLC–JKP. Invite Polk to a celebration in Evansville, Indiana, on October 28, honoring Richard M. Johnson.
4 Oct	From Joseph G. Barclift. ALS. DLC–JKP. Seeks to obtain a correction of an error in the deed to his land.
4 Oct	From Logan D. Brandon. ALS. DLC–JKP. Wishes to know if Democrats will carry Tennessee in the coming presidential election.
4 Oct	*From John J. Garner.*
5 Oct	From John H. Dew. ALS. DLC–JKP. Accepts appointment as special judge to hold the court at Lawrenceburg on the second Monday in October.
6 Oct	From H. S. Garland et al. LS. DLC–JKP. Acknowledge Polk's acceptance of an invitation to a public dinner at Clarksville.
7 Oct	From Timothy Childs. ALS. DLC–JKP. Introduces James G. Shephard.
7 Oct	From Edwin A. Keeble. ALS. T–GP. Recommends pardon for William Summerville.
7 Oct	From Henry Trott, Jr. ALS. DLC–JKP. Advises that the public dinner in Woodbury has been canceled.
7 Oct	From Thomas C. Whiteside et al. LS. T–GP. Request a pardon for William Summerville.
[8 Oct 1840]	From William M. Dunaway. ALS. DLC–JKP. Wishes to hire Harry for the following year.
8 Oct	From William H. Wood et al. LS. DLC–JKP. Invite Polk to a public dinner at Bolivar on October 15.
9 Oct	From Wesley Nixon. ALS. DLC–JKP. Writes from Mount Pleasant that "expectation is on tiptoe, to See, & greet, our 'Old Hero' and your Self."
9 Oct	From Wesley Nixon et al. LS. DLC–JKP. Invite Polk to a public dinner at Mount Pleasant on October 14.
9 Oct	From R. V. Thorne et al. L. DLC–JKP. Invite Polk to a

celebration in Brooklyn, New York, commemorating the surrender of the British at Yorktown.

11 Oct — *From John S. Young.*

12 Oct — From Alexander O. Anderson. ALS. DLC–JKP. Introduces James A. Lyon, a Presbyterian minister.

12 Oct — *From Alexander O. Anderson.*

12 Oct — From Cave Johnson. ALS. DLC–JKP. Advises that the people at Clarksville have changed the day of the dinner to Tuesday the 20th, "because the 19th would have produced the necessity of cooking on the Sabbath."

12 Oct — From Hugh Kirk et al. LS. DLC–JKP. Extends invitation from the Whigs to attend a public dinner in Murfreesboro on October 21.

13 Oct — From William Wallace. ALS. T–GP. Asks for the release of Thomas Davis from the penitentiary.

13 Oct — From William Williams et al. LS. DLC–JKP. Invite Polk to a public barbecue at Cainesville in Wilson County.

14 Oct — From H. J. Anderson. ALS. T–GP. Recommends commuting the prison sentence of Allen Jarnagin.

15 Oct — From Lunsford M. Bramlett. ALS. T–GP. Requests release of Joseph P. Eliff, convicted of carrying a bowie knife.

15 Oct — From Robert Farquharson. ALS. T–GP. Asks Polk to remit the fine paid by William Moffett and to release him from confinement.

16 Oct — From James Rose. ALS. T–GP. Transmits statement of the affairs of the Southwestern Railroad Bank, including its branch in Tennessee.

17 Oct — To Arthur P. Bagby. Copy. T–GP. Advises that Daniel Young of Nashville, accused of slave stealing in Alabama, will be released to that state's agent as soon as a certified copy of John B. Morrow's affidavit of complaint is received; explains that he cannot act on the basis of the uncertified copy accompanying Bagby's request.

17 Oct — From Robert M. Burton. ALS. DLC–JKP. Invites Polk to a public meeting at Silver Springs on October 24.

17 Oct — To Buckley Kimbrough. Copy. T–GP. Discusses the case of two men detained in Louisiana for slave stealing in Shelby County.

17 Oct — To Eastin Morris. Copy. T–GP. Discusses issuance of state bonds for the benefit of the LaGrange & Memphis Railroad Company.

17 Oct — From Isaac Roberson. ALS. T–GP. Certifies election of officers for the 36th regiment of Tennessee militia; requests that their commissions be sent to him.

19 Oct — From Rolla P. Raines. ALS. T–GP. Urges that Wiley Melton be pardoned.

19 Oct — From Henderson K. Yoakum. ALS. DLC–JKP. Advises that he will "have arrangements made in due order for the affair at Millersburg"; complains that Whig propaganda is discouraging Democrats in Murfreesboro.

20 Oct	From Grant Allen et al. LS. DLC–JKP. Invite Polk to a public dinner in Smith County on October 31.
20 Oct	From Silas M. Caldwell. ALS. DLC–JKP. Advises that Polk's slave, Henry, has surrendered himself to Caldwell, saying that he ran away because the overseer threatened to shoot him; says that he will retain Henry and await instructions from Polk.
20 Oct	From Robert Farquharson and James Fulton. LS. T–GP. Discuss the case of William Moffett.
20 Oct	From Josephus C. Guild. ALS. DLC–JKP. Reports on preparations for the Smith County meeting on the Saturday before the election.
20 Oct	From R. L. Mason et al. LS. DLC–JKP. Invite Polk to a public dinner at Silver Springs in Wilson County "on Saturday next."
20 Oct	From J. G. M. Ramsey. ALS. DLC–JKP. Urges Polk to give a proxy commission to someone to represent the state at the annual meeting of the stockholders of the Louisville, Cincinnati and Charleston Railroad Company.
21 Oct	From I. A. Duncan. ALS. DLC–JKP. Urges Polk to accept an invitation to a public dinner at Spring Hill on October 29.
21 Oct	From William Estill. ALS. DLC–JKP. Advises that Democratic friends have designated Winchester "as the most advisable place for your appointment for Monday next, and have sent . . . printed notices of it."
21 Oct	From A. V. S. Lindsley. ALS. T–GP. Encloses petition and adds his endorsement of same. (Enclosure not found.).
21 Oct	From William S. Watterson. ALS. DLC–JKP. Recommends Erwin J. Frierson of Shelbyville to be judge for Tennessee's Fifth Judicial District.
22 Oct	From Levin H. Coe. ALS. T–GP. Writes in behalf of Thomas Wilson, sentenced to the penitentiary for horse stealing.
22 Oct	*To Boling Gordon.*
22 Oct	From A. W. Potter et al. LS. DLC–JKP. Invite Polk to a public barbecue at Spring Hill on October 29.
22 Oct	*From Robert B. Reynolds.*
23 Oct	From Thomas W. Gilmer. ACS. T–GP. Transmits preamble and resolutions adopted by the General Assembly of Virginia regarding demands made upon the governor of New York to surrender certain fugitives from justice.
24 Oct	From Aaron V. Brown. ALS. T–GP. Vouches for the good character of Joseph P. Eliff, convicted of carrying a bowie knife.
24 Oct	From Eastin Morris et al. LS. T–GP. Request that additional state bonds totaling $18,750 be issued for the benefit of the LaGrange & Memphis Railroad Company.
24 Oct	From Gideon J. Pillow. ALS. T–GP. Requests appointment of three commissioners to examine the progress of the Columbia Central Turnpike Company.

25 Oct	From Robert M. Burton. ALS. DLC–JKP. Advises that he has accepted for Polk an invitation to a public dinner in Wilson County on October 30; discusses arrangements for the meeting.
25 Oct	From Armistead Moore et al. LS. DLC–JKP. Invite Polk to a public dinner at Big Spring in Wilson County on October 30.
26 Oct	From T. A. Campbell. ALS. DLC–JKP. Requests loan to enable him to complete his studies at East Tennessee University.
27 Oct	From Ephraim D. Dickson. ALS. DLC–JKP. Asks Polk to recommend him to the secretary of war for the appointment of public storekeeper at Fayetteville, Arkansas.
27 Oct	From James L. Garrett. ALS. T–GP. Discusses character of Joseph P. Eliff.
27 Oct	*From J. G. M. Ramsey.*
27 Oct	*From John S. Young.*
28 Oct	From Robert M. Burton. ALS. DLC–JKP. Asks Polk to meet him and Andrew Jackson at Burton's house on the following evening; together they will go to the dinner at Big Spring on Friday.
29 Oct	*From John S. Young.*
30 Oct	From Edward S. Walton. ALS. DLC–JKP. Introduces A. Bradly.
[Nov 1840]	From William L. Williamson et al. LS. T–GP. Request release of John Busby.
1 Nov	*From John J. Garner.*
1 Nov	From R. L. W. Hogg. ALS. DLC–JKP. Solicits appointment as messenger to carry Tennessee's electoral votes to Washington City.
3 Nov	From Howell Taylor. ALS. DLC–JKP. Encloses report of commissioners and requests payment for services. (Enclosure not found.)
4 Nov	From William Estill. ALS. DLC–JKP. Reports that the Whigs have gained ground in Manchester and that from 75 to 100 Democrats were absent from Franklin County.
4 Nov	From William Gammon. ALS. DLC–JKP. Reports that Sullivan County has supported Martin Van Buren 1,386 to 327 for William H. Harrison.
4 Nov	From J. T. Leath. ALS. T–GP. Authorizes Polk to initiate action to release from prison in New Orleans two prisoners.
4 Nov	*From Samuel P. Walker.*
4 Nov	From John S. Young. ALS. DLC–JKP. Reports that the Cannon County civil districts formerly a part of Warren County have given Martin Van Buren a majority of 250 votes.
5 Nov	From John Kennedy. ALS. DLC–JKP. Reports that Polk County has given Martin Van Buren a 150-vote majority.
5 Nov	To the President and Directors of the LaGrange & Memphis Railroad Company. ALS, copy. T–GP. Notifies them that

	$18,750 in state bonds have been issued for the benefit of their company.
5 Nov	To R. P. Raines. ALS, copy. T–GP. Discusses petition for the pardon of Wiley Melton.
5 Nov	To John W. Richardson et al. ALS, copy. T–GP. Discusses appointment of commissioners to examine the Jefferson Turnpike.
5 Nov	From John S. Young. ALS. DLC–JKP. Reports that Warren County has given Martin Van Buren a majority of 1,419 votes; observes that Van Buren's majority is 296 votes less than that received by Polk in 1839; and adds that the Whigs have reduced the 1839 electoral majority in White County by 270 votes.
6 Nov	*From A. O. P. Nicholson.*
6 Nov	*From Robert B. Reynolds.*
6 Nov	*From Samuel P. Walker.*
7 Nov	From anonymous writer. L. DLC–JKP. Boasts of Whig victory in presidential election.
7 Nov	*To David Burford.*
7 Nov	*To George W. Jones.*
7 Nov	*To A. O. P. Nicholson.*
8 Nov	*From Miner K. Kellogg.*
8 Nov	*From David Lynch.*
8 Nov	*To A. O. P. Nicholson.*
8 Nov	From Henderson K. Yoakum. ALS. DLC–JKP. Observes that Whig election tactics could not have been counteracted without adopting a similar system, which must in time fall from the weight of having promised too much.
9 Nov	From Isaac Golladay. ALS. DLC–JKP. Expresses great disappointment in the election defeat.
9 Nov	From Edwin A. Keeble. ALS. DLC–JKP. Attributes Whig victory to superior organization and describes plans to prepare Rutherford County for the 1841 election contest.
10 Nov	From Silas H. Jenison. LS. T–GP. Forwards copies of resolutions by the Vermont legislature, which favors restricting presidents to a single term.
10 Nov	From John Pearce, Jr. ALS. DLC–JKP. Explains that the delay in shipping Polk's mill was caused by the low water level of the Ohio River.
10 Nov	To the President and Directors of the Ashport Turnpike Company. ALS, copy. T–GP. Informs them that he has issued $20,000 in state bonds for the benefit of their company.
10 Nov	To Howell Taylor. ALS, copy. T–GP. Discusses Taylor's examination of the Ashport Turnpike.
11 Nov	From James Goodner. ALS. T–RG 5. Encloses report of the commissioners appointed to examine the Lebanon & Sparta Turnpike.
11 Nov	To Buckley Kimbrough. ALS, copy. T–GP. Discusses case

	of two fugitives from justice detained in a prison at New Orleans.
11 Nov	To J. T. Leath. ALS, copy. T–GP. Discusses case of two fugitives from justice confined in a prison at New Orleans.
11 Nov	From J. W. Norris. ALS. DLC–JKP. Reports voting frauds by Hardeman County Whigs and attributes Democratic defeat to hard times and Whig promises of economic recovery.
11 Nov	From Robert Wilson et al. LS. T–RG 5. Report upon their examination of the Columbia Central Turnpike.
12 Nov	From Thomas W. Gilmer. CS. T–GP. Discusses refusal of the governor of New York to surrender fugitives from justice to Virginia.
12 Nov	From Gideon J. Pillow. ALS. T–GP. Transmits report of the commissioners appointed to examine ten miles of the Columbia Central Turnpike.
12 Nov	*From Hopkins L. Turney.*
13 Nov	From Thomas Boyd. ALS. DLC–JKP. Solicits support for starting a newspaper in Charlotte, North Carolina; observes need to counteract Whig influence on the younger generation of voters.
13 Nov	*From Archibald Wright.*
14 Nov	*From David Burford.*
14 Nov	To James Goodner. ALS, copy. T–GP. Discusses the report of the commissioners appointed to examine the work performed on the Lebanon & Sparta Turnpike.
14 Nov	*From Harvey M. Watterson.*
15 Nov	From John W. Childress. ALS. DLC–JKP. Recommends Greenville T. Henderson, a Democrat, to be postmaster of Murfreesboro.
15 Nov	*From A. O. P. Nicholson.*
15 Nov	From J. W. Thompson. ALS. DLC–JKP. Reports election defeat of Shelbyville Democrats and requests information on state-wide returns.
15 Nov	*From Richard Warner.*
15 Nov	From Henderson K. Yoakum. ALS. DLC–JKP. Recommends Greenville T. Henderson to be postmaster of Murfreesboro.
16 Nov	*From Boling Gordon.*
17 Nov	*From Samuel H. Laughlin.*
17 Nov	From William A. Maxwell. ALS. DLC–JKP. Requests information on the administration of Jacob Fous' estate.
18 Nov	From anonymous writer. L. DLC–JKP. Boasts of Whig election victory.
18 Nov	To A. R. Cartwright. ALS, copy. T–GP. Encloses commissions for two state directors for the Franklin & Columbia Turnpike Company.
18 Nov	*To Robert B. Reynolds.*
19 Nov	To the President and Directors of the Clarksville & Russellville Turnpike Company. ALS, copy. T–GP. Informs them

that $10,000 in state bonds have been issued for the benefit of their company.

20 Nov — From James Goodner. ALS. T–RG 5. Discusses report of the commissioners appointed to examine the Lebanon & Sparta Turnpike Company.

20 Nov — To William W. Lea. Copy. T–GP. Discusses appointment of commissioners to examine the progress of the Fulton Turnpike Company.

20 Nov — *From William H. Polk and Samuel P. Walker.*

20 Nov — To the President and Directors of the Fulton Turnpike Company. Copy. T–GP. Forwards commissions for state directors of their company.

22 Nov — *From Samuel H. Laughlin.*

23 Nov — From Medicus A. Long. ALS. DLC–JKP. Reviews Bedford county politics.

24 Nov — From anonymous writer. L. DLC–JKP. Berates Polk's partisan dogmatism.

27 Nov — From John W. Goode. ALS. T–RG 5. Requests appointment of commissioners to examine the progress of the Columbia, Pulaski, Elkton & Alabama Turnpike Company.

28 Nov — From John Harwell. ANS. T–GP. Certifies capture of George W. Rogers and Russell Rogers, for whom a reward had been offered.

29 Nov — From Reuben Smith. ALS. T–RG 5. Declines to serve as a state director for the Franklin & Columbia Turnpike Company.

30 Nov — *From Alexander O. Anderson.*

30 Nov — To A. M. Ballentine. ALS, copy. T–GP. Discusses election of directors of the Columbia, Pulaski, Elkton & Alabama Turnpike Company.

30 Nov — To William Conner. ALS, copy. T–GP. Discusses election of directors of the Ashport Turnpike Company.

30 Nov — To Gideon J. Pillow. ALS, copy. T–GP. Discusses election of directors of the Columbia Central Turnpike Company.

30 Nov — To the President and Directors of the Big Hatchie Turnpike Company. ALS, copy. T–GP. Discusses election of directors of their company.

[Dec 1840] — From Nathan Green, William B. Reese, and William B. Turley. LS. T–GP. Certify cases in which Green has recused himself.

[Dec 1840] — From William F. Kizer et al. LS. T–GP. Request pardon for Henry R. Mooring.

1 Dec — To Ephraim H. Foster et al. ALS, copy. T–GP. Forwards names of Tennessee's presidential electors.

1 Dec — From W. F. R. Hamilton. ALS. T–GP. Reports election of officers for the 54th regiment of Tennessee militia.

1 Dec — From Gideon J. Pillow. ALS. T–GP. Discusses composition of the board of directors of the Columbia Central Turnpike Company.

1 Dec	To the President and Directors of the Harpeth Turnpike Company. ALS, copy. T–GP. Discusses election of directors of their company.
1 Dec	To the President and Directors of the Pelham & Jasper Turnpike Company. ALS, copy. T–GP. Discusses election of directors of the company.
1 Dec	From Joseph H. Talbot. ALS. T–GP. Tells of an intrigue to collect the reward posted for two murder suspects, George and Russell Rogers.
2 Dec	*From Ezekiel P. McNeal.*
2 Dec	To the President and Directors of the Chambers & Purdy Turnpike Company. ALS, copy. T–GP. Discusses election of directors of their company.
2 Dec	To the President and Directors of the Forked Deer Turnpike Company. ALS, copy. T–GP. Discusses election of directors of their company.
2 Dec	*From Robert B. Reynolds.*
3 Dec	To the President and Commissioners of the Shelbyville & Fayetteville Turnpike Company. Copy. T–GP. Discusses election of commissioners of the company.
4 Dec	From James Goodner. ALS. T–RG 5. Discusses report of the commissioners appointed to examine the Lebanon & Sparta Turnpike.
4 Dec	To Gideon J. Pillow. ALS, copy. T–GP. Discusses appointment of state directors for the Columbia Central Turnpike Company.
4 Dec	*From William H. Polk.*
4 Dec	From W. M. Warner. ALS. T–GP. Resigns as director of the LaGrange and Memphis Railroad Company; recommends Curtis Winfield of Moscow to take his place.
5 Dec	From H. J. Anderson. ALS. T–GP. Reports on the physical condition of Larkin Thurman, a prisoner in the Tennessee penitentiary.
5 Dec	To William R. Caswell. Copy. T–GP. Discusses supplying arms to the 23rd regiment of the Tennessee militia.
5 Dec	From L. C. Chitwood. ALS. T–GP. Reports election of officers of the 143rd regiment of Tennessee militia and requests commissions for those elected.
5 Dec	From Thomas Maxwell. ALS. DLC–JKP. Introduces B. Shipman, a Methodist minister from New York.
5 Dec	To Joseph H. Talbot. ALS, copy. T–GP. Discusses reward paid for the capture of George and Russell Rogers.
[7 Dec 1840]	From Nathan Green, William B. Reese, and William B. Turley. LS. T–GP. Certify that Green has recused himself in the case of Thomas Green *vs.* the Bank of the State of Tennessee.
7 Dec	To Buckley Kimbrough. ALS, copy. T–GP. Discusses case of two fugitives from justice confined in the prison at New Orleans.

7 Dec	From John H. Weeks. ALS. T–GP. Certifies militia returns of 108th regiment of Tennessee militia in which John N. Bornhill and Mark H. Wilson were elected captains.
8 Dec	From Nathan P. Akins. ALS. T–GP. Requests that Polk send him commissions for John Edmondson and Noah Hubbard as captains in the 142nd regiment of Tennessee militia.
[8 Dec 1840]	From Nathan Green, William B. Reese, and William B. Turley. LS. T–GP. Certify cases in which Reese and Turley have recused themselves.
8 Dec	From Isaac Rains et al. LS. T–GP. Request the release of Benson Williams from jail.
9 Dec	From J. B. Anthony. ALS. DLC–JKP. Introduces B. Shipman, a minister who is traveling south for reasons of health.
9 Dec	From A. M. Ballentine. ALS. T–RG 5. Reports individuals selected by stockholders to be directors of the Columbia, Pulaski, Elkton & Alabama Turnpike Company; suggests persons who might be appointed as directors by the state.
9 Dec	To Johoyle Fugate. Copy. T–GP. Discusses issuance of arms to a militia unit under his command.
9 Dec	To the President and Directors of the Lebanon & Sparta Turnpike Company. Copy. T–GP. Discusses capitalization of their company and issuance of state bonds.
10 Dec	From E. S. Davis. ALS. T–GP. Declines to serve another term as a director of the LaGrange & Memphis Railroad Company.
10 Dec	To Thomas W. Gilmer. Copy. T–GP. Concurs with Gilmer's position in his dispute with the governor of New York over the surrender of fugitives from justice.
10 Dec	To Eastin Morris. Copy. T–GP. Appoints new director to the LaGrange & Memphis Railroad Company.
10 Dec	From J. G. M. Ramsey. ALS. T–GP. Reports on the annual meeting in Charleston of the Louisville, Cincinnati and Charleston Railroad Company.
10 Dec	From Jacob A. Tully. ALS. T–GP. Forwards petition in behalf of Henry R. Mooring, convicted of wearing a bowie knife.
11 Dec	From William M. C. Barr. ALS. T–GP. Suggests that a reward be offered for the capture of Malkijah D. Vaughan, accused of murdering John A. Hopkins.
11 Dec	*From Daniel Graham.*
11 Dec	From James H. Reagan. ALS. T–GP. Reports elections of John Hix as captain and William O'Conar as first lieutenant in the 31st regiment and requests that their commissions be forwarded to him.
11 Dec	From R. L. Sanders. ALS. T–GP. Reports elections of officers for the 8th regiment of Tennessee militia.
11 Dec	From John S. Young. ALS. DLC–JKP. Reports that Felix Grundy is near death.

13 Dec	From Daniel Graham. ALS. DLC–JKP. Advises that Felix Grundy is dangerously ill and has shown no improvement.
14 Dec	From Leonard L. Fields. ALS. T–GP. Reports names of directors of the Forked Deer Turnpike Company; encloses list of men available for selection as managers for the state; and adds that the road yet remains unfinished.
14 Dec	From Daniel Graham. ALS. DLC–JKP. Reports that Felix Grundy's condition is unchanged; advises that if Polk cannot persuade James Walker to go to Mississippi, "you should perhaps go on yourself & hope for the best here."
14 Dec	From John C. McLemore. ALS. DLC–JKP. Suggests Maurace Smith or Samuel J. Hayes as director of the LaGrange and Memphis Railroad Company.
15 Dec	*From Cave Johnson.*
17 Dec	To A. M. Ballentine. ALS, copy. T–GP. Informs him of persons selected to be state directors of the Columbia, Pulaski, Elkton & Alabama Turnpike Company.
17 Dec	To William M. C. Barr. Copy. T–GP. Requests additional information regarding the alleged murderer, Malkijah D. Vaughan.
17 Dec	To James H. Wilson. Copy. T–GP. Informs him of the state directors appointed to the board of the Harpeth Turnpike Company.
18 Dec	From William M. C. Barr. ALS. T–GP. Discusses case of Malkijah D. Vaughan, charged with the murder of John A. Hopkins.
18 Dec	From Levin H. Coe. ALS. DLC–JKP. Reports on the political situation in several counties, including Shelby, Hardeman, Haywood, Perry, and Tipton.
18 Dec	From Adam Huntsman. ALS. T–GP. Encloses petition requesting a pardon for John Busby of Henderson County.
18 Dec	To the President and Directors of the Clarksville & Russellville Turnpike Company. ALS, copy. T–GP. Transmits commissions for persons selected to be state directors of the company.
19 Dec	*From Andrew Jackson.*
20 Dec	From Amos David. ALS. DLC–JKP. Complains of mismanagement in the LaGrange and Memphis Railroad Company; recommends that William Stedham of Fayette County be appointed as a director.
20 Dec	*From Andrew Jackson.*
21 Dec	*From Aaron V. Brown.*
21 Dec	From S. W. Fowler. ALS. DLC–JKP. Requests that his name be withdrawn as a candidate for director of the LaGrange and Memphis Railroad Company; suggests that Dudley Dunn be considered instead.
21 Dec	From John C. McLemore. ALS. DLC–JKP. Recommends that John J. Potts, David Jernigan, George Anderson, Daniel Johnson, Miles Owen, and Maurace Smith be appointed state directors of the LaGrange and Memphis

Railroad Company; urges that he or someone else friendly to the railroad and Fort Pickering be consulted on these appointments.

21 Dec *From Hopkins L. Turney.*

22 Dec To Gustavus A. Henry. ALS, copy. T–GP. Discusses appointment of directors and commissioners of the Clarksville & Russellville Turnpike Company.

22 Dec From Felix Grundy Mayson. ALS. DLC–JKP. Requests recommendation for the position of navy purser.

22 Dec From William E. Owen. ALS. DLC–JKP. Requests pardon for David Osment.

23 Dec From John C. McLemore. ALS. DLC–JKP. Warns that persons named in a Memphis petition, recommending directors for the LaGrange and Memphis Railroad Company, are opponents of the railroad and will do much harm if appointed.

23 Dec *From A. O. P. Nicholson.*

23 Dec To George Talcott. ALS, copy. T–GP. Discusses arms for the Tennessee militia.

23 Dec To Jacob A. Tully. ALS, copy. T–GP. Declines acting on the petition in behalf of Henry R. Mooring until additional information is provided.

23 Dec From Josiah Walton. ALS. T–RG 5. Resigns as state director of the Nashville & Kentucky Turnpike Company.

24 Dec From H. J. Anderson. ALS. T–GP. Recommends commutation of the sentence of John Huffman, convicted of horse stealing.

24 Dec From H. J. Anderson. ALS. DLC–JKP. Reports that 90 boxes containing 20 muskets each and 32 boxes of infantry accoutrements were received and stored in the arsenal on November 3 and 4, 1840.

24 Dec From Pendleton G. Gaines. ALS. DLC–JKP. Complains of extravagance among the directory of the LaGrange and Memphis Railroad Company and makes six recommendations for new state directors for the railroad.

24 Dec *To A. O. P. Nicholson.*

25 Dec From Ezekiel Brown. ALS. DLC–JKP. Returns ten dollars that he borrowed when in Nashville; reports on his travels to Fort Pickering and Memphis while en route to New Orleans.

25 Dec From John W. Ford. ALS. DLC–JKP. Recommends Samuel H. Laughlin to fill the unexpired U.S. Senate term of Felix Grundy, deceased.

25 Dec From William R. Saunders. ALS. T–GP. Discusses murder of Isaac Lindsey, a minister, by Willis G. Carroll.

27 Dec From William M. C. Barr. ALS. T–GP. Encloses copy of the coroner's report concerning the body of John A. Hopkins.

27 Dec From E. R. Hammond. ALS. DLC–JKP. Requests Polk's autograph.

27 Dec	From John C. McLemore. ALS. DLC–JKP. Urges early and economical completion of the LaGrange and Memphis Railroad; defends directors from attacks that he feels are unfair.
[27 Dec 1840]	From A. O. P. Nicholson. ALS. DLC–JKP. States that he has decided to take the stage because of inclement weather.
28 Dec	From Stephen C. Pavatt. ALS. DLC–JKP. Reports on Democratic prospects in West Tennessee.
28 Dec	From James R. Robertson. ALS. DLC–JKP. Requests financial assistance.
29 Dec	From John Lanier, Samuel E. Gilliland, and Matt Marshall. LS. T–RG 5. Discuss issuance of state bonds for the benefit of the Shelbyville & Fayetteville Turnpike Company.
31 Dec	From Joel R. Poinsett. Copy. DNA–RG 107. Acknowledges receipt of recommendation of Paul H. Otey for an appointment as cadet in the U.S. Military Academy.
31 Dec	*From Sarah C. Polk.*

1841

Jan	From Mark Bradley et al. LS. T–GP. Request pardon for Matthew Murphey, convicted of larceny.
[Jan 1841]	From Samuel Martin. ALS. DLC–JKP. Claims that Polk cannot be reelected governor without his support.
1 Jan	From William H. Beavers. ALS. T–GP. Reports on the condition of the Chambers & Purdy Turnpike and on his own financial difficulties; requests that Polk advise him soon what to do about the road.
1 Jan	From Mark Black et al. LS. T–GP. Request pardon for Elizabeth Henderson.
[1 Jan 1841]	From Dudley Dunn et al. LS. DLC–JKP. Urges prompt completion of the LaGrange and Memphis Railroad.
3 Jan	From William R. Harris. ALS. DLC–JKP. Declines to run for Congress, citing as a primary reason his wife's poor health; suggests William Fitzgerald as the best Democratic candidate.
3 Jan [1841]	*From Harvey M. Watterson.*
4 Jan	From Daniel Graham. ALS. DLC–JKP. Reports that state governmental affairs are going well during Polk's absence.
4 Jan	From A. N. Sabin. ALS. DLC–JKP. Solicits backing for an important philosophical discovery that "fully explains the movement of material matter."
[4 Jan 1841]	From A. N. Sabin. ALS. DLC–JKP. Requests small donation that would justify naming Polk as one of the patrons of his invention.
5 Jan	From Solomon D. Jacobs et al. NS. T–GP. Certify stockholders' payments into the treasury of the Hiwassee Railroad Company.

6 Jan	From James W. Smith. ALS. DLC–JKP. Declines to run for the legislature; cites reasons of ill health.
6 Jan	*From Richard M. Woods.*
7 Jan	From Sackfield Maclin. ALS. DLC–JKP. Offers to meet Polk near La Grange and accompany him to Somerville.
8 Jan	From William R. Caswell. ALS. T–GP. Reports quantities and types of arms stored in Knoxville.
9 Jan	From D. C. Gaskill. ALS. DLC–JKP. Solicits appointment as postmaster at Gallatin, Tennessee.
10 Jan	From Pierce B. Anderson. ALS. DLC–JKP. Suggests that many persons in East Tennessee who voted for William H. Harrison will have no problem supporting Polk.
11 Jan	From Arthur P. Bagby. ACS. T–GP. Transmits report and joint resolution of the General Assembly of Alabama on the Georgia-Maine controversy.
11 Jan	From Frederick R. Smith. ALS. T–RG 5. Reports election of directors by stockholders; names individuals nominated as directors by the state for the Big Hatchie Turnpike & Bridge Company.
12 Jan [1841]	From Alexander O. Anderson. ALS. DLC–JKP. Reports that he has obtained passage in the Senate of a bill providing for the final disposition of the public lands in Tennessee.
13 Jan	From I. W. Callon. ANS. T–GP. Reports election of officers in the 34th regiment of Tennessee militia.
13 Jan [1841]	*From Cave J. Couts.*
13 Jan	From Eastin Morris. ALS. T–RG 5. Names directors elected by the stockholders of the LaGrange & Memphis Railroad Company.
13 Jan	*From A. O. P. Nicholson.*
14 Jan	From Sam Bigger. CS. T–GP. Forwards joint resolution of the Indiana legislature on amending the U.S. Constitution.
14 Jan	From Green Pryor. ALS. DLC–JKP. Requests information pertaining to a lawsuit involving his security bond for Shelby Polk; recalls that the suit was tried some twenty years ago.
17 Jan	From R. D. Caldwell. ANS. T–GP. Requests lieutenant's commission for Thomas A. Randle in the 114th regiment of Tennessee militia.
19 Jan	From Sam Bigger. CS. T–GP. Forwards joint resolution of the Indiana legislature concerning the election of president and vice-president.
20 Jan	From William H. Beavers. ALS. T–GP. Asks Polk to examine the charter of the Chambers & Purdy Turnpike Company and to let him know what to do about toll gates; wants to surrender the charter to the state due to financial difficulties.
20 Jan	From John Hearn. ALS. T–GP. Asks if the stock certification for the Lebanon & Sparta Turnpike Company is on file.

21 Jan	*From Isaac H. Dismukes.*
21 Jan	*From E. G. Eastman.*
21 Jan	From M. McLaurine. ALS. T–GP. Requests that a reward be offered for the capture of Charles J. Sowel, charged with the murder of Jesse Turner.
22 Jan	From Hopkins L. Turney. ALS. DLC–JKP. Asks that Polk assist William McClellan to obtain payment for duties performed as a census taker.
24 Jan	From William Aymett. ALS. T–GP. Asks for pardon of his prison sentence for carrying a bowie knife and for remission of his fine.
24 Jan	From Silas M. Caldwell. ALS. DLC–JKP. Requests payment of the $50 note that Polk owes him.
26 Jan	From A. R. Cartwright. ALS. T–RG 5. Suggests several persons as suitable replacements for M. D. Thompson as a state director of the Franklin & Columbia Turnpike Company.
26 Jan	To John Hearn. ALS, copy. T–GP. Discusses capitalization of the Lebanon & Sparta Turnpike Company.
27 Jan	From H. J. Anderson. ALS. T–GP. Recommends commutation of the sentence of William M. Duke, convicted of horse stealing.
27 Jan	From E. R. Feild. ALS. T–GP. Reports on the physical condition of William Aymett, confined in the Giles County jail.
27 Jan	To E. R. Feild. ALS, copy. T–GP. Requests additional information about the health of William Aymett.
27 Jan	From P. Hay. ALS. T–GP. Requests that Polk consider the case of William Aymett as soon as possible.
27 Jan	From Solomon D. Jacobs. ALS. T–GP. Protests application of a law passed in 1840 to the Hiwassee Railroad Company.
27 Jan	To Thomas Martin and Archibald Wright. ALS, copy. T–GP. Denies pardon for William Aymett; requests additional information on the case.
27 Jan	To Jacob A. Tully. ALS, copy. T–GP. Declines to intervene in behalf of Henry R. Mooring.
28 Jan	To W. C. Reedman, Jr. ALS, copy. T–GP. Declines to intervene in behalf of Benson Williams.
29 Jan	To William H. Beavers. ALS, copy. T–GP. Describes procedures whereby the Chambers & Purdy Turnpike Company might surrender their charter to the state.
29 Jan	To Maclin Cross. ALS, copy. T–GP. Discusses appointment of directors of the Chambers & Purdy Turnpike Company.
29 Jan	From William Garrett. ACS. T–GP. Forwards copies of a joint resolution of the General Assembly of Alabama and of the decisions of the Alabama Supreme Court; requests that Polk send copies of Tennessee's supreme court decisions.
30 Jan	*To William Moore.*

30 Jan	From David R. Porter. ACS. T–GP. Forwards copy of the joint resolutions of the legislature of Pennsylvania regarding the public lands.
30 Jan	To Daniel Ragan. ALS, copy. T–GP. Acknowledges receipt of arms for the Tennessee militia.
[31] Jan	From C. R. Bedford. ALS. DLC–JKP. Gives account of an attack made on him while traveling through Tennessee and warns that he will not travel the state again without being armed.
[Feb 1841]	From Jonas E. Thomas et al. LS. T–GP. Request pardon for Nathan G. Johnston, confined in the state penitentiary for horse stealing.
1 Feb	*From Isaac H. Dismukes.*
1 Feb	To Gustavus A. Henry. ALS, copy. T–GP. Refuses to authorize the erection of toll gates on the Clarksville & Russellville Turnpike.
1 Feb	From West H. Humphreys. ALS. DLC–JKP. Requests copy of an article attacking the Democratic party; urges Polk to come to Nashville as soon as possible.
1 Feb	From Leonard W. Marbury. ALS. DLC–JKP. Requests payment for subscription to the Shelbyville *Peoples Advocate*.
1 Feb	*From Harvey M. Watterson.*
2 Feb	*To David Burford.*
2 Feb	To E. R. Feild. ALS, copy. T–GP. Notifies him of a pardon granted to William Aymett.
2 Feb	*From A. O. P. Nicholson.*
3 Feb	From Maclin Cross. AL. T–GP. Recommends several persons for the directorship of the Purdy & Chambers Turnpike Company.
3 Feb	To Adam Huntsman. ALS, copy. T–GP. Suspends action on the request of a pardon for John Busby pending the receipt of additional information.
4 Feb	*To Robert B. Reynolds.*
6 Feb	From Sam Bigger. CS. T–GP. Transmits copy of a joint resolution passed by the Indiana legislature concerning the public lands.
6 Feb	From John W. Houston. ACS. T–GP. Transmits copy of resolutions adopted by the General Assembly of Delaware concerning the public lands.
6 Feb	*From William C. Tate.*
6 Feb	From Henderson K. Yoakum. ALS. DLC–JKP. Prefers that should a special session of the legislature be called, the meeting should be held as early as possible.
7 Feb	From Richard H. Allen. ALS. DLC–JKP. Declines to run for the Tennessee Senate; expresses confidence that Polk will receive many Whig votes in the coming election.
8 Feb	*From Andrew Jackson.*
9 Feb	To Gustavus A. Henry. Copy. T–GP. Authorizes erection of one toll gate by the Clarksville & Russellville Turnpike Company.

9 Feb   From Joel R. Poinsett. Copy. DNA–RG 107. Acknowledges receipt of the recommendation of James Trooper Armstrong for appointment to the U.S. Military Academy.

10 Feb   From Robert P. Letcher. C. T–GP. Forwards copy of resolutions passed by the Kentucky legislature, which propose to limit presidents to a single term.

10 Feb   From Samuel Ward King. CS. T–GP. Transmits copies of resolutions expressing the Rhode Island legislature's views on the public lands, the Sub-Treasury, and a national bank.

10 Feb   From Daniel Ragan. ALS. T–GP. Requests Polk's signature on papers acknowledging receipt of an arms shipment.

12 Feb   *From John F. Gillespy.*

12 Feb   *From A. O. P. Nicholson.*

12 Feb   *From A. O. P. Nicholson.*

12 Feb   From N. B. Shelby. ALS. DLC–JKP. Gives information pertaining to the apprehension and transportation of a prisoner from Galveston to Tennessee; discusses question of who is entitled to receive the reward.

13 Feb   To A. M. Coffee. ALS, copy. T–GP. Transmits commissions for state directors of the Hiwassee Railroad Company.

13 Feb   To Maclin Cross. ALS, copy. T–GP. Transmits commissions for the state directors of the Chambers & Purdy Turnpike Company.

13 Feb   To Herndon Haralson. ALS, copy. T–GP. Refuses to pardon David Osment.

13 Feb   From Pitser Miller and John H. Bills. LS. DLC–JKP. Enclose $104 to pay the board for two inmates in the state lunatic asylum at Nashville.

13 Feb   To David Street et al. ALS, copy. T–GP. Asks them, in their capacity as state directors of the Chambers & Purdy Turnpike Company, to report on the progress of the road.

14 Feb   *From John C. McLemore.*

15 Feb   From Cave Johnson. ALS. DLC–JKP. Advises that the Tennessee land bill has passed the U.S. House by a vote of 136 to 45; thinks that the bill will pass the Senate, which has approved the measure twice before.

15 Feb   From A. O. P. Nicholson. ALS. DLC–JKP. Advises that the Tennessee land bill has passed the U.S. House.

15 Feb   To the President of the United States. ALS. DNA–RG 59. Also ALS, copy, in T–GP. Asks assistance in returning Zebulon Payne, accused of murdering William Coltart, from the Republic of Texas.

[15] Feb   *From Robert B. Reynolds.*

16 Feb   To the President of the United States. ALS. DNA–RG 59. Also ALS, copy, in T–GP. Advises that Zebulon Payne is now imprisoned in New Orleans and that a request for extradition is no longer needed.

16 Feb   To Jonas E. Thomas. ALS, copy. T–GP. Declines to pardon Nathan G. Johnston.

16 Feb   From William Wallace. ALS. DLC–JKP. Offers opinions regarding Democratic strategy in Blount County.

17 Feb	*From Alexander O. Anderson.*
17 Feb	From Levin H. Coe. ALS. DLC–JKP. Discusses Democratic campaign strategies in West Tennessee.
17 Feb	From Francis Duffy. ALS. DLC–JKP. Discusses Democratic prospects in Middle Tennessee.
17 Feb	From James Goodner. ALS. T–GP. Transmits report of the president and directors of the Lebanon & Sparta Turnpike Company, who propose an additional issue of state bonds.
17 Feb	From John W. Houston. CS. T–GP. Transmits resolutions expressing the views of the Delaware legislature on limiting presidents to a single term.
17 Feb	From William Moore. ALS. DLC–JKP. Reports that he is leaving for home and will relate the news from Lincoln County upon his return to Nashville.
17 Feb	From Charles Taliaferro. ALS. DLC–JKP. Reports that citizens of Roane County have circulated a petition calling for a special session of the legislature to pass stay laws.
18 Feb	From Joseph Thompson. ALS. DLC–JKP. Offers to assist in returning an escaped felon, Zebulon Payne, to Tennessee; wishes to know if the state will assume responsibility for expenses incurred in the undertaking.
19 Feb	To Jacob D. Donaldson. ALS, copy. T–GP. Discusses issuance of state bonds for the benefit of the Jefferson Turnpike Company.
19 Feb	*From Hopkins L. Turney.*
20 Feb	To James Goodner. ALS, copy. T–GP. Notifies him that $5,000 in additional state bonds have been issued for the benefit of the Lebanon & Sparta Turnpike Company.
20 Feb	To the President and Directors of the Columbia, Pulaski, Elkton & Alabama Turnpike Company. ALS, copy. T–GP. Forwards copy of the opinion of the comptroller, attorney general, and governor denying the issuance of additional state bonds.
20 Feb	To Joseph Thompson. ALS, copy. T–GP. Declines to appoint him agent to convey the fugitive, Zebulon Payne, from Louisiana to Tennessee.
22 Feb	To A. B. Roman. ALS, copy. T–GP. Discusses case of Zebulon Payne, fugitive from justice.
22 Feb	From Felix K. Zollicoffer. ALS. DLC–JKP. Requests information regarding Polk's subscription to the *Columbia Observer.*
23 Feb	To the President and Directors of the Jefferson Turnpike Company. ALS, copy. T–GP. Refuses application for additional state bonds.
23 Feb	From John W. Stephenson et al. LS. DLC–JKP. Requests assistance in obtaining Miss E. C. Foster's admission to the state lunatic asylum at Nashville.
24 Feb	From E. G. Eastman. ALS. DLC–JKP. Advises that he has sent Robert Armstrong a promissory note for a loan to be arranged in Nashville and that this accommodation would

	place the Knoxville *Argus* "on a firm and permanent footing."
24 Feb	From Elias Pharr et al. LS. T–GP. Request pardon for John Robertson.
24 Feb	*From James Walker.*
25 Feb	From B. M. Bayly. ALS. DLC–JKP. Discusses Democratic prospects in East Tennessee.
27 Feb	From A. M. Coffee. ALS. T–GP. Lists directors elected by the stockholders of the Hiwassee Railroad Company for the current year.
27 Feb	From J. B. Dickerson. ALS. T–GP. Requests that a reward be offered for Madison Wilks, indicted for the murder of a slave named Jim.
27 Feb	*To Thomas L. Hamer.*
March	From John H. Griscom et al. C. DLC–JKP. Requests that copies of Tennessee's laws be placed in the New York Lyceum Library.
[March 1841]	From P. M. Neal et al. LS. T–GP. Request pardon for John Venable.
[1 March 1841]	From William H. Seward. CS. T–GP. Transmits copies of a joint resolution expressing the views of the New York legislature on the public lands.
1 March	From Henry A. Miller. ALS. DLC–JKP. Asks if Polk recalls witnessing the transfer of a deed from George Briscoe to Robert Wortham and John Briscoe.
4 March	*From Andrew Johnson.*
6 March	*From Thomas L. Hamer.*
6 March	*From Andrew Jackson.*
7 March	*From William H. Polk.*
8 March	From John Hughes et al. LS. T–GP. Request Isaac Hamilton's release from the penitentiary.
8 March	*From A. O. P. Nicholson.*
8 March	From Gideon J. Pillow. ALS. T–GP. Requests appointment of three commissioners to examine the progress of the Columbia Central Turnpike Company.
9 March	*From Robert M. Burton.*
9 March	*From Isaac H. Dismukes.*
9 March	From E. B. Duncan et al. LS. T–GP. Request release of Presley L. Smith from the state penitentiary.
9 March	From Adam Huntsman. ALS. DLC–JKP. Discusses candidates in several counties and their prospects for success; suggests that calling a special session of the legislature would make Polk vulnerable to much criticism.
9 March	*To Samuel H. Laughlin.*
9 March	*From A. O. P. Nicholson.*
9 March	From Gideon J. Pillow. ALS. T–GP. Discusses appointment of another commissioner to examine the progress of the Columbia Central Turnpike Company.
9 March	To the President and Directors of the Columbia, Pulaski, Elkton & Alabama Turnpike Company. ALS, copy. T–GP.

Discusses application for an additional issuance of state bonds.

10 March [1841]   *From A. O. P. Nicholson.*

10 March   *From James Walker.*

11 March   From James Gadsden. ALS. T–GP. Encloses copy of the proceedings of the stockholders of the Louisville, Cincinnati & Charleston Railroad Company; reports that the stockholders in South Carolina will allow the state of Tennessee to withdraw.

11 March   To Gideon J. Pillow. ALS, copy. T–GP. Discusses appointment of commissioners to examine the progress of the Columbia Central Turnpike Company.

12 March   From Hays Blackman. ANS. T–GP. Reports that Robert Currin, a state director in the Nolensville Turnpike Company, has removed from the state.

12 March   From Samuel H. Laughlin. ALS. DLC–JKP. Discusses Democratic prospects in several county and district election races.

13 March   From A. M. Coffee. ALS. T–GP. Notifies Polk that William Lyon has declined to serve as commissioner of the Hiwassee Railroad Company and encloses a copy of his declination.

14 March   From Daniel Graham. ALS. DLC–JKP. Discusses legislative candidates from counties in southwest Tennessee.

14 March   From Joseph H. Talbot. ANS. T–GP. Reports murder of James Bird by William Stewart and Richard Baily; suggests that a reward be offered for the capture of Stewart, Baily having already been apprehended.

15 March [1841]   From John W. Childress. ALS. DLC–JKP. Reports on campaign strategy and movements of James C. Jones.

15 March   *To James C. Jones.*

15 March   From William M. Lowry. ALS. DLC–JKP. Encloses $3 for three subscriptions to the Nashville *Plain Dealer*, which he asks Polk to forward to J. George Harris; discusses candidates for the legislature from East Tennessee.

15 March   From Henry Van Pelt and Pendleton G. Gaines. ALsS. DLC–JKP. Discuss arrangements for publishing a Democratic newspaper in Memphis; express confidence that Polk will carry Shelby County.

15 March   From Henderson K. Yoakum. ALS. DLC–JKP. Reports on a campaign speech given in Murfreesboro by James C. Jones.

17 March   From Jonathan P. Hardwicke. ALS. DLC–JKP. Urges Polk to debate James C. Jones "fully and freely on all the Subjects connected with the Banks and currency."

18 March   *From James C. Jones.*

18 March   *From James Walker.*

19 March   *To Robert J. Chester.*

19 March   *From Edwin Croswell.*

19 March   From R. W. Sanford. ALS. T–RG 5. Resigns as director of the Big Hatchie Bridge & Turnpike Company.

20 March	From John Briscoe. ALS. DLC–JKP. Requests information regarding the transfer of a deed from George Briscoe to Robert Wortham and John Briscoe.
20 March	*From Andrew Jackson.*
21 March	From Ezekiel Brown. ALS. DLC–JKP. Requests acknowledgement of the receipt of a bank note sent in December to Polk as payment of a loan.
21 March	From Robert C. Foster. ALS. T–GP. Requests executive clemency on behalf of John Venable.
21 March	*From James Walker.*
22 March	From John W. Childress. ALS. DLC–JKP. Believes that there is a Whig sympathizer in the *Nashville Union* office who is leaking information; urges Polk to be "well supplied with Documents" when he meets James C. Jones in Murfreesboro.
22 March	To A. M. Coffee. ALS, copy. T–GP. Discusses William Lyon's appointment as commissioner to examine the Hiwassee Railroad Company.
22 March	From John W. Lide. ALS. DLC–JKP. Explains why he cannot be a candidate for the Tennessee Senate.
22 March	To William Lyon. ALS, copy. T–GP. Discusses his appointment as a commissioner to examine the Hiwassee Railroad Company.
22 March	From Thomas Maney. ALS. T–GP. Discusses the case of John Venable.
22 March	From James Walker. ALS. DLC–JKP. Advises that he cannot assist Polk in obtaining a horse.
23 March	From James Goodner. ALS. T–RG 5. Requests appointment of commissioners to examine the progress of the Lebanon & Sparta Turnpike Company pursuant to obtaining state bonds.
23 March	From Adam Huntsman. ALS. T–GP. Discusses the case of John Busby, convicted of manslaughter.
24 March	To Robert C. Foster. ALS, draft. T–GP. Declines request to intervene on behalf of John Venable, convicted of grand larceny.
25 March	From Hervey Hoge. ALS. DLC–JKP. Requests "favor of your attention to the within. You will pleas exermin it & Send a reply to me." (Enclosure not found.)
25 March	From Abraham McClellan. ALS. DLC–JKP. Reports that family illnesses prevent his conducting an extensive campaign for the U.S. House; urges Polk to spend as much time as possible in East Tennessee.
25 March	From Blake Sageby. ALS. DLC–JKP. Requests that Leonard Eadins be released from the penitentiary.
26 March	From William S. Scott. ALS. T–GP. Requests that a reward be offered for the capture of Wilkerson Fletcher and J. John Fletcher, charged with the murder of John Pryor.
27 March	From W. W. C. Kelley. ALS. DLC–JKP. Requests letter of introduction to the chargé d'affaires of Colombia, S.A.

[*28 March 1841*] *From Robert Armstrong.*
28 March From Pendleton G. Gaines. ALS. DLC–JKP. Discusses issues that he would like to have presented to the legislature, in the event that Polk calls a special session.
28 March *From Sarah C. Polk.*
28 March *From Robert B. Reynolds.*
28 March *From Archibald Yell.*
29 March From John Hearn. ALS. DLC–JKP. Requests appointment of commissioners for the Lebanon and Sparta Turnpike Company.
29 March To the Jonesboro *Tennessee Sentinel.* C, copy. T–GP. Requests publication of a proclamation. (Circular also sent to eight other Tennessee papers.)
30 March From William E. Butler. ALS. DLC–JKP. Requests certification of John Read.
30 March From George W. Jones. ALS. DLC–JKP. Urges that Polk call a special session of the Tennessee legislature.
30 March From William Lyon. ALS. DLC–JKP. Accepts appointment as commissioner of the Hiwassee Railroad Company.
30 March From Gideon C. Matlock. ALS. DLC–JKP. Urges that Polk visit Carthage to campaign and discuss politics.
30 March *From Edwin Polk.*
31 March From anonymous writer. L. DLC–JKP. Urges that James Claxton not be released from the penitentiary.
31 March From John McGaughey. ALS. DLC–JKP. Expresses pleasure that Polk does not plan to call a special session of the legislature.
1 April *From Isaac H. Dismukes.*
1 April From William Lyon. ALS. T–GP. Resigns as commissioner of the Hiwassee Railroad Company and suggests that Arthur R. Crozier of Knoxville be appointed his replacement.
1 April From John S. Young. ALS. T–GP. Sends copy of a letter from William S. Scott, who requests a reward for Wilkerson Fletcher and J. John Fletcher.
[2 April 1841] From Robert Armstrong. ALI. DLC–JKP. Advises that J. George Harris is slow in publishing Polk's "Address to the People of Tennessee."
2 April From G. F. Benton et al. LS. DLC–JKP. Invite Polk to a public dinner in Savannah on April 22.
2 April From Eastin Morris et al. NS. T–GP. Apply for an additional $37,500 in state bonds for the LaGrange & Memphis Railroad Company.
3 April From John C. Claiborne. ALS. DLC–JKP. Urges special session of the Tennessee legislature; requests that the Chancery Court session at Trenton be rescheduled to avoid conflicting with the court at Savannah.
5 April [1841] *From Robert Armstrong.*
5 April From William Bobbitt. ALS. DLC–JKP. Discusses business pertaining to Polk's plantation.

5 April	From Joseph B. Boyd. ALS. DLC–JKP. Requests Polk's autograph.
5 April	From Nathan Green, William B. Reese, and William B. Turley. LS. T–GP. Certify that Turley has recused himself in a case to be tried in Jackson in April 1841.
5 April	From L. W. Jordan. ALS. DLC–JKP. Wishes to know the expiration date for the terms of congressmen elected to the special session.
6 April	From Albert T. McNeal. ALS. DLC–JKP. Introduces R. S. Graves, Democratic candidate for treasurer in Mississippi.
8 April	*From Sarah C. Polk.*
[9 April 1841]	From Sarah C. Polk. ANS. DLC–JKP. Encloses letter (not found) from Edwin Polk containing a statement from George Alexander.
10 April	From Robert Armstrong. ALS. DLC–JKP. Advises that he is sending a confidential messenger, "Mr. Penticost," to return to Nashville with Polk's appointment of a special judge.
10 April	From J. George Harris. ALS. DLC–JKP. Discusses political matters in Nashville.
10 April	*From Sarah C. Polk.*
10 April	From William H. Seward. CS. T–GP. Forwards proceedings of the legislature of New York regarding the death of William H. Harrison.
10 April	From Nathan Vaught. ALS. DLC–JKP. Wishes to lease land belonging to the heirs of Marshall T. Polk.
11 April	*To Sarah C. Polk.*
12 April	From Robert Armstrong. ALI. DLC–JKP. Advises that he has sent a messenger to meet Polk at Washington in Rhea County; reports the death of William H. Harrison.
12 April	From Ephraim Beanland. ALS. DLC–JKP. Requests payment of money owed to him.
[12 April 1841]	From Sarah C. Polk. ANS. DLC–JKP. Encloses clipping from the Washington *Globe* announcing the death of William H. Harrison.
13 April	From James R. Butler. ALS. T–GP. Requests signed receipt for arms issued.
14 April	*From Sarah C. Polk.*
15 April	From William B. Lenoir. ALS. T–GP. Resigns as commissioner of the Hiwassee Railroad Company.
16 April	From Graham H. Chapin. ALS. DLC–JKP. Introduces Benjamin F. Graves, who may leave Rochester, New York, in favor of Tennessee.
16 April	*To Sarah C. Polk.*
17 April	From Timothy Childs. ALS. DLC–JKP. Introduces Benjamin F. Graves.
17 April	From William Grason. CS. T–GP. Transmits report and resolutions expressing the views of the Maryland House on the surrender of fugitives from justice.
17 April	From Frederick Whittlesey. ALS. DLC–JKP. Introduces Benjamin F. Graves.

[19 April 1841]   From West H. Humphreys. ALS. DLC–JKP. Discusses political machinations of congressional candidates; thinks that Polk is gaining support.

19 April   From Samuel P. Walker. ALS. DLC–JKP. Discusses Maury County politics; relates news of his mother's illness.

20 April   From A. R. Cartwright. ALS. T–RG 5. Names directors elected by the stockholders of the Franklin & Columbia Turnpike Company.

21 April   From John S. Young. ALS. DLC–JKP. Reports news and activities from Nashville.

23 April   From John S. Young. ALS. DLC–JKP. Discusses state business matters that will need Polk's attention.

24 April   From John P. Bigelow. CS. T–GP. Forwards copies of resolutions passed by the legislature of Massachusetts.

24 April   From E. B. Mason et al. LS. DLC–JKP. Invite Polk to a public dinner at Mason's Grove in Madison County.

24 April   *To Sarah C. Polk.*

25 April   From anonymous writer. L, signed "A Freand Gibson Cty Tenn." DLC–JKP. Reports local Whig charges that Polk's father was a Tory during the revolution.

25 April   From Levin H. Coe. ALS. DLC–JKP. Discusses candidates for the Tennessee legislature from the Western District.

25 April   *To Cave Johnson.*

25 April   *From Sarah C. Polk.*

27 April   From J. G. M. Ramsey. ALS. DLC–JKP. Gives account of the events leading to the British capture and execution of Robert Y. Hayne, a patriot of the Revolutionary War.

27 April   From Benjamin Sharpe. ALS. T–RG 5. Names directors elected by the stockholders of the Nashville & Charlotte Turnpike Company.

29 April   From Joseph S. Lake et al. C. T–GP. Transmit statement "of the financial condition and resources of the State of Ohio."

29 April   From Andrew Taylor et al. LS. DLC–JKP. Invite Polk to a public dinner at Middleburg in Hardeman County.

30 April   From John Blair. ALS. DLC–JKP. Urges Polk to visit Jonesboro.

30 April   From Edward Kent. CS. T–GP. Transmits copy of a report and resolutions of the legislature of Maine on the northeastern boundary dispute.

30 April   From Edward Kent. CS. T–GP. Transmits copy of a resolution expressing the views of the Maine legislature on restricting presidents to a single term.

[1 May 1841]   From John P. Chester. ALS. DLC–JKP. Advises that he will be unable to meet Polk at Rheatown, but that he will send his son, Thomas, to deliver Polk's letters.

2 May   From Daniel Graham. ALS. DLC–JKP. Reports on requests for state aid submitted by internal improvement companies; discusses Democratic election prospects in various Middle Tennessee counties.

2 May   *From Sarah C. Polk.*
2 May   *To Sarah C. Polk.*
3 May   From W. M. Green. ALS. DLC–JKP. Introduces James H.
                 Viser, recent graduate of the University of North Carolina,
                 who is spending the next year in Columbia.
4 May   From Daniel Graham. ALS. DLC–JKP. Discusses applica-
                 tions for state aid from internal improvement companies in
                 La Grange, Charlotte, and Pulaski.
5 May   From Samuel Powel. ALS. DLC–JKP. Asks Polk to write
                 and give his opinions "of the public pulse in Tennessee at this
                 time."
5 May   From Samuel Powel. ALS. T–GP. Discusses case of
                 Elizabeth Boatman.
5 May   From Joseph H. Talbot. ALS. T–GP. Reports that the
                 grand jury has returned a true bill against William Stewart
                 and Richard Baily for the murder of James Bird.
6 May   From Richard G. Dunlap. ALS. DLC–JKP. Solicits alloca-
                 tion of state bonds for investment in a railroad project in
                 Memphis.
6 May [1841]   From Lawson Gifford. ALS. DLC–JKP. Encloses newspa-
                 per articles that he attributes to William G. Brownlow.
6 May   From Eastin Morris. ALS. DLC–JKP. Sends messenger to
                 try to obtain allocation of state bonds.
6 May   To Elisha Thomason. Copy. T–GP. Transmits pardon for
                 Elizabeth Boatman.
7 May   From Alvin Cullom. ALS. DLC–JKP. Urges Polk to attend
                 a meeting in Livingston on May 26.
7 May   *From James Walker.*
8 May   From John P. Chester. ALS. DLC–JKP. Urges Polk to stay
                 as long as possible when he visits Jonesboro; discusses dis-
                 sention within the Whig ranks.
9 May   *To Sarah C. Polk.*
9 May   From Alexandre Vattemare. ALS. DLC–JKP. Encloses re-
                 port proposing a system of international exchanges in nat-
                 ural history, art, science, and literature; requests that this
                 report be submitted to the joint committee on the library for
                 their consideration.
10 May   From Daniel Graham. ALS. DLC–JKP. Reports on re-
                 quests for state aid from internal improvement companies.
10 May   *From Samuel H. Laughlin.*
10 May   From William S. Scott and David P. Caldwell. LS. T–GP.
                 Advise Polk to increase the reward offered for Wilkerson
                 Fletcher and J. John Fletcher; suggest that a more complete
                 description of them be published.
11 May   From H. J. Anderson. ALS. T–GP. Recommends commut-
                 ing the prison sentences of several inmates in the state
                 penitentiary.
11 May   *From Levin H. Coe.*
12 May   *From Alexander O. Anderson.*
[13 May 1841]   From Benjamin T. Hollins. ALS. T–RG 5. Resigns as one of

the state directors of the Pelham & Jasper Turnpike Company; recommends that Stephen Clark be appointed his replacement.

13 May   From Solomon D. Jacobs. ALS. T–GP. Encloses report of the commissioners appointed to examine the books and the work done by the Hiwassee Railroad Company; discusses issuance of state bonds.

13 May   From Lindsey Sanders et al. NS. T–GP. Report condition of the Chambers & Purdy Turnpike.

13 May   From Christopher H. Williams. ALS. DLC–JKP. Asks that a commission certifying his election to the U.S. House be sent to Washington City.

14 May   From Josephus C. Guild. ALS. DLC–JKP. Introduces George F. Crockett.

14 May   From Thomas J. Matthews. ALS. DLC–JKP. Wants proof that Franklin Buchanan received double pay as both a member of the General Assembly and an assistant clerk.

15 May   From Milton Brown. ALS. DLC–JKP. Asks that a commission certifying his election to the U.S. House be sent to Washington City.

16 May   From W. R. Burditt. ALS. DLC–JKP. Requests appointment as director of the Bank of Tennessee at Shelbyville.

16 May   From Adam Huntsman. ALS. DLC–JKP. Reports from Lexington on his campaign efforts; urges Polk to spend a couple of days in Henderson County.

16 May   From Cave Johnson. ALS. DLC–JKP. Requests receipt for $365 "to be applied to the payment of three notes given by A V Brown, C Johnson, Jas Walker, W A Polk & Joseph Guild each for Six hundred dollars due & payable in six, twelve & 18 mos from about 7th Oct 1837 to J. M Smith."

16 May   From Edward Scott. ALS. T–GP. Reports inability to hold courts in the Second Judicial District and suggests that Spencer Jarnagin be appointed as temporary judge in his place.

17 May   *To James C. Jones.*

17 May   To the President and Directors of the Columbia, Pulaski, Elkton & Alabama Turnpike Company. Copy. T–GP. Notifies them that he has issued $15,000 in state bonds for the benefit of their company.

18 May   To N. A. Evans. Copy. T–GP. Notifies him that arms for his militia company are presently available.

20 May   To the President and Directors of the Hiwassee Railroad Company. Copy. T–GP. Notifies them that he has issued $97,000 in state bonds for the benefit of their company.

21 May   From Andrew M. Ballentine. ALS. T–RG 5. Discusses state bonds for the Columbia, Pulaski, Elkton & Alabama Turnpike Company.

21 May   From Joseph Brown et al. LS. T–RG 5. Discuss capitalization of the Columbia Central Turnpike Company.

22 May	From Henry M. Smith. L. DLC–JKP. Proposes plan for merging state banks into a new system.
25 May	From O. R. Watkins. ALS. DLC–JKP. Regrets that illness prevented his seeing Polk at Dandridge; thinks that Polk is gaining in East Tennessee; and urges him to consider another visit to the area before the election.
27 May	From Andrew M. Ballentine. ALS. T–RG 5. Discusses financial affairs of the Columbia, Pulaski, Elkton & Alabama Turnpike Company.
28 May	From Samuel W. Adkisson. ALS. DLC–JKP. Professes allegiance to the Democratic party; discusses efforts to explain Democratic principles to others; and denounces the BUS.
30 May	From Alexander O. Anderson. ALS. DLC–JKP. Encloses list of recommendations for directors of the Bank of Tennessee at Rogersville.
31 May	From Gideon C. Matlock. ALS. DLC–JKP. Reports that in 1839 James C. Jones advocated making state bonds redeemable in sterling; maintains that if the bonds were sold in Europe, the interest could be paid with cotton.
31 May	From Edward Shegog. ALS. DLC–JKP. Requests letters of introduction to Andrew Jackson, Martin Van Buren, and "some of your friends in Washington or New York."
31 May	From James Walker. ALS. DLC–JKP. Submits recommendations for a new board of directors for the Bank of Tennessee.
[June 1841]	From James H. Carson. ALS. T–GP. Requests that a reward be offered for the capture of Frederick Benson, charged with the murder of Alonzo D. Pickett.
[June 1841?]	To Eastin Morris. Copy. T–GP. Transmits commission for a state director of the LaGrange & Memphis Railroad Company.
1 June	*From Isaac H. Dismukes.*
2 June	To Andrew M. Ballentine. ALS, copy. T–GP. Discusses state bonds for the Columbia, Pulaski, Elkton & Alabama Turnpike Company.
2 June	From Edwin A. Keeble. ALS. DLC–JKP. Reports on campaign efforts in Cannon County.
2 June	From Gideon C. Matlock. ALS. DLC–JKP. Discusses debates of the 1839 campaign in which James C. Jones advocated making state bonds redeemable in sterling.
4 June	From John B. Johnson. ALS. DLC–JKP. Urges Polk to speak at Carrollsville in Wayne County.
4 June	From George W. Smith. ALS. DLC–JKP. Reports that Democratic prospects in West Tennessee are very promising; says that Democrats in Memphis look forward to Polk's visit on the 20th.
7 June	*To Sarah C. Polk.*
8 June	From David Dobbins. ALS. DLC–JKP. Asks Polk to assist in locating his pension papers.

9 June [1841]   From Robert Armstrong. ALI. DLC–JKP. Forwards copy of John Tyler's message and informs Polk of efforts to secure local legislative candidates.

10 June   From William W. Ellsworth. CS. T–GP. Forwards copy of resolutions expressing the Connecticut legislature's views on limiting presidents to a single term.

10 June   *From Daniel Graham.*

10 June   From Benjamin Sharpe. ALS. T–RG 5. Requests appointment of commissioners to examine the progress of the Nashville & Charlotte Turnpike Company.

12 June   From William C. Blake et al. LS. T–GP. Request pardon for William H. Moffett, convicted of assault and battery.

12 June   *From Aaron V. Brown.*

12 June   From Daniel Graham. ALS. DLC–JKP. Reports on requests by internal improvement companies for state aid; complains that he has been trying for three days to draw the attention of West H. Humphreys to the Gallatin Turnpike Company papers; and notes that John S. Young is recovering and has signed all the bonds.

12 June   From Joseph Sinow. ALS. DLC–JKP. Invites Polk to speak at Hickory Withe in Fayette County on June 25.

13 June   From Robert M. Anderson. ALS. T–GP. Encloses petition in behalf of Zachariah Herrel, convicted of larceny.

13 June [1841]   From Robert Armstrong. ALS. DLC–JKP. Relates local political news and notes requests for financial assistance needed by political friends in East Tennessee.

13 June   *To Sarah C. Polk.*

14 June   From Andrew M. Ballentine. ALS. T–RG 5. Discusses appointment of commissioners to examine the progress of the Columbia, Pulaski, Elkton & Alabama Turnpike.

14 June   From Boling Gordon. ALS. DLC–JKP. Declines to run for the Tennessee Senate; declares his support for Thomas J. Matthews.

14 June   *From A. O. P. Nicholson.*

14 June   From John Parshall. ALS. T–GP. Resigns as director of the Hiwassee Railroad Company.

15 June   From John H. Griscom. LS. DLC–JKP. Encloses annual report of the board of directors of the New York Lyceum and memorial stating the goals and purpose of the Lyceum. (Enclosures not found.)

15 June   *To Sarah C. Polk.*

16 June   From Levin H. Coe. ALS. DLC–JKP. Forwards invitation for Polk to stay at William Guerrant's home en route to Raleigh.

17 June   From Daniel Graham. ALS. DLC–JKP. Encloses papers of the Gallatin Turnpike Company.

18 June   *From J. George Harris.*

18 June   *From Sarah C. Polk.*

21 June	From James Cowan. ALS. DLC–JKP. Invites Polk to visit Mount Holyoke the day after he visits Dresden; asks Polk to extend the invitation to James C. Jones also.
23 June	From Lemuel Rudd. LS. DLC–JKP. Requests preparation of a deed.
24 June	From William Guerrant. ALS. DLC–JKP. Expresses pleasure that Polk is planning to stay at his house after leaving Somerville.
25 June	From Jonathan P. Hardwicke. ALS. DLC–JKP. Discusses whether Polk should spend his time in Middle or East Tennessee; feels that Polk could do some good in Hickman, Dickson, Humphreys, and Stewart counties; but allows that if Polk can effect many changes in East Tennessee, he should concentrate on that area.
25 June	*From Sarah C. Polk.*
25 June	*To Sarah C. Polk.*
25 June	From John S. Young. ALS. DLC–JKP. Encloses J. Parshall's letter of resignation as a director of the Hiwassee Railroad Company; suggests Joseph W. McMillin as a replacement.
27 June	From Samuel H. Laughlin. ALS. DLC–JKP. Believes that Polk is gaining in Franklin, Warren, and White counties; discusses various races in that area of the state; and approves of Polk's plan to visit East Tennessee before the campaign ends.
28 June	From N. A. McNairy and Orville Ewing. NS. T–RG 5. Report results of their examination of the Nashville & Charlotte Turnpike Company.
29 June [1841]	From Cave Johnson. ALS. DLC–JKP. Urges Polk to arrange a visit to Clarksville; observes that many will be disappointed if he does not come.
30 June [1841]	*From Sarah C. Polk.*
1 July	*To Sarah C. Polk.*
5 July	*From Alexander O. Anderson.*
5 July	*From Sarah C. Polk.*
5 July	From James Trezevant. ALS. T–GP. Declines appointment as a director of the LaGrange & Memphis Railroad Company.
6 July	*From Robert Armstrong.*
6 July	From Levin H. Coe. ALS. DLC–JKP. Complains that J. Hotchkiss, postmaster at Somerville, was fired solely because he is a Democrat; believes that Polk is gaining in West Tennessee and "the State may yet be saved."
6 July	*To Sarah C. Polk.*
8 July	*From Alexander O. Anderson.*
8 July	From John Blair. ALS. DLC–JKP. Observes that some of the Whigs in East Tennessee are unhappy over the appropriation to William H. Harrison's family; thinks that if Polk

could visit the area before the election, it would help his cause.

8 July
From Nicholas Fain. ALS. DLC–JKP. Urges Polk to speak in Kingsport when he returns to East Tennessee; discusses legislative races in the area.

10 July [1841]
From Lawson Gifford. ALS. DLC–JKP. Urges Polk to visit East Tennessee; discusses local legislative races.

13 July
From Brookins Campbell. ALS. DLC–JKP. Urges Polk to visit upper East Tennessee before the election; feels that the Whigs are disheartened.

13 July
From Robert J. Chester. ALS. DLC–JKP. Expresses confidence that James C. Jones injures the Whig cause by defending Daniel Webster and the "corrupt bargain" between John Q. Adams and Henry Clay.

13 July
From [W. N. Kentrick]. ALS. DLC–JKP. Proposes banking system that he believes will "remove all present difficulties & insure future prosperity."

14 July
From Samuel H. Love et al. LS. T–GP. Request release of Edward Tyler from the penitentiary.

14 July
From W. G. Roulhac et al. LS. DLC–JKP. Extend invitation to a public dinner in Rutherford County.

14 July
From William R. Rucker. ALS. DLC–JKP. Urges that Polk issue state bonds to the Stones River & Cumberland Turnpike Company before he leaves for East Tennessee.

14 July
From James Walker.

15 July
From Willie B. Johnson. ALS. DLC–JKP. Sends papers pertaining to the pardon of John Heathcock; urges action in the matter.

16 July
From William Bobbitt. ALS. DLC–JKP. Reports on several items of business pertaining to Polk's plantation; feels that Isaac Dismukes has done a good job with the crops; but worries that unless the current drought is lifted, there will be no profit.

17 July
From Cave Johnson.

18 July
From William Welch. ALS. T–RG 30. Requests commission as sheriff of Perry County.

19 July
To the President and Directors of the Cumberland & Stones River Turnpike Company. Copy. T–GP. Discusses application for state bonds.

19 July
To the President and Directors of the Gallatin Turnpike Company. Copy. T–GP. Notifies them that $22,000 in state bonds have been issued for the benefit of their company.

20 July
From Thomas Dodson. ALS. DLC–JKP. Forwards title bonds as requested.

21 July
From Alexander O. Anderson. ALS. DLC–JKP. Reports that he is going to McMinn and Bradley counties to try to resolve differences between Democratic candidates there; refers to a division in Democratic ranks in Washington County; and asks Polk to compose these quarrels.

21 July	From H. J. Anderson. ALS. T–GP. Recommends commuting the prison sentence of James W. Duncan.
22 July	From John Sommerville. ALS. T–GP. Encloses resignation of William G. Childress as a state director of the Union Bank of Tennessee.
23 July	*From Silas M. Caldwell.*
25 July	From Oliver Alexander. ALS. DLC–JKP. Wishes to form a partnership with Polk to manage his plantation in Mississippi.
25 July [1841]	*From Sarah C. Polk.*
25 July	*To Sarah C. Polk.*
29 July	*From Sarah C. Polk.*
29 July	From David Shaver, Jr. ALS. DLC–JKP. Reports on campaign strategy and preparations for Polk's visit to upper East Tennessee.
[Aug 1841]	From Willie B. Johnson. ANS. T–GP. Discusses pardon petition on behalf of John Heathcock.
[Aug 1841]	From Samuel McClanahan and Adam Huntsman. LS. T–GP. Ask for executive clemency for Stephen Snell.
[Aug 1841]	From William K. Turner. ALS. T–GP. Presents statement of facts in the case of John Heathcock, alias John Young.
2 Aug	*To Robert Armstrong.*
2 Aug	*From Isaac H. Dismukes.*
[2] Aug	From Philip Lindsley. ALS. DLC–JKP. Advises of meeting of the trustees for the University of Nashville.
2 Aug	From Richard M. Woods. ALS. DLC–JKP. Suggests that many who hear Polk in East Tennessee will be Whigs and that Polk should "handle them with gloves off."
2 Aug	From Kavanaugh Yancy. ALS. DLC–JKP. Solicits employment as an overseer.
3 Aug	From William S. Plumer. ALS. DLC–JKP. Submits bill for $7 for subscription to the Richmond *Watchman of the South.*
4 Aug	From Thomas A. Anderson. ALS. DLC–JKP. Advises that he has procured a horse and buggy for Polk's use between Panther Springs, Jefferson County, and Tazewell.
5 Aug	From James T. Armstrong. NS. DLC–JKP. Invites Polk to a ball at the United States Military Academy.
6 Aug	From John Corbitt. ALS. T–GP. Encloses copy of the report of inquest held in the death of George Eubank.
6 Aug	From I. C. Lane. ALS. DLC–JKP. Gives election returns for Claiborne County.
6 Aug	From James R. McMeans. ALS. DLC–JKP. Gives election returns for Henry County.
6 Aug	From Green Moore. ALS. DLC–JKP. Gives election returns for Johnson County.
6 Aug	From Robert W. Powell. ALS. DLC–JKP. Gives election returns for Carter and Johnson counties.
7 Aug	From William Houston. ALS. DLC–JKP. Gives election returns for Claiborne County.

7 Aug	From Lewis P. Roberts. ALS. DLC–JKP. Introduces Stamos S. Trikaliotes, a native of Athens, Greece, who is on his way home via Nashville, Pittsburgh, and New York.
7 Aug	From Richard M. Woods. ALS. DLC–JKP. Gives election results for Greene County.
8 Aug	*From Aaron V. Brown.*
8 Aug	From [Samuel Martin]. L. DLC–JKP. Lists the articles needed for the Manual Labor School of Knox County.
8 Aug	From William Welch. ALS. T–RG 30. Discusses request for a commission.
9 Aug	From L. W. Jordan. ALS. DLC–JKP. Gives incomplete election returns for several counties in the southeast part of the state.
9 Aug	From John Kennedy. ALS. DLC–JKP. Solicits appointment as judge of the First Judicial District in place of William Powel, deceased.
[9] Aug	From Samuel Martin. ALS. DLC–JKP. Requests state assistance in providing arms with which to train students attending a manual labor and military school that he plans to establish at Campbell's Station.
10 Aug	From Levin H. Coe. ALS. DLC–JKP. Analyzes the vote in Hardeman, Fayette, and Shelby counties; discusses national political issues.
10 Aug	From William H. Cooke. ALS. T–GP. Resigns as director of the Hiwassee Railroad Company.
[10 Aug 1841?]	From J. George Harris. ALS. DLC–JKP. Requests financial support for the *Nashville Union*.
10 Aug	From Moses G. Reeves. ALS. DLC–JKP. Urges delay in the release of state bonds earmarked for the Lebanon & Murfreesboro Turnpike Company.
11 Aug	From William C. Dunlap. ALS. T–GP. Requests pardon for Stephen Snell.
12 Aug	From Enoch Ensley and Hays Blackman. NS. T–RG 5. Recommend several persons to serve as directors of the Nolensville Turnpike Company.
12 Aug	*From Hopkins L. Turney.*
13 Aug	*From Levin H. Coe.*
13 Aug	To the President and Directors of the Cumberland & Stones River Turnpike Company. ALS, copy. T–GP. Notifies them that additional state bonds cannot be issued at the present time.
14 Aug	From H. J. Anderson. ALS. T–GP. Recommends commuting the prison sentence of George Mezell.
14 Aug	To T. L. Green. ALS, copy. T–GP. Refuses to pardon Isaac Young.
14 Aug	From Samuel P. Walker. ALS. DLC–JKP. Reports on public meeting held in Columbia to consider who might be named his successor as postmaster.
14 Aug	From Hugh Wallace Wormsley. ALS. T–GP. Urges pardon for Stephen Snell.

15 Aug   *From Cave Johnson.*

15 Aug [1841]   *From A. O. P. Nicholson.*

16 Aug   From E. G. Eastman. ALS. DLC–JKP. Discusses voting results in East Tennessee; solicits appointment to a clerkship in the federal court.

16 Aug   From William Lacewell. ALS. T–GP. Requests that a reward be offered for the capture of a slave named Jacob and of John Rogers, Jr., both of whom are accused of felonious acts.

16 Aug   From A. O. P. Nicholson. ALS. DLC–JKP. Reports that John Tyler's Fiscal Bank bill veto has been received by the Congress and read "amidst a tremendous excitement."

17 Aug   From William G. Childress. ALS. DLC–JKP. Requests names of the Democratic members of the Tennessee Senate, the clerkship of which he is seeking.

17 Aug   From Leonard Jones. ALS. DLC–JKP. Urges prayer and fasting for unjust convictions recently rendered against several of his clients tried for murder in Greensburg, Kentucky.

17 Aug   From Ezra Keyser. ALS. DLC–JKP. Asks assistance in obtaining the office of engrossing clerk to the Tennessee Senate.

18 Aug   From Gladin Gorin. ALS. T–GP. Asks for pardon of Stephen Snell.

18 Aug   From John B. Hays. ALS. DLC–JKP. Requests assistance in obtaining a renewal of his note to the Planter's Bank of Nashville.

18 Aug   To Willie B. Johnson. ALS, copy. T–GP. Requests additional information in the case of John Heathcock.

18 Aug   To John H. Thomas. ALS, copy. T–GP. Requests additional information in the case of Will Bird.

18 Aug   From John S. Young. ALS. DLC–JKP. Advises that his wife's poor health prevents his traveling to Nashville at this time.

19 Aug   To Alexander A. Clingan. ALS, copy. T–GP. Describes proper procedure for reporting the results of the recent election.

19 Aug   *To Robert B. Reynolds.*

19 Aug   To the Speaker of the Tennessee Senate. ALS, copy. T–GP. Transmits election returns from Bradley County.

20 Aug   *From Alexander O. Anderson.*

20 Aug   From H. J. Anderson. ALS. T–GP. Describes physical and mental condition of convict Thomas Wilson.

20 Aug   From H. J. Anderson. ALS. T–GP. Informs Polk that John Robertson has not yet been received at the penitentiary.

20 Aug   From H. J. Anderson. ALS. T–GP. Forwards statement of the court in the case of Elizabeth Henderson, convicted of larceny in Bradley County.

20 Aug   From John Corbitt et al. LS. T–GP. Request that a reward be offered for James Henderson, alias James Earl.

20 Aug	From G. B. Hughes. ALS. T–GP. Encloses petition asking for the release of P. L. Smith from the state penitentiary.
20 Aug	From L. W. Jordan. ALS. DLC–JKP. Asks about prospects for electing one Democrat to the U.S. Senate; advises that Thomas I. Read will seek the position of doorkeeper for the Tennessee Senate, provided that Polk thinks Read can secure the necessary votes from west of the Cumberland Mountain.
20 Aug	To the President and Directors of the Columbia, Pulaski, Elkton & Alabama Turnpike Company. ALS, copy. T–GP. Notifies them that $14,000 in state bonds have been issued for the use of their company.
20 Aug	*From Isaac Wright.*
20 Aug	From Henderson K. Yoakum. ALS. DLC–JKP. Praises Polk for political gains in Rutherford County.
21 Aug	To Robert M. Anderson. ALS, copy. T–GP. Requests that he hold the upcoming courts in Hawkins and Green counties; informs him that Zachariah Herrel recently died in the penitentiary.
21 Aug	From John Blair. ALS. DLC–JKP. Advises Polk not to appoint a replacement for Samuel Powel, deceased; discusses effects of John Tyler's veto of Henry Clay's bank bill.
21 Aug	From William Carroll et al. LS. T–GP. Request pardon for Elizabeth Henderson, confined in the state penitentiary.
21 Aug	From Henderson K. Yoakum. ALS. DLC–JKP. Claims moral victory in the recent election defeat.
22 Aug	From J. W. Kendall. ALS. DLC–JKP. Discusses shipment and possible sale of sheep.
22 Aug	From George A. Sublett. ALS. DLC–JKP. Gives opinion as to the character of a Negro named Pleasant, who is under a death sentence for housebreaking.
23 Aug	From Beverly S. Allen. ALS. T–GP. Discusses the case of Stephen Snell.
23 Aug	From Samuel Eskridge. ALS. DLC–JKP. Urges that Polk see Thomas Brown when he visits Nashville; says that Brown wishes to run Polk for the U.S. Senate.
23 Aug	From John B. Hays. ALS. DLC–JKP. Asks Polk's assistance in a financial matter.
23 Aug	To Thomas A. Pasteur. ALS, copy. T–GP. Refuses to pardon Henry Norwood.
23 Aug	From William H. Polk. ALS. DLC–JKP. Encloses note for $225, as requested; states that "Our friends are in fine spirits. They look on your defeat, as a *triumph*, and are animated with the full belief that Tennessee is Democratic, and that your election went by default."
24 Aug	*To Samuel H. Laughlin.*
24 Aug	From H. D. Rogers. ALS. DLC–JKP. Wants to know if Polk will allow his name to be run as a candidate for the U.S. Senate.

24 Aug	*From Hopkins L. Turney.*
25 Aug	From Elijah Boddie et al. LS. DLC–JKP. Extend invitation to a public dinner in Gallatin.
25 Aug	From Arthur R. Crozier. ALS. DLC–JKP. Asks Polk to speak to John Catron about appointing E. G. Eastman clerk of the federal court.
25 Aug	From Josephus C. Guild. ALS. DLC–JKP. Urges Polk to accept the invitation to the public dinner at Gallatin; invites him to stay at his home.
25 Aug	From Willie B. Johnson. ALS. DLC–JKP. Sends records in the case of John Heathcock, along with a "short statement of the facts." (Enclosures not found.)
25 Aug	*From J. G. M. Ramsey.*
26 Aug	From Jonathan P. Hardwicke. ALS. DLC–JKP. Reports that Isaac Goodall and Henry Marable are likely to vote with the Democrats in the state legislature.
27 Aug	From Alvin Cullom. ALS. DLC–JKP. Believes that John England, legislator-elect from White County, will be sympathetic to Democratic interests, especially in the U.S. Senate elections.
28 Aug	From Robert M. Anderson. ALS. DLC–JKP. Explains why he cannot hold the courts at Rogersville on the fourth Monday of September and at Greeneville on the second Monday of October.
29 Aug	From William Bobbitt. ALS. DLC–JKP. Discusses business pertaining to Polk's plantation; urges Polk to attend a Democratic rally in Yalobusha County on October 5.
30 Aug	*From Alexander O. Anderson.*
30 Aug	From Robert A. Campbell. ALS. DLC–JKP. Reports on rumors from Van Buren County that John England intends to vote for Polk for the U.S. Senate.
30 Aug	From Nicholas Fain. ALS. DLC–JKP. Introduces W. James Fulkerson, a visitor to Nashville.
30 Aug	From John B. Hays. ALS. DLC–JKP. Requests assistance in a business matter.
30 Aug	From G. L. Lenard. ALS. DLC–JKP. Extends invitation to a public dinner in Petersburg, Lincoln County.
31 Aug	From Andrew M. Ballentine. ALS. T–RG 5. Reports names of the directors elected by the stockholders of the Columbia, Pulaski, Elkton & Alabama Turnpike Company.
31 Aug	*To Elijah Boddie et al.*
31 Aug	To Michael Doyles and T. L. Green. ALS, copy. T–GP. Transmits pardon for Isaac Young.
31 Aug	*From Sackfield Maclin.*
1 Sept	*From Julius W. Blackwell.*
1 Sept	*From Isaac H. Dismukes.*
1 Sept	*From Samuel H. Laughlin.*
1 Sept	From J. W. White. ALS. DLC–JKP. Sends bill for subscription to the Shelbyville *Whig Advocate*.

2 Sept	From Alexander O. Anderson. L, fragment. DLC–JKP. Discusses possible Whig choices for the U.S. Senate and Whig attitudes in Washington City concerning John Tyler.
2 Sept	From John M. Bailey. ALS. DLC–JKP. Wishes to know the result of the Tennessee gubernatorial election, as he has heard conflicting reports.
2 Sept	From George Bomford. ANS. T–GP. Renders statement regarding arms to be furnished to the Tennessee militia.
2 Sept	To B. W. D. Carty. ALS, copy. T–GP. Refuses to reduce the prison sentence of William Moffett.
2 Sept	From Julian Frazier. ALS. DLC–JKP. Declares that "under the circumstances" Polk's election defeat was "a great triumph."
2 Sept	*To Samuel H. Laughlin.*
2 Sept	*From George W. Smith.*
2 Sept	From Archibald Wright, John W. Goode, and Samuel Moseley. LS. T–RG 5. Discuss issuance of state bonds for the benefit of the Columbia, Pulaski, Elkton & Alabama Turnpike Company.
3 Sept	*From J. George Harris.*
3 Sept	From Samuel D. Morgan. ALS. T–GP. Testifies to the good character of Eli M. Driver.
3 Sept	From Samuel Seay and Joseph H. Shepherd. LS. T–GP. Express confidence in Eli M. Driver of Pontotoc, Mississippi.
4 Sept	From Eli M. Driver. ALS. T–GP. Promises that he will prevent his slave, Pleasant, from returning to Tennessee.
4 Sept	From Samuel Eskridge. ALS. DLC–JKP. Endorses Thomas A. Brown, candidate for engrossing clerk to the Tennessee House.
4 Sept	From David Hubbard. ALS. T–GP. Attests to the integrity of Eli M. Driver.
6 Sept	From Felix Bosworth. ALS. DLC–JKP. Sends evidence of his defense before the Louisiana legislature. (Enclosure not found.)
6 Sept	From Robert B. Reynolds. ALS. DLC–JKP. Discusses possible candidates to replace the late Samuel Powel, judge of the First Judicial District.
7 Sept	*From Ann S. Johnson.*
7 Sept	To Charles F. Keith. ALS, copy. T–GP. Asks him to hold upcoming courts in Hawkins and Greene counties.
7 Sept	To William Lacewell. ALS, copy. T–GP. Asks for additional information in the cases of Jacob, a slave indicted for the murder of Daniel Lacewell, and of John Rogers, Jr., indicted as an accessory to the crime.
7 Sept	From G. C. McBee. ALS. DLC–JKP. Recommends John Blevins, candidate for clerk in the legislature.
7 Sept	From John L. McCarty. ALS. T–GP. Resigns as director of the Hiwassee Railroad Company.
7 Sept	From G. W. L. Marr. ALS. DLC–JKP. Advises that he

does not intend to contest the election of representative from his district; explains that fraud would be difficult to prove.

7 Sept	*From A. O. P. Nicholson.*
7 Sept	*From William H. Polk.*
7 Sept	*From Bromfield L. Ridley.*
7 Sept	To the Speaker of the Tennessee Senate. ALS, copy. T–GP. Encloses election returns for Davidson County.
7 Sept	From James H. Thomas. ALS. T–GP. Requests pardon for Richard Rail.
8 Sept	From John M. Bell. ACS. T–GP. Requests information regarding the number of small arms owned by the state.
8 Sept	From Robert A. Campbell. ALS. DLC–JKP. Requests pardon for Alexander Webb, convicted of the murder of Shadrack M. Taylor.
8 Sept	From M. D. Cardwell. ALS. DLC–JKP. Wishes advice on running for engrossing or reading clerk in the next legislature.
8 Sept	To G. L. Lenard et al. ALS, draft. DLC–JKP. Accepts invitation to a public dinner in Petersburg, the date of which is to be designated later.
8 Sept	From Yandell S. Patton. ALS. DLC–JKP. Solicits loan of $100.
8 Sept	From George R. Powel. ALS. DLC–JKP. Suggests that the vacancy in the First Judicial District, caused by his father's death, should be filled as soon as possible; recommends no particular candidate; and discusses Tyler's Fiscal Bank bill veto and other political issues.
8 Sept	From W. G. Roulhac. ALS. DLC–JKP. Seeks advice on the propriety of running for the office of engrossing clerk to the Tennessee Senate.
9 Sept	From H. J. Anderson. ALS. T–GP. Recommends commuting the prison sentence of William Campbell.
9 Sept	To the President and Directors of the Columbia, Pulaski, Elkton & Alabama Turnpike Company. Copy. T–GP. Notifies them that $4,000 in state bonds have been issued for the benefit of their company.
9 Sept	To the President and Directors of the Nolensville Turnpike Company. Copy. T–GP. Notifies them that $8,000 in state bonds have been issued for the benefit of their company.
10 Sept	From John W. Lide. ALS. T–GP. Recommends several men from both parties as possible directors of the Hiwassee Railroad Company.
10 Sept	*From Nathan Vaught.*
11 Sept	From James Goodner. ALS. T–RG 5. Encloses report by the commissioners appointed to examine the Lebanon & Sparta Turnpike Company and discusses the issuance of state bonds.
11 Sept	From J. C. Napier. ALS. DLC–JKP. Extolls virtues of the Polk administration and denounces Whig opponents.

12 Sept	*From Samuel H. Laughlin.*
15 Sept	*From Adam Huntsman.*
15 Sept	From Charles F. Keith. ALS. DLC–JKP. Explains that the Circuit Court in Polk County will occupy his time and that he must decline the request to hold the Circuit courts in Hawkins and Greene counties.
17 Sept	To James Gadsden. Copy. T–GP. Requests information concerning the Louisville, Cincinnati and Charleston Railroad Company.
17 Sept	*From David Hubbard.*
17 Sept	To J. G. M. Ramsey. Copy. T–GP. Requests information on the Louisville, Cincinnati and Charleston Railroad Company.
18 Sept	To the President and Directors of the Hiwassee Railroad Company. Copy. T–GP. Forwards commissions for state directors of the company.
18 Sept	To J. G. M. Ramsey. Copy. T–GP. Requests information regarding specie payments by the Knoxville branch of the Southwestern Railroad Bank.
18 Sept	From Samuel P. Walker. ALS. DLC–JKP. Encloses Polk's note held by James Walker; reports that local Whigs are indignant with John Tyler's second bank bill veto. (Enclosure not found.)
20 Sept	From W. J. Dale. ALS. DLC–JKP. Encloses letter to A. O. P. Nicholson informing him of his daughter's death; asks Polk to find an appropriate way to deliver the news.
21 Sept	From C. B. Fletcher. ALS. DLC–JKP. Suggests that it is "the wish of a number of Democratic friends in Missouri that you should be a Candidate for President of the United States."
21 Sept	*To Cave Johnson.*
21 Sept	From D. B. Stockholm. ALS. T–GP. Conveys information on chemical guano and asks Polk to communicate the same to leading planters.
22 Sept	From James T. Dunlap. ALS. DLC–JKP. Solicits appointment as attorney general for the Seventh Judicial District, replacing James R. McMeans, deceased.
24 Sept	*From N. S. Anderson.*
24 Sept	From Robert Campbell, Jr. ALS. DLC–JKP. Recommends James O. Potter as engrossing clerk for the Tennessee Senate.
24 Sept	*To William Moore.*
24 Sept	From J. G. M. Ramsey. ALS. T–GP. States that specie is paid for all notes of the Knoxville branch of the Southwestern Railroad Bank.
24 Sept	From J. G. M. Ramsey. ALS. T–GP. Encloses pamphlet of the stockholders meeting of the Louisville, Cincinnati and Charleston Railroad Company; discusses withdrawal of Tennessee as a stockholder in the company.

24 Sept	From J. G. M. Ramsey. ALS. DLC–JKP. Urges that the state pay interest on state bonds issued for the Louisville, Cincinnati and Charleston Railroad Company.
25 Sept	From Wallace Estill. ALS. DLC–JKP. Reports that an unusual amount of illness demanding his professional services at home will prevent his coming to Nashville so early as planned.
25 Sept	From William Fitzgerald. ALS. DLC–JKP. Suggests that "it will save any feeling which might arise among your friends if it was left for the General Assembly to act" in the matter of filling the vacant attorney generalship in the Ninth Judicial District.
25 Sept	From Adam Gardenhire. ALS. DLC–JKP. Introduces son, E. L. Gardenhire, candidate for attorney general in the Fourth Judicial District.
25 Sept	From Philip B. Glenn. ALS. DLC–JKP. Urges political friends to assist James L. Green until "he gets into the *run of things.*"
26 Sept	From Sackfield Maclin. ALS. T–GP. Advises Polk to appoint Seth Wallard a director of the LaGrange & Memphis Railroad Company.
26 Sept	From Henderson K. Yoakum. ALS. DLC–JKP. Discusses Democratic positions and strategies.
27 Sept	*From Isaac H. Dismukes.*
27 Sept	From A. M. Gaines. ALS. DLC–JKP. Solicits appointment as attorney general of the First Judicial District, replacing James R. McMeans, deceased.
27 Sept	From J. G. M. Ramsey. ALS. T–GP. Discusses withdrawal of Tennessee as a stockholder in the Louisville, Cincinnati and Charleston Railroad Company.
27 Sept	From J. G. M. Ramsey. ALS. DLC–JKP. Discusses banking issue, composition of the state legislature, and possibility of Polk's appointment to the U.S. Senate.
27 Sept	*From Robert B. Reynolds.*
28 Sept	*From Alexander O. Anderson.*
28 Sept	From R. L. Brown et al. LS. T–GP. Ask Polk to post a reward for Lewis H. Moore and Robert Montgomery, alleged murderers of Samuel Caskey.
28 Sept	From Robert J. Chester. ALS. DLC–JKP. Discusses effect in Perryville of the reading of John Tyler's Fiscal Corporation veto; discusses candidacies of Timothy P. Scurlock and Joseph H. Talbot for the attorney generalship of the Tenth Judicial District; and asks Polk to "take no part against Scurlock."
29 Sept	*From Alexander O. Anderson.*
29 Sept	From William E. Butler. ALS. DLC–JKP. Asks Polk to take no part in the election between Joseph H. Talbot and Timothy P. Scurlock, candidates for attorney general of the Tenth Judicial District.

29 Sept	From David Cleage. ALS. T–GP. Declines appointment as state director of the Hiwassee Railroad Company; suggests John McGaughey for the position.
29 Sept	To Robert Walker. Copy. T–GP. Informs him that he is unable to pardon Isham Walker.
30 Sept	To Daniel Graham. Copy. T–GP. Directs him to issue to Robert A. Campell a warrant upon the treasury for $200 as reward for the capture of Samuel Earthman.
30 Sept	From Adam Huntsman. ALS. DLC–JKP. Supports candidacy of Timothy P. Scurlock for attorney general of the Tenth Judicial District; asks Polk not to intervene in the election.
30 Sept	From Cave Johnson. ALS. DLC–JKP. Reports that his arrival in Nashville will be delayed.
30 Sept	From David B. Molloy. ALS. DLC–JKP. Reports that Polk's slave, Gilbert, has been found and is jailed at Holly Springs, Mississippi.
30 Sept	To the President and Directors of the Lebanon & Sparta Turnpike Company. Copy. T–GP. Notifies them that the Board of Internal Improvement has rejected their application for additional state bonds.
[Oct 1841]	To James H. Thomas. Copy. T–GP. Refuses to pardon Thomas Rail.
[1 Oct]	*From John F. Gillespy.*
1 Oct	From John B. Hays. ALS. DLC–JKP. Advises that he has not been able "to ascertain any thing on the subject, to which, you alluded the other day in your last. But I guess that he will be a candidate if there is a reasonable prospect."
1 Oct	To the Secretary of War. Copy. T–GP. Reports number of small arms received from the federal government for the Tennessee militia.
1 Oct	From Robert Walker. ALS. DLC–JKP. Expresses deep disappointment that Polk declines to pardon Isham Walker.
2 Oct	From H. J. Anderson. ALS. DLC–JKP. Reports number of convicts received at the state penitentiary since September 30, 1839, totals 116.
2 Oct	From H. J. Anderson. ALS. DLC–JKP. Submits report on the number of convicts at the state penitentiary discharged in the previous two years.
3 Oct	From H. J. Anderson. ALS. DLC–JKP. Advises that "the information desired relative to the recpts. and Expenditures of the Prison cannot be furnished in time for your message."
3 Oct	From Abram Caruthers. ALS. T–GP. Reports inability to hold the Circuit Court at Sparta; asks that someone be appointed to take his place.
5 Oct	To Abram Caruthers. Copy. T–GP. Notifies him that he has appointed Alvin Cullom as a special judge.
5 Oct	To Alvin Cullom. Copy. T–GP. Transmits commission as special judge to hold the upcoming Circuit Court in White County.

6 Oct	*From Alexander O. Anderson.*
6 Oct	From Garrett Lane et al. LS. DLC–JKP. Invite Polk to a public dinner in Hickman County honoring Cave Johnson.
7 Oct	From Cothran & Neill. LS. DLC–JKP. Reports that Polk's slave, Harry, has asked to be placed in the firm's custody, should he be granted his own time for the coming year; requests instructions in the matter.
7 Oct	From John S. Potter. ALS. DLC–JKP. Invites Polk to attend the Nashville Theatre on October 8.
[13] Oct	*To Andrew Jackson Donelson.*
14 Oct	*From Andrew Jackson.*
17 Oct [1841]	From David M. Hunter. ALS. DLC–JKP. Discusses arrangements for his son, William, to attend school in Columbia.
18 Oct	*To J. P. Hardwicke, G. W. Campbell et al.*
19 Oct	*From Harvey M. Watterson.*
20 Oct	From David B. Molloy. ALS. DLC–JKP. Wishes to know when Polk will be in Holly Springs en route to his farm; says that many friends would like to greet him there.
23 Oct	From Egbert Haywood. ALS. DLC–JKP. Recommends Charles P. Taliaferro to be postmaster at Brownsville.
25 Oct	From George S. Houston. ALS. DLC–JKP. Wishes to know about the navigability of the Cumberland and Ohio rivers; also wishes to know who will be elected to the U.S. Senate from Tennessee.
26 Oct	*From Levin H. Coe.*
30 Oct	*To Andrew Jackson.*
31 Oct	From Joseph G. Barclift. ALS. DLC–JKP. Seeks information regarding the disposition of a deed.
31 Oct	From Andrew Jackson. ALS. DLC–JKP. Advises that in accordance with Polk's request, he has written a note to Charles Wickliffe recommending Charles P. Taliaferro to be postmaster at Brownsville.
1 Nov	From Edward L. Crain. ALS. DLC–JKP. Regrets Polk's defeat for the governorship; suggests that Polk would be an admirable presidential candidate.
1 Nov	*To William C. Tate.*
6 Nov	From Pitser Miller. ALS. DLC–JKP. Advises that he knows nothing about the land Nathan Roberts proposes to trade to Polk; recalls that "Mr. Hans Finley wrote me in Octr. 1839 that it ought to Sell or be disposed of at $3 pr. acre."
6 Nov	From Nathan Roberts. ALS. DLC–JKP. Proposes making an exchange of land with Polk.
9 Nov	*From J. G. M. Ramsey.*
12 Nov	From William L. Berry. ALS. DLC–JKP. Submits bill in the amount of $16.50 for past subscriptions to the Fayetteville *Independent Yeoman*, the Fayetteville *Standard of the Union* and the Fayetteville *Lincoln Journal*.
12 Nov	*From Jonathan P. Hardwicke.*

13 Nov	*From Samuel H. Laughlin.*
14 Nov	From James Brown. ALS. DLC–JKP. Advises that he has just learned that Polk is in Oxford, Mississippi; hopes to call in the morning.
15 Nov	From George Long. ALS. DLC–JKP. Endorsed by Polk as being "Anonymous & illegible."
19 Nov	From Marcus B. Winchester. ALS. DLC–JKP. Advises that on November 13 he forwarded notice of the receipt of a wagon; adds that he will retain the wagon until Polk sends a team of horses.
22 Nov	From William H. Polk. ALS. DLC–JKP. Discusses political maneuvers pertaining to the U.S. Senate election.
23 Nov	From Jonathan P. Hardwicke. ALS. DLC–JKP. Reports on Samuel Turney's actions, which are said to run counter to party strategy.
23 Nov	From Sackfield Maclin. ALS. DLC–JKP. Reports that Samuel Turney has deserted the party in relation to the U.S. Senate elections.
24 Nov	*From Samuel H. Laughlin.*
24 Nov	From Sackfield Maclin. ALS. DLC–JKP. Reports that Samuel Turney has deserted the party in relation to the U.S. Senate elections; regrets Polk's absence from Nashville, for "it is most likely you could influence him to do right."
24 Nov	From Marcus B. Winchester. ALS. DLC–JKP. Sends bill for farm equipment.
25 Nov	From Samuel P. Walker. ALS. DLC–JKP. Discusses plans for a public dinner to be given on Polk's arrival home at Columbia; wants to know the exact day when Polk will return.
1 Dec	From W. T. Caruthers. ALS. DLC–JKP. Requests copy of Polk's speech at Holly Springs, Mississippi; plans to publish the address.
2 Dec	From William Shapard. ALS. DLC–JKP. Transmits inquiry from J. Davis, who is interested in purchasing Polk's farm in Mississippi.
12 Dec	From Jesse Speight. ALS. DLC–JKP. Reports that he has never seen the land about which Polk in inquiring, but that others say it is worth about $5 per acre.
13 Dec	From Jonathan P. Hardwicke. ALS. DLC–JKP. Urges Polk to return to Nashville to attend to party business.
13 Dec	*From J. George Harris.*
15 Dec	*From Jonathan P. Hardwicke.*
15 Dec	*From J. George Harris.*
15 Dec	From William H. Polk. ALS. DLC–JKP. Advises that if Polk were in Nashville the U.S. Senate elections might be accomplished successfully.
16 Dec	From William H. Bayne. ALS. DLC–JKP. Wishes to know if Polk has paid for his subscription to the Fayetteville *North Carolinian*.

20 Dec	From Jesse Speight. ALS. DLC–JKP. Discusses advisability of buying land in central Mississippi; comments on the political situation at the state and national levels.
22 Dec	From W. P. Rowles. ALS. DLC–JKP. Solicits help in obtaining the position of principal of the Knoxville Female Academy.
23 Dec	From Aaron V. Brown. ALS. DLC–JKP. Discusses issues under debate in the U.S. House; comments on the U.S. Senate elections in Tennessee.
25 Dec	To A. R. Wynne. ALS. T–ARW. Describes procedure for requesting an appointment to the U.S. Military Academy at West Point in behalf of Wynne's son; advises that he has talked with Hopkins L. Turney about the matter and will write to Cave Johnson.
26 Dec	*From Hopkins L. Turney.*
29 Dec	*To Samuel H. Laughlin.*
30 Dec	From Thomas H. Benton. ALS. DLC–JKP. Acknowledges receipt of Polk's letter concerning Samuel Hogg's application for a pension and promises to assist in expediting the matter.
30 Dec	From William S. Fulton. ALS. DLC–JKP. Agrees to assist Samuel Hogg in his claim for a pension.
31 Dec	*From Jonathan P. Hardwicke.*
31 Dec	*To Andrew Jackson.*
31 Dec	From Andrew A. Kincannon. ALS. DLC–JKP. Advises that the land about which Polk inquired is of little value; thinks that a majority of the people of Tennessee would like to see Polk in the U.S. Senate.
31 Dec	From Henderson K. Yoakum. ALS. DLC–JKP. Gives reflections on Polk's defeat, the U.S. Senate elections, John Tyler's policies, and other political issues.

1842

2 Jan	*From John Catron.*
2 Jan	*From Hopkins L. Turney.*
4 Jan	*To Andrew Jackson Donelson.*
6 Jan	*From William H. Polk.*
7 Jan	From Andrew Jackson. ALS. DLC–JKP. Acknowledges receipt of three letters and will "duly attend to them" as soon as his health will permit.
8 Jan	From Seay & Shepherd. LS. DLC–JKP. Forwards account for commission and drayage charges incurred in February 1841.
9 Jan	From Jonathan P. Hardwicke. ALS. DLC–JKP. Relates current political movements of Nashville Whigs and John Bell's attempts to win a Senate seat.
[10 Jan 1842]	From W. F. Baug & Co. LS. DLC–JKP. Forwards Polk's account with S. Nye and Co. for subscriptions to the Nashville *Republican Banner*.

10 Jan	*From John H. Dew.*
10 Jan	From Samuel H. Laughlin. ALS. DLC–JKP. Reports that the Rutherford and Wilson legislative delegations will support Hopkins L. Turney if "we will unite with them and elect John Bell" to the U.S. Senate.
10 Jan	From Hopkins L. Turney. ALS. DLC–JKP. Acknowledges receipt of Polk's letter of December 29, 1841, with enclosure; relates that Nashville Democrats will refuse a portion of Tennessee's proceeds under the distribution law of 1842; and advises that Democrats in Washington are unorganized on the Treasury note bill, which some will reject unless the land bill is first repealed.
11 [Jan]	*From J. George Harris.*
13 Jan	From Thomas Robley. ALS. DLC–JKP. Seeks legal advice and assistance in retaining an interest for his wife, Jane S. Wilkes, in the distribution of John Wilkes' estate.
13 Jan	*From James Walker.*
16 Jan	From Jonathan P. Hardwicke. ALS. DLC–JKP. Writes that there is an "unholy alliance" between Foster and Nicholson in the U.S. Senate election; notes that Barkly Martin has promoted the election of Nicholson and has engendered "strong prejudices" against Hopkins L. Turney's election; and expresses his view that if all else fails, Democrats may have to elect Polk to the Senate.
16 Jan	From Hopkins L. Turney. ALS. DLC–JKP. Encloses letter received from R. B. Moore.
16 Jan	From James Walker. ALS. DLC–JKP. Declares that John Bell's election "under *any circumstances* would be endorsing his treachery" and that Bell's candidacy "will not take"; states that Ephraim H. Foster cannot be elected, although Barkly Martin wishes to compromise on Foster and A. O. P. Nicholson.
17 Jan	*To Sackfield Maclin.*
17 Jan	*From William H. Polk.*
17 Jan	*To James Walker.*
18 Jan	From Seay & Shepherd. LS. DLC–JKP. Encloses an account for goods shipped from New Orleans.
20 Jan	From William Bobbitt. ALS. DLC–JKP. Reports that he has purchased 3,000 pounds of pork for Polk's Mississippi plantation.
20 Jan	From Eunice O. Polk. ALS. DLC–JKP. Relates news received from the family of Polk's deceased brother, Marshall T. Polk.
20 Jan	From Harvey M. Watterson. ALS. DLC–JKP. Observes that Tennessee will have eleven members of the U.S. House under the new apportionment law and that the power to deal in bills of exchange has been removed from Walter Forward's exchequer scheme by the House Select Committee on Finance and the Currency; reports that the House has voted to repeal the bankruptcy act, but that its passage in the Senate is in doubt.

22 Jan	From Robert Armstrong. ALS. DLC–JKP. Urges that Polk come to Nashville and "put things right," for A. O. P. Nicholson is dividing the party and selling himself to the Whigs.
22 Jan	From Archibald Yell. ALS. DLC–JKP. Acknowledges two letters from Polk concerning proposed land sales; reports that he is unable to sell Polk's land "at any price," as there is "no money in the country."
24 Jan	From Thomas Ewell. ALS. DLC–JKP. Relates that he is contemplating a move to Little Rock, Arkansas; requests letters of introduction to Archibald Yell and to "other influential men of your acquaintance."
25 Jan	From Samuel H. Laughlin. ALS. DLC–JKP. Urges Polk to come to Nashville, for Democratic losses on the specie resumption and bond questions have left him in a state of despair.
26 Jan	*From Jonathan P. Hardwicke.*
26 Jan	*From Sackfield Maclin.*
28 Jan	*From Thomas Fletcher.*
29 Jan	From Robert Armstrong. ALS. DLC–JKP. Lists names of James C. Jones' appointees to the directorship of the Bank of Tennessee; urges Polk to "come in on *Monday*," as "all the movements of the Whig party are made with a view to effect *you.*"
29 Jan	*From Samuel H. Laughlin.*
1 Feb	From Isaac H. Dismukes. ALS. DLC–JKP. Discusses business of Polk's Mississippi plantation.
2 Feb	From J. G. M. Ramsey. ALS. DLC–JKP. Encloses circular from the East Tennessee Historical and Antiquarian Society; discusses Polk's political strength in East Tennessee and North Carolina; and urges prompt movement for a Calhoun-Polk ticket in 1844.
3 Feb	From James McAlister. ALS. DLC–JKP. Requests letter of recommendation for a military appointment.
5 Feb	From Lewis J. Cist. ALS. DLC–JKP. Requests Polk's autograph.
11 Feb	From Jackson Leggett. ALS. DLC–JKP. Requests information on the disposition of the pension papers of Thomas Fisher.
15 Feb	From Robert Armstrong. ALS. DLC–JKP. Acknowledges receipt of Polk's "covering Letter" to John Tyler and William S. Fulton; urges confidentiality of his interest in a military appointment.
15 Feb	To Aaron V. Brown, ALS. DNA–RG 59. Transmits letter from D. A. Alexander to John Tyler requesting assistance in securing the release of F. H. Alexander from prison in Texas.
15 Feb	*From James M. Howry.*
18 Feb	From Robert Armstrong. ALS. DLC–JKP. Advises Polk of a suit against Josephus C. Guild.
18 Feb	From William McCalester. ALS. DLC–JKP. Seeks assis-

tance in securing pay for executing warrant against G. W. McLawson.

18 Feb   From Ezekiel P. McNeal. ALS. DLC–JKP. Acknowledges receipt of Polk's letters of February 11 and "your favor of last month"; advises Polk of financial business.

21 Feb   *From Joseph W. Horton.*

21 Feb   From James Irwin. ALS. DLC–JKP. Discusses Polk's financial affairs.

21 Feb   From John J. Scuitall. ALS. DLC–JKP. Requests exposition of Polk's political ideas.

22 Feb   From Daniel Graham. ALS. DLC–JKP. Apprises Polk of political activities in Summer and Smith counties.

23 Feb   *From Robert Armstrong.*

23 Feb   From John M. Bass. ALS. DLC–JKP. Acknowledges receipt of Polk's letter of February 21, which requested renewal of a note held by the Union Bank of Tennessee.

24 Feb   From G. W. Rogers. ALS. DLC–JKP. Inquires about a reward due Hezekiah Bradbury of Henderson County.

24 Feb   *From Hopkins L. Turney.*

25 Feb   From John Ray. ALS. DLC–JKP. Discusses efforts to recover a debt of $303 owed the estate of Samuel Polk for the sale of 274 acres of land in Carroll County.

26 Feb   From Silas M. Caldwell. ALS. DLC–JKP. Wishes Polk to collect and forward a small sum of money held by Terry H. Cahal and A. O. P. Nicholson.

26 Feb   From J. G. M. Ramsey. ALS. DLC–JKP. Urges Polk's early nomination for the vice-presidency on a ticket with John C. Calhoun; says that he has written to J. W. Hampton of North Carolina urging the Charlotte *Jeffersonian* to endorse such a ticket.

27 Feb   *From Cave Johnson.*

28 Feb   From Adlai O. Harris. ALS. DLC–JKP. Acknowledges Polk's letter of February 21 and states that he will reply to Polk's financial inquiries "in a few days," if West H. Humphreys does not write Polk at Bolivar.

28 Feb   From Cave Johnson. ALS. DLC–JKP. Inquires about pension claims for the father and uncle of Robert J. Nelson; reports that Martin Van Buren is on the way to the Hermitage via South Carolina.

28 Feb   From H. W. Noe. ALS. DLC–JKP. Solicits Polk's support in securing a contract to deliver journals and public documents in Middle Tennessee.

1 March   From John M. Bass. ALS. DLC–JKP. Returns Polk's cancelled note for $800, paid at the Union Bank of Tennessee at Nashville.

4 March   From Robert J. Nelson. ALS. DLC–JKP. Polk's assistance in securing pension claims for his father, John Nelson.

6 March   *From Archibald Yell.*

11 March *To Sarah C. Polk.*

11 March   From John A. Thomas. ALS. DLC–JKP. Appeals to Polk for a statement of his family "character and standing in society," to be directed to Troy, New York, where he is aide-de-camp to John Ellis Wool.

12 March [1842]   *From John C. Calhoun.*

17 March   From W. F. Davidson. ALS. DLC–JKP. Desires information on Tennessee's statute of limitations.

18 March   *From E. G. Eastman.*

18 March   From James Irwin. ALS. DLC–JKP. Informs Polk of personal financial business.

20 March   From Cave Johnson. ALS. DLC–JKP. Acknowledges Polk's letter of March 5; describes political movements of Richard M. Johnson, David R. Porter, Robert J. Walker, John C. Calhoun, Thomas H. Benton, etc.; maintains that he and a majority of Democratic members of Congress favor a Martin Van Buren-Polk ticket; states that the Board of Exchequer proposal creates division in the party; and sees nothing to be gained in attacking John Tyler.

22 March   *From Aaron V. Brown.*

24 March   From Sarah C. Polk. ALS. DLC–JKP. Forwards letter from E. G. Eastman on East Tennessee politics.

[30 March 1842]   *From J. G. M. Ramsey.*

2 April   From Ezekiel P. McNeal. ALS. DLC–JKP. Has been unable to sell any of Polk's land in the Western District.

5 April   From Barnet Hardy. ALS. DLC–JKP. Wishes to know the price of a 240-acre tract of Polk's land located near John Henning's farm in Madison County.

6 April   From Sackfield Maclin. ALS. DLC–JKP. Expresses confidence that Polk could now carry his senatorial district in a contest with James C. Jones; reports that volunteers from the Western District and North Mississippi have gone to Texas.

9 April   *From Aaron V. Brown.*

9 April   From Isaac H. Dismukes. ALS. DLC–JKP. Informs Polk of spring planting on his Mississippi plantation.

13 April   *From Robert Armstrong.*

14 April   From Robert Armstrong. ALS. DLC–JKP. Suggests that Polk will be accused of a "Bargain" with Martin Van Buren if Polk seeks a place on the presidential ticket while Van Buren is in Tennessee.

14 April   From I. H. Rawlings. ALS. DLC–JKP. Wishes Polk to examine the land office register in his behalf.

15 April   *From Robert Armstrong.*

[April 16]   From Robert Armstrong. ALI. DLC–JKP. Reports that the Democrats have carried Connecticut; expects an early calling of the Tennessee legislature.

[18 April 1842]   *From J. G. M. Ramsey.*

19 April   *From Samuel H. Laughlin.*

22 April   *From Robert Armstrong.*

25 April [1842]   *From Robert Armstrong.*

25 April	From Joseph W. Horton. ALS. DLC–JKP. Acknowledges receipt of Polk's letter of April 22, enclosing $332; has applied that sum to Polk's note, which is due the Bank of Tennessee at Nashville on April 25.
26 April [1842]	From Samuel P. Caldwell. ALS. DLC–JKP. Recalls that a 500-acre tract of Polk lands in the Western District was sold at sheriff's sale in 1836 or 1837.
26 April	From Robert Desha. ALS. DLC–JKP. Acknowledges receipt of Polk's letter of April 14; discusses payment of Polk's fees for his legal services.
[26] April	*From Hopkins L. Turney.*
27 April	From Isaac H. Dismukes. ALS. DLC–JKP. Informs Polk of plantation business.
27 April	From Daniel Webster. LS. DLC–JKP. Also copy in DNA–RG 59. Acknowledges receipt of Polk's letter of April 13, inquiring into the release of Samuel G. Narvell from Mexican authorities.
29 April	*From Cave Johnson.*
29 April	From John Pearce, Jr. ALS. DLC–JKP. Complains that he is due a proper explanation for Polk's failure to arrange payment of his debt.
30 April	*From Levin H. Coe.*
30 April	*From Archibald Yell.*
2 May	From William T. Ross. ALS. DLC–JKP. Encloses receipt for subscription payment.
2 May	*From Harvey M. Watterson.*
3 May	From Granville S. Crockett. ALS. DLC–JKP. Invites Polk and Martin Van Buren to visit Murfreesboro on Van Buren's return from Columbia to Nashville.
3 May	From Arthur Davis. ALS. DLC–JKP. Inquires about the price of a tract of Polk's land located near John Henning's farm in Madison County.
4 May	*From Robert Armstrong.*
4 May	From John P. Heiss. ALS. DLC–JKP. Wishes letters of introduction to carry to Washington City.
4 May	From Isaac Lewis. ALS. DLC–JKP. Desires Polk's support for an appointment as postmaster at Knoxville.
4 May	From Sackfield Maclin. ALS. DLC–JKP. Acknowledges receipt of Polk's letter of April 30; observes that he has urged a Democratic convention in North Mississippi to nominate Martin Van Buren and Polk; and desires copies of Polk's "printed speeches and reports while a member of Congress."
5 May	To John P. Heiss. ALS. T–JPH. Acknowledges receipt of Heiss' letter of May 4; encloses letter of introduction to Cave Johnson in Washington City.
5 May	From Malinda Wilder. ALS. DLC–JKP. States that she is a resident of Marshall County, that she has been abandoned by her husband, and that she needs assistance.
6 May	From Thomas Martin. ALS. DLC–JKP. Introduces his son, William M. Martin, and requests that a letter addressed to

	Martin Van Buren by Pulaski citizens be forwarded to him "in the manner you may think most effectual."
6 May	From Gideon J. Pillow. ALS. DLC–JKP. Will be in Columbia before noon, but then must leave immediately for Decatur, Alabama.
6 May	From Henderson K. Yoakum and Edwin A. Keeble. LS. DLC–JKP. Urge Polk to bring Martin Van Buren to Murfreesboro.
7 May	From Robert Armstrong. ALS. DLC–JKP. Advises Polk that Martin Van Buren left for Columbia "this morning," but will be unable to go via Shelbyville and Murfreesboro; says that he has no word on the vice-presidential question.
7 May	From Terrell Brooks. ALS. DLC–JKP. Requests Polk's legal assistance with a case in the Hardin County Court.
7 May	From Henry W. McCorry. ALS. DLC–JKP. Acknowledges receipt of Polk's letter of May 3; states that William T. Haskell has resigned his seat in the Tennessee House; and adds that he is unwilling to run.
9 May	From Eli Shelby. ALS. DLC–JKP. Wishes to pay Polk in Alabama money "at par now for the debt which is due next Christmas."
10 May	*From Harry.*
10 May	*From J. G. M. Ramsey.*
10 May	From John A. Thomas. ALS. DLC–JKP. Acknowledges receipt of Polk's letter of April 18, with enclosure.
12 May	*From Franklin H. Elmore.*
12 May	From Howell Taylor and James Meriwether. LS. DLC–JKP. Ask in behalf of Arthur Davis what terms might be given on the purchase of Polk's 230–acre tract located near John Henning's farm in Madison County.
16 May	From John P. Campbell. ALS. DLC–JKP. Solicits Polk's support in the appointment of Joshua James as receiver for a new land district in Missouri.
17 May	From Isaac H. Dismukes. ALS. DLC–JKP. Informs Polk of business affairs relating to his Mississippi plantation.
19 May	From Samuel P. Caldwell. ALS. DLC–JKP. Acknowledges receipt of Polk's letter of May 5 concerning Samuel W. Polk's lands in Fayette County which were sold for taxes in 1836 and 1837.
20 May	*From Cave Johnson.*
22 May	From William R. Rucker. ALS. DLC–JKP. Extends invitation to attend the marriage of his daughter Elizabeth on June 1.
23 May	From Joseph S. Douglas. ALS. DLC–JKP. Acknowledges receipt of Polk's letter of May 4 and informs Polk that his land in Perry County was sold for taxes in 1835.
25 May	From Vernon K. Stevenson. LS. DLC–JKP. Requests payment of note in amount of $324.18 by June 2, 1842.
28 May	From James Caruthers. ALS. DLC–JKP. Acknowledges receipt of Polk's letters of May 4 and 16, and informs Polk

that his two tracts of land in Madison County have not yet sold.

29 May — From Elbridge G. Sevier. ALS. DLC–JKP. Solicits Polk's support for appointment as assigner for bankruptcy proceedings filed in the District of East Tennessee.

30 May — From Levin H. Coe. ALS. DLC–JKP. Reports on Democratic movements in North Mississippi and Arkansas.

1 June — From Litle Choat. ALS. DLC–JKP. Wishes to exchange a Negro woman and child for Polk's land in Wayne county.

1 June — From Isaac H. Dismukes. ALS. DLC–JKP. Informs Polk of business affairs relating to his Mississippi plantation.

1 June — *To Samuel H. Laughlin.*

2 June — From Levin H. Coe. ALS. DLC–JKP. Objects to an article in the *Nashville Union* of May 27 "throwing cold water upon a movement in the Holly Springs paper."

2 June — *From George R. Powel.*

6 June — From John Vinson. ALS. DLC–JKP. Wishes to purchase tract of Polk's land adjoining his own in Denmark, Tennessee.

9 June — From John H. Bills. ALS. DLC–JKP. Acknowledges receipt of Polk's letter of May 4 and advises him on land sales in Perry and Fayette counties.

12 June — From Isaac H. Dismukes. ALS. DLC–JKP. Informs Polk of business affairs relating to his Mississippi plantation.

12 June — From Leonard H. Sims. ALS. DLC–JKP. Solicits Polk's support for the appointment of Nicholas R. Smith to be receiver of public moneys at Springfield, Missouri.

13 June — *To Franklin H. Elmore.*

17 June — From Adlai O. Harris. ALS. DLC–JKP. Wishes Polk's assistance in obtaining a copy of a Chancery Court decree in Dyer County.

19 June — From Sarah C. Polk. ALS. DLC–JKP. Writes personal news; encloses copy of John Vinson's letter of June 6.

20 June — From Cave J. Couts. ALS. DLC–JKP. Gives news from the U.S. Military Academy at West Point.

21 June — From James Walker. ALS. DLC–JKP. Requests promotion of his mail contract claims when Polk is in Washington City.

22 June — To Sarah C. Polk. ALS. DLC–JKP. Advises his wife of progress on his trip to Washington City.

24 June — From Ezekiel P. McNeal. ALS. DLC–JKP. Acknowledges receipt of Polk's letters of April 13 and May 5; details business affairs concerning taxes and land sales in Madison, Fayette, and Perry counties.

24 June — *From Sarah C. Polk.*

25 June — From Silas M. Caldwell. ALS. DLC–JKP. Discusses accounts with Armour, Lake & Morton of Grenada, Mississippi.

25 June — *From Archibald Yell.*

26 June — From Isaac H. Dismukes. ALS. DLC–JKP. Informs Polk of business affairs relating to his Mississippi plantation.

30 June	From Helen M. Newton. ALS. DLC–JKP. Explains that she is a widow and wishes to borrow $100 from Polk.
1 July	*To Andrew Jackson.*
1 July	*From Sarah C. Polk.*
3 July	From George Long. ALS. DLC–JKP. AE by Polk reads, "Illegible & Incomprehensible."
4 July	From Robert A. Dabney. ALS. DLC–JKP. Expresses strong support for Polk's political principles.
4 July	From F. H. Knapp. ALS. DLC–JKP. Wishes testimonial letter as to his skills as a dental surgeon; explains that he must go to Cuba to recover his health.
4 July	From John Vinson. ALS. DLC–JKP. Offers to purchase 244 acres of land adjoining his farm in Madison County.
6 July	*From Henry Horn.*
7 July	From Lawson Gifford. ALS. DLC–JKP. Solicits Polk's support in securing a provisioning contract should the Florida armed occupation bill pass in the U.S. House.
7 July	From A. B. Smith. ALS. DLC–JKP. Inquires about land grants in Tennessee.
9 July	From John P. Campbell. ALS. DLC–JKP. Solicits Polk's support for the appointment of James McBride as register of the Platt Land District in Missouri.
9 July	From Campbell P. White. ALS. DLC–JKP. Regrets that he was away from his residence when Polk called.
11 July	From Lucius J. Polk. ALS. DLC–JKP. Solicits letters of introduction to Polk's New York acquaintances, from whom he wishes to borrow money.
12 July	From Rasha Cannon. ALS. DLC–JKP. Desires information respecting the Columbia Female Academy.
13 July	From Isaac H. Dismukes. ALS. DLC–JKP. Informs Polk of business affairs relating to his Mississippi plantation.
13 July	From A. M. Young and Felix Bosworth. LS. DLC–JKP. Report Democratic victories in the Louisiana elections.
14 July	From Joseph S. Douglas. ALS. DLC–JKP. Acknowledges receipt of Polk's letter of June 4 and gives Polk information on his Perry County land that was sold for taxes.
16 July	From Aaron V. Brown. ALS. DLC–JKP. Reports that a tariff bill has just passed the U.S. House.
17 July	*From Hopkins L. Turney.*
20 July	*From Cave Johnson.*
20 July	From Cave Johnson. ALS. DLC–JKP. Informs Polk of business in the U.S. House and concludes that "the matter is *certain* that Van B. will be the nominee—& of course the Vice will be in the S.W."
21 July	From William Bobbitt. ALS. DLC–JKP. Acknowledges receipt of Polk's letter of June 15 and his enclosed $50 check.
22 July	*From Robert Armstrong.*
22 July	*To Samuel H. Laughlin.*
[23 July]	From Robert Armstrong. ALI. DLC–JKP. Relates political news centering on legislative resignations.

23 July	From Amos Phips and James Y. Caudle. LS. DLC–JKP. Solicit Polk's assistance in securing patent rights for an "inclined wheel."
23 July	From Isaac J. Thomas. ALS. DLC–JKP. Discusses Polk's personal financial business.
24 July	*From Alexander O. Anderson.*
24 July	From Isaac H. Dismukes. ALS. DLC–JKP. Informs Polk of business affairs relating to his Mississippi plantation.
25 July	*From E. G. Eastman.*
25 July	From F. H. Knapp. ALS. DLC–JKP. Wishes Polk to return the testimonials forwarded to him on July 4; asks again for a favorable letter regarding his skills as a dental surgeon.
25 July	From Thomas Martin. ALS. DLC–JKP. Invites Polk to visit Pulaski next week and address the citizens of Giles County.
25 July	*From J. G. M. Ramsey.*
[26 July 1842]	From Robert Armstrong. ALI. DLC–JKP. Reports that Brookins Campbell and Thomas J. Matthews have resigned their seats in the Tennessee House, subject to a mass resignation by the members of both parties.
[27 July 1842]	From Alexander O. Anderson. ALS. DLC–JKP. Advises that measures have been taken to secure the prompt submission of resignations by the Democratic members of the legislature from East Tennessee.
27 July	From Robert Armstrong. ALS. DLC–JKP. Reports further legislative resignations; discusses politics in Louisiana.
27 July	From Arthur R. Crozier. ALS. DLC–JKP. Reports on legislative resignations in his district; solicits Polk's aid in urging Thomas C. Lyon to run for the Tennessee Senate.
28 July	From Boling Gordon. ALS. DLC–JKP. Seeks Polk's advice on making travel arrangements to Richmond, Virginia; includes brief political news.
28 July	*From Samuel H. Laughlin.*
30 July	*From Levin H. Coe.*
31 July	From William Nichol. ALS. DLC–JKP. Calls on Polk for a note due.
2 Aug	*To William McNeill.*
3 Aug	From Robert Armstrong. ALI. DLC–JKP. Advises Polk of current political news in Nashville.
[3 Aug 1842]	From Sarah C. Polk. ALS. DLC–JKP. Discusses personal matters; notes that the *Columbia Observer* has alluded to Polk's experiencing "some disappointments as to the V.P."
5 Aug	From William Lyon. ALS. DLC–JKP. Extends invitation to stay at his home.
5 Aug	From J. G. M. Ramsey. ALS. DLC–JKP. Extends invitation to stay at his home.
9 Aug	From Thomas J. Read & Son. LS. DLC–JKP. Encloses bill of exchange to be forwarded to Polk's commission house in New Orleans. (Enclosure not found.)
11 Aug	From John W. Ford. ALS. DLC–JKP. Acknowledges re-

	ceipt of Polk's letter of August 7; reports that Thomas Grisham of Fentress County and James Walker of McMinn County have sent their resignations to Nashville.
11 Aug	*From Daniel Graham.*
11 Aug	*From Samuel H. Laughlin.*
14 Aug	From Charles A. Warland. ALS. DLC–JKP. Wishes Polk's autograph.
15 Aug	From William Lyon. ALS. DLC–JKP. Invites Polk to "dine with us tomorrow" at Union Mills.
16 Aug	From Isaac H. Dismukes. ALS. DLC–JKP. Informs Polk of business affairs relating to his Mississippi plantation.
16 Aug	From Robert B. Reynolds. ALS. DLC–JKP. Forwards letter from Daniel Graham; notes general resignation of the legislature; and reports Democratic victories in North Carolina.
19 Aug [1842]	*From Cave Johnson.*
19 Aug	From Hopkins L. Turney. ALS. DLC–JKP. Encloses account for book purchases; thinks no tariff bill will pass at the present session of Congress.
24 Aug	From Isaac H. Dismukes. ALS. DLC–JKP. Informs Polk of business affairs relating to his Mississippi plantation.
24 Aug	*From J. George Harris.*
25 Aug	From Robert Armstrong. ALS. DLC–JKP. Reports that William P. Rowles has suggested establishing another newspaper in Nashville.
26 Aug	From Levin H. Coe. ALS. DLC–JKP. Acknowledges receipt of Polk's letters of August 2 and 15; reports Democratic gains in the Western District; and suggests that Polk make appointments to speak at places en route to or from his plantation in North Mississippi.
27 Aug	*From William M. Gwin.*
[27 Aug 1842]	From William P. Rowles. ALS. DLC–JKP. Wishes Polk's advice on establishing a new Democratic press in Nashville.
28 Aug	*From Cave Johnson.*
30 Aug	From Robert Armstrong. ALS. DLC–JKP. Expects Polk to come to Nashville soon; thinks that Whig posturing on the relief question will come to nothing.
30 Aug	*From J. George Harris.*
4 Sept	*From Hopkins L. Turney.*
9 Sept	*From James M. Howry.*
9 Sept	*From Samuel H. Laughlin.*
10 Sept	From Robert J. Chester. ALS. DLC–JKP. Acknowledges receipt of Polk's letter of September 7 and makes arrangements for William P. Rowles to visit the *Jackson Republican.*
10 Sept	From C. B. Raines. ALS. DLC–JKP. Wishes letters of introduction to Polk's friends in Texas, to which country he will soon remove.
11 Sept	*From Jonathan P. Hardwicke.*
12 Sept	From Amos David. ALS. DLC–JKP. Urges support of

Lewis Cass in lieu of Martin Van Buren.

13 Sept   From Isaac H. Dismukes. ALS. DLC–JKP. Informs Polk of business affairs relating to his Mississippi plantation.

14 Sept   *From Alexander O. Anderson.*

14 Sept   From Thomas Martin. ALS. DLC–JKP. Confirms Polk's acceptance of a public barbecue to be given in Pulaski on September 29.

14 Sept   From Harvey M. Watterson. ALS. DLC–JKP. Has recently returned from Washington; reports on John C. Calhoun's efforts for a presidential nomination; and states that Thomas H. Benton supports Polk for the vice-presidency.

14 Sept   From John S. Young. ALS. DLC–JKP. Acknowledges receipt of Polk's letter of September 13; expects that relief measures, including the issuance of post notes, will come before the next legislature.

15 Sept   From Thomas Martin. ALS. DLC–JKP. Acknowledges receipt of Polk's letter of September 14; states that A. O. P. Nicholson has been invited to the dinner in Pulaski on September 29.

18 Sept   From Cave Johnson. ALS. DLC–JKP. Acknowledges receipt of Polk's invitation; regrets that he will be unable to accompany Polk to Pulaski on September 29.

20 Sept   *From Hopkins L. Turney.*

21 Sept   *From Abbott Lawrence.*

22 Sept   From Robert Armstrong. ALS. DLC–JKP. Advises Polk on personal financial business.

22 Sept   From J. G. M. Ramsey. ALS. DLC–JKP. Regrets that his daughter may be unable to attend the Columbia Female Academy this fall; states that he has urged Thomas Ritchie and others to support Polk for the vice-presidential nomination.

23 Sept   *To Samuel H. Laughlin.*

24 Sept   From Clement C. Clay. ALS. DLC–JKP. Acknowledges receipt of Polk's "favor of yesterday"; regrets that he will be unable to meet Polk at Pulaski on September 29.

24 Sept   From William Lyon. ALS. DLC–JKP. Encloses J. G. M. Ramsey's recommendation of William Lyon, Jr., to be postmaster at Knoxville.

24 Sept   From J. G. M. Ramsey. ALS. DLC–JKP. Recommends William Lyon, Jr., to be postmaster at Knoxville.

26 Sept   From Robert Armstrong. ALS. DLC–JKP. Advises Polk on personal financial business.

26 Sept   From William P. Rowles. ALS. DLC–JKP. Requests Polk's assistance in acquiring, through A. O. P. Nicholson, part of the Wayne County legal practice of Russell Houston.

27 Sept   *From Robert Armstrong.*

27 Sept   From Adam Huntsman. ALS. DLC–JKP. Notes unaccountable apathy among Democrats in the Western District.

27 Sept   *From William Wallace.*

28 Sept	From John T. Leigh. ALS. DLC–JKP. Observes that Polk's cotton crop is the best that he has seen in North Mississippi.
29 Sept	From Silas M. Caldwell. ALS. DLC–JKP. Discusses personal financial business.
29 Sept	From William H. Polk. ALS. DLC–JKP. Discusses political situation in advance of the legislature's meeting.
30 Sept	From John B. Fowler. ALS. DLC–JKP. Requests Polk's assistance in obtaining and registering a land title in McNairy County.
30 Sept	*From William H. Polk.*
1 Oct	*From Levin H. Coe.*
4 Oct	From Isaac H. Dismukes. ALS. DLC–JKP. Informs Polk of business affairs relating to his Mississippi plantation.
5 Oct	To Sarah C. Polk. ALS. DLC–JKP. Sends brief personal and political news from Nashville.
6 Oct	From Harvey M. Watterson. ALS. DLC–JKP. States that he spoke to a large crowd at Columbia "on last Monday"; urges Polk's presence at a barbecue to be held at Davis' Mills on October 21.
8 Oct	From Henderson K. Yoakum. ALS. DLC–JKP. Reminds Polk of their discussion on congressional redistricting; maintains that if Rutherford County is placed in Whig legislative or congressional districts, "you may readily see that we must fail."
10 Oct	To Sarah C. Polk. ALS. DLC–JKP. Sends personal news.
11 Oct	*From Samuel H. Laughlin.*
11 Oct	From Harvey M. Watterson. ALS. DLC–JKP. Acknowledges receipt of "yours of yesterday"; encloses invitation to a barbecue at Davis' Mills on October 21. (Enclosure not found.)
12 Oct	From Moses Dawson. ALS. DLC–JKP. Reports Democratic victories in the Ohio elections; concludes that Henry Clay's prospects "are by this election completely prostrated."
12 Oct	From Isaac H. Dismukes. ALS. DLC–JKP. Informs Polk of business affairs relating to his Mississippi plantation.
12 Oct	From J. Parshall. ALS. DLC–JKP. Proposes bank plan that he thinks should be acceptable to Congress and the states.
12 Oct	*From William H. Polk.*
12 Oct	*From J. G. M. Ramsey.*
13 Oct	From William H. Polk. ALS. DLC–JKP. Acknowledges receipt of Polk's letter and writes of personal business.
13 Oct	*From William C. Tate.*
15 Oct	From Charles Graham. ALS. DLC–JKP. Relinquishes rights to 110 acres of land in Perry County, which were obtained at sheriff's sale in 1835.
16 Oct	From William H. Polk. ALS. DLC–JKP. Reports Democratic election victories in Maryland and Ohio.
16 Oct	*From Harvey M. Watterson.*

17 Oct   From William H. Polk. ALS. DLC–JKP. Sends political news from Nashville and concludes that "Maury, Marshall, Bedford and Giles will compose a district," if any congressional redistricting bill is passed during the session.

18 Oct   *From William H. Polk.*

[19 Oct 1842]   From Thomas B. Jones. ALS. DLC–JKP. Solicits letter of recommendation to be directed to the governor of Louisiana.

19 Oct   *To Samuel H. Laughlin.*

20 Oct   From P. B. Cobb. ALS. DLC–JKP. Urges Polk to accept an invitation to a barbecue in Mifflin on November 11.

20 Oct   *From Adam Huntsman.*

21 Oct   *From Cave Johnson.*

24 Oct   To P. B. Cobb. ALS. Pvt Ms of Clarence Clifton, Memphis, Tennessee. Acknowledges receipt of Cobb's letter of October 20 and requests that the public barbecue in Mifflin be arranged for November 5.

25 Oct   From Matthew D. Cooper. ALS. DLC–JKP. Advises Polk on personal financial business.

27 Oct   *From Alexander O. Anderson.*

30 Oct   From Matthew M. Brown. ALS. DLC–JKP. Wishes to borrow money from Polk.

1 Nov   From D. S. Pickett. ALS. DLC–JKP. Encloses Polk's discounted note, which has been renewed by the Union Bank of Tennessee.

2 Nov   From A. P. Grant. ALS. DLC–JKP. Directs letter of introduction to Polk for William H. Eagle of Oswego, New York.

5 Nov   From Thomas Beekman. ALS. DLC–JKP. Introduces William H. Eagle of Oswego, New York.

5 Nov   *From William M. Gwin.*

7 Nov   *From Sarah C. Polk.*

11 Nov   *From Martin Van Buren.*

13 Nov   *From Jonathan P. Hardwicke.*

13 Nov   From Nicholas R. Smith. ALS. DLC–JKP. Solicits support in correcting his appointment as receiver of public moneys at Springfield, Missouri.

14 Nov   *From W. L. D. Ewing.*

14 Nov   From Joel Turrill. ALS. DLC–JKP. Introduces William H. Eagle of Oswego, New York.

17 Nov   From Sarah C. Polk. ALS. DLC–JKP. Sends personal and political news.

20 Nov   *From Jonathan P. Hardwicke.*

23 Nov   From John H. Bills. ALS. DLC–JKP. Awaits Polk's arrival and will accompany him to Jackson.

29 Nov   From Robert Josselyn. ALS. DLC–JKP. Advises Polk on personal financial business in Holly Springs.

29 Nov   *From J. G. M. Ramsey.*

5 Dec   From Isaac H. Dismukes. ALS. DLC–JKP. Informs Polk of business affairs relating to his Mississippi plantation.

5 Dec   From Thomas J. Read & Son. LS. DLC–JKP. Acknowl-

edges receipt of Polk's letter of November 19; encloses Polk's account. (Enclosure not found.)

8 Dec   From Adam Huntsman. ALS. DLC–JKP. Informs Polk of politics in the Western District; expresses great disappointment over the elections in Massachusetts.

8 Dec   *From Williamson Smith.*

8 Dec   *From Hopkins L. Turney.*

8 Dec   *To Martin Van Buren.*

9 Dec   From John H. Bills. ALS. DLC–JKP. Reports party movements in the Tenth Congressional District.

11 Dec   From St. Clair F. Caldwell. ALS. DLC–JKP. Acknowledges receipt of Polk's note of December 7; regrets that he will be unable to accommodate Polk's request for a loan.

12 Dec   *From Robert Armstrong.*

13 Dec   From Ezekiel P. McNeal. ALS. DLC–JKP. Acknowledges receipt of Polk's letter of December 7; accounts for finances of the heirs of Marshall T. Polk.

14 Dec   *From Levin H. Coe.*

16 Dec   From Richard W. Gardner. ALS. DLC–JKP. States that he is poverty stricken; offers to let Polk rear one of his six sons.

16 Dec   From Joel M. Smith. ALS. DLC–JKP. Solicits assistance in closing the accounts for printing J. George Harris' campaign pamphlet, the *Looking Glass.*

16 Dec   From Samuel P. Walker. ALS. DLC–JKP. Advises Polk on personal financial business.

17 Dec   From Mahlon Prim. ALS. DLC–JKP. Wishes personal loan from Polk.

18 Dec   *From Jonathan P. Hardwicke.*

18 Dec   *From Cave Johnson.*

19 Dec   *From E. G. Eastman.*

20 Dec   *From Robert Armstrong.*

20 Dec   *From William C. Dunlap.*

20 Dec   *From J. George Harris.*

22 Dec   From Henry W. Anderson. ALS. DLC–JKP. Solicits support for the appointment of James H. Murray to be agent for the Chickasaw Indians west of the Mississippi River.

22 Dec   From David Craighead. ALS. DLC–JKP. Requests payment of Polk's note in the amount of $594.

22 Dec   *From Henderson K. Yoakum.*

23 Dec   *From Samuel H. Laughlin.*

23 Dec   *From Sackfield Maclin.*

25 Dec   *From John Catron.*

25 Dec   From Isaac H. Dismukes. ALS. DLC–JKP. Informs Polk of business affairs relating to his Mississippi plantation.

25 Dec   From William Fitzgerald. ALS. DLC–JKP. Solicits Polk's assistance in persuading William R. Harris to run, should Cave Johnson decide to retire from Congress.

26 Dec   *From John W. Childress.*

27 Dec   *From Aaron V. Brown.*

28 Dec	*From J. G. M. Ramsey.*
29 Dec	From John W. Childress. ALS. DLC–JKP. Reports that Edwin A. Keeble is quitting the Democratic party over the removal of the postmaster at Murfreesboro.
29 Dec	*From William Fitzgerald.*
31 Dec	From James B. Craighead. ALS. DLC–JKP. Forwards David Craighead's letter to Polk of December 22.

1843

[1843]	From Robert Armstrong. ALI. DLC–JKP. Sends mail bag filled with documents, some of which are "on the Bargain."
[1843]	From Edward Sheegog. ALS. DLC–JKP. Encloses letter for James Houston Thomas from Thomas Jones. (Enclosure not found.)
1 Jan [1843]	*From Timothy Kezer.*
2 Jan	From Robert Armstrong. ALS. DLC–JKP. Acknowledges receipt of Polk's letter and states that he will give an answer soon on the hire of the Negro boy, John.
2 Jan	From John N. Charter. ALS. DLC–JKP. Solicits Polk's support for an appointment as postmaster at Franklin.
2 Jan	To the Democrats of Philadelphia. PL, Philadelphia *Pennsylvanian*. Acknowledges receipt of the invitation dated December 25, 1842; regrets that he cannot attend their Battle of New Orleans celebration.
2 Jan	From Isaac H. Dismukes. ALS. DLC–JKP. Informs Polk of business affairs relating to his Mississippi plantation.
3 Jan	From James Caruthers. ALS. DLC–JKP. Advises Polk on the sale of his land in Madison County.
4 Jan	From Isaac H. Dismukes. ALS. DLC–JKP. Informs Polk of business affairs relating to his Mississippi plantation.
4 Jan	*From Cave Johnson.*
4 Jan	*From Hopkins L. Turney.*
5 Jan	*From George W. Rowles.*
5 Jan	From Joseph Thompson. ALS. DLC–JKP. Acknowledges receipt of Polk's letter of December 30, 1842; gives assurances of his friendship for Polk.
6 Jan	*From Julius W. Blackwell.*
6 Jan	*From Aaron V. Brown.*
6 Jan	*To Samuel H. Laughlin.*
7 Jan	From Robert Armstrong. ALS. DLC–JKP. Advises of arrangements for the hire of the Negro boy, John; wishes to know Polk's desires in the matter.
8 Jan	From John C. Blackburn. ALS. DLC–JKP. Acknowledges receipt of Polk's letter of last December 7; encloses letter received from Samuel Cade, December 3, 1842, concerning the purchase of a tract of Polk's land in Wayne County; and identifies the Polk acreage as that located next to his own farm. (Enclosure not found.)
10 Jan	*From Williamson Smith.*

11 Jan   From Robert Armstrong. ALS. DLC–JKP. Encloses note regarding the hire of the Negro boy, John. (Enclosure not found.)

12 Jan   From Henderson K. Yoakum. ALS. DLC–JKP. Informs Polk of the agenda of a Democratic meeting to be held in Murfreesboro on January 28; requests Polk's views on the issues, particularly on the "location of the seat of government."

15 Jan   From Aaron V. Brown. ALS. DLC–JKP. States that his determination not to run for reelection is genuine; denies losing interest in or zeal for the Democratic cause.

16 Jan   *From J. George Harris.*

16 Jan   *From Henry Simpson.*

17 Jan   *From Thomas Hogan.*

17 Jan   From Thomas Martin. ALS. DLC–JKP. Acknowledges receipt of Polk's letter of last December 8; advises Polk that Giles County will support James H. Thomas for the Tennessee Senate since he has "found none who wish to aspire to the office" in that county; and plans to urge A. V. Brown to seek reelection to Congress.

20 Jan   From Robert Armstrong. ALS. DLC–JKP. Details political management involved in the selection of a candidate for the Eighth Congressional District.

20 Jan   From Edwin F. Polk. ALS. DLC–JKP. Reports political affairs in the Western District; states that he will run for the legislature.

20 Jan   *From John A. Thomas.*

20 Jan   *From Joseph R. A. Tomkins.*

22 Jan   *From Cave Johnson.*

22 Jan   From Samuel Martin. ALS. DLC–JKP. Offers Polk his support for governor "this Coming Election."

23 Jan   From Willie B. Johnson. ALS. DLC–JKP. Acknowledges receipt of Polk's letter and advises him on political movements in the Ninth Congressional District.

24 Jan   From George L. Boutwell et al. LS. DLC–JKP. Invite Polk to a Democratic festival in Boston honoring Marcus Morton on February 9.

25 Jan   From Sarah Polk. ALS. DLC–JKP. Requests copy of agreement for "5000 Acre tract in the western district formerly belonging to the heirs of Rice."

26 Jan   From Isaac H. Dismukes. ALS. DLC–JKP. Informs Polk of business affairs relating to his Mississippi plantation.

26 Jan   *From Granville C. Torbett.*

27 Jan   From H. Talbot Cox. ALS. DLC–JKP. Advises Polk of political affairs in Blount County; hopes for a Democratic victory in the August election; and urges Polk to speak at Louisville, Tennessee, on his trip to East Tennessee.

27 Jan   *To Samuel H. Laughlin.*

28 Jan   From William T. Leacock. ALS. DLC–JKP. States that he will be unable to deliver Polk's stock to market.

28 Jan   From Ezekiel P. McNeal. ALS. DLC–JKP. Reviews financial business; encloses checks from John H. Bills; and discusses political affairs in the Tenth Congressional District. (Enclosures not found.)

29 Jan   *From Cave Johnson.*
30 Jan   *From Thomas R. Barry.*
31 Jan   *From Hopkins L. Turney.*
1 Feb   *From Samuel H. Laughlin.*
2 Feb [1843]   From Lewis P. Roberts. ALS. DLC–JKP. Reports that he is unable to pay a note endorsed for E. G. Eastman at the Bank of Tennessee at Athens; observes that without assistance, the *Argus* "will have to be sold to make the money—consequently the Democratic Party will have no organ in E. Tenn. that can be relied on in the coming elections."

4 Feb   *From Aaron V. Brown.*
4 Feb   From Willie B. Johnson. ALS. DLC–JKP. Reports support for Polk's gubernatorial candidacy in Clarksville; fears Democratic split at the Dover Convention.

5 Feb   From John W. Ford. ALS. DLC–JKP. Acknowledges receipt of Polk's letter of January 30; notes that the Fourth Congressional District is troubled by the split between Samuel H. Laughlin and Alvin Cullom, rivals for the party's congressional nomination.

5 Feb   *From Cave Johnson.*
6 Feb   From J. G. M. Ramsey. ALS. DLC–JKP. Expresses concern for the date of the National Democratic Convention; reports on candidates coming out in East Tennessee for the August elections.

7 Feb   From Elijah Boddie. ALS. DLC–JKP. Acknowledges receipt of Polk's letters of January 11 and 21; relates that Josephus C. Guild and David Burford will run for Congress and the Tennessee Senate respectively; and notes that on February 11 Democrats will hold county meetings to choose delegates to the Gallatin meeting called for February 20.

8 Feb   From Aaron V. Brown. ALI. DLC–JKP. Expresses confusion over Maury and Giles county politics; asks why William H. Polk cannot run for Congress; and concludes that if no other candidate will do, he will run for reelection.

8 Feb   *From John A. Gardner.*
8 Feb   From William Wallace. ALS. DLC–JKP. Acknowledges receipt of Polk's letter of January 19; explains difficulties in finding suitable candidates to run for the legislature from Blount County; predicts that Democrats will not nominate a candidate to run from the Second Congressional District; and notes that the Whigs are trying to mitigate Henry Clay's responsibility for the bankruptcy law by claiming that Martin Van Buren also supported passage of the measure.

10 Feb   From Aaron V. Brown. ALS. DLC–JKP. States that if he runs for reelection to Congress he will delay his move to

	Columbia, thus obviating the need to rent a house there at present.
12 Feb	From Silas M. Caldwell. ALS. DLC–JKP. Discusses family business.
13 Feb	From Pierce B. Anderson. ALS. DLC–JKP. Answers Polk's inquiry of January 27 concerning local Democratic politics in East Tennessee.
13 Feb	*To E. G. Eastman.*
14 Feb	*From William H. Polk.*
15 Feb	From Robert Armstrong. ALS. DLC–JKP. Reports on Davidson County politics.
15 Feb	*From Aaron V. Brown.*
16 Feb [1843]	*From Robert Armstrong.*
16 Feb	*From Jonathan P. Hardwicke.*
16 Feb	From William Houston. ALS. DLC–JKP. Acknowledges receipt of Polk's letter of January 30; answers Polk's inquiries concerning the local Democratic slate in the Second Congressional District.
17 Feb	*From Cave Johnson.*
[17 Feb 1843]	From J. G. M. Ramsey. ALS. DLC–JKP. Wishes Polk's support for an appointment as "visitor to West Point"; reports local political movements.
18 Feb	*From Robert M, Burton.*
18 Feb	*From Isaac Taylor.*
20 Feb	From David Burford. ALS. DLC–JKP. Answers Polk's inquiry of January 21, concerning the local Democratic slate.
20 Feb	*From Andrew Johnson.*
20 Feb	From Thomas Martin. ALS. DLC–JKP. Has received Polk's "favor of this date" and "will be in Columbia on Wednesday morning."
20 Feb	*From Abraham McClellan.*
20 Feb	*From Sam Milligan.*
20 Feb	*From Robert B. Reynolds.*
20 Feb	From William P. Rowles. ALS. DLC–JKP. Has announced himself a candidate for the Tennessee Senate from Maury and Giles counties; wishes Polk's advice.
21 Feb [1843]	From Robert Armstrong. ALS. DLC–JKP. Informs Polk of the Democratic slate for the Eighth Congressional District.
21 Feb	From George C. Conrad. ALS. DLC–JKP. Sends political news from the Ninth Congressional District.
21 Feb	From Joseph Linow. ALS. DLC–JKP. Wishes Polk to speak at Hickory Withe in Fayette County.
23 Feb	*To John C. Spencer.*
24 Feb	From Benjamin Adams. ALS. DLC–JKP. Inquires about personal business with Polk.
24 Feb	*From Robert Armstrong.*
[24 Feb 1843]	*From W. L. D. Ewing.*
25 Feb	*From Jonathan P. Hardwicke.*
27 Feb	*From Sackfield Maclin.*

28 Feb	*From Cave Johnson.*
1 March	From Joseph W. Horton. ALS. DLC–JKP. Acknowledges receipt of Polk's letter of February 23 and its enclosure; states that he has renewed Polk's note with the Bank of Tennessee at Nashville.
2 March	*From George W. Smith.*
3 March	*From James M. Howry.*
3 March	*From Sarah C. Polk.*
3 March	*To Sarah C. Polk.*
3 March	From John Sommerville. ALS. DLC–JKP. Acknowledges Polk's request of February 23 for renewal of his $600 note with the Union Bank of Tennessee; encloses cancelled note. (Enclosure not found.)
5 March	From Lewis Shepherd. ALS. DLC–JKP. Answers Polk's inquiry of January 28 concerning local Democratic politics in the Third Congressional District; states that he is the candidate for the Tennessee House from Hamilton County.
6 March	From Levin H. Coe. ALS. DLC–JKP. Reports on congressional and senatorial candidates in West Tennessee; wishes Polk's assistance in obtaining affidavits in Nashville for James H. Walker.
6 March	From Christopher H. McGinnis. ALS. DLC–JKP. Names candidates nominated this date at a Democratic meeting in Savannah, Tennessee.
7 March	*From Thomas Martin.*
9 March	From Alexander McCulloch, Jr. ALS. DLC–JKP. Wishes letter of introduction from Polk directed to the surveyor of Iowa.
11 March [1843]	*From John Blair.*
13 March	From Robert Armstrong. ALS. DLC–JKP. Names Davidson County ticket for the state legislature.
13 March	From Argyle Campbell. ALS. DLC–JKP. Introduces John Huddleston, a friend from Mississippi.
13 March	*From William G. Childress.*
13 March	From Thomas Hogan. ALS. DLC–JKP. Reports on proceedings of the Davidson County nominating convention.
15 March	From William Wallace. ALS. DLC–JKP. Discusses Blount County legislative nominations.
16 March	*From Cave Johnson.*
17 March	From Joseph Powell. ALS. DLC–JKP. (Text largely illegible.)
18 March	To James H. Thomas. ALS. DLC–JKP. Orders payment of a cash note in favor of Samuel P. Walker.
19 March	*From George C. Conrad.*
19 March	*From John A. Thomas.*
19 March	From William Wallace. ALS. DLC–JKP. Prefers that Polk speak in Maryville rather than in Louisville.
20 March	To Alvin Cullom. AL, copy. DLC–JKP. Appeals to Cullom to compose his differences amicably with Samuel H.

	Laughlin in their dispute over who is to run from the Fourth Congressional District.
20 March	*From Timothy Kezer.*
20 March	*To Samuel H. Laughlin.*
25 March	*From Adam Huntsman.*
25 March	*From William Wallace.*
27 March	From E. G. Eastman. ALS. DLC–JKP. Sends newspaper clipping detailing James C. Jones' stand on the U.S. Senate election in Tennessee.
27 March	*From Samuel H. Laughlin.*
27 March	*From J. G. M. Ramsey.*
29 March	From James N. Dortch. ALS. DLC–JKP. Requests campaign material proving that Hugh L. White had denied charge of political trimming.
29 March	*From Sarah C. Polk.*
30 March	From William R. Harris. ALS. DLC–JKP. Assures Polk that a Democratic candidate from Henry County will be amicably selected.
31 March	*From Robert Armstrong.*
31 March	From Henry Talbot Cox. ALS. DLC–JKP. Acknowledges Polk's letter of March 14; expresses pleasure that Polk will speak in Louisville, Tennessee, on June 16.
1 April	*From Hopkins L. Turney.*
2 April	From Benjamin Totten. ALS. DLC–JKP. Wishes Polk to speak at Tottens Wells in Obion County on May 4, 1843.
3 April	From James A. Tullas. ALS. DLC–JKP. Wishes Polk to visit Pikeville during his tour of East Tennessee.
3 April	*From Henderson K. Yoakum.*
4 April	From William T. Brown. ALS. DLC–JKP. Acknowledges receipt of Polk's letters from Somerville and Bolivar; regrets circumstances that prevent his running in the Tenth Congressional District.
4 April	From William R. Harris. ALS. DLC–JKP. Relates that Henry County will hold a Democratic convention.
4 April	*To Sarah C. Polk.*
5 April	From John C. Mullay et al. LS. DLC–JKP. Solicit Polk's support for the appointment of Henry H. Stephens as attorney general for East Tennessee.
6 April	From John W. Childress. ALS. DLC–JKP. Reports on the canvass in Rutherford and Williamson counties.
6 April	From John W. Childress. ALS. DLC–JKP. Solicits assistance in obtaining a pardon for Littleberry Bostick.
7 April	*From Sarah C. Polk.*
7 April	*To Sarah C. Polk.*
[8 April 1843]	From Adam Huntsman. AL, fragment. DLC–JKP. States that Samuel McClanahan has withdrawn as the Democratic candidate for the Tennessee Senate.
9 April	From Robert W. Powell. ALS. DLC–JKP. Responds to Polk's request of October 15, 1842, for a copy of Spencer

Jarnagin's answers to the interrogatories posed by the Democratic members of the Tennessee Senate.

10 April   *From John J. Goodman.*

10 April   *To Sarah C. Polk.*

10 April   *From William H. Polk.*

11 April   *From Sarah C. Polk.*

13 April [1843]   From Thomas Ewell. ALS. DLC–AJD. Reports on the Democratic canvass in Madison County.

14 April   *To Sarah C. Polk.*

16 April   *From William Fitzgerald.*

17 April   *From Sarah C. Polk.*

18 April   From Howell Taylor. ALS. DLC–JKP. Wishes Polk to call at Edmund Taylor's "very early in the morning & we will accompany you to Dancyville."

19 April   *From James M. Howry.*

20 April   From Robert J. Nelson. ALS. DLC–JKP. Entreats Polk to handle the military claims of John Nelson.

20 April   From William M. Warner. ALS. DLC–JKP. Acclaims Polk's political principles.

26 April   From Sackfield Maclin et al. LS. DLC–JKP. Certify that on April 22 James C. Jones spoke in Memphis and made insulting remarks about Arthur R. Crozier.

3 May   From Pendleton G. Gaines. ALS. DLC–JKP. Declares that Polk's speech in Memphis on April 22 "has given a new and I think an irresistable impetus to the cause of Democracy and made '*Polk*' the great man of the nation in the estimation of this people"; urges Polk to answer the Memphis interrogatories.

3 May   *From Sarah C. Polk.*

3 May   *From George W. Smith.*

4 May   From John Ray. ALS. DLC–JKP. Wishes a letter of introduction to Polk's "political or personal acquaintances in the state of South Carolina."

6 May   *From Levin H. Coe.*

6 May   *From William M. Lowry.*

8 May   *To Samuel H. Laughlin.*

8 May   *To Sarah C. Polk.*

9 May   From John W. Campbell. ALS. DLC–JKP. Discusses Polk's financial affairs with the Union Bank of Tennessee's Jackson branch.

10 May   From William S. Harris. ALS. DLC–JKP. Requests republication of Polk's congressional speech on Gulian C. Verplanck's compromise tariff bill of 1833.

10 May   *From Cave Johnson.*

11 May   *From J. G. M. Ramsey.*

11 May   *From Henderson K. Yoakum.*

12 May   From Aaron V. Brown. ALS. DLC–JKP. Reports on his local canvass.

12 May   From Thomas Ewell. ALS. DLC–JKP. Reports on the political canvass in the Eleventh Congressional District.

12 May	*From Henry Strange.*
13 May	From Thomas E. S. Russwurm. ALS. DLC–JKP. Encloses clipping from this day's Murfreesboro *Tennessee Telegraph*; urges Polk to answer the newspaper's charge that he opposed the removal of the seat of Tennessee government to Murfreesboro in 1841.
13 May	From George Winchester. ALS. DLC–JKP. Reports on the political canvass in Haywood County.
13 May	From Henderson K. Yoakum. ALS. DLC–JKP. Urges Polk to deny the falsehoods published in the enclosed issue of the Murfreesboro *Tennessee Telegraph*; suggests that Polk give Thomas E. S. Russwurm a brief answer. (Enclosure not found.)
14 May [1843]	From Robert Armstrong. ALS. DLC–JKP. Reports on Davidson County Democratic Convention.
14 May	From Levin H. Coe. ALS. DLC–JKP. Reports on the local canvass as well as on Richard M. Johnson's speech at Memphis.
14 May	From Boling Gordon. ALS. DLC–JKP. Solicits Polk's assistance in inciting T. J. Matthews "to active exertions in our cause."
15 May	*From Robert Armstrong.*
15 May	From M. D. Cardwell. ALS. DLC–JKP. Reports on Weakley County politics.
15 May	*From John W. Childress.*
15 May	*To Wyatt Christian et al.*
15 May	From Thomas Hogan. ALS. DLC–JKP. States that he will visit Polk in Columbia "on Wednesday morning."
15 May	From James Park et al. LS. DLC–JKP. Invite Polk to speak at Franklin.
[15 May 1843]	*To George W. Smith et al.*
15 May	*To Henry Van Pelt.*
16 May	From J. Robinson. ALS. DLC–JKP. Names Democratic candidates running in the Tenth Congressional District.
20 May	*From Henry Clay.*
22 [May 1843]	*From Robert Armstrong.*
22 May	From George Batey. ALS. DLC–JKP. Solicits Polk's assistance in locating T. W. Batey, former deputy sheriff of Marshall County.
22 May	From James Gamble. ALS. DLC–JKP. Discusses Roane and Knox county canvass; wishes Polk to visit his home while in Roane County.
23 May	*From Sarah C. Polk.*
25 May	*From Robert Armstrong.*
29 May	From William H. Polk. ALS. DLC–JKP. Discusses political canvass in the Western District and in Maury County.
31 May	From Cave Johnson. ALS. DLC–JKP. Discusses political canvass in the Ninth Congressional District.
31 May	From J. G. M. Ramsey. ALS. DLC–JKP. Reports on the canvass in East Tennessee; claims that the *Charleston Mer-*

cury endorsed Levi Woodbury for vice-president without authority; that John C. Calhoun wants his friends to avoid interfering in the vice-presidential question; and that Tennessee also must leave that matter to the National Democratic Convention.

31 May   From Robert B. Reynolds. ALS. DLC–JKP. Discusses the political canvass in East Tennessee.

3 June   From Henry Simpson et al. LS. DLC–JKP. Enclose an address of the Philadelphia Democratic Hickory Club seeking concerted action for the next presidential election.

5 June   From Christopher H. McGinnis. ALS. DLC–JKP. Reports on the campaign in Hardin County and wishes Polk's opinion "as to the prospects of your Election."

7 June   From Lucien B. Chase. ALS. DLC–JKP. Discusses the campaign and "system of organisation" in the Ninth Congressional District.

7 June   From Edwin F. Polk. ALS. DLC–JKP. Discusses campaign in the Western District.

9 June   *To Sarah C. Polk.*

12 June   *From Robert Armstrong.*

14 June   From George W. Mayo et al. LS. DLC–JKP. State that McMinn County mechanics wish to know Polk's views "in relation to the system of labor as at present conducted in our state penitentiary."

15 June   From Nathaniel W. Williams et al. LS. DLC–JKP. Extends an invitation from the Chi-Delta Society of East Tennessee University to a public debate "on Saturday evening the 17th instant."

16 June   *From William Wallace.*

16 June   From William Wallace. ALS. DLC–JKP. Urges Polk to keep his appointment in Maryville.

17 June   From Robert Armstrong. ALS. DLC–JKP. Acknowledges receipt of Polk's letters from Kingston and Athens; urges Polk to compose factional disputes in his passage through East Tennessee.

17 June   *To George W. Mayo et al.*

18 June   *To Sarah C. Polk.*

19 June   From Joseph L. Thomas et al. LS. DLC–JKP. Invite Polk to a Fourth of July celebration to be given by the Democracy of the Northern Liberties of Philadelphia.

24 June   From William F. Hosea. ALS. DLC–JKP. Wishes personal favor.

24 June   From J. G. M. Ramsey. ALS. DLC–JKP. Reports campaign news from East Tennessee.

27 June   From W. Norton. ALS. DLC–JKP. Warns Polk that the Whigs will make a concerted effort against him at Bean's Station on July 3.

29 June   *To Sarah C. Polk.*

7 July   From John McGaughey. ALS. DLC–JKP. Answers Polk's inquiry for election news from Greene County.

8 July   From John D. Grant. ALS. DLC–JKP. Inquires into the

purchase of a tract of land adjoining Thomas Read's farm in Madison County.

10 July   From W. W. Gleeson. ALS. DLC–JKP. Reports on the campaign in the Eleventh Congressional District; encloses affidavit of James Summers attesting to James C. Jones' position on disposing of state bonds. (Enclosure not found.)

12 July   From Powhatan Gordon. ALS. DLC–JKP. Relates campaign news from Maury County.

12 July   From John C. Mullay. ALS. DLC–JKP. Reports Democratic prospects in East Tennessee and assures Polk "that we shall increase your vote in East Tennessee from 1500 to 2000 votes."

12 July   *From William H. Polk.*

12 July   From Lycurgus Winchester. ALS. DLC–JKP. Names candidates in Henderson County and the Eleventh Congressional District.

14 July   From William C. Hazen. ALS. DLC–JKP. Gives county-by-county report of party strength in the Tenth Congressional District; expects that Polk will lose the Western District by no more than 1,200 votes.

15 July   From William McClellan. ALS. DLC–JKP. Answers Polk's inquiry about the campaign in Sullivan County; predicts that Andrew Johnson will carry the First Congressional District by at least 1,000 votes.

16 July   *From Thomas Davis.*

18 July   From John H. Bills. ALS. DLC–JKP. Reports that Democratic prospects in the Tenth Congressional District are favorable.

18 July   From George W. Mayo. ALS. DLC–JKP. Reports favorable gains in the Third Congressional District.

18 July   *From Austin Miller.*

19 July   From Thomas B. Claiborne. ALS. DLC–JKP. Names candidates and discusses campaign in the Western District.

19 July   From Lycurgus Winchester. ALS. DLC–JKP. Discusses campaign in the Eleventh Congressional District; declares that Stephen Pavatt "is really doing battle like a trojan" against Milton Brown.

20 July   *From A. W. Goodrich.*

20 July   From R. M. Hooke. ALS. DLC–JKP. Acknowledges receipt of Polk's letter from Jacksboro and reports that prospects "are beginning to brighten up" in the Third Congressional District.

20 July   *From Robert B. Reynolds.*

22 July   From Robert Armstrong. ALS. DLC–JKP. Relates case of Gideon Matlock.

22 July   *From James Fulton.*

22 July   *From Cave Johnson.*

22 July   From Joel L. Jones. ALS. DLC–JKP. Acknowledges receipt of Polk's letter of July 9; assures him of Democratic strength in the Tenth Congressional District.

22 July   *From William M. Lowry.*

23 July	*From Sarah C. Polk.*
29 July	From Thomas Newsom. ALS. DLC–JKP. Wishes Polk's opinion "concerning your election, particularly in East Tennessee."
31 [July 1843]	From Robert Armstrong. ALS. DLC–JKP. Sketches late political news.
31 July	From Aaron V. Brown. ALS. DLC–JKP. Gives news of his campaign for reelection to Congress.
1 Aug	From William H. Polk. ALS. DLC–JKP. Urges Polk to be "at Columbia on Wednesday, by the time Jones finishes his speech."
[4 Aug 1843]	From Andrew Jackson. ALS. DLC–JKP. Extends sentiments of consolation.
5 Aug	From J. Lancaster ALS. DLC–JKP. Wishes Polk to "write out views upon the Great Questions that are now dividing the two political parties," to be printed in a circular by Mississippi Democrats in the Choctaw Purchase.
7 Aug	*To Robert Armstrong.*
18 Aug	*To Martin Van Buren.*
31 Aug	From Benjamin S. Brooks. ALS. DLC–JKP. Answers Polk's inquiry concerning the balance of a note at the Union Bank at Jackson.
4 Sept	From John C. Blackburn. ALS. DLC–JKP. Inquires about the sale of Polk's land in Wayne County.
9 Sept	From H. A. Cole et al. LS. DLC–JKP. Invite Polk to attend a convention of Montgomery County Democratic Young Men at Clarksville on November 9, 1843.
13 Sept	From James Cone. ALS. DLC–JKP. Acknowledges receipt of Polk's letter of August 11; regrets that he is unable to pay Polk the note due him.
14 Sept	*To John H. Bills.*
16 Sept	From James Sanfley. ALS. DLC–JKP. Solicits letters of recommendation to the governors of Louisiana and Kentucky.
22 Sept	*From George W. Rice.*
28 Sept	From Gardiner Frierson. ALS. DLC–JKP. Acknowledges receipt of Polk's letter of September 22; promises services of Frierson & Co. in selling Polk's cotton.
29 Sept [1843]	From Marshall T. Polk, Jr. ALS. DLC–JKP. Sends personal news.
5 Oct	*From Julius W. Blackwell.*
5 Oct	*From Archibald Yell.*
8 Oct	*To Edmund Burke.*
9 Oct	From Gideon J. Pillow. ALS. DLC–JKP. Solicits Polk's support in the election of William P. Martin over Edmund Dillahunty as judge of the Eighth Judicial Circuit.
10 Oct	From Levin H. Coe. ALS. DLC–JKP. Acknowledges receipt of Polk's letter of September 11; reports on the recent Democratic meeting at Jackson that was held to appoint

delegates to the State Convention; will make plans to attend the Baltimore Convention, if elected as a delegate; and intends to push for the nomination of Martin Van Buren and Polk.

10 Oct   From William J. Whitthorne. ALS. DLC–JKP. States that he plans to send his son to Columbia to school.

12 Oct   *From Henry Ewing.*

12 Oct   *From Samuel H. Laughlin.*

12 Oct   From William B. Preston. ALS. DLC–JKP. Requests instructions arising from Andrew J. Donelson's recent correspondence with Polk.

12 Oct   *From J. G. M. Ramsey.*

13 Oct   From Felix Robertson. ALS. DLC–JKP. Discusses financial business of Polk and William H. Polk with the Bank of Tennessee.

14 Oct   From Thomas Smith. ALS. DLC–JKP. Solicits Polk's recommendation to the governor of Louisiana for the appointment of James D. Smith as tobacco inspector at New Orleans.

14 Oct   From William C. Tate. ALS. DLC–JKP. Acknowledges receipt of Polk's letter; says that Polk's nephew, Marshall T. Polk, Jr., has permission to live with him and Sarah in Columbia.

16 Oct   *To H. A. Cole, David Howell, et al.*

16 Oct   *From William H. Polk.*

17 Oct   *From John W. Davis.*

17 Oct   From Thomas B. Eastland. ALS. DLC–JKP. Solicits Polk's support in the appointment of Thomas W. Essex as tobacco inspector at New Orleans.

17 Oct   *From William H. Polk.*

19 Oct   *To Andrew Jackson Donelson.*

20 Oct   *From Samuel H. Laughlin.*

20 Oct   *To Samuel H. Laughlin.*

21 Oct   From J. B. Boyd, Jr. ALS. DLC–JKP. Wishes advice on whether he should read law in Columbia or in Nashville.

21 Oct   From William M. Lowry. ALS. DLC–JKP. Thinks Lewis Cass is the best compromise candidate to compose the differences between Martin Van Buren and John C. Calhoun; favors Polk as the vice-presidential choice, for that ticket would be "as strong in the North as Van and much stronger in the Western States & Tennessee & Southern States."

22 [Oct]   From Daniel Kenney. ALS. DLC–JKP. Requests assistance in bringing Polk's vice-presidential aspirations to public notice in western Virginia.

22 Oct   *From William H. Polk.*

23 Oct   From John S. Young. ALS. DLC–JKP. Introduces J. W. Dolleur of New Orleans.

25 Oct   From Thomas C. Caldwell. ALS. DLC–JKP. Solicits Polk's assistance in procuring a consulship in Chihuahua, Mexico.

25 Oct	From William Fitzgerald. ALS. DLC–JKP. Solicits Polk's support for the appointment of Isaac B. Williams as attorney general for the Ninth Judicial District.
26 Oct	From Levin H. Coe. ALS. DLC–JKP. Acknowledges receipt of Polk's letter of October 20; states that professional obligations may prevent his attending the Baltimore Convention.
26 Oct	*To Sarah C. Polk*
27 Oct	From Samuel P. Walker. ALS. DLC–JKP. Acknowledges receipt of Polk's letter from Bolivar and reports on the cotton market at Memphis.
28 Oct	From Felix Bosworth. ALS. DLC–JKP. Bestows on Polk an honorary membership in the Democratic Association of Carroll Parish, Louisiana.
30 Oct	*From Edmund Burke.*
30 Oct	From David C. Skerrett et al. C. DLC–JKP. Seek support for the presidential candidacy of Martin Van Buren.
31 Oct	*From Archibald Yell.*
3 Nov	From John W. Ford. ALS. DLC–JKP. Solicits payment of Polk's account with the McMinnville *Central Gazette*.
4 Nov	From William Parmenter. ALS. DLC–JKP. Acknowledges receipt of Polk's letter of October 8; states that he would be pleased should members of the U.S. House elect Cave Johnson their Speaker.
4 Nov	From William J. Whitthorne. ALS. DLC–JKP. Solicits Polk's support for an appointment as clerk and master of Bedford County.
[6 Nov]	*From David Craighead.*
6 Nov	*From W. S. Pickett.*
8 Nov	To B. F. Fitzhugh. ALS. DLC–JKP. Encloses letter received from James W. Moore, who is seeking settlement of a personal debt. (Enclosure not found.)
10 Nov	*From Cave Johnson.*
11 Nov	From William Bobbitt. ALS. DLC–JKP. Reports Democratic victories in Yalobusha County, Mississippi.
16 Nov	From William H. Polk. ALS. DLC–JKP. Urges Polk to come to Nashville by Monday "to spur our friends up to *action*" before the state convention.
17 Nov	*From Samuel H. Laughlin.*
17 Nov	*To Samuel H. Laughlin.*
17 Nov	From Hopkins L, Turney. ALS. DLC–JKP. Acknowledges receipt of Polk's letter of October 20; regrets that professional obligations will prevent his attending the state convention; and adds that adverse financial affairs will prevent his being a delegate to the Baltimore Convention.
18 Nov	From William Pope. ALS. DLC–JKP. Seeks Polk's assistance in obtaining bail for J. H. Pope, who is in the Lawrenceburg jail.

18 Nov	*To William C. Tate.*
24 Nov	From William V. Voorhies. ALS. DLC–JKP. Wishes appointment as Columbia postmaster.
25 Nov	From George N. Sanders et al. LS. DLC–JKP. Enclose proceedings of a mass meeting in Carroll County, Kentucky; request Polk's views "as to the policy of admitting Texas into the United States."
26 Nov	From John C. Whitsitt. ALS. DLC–JKP. Introduces S. Giles of Gainesville, Alabama.
28 Nov	From Samuel P. Caldwell. ALS. DLC–JKP. Regrets that he is unable to accept Polk's "propositions with regard to selling me a part of your land, and hiring my negroes upon terms to be agreed upon between us."
28 Nov	*From Lucien B. Chase.*
28 Nov	*From Cave Johnson.*
30 Nov	*To Martin Van Buren.*
3 Dec	*From J. George Harris.*
4 Dec	From Aaron V. Brown. ALS. DLC–JKP. Reports that the organization of the U.S. House has been completed "peaceably and orderly"; fears no "serious disunion" of the party; and expects that the vice-presidency will be offered to Richard M. Johnson as a compromise.
4 Dec	*To Samuel H. Laughlin.*
5 Dec	From John W. Childress. ALS. DLC–JKP. Reports on efforts to sell his lands near Murfreesboro and remove to Mississippi "in time for the coming crop"; and states that if he sells his Tennessee lands at a good price, he would be pleased to accept Polk's proposition to purchase his Yalobusha County plantation.
5 Dec	From J. Mortimer Willis et al. LS. DLC–JKP. Invite Polk to deliver the annual address to the Agatheridan and Erosophian societies of Nashville University.
5 Dec	From Archibald Yell. ALS. DLC–JKP. Reports that the Arkansas Democratic Convention has endorsed a Martin Van Buren-Polk ticket; and adds that the convention also nominated Elias N. Conway for governor and Daniel J. Chapman for Congress.
7 Dec	From West H. Humphreys. ALS. DLC–JKP. Sends political news from the Western District.
7 Dec	*From Samuel H. Laughlin.*
8 Dec	From Robert Armstrong. ALS. DLC–JKP. Urges Polk to come to Nashville; believes that Samuel H. Laughlin will agree to take over the *Nashville Union.*
9 Dec	*From Aaron V. Brown.*
9 Dec	From Joseph W. Horton. ALS. DLC–JKP. Requests statement on the financial status of John A. Tanner and James Olney for use by the Bank of Tennessee.
9 Dec	*From Cave Johnson.*

9 Dec	From Charles Mapes et al. N. DLC–JKP. Invite Polk to a ball to be held by the New York Tammany Society on January 8.
11 Dec	*From Cave Johnson.*
13 Dec	From A. W. Smith. ALS. DLC–JKP. Suggests that the *Nashville Union* "wants life & spirit, it is not able to cope with the opposition it has."
15 Dec	*From Cave Johnson.*
15 Dec	From Samuel Mitchell. ALS. DLC–JKP. Reports that the Arkansas Democratic Convention preferred a Martin Van Buren-Polk ticket; seeks Polk's assistance in financial affairs.
15 Dec	From Daniel Sheffer. ALS. DLC–JKP. Apprises Polk of Pennsylvania's support for James Buchanan for the presidency; details intricacies of state politics and nominees.
18 Dec	*From Samuel H. Laughlin.*
19 Dec	From Leonard P. Cheatham. ALS. DLC–JKP. Encloses letter from Cave Johnson, who writes that the nomination by Tennessee Democrats of any man other than Martin Van Buren "would be *destructive* to the prospects of *Govr. Polk.*" (Enclosure not found.)
19 Dec	*From Samuel H. Laughlin.*
19 Dec	From R. L. Lloyd et al. LS. DLC–JKP. Invite Polk to a public dinner to be given on January 8 by Philadelphia's Third District Democrats in celebration of the Battle of New Orleans.
20 Dec	*To Andrew J. Donelson.*
[20] Dec	*From John P. Heiss.*
20 Dec	From William H. Polk. ALS. DLC–JKP. Requests copy of William O. Butler's speech on Andrew Jackson's contempt of court conviction; reports that the Address of the Democratic State Convention will appear in the *Nashville Union* on Saturday.
21 Dec	*From Robert Armstrong.*
21 Dec	*To John P. Heiss.*
21 Dec	*From Samuel H. Laughlin.*
22 Dec [1843]	*From Robert Armstrong.*
22 Dec	*From Leonard P. Cheatham.*
[22] Dec	*From John P. Heiss.*
22 Dec	From West H. Humphreys. ALS. DLC–JKP. Seeks Polk's assistance in completing new arrangements for publication of the *Nashville Union.*
22 Dec	From Rody Patterson et al. LS. DLC–JKP. Invite Polk to Battle of New Orleans celebration at Pittsburgh, Pennsylvania.
23 Dec	From R. U. Hale et al. LS. DLC–JKP. Seeks financial backing for the Callispean Society of Washington College.
24 Dec	From James L. Totten. ALS. DLC–JKP. Informs Polk that B. F. Fitzhugh has declared bankruptcy; encloses "the paper against him which you left with me."

25 Dec	*To Andrew Jackson.*
25 Dec	*From Samuel H. Laughlin.*
26 Dec	From Joseph Thompson. ALS. DLC–JKP. Complains that William J. Whitthorne of Nashville has been appointed Chancery Court clerk, a position for which he had made application; wishes to know what part Polk took in Whitthorne's selection.
26 Dec	From Hopkins L. Turney. ALS. DLC–JKP. Acknowledges receipt of Polk's letter of December 22; states that if possible he will meet Polk in Nashville on January 1.
26 Dec	From Hugh W. Wormsley. ALS. DLC–JKP. Solicits support for his claim before Congress.
27 Dec	From Robert Armstrong. ALS. DLC–JKP. Encloses letter received from Arthur R. Crozier, who urges that A. O. P. Nicholson be named an at-large presidential elector.
27 Dec	To W. S. Pickett & Co. ALS. T–JKP. Inquires into the marketing of his cotton crop.
27 Dec	*From Martin Van Buren.*
28 Dec	To R. L. Lloyd et al. ALS, draft. DLC–JKP. Regrets that he is unable to accept their invitation.
29 Dec	*From Samuel H. Laughlin.*
29 Dec	*To Samuel H. Laughlin.*
30 Dec	From John W. Campbell. ALS. DLC–JKP. Encloses account with the Jackson branch of the Union Bank of Tennessee.
30 Dec	*From Levin H. Coe.*
30 Dec	*From Cave Johnson.*
30 Dec	*To Samuel H. Laughlin.*
30 Dec	From Gideon J. Pillow. ALS. DLC–JKP. Regrets that family illness will prevent his accompanying Polk to Nashville.
30 Dec	From William J. Whitthorne. ALS. DLC–JKP. Expresses appreciation for Polk's supporting his appointment as Bedford County Chancery Court clerk.
31 Dec	From Robert Armstrong. ALS. DLC–JKP. Discusses arrangements for Hopkins L. Turney's trip to Columbus, Ohio; states that Turney and Samuel H. Laughlin are at the Hermitage getting letters from Andrew Jackson and Andrew J. Donelson.
31 Dec	*From William H. Polk.*

INDEX

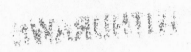